Le-ma'an Ziony

Le-ma'an Ziony:
Essays in Honor of Ziony Zevit

edited by
FREDERICK E. GREENSPAHN
& GARY A. RENDSBURG

CASCADE *Books* • Eugene, Oregon

LE-MA'AN ZIONY
Essays in Honor of Ziony Zevit

Copyright © 2017 Wipf and Stock Publishers. All rights reserved. Except for brief quotations in critical publications or reviews, no part of this book may be reproduced in any manner without prior written permission from the publisher. Write: Permissions, Wipf and Stock Publishers, 199 W. 8th Ave., Suite 3, Eugene, OR 97401.

Cascade Books
An Imprint of Wipf and Stock Publishers
199 W. 8th Ave., Suite 3
Eugene, OR 97401

www.wipfandstock.com

PAPERBACK ISBN: 978-1-4982-0691-4
HARDCOVER ISBN: 978-1-4982-0693-8
EBOOK ISBN: 978-1-4982-0692-1

Cataloguing-in-Publication data:

Names: Greenspahn, Frederick E. | Rendsburg, Gary A.

Title: Le-ma'an Ziony : essays in honor of Ziony Zevit / edited by Frederick E. Greenspahn and Gary A. Rendsburg.

Description: Eugene, OR: Cascade Books, 2016 | Includes bibliographical references and indexes.

Identifiers: ISBN 978-1-4982-0691-4 (paperback) | ISBN 978-1-4982-0693-8 (hardcover) | ISBN 978-1-4982-0692-1 (ebook)

Subjects: LCSH: Zevit, Ziony. | Bible. O.T.—Criticism, interpretation, etc.

Classification: DS111 L44 2017 (print) | DS111 (ebook)

Manufactured in the U.S.A.   FEBRUARY 24, 2017

Contents

List of Figures and Tables | vii
List of Contributors | xi
Acknowledgments | xiv
Abbreviations | xv
Introduction | xxi
Publications of Ziony Zevit | xxv

Part 1: History and Archaeology

1. History from Things: On Writing New Histories of Ancient Israel | *William G. Dever* | 3
2. Tel 'Eton Excavations and the History of the Shephelah during the Iron Age | *Avraham Faust* | 21
3. Jerusalem in Rome: Moses Mendelssohn on the Arch of Titus Menorah | *Steven Fine* | 44
4. Ekron of the Philistines: A Response to Issues Raised in the Literature | *Seymour Gitin* | 60
5. Regional and Local Museums for Archaeology in the First Years of the State of Israel | *Raz Kletter* | 77
6. Disks and Deities: Images on Iron Age Terracotta Plaques | *Carol Meyers* | 116
7. An Early Iron Age Phase to Kuntillet 'Ajrud? | *William M. Schniedewind* | 134

Part 2: Bible

8. Psalm 122: The Idealized Jerusalem | *Adele Berlin* | 149
9. The *Qeré* in the Context of the Masorah Parva | *Michael V. Fox* | 156

10. The Odd Prophet Out and In | *Zev Garber and Bruce Zuckerman* | 175

11. Canon, Codex, and the Printing Press | *Frederick E. Greenspahn* | 203

12. Piercing God's Name: A Mythological Subtext of Deicide Underlying Blasphemy in Leviticus 24 | *Theodore J. Lewis* | 213

13. Varia on Crowns and Diadems in the Bible and Mesopotamia | *Shalom M. Paul* | 239

14. Psalm 20 and Amherst Papyrus 63, XII, 11–19: A Case Study of a Text in Transit | *Karel van der Toorn* | 244

Part 3: Hebrew (and Aramaic) Language

15. Two Maskilic Explanations of the Difference between the Causative *Pi'el* and the *Hiph'il* in Biblical Hebrew | *Steven E. Fassberg* | 263

16. Kissing through a Veil: Translating the Emphatic in Biblical Hebrew | *Richard Elliott Friedman* | 281

17. H. H. Rowley's *Aramaic of the Old Testament* after (Almost) a Century | *Lester L. Grabbe* | 294

18. Visual Grammar: An Eye-Tracking Perspective on Cognitive Complexity in Biblical Hebrew Pronunciation | *Cynthia L. Miller-Naudé, Jacobus A. Naudé, Tanya Beelders, and Luna Bergh* | 316

19. Syntactic-Stylistic Aspects of the So-Called 'Priestly' Work in the Torah | *Frank H. Polak* | 345

20. שֶׁמֶן תּוּרַק *šemen tūraq* (Song 1:3) | *Gary A. Rendsburg and Ian Young* | 383

21. On the Tolerative/Permissive *Hiph'il* | *Jeffrey H. Tigay* | 397

Index of Scholars Cited | 415

Index of Biblical Passages | 424

List of Figures and Tables

Figures

Faust

1 Location Map of Tel 'Eton
2 Excavation Areas at Tel 'Eton
3 The Assyrian Destruction Layer in Room 101C, Area A
4 The Assyrian Destruction Layer in Area B (Square S48)
5 Area A—up-to-date plan of the excavations, reflecting the current state of the area
6 Part of the 8th-Century Ceramic Assemblage

Fine

1 Spoils of Jerusalem relief, Arch of Titus
2 Menorah base of the Arch of Titus Menorah relief
3 Drawing of the Menorah from Adriaan Reland, *De spoliis templi Hierosolymitani*, 1716
4 Mosaic Pavement from Maon (Nirim), 6th-century
5 Raphael, The Expulsion of Heliodorus from the Temple, 1512, Vatican Museums
6 Fountain from the Jewish ghetto of Rome, 1614

Kletter

1 Dan, Ussishkin House: archaeological exhibition
2 Letter by Amiran on museums, September 1948, GL44872/4

3 Memorandum by Kahane, November 1951, GL44872/4
4 The remains of the Gevim archaeological collection
5 Form for Registering Museum finds, October 1948, GL44872/4
6 Chana Benyamini in the archaeological exhibition of underwater finds

Schniedewind

1 Map by Amy Karoll based on data publically available

Lewis

1 A warrior deity piercing a seven-headed dragon from Tell Asmar
2 A god cuts the throat of another god

Miller-Naudé et al.

1 Gaze plot for English reader reading (a) English and (b) Hebrew passages
2 Gaze plot for Afrikaans readers reading (a) Afrikaans and (b) Hebrew passages
3 Gaze plot for Sesotho reader reading (a) Sesotho and (b) Hebrew passages

Tables

Schniedewind

1 Phoenician Scripts

Fox

1 Psalms
2 Job
3 Proverbs

Miller-Naudé et al.

1 Participants in the eye-tracking study
2 Fixations in home language and in Biblical Hebrew

Polak

1 P-Narrative (IES)
2 P-Narrative (VoLB
3 Lev 18–26; 27: The Voiced, Lean, Brisk Style
4 Lev 17; 22–26; Num 15: The Intricate Style
5 Lev 11–15 - VoLB and IES
6 The Cultic Precepts
7 The *Miškan*

List of Contributors

Tanya R. Beelders, Senior Lecturer, Computer Science and Informatics, University of the Free State, Bloemfontein, South Africa

Luna Bergh, Lecturer, University of the Free State Business School, Bloemfontein, South Africa

Adele Berlin, Robert H. Smith Professor of Bible Emerita, University of Maryland, College Park, MD, U.S.A.

William G. Dever, Distinguished Visiting Professor, Lycoming College, Williamsport, PA, U.S.A.; and Professor Emeritus of Judaic Studies and Near Eastern Studies, University of Arizona, Tucson, AZ, U.S.A.

Steven E. Fassberg, Caspar Levias Chair in Ancient Semitic Languages, The Hebrew University of Jerusalem, Israel

Avraham Faust, Professor of Archaeology, The Institute of Archaeology, The Martin (Szusz) Department of Land of Israel Studies and Archaeology, Bar-Ilan University, Ramat-Gan, Israel

Steven Fine, Dean Pinkhos Churgin Professor of Jewish History, Yeshiva University, New York, NY, U.S.A.

Michael V. Fox, Halls-Bascom Professor of Hebrew Emeritus, University of Wisconsin, Madison, WI, U.S.A.

Richard Elliott Friedman, Ann & Jay Davis Professor of Jewish Studies, University of Georgia, Athens, GA, U.S.A.; and Katzin Professor of Jewish Civilization Emeritus, University of California at San Diego, San Diego, CA, U.S.A.

List of Contributors

Zev Garber, Professor Emeritus and Chair of Jewish Studies and Philosophy, Los Angeles Valley College, Valley Glen, CA, U.S.A.

Seymour Gitin, Dorot Director and Professor of Archaeology, Emeritus, W. F. Albright Institute of Archaeological Research, Jerusalem, Israel.

Lester L. Grabbe, Professor Emeritus of Hebrew Bible and Early Judaism, University of Hull, Hull, England, U.K.

Frederick E. Greenspahn, Gimelstob Eminent Scholar of Judaic Studies, Florida Atlantic University, Boca Raton, FL, U.S.A.

Raz Kletter, Docent for Near-Eastern Archaeology, University of Helsinki, Helsinki, Finland

Theodore J. Lewis, Blum-Iwry Professor of Near Eastern Studies, Johns Hopkins University, Baltimore, MD, U.S.A.

Carol Meyers, Mary Grace Wilson Professor Emerita of Religious Studies, Duke University, Durham, NC, U.S.A.

Cynthia L. Miller-Naudé, Senior Professor, Department of Hebrew, University of the Free State, Bloemfontein, South Africa

Jacobus A. Naudé, Senior Professor, Department of Hebrew, University of the Free State, Bloemfontein, South Africa

Shalom M. Paul, Yehezkel Kaufman Professor Emeritus of Biblical Studies, Hebrew University of Jerusalem, Israel

Frank H. Polak, Professor Emeritus of Bible, Department of Bible, Tel-Aviv University, Ramat-Aviv, Israel

Gary A. Rendsburg, Blanche and Irving Laurie Professor of Jewish History, Rutgers University, New Brunswick, NJ, U.S.A.

William M. Schniedewind, Kershaw Chair of Ancient Eastern Mediterranean Studies, University of California at Los Angeles, Los Angeles, CA, U.S.A.

Jeffrey H. Tigay, Emeritus Ellis Professor of Hebrew and Semitic Languages and Literatures, University of Pennsylvania, Philadelphia, PA, U.S.A.

Karel van der Toorn, Professor of Religion and Society, University of Amsterdam, Netherlands

Ian Young, Associate Professor, Department of Hebrew, Biblical and Jewish Studies, University of Sydney, Sydney, N.S.W., Australia

Bruce Zuckerman, Professor of Religion and Linguistics, University of Southern California, Los Angeles, CA, U.S.A.

Acknowledgments

The editors would like to thank their respective endowed chairs, which continue to support their research, writing, and editing on an ongoing basis. Rendsburg, accordingly, expresses his gratitude to the Blanche and Irving Laurie Chair of Jewish History at Rutgers University; while Greenspahn does likewise to the Gimelstob Eminent Scholar Chair of Judaic Studies at Florida Atlantic University.

Charles Loder, a graduate student at Rutgers University, was exceedingly helpful in preparing the final manuscript, assuring all manner of accuracy and consistency in the present volume. The editors are greatly indebted to Charles for all his excellent work and wish to extend to him a heartfelt תודה רבה—even if those two simple words do not begin to capture our deep appreciation for all that he has done.

We also thank American Jewish University, the home institition of our honoree, for a subvention which helped defray some of the production costs.

Finally, it has been a pleasure to work with K. C. Hanson and the excellent staff at Wipf and Stock, with their clear commitment to producing first-rate scholarly publications.

Bibliographic Abbreviations

AB	Anchor Bible
ABD	*Anchor Bible Dictionary*
AJA	*American Journal of Archaeology*
AJS	Association for Jewish Studies
ANESSup	Ancient Near Eastern Studies Supplement Series
ANET	James B. Pritchard, ed. *Ancient Near Eastern Texts Relating to the Old Testament.* 3rd ed. Princeton: Princeton University Press, 1969
AOAT	Alter Orient und Altes Testament
ARAB	Daniel David Luckenbill. *Ancient Records of Assyria and Babylonia.* 2 vols. Chicago: University of Chicago Press, 1926–27
ARM	Archives Royales de Mari
ARMT	Archives Royales de Mari, transcrite et traduite
ASOR	American Schools of Oriental Research
BA	*Biblical Archaeologist*
BAR	*Biblical Archaeology Review*
BASOR	*Bulletin of the American Schools of Oriental Research*
BDB	Francis Brown, S. R. Driver, and Charles A. Briggs, *Hebrew and English Lexicon of the Old Testament.* Oxford: Clarendon, 1907
BO	*Bibliotheca Orientalis*
BZAW	Beihefte zur Zeitschrift für die alttestamentliche Wissenschaft
CAD	A. Leo Oppenheim, Erica Reiner, Martha T. Roth, et al. *The Assyrian Dictionary of the Oriental Institute of the University of Chicago.* 21 vols. Chicago: University of Chicago, 1956–2006

CAL	*Comprehensive Aramaic Lexicon*, online at: http://cal1.cn.huc.edu/
CAT	Oswald Loretz and Joaquín Sanmartín. *The Cuneiform Alphabetic Texts from Ugarit, Ras Ibn Hani and Other Places / Die keilalphabetischen Texte aus Ugarit, Ras Ibn Hani und anderen Orten*. 3rd ed. Alter Orient und Altes Testament 360/1. Münster: Ugarit-Verlag, 2013
CBQ	*Catholic Biblical Quarterly*
CDA	Jeremy Black, Andrew George, and Nicholas Postgate, eds. *A Concise Dictionary of Akkadian*. 2nd corrected printing. Wiesbaden: Harrassowitz, 2000
CT	*Cuneiform Texts from Babylonian Tablets in the British Museum*
DCH	David J. A. Clines. *Dictionary of Classical Hebrew*. 8 vols. Sheffield: Sheffield Phoenix, 1993–2011
DDD^2	Karel van der Toorn, Bob Becking, and Pieter Willem van der Horst, eds. *Dictionary of Deities and Demons in the Bible*. 2nd ed. Leiden: Brill, 1999
DJBA	Michael Sokoloff. *A Dictionary of Jewish Babylonian Aramaic of the Talmudic and Geonic Periods*. Ramat-Gan: Bar-Ilan University Press / Baltimore: Johns Hopkins University Press, 2002
DJD	Discoveries in the Judaean Desert
DNWSI	J. Hoftijzer and K. Jongeling. *Dictionary of North-West Semitic Inscriptions*. 2 vols. Handbuch der Orientalistik 1.21. Leiden: Brill, 1995
DULAT	Gregorio del Olmo Lete and Joaquín Sanmartín. *A Dictionary of the Ugaritic Language in the Alphabetic Tradition*. 2 vols. Translated by W. G. E. Watson. Handbuch der Orientalistik 1.67. Leiden: Brill, 2003
EHLL	Geoffrey Khan, ed. *Encyclopedia of Hebrew Language and Linguistics*. 4 vols. Leiden: Brill, 2013
EncJud	*Encyclopaedia Judaica*
ET	English Translation
FAT	Forschungen zum Alten Testament

GAG	Wolfram von Soden. *Grundriss der Akkadischen Grammatik*. Analecta Orientalia 33. Rome: Pontificium Institutum Biblicum, 1952
GKC	*Gesenius' Hebrew Grammar*. Edited by Emil Kautzsch. Translated by A. E. Cowley
GLECS	*Comptes rendus du Groupe Linguistique d'études Chamito-Sémitiques*
HAR	*Hebrew Annual Review*
HdO	*Handbuch der Orientalistik*
HUCA	*Hebrew Union College Annual*
HS	*Hebrew Studies*
IEJ	*Israel Exploration Journal*
JANES	*Journal of the Ancient Near Eastern Society*
JANER	*Journal of Ancient Near Eastern Religions*
JAOS	*Journal of the American Oriental Society*
JBL	*Journal of Biblical Literature*
JCS	*Journal of Cuneiform Studies*
JHS	*Journal of Hebrew Scriptures*
JNES	*Journal of Near Eastern Studies*
JNSL	*Journal of Northwest Semitic Languages*
JQR	*Jewish Quarterly Review*
JSNT	*Journal for the Study of the New Testament*
JSOT	*Journal for the Study of the Old Testament*
JSOTSup	Journal for the Study of the Old Testament Supplement Series
JSS	*Journal of Semitic Studies*
JSSEA	*Journal of the Society for the Study of Egyptian Antiquities*
JTS	*Journal of Theological Studies*
KAI	Herbert Donner and Wolfgang Röllig. *Kanaanäische und aramäische Inschriften*. 3 vols. Wiesbaden: Harrassowitz, 1962–1964
KTU	see CAT
LCL	Loeb Classical Library

MGWJ	*Monatsschrift für die Geschichte und Wissenschaft des Judenthums*
NAPH	National Association of Professors of Hebrew
NEA	*Near Eastern Archaeology*
NEAEHL	Ephraim Stern, ed. *The New Encyclopedia of Archaeological Excavations in the Holy Land.* 5 vols. Jerusalem: Israel Exploration Society, 1993 [vols. 1–4], 2008 [vol. 5].
NETS	Albert Pietersma and Benjamin G. Wright, eds. *A New English Translation of the Septuagint.* New York: Oxford University Press, 2007
OED	*Oxford English Dictionary*
PEQ	*Palestine Exploration Quarterly*
PL	*Patrologia Latina*
RB	*Revue biblique*
RBL	*Review of Biblical Literature*
SBL	Society of Biblical Literature
SBLWAW	Society of Biblical Literature Writings from the Ancient World
SJOT	*Scandinavian Journal of the Old Testament*
TAD	Bezalel Porten and Ada Yardeni. *Textbook of Aramaic Documents from Ancient Egypt.* 4 vols. Jerusalem: Department of the History of the Jewish People, Hebrew University, 1986–1999
TDOT	*Theological Dictionary of the Old Testament.* Edited by G. Johannes Botterweck, Helmer Ringgren, and Heinz-Josef Fabry. Translated by John T. Willis et al. 15 vols. Grand Rapids: Eerdmans, 1974–2015
UF	*Ugarit-Forschungen*
VT	*Vetus Testamentum*
VTSup	Supplements to Vetus Testamentum
ZAH	*Zeitschrift für Althebräistik*
ZAW	*Zeitschrift für die alttestamentliche Wissenschaft*
ZDMG	*Zeitschrift der deutschen morgenländischen Gesellschaft*
ZDPV	*Zeitschrift des deutschen Palästina-Vereins*

Abbreviations of Ancient Sources

'Abod. Zar.	'Abodah Zarah
'Abot	'Abot
b.	Babylonian Talmud
B. Bat.	Baba Batra
B. Qam.	Baba Qamma
Ber.	Berakot
'Erub.	'Erubin
Gen. Rab.	Genesis Rabbah
Giṭ.	Giṭṭin
Ḥag.	Ḥagigah
Jas	James
Jub.	Jubilees
Kallah Rab.	Kallah Rabbati
Ketub.	Ketubbot
LE	Laws of Eshnunna
LXX	Septuagint
m.	Mishnah
Matt	Matthew
Meg.	Megillah
Me'il.	Me'ilah
Menaḥ.	Menaḥot
MT	Masoretic Text
Naz.	Nazir
Nid.	Niddah
P.	Papyrus

Q	Qumran text
Šabb.	Šabbat
Sanh.	Sanhedrin
Sir	Ben Sira / Sirach
t.	Tosefta
Taʿan.	Taʿannit
y.	Jerusalem Talmud
Yebam.	Yebamot
Yoma	Yoma

Introduction

Ziony Zevit: A Scholar of Breadth and Depth

In an age of ever-increasing specialization, Ziony Zevit has swum against the tide with a breadth and depth to his scholarship not typically encountered nowadays. He is that rare scholar who is expert in both the written word and the archaeological artifact. In the former realm, he is able to analyze with fine linguistic skill both the biblical text and ancient Hebrew epigraphs. In the latter realm, he brings new insights to both mundane objects and those which served a cultic or religious function. One thinks of the great synthesizers of the past such as W. F. Albright, Yigael Yadin, and Anson Rainey in such vein—and yet here is a contemporary scholar who carries on that glorious tradition.

Ziony Zevit was born in 1942 in Winnipeg, Manitoba, Canada, to a family devoted to both traditional Jewish life and liberal education. Our honoree's parents could not have realized the prescient nature of their naming their oldest child Ziony, for the city of Jerusalem was to play a major part in his life for decades to come, עד היום הזה.

The Zevit family actually moved back-and-forth between Winnipeg and Los Angeles during Ziony's grade-school years, but his virtually unbroken connection to the latter city began in earnest in 1959. Did he know then that his enrollment as an undergraduate student at the University of Southern California would commence a 57-year (and counting!) association with the city? Ziony received his B.A. in Religion from the University of Southern California in 1964, though this represented only the start of his studies at leading academic centers.

While an undergraduate at USC, Ziony took a year off to study in Jerusalem at both the Hayim Greenberg Teachers Institute and the Hebrew University. His teachers that year included David Flusser, Moshe Greenberg, Menaham Haran, and Yigael Yadin. Thus began a long and fruitful association with the Hebrew University, to which Ziony would return again and again, once more עד היום הזה.

Back in Los Angeles, and immediately upon receiving his B.A., Ziony began his graduate studies at the University of California at Los Angeles (UCLA), with his primary teachers being Jonas Greenfield and Wolf Leslau. One year later, when Jonas[1] left UCLA for the University of California at Berkeley, he arranged for Ziony to transfer his fellowship and continue his studies at Berkeley. Among his other teachers at Berkeley were Jacob Milgrom, Ariel Bloch, Anne Drafkorn Kilmer, and Joshua Blau (visiting from the Hebrew University), along with Victor Gold, James Muilenberg, and David Noel Freedman, all of whom were associated with the Graduate Theological Union at the time. Ziony emerged from these studies with his M.A. in 1967 and his Ph.D. in 1973.

During the years of his graduate study, Ziony also spent two summers in Ann Arbor, one at the Summer Institute for Near Eastern Languages (1965), where he studied Arabic, and one at the Summer Institute of Linguistics (1967), where he studied with Charles Hockett and Gene Schramm.

More importantly, however, were his two academic years (1968–1969 and 1970–1971) at the Hebrew University in Jerusalem, where once more he studied with Haran, along with a host of other great scholars of those years, including E. Y. Kutscher, Samuel Loewenstamm, Chaim Rabin, Shemaryahu Talmon, and Meir Weiss.

As we reflect back on Ziony's career, research interests, and emerging publications, one sees the influence of so many of his primary professors mentioned here: Greenfield in philology; Blau, Rabin, and Kutscher in language; Milgrom in priestly matters; Haran and Greenberg in Israelite religion; Yadin in archaeology; and so on.

On a personal level, we note that Ziony met his wife-to-be, Rachel Elkarat, in 1962, during his undergraduate year at the Hebrew University, and that the two then married in 1966. Three children followed, Zehava, Noam, and Yonatan; and ten grandchildren in their wake. The entire Zevit progeny lives in Israel, and thus Ziony and Rachel spend as much time as possible (summers, sabbaticals, etc.) in the country that they know so well and love so much.

Back to academics: given his strong training both at Berkeley and in Jerusalem, and given the talent evident already at an early stage in his career (note that he published his first two articles in 1968 and 1969), it was no surprise that Ziony landed his first professorial position shortly

---

1. He will forever be "Jonas" to everyone; "Greenfield" somehow does not ring properly.

after graduating from Berkeley with the Ph.D.[2] First, and only, that is! For in 1974, Ziony began teaching at the University of Judaism, renamed the American Jewish University in 2007, where he rose through the ranks from assistant professor to his current title as Distinguished Professor of Biblical Literature and Northwest Semitic Languages and Literatures. In this position, Ziony has introduced several generations of rabbis and educators to modern biblical studies, teaching them how to read the text, how to understand its language, and how to interpret it against the cultural background of the ancient Near East.

Over the years Ziony has held prestigious visiting positions at a host of academic institutions: Hebrew University, Pontifical Biblical Institute, W. F. Albright Institute of Archaeological Research, the Center for Advanced Judaic Studies at the University of Pennsylvania, and the Bellagio Center of the Rockefeller Foundation. The two places to which he has returned again and again are those located in Jerusalem: the Hebrew University and the Albright Institute. Here he developed close ties not only with the local scholars, but also with many visiting scholars whose appointments at the two institutions overlapped with Ziony's.

Given his location in Los Angeles, colleagues in the area have turned to Ziony to serve as visiting or adjunct professor throughout his career. Thus, he has also taught at the University of California at Los Angeles, the University of California at San Diego (UCSD), Hebrew Union College (Los Angeles), California State University at Northridge, the Claremont Graduate School, and his alma mater the University of Southern California.

Ziony's collegial nature is further witnessed by his active involvement in a variety of scholarly associations, though none more so than the National Association of Professors of Hebrew (NAPH). Through the years, Ziony has served as President (2009–2011), Vice-President (2007–2009), on the Executive Board (2011–2016), and on the Executive Council (1998–2011)—plus he served as Editor-in-Chief of its journal, *Hebrew Studies*, for eight years (1998–2005), during which time the annual publication expanded its size, breadth, and coverage remarkably.

As if this were not enough involvement, just as his tenure as Editor-in-Chief was coming to an end, Ziony organized two panels at NAPH meetings (held in conjunction with the Society of Biblical Literature) devoted to the question "Can Biblical Texts Be Dated Linguistically?" (2004, 2005), the results of which were then published in *Hebrew Studies*, volumes 46 (2005) and 47 (2006), under Ziony's special editorship. Most significantly, whereas

---

2. First, fulltime, tenure-track position, that is, since Ziony taught as a lecturer both at the University of Haifa and at the University of the Negev (before its name change to Ben-Gurion University) during the years 1971–1974.

most scholars on different sides of this crucial issue within biblical studies were simply talking past each other, Ziony brought them together to serve on the panels in order to engage in real dialogue. Such is the make of the man.

At the outset we referred to Ziony's breadth and depth. As we survey his career, we are able to identify three distinct areas to which he has made lasting contributions. These are: a) Hebrew language; b) Bible *per se*; and c) the history and archaeology of ancient Israel, with a special emphasis on religious life. Consider, for example, his two monographs, *Matres Lectionis in Ancient Hebrew Epigraphs* (1980) and *The Anterior Construction in Classical Hebrew* (1998), which belong to the first subject area; his most recent book *What Really Happened in the Garden of Eden?* (2013), with a focus on a well-known and important narrative in the book of Genesis; and his *magnum opus*, *The Religions of Ancient Israel: A Synthesis of Parallactic Approaches* (2001), replete with 135 images (yes, we counted) presenting archaeological material relevant to the subject.

Alongside these books are numerous articles which surely will be read for decades to come, including "The So-Called Interchangeability of the Prepositions *b*, *l*, and *m(n)* in Northwest Semitic"; "Converging Lines of Evidence Bearing on the Date of P"; "A Chapter in the History of Israelite Personal Names"; "The Common Origin of the Aramaicized Prayer to Horus and of Psalm 20"; "Roman Jakobson, Psycholinguistics, and Biblical Poetry"; "Philology, Archaeology, and a *terminus a quo* for P's *ḥaṭṭaʾt* Legislation"; and many more—along with his "Introduction and Annotations to the Books of Kings," contributed to *The Jewish Study Bible* (2003/2014). If we highlight these specific essays, it is because the editors have continued to return to these writings in their own research, and/or have assigned them to students throughout the years.

The contributions to and the organization of this *Festschrift* reflect the honoree's breadth and depth. We have divided the individual contributions into three areas, aligned with the aforementioned purviews of Ziony's research interests—see further the Table of Contents and of course the essays themselves. The international scope of the present volume, corresponding to the international reputation of our jubilarian, is indicated by the fact that the contributors come from five continents.

All who have participated in this volume honor Ziony Zevit greatly as both friend and colleague, as we wish him many more years of productive teaching, editing, research, and writing.

Gary A. Rendsburg and Frederick E. Greenspahn

Publications of Ziony Zevit

DISSERTATION

1. *Studies in Biblical Poetry and Vocabulary in Their Northwest Semitic Setting* (University of California at Berkeley, 1973)—supervised by Jonas C. Greenfield (chair), Joshua Blau, and Ariel Bloch.

BOOKS AUTHORED

1. *Matres Lectionis in Ancient Hebrew Epigraphs.* ASOR Monograph Series 2. Cambridge, MA: American Schools of Oriental Research, 1980.

2. *The Anterior Construction in Classical Hebrew.* SBL Monograph Series 50. Atlanta: Scholars, 1998.

3. *The Religions of Ancient Israel: A Synthesis of Parallactic Approaches.* London: Continuum, 2001.

4. *What Really Happened in the Garden of Eden?* New Haven: Yale University Press, 2013.

BOOKS EDITED

1. *Solving Riddles and Untying Knots: Biblical, Epigraphic, and Semitic Studies Presented to Jonas C. Greenfield*, co-edited with Seymour Gitin and Michael Sokoloff. Winona Lake, IN: Eisenbrauns, 1995.

2. *The Jewish Bible: A JPS Guide*, co-edited with Shalom M. Paul and Frederick E. Greenspahn. Philadelphia: Jewish Publication Society, 2008.

3. *Diachrony in Biblical Hebrew*, co-edited with Cynthia Miller-Naudé. Winona Lake, IN: Eisenbrauns, 2012.

4. *Subtle Citation, Allusion, and Translation in the Hebrew Bible*. London: Equinox, 2017.

ARTICLES

1. "The Structure and Individual Elements of Daniel 7." *ZAW* 80 (1968) 385–96.

2. "The Use of '*ebed* as a Diplomatic Term in Jeremiah." *JBL* 88 (1969) 74–77.

3. "A Misunderstanding at Bethel—Amos VII, 12–17." *VT* 25 (1975) 783–90.

4. "The So-Called Interchangeability of the Prepositions *b*, *l*, and *m (n)* in Northwest Semitic." *JANES* 7 (1975) 103–12.

5. "The '*Eglah* Ritual of Deut 21:1–9." *JBL* 95 (1976) 377–90.

6. "The Priestly Redaction and Interpretation of the Plague Narrative in Exodus." *JQR* 66 (1976) 193–211.

7. "A Phoenician Inscription and Biblical Covenant Theology." *IEJ* 27 (1977) 110–18.

8. "The Linguistic and Contextual Arguments in Support of a Hebrew 3 m.s. Suffix –*y*." *UF* 9 (1977) 315–28.

9. "The Exegetical Implications of Dan VIII, 1; IX, 21." *VT* 28 (1978) 488–92.

10. "Expressing Denial in Biblical and Mishnaic Hebrew and in Amos." *VT* 29 (1979) 505–9.

11. "The Ten Plagues: A Biblical Midrash." *Proceedings of the Rabbinical Assembly* 41 (1979) 181–85.

12. "Two Hapax Legomena in Ugaritic: *tʿlgt* and *pš*." *UF* 13 (1981) 194–97.

13. "Converging Lines of Evidence Bearing on the Date of P." *ZAW* 94 (1982) 481–511.

14. "A Chapter in the History of Israelite Personal Names." *BASOR* 250 (1983) 1–16.

15. "Archaeological and Literary Stratigraphy in Joshua 7–8." *BASOR* 251 (1983) 23–35.
16. "Nondistinctive Stress, Syllabic Constraints, and *Wortmetrik* in Ugaritic Poetry." *UF* 15 (1983) 291–98.
17. "A Supplementary Note on Ugaritic '*lg*.'" *UF* 15 (1983) 319.
18. "The Question of Case Endings on Ugaritic Nouns in *Status Constructus*." *JSS* 28 (1983) 225–32.
19. "The Khirbet el-Qom Inscription Mentioning a Goddess." *BASOR* 255 (1984) 39–47.
20. "The Problem of Ai." *BAR* 11/2 (1985) 58–69.
21. "Deuteronomistic Historiography in I Ki 12–II Ki 17 and the Reinvestiture of the Israelite Cult." *JSOT* 32 (1985) 57–73.
22. "Clio, I Presume." *BASOR* 260 (1985) 71–82.
23. "Psalms at the Poetic Precipice." *HAR* 10 (1986) 351–66.
24. "Underground Religion." *American Schools of Oriental Research Newsletter* 39 (1988) 2–4.
25. "Onomastic Gleanings from Recently Published Judahite Bullae." *IEJ* 38 (1988) 227–34.
26. "Talking Funny in Biblical Henglish and Solving a Problem of the YAQTUL Past Tense." *HS* 29 (1988) 25–31.
27. "Phoenician *nbš/npš* and Its Hebrew Semantic Equivalents." In *Sopher Mahir: Northwest Semitic Studies Presented to Stanislav Segert*, edited by Edward M. Cook, 337–44 = *Maarav* 5–6 (1990) 337–44.
28. "The Common Origin of the Aramaicized Prayer to Horus and of Psalm 20." *JAOS* 110 (1990) 213–28.
29. "Roman Jakobson, Psycholinguistics, and Biblical Poetry." *JBL* 109 (1990) 385–401.
30. "Three Ways to Look at the Ten Plagues." *BR* 6/3 (1990) 16–23, 42. [See also no. 84 below.]
31. "Yahweh and Yahweh Worshippers in 8th-Century Syria." *VT* 41 (1991) 363–66.
32. "How Do You Say 'Noble' in Phoenician, Biblical Hebrew, and Ugaritic?" In *Semitic Studies in Honor of Wolf Leslau on the Occasion of His 85th Birthday*, edited by Alan S. Kaye, 1704–15. Wiesbaden: Harrassowitz, 1991.

33. "Timber for the Tabernacle: Text, Tradition, and *Realia*." In *Eretz Israel 23: The Avraham Biran Volume*, edited by Ephraim Stern and Thomas E. Levy, 136–43. Jerusalem: Israel Exploration Society, 1992.

34. "Cognitive Theory and the Memorability of Biblical Poetry." In *Let Your Colleagues Praise You: Studies in Memory of Stanley Gevirtz*, edited by Robert J. Ratner, et al., 199–212 = *Maarav* 8/2 (1992) 199–212.

35. "Two Inscribed Punic Seals from the J. Paul Getty Museum." *Studi Epigrafici e Linguistici* 10 (1993) 85–91. [See also below, Miscellaneous, no. 3.]

36. "Philology, Archaeology, and a *terminus a quo* for P's *ḥaṭṭā't* Legislation." In *Pomegranates and Golden Bells: Studies in Biblical, Jewish, and Near Eastern Ritual, Law, and Literature in Honor of Jacob Milgrom*, edited by David P. Wright, David N. Freedman, and Avi Hurvitz, 29–39. Winona Lake, IN: Eisenbrauns, 1995.

37. "In Memoriam—Jonas C. Greenfield." *BASOR* 298 (1995) 3–5.

38. "Report—Religions of Ancient Israel: A Synthesis of Parallactic Approaches." *BASOR* 298 (1995) 74.

39. "Jonas C. Greenfield: An Appreciation" (in Hebrew). In *Le-Zikro šel Ḥayyim Yonah Greenfield: Devarim še-Ne'emeru bi-Mle'ot Šelošim le-Moto*, 25–30. Jerusalem: Israel Academy of the Sciences and Humanities, 1996.

40. "The Earthen Altar Laws of Exod 20:24-26 and Related Sacrificial Restrictions in their Cultural Context." In *Texts, Temples, and Traditions, A Tribute to Menahem Haran*, edited by Michael V. Fox, et al., 53–62. Winona Lake, IN: Eisenbrauns, 1996.

41. "Greenfield, Jonas Carl." In *The Oxford Encyclopedia of Archaeology in the Near East*, edited by Eric M. Meyers, 2:440–41. New York: Oxford University Press, 1997.

42. "Ha-'Etos ha-Yiśra'eli še-bo Ṣamaḥ Sefer Devarim" ("The Israelite Ethos in which Deuteronomy Developed" [in Hebrew]). *Shnaton: An Annual for Biblical and Ancient Near Eastern Studies* 11 (5757 / 1997) 103–13.

43. "The Gerizim-Samarian Community in and between Texts and Times: An Experimental Study." In *The Quest for Context and Meaning: Studies in Biblical Intertextuality in Honor of James A. Sanders*, edited by Craig A. Evans and Shemaryahu Talmon, 547–72. Biblical Interpretation Series 28. Leiden: Brill, 1997.

44. "Proclamations to the Fruitful Tree and the Spiritualization of Androgyny." In *The Echoes of Many Texts: Reflections on Jewish and Christian Traditions: Essays in Honor of Lou H. Silberman*, edited by William G. Dever and J. Edward Wright, 43–50. Brown Judaica Studies 313. Atlanta: Scholars, 1997.

45. "Discussion." In *Mediterranean Peoples in Transition: Thirteenth to Early Tenth Centuries BCE*, edited by Seymour Gitin, et al., 265–66. Jerusalem: Israel Exploration Society, 1998.

46. "The Second-Third Century Canonization of the Hebrew Bible and Its Influence on Christian Canonizing." In *Canonization and Decanonization: Papers Presented to the International Conference of the Leiden Institute for the Study of Religions (LISOR), held at Leiden 9–10 January 1997*, edited by Arie van der Kooij and Karel van der Toorn, 133–60. Leiden: Brill, 1998.

47. "Congenital Human Baculum Deficiency: The Generative Bone of Genesis 2:21-23." *American Journal of Medical Genetics* 101:3 (2001) 284–85 [co-authored with Scott F. Gilbert]—republished in *Cabinet: A Quarterly of Art and Culture* 28 (January 2008) 76–77.

48. "Philology and Archaeology: Imagining New Questions, Begetting New Ideas." In *Sacred Time, Sacred Space: Archaeology and the Religion of Israel*, edited by Barry M. Gittlin, 35–42. Winona Lake, IN: Eisenbrauns, 2002.

49. "Preamble to a Temple Tour." In *Sacred Time, Sacred Space: Archaeology and the Religion of Israel*, edited by Barry M. Gittlin, 73–81. Winona Lake, IN: Eisenbrauns, 2002.

50. "Three Debates about the Bible and Archaeology." *Biblica* 83 (2002) 1–27.

51. "Anatomy of An Impending Divorce." *AJS Perspectives* (Fall/Winter 2002) 5–8.

52. "False Dichotomies in Descriptions of Israelite Religion: A Problem, Its Origin, and A Proposed Solution." In *Symbiosis, Symbolism and the Power of the Past: Canaan, Ancient Israel, and their Neighbors from the Late Bronze Age through Roman Palaestina*, edited by William G. Dever and Seymour Gitin, 223–35. Winona Lake, IN: Eisenbrauns, 2003.

53. "Introduction and Annotations to the Books of Kings." *The Jewish Study Bible*, edited by Adele Berlin and Marc Z. Brettler, 668–779. New York: Oxford University Press, 2003. [See also below, no. 83.]

54. "Invisible and Unheard in Translation: How New Discoveries in Hebrew Grammar Affect Our Understanding of Tanakh." *Conservative Judaism* 55/2 (2003) 38–48.

55. "The Biblical Archaeology versus Syro-Palestinian Archaeology Debate in its American Institutional and Intellectual Contexts." In *The Future of Biblical Archaeology: Reassessing Methodologies and Assumptions*, edited by James K. Hoffmeier and Alan R. Millard, 3–19. Grand Rapids: Eerdmans, 2004.

56. "The Prophet versus Priest Antagonism Hypothesis: Its Origins and History." In *The Priests in the Prophets: The Portrayal of Priests, Prophets and Other Religious Specialists in the Latter Prophets*, edited by Lester L. Grabbe and Alice O. Bellis, 189–217. London: T. & T. Clark, 2004.

57. "Introductory Remarks: Historical Linguistics and the Dating of Hebrew Texts ca. 1000–300 BCE." *HS* 46 (2005) 321–26.

58. "Symposium Discussion Session: An Edited Transcription." *HS* 46 (2005) 371–76.

59. "Dating Ruth: Legal, Linguistic and Historical Observations." *ZAW* 117 (2005) 574–600.

60. "Jewish Biblical Theology: What? Whence? Whither?" *HUCA* 76 (2005) 289–340.

61. "Implicit Population Figures and Historical Sense: What Happened to 200,150 Judahites in 701 BCE?" In *Confronting the Past: Archaeological and Historical Essays on Ancient Israel in Honor of William G. Dever*, edited by Seymour Gitin, et al., 357–66. Winona Lake, IN: Eisenbrauns, 2006.

62. "Israel's Royal Cult in the Ancient Near Eastern *Kulturkreis*." In *Text, Artifact and Image: Revealing Ancient Israelite Religion*, edited by Gary M. Beckman and Theodore J. Lewis, 189–200. Brown Judaic Studies 346. Providence: Brown University, 2006.

63. "What A Difference A Year Makes: Can Biblical Texts Be Dated Linguistically?" *HS* 47 (2006) 83–91.

64. "The First Halleluyah." in *Milk and Honey: Essays on Ancient Israel and the Bible in Appreciation of the Judaic Studies Program at the University of California, San Diego*, edited by Sarah Malena and David Miano, 157–64. Winona Lake, IN: Eisenbrauns, 2007.

65. "Scratched Silver and Painted Walls: Can We Date Biblical Texts Archaeologically?" *HS* 48 (2007) 23–37.

66. "Text Traditions, Archaeology, and Anthropology: Uncertainties in Determining the Populations of Judah and Yehud from ca. 734 to ca. 400 BCE." In *"Up to the Gates of Ekron": Essays on the Archaeology and History of the Eastern Mediterranean in Honor of Seymour Gitin*, edited by Seymour Gitin, et al., 436–43. Jerusalem: W. F. Albright Institute of Archaeological Research and Israel Exploration Society, 2007.

67. "The Search for Violence in Israelite Culture and in the Bible." In *Religion and Violence: The Biblical Heritage*, edited by David A. Bernat and Jonathan Klawans, 16–37. Recent Research in Biblical Studies 2. Sheffield: Sheffield Phoenix Press, 2007.

68. "From Judaism to Biblical Religion and Back Again." In *The Hebrew Bible: New Insights and Scholarship*, edited by Frederick E. Greenspahn, 164–90. New York: New York University Press, 2008.

69. "The Davidic-Solomonic Empire from the Perspective of Archaeological Bibliology." In *Birkat Shalom: Studies in the Bible, Ancient Near Eastern Literature, and Postbiblical Judaism Presented to Shalom M. Paul on the Occasion of His Seventieth Birthday*, edited by Chaim Cohen, et al., 201–24. Winona Lake, IN: Eisenbrauns, 2008.

70. "Deuteronomy in the Temple: An Exercise in Historical Imagining." In *Mishneh Todah: Studies in Deuteronomy and Its Cultural Environment in Honor of Jeffrey H. Tigay*, edited by Nili S. Fox, et al., 201–18. Winona Lake, IN: Eisenbrauns, 2009.

71. "The Two-Bodied People, Their Cosmos, and The Origin of the Soul." In *Maven in Blue Jeans: A Festschrift in Honor of Zev Garber*, edited by Steven L. Jacobs, 465–75. West Lafayette, IN: Purdue University Press, 2009.

72. "Is There an Archaeological Case for Phantom Cities in the Persian Period?" *PEQ* 141 (2009) 124–37.

73. "Jesus, God of the Hebrew Bible." *Shofar* 28/3 (2010) 14–32.

74. "What's New About What's Old?" *Iggeret: Newsletter of the National Association of Professors of Hebrew* 82 (Fall 2010) 1–4.

75. "Jesus Stories, Jewish Liturgy and Some Evolving Theologies Until ca. 200 CE: Stimuli and Responses." In *Jesus in the Context of Judaism: Revelation, Reflection, Reclamation*, edited by Zev Garber, 65–92. Shofar Supplements in Jewish Studies Series. West Lafayette, IN: Purdue University Press, 2011.

76. "Syntagms in Biblical Hebrew: Four Short Studies." In *En pase grammatike kai sophia: Saggi di linguistica ebraica in onore di Alviero Niccacci, ofm*, ed. Gregor Geiger and Massimo Pazzini, 393–403. Studium Biblicum Franciscanum, Analecta 78. Jerusalem / Milano: Terra Santa, 2011.

77. "Biblical Histories Yesterday and Tomorrow." *Iggeret: Newsletter of the National Association of Professors of Hebrew* 83 (Fall 2011) 1–4.

78. "Mesha's *ryt* in the Context of Moabite and Israelite Bloodletting." In *Puzzling out the Past: Studies in the Northwest Semitic Languages and Literatures in Honor of Bruce Zuckerman*, edited by Marilyn J. Lundberg, et al., 235–38. Culture and History of the Ancient Near East 55. Leiden: Brill, 2012.

79. "Not-so-random Thoughts About Linguistic Dating and Diachrony in Biblical Hebrew." In *Diachrony in Biblical Hebrew*, edited by Cynthia Miller-Naudé and Ziony Zevit, 453–87. Linguistic Studies in Ancient West Semitic 8. Winona Lake, IN: Eisenbrauns, 2012.

80. "Of What Was Eve Guilty (Gen 3:16)?" In *"Built by Wisdom, Established by Understanding": Essays in Honor of Adele Berlin*, edited by Maxine L. Grossman, 29–38. Studies and Texts in Jewish History and Culture 23. Bethesda, MD: University of Maryland Press, 2013.

81. "The Textual and Social Embeddedness of Israelite Family Religion: Who Were the Players? Where Were the Stages?" In *Family and Household Religion: Toward a Synthesis of Old Testament Studies, Archaeology, Epigraphy, and Cultural Studies*, edited by Rainer Albertz and Rüdiger Schmitt, 287–314. Winona Lake, IN: Eisenbrauns, 2014.

82. "Dating Torah Documents: From Wellhausen to Polak." In *Discourse, Dialogue, and Debate in the Bible: Essays in Honour of Frank H. Polak*, edited by Athalya Brenner-Idan, 258–91. Hebrew Bible Monographs 63. Amsterdam Studies in the Bible and Religion 7. Sheffield: Sheffield Phoenix Press, 2014.

83. "Introduction and Annotations to the Books of Kings." In *The Jewish Study Bible*, 2nd edition, edited by Adele Berlin and Marc Z. Brettler, 653–761. New York: Oxford University Press, 2014. [See also above, no. 53.]

84. "Exodus in the Bible and the Egyptian Plagues." Online at *Bible History Daily*, www.biblicalarchaeology.org/daily/biblical-topics/exodus/exodus-in-the-bible-and-the-egyptian-plagues/. (March 31, 2015). [See also no. 30 above.]

85. "Einführung in das Buch Bereschit / Genesis." In *Die Tora: Die Fünf Bücher Mose und die Prophetenlesungen (hebräisch-deutsche) in der revidierten Übersetzung von Ludwig Philippson*, edited by Walter Homolka, et al., 63–76. Freiburg: Herder, 2015.

86. "Was Eve Made from Adam's Rib—or His Baculum?" *BAR* 41/5 (September/October 2015) 33–35.

87. "Taking the Measure of the Ten Cubit Gap, Isaiah's Vision, and Iron Age Bones." In *Marbeh Ḥokma: Essays in Memory of Victor Avigdor Hurowitz*, edited by Shamir Yona, et al., 631–53. Winona Lake, IN: Eisenbrauns, 2015.

88. "Weber's *Ancient Judaism*: How Well Has It Worn?" In *Weber's Economic Ethics of the World Religions, New Perspectives*, edited by Tom Ertman and Detlef Pollack. Cambridge: Cambridge University Press, forthcoming.

89. "Echoes of Texts Past." In *Subtle Citation, Allusion, and Translation in the Hebrew Bible*, edited by Ziony Zevit. London: Equinox, forthcoming.

90. "Yehezkel Kaufmann: Observations about His Major Ideas in the Past, Almost Present, and the Immediate Future." *Yehezkel Kaufmann and the Reinvention of Jewish Exegesis of the Bible*, edited by Thomas Staubli, Benjamin Sommer, and Job Jindo. Orbis Biblicus et Orientalis. Freiburg: Universitätsverlag Freiburg / Göttingen: Vandenhock & Ruprecht, forthcoming.

REVIEW ESSAY

1. "Timing Is Everything: A Review Essay of *Biblical Hebrew: Studies in Chronology and Typology*, edited by Ian Young. *Review of Biblical Literature* 8 (2004) 1–15. Online at www.bookreviews.org/pdf/4084_3967.pdf.

REVIEWS

1. Richard V. Bergren, *The Prophets and the Law*, in *AJS Newsletter* 16 (1975) 22, 24.

2. Joseph Blenkinsopp, *Gibeon and Israel: The Role of the Gibeonites in the Political and Religious History of Early Israel*, in Hebrew Abstracts 16 (1975) 61–62.

3. James L. Crenshaw, *Prophetic Conflict*, in AJS Newsletter 16 (1975) 22.

4. Judah Goldin, *The Song at the Sea: Being a Commentary on a Commentary in Two Parts*, in Hebrew Abstracts 16 (1975) 59–60.

5. R. N. Whybray, ed., *The Intellectual Tradition in the Old Testament*, in AJS Newsletter 16 (1975) 24.

6. Alexander Rofé, *Introduction to Deuteronomy* (in Hebrew), in JBL 95 (1976) 646–47.

7. Moshe Garsiel, *The Kingdom of David: Studies in History and Inquiries in Historiography* (in Hebrew), in JBL 96 (1977) 116–18.

8. E. Y. Kutscher, *Studies in Galilean Aramaic* in JAOS 98 (1978) 512–13.

9. Douglas A. Knight, ed., *Tradition and Theology in the Old Testament*, in JAOS 99 (1979) 376–78.

10. William H. Irwin, *Isaiah 28–33: Translation with Philological Notes*, in JAOS 99 (1979) 378–79.

11. Menahem Haran, ed., *Eretz Israel 14 (The H. L. Ginsberg Volume)*, in BASOR 249 (1983) 91–92.

12. Robert B. Coote, *Amos among the Prophets: Composition and Theology*, in JBL 102 (1983) 308–10.

13. Dennis Pardee, *Handbook of Ancient Hebrew Letters*, in JQR 74 (1984) 431–33.

14. R. J. Coggins et al., eds., *Israel's Prophetic Tradition: Essays in Honor of Peter Ackroyd*, in HS 25 (1984) 198–99.

15. Frederick E. Greenspahn, *Hapax Legomena in Biblical Hebrew: A Study of the Phenomenon and Its Treatment since Antiquity with Special Reference to Verbal Forms*, in CBQ 47 (1985) 701–3.

16. Adele Berlin, *The Dynamics of Hebrew Parallelism*, in HS 27 (1986) 96–99.

17. Foster R. McCurley, *Ancient Myths and Biblical Faith: Scriptural Transformations*, in BA 49 (1986) 61–62.

18. Brevard S. Childs, *Old Testament Theology in a Canonical Context*, in CBQ 50 (1988) 491–93.

19. William H. Stiebing, Jr., *Out of the Desert? Archaeology and the Exodus/Conquest Narratives*, in *Shofar* 8 (1989) 83–84.

20. Jeaneane D. Fowler, *Theophoric Personal Names in Ancient Hebrew: A Comparative Study*, in *CBQ* 52 (1990) 115–18.

21. Jon D. Levenson, *Creation and the Persistence of Evil: The Jewish Drama of Divine Omnipotence*, in *Journal of Reform Judaism* 37/2 (Spring 1990) 80–82.

22. James Barr, *The Variable Spellings of the Hebrew Bible*, in *JAOS* 111 (1991) 647–50.

23. Gary A. Rendsburg, *Linguistic Evidence for the Northern Origin of Selected Psalms*, in *CBQ* 54 (1992) 126–29.

24. Silvia Schroer, *In Israel gab es Bilder: Nachrichten von darstellender Kunst im Alten Testament*, in *BASOR* 285 (1992) 85–86.

25. Mark S. Smith, *The Early History of God: Yahweh and the Other Deities in Ancient Israel*, in *AJS Review* 17 (1992) 93–97.

26. Graham I. Davies, *Ancient Hebrew Inscriptions: Corpus and Concordance*, in *CBQ* 55 (1993) 753–54.

27. Philip R. Davies, *In Search of "Ancient Israel"*, in *AJS Review* 20 (1995) 153–56.

28. Karel van der Toorn, *Family Religion in Babylonia, Syria and Israel: Continuity and Change in the Forms of Religious Life*, in *JQR* 86 (1996) 519–22.

29. Hans M. Barstad, *The Myth of the Empty Land. A Study in the History and Archaeology of Judah During the "Exilic" Period*, in *BASOR* 308 (1997) 106–8.

30. Simon B. Parker, *Stories in Scripture and Inscriptions: Comparative Studies on Narratives in Northwest Semitic Inscriptions and the Hebrew Bible*, in *BASOR* 312 (1998) 82–84.

31. Robert Chazan, William W. Hallo, and Lawrence H. Schiffman, eds., *Ki Baruch Hu: Ancient Near Eastern, Biblical, and Judaic Studies in Honor of Baruch A. Levine*, in *BASOR* 316 (1999) 118.

32. Sandra L. Gogel, *A Grammar of Epigraphic Hebrew*, in *RBL* (online at www.bookreviews.org/pdf/163_633.pdf, published October 1999), and in *JBL* 120 (2001) 347–48.

33. Avraham Negev and Shimon Gibson, eds., *Archaeological Encyclopedia of the Holy Land*, in *Shofar* 21 (2002) 156–57.

34. Bernhard Lang, *The Hebrew God: Portrait of an Ancient Deity*, in *RBL* (online at www.bookreviews.org/pdf/2835_2785.pdf, published January 2003).

35. Dennis Pardee, *Ritual and Cult at Ugarit*, in *RBL* (online at www.bookreviews.org/pdf/2976_3068.pdf, published May 2003).

36. Meir Malul, *Knowledge, Control and Sex: Studies in Biblical Thought, Culture and Worldview*, in *JAOS* 123 (2003) 671–72.

37. William G. Dever and Seymour Gitin, eds., *Symbiosis, Symbolism, and the Power of the Past: Canaan, Ancient Israel, and Their Neighbors from the Late Bronze Age through Roman Palestina: Proceedings of the Centennial Symposium W. F. Albright Institue of Archaeological Research and the American Schools of Oriental Research Jerusalem, May 29–31, 2000*, in *RBL* (online at http://www.bookreviews.org/pdf/4100_3983.pdf, published July 2004).

38. Ian Young, ed., *Biblical Hebrew: Studies in Chronology and Typology* in *RBL* (online at www.bookreviews.org/pdf/4084_3967.pdf, published August 2004).

39. Ronald Handel, *Remembering Abraham: Culture, Memory and History in the Hebrew Bible*, in *Shofar* 24 (2006) 186–89.

40. Richard C. Steiner, *Stockman from Tekoa, Sycomores from Sheba: A Study of Amos' Occupations*, in *JNES* 66 (2007) 66–68.

41. André Lemaire, *The Birth of Monotheism: The Rise and Disappearance of Yahwism*, in *HS* 49 (2008) 331–33.

42. Deborah O'Daniel Cantrell, *The Horsemen of Israel: Horses and Chariotry in Monarchic Israel (Ninth–Eighth Centuries B.C.E.*, in *BAR* 38/2 (March/April 2012) 62–63.

43. Beate Pongratz-Leisten, ed., *Reconsidering the Concept of Revolutionary Monotheism*, in *BASOR* 369 (2013) 237–40.

MISCELLAENOUS

1. "Response to letter of Jeffrey Chadwick." *BAR* 11/4 (1985) 22–23.
2. "Response to letter of John J. Bimson." *BAR* 11/5 (1985) 79–80.
3. Decipherments of two Punic seals cited in Jeffrey Spier, *Ancient Gems and Finger Rings* (Malibu, CA: J. Paul Getty Museum, 1992), 83 and 119. [See also above, Article no. 35.]

4. "Response to letter of Jean-Daniel Stanley." *BAR* 31/1 (2005) 63.

5. "Before the Beginning: Appreciating the Thought of an Ancient Cosmologist," online at http://thetorah.com/before-the-beginning/ (October 14, 2014).

6. "Seeing God(s) in Temples, the Heavens, and in Model Shrines, A Problem in Ancient Metaphysics." *ASOR Blog*, online at http://asor-blog.org/seeing-gods-in-temples-the-heavens-and-in-model-shrines-a-problem-in-ancient-metaphysics/ (October 1, 2014) = *Albright News* 19 (November 2014) 16.

7. "The Ten Plagues and Egyptian Ecology" (a popular and slightly revised version of Articles nos. 30 and 84 above), online at http://thetorah.com/ten-plagues-and-egyptian-ecology/ (January 15, 2015).

8. "Invoking Creation in the Story of the Ten Plagues," online at http://thetorah.com/invoking-creation-in-the-story-of-the-ten-plagues/ (March 27, 2015).

Part 1: History and Archaeology

1

History from Things: On Writing New Histories of Ancient Israel

William G. Dever

LYCOMING COLLEGE

Introduction

Twenty-five years ago (1991) Max Miller famously asked: "Is it possible to write a history of Israel without relying on the Hebrew Bible?"[1] His answer was that it might be possible; but it would be undesirable. Four years earlier, Miller's own history of Israel, written with John Hayes, had been published, and not unexpectedly it made only scant use of archaeological data. Miller and Hayes' *A History of Ancient Israel and Judah* in its second edition (2006), although in my judgment deficient, is still the standard work in the English-speaking world.

Meanwhile, in the past 25 years *no* new, mainstream history of ancient Israel has been written by *any* scholar anywhere in the world. Provan, Long, and Longman's *A Biblical History of Israel* (2003) is largely uncritical, essentially a fundamentalist work. Mario Liverani's *Israel's History and*

---

1. Thus the title of his article: Miller, "Is It Possible."

the History of Israel (2005) is a learned revisionist work, but Marxist and scarcely mainstream.

Twenty-five years in the progress of our branch of archaeological research marks a long, revolutionary era that has seen dramatic, profound changes. Yet the majority of biblical scholars seem oblivious to the new potential of material culture data as a source for writing history. The latest handbook (so-called), Moore and Kelle's *Biblical History and Israel's Past: The Changing Study of the Bible and History* (2011) betrays no overall comprehension of the discipline of modern archaeology. It uncritically cites mavericks and authorities side-by-side; it completely ignores many major works; and it makes grandiose claims that are groundless.

This is what happens when amateurs meddle in fields in which they have no credentials. A single statement of Moore and Kelle will illustrate my point. They claim: "Without the Bible, archaeologists would never have been able to name the ancient names of many ruins, or know the names of rulers in the area or the general circumstances of their reigns, particularly their building activities . . . Also, without the Bible, it would be very difficult to construct a time line of the important events in the region."[2]

Each of these claims is grossly overstated. Anyone who makes such claims can be dismissed immediately as a reliable guide. (When the blind lead the blind, both fall into a ditch.) This "guidebook" to the Bible and history-writing leads nowhere.

The "Literary Turn" and a Historiographical Crisis

What went wrong? What provoked the crisis in history-writing in both archaeology and biblical studies, which we all know has plagued both our disciplines for more than a generation now? The short answer lies in what is often called the "literary turn." Notwithstanding the major contributions from the likes of Robert Alter and Meir Sternberg (who actually said little or nothing about the historicity of the biblical text), other scholars latched on to the literary turn, abused the methodology, and took it to extremes—thereby spawning an increasingly skeptical attitude toward the credibility of the texts of the Hebrew Bible as a historical source. That was presumably because these texts were all too late (i.e., Persian or even Hellenistic in date), or too tendentious to contain any reliable historical information about any "Israel" in the Iron Age.

The gauntlet was thrown down in Philip R. Davies' *In Search of "Ancient Israel"* (1992). Davies found three "Israels" (1) The first was a putative

---

2. Moore and Kelle, *Biblical History and Israel's Past*, 21.

"historical" Israel, about which little could be said. (2) The second was "biblical Israel," a late, Jewish literary construct, in effect a foundation-myth. (3) The third was "ancient Israel," a concoction of modern scholars, especially Americans and Israelis who had bought into the Zionist program.

Davies' diatribe cites *none* of the available archaeological data except Amihai Mazar, *Archaeology of the Land of the Bible* (1990), and that in a single footnote,[3] claiming that since Mazar's work deals with the Iron Age and stops there, it is "irrelevant" (his word) to the *real* Israel, that is, Davies' Persian-Hellenistic "literary Israel."

Davies' deliberately provocative book was soon followed by other works of the Sheffield and Copenhagen axis who were by now coming to be regarded as "revisionists" (their term originally, adopted by me); "minimalists"; or even "nihilists." In short order there appeared Keith Whitelam's *The Invention of Ancient Israel: The Silencing of Palestinian History* (1996), whose anti-Israel (and potentially anti-Semitic) bias was evident already in the title. This was followed in a similar vein by Thomas L. Thompson's *The Mythic Past: Biblical Archaeology and the Myth of Israel* (1999). Here the "myth" was that Thompson's work had anything whatsoever to do with archaeology. Both volumes are simply caricatures of archaeology and archaeologists, written by authors with little or no field experience.

The deepening of the historiographical crisis in the 1990s and into the early twenty-first century can best be followed by skimming through the pages of the dozen or so volumes published from a series of symposia sponsored by the "European Seminar on Method in Israel's History." The first was a volume edited by the seminar's founder, Lester L. Grabbe, titled appropriately *Can a "History of Israel" Be Written?* (1997). Subsequent volumes dealt with several case-studies: the exile and the "myth of the empty land" (1998); the prophets as putative historical figures (2001); the presumed Hellenistic date of the biblical texts (2001); the campaign of Sennacherib in 701 BCE (2003); the kings of Israel and Judah (2006); Ahab and the Omride dynasty (2007); and finally, two volumes on the Late Bronze-Iron I horizon and the rise of ancient Israel (2008; 2010), where for the *first* time archaeologists were included in the discussion and their data taken seriously.[4]

As an example of how oblivious the seminar's members were to the potential of archaeology for history-writing I note that the 2003 volume, *"Like a Bird in a Cage,"* a study of the famous campaign of Sennacherib to Judah in 701 BCE, did not contain a chapter by an archaeologist.

---

3. Davies, *In Search of "Ancient Israel,"* 24.

4. In the interest of brevity, I have not included the bibliographic details of these various volumes, neither here nor in the Bibliography collected at the end of this essay.

To put this deficiency in perspective, the books of Kings and Chronicles confine their references to any of the "46 walled towns," which Sennacherib claims to have destroyed, to one or two sites. Lachish is one, which they mention in a single verse, noting only that Sennacherib "was there." (Libnah is the other site, but no information is provided.) Then the biblical writers go on to devote three long chapters to the miraculous lifting of the siege of Jerusalem—obviously their only concern, given their theocratic program.

Lachish has been extensively excavated in several large projects, and 10 sumptuous volumes of final reports are now available. Which source do you think more promising for writing a history of the Neo-Assyrian campaigns: the tendentious biblical account of events or the vast and detailed archaeological evidence? Yet the foremost European biblical historians saw no problem in focusing almost exclusively on the biblical texts—despite their own declared pessimism regarding these texts as historical sources. That is an example of the dilemma we face, which as an archeologist I confess I find inexplicable.

Thus far I have illustrated what the much-discussed "literary turn" in biblical (Old Testament) scholarship has produced over the past 25 years. The "turn," as it is called, was clearly a moving *away* from historical considerations (and, of course, theological issues), and *toward* the kind of strictly *textual* analysis. This was the tactic favored by New Literary criticism and other more extreme approaches such as semiotics, post-Colonialism, liberation theology, the New Historicism, radical feminist critiques, queer theory, and the like.

The latest fad is "cultural memory" or "reception history" which is said to be the *sine qua non* of modern Old Testament/Hebrew Bible scholarship. Here one no longer asks what the text "says," but only how it is *able* to say anything at all, what it "signifies." What really happened need not concern us, since it is impossible to know, and irrelevant in any case. What matters is only what the "story" has come to *mean* over time. But this is what I would call simply "the history of the *history*," that is, an appraisal of the biblical writers' reconstruction of ancient Israel, regardless of whether it is fictitious or not.

Hans Barstad, one of the European Seminar's prominent members, points out that acceptance of radical "cultural memory" methods "would mean the end of history." He goes on to say that "If we want to retain the term 'history' at all, we cannot refrain from discussing whether or not past events are 'true' in a positivist sense."[5]

---

5. Barstad, *History and the Hebrew Bible*, 8.

Postmodernism and Its Impact on History-writing

In a series of publications over the past twenty years, I have argued that the radical critique of the biblical revisionists is only a belatedly borrowed and thinly disguised form of postmodernism.[6] Look at their repeated assertions: (1) The biblical texts do not refer to any external reality, only to other texts. (2) These texts are all propaganda, ideological manifestos, really about race, class, power, and, above all, politics. (3) We must treat the biblical view of Israel's history skeptically, as a "metanarrative" to be delegitimized, simply a "social construct" and therefore to be "*de*-constructed."

These are the revisionist's fundamental methological and historiographical (!) presuppositions. And I have shown that they are all derived directly from postmodernist gurus like Roland Barthes, Jacques Derrida, Michel Foucault, Jacques Lacan, Jean Francois Lyotard, and others (even if never acknowledged). I made that point as early as 1995, then developed it fully in *What Did the Biblical Writers Know and When Did They Know It?* (2001).

James Barr in his magisterial *History and Ideology in the Old Testament: Biblical Studies at the End of a Millennium* (2001) agreed with me and then devoted some 70 pages to documenting further the revisionists' fundamental postmodern stance. As Barr concluded, these radically skeptical Biblicists were "ideologically driven"; "incredibly naïve"; "without factual evidence"; "too absurd to be taken seriously"; "simply wrong." All this by one of Europe's leading Old Testament scholars.[7]

In a later state-of-the-art analysis, John Collins' *The Bible after Babel: Biblical Studies in a Postmodern Age* (2005) notes my documentation of the revisionists' postmodernist biases; but he thinks that postmodernism is here to stay. On the contrary, I think it is *passé*, as I shall show.

However crucial the postmodern challenge to writing any history of Israel turned out to be, the implications were ignored by most biblical scholars in America and Israel. And archaeologists responded to revisionism, if at all, by simply quoting me, as though this were an issue only in Europe, or in the American religious communities (which they had never really understood).

6. See in particular Dever, *What Did the Biblical Writers Know*, 13–21, 25–34; and Dever, *Lives of Ordinary People*, 23–40, 245–66, both with full references. See also nn. 7, 19, and 22 below and works cited there.

7. See Barr, *History and Ideology*, 59–101, 141–80. Lemche, "Conservative Scholarship," has acknowledged that Barr is indeed a leading European Old Testament scholar; but he has not responded to his critique of the revisionists. As for my numerous critiques, he dismisses me as a rustic—presumably because I am an American and thus peripheral.

There were, however, a few notable exceptions to the general malaise. Hans Barstad, whose sensible caution we have noted, produced a thoughtful prolegomenon in his *History and the Hebrew Bible: Studies in Ancient Israelite and Ancient Near Eastern Historiography* (2008).

An even more promising work, although admittedly also a prolegomenon, was Grabbe's work *Ancient Israel: What Do We Know and How Do We Know It?* (2007). Grabbe had all along been unique among Seminar members in demonstrating a familiarity with the archaeological data that was commendable for a non-specialist, arguing not only that archaeology was important, but that the archaeological data now constituted our *primary* source for writing any new histories of ancient Israel. A few other Biblicists had earlier recognized that fact in principle, such as Ernst Axel Knauf, who observed that "history can be written on the basis of archaeology, and, if need be, on the basis of archaeology alone."[8] Knauf went on to say that much depends on what *kind* of history one wanted—a point that I had long made.[9]

I wrote a rave review of Grabbe's 2007 book (Dever 2010), which I dare to think may have been partly a response (even the title) to my 2001 book *What Did the Biblical Writers Know?* For some time I had been characterizing the more extreme revisionists (Thompson and Whitelam) as in effect "nihilist," with extensive documentation from their own writings. But I did so advisedly (not "mere polemics"), having looked in some detail at the founders of the nihilistic school of thought, the ancient Greek philosophers, and more modern proponents, 19th-century thinkers like Nietzsche, Spengler, and other prophets predicting the impending doom of the Western cultural tradition—the "modernism," of course, that the postmodernists proclaim obsolete. Its fundamental principles—rationalism, egalitarianism, the pursuit of truth, progress in history—are precisely what the postmodernists and their imitators the biblical revisionists ridiculed and rejected.[10]

Was my critique simply *ad hominem* polemics, as critics charged? Hardly. In identifying nihilism I was basing myself on numerous assertions like this, by Thompson: "This is no more 'ancient Israel.' History no longer has room for it. This we do know. And now as one of the first conclusions of this knowledge, 'biblical Israel' was in its origin a Jewish concept."[11]

Elsewhere, he specifies "a Jewish *construct.*" If this is not nihilism, I don't know what it is. "*No Israel*" equals nothing. As Baruch Halpern

---

8. Knauf, "From Archaeology to History," 85.

9. Ibid., 84. For my expansion of the idea of several types of history—and archaeology's potential, even its superiority in writing some of these histories—see Dever, "On Listening to the Texts."

10. See further n. 15 below.

11. Thompson, "Neo-Albrightian School," 98.

correctly pointed out, the aim of the revisionists from the beginning was to "erase Israel from history"[12]—both ancient and modern Israel, as a bit of detective work will confirm.

Constructivism and Ethnicity; Writing Israel Out of History

Running through *all* the publications of the "European Seminar on Method in Israel's History" over twenty years (by 2007 the name had changed to simply "Method"—no longer any "Israel"), one discovers a scarlet thread: "ethnicity is only a social construct," i.e., a *fiction* concocted by writers (ideologues) to create a tortured sense of self-identify for a beleaguered people.

Already in the first European Seminar volume in 1997, Thompson had attacked my several earlier publications identifying an "early Israel" in the *Iron Age* as essentially a Zionist enterprise. As he put it:

> Ethnicity, however, is an interpretive historigraphical fiction: a concept construing human relationships, before it is a term. Ethnicity is hardly a common aspect of human existence at this early period [i.e., in the era of ancient Israel—W.G.D.].[13]

Thus, again there *was* no identifiable "ancient Israel," so scholars like me have invented it in order to legitimize the *modern* state of Israel. Lemche made the same charge as Thompson, labeling me a Zionist because I worked in Israel, but at the same time declaring that my repeated claims about ethnicity sounded like those of the Nazis in Germany about "race."[14]

The culmination of this scandalous libel finally came in a book by a Swedish woman, Terje Oestigaard, a student of Thompson and Lemche. The book was titled *Political Archaeology and Holy Nationalism: Archaeological Battles over the Bible and Land in Israel and Palestine from 1967–2000* (2007). The chief target is me, supposedly a practitioner of "Biblical archaeology and Israel nationalistic archaeology." She says upfront that her subject is ethnicity, quoting Thompson, Lemche, and Whitelam on its illegitimacy. The Israelis and I are "extremists who misuse knowledge for political purposes." Oestigaard likens me to Gustav Kossina, the notorious Nazi racist who tried to use archaeology to validate a Super Race.

She quotes extensively from my writing, but only to distort what I wrote into the exact *opposite* of what I said. It is clear that for Oestigaard and the biblical revisionists, who are her mentors, that there cannot have

---

12. Halpern, "Erasing History."
13. Thompson, "History and Ethnicity," 175.
14. Lemche, "Response to William G. Dever," 12.

been an "ancient Israel" or a modern state of Israel: it is inconvenient for their theories. *Now who* are the "racists"?

The point of the foregoing excursus is that the biblical revisionists and all who unwittingly buy into their nihilist notions cannot possibly write any history of an ancient Israel in the Iron Age, because they deny the existence of any such entity (or at least its recovery). Theirs would be what Ernst Axel Knauf aptly described as "a pseudo-history of non-events."[15]

Already in 1997 the distinguished historian George Iggers had published his work *Historiography in the Twentieth Century: From Scientific Objectivity to the Postmodern Challenge* (the German original in 1993). Iggers argued persuasively that despite some caveats, writing history is not all about ideology, that good historians in practice still assume that an account of actual events is their goal and that it is obtainable within reason. As Iggers puts it:

> This distinction between truth and falsehood remains fundamental to the work of the historian. The concept of truth has become immeasurably more complex in the course of recent critical thought. To be sure the postulate of "an absolute objectivity and scientificity of historical knowledge is no longer accepted without reservation." Nevertheless the concept of truth and with it the duty of the historian to avoid and to uncover falsification has by no means been abandoned. As a trained professional he continues to work critically with the sources that make access to the past reality possible.[16]

All this means that it is up to the rest of us to write a history of events, based on *our* sources, based this time not on ideology, biblical or otherwise, but upon archaeology as a source of knowledge concerning a real-life Israel in the Iron Age.

Fortunately, the time is ripe for just such an effort. That is partly because in real intellectual circles postmodernism is *passé*. Radical skepticism is being discredited as bankrupt; and anthropology, archaeology, and the social sciences are turning their attention once again to history. And this time, our branch of archaeology is poised to make a contribution, because we now have a vast and varied data base, and we are newly aware that we are *historians* or nothing—"historians of things." Let me expand on these notions.

---

15. Knauf, "From History to Interpretation," 49.
16. Iggers, *Historiography in the Twentieth Century*, 12.

Changing Pardigms: Back to History

One of the most comprehensive and up-to-date surveys of anthropological and archaeological theory is Robert Preucel and Stephen Mrozowski's work *Contemporary Archaeology in Theory: The New Pragmatism* (2010). They show that one of the most promising trends now, after some 40 years of abstract theory, is the revival of interest in history-writing. As they say:

> It is no longer possible to justify archaeology on some abstract terms; rather, the ethics of archaeology now require that we join diverse interest groups in the common project of understanding the multiple meanings of the past for the present.[17]

A borrowing of the idea of a "new pragmatism" by an archaeologist in our field, Tom Levy, is by contrast rather naïve. It amounts to little more than scientism—the notion that the future lies in cyber-archaeology—which only improves data-collection and neglects the epistemological issues that are critical to history-writing. Deciding "what works" all depends on what you *want* to work.[18]

Two books on archaeology published last year already embodied the renewed interest in history. The first is by Andrew M. Martin, *Archaeology beyond Postmodernity: A Science of the Social* (2013). The publisher describes this book as follows:

> In the last decade, a new conception of culture has emerged in sociology, out of the *ashes* of modernism and postmodernism, that has the potential to change how we think about cultural objects and groups in archaeology.[19]

---

17. Preucel and Mrozowski, *Contemporary Archaeology in Theory*, 4.

18. See Levy, "New Pragmatism," 9, the only place where he discusses pragmatism, despite choosing the term for the book's title. He cites Pierce as the founder of the movement, but does not cite any of his work. His citation of other pragmatists, like William James and John Dewey, is likewise secondary. Levy's "authority" is the contemporary California social commentator Daniel Yankelovich. Levy's writings here and elsewhere demonstrate his own pragmatism, i.e., cyber-archaeology. Yet that only showcases technology; it glosses over the fundamental *epistemological* issues. For substantive discussions of the much-debated topic of ethnicity and material culture (i.e., archaeology), see Dever, "Ceramics, Ethnicity"; Dever, *Who Were the Early Israelites*, 191–2, 219–21; Faust, *Israel's Ethnogenesis*; and Faust, "Future Directions." All the latter have full references to the wider literature.

19. This is an unnamed quotation from a book catalog; italics are mine. Despite its claim to have moved beyond postmodernism (and thus modernism as well), Martin's work offers little more than a critique. Moreover, it is marred by absurd notions that objects—even inanimate objects—can act on their own as "agents" (now called ANT, "agent network theory"). Olsen's work (below and n. 7) also looks at now-faddish

The second volume is by Bjørnar Olsen, *In Defense of Things: Archaeology and the Ontology of Objects* (2013). One reviewer hails it as: "both an unequivocal sign of paradigm change and the maturity achieved by archaeological thinking ... One of the three most important works in the last decade."[20]

The above comments are particularly significant because during the heyday of postmodernism in the 1980s–1990s, few anthropologists and archaeologists seemed aware of its potential threat. That was certainly true in our branch of archaeology (above). In Americanist archaeology, one of the few statements about postmodernism that I could find was that of the distinguished Michigan scholars Kent Flannery and Joyce Marcus. In chapter 3 of John Bintliff and Mark Pearce's *The Death of Archaeological Theory?* (2011), they observe, "Only if post-modernism were to endure forever—which we do not expect—will there be cause for a memorial service."[21] Precisely.

My point, however, is that postmodernism has *not* prevailed. Postmodernism was learned nonsense—a fad that after a generation or so could not reproduce itself: it has proven to be sterile. David Gress has deftly skewered its pretensions.

> But if postmodernism were merely nihilism, it offered nothing other than a new name to distinguish itself from the far more serious and better-defined nihilism analyzed by Nietzsche and Spengler ... If postmodernism concealed, under a façade of nihilism, yet another version of the radical attack on the legitimacy of the West, that again was nothing new, merely a tedious and repetitive recital of the same grievances and errors denounced by Rousseau, Marx, and their followers for two centuries. The sole contribution of postmodernism as a label or a movement was to sow further confusion by combining anticapitalist and antimodern resentments.[22]

---

agency theory, along with poststructuralism, postmodernism, phenomenology, and various other recent philosophies. But it offers a few more productive theories about objects and artifacts that might actually apply to archaeology. The value of both works, despite limitations, lies primarily in calling attention again to things and their potential superiority over texts as a representation of reality present and past. For a commonsense assessment of where we are after forty years of attempting to borrow theory from anthropology and sociology, see Bintliff and Pearce, *The Death of Archaeological Theory?*

20. This is an unnamed quotation from a book catalog. Cf. n. 18 above.

21. Bintliff and Pearce, *The Death of Archaeological Theory?*, 29.

22. Gress, *From Plato to NATO*, 477. Gress, a well-trained Classicist (Ph.D., Bryn Mawr), provides a thorough history of the Western cultural tradition and defends its virtues ably but critically. See also Tarnas, *Passion of the Western Mind*, an even more comprehensive critique, with due attention to the postmodern challenge. With specific reference to the central notion of "deconstruction" and history, see the rebuttal of Ellis, *Against Deconstruction*. For an about-face of a leading postmodernist, see Eagleton,

Postmodernism's demise as a driving force in recent intellectual life opens the way for a return to more productive approaches to history-writing. This will involve emphasizing once again rational methods for investigating the past; the importance of striving for as much objectivity as possible; and a modest optimism that our efforts can produce meaning—the meaning of both texts and artifacts. And the New History (if we can call it that) will embrace both our sources, texts and artifacts, but it will give priority to the archaeological data—material culture—as our primary source.

"History from Things": the Truth of Objects in History

Archaeology is obviously a discipline that deals primarily with material culture, or with human culture as it is reflected in artifacts. By definition, that has usually meant studying artifacts from the remote past. But in the last two decades or so, there has developed a discipline that studies more recent and even contemporary material culture—not relics, the artifactual remains from extinct societies, but objects from living cultures. Here the objective is to write recent or contemporary history largely *without* texts.

Two volumes that appeared in 1993 signaled the growing maturity of a real discipline of material culture studies. Both were published significantly as the results of conferences held at the Smithsonian Institution and its Museum of Natural History. One volume is a series of essays edited by the distinguished historian of technology W. David Kingery: *Learning from Things: Method and Theory of Material Culture Studies*.

Its methodological approach was ably summarized by Kingery in the Preface:

> At the heart of the conference was the conviction that the things humankind makes and uses at any particular time and place are probably the truest representations we have of the values and meanings within a society. The study of things, material culture, is thus capable of piercing interdisciplinary boundaries

---

Illusions of Postmodernism. Perhaps the most devasting exposure of postmodernism's anti-historical stance is Windschuttle, *Killing of History*, 154:
> Foucault's histories of institutions, therefore, are demonstrations of the falsity of his own theories. History is not fiction, nor is it merely 'perspective.' The core of history—the basis for the conclusions that individual historians reach and the basis of the debates that historians conduct between each other—is factual information. Despite the speculations of Foucault and his followers, history remains a search for truth and the construction of knowledge about the past.

and bringing forward meaningful discussions and interactions among scholars in many disparate fields.[23]

Kingery calls this enterprise a relatively new and distinct discipline. In his own essay, Kingery speaks of "the grammar of things," noting that artifacts are signals, signs, and symbols. That is an independent insight into what Ian Hodder saw in his work *Reading the Past* (1986). Hodder argued that one should "read" artifacts just like texts—with the same hermeneutical methods. Once one learned the vocabulary, grammar, and syntax of artifacts, one could then search for their meaning, and thus could begin to *write history from things*, as well as from texts. Here Hodder employed a word-play: "con-textual" archaeology, "with texts." The ultimate goal of his contextual archaeology came to be called "the archaeology of mind." As Hodder put it, "to study history is to try to get at purpose and thought, at the inside of events" (1986). Ambitious though it is, that is my goal.

A prior Smithsonian volume was co-edited by Kingery and Steven Lubar, Curator of Engineering and Industry at the Smithsonian's National Museum of American History. It is a series of essays entitled *History from Things: Essays on Material Culture*. One of the most provocative discussions is that of Jules David Prown, "Truth of Material Culture: History or Fiction?" (1993). That question has astonishingly close parallels to the question that biblicists, always logocentric, have been asking of their texts since the dawn of modern critical scholarship. Biblical and Levantine archaeologists, on the other hand, always pragmatic and often inimical to theory—to epistemology—have tended näively to avoid the issue. This chapter by Prown would be an eye-opener to scholars in both disciplines, and it should be required reading.

Several authors in these two volumes expand on the potential of artifacts as a primary source for history-writing, applauding archaeologists for being "unfettered by textual evidence." Prown argues that the potential of objects in providing an entré into cultural beliefs lies in the universality of many human experiences. "In the end, reality rests on the vision seen through the culturally conditioned eyes of the analyst."[24] Nevertheless, philosophers and historians of technology have too often worked in isolation, the latter usually dismissed as inferior in their grasp of reality. But now, we "historians of material culture" can come into our own as *real* historians.

Lubar expands on the idea of artifacts as a primary source. Because cultural meaning is carried by a variety of vehicles, all of which must

---

23. Kingery, *Learning from Things*, ix.
24. Prown, "Truth of Material Culture," 4.

be expressed in words to be understood, objects have "an inescapable textuality."[25] Historians of technology are distinguished by the texts they read—objects. This follows Geertz's argument that a technological artifact should be regarded as a "cultural phenomenon," which is like any other cultural phenomenon, but can make for better historical explanation. Objects then, like texts, must be deciphered. What is required is research outside the library, the hands-on scrutiny of three-dimensional objects. That is precisely what we archaeologists do, and have long done—but without adequate training in history or any self-conscious historiographical focus. But biblical scholars could nevertheless follow us out of the library into the field.

Among the few archaeologists in these two volumes is Michael Schiffer, a well-known New World archaeological theorist. He acknowledges that the past is past. It no longer exists as part of the phenomenological world, and thus it can never be fully known. Nevertheless, "the study of the human past is made possible by the fact that some objects made and used long ago survive into the present and so can serve as evidence."[26] That evidence can be interpreted by inferences we make about past human behavior. Depending upon the weight of the evidence and of the relevant generalizations, this process of archaeological reasoning can be not only systematic, but even scientific. This "positivist" claim for archaeology may seem astounding to many text-based historians. But it is tacitly assumed by most archaeologists, because otherwise our enterprise is little more than treasure hunting. Formidable as that goal of archaeology and history may be, I would argue that it is no more formidable than the task that text-based biblical historians take on. It all depends on adequate hermeneutical principles that enable us (1) to sift out from a mass of data reliable and relevant facts; and (2) to place these facts in a larger cultural context that gives them meaning. The fact that absolute Truth is not obtained does not imply that all history-writing is futile—mere "fiction," as biblical revisionists and other postmodernists assert.

Prown, whom we have already quoted, is perhaps the most positivist of all the contributors to the above volumes. For him artifacts are "historical evidence." That is uniquely so because, unlike other historical events that happened in the past, "Artifacts constitute the only class of historical events that occurred in the past but survive into the present. They can be re-experienced: they are authentic, primary historical material available for firsthand study."[27]

25. Lubar, in Lubar and Kingery, *History from Things*, 32–35.
26. Schiffer, "Formation Processes," 73.
27. Prown, "Truth of Material Culture," 3, 5.

Furthermore, objects are in some respects "truer" than texts, since "the questions that artifacts pose are authentic" ones, and they "do not lie." To put it another way, artifacts are indeed fabrications, but they are not fictitious in the same way that texts may be. Objects can communicate to us directly, unedited, if we come to understand the universal beliefs, emotions, and values that they connote. Artifacts, like texts, are thus metaphysical expressions of human culture.

Regarding the archaeological data, rather than the textual data, as our "primary" source for history-writing seems obvious to me (and perhaps to a few others), but that may require some justification. Simply put, I would argue that material culture remains—artifacts—are superior to texts, in this case primarily the biblical texts, for several reasons.

1. The artifacts are by definition a contemporary witness to events, whereas the biblical texts are later, often much later.

2. The artifacts are far more numerous and varied, more representative of the lives of the majority. The biblical texts are deliberately selective, representing the biases of elites, and heavily edited and re-edited over time.

3. While both sources require interpretation (hermeneutics), the reading of artifacts is more straightforward, since the makers had no ideology to intervene. The "truth" of things is more directly accessible.

4. Finally new archaeological evidence is constantly coming to light, a source more dynamic than the biblical texts, for which the canon is closed. We cannot wring out of the texts any more information than they happen to contain.

Toward New, Archaeological Portraits of Ancient Israel and Judah

Having argued that previous histories of ancient Israel are deficient and that new, *archaeologically*-based histories are now needed, and are possible, where do we go from here? My response to the challenge is that I have just completed a massive, heavily documented and illustrated work entitled *"History from Things": An Archaeological Portrait of Ancient Israel and Judah*. This work differs from all previous histories by taking the archaeological data consistently as the *primary* source, regarding the biblical texts as secondary and useful for the historian only when corroborated by material culture data. Inspired by Grabbe's 2007 prolegomenon (see above),

I have arranged all the narratives of events in the book of Kings (and some of the prophetic works) along a continuum, from "proven" to "disproven," with several intermediate stages such as "possible," "probable," and in some cases "insufficient evidence." I would estimate that only in about 20 percent of case-studies were the biblical texts useful, and rarely were they primary data, i.e., *prima facie* evidence.

The overall structure of this work is provided by General Systems Theory (GST). This theory was once widespread during the heyday of the "New Archaeology" in the 1970s, when models were often borrowed from the natural sciences. Simply put, the GST model assumes that *social* systems, like biological systems, are made up of several sub-systems, cooperating together to create an equilibrium, which is what sustains the organism. When one or more sub-systems fails, however, disequilibrium gradually ensues, and a subsequent downward spiral eventually results in collapse, or the death of the organism.

Using this model, in each chapter I look at the archaeological evidence for sub-systems like (1) settlement type and pattern; (2) demography; (3) socio-economic structure; (4) political structure; (5) technology; (5) aesthetics, including art, literature, and religion; and (6) foreign relations. Every chapter attempts to chart and explain *changes* over time, which is what history-writing is all about. And every chapter is concerned with the question "What was it *really* like to live in that time and place?"

The above are the elements that I find missing in nearly all previous histories of ancient Israel, and they provide the rationale for undertaking such a formidable project—a synthesis of virtually of all we know that is relevant for understanding ancient Israel and Judah in the Iron Age. The book will be controversial because it is innovative. Nothing like it has been previously undertaken, despite a few forays. Whether my effort is bold or foolish, time will tell. But it is time someone tried. Unless archaeology results in new and better histories of both Israel and her neighbors,[28] it is a monumental waste of time and resources.

---

28. Happily, a few other scholars have also pointed the way. Already in 2007, Rendsburg, "Israel without the Bible," 7, declared, "Let us reconstruct the history of ancient Israel based solely on the information provided by archaeology ... Only when we are done with this exercise will we bring the Bible back into the picture, to see to what extent the two overlap."

BIBLIOGRAPHY

Barr, James. *History and Ideology in the Old Testament: Biblical Studies at the End of a Millennium.* Oxford: Oxford University Press, 2000.

Barstad, Hans. "History and Memory: Some Reflections on the 'Memory Debate' in Relation to the Hebrew Bible." In *The Historian and the Bible: Essays in Honour of Lester L. Grabbe,* edited by Philip R. Davies and Diana V. Edelman, 1–10. Library of Hebrew Bible/Old Testament Studies 530. London: T. & T. Clark, 2010.

———. *History and the Hebrew Bible: Studies in Ancient Israelite and Ancient Near Eastern Historiography.* FAT 61. Tübingen: Mohr Siebeck, 2008.

Barton, John. *Reading the Old Testament: Method in Biblical Study.* 2nd ed. London: Darton, Longman & Todd, 1996.

Bintliff, John L., and Mark Pearce, eds. *The Death of Archaeological Theory?* Oxford: Oxbow Books, 2011.

Collins, John J. *The Bible after Babel: Historical Criticism in a Postmodern Age.* Grand Rapids: Eerdmans, 2005.

Davies, Philip R. *In Search of 'Ancient Israel.'* JSOTSup 148. Sheffield: Sheffield Academic, 1992.

Dever, William G. "Ceramics, Ethnicity, and the Question of Israel's Origins." BA 58 (1995) 200–213.

———. "*History from Things*": *An Archaeological Portrait of Ancient Israel and Judah.* Forthcoming.

———. *The Lives of Ordinary People in Ancient Israel: Where Archaeology and the Bible Intersect.* Grand Rapids: Eerdmans, 2012.

———. "On Listening to the Texts—and the Artifacts." In *The Echoes of Many Texts: Reflections on Jewish and Christian Traditions: Essays in Honor of Lou H. Silberman,* edited by William G. Dever and J. Edward Wright, 1–23. Brown Judaic Studies 313. Atlanta: Scholars, 1997.

———. Review of Lester L. Grabbe, *Ancient Israel: What Do We know and How Do We Know It?* BASOR 357 (2010) 77–83.

———. *What Did the Biblical Writers Know and When Did They Know It? What Archaeology Can Tell Us about the Reality of Ancient Israel.* Grand Rapids: Eerdmans, 2001.

———. *Who Were the Early Israelites and Where Did They Come From?* Grand Rapids: Eerdmans, 2003.

Eagleton, Terry. *The Illusions of Postmodernism.* Oxford: Blackwell, 1996.

Ellis, John M. *Against Deconstruction.* Princeton: Princeton University Press, 1989.

Faust, Avraham. "Future Directions in the Study of Ethnicity in Ancient Israel." In *Historical Biblical Archaeology and the Future: The New Pragmatism,* edited by Thomas E. Levy, 55–68. London: Equinox, 2010.

———. *Israel's Ethnogenesis: Settlement, Interaction, Expansion, and Resistance.* London: Equinox. 2006.

Grabbe, Lester L. *Ancient Israel: What Do We Know and How Do We Know It?* London: T. & T. Clark, 2007.

———, ed. *Can a "History of Israel" Be Written?* JSOTSup 245. Sheffield: Sheffield Academic, 1997.

Gress, David. *From Plato to NATO: The Idea of the West and Its Opponents.* London: Free Press, 1998.

Halpern, Baruch. "Erasing History: The Minimalist Assault on Ancient Israel." *Bible Review* 11/6 (Dec. 1995) 26–35, 47.
Hodder, Ian, and Scott Hutson. *Reading the Past: Current Approaches to Interpretation in Archaeology*. Cambridge: Cambridge University, 1986.
Iggers, George G. *Historiography in the Twentieth Century: From Scientific Objectivity to the Postmodern Challenge*. Hanover, NH: Wesleyan University Press, 1997.
Kingery, W. David., ed. *Learning from Things: Method and Theory of Material Cultural Studies*. Washington, DC: Smithsonian Institution Press, 1996.
Knauf, Ernst Axel. "From Archaeology to History, Bronze and Iron Ages, with Special Regard to the Year 1200 BCE, and the Tenth Century." In *Israel in Transition: From Late Bronze II to Iron IIa (c. 1250–850 BCE)*, vol. 1: *The Archaeology*, edited by Lester L. Grabbe, 72–85. Library of Hebrew Bible/Old Testament Studies 491. London: T. & T. Clark, 2008.
———. "From History to Interpretation." In *The Fabric of History: Text, Artifact and Israel's Past*, edited by Diana V. Edelman, 26–64. JSOTSup 127. Sheffield: JSOT Press, 1991.
Lemche, Niels Peter "Conservative Scholarship on the Move." *SJOT* 19 (2005) 203–52.
———. *The Israelites in History and Tradition*. Library of Ancient Israel. Louisville: Westminster John Knox, 1998.
———. "Response to William G. Dever: 'Revisiting Israel Revisited.'" *Currents in Research: Biblical Studies* 5 (1997) 9–14.
Levy, Thomas E. "The New Pragmatism: Integrating Anthropological, Digital, and Biblical Archaeologies." In *Historical Biblical Archaeology and the Future: The New Pragmatism*, edited by Thomas E. Levy, 3–43. London: Equinox, 2010.
Liverani, Mario. *Israel's History and the History of Israel*. London: Equinox, 2005.
Lubar, Steven D., and W. David Kingery, eds. *History from Things: Essays on Material Culture*. Washington DC: Smithsonian Institution Press, 1993.
Martin, Andrew M. *Archaeology beyond Postmodernity: A Science of the Social*. Archaeology in Society Series. New York: AltaMira, 2013.
Mazar, Amihai. *Archaeology of the Land of the Bible, 10,000–586 B.C.E*. Anchor Bible Reference Library. New York: Doubleday, 1990.
Miller, J. Maxwell, "Is It Possible to Write a History of Israel without Relying on the Hebrew Bible." In *The Fabric of History: Text, Artifact and Israel's Past*, edited by Diana V. Edelman, 93–102. JSOTSup 127. Sheffield: JSOT Press, 1991.
Miller, J. Maxwell, and John H. Hayes. *A History of Ancient Israel and Judah*. 2nd ed. Louisville; Westminster John Knox, 2006.
Moore, Megan B, and Brad E. Kelle. *Biblical History and Israel's Past: The Changing Study of the Bible and History*. Grand Rapids: Eerdmans, 2011.
Oestigaard, Terje. *Political Archaeology and Holy Nationalism: Archaeological Battles over the Bible and Land in Israel and Palestine from 1967–2000*. GOTARC ser. C 67. Göteborg: Göteborg University, Dept. of Archaeology, 2007.
Olsen, Bjørnar. *In Defense of Things: Archaeology and the Ontology of Objects*. Archaeology in Society Series. New York: AltaMira, 2013.
Preucel, Robert W., and Stephen A. Mrozowski, eds. *Contemporary Archaeology in Theory: The New Pragmatism*. Oxford: Wiley-Blackwell, 2010.
Provan, Iain W., V. Phillips Long, and Tremper Longman. *A Biblical History of Israel*. Louisville: Westminster John Knox, 2003.

Prown, Julius D. "The Truth of Material Culture: Truth or Fiction?" In *History from Things: Essays on Material Culture*, edited by Steven D. Lubar and W. David Kingery, 1–19. Washington, DC: Smithsonian Institution Press, 1993.

Rendsburg, Gary A. "Israel without the Bible." In *The Hebrew Bible: New Insights and Scholarship*, edited by Frederick E. Greenspahn, 3–23. Jewish Studies in the Twenty-First Century Series. New York: New York University Press, 2007.

Schiffer, Michael B. "Formation Processes of the Historical and Archaeological Records." In *Learning from Things: Method and Theory of Material Culture Studies*, edited by W. David Kingery, 73–80. Washington, DC: Smithsonian Institute Press, 1996.

Tarnas, Richard. *The Passion of the Western Mind: Understanding the Ideas that Have Shaped Our World View*. New York: Ballantine, 1991.

Thompson, Thomas L. "Defining History and Ethnicity in the South Levant." In *Can a 'History of Israel' Be Written*, edited by Lester L. Grabbe, 166–87. JSOTSup 245. Sheffield: Sheffield Academic, 1997.

———. *The Mythic Past: Biblical Archaeology and the Myth of Israel*. London: Basic Books, 1999.

———. "A Neo-Albrightian School in History and Biblical Scholarship?" *JBL* 114 (1995) 683–98.

Whitelam, Keith W. *The Invention of Ancient Israel: The Silencing of Palestinian History*. London: Routledge, 1996.

Windschuttle, Keith. *The Killing of History: How Literary Critics and Social Theorists Are Murdering Our Past*. New York: Free Press, 1996.

Zevit, Ziony. *The Religions of Ancient Israel: A Synthesis of Parallactic Approaches*. London: Continuum, 2001.

2

Tel 'Eton Excavations and the History of the Shephelah during the Iron Age

Avraham Faust

BAR-ILAN UNIVERSITY

The Shephelah was one of the most important regions in the kingdom of Judah, and Tel 'Eton is a central site in its eastern part, near the trough valley which separates it from the Judean highlands (Fig. 1). In this article I will discuss the history of the settlement at Tel 'Eton during the Iron Age, its relations with its surroundings at the time, and the implications for our understanding the overall history of the Shephelah.[1]

Background: Tel 'Eton and its Exploration

Tel 'Eton is an important site, located in a strategic position, controlling a major junction and large tracts of good agricultural lands. Most scholars identify the site as biblical Eglon (Josh 10:34–36; 12:12; 15:39).[2]

---

1. This article updates, develops, and combines, some of the ideas presented in previous publications of the Tel 'Eton expedition. Copyright for all figures used herein held by the Tel 'Eton Archaeological Expedition, Avraham Faust, director.

2. See Noth, *Das Buch Joshua*, 95; and Rainey, "Administrative Division," 197; for a different view, see Galil, "Administrative Division," 67–71; and Na'aman, "Date of the List of Towns," 180.

A brief salvage excavation was conducted on the mound during the 1970s by the Lachish expedition, headed by David Ussishkin and directed in the field by Etan Ayalon and Rachel Bar-Nathan,[3] and additional digs were conducted at several tombs in the hills surrounding the site.[4]

The current project, which includes large-scale excavations at Tel ʿEton and a survey of its surroundings, was initiated in 2006.[5] The excavations focus on six areas (Fig. 2), and the findings suggest that the site was settled throughout much of the Bronze and Iron Ages, as well as in the Persian-Hellenistic period.[6]

While this article focuses on the Iron Age, we will begin with a brief review of the situation during the Late Bronze Age, in order to set the scene for the discussion:

The Late Bronze Age

The Late Bronze Age is one of the peaks in the settlement of the Shephelah. The overall number of Late Bronze Age sites unearthed in the Shephelah

---

3. Ayalon, "Trial Excavation"; and Zimhoni, "Iron Age Pottery."
4. E.g., Edelstein and Auraunt, "Necropolis"; and Faust and Katz, "Cemetery."
5. The excavations (permit nos. G45/2006, G69/2007, G47/2008, G47/2009, G53/2010, G51/2011, G59/2012, G82/2013, G51/2014, and G48/2015) and the survey (G46/2006, G15/2007, S28/2008, S130/2009, S197/2010, S-286/2011, S363/2012 and S470/2014) were directed by Avraham Faust. Hayah Katz serves as associate director and is responsible for ceramics analysis. Petrography was done by David Ben-Shlomo of the Hebrew University; the sample of bones discussed here was examined by Ram Bouchnic of Haifa University and Bar-Ilan University (the rest of the assemblage is currently studied by Tehilah Sadiel and Guy Bar-Oz); the spatial GIS analysis was conducted by Yair Sapir; and the Persian-Hellenistic period material was studied by Pirchiya Eyal as part of her M.A. thesis. The excavation was carried out with the help of students from Bar-Ilan University, the Open University of Israel, Franklin and Marshall College, Wheaton College, SPNI trailblazers, and volunteers. The excavation received support from the Lachish Regional Council and residents from Moshav Shekef. Different aspects of the research were supported by various grants, including the Israel Science Foundation ("Tel ʿEton and Judah's Southern Trough Valley: a Bridge or a Barrier," grant #884/08; "The Birth, Life and Death of a Four-Room House at Tel ʿEton," grant #284/11), the Jewish National Fund ("Archaeological Sites and the 'Open' Landscape—the Landscape around Tel ʿEton as a Test-Case"), and the Open University of Israel ("The Iron Age IIa Tomb from the vicinity of Tel ʿEton"; "Death at Tel ʿEton: Final publication of four tombs in the vicinity of Tel ʿEton"; "The ceramic sequence at Tel ʿEton and other trough valley sites, and its implications for understanding the settlement history in the region during the third and second millennia BCE").
6. Faust, "Tel ʿEton Excavations (2006–2009)"; Faust, "History of Tel ʿEton," Faust et al., "Interregional Contacts"; Faust, "Late Persian"; and Faust and Katz, "Canaanite Town."

survey is about twenty-five settlements—many of which have been excavated—plus there are additional "find spots."[7] The settlement that existed at Tel 'Eton in the Late Bronze Age was quite large, as remains were unearthed in the slopes, including the western part of the section in Area B, as well as in Area C, on the far, northern part of the mound (cf., Fig. 2). This is in line with the overall settlement situation in the Shephelah, and it appears that Tel 'Eton was a field town in the territory of the city-state of Lachish, and it is possible that it was even an independent city during part of the time.[8]

The Iron Age I

During the transition to the Iron Age I, most of the sites in the Shephelah were destroyed, and the majority of them did not immediately recover and were therefore not settled during most of this era. Thus, the major city that existed at Lachish,[9] as well as the towns of Goded,[10] Tel Zayit,[11] Tel Burna,[12] Tel Harasim,[13] Tel Azekah[14] and others, were apparently destroyed and abandoned.[15] Only in a few sites, like Tell Beit Mirsim and Beth-Shemesh, were remains from this period identified, and those will be discussed in more detail below.

At Tel 'Eton, unlike most of the Shephelah, Iron I remains were unearthed. These, however, were discovered in more limited areas than the remains from the Late Bronze Age. Thus, for example, no *in situ* remains were unearthed down the slope in the long section that cut through the mound in Area B, nor in Area C (in one square in this area a few Iron I sherds were unearthed, but out of context). This apparently indicates that the site was somewhat smaller than that of the Late Bronze Age. Occupation, however, was relatively massive (in square W46, for example, the 12th-century accumulation was about 1 m thick).

---

7. E.g., Dagan, "Settlement in the Judean Shephelah," 163, and fig. 15. The settlement in Shephelah during the Late Bronze Age even exceeds that of the Middle Bronze Age; see Dagan, "Settlement in the Judean Shephelah," 144.

8. Faust et al., "Interregional Contacts"; and Na'aman, "Shephelah," 285, 287.

9. Ussishkin, *Biblical Lachish*.

10. Gibson, "Tel Goded."

11. Tappy, "Zayit"; Tappy, "East of Ashkelon."

12. Shai et al., "Fortifications at Tel Burna."

13. Givon, "Harasim."

14. Lipschits et al., "Tel Azekah," 200.

15. See also Faust et al., "Interregional Contacts."

As noted, the settlement system of the Iron I was strikingly different from that of the Late Bronze Age. The Shephelah was almost completely devoid of settlements, and the existing settlement concentrated in its eastern part, in or near the trough valley. Of the excavated sites, remains from this period were unearthed in Tel Beth-Shemesh in the north,[16] Tel Yarmouth near the valley of Elah,[17] Tel 'Eton (above) and Tell Beit Mirsim, about 4 km. southwest of Tel 'Eton.[18]

The settlement at Tel 'Eton is therefore part of a small group of sites which existed in the Iron I in or near the trough valley, the easternmost part of the Shephelah.[19] The Iron Age I is the period in which the Philistines consolidated in the coastal plain to the west of the trough valley, while the Israelites emerged in the highlands to its east, but who were the settlers in the small group of sites in the trough valley? The finds in these sites are quite confusing when trying to connect them with any specific cultural system in the coast or the highlands. The issue was developed elsewhere, and I will therefore only summarize here some of the main arguments.[20] Unlike the highlands, where collared rim jars for example are abundant, such are hardly found in the trough valley sites.[21] In addition, the number of pottery forms is quite large, in sharp contrast to the reality in the highlands,[22] and Philistine pottery is present, even if in limited quantities.[23] The pottery is,

16. Bunimovitz and Lederman, "Beth-Shemesh"; Border Communities."

17. De Miroschedji, *Yarmouth I*, 92; de Miroschedji, "Yarmuth," 17.

18. Albright, "Excavations of Tell Beit Mirsim I"; Albright, "Excavations of Tell Beit Mirsim III"; and Greenberg, "New Light." In addition, a few Philistines sites on the western edge of the Shephelah, e.g., Tell es-Safi/Gath and Tel Batash were excavated, but they were clearly part of Philistia at the time (Faust and Katz, "Philistines," and the references cited there). Notably, the detailed Shephelah survey did not add any settlement to this list; see Dagan, "Settlement in the Judean Shephelah," 191.

19. Faust and Katz, "Philistines;" see also Faust, "Between Israel and Philistia"; Faust et al., "Interregional Contacts."

20. See, e.g., Faust and Katz, "Philistines."

21. We found one or two such sherds in the main Iron I level at Tel 'Eton; for the others sites, see for example, Bunimovitz and Lederman, "Archaeology of Border Communities," 123; Greenberg, "New Light," 64, 71.

22. See also Greenberg, "New Light," 76; Bunimovitz and Lederman, "Archaeology of Border Communities," 23; de Miroschedji "Yarmuth," 17.

23. Albright, "Excavations of Tell Beit Mirsim I," 61–64; Albright, "Excavations of Tell Beit Mirsim III," 1, 4, 9–10, 25, 36; Greenberg, "New Light," 76; Bunimovitz and Lederman, "Border Case," 24; "Archaeology of Border Communities," 123; de Mirocheji, "Yarmuth," 17; see also Dagan, "Settlement in the Judean Shephelah," 180; Edelstein and Aurant, "'Philistine' Tomb"; Faust, "'Philistine Tomb." A relatively large number of Philistine wares was unearthed in the "Philistine tomb" (Edelstein and Aurant, "'Philistine' Tomb"). This was an elite tomb, and the imported pottery found in it

therefore, similar to non-Israelite sites outside the highlands, and is much more similar to the coast (only that Philistine pottery is much rarer) than to that unearthed in the nearby highlands. All those traits seem to have been culturally and even ethnically sensitive at the time,[24] and those differences are sufficient to disconnect the trough valley settlers from those of the highlands. It must be noted that pig bones are practically absent in the trough valley sites,[25] and in this respect those sites differ dramatically from the central sites in Philistia, and the finds are similar to that of the highlands.[26]

Elsewhere we have suggested that the settlers in the trough valley used meaningful symbols of the Iron I era in order to show that they were neither Israelites nor Philistines.[27] They were most likely Canaanites, descended of the "local" Late Bronze Age population that found refuge in the trough valley,[28] and they "played" with the ethnically sensitive symbols of the time, in order to carve their own identity in contrast to the other groups which were active and dominant in the region.

The changes in settlement patterns during the Iron I can explain this process, which led to the creation of a Canaanite enclave in the trough valley. As noted by many,[29] the number of settlements in Philistia declined dramatically in the Iron I, and various scholars attributed this decrease to a Philistine policy of urban imposition or forced settlement.[30] It appears that the disappearance of settlements in the Shephelah should indeed be attributed to this policy, and once the region was colonized by the Philistines, the remaining inhabitants (those who did not die in the wars and destructions that accompanied the early part of the Iron I, regardless of the question

---

throws some light on the site's elite at the time (the issue is discussed at length in Faust, "'Philistine Tomb'").

24. E.g., Bunimovitz and Faust, "Chronological Separation"; Bunimovitz and Lederman, "Canaanite Resistance"; Faust, *Ethnogenesis*; Faust and Lev-Tov, "Construction"; Faust and Lev-Tov, "Philistia and the Philistines"; Gilboa et al., "Philistine Bichrome Pottery"; Killebrew and Lev-Tov, "Early Iron Age Feasting"; Bunimovitz and Yasur-Landau, "Philistine and Israelite Pottery."

25. Bunimovitz and Lederman, "Archaeology of Border Communities," 123; Faust and Katz, "Philistines."

26. For the situation in Philistia, see also Sapir-Hen et al., "Pig Husbandry," 10–11; Faust and Lev-Tov "Philistia and the Philistines," 6–7, 10–11; Faust, "Pottery and Society."

27. Faust and Katz, "Philistines"; Faust, "Between Israel and Philistia."

28. Already Greenberg, "New Light," 76, 78; see also Bunimovitz and Lederman, "Canaanite Resistance."

29. Finkelstein, "Date of the Settlement"; Finkelstein, "Philistine Settlements"; Shavit, "Settlement Patterns."

30. E.g., Bunimovitz, "Sea Peoples," 107–8.

who was responsible for them) were either transferred to the Philistine centers or fled to other regions, and especially to the trough valley sites. Those refugees, along with some of the local population of the trough valley, renegotiated their identity vis-à-vis the Philistines of the coastal plain and the Israelites of the highlands, and manipulated the material symbols of the time in order to express their own identity.[31]

Given the above background, it is quite clear that the settlement at Tel 'Eton was part of the local phenomenon in the trough valley. The relative isolation is evident also by the petrographic analysis, whereas ten of the fourteen sherds that were tested are attributed either to the site itself or to its immediate vicinity. This is the peak of all times as far as the locality of the pottery is concerned—71 percent of the examined sherds were locally produced, while in all other periods it varies from 26–56 percent of the assemblage. Clearly, interaction with the surrounding settlements and sub-regions was more limited than in the previous Late Bronze Age period, mainly because there really was no one with whom to interact. The Shephelah—the natural hinterland of the site—was devastated,[32] and the Philistines in the coastal plain and the Israelites in the highlands were the "other" against whom the local population defined itself. It appears, therefore, that interaction by the inhabitants of Tel 'Eton was limited to sites like nearby Tell Beit Mirsim and probably also Tel Halif further south.[33] These settlements were part of the same enclave, although the elite had connections with other regions, as reflected in tomb C1 (also known as the Philistine tomb),[34] and its members served as agents of change.[35]

---

31. For an extended discussion, see Faust and Katz, "Philistines"; Faust, "Between Israel and Philistia"; Faust, "'Philistine Tomb.'"

32. Interestingly the number of wild species in the faunal assemblage of the 12th century was some 4.6 percent (including loci from all parts of the 12th century; 12 bones of Dama mesopotamica and Gazella gazelle were identified, out of 264 identified bones; based on a report by Ram Bouchnik). Just for comparison, wild animals comprised some 1.1 percent at Late Bronze Age Lachish (based on Croft, "Archaeozoological Studies," 2257). If this is not a result of the limited sample that was examined, than the large percentage of wild animals at Iron I 'Eton it might be a result of the emptiness of the region. This suggestion, however, is only preliminary and should await more data from Tel 'Eton and other sites.

33. Seger, "Halif."

34. Edelstein and Aurant, "'Philistine' Tomb."

35. Faust, "'Philistine Tomb.'"

The Iron Age IIA

Only a few studies have examined in detail the processes the Shephelah experienced at this time, perhaps because, among other reasons, most past studies did not identify the scope of abandonment of the region during Iron I.[36] Generally speaking, it appears that sites were gradually resettled during the Iron IIA, e.g., at Lachish,[37] Tel Goded,[38] Tel Burna,[39] Tel Zayit,[40] Tel Harasim,[41] and others (below). How does Tel 'Eton fit into this process?

Unlike most other sites, the settlement in Tel 'Eton did not have to be "resettled," as it continued to exist and was even significantly expanded in its size in Iron IIA. Remains from this period were unearthed below the 8th century remains and above those of the Late Bronze Age in Area C and relatively down the slope in Area B, showing that the site expanded significantly in comparison to that of Iron I. The available evidence also suggests that fortifications were erected at this time. Although it expanded in size, it appears that the settlement continued its predecessor, and there was no gap or cultural break between the two.

It is quite clear that the resettlement of the Shephelah was done mostly by Judah (or, in the 10th century, the United Monarchy; we will not discuss the latter's historicity in this article and will simply refer to the kingdom of Judah for convenience). This is indicated by the excavators of practically all the sites,[42] as well as by the overall settlement process.[43] It appears that the construction of fortifications at Tel 'Eton, as with other sites such as Beth-Shemesh[44] and Tell Beit Mirsim,[45] was part of the process in which the

---

36. The Iron Age IIA had received a great deal of scholarly attention in recent years mainly as a result of the heated debate over the Iron Age chronology, and the related issue of the historicity of the United Monarchy (which was supposed to have existed in the 10th century BCE). Following Mazar (see, e.g., Mazar, "Debate over the Chronology"; and Mazar, "Iron Age Chronology"), we date most of the 10th–9th centuries (from some point in the first half of the 10th to some point in the second half of the 9th century) within the Iron Age IIA (see also Katz and Faust, "The Chronology").

37. Ussishkin, "Synopsis."

38. Gibson, "Goded," 230.

39. Shai et al., "Fortifications at Tel Burna."

40. Tappy, "Zayit"; Tappy, "East of Ashkelon."

41. Givon, "Harasim."

42. E.g., Lachish (see Ussishkin, "Synopsis," 93); Tel Zayit (see Tappy, "East of Ashkelon," 459–61); Tel Burna (see Shai et al., "Fortifications at Tel Burna"); and more.

43. See also Dagan, "Settlement in the Judean Shephelah," 257; Faust, "Shephelah in the Iron Age," 209–11; Faust, "Iron I–Iron II Transition."

44. Bunimoviz and Lederman, "Canaanite Resistance."

45. Albright, "Excavations of Tell Beit Mirsim III"; see also Katz and Faust, "tomb,"

area was integrated into Judah, regardless of the exact mechanism of this incorporation—conquest or, much more likely, through alliances with the local elites. Thus, Tel 'Eton and the other trough valley sites became part of Judah, as part of the colonization of the Shephelah by Judah.[46] Many new sites were gradually established in the process, for example at Lachish (initially level V, and subsequently the more impressive stratum IV), Tel Zayit, Tel Burna, Tel Azeka, Tel Harasim, and others, and the existing sites, like Tel 'Eton, were "swallowed" by Judah, its inhabitants gradually assimilated into Judahite society (for the Judahite/Israelite [for simplicity we will use in this article the term Judahite, although for some purposes Israelite could be a better term] identity of the inhabitants in the 8th century, see below).[47]

We also must note the discovery of a unique Iron Age IIA tomb by Trude Dothan in salvage excavations in 1968.[48] This was an elite tomb, which yielded some 200 pottery vessels and many other artefacts contained therein. The tomb is very unique in Judah's Iron IIA landscape, and bears clear similarity with the Iron I tomb uncovered nearby (the "Philistine tomb," above) in terms of its architecture. The finds unearthed in it, however, are more in line with the Judahite tradition (known from the later, Iron Age IIB-C Judahite tombs), thus exemplifying the intricate process by which the region gradually became part of Judah.

The Iron Age IIB

The Iron Age in general was a period of flourishing settlement throughout most of the country, and the Iron Age IIB—the 8th century BCE—is usually regarded as constituting an unprecedented settlement peak in this era.[49] Both the highlands[50] and lowlands[51] reached a settlement peak at this time, and the same is true for the northern Negev.[52] In the Shephelah, as a whole,

---

117, 120–21.

46. Faust, "Iron I–Iron II Transition," with extended discussion.

47. Nine Iron Age IIA samples were examined petrographically. Of those, five were manufactured at Tel 'Eton, three at the southern Shephelah, and one in the central Shephelah. Clearly, while the available evidence on the site's regional and interregional connections are still limited, this indicates interaction only with its immediate vicinity, though (with the exception of the Philistine sherd and the collared rim jar sherd) it is wider than in the Iron Age I, and includes the newly established sites in the Shephelah.

48. Katz and Faust, "tomb."

49. E.g., Broshi and Finkelstein, "Population of Palestine."

50. Ofer, "Judean Hills," 46, 51.

51. Dagan, "Settlement in the Judean Shephelah," 203.

52. Herzog, "Arad Fortresses," 237–9; Finkelstein, "Date of the Settlement." Whether

Dagan identified 277 settlements from this period (and many additional find spots, see below).[53] He estimated the total settled area of 4187 dunams, and the population as 108,000 people.

Tel 'Eton fits nicely into the general picture. The 8th century appears to be the peak of settlement at the site, as it probably reached its maximum size—over 60 dunams, making it one of the largest sites in Judah. Notably, the vast majority of the finds in the survey and shovel tests that were conducted at Tel 'Eton belong to this period (72 percent and 62 percent respectively),[54] and this further supports the importance of this phase in the history of the site (although this is also influenced by formation processes). On the basis of the finds, which include massive fortifications, an impressive four-room governor's residency (built partially with ashlar stones) with a unique collection of bullae and sealings, it is clear that the site was a regional center at the time.[55] This phase ended in a violent destruction in the late 8th century BCE, most likely inflicted by Sennacherib in his 701 BCE campaign.[56]

The massive destruction preserved the finds (Figs. 3, 4), and the fact that the 8th century was one of uppermost levels in the site enabled a wide exposure. In Area A, parts of a number of structures were uncovered (Fig. 5), including Structure 101. This was a large building (circa 230 sq.m. on the ground floor only) whose opening was to the east and whose construction made use of stones, usually with mud-brick superstructure, and in whose corners and some doorways ashlar stones were used. The house was built following the four-room house plan. The central space was an unroofed courtyard, and to its north, south and west were systems of rooms, with openings to the central yard. We must also note that parts of a few additional buildings, dated to the same time, were unearthed in the same area, but the exposure is too limited, and we cannot discuss their plan or function. In the upper part of Area B we uncovered parts of five buildings. Despite the partial exposure it is clear that the buildings were apparently quite large and some of the floors are made of high quality plaster. In many cases the preservation was good, and we found many vessels *in situ*. In the lower part of Area B the exposure was limited to a series of squares, and we found parts of buildings

---

settlement in all those areas increased or decreased in the 7th century (Iron IIC) is a different issue; see Finkelstein, "Archaeology of the Days of Manasseh"; Faust, "Settlement and Demography," and the references cited there.

53. Dagan, "Settlement in the Judean Shephelah," 203.

54. Faust and Katz, "Survey."

55. E.g., Faust, "Tel 'Eton Excavations (2006–2009)"; Faust, "History of Tel 'Eton"; Faust and Eshel, "Inscribed Bulla"; more below.

56. Katz and Faust, "Assyrian Destruction Layer."

and *in situ* pottery from this period down the slope, indicating that the site was quite large at the time. A massive wall, unearthed down the slopes in the section, probably defended the Iron Age city. The finds from this period in Area C were damaged by the Persian-Hellenistic pits, and the remains included a clay installation of an unclear nature and remains of walls, along with a city wall. The finding of these remains in this northern and low part of the mound indicate that occupation was significant, and that it covered the entire area of the tell. In Area D we unearthed the city's massive fortifications, along with parts of domestic buildings that were built parallel to the city wall (the building and the wall were separated by a small street). At least one of the structures was clearly dated to the 8th century BCE. Although it appears that the city wall was first erected before the time discussed here, most likely it continued to serve during the 8th century BCE.

The Tel 'Eton pottery assemblage (Fig. 6) is similar to those uncovered at Judahite sites such as Level III at Lachish, Stratum A2 at Tel Beit-Mirsim, and Stratum II at Beersheba. The pottery is simple, and decorations are rare to non-existent. The assemblage is no doubt Judahite, and only a few non-Judahite vessels were unearthed.[57] A comparison of the finds at Tel 'Eton with those at the nearby sites of Lachish and Tell Beit Mirsim is very revealing,[58] as it allows one to assess the amount of non-local pottery. Interestingly, although Tel 'Eton is the easternmost site of all three, it had about the same percentage of vessels produced in non-local style as Tel Lachish, and far more than at Tell Beit Mirsim. Given the position of Lachish in Judah's settlement hierarchy,[59] in addition to its more westerly location, this is very surprising. This shows clearly the central position of Tel 'Eton, which had relatively many connections with the outside world, and was not a simple "field town." This clearly stands out when compared with Tell Beit Mirsim, which seem to have been on a lower step on the settlement hierarchy. In addition, thirty pottery samples were petrographically examined. About twelve vessels seem to have their origin at the site or its immediate environment, two appear to have come from the highlands, and one vessel could have come from either of these regions. Twelve vessels appear to have originated from the central Shephelah, and two from the coastal plain (the origins of one vessel are unknown). Clearly, the site was embedded within the local extensive settlement, and was oriented mainly toward the central Shephelah. Interestingly, despite the large sample not a single vessel came from the northern Negev, and it is clear that the orientation of the site's

---

57. Ibid.
58. See Faust et al., "Interregional Contacts," 62–64.
59. E.g., Barkay, "Iron Age II–III," 344.

interaction within the Shephelah shifted northward when compared with earlier periods (a tendency that might be traced already in the Iron Age IIA, though the sample is too small and further research is needed in order to verify this suggestion).

In the 8th century, therefore, Tel 'Eton "behaves" just like the rest of the Shephelah, which peaked at the time, and with denser settlement than ever before. Tel 'Eton was embedded within a dense system of settlements, and interacted mainly with its neighbors, and with the central Shephelah.

As far as the identity of the inhabitants is concerned, it is quite clear that at this stage they were Judahites. This is clear not only from biblical (and Assyrian) texts which clearly affiliate the region with Judah, its location in the eastern Shephelah near the highlands, and its fate during the Assyrian campaigns (below), but also from the archaeological evidence itself. The presence of four-room houses, which were very prevalent amongst the Judahite population, clearly hint at this direction, and so does the lack (or extreme rarity) of decoration on the local pottery, as well as the almost complete absence of imported (from outside the country) pottery.[60] It is likely that the assimilation process of the local population started already in Iron Age IIA,[61] and that by the 8th century the process ended and the residents' Judahite identity was clear. Indeed, many tombs were unearthed in the mound's vicinity, some similar to their predecessors and some more akin to the general "Judahite" type. It seems as if in this period the incorporation of Tel 'Eton within Judah was complete also from an ethnic perspective (the issue will be addressed in detail elsewhere).

The size of the site (over 60 dunams), the relatively high percentage of non-local pottery (i.e., not from region itself, as compared with the finds in other nearby sites, above), along with additional finds such as the only 8th-century collection of bullae and sealings discovered (or at least published) in Judah[62] and the unique characteristics of the governor's residency (where the bullae and sealings were unearthed) seem to indicate that the site had a central role within the Judahite settlement system and administration. Elsewhere we suggested that perhaps the highlands were the center of administration, and the Shephelah was only the periphery, and that as a result of Tel 'Eton's location in the trough valley it was more central than most other sites in the Shephelah. For this reason, then, Tel 'Eton had a prominent role

---

60. For discussion of those ethnically sensitive traits, see Bunimovitz and Faust, "Ideology in Stone"; Faust and Bunimovitz, "Four Room House"; Faust, *Ethnogenesis*, and references.

61. Also Faust and Katz, "Philistines."

62. Faust, "Assemblage of Bullae"; the issue will be developed elsewhere.

within both the colonization of the Shephelah (above) and (subsequently) the administrative structure of Judah.[63]

The Iron Age IIC

Tel ʿEton was destroyed in the late 8th century, most likely by Sennacherib during his 701 campaign. Evidence for the destruction was unearthed in practically every excavation area. The houses in Area A and the upper part of Area B were devastated in the campaign (Figs. 3, 4), and despite the more limited exposure it is clear that this was also the case in the lower part of Area B. At least one of the houses in Area D was apparently also destroyed at this time, and this seems to be the case in Area C too.

Tel ʿEton was not resettled after its destruction. There is evidence for very limited reoccupation after the destruction by squatters, but this was very limited and short lived, and happened probably immediately after the devastation. Some evidence of later occupation was uncovered in 2015 in the plain to the northwest of the mound, but its nature and scope remain unclear.

As far as its fate in the 7th century, Tel ʿEton is in line with the rest of the Shephelah. While other parts of Judah were only partially destroyed by Sennacherib, and quickly recovered,[64] the Shephelah was thoroughly devastated and did not recover. Most sites, e.g., Khirbet el-Qom and Beth-Shemesh, did not recover at all, while sites like Lachish were rebuilt at some point, but on a much more moderate scale than their 8th-century predecessors. It is likely that much of the region was indeed transferred to Philistine hands by the Assyrians.[65]

Summary and Conclusions

During the Late Bronze Age Tel ʿEton flourished, like many other sites in the Shephelah. The site was of regional importance at the time, maybe as a central city at the edge of the realm of Lachish, and perhaps even (during part of the time) as an independent city in the southeastern Shephelah. The flourishing settlement system of the Late Bronze collapsed in the 12th century BCE, and during the Iron Age I period Tel ʿEton was a central

---

63. Ibid.; also Faust, "Tel ʿEton Excavations (2006–2009)," 221.

64. Faust, "Settlement and Demography."

65. Dagan, "Settlement in the Judean Shephelah," 210; Faust, "Settlement and Demography"; "Shephelah in the Iron Age," and references.

settlement in the Canaanite enclave that survived in the trough valley. Most of the Shephelah was abandoned at this time, and Tel ʿEton was relatively isolated from its surrounding, with very limited connections to both the Philistine settlement to the west and the Israelite region to the east. This is manifested, for example, in the amount of pottery manufactured at the site and its immediate vicinity, which reached a peak of more than 70 percent!

With the transition to the Iron Age IIA the site again grew in size, and probably also in importance. The site was fortified and it is likely that it become part of Judah, probably as a result of an alliance between the site's leaders and the Israelites. This was in tandem with the gradual process of colonization of the Shephelah by Judah (and maybe even preceded it). It appears that a process of cultural change at the site was underway at this stage, and the inhabitants were in the process of assimilation i.e., of losing their unique identity and eventually becoming Judahites. During the settlement peak of Iron Age IIB the site served as a regional center in the southern trough valley. This was a large and fortified city, and the finds include parts of many dwellings, including what we call the governor's residency, a rich ceramic assemblage, bullae, and more. The inhabitants were clearly Judahites at the time. Tel ʿEton interacted mainly with its immediate surroundings (the percentage of the pottery produced in the site and its immediate vicinity is about 40 percent, quite similar to that of the Late Bronze Age), but at this time the weight shifted more to the north (the central Shephelah). The evidence suggests that the site was one of the central cities of Judah at the time, and that it was perhaps one of the "gateways" through which the highland center managed the Shephelah. Like most of the Shephelah, the site was devastated in Sennacherib's campaign and did not recover. The mound was desolate for over 300 years, until a fort and a village were erected on it in the 4th century BCE.[66]

List of Figures (see after Bibliography)

1. Location Map of Tel ʿEton (prepared by Yair Sapir)
2. Excavation Areas at Tel ʿEton (prepared by Tamar Olenick)
3. The Assyrian Destruction Layer in Room 101C, Area A
4. The Assyrian Destruction Layer in Area B (Square S48)
5. Area A—up-to-date plan of the excavations, reflecting the current state of the area (prepared by Segev Ramon, Yair Sapir and Tamar Olenick)

66. Faust et al., "Late Persian."

6. Part of the 8th-Century Ceramic Assemblage

BIBLIOGRAPHY

Albright, William F. "The Excavations of Tell Beit Mirsim I: The Pottery of the First Three Campaigns." *Annual of the American Schools of Oriental Research* 12 (1931).
———. "The Excavations of Tell Beit Mirsim III: The Iron Age." *Annual of the American Schools of Oriental Research* 21–22 (1943).
Ayalon, Etan. "Trial Excavation of Two Iron Age Strata at Tel 'Eton." *Tel Aviv* 12 (1985) 54–62.
Barkay, Gabriel. "The Iron Age II–III." In *The Archaeology of Ancient Israel*, edited by Amnon Ben-Tor, 302–73. New Haven: Yale University Press, 1992.
Broshi, Magen, and Israel Finkelstein. "The Population of Palestine in the Iron Age II." *BASOR* 287 (1992) 47–60.
Bunimovitz, Shlomo. "Sea Peoples in Cyprus and Israel: A Comparative Study of Immigration Process." In *Mediterranean Peoples in Transition: Thirteenth to Early Tenth Centuries B.C.E.*, edited by Seymour Gitin et al., 103–13. Jerusalem: Israel Exploration Society, 1998.
Bunimovitz, Shlomo, and Avraham Faust. "Chronological Separation, Geographical Segregation, or Ethnic Demarcation? Ethnography and the Iron Age Low Chronology." *BASOR* 322 (2001) 1–10.
———. "Ideology in Stone, Understanding the Four Room House." *BAR* 28/4 (2002) 32–41, 59–60.
Bunimovitz, Shlomo, and Lederman, Zvi. "A Border Case: Beth-Shemesh and Rise of Ancient Israel." In *Israel in Transition: From the Late Bronze II to the Iron Age IIa (c. 1250–850 B.C.E.)*, edited by Lester L. Grabbe, 1:21–31. Library of Hebrew Bible/Old Testament Studies 491. New York: T. & T. Clark, 2008.
———. "Beth-Shemesh." In *NEAEHL* 1.249–53.
———. "Canaanite Resistance: The Philistines and Beth-Shemesh—A Case Study from Iron Age I." *BASOR* 364 (2011) 37–51.
———. "The Archaeology of Border Communities: Renewed Excavations at Tel Beth-Shemesh (part I, the Iron Age)." *NEA* 72 (2009) 114–42.
Bunimovitz, Shlomo, and Assaf Yasur-Landau. "Philistine and Israelite Pottery: A Comparative Approach to the Question of Pots and People." *Tel Aviv* 23 (1996) 88–101.
Croft, Paul. "Archaeozoological Studies." In *The Renewed Archaeological Excavations at Lachish (1973–1994)*, edited by David Ussishkin, 2254–348. 5 vols. Tel-Aviv: Tel-Aviv University, 2004.
Dagan, Yehuda. "The Settlement in the Judean Shephelah in the Second and First Millennium B.C.: A Test-case of Settlement Processes in a Geographic Region." PhD diss., Tel Aviv University, 2000 (Hebrew).
Edelstein, Gershon, and Sarah Aurant. "The 'Philistine' Tomb at Tell 'Eitun." *Atiqot* 21 (1992) 23–41.
Edelstein, Gershon, et al. "The Necropolis of Tell 'Aitun." *Qadmoniot* 15 (1971) 86–90 (Hebrew).
Faust, Avraham. "An Assemblage of Bullae from Tel 'Eton and the Development of Administration in Judah." Paper presented at the 30th Annual Meeting of the

Department of Land of Israel Studies and Archaeology, Bar-Ilan University (and the J. M. Alkow Department of Archaeology and Near Eastern Cultures, Tel Aviv University), "And They Went Up and Toured the Land," in honor of Professor Anson F. Rainey on the occasion of his 80th birthday (held at Bar-Ilan University on May 6, 2010).

———. "Between Israel and Philistia: Ethnic Negotiations in the Iron Age I." In *The Ancient Near East in the 12th–10th Centuries BCE: Culture and History*, edited by Gershon Galil et al., 121–35. Münster: Ugarit-Verlag, 2012.

———. "The History of Tel 'Eton Following the Results of the First Seven Seasons of Excavations (2006–2012)." In *Proceedings of the 8th International Congress on the Archaeology of the Ancient Near East (ICAANE): 30 April–4 May 2012, University of Warsaw (Volume 2, Excavations and Progress Reports)*, edited by Piotr Bieliński et al., 585–604. Wiesbaden, Harrassowitz: 2014.

———. "The Iron I–Iron II Transition in the South: Settlement, Demography and Political Changes." *New Studies on Jerusalem* 20 (2014) 35–65 (Hebrew).

———. *Israel's Ethnogenesis: Settlement, Interaction, Expansion and Resistance*. London: Equinox, 2006.

———. "The 'Philistine Tomb' at Tel 'Eton: Cultural Contact, Colonialism, and Local Responses in the Iron Age Shephelah, Israel." *Journal of Anthropological Research* 71 (2015) 195–230.

———. "Pottery and Society in Iron Age Philistia: Feasting, Identity, Economy and Gender." *BASOR* 373 (2015) 167–98.

———. "Settlement and Demography in Seventh Century Judah and the Extent and Intensity of Sennacherib's Campaign." *PEQ* 140 (2008) 168–94.

———. "The Shephelah in the Iron Age: A New Look on the Settlement of Judah." *PEQ* 145 (2013) 203–19.

———. "Tel 'Eton Excavations (2006–2009): A Preliminary Report." *PEQ* 143 (2011) 198–224.

Faust, Avraham, and Shlomo Bunimovitz. "The Four Room House: Embodying Israelite Society." *NEA* 66 (2003) 22–31.

Faust, Avraham, and Esther Eshel. "An Inscribed Bulla with Grazing Doe from Tel 'Eton." In *Puzzling Out the Past: Studies in the Northwest Semitic Languages and Literatures in Honor of Bruce Zuckerman*, edited by Marilyn J. Lundberg et al., 63–70. Culture and History of the Ancient Near East 55. Leiden: Brill, 2012.

Faust, Avraham, and Hayah Katz. "Philistines, Israelites and Canaanites in the Southern Trough Valley During the Iron Age I." *Egypt and the Levant* 21 (2011) 231–47.

———. "A Canaanite Town, Judahite Center, and a Persian Period Fort: Excavating Over Two Thousand Years of History at Tel 'Eton." *NEA* 78 (2015) 88–102 (with contributions by Zev Farber, Yair Sapir, Assaf Avraham and Shani Libi).

———. "Survey, Shovel Tests and Excavations at Tel 'Eton: on Methodology and Site History." *Tel Aviv* 39 (2012) 158–85.

———. "Tel 'Eton Cemetery: An Introduction." *Hebrew Bible and Ancient Israel* 5 (2016) 171–86.

Faust, Avraham, and Justin Lev-Tov. "The Construction of Philistine Identity: Ethnic Dynamics in 12th–10th Centuries Philistia." *Oxford Journal of Archaeology* 30 (2011) 13–31.

———. "Philistia and the Philistines in the Iron Age I: Interaction, Ethnic Dynamics and Boundary Maintenance." *HIPHIL Novum* 1 (2014) 1–24.

Faust, Avraham, et al. "Tel ʿEton / Tell ʿEtun and its Interregional Contacts from the Late Bronze Age to the Persian-Hellenistic Period: Between Highlands and Lowlands." *ZDPV* 130 (2014) 43–76.

———. "Late Persian–Early Hellenistic Remains at Tel ʿEton: A Preliminary Report (2006–2014)." *Tel Aviv* 42 (2015) 103–26.

Finkelstein, Israel. "The Archaeology of the Days of Manasseh." In *Scripture and Other Artifacts: Essays on the Bible and Archaeology in Honor of Philip J. King*, edited by Michael D. Coogan et al., 169–87. Louisville: Westminster John Knox, 1994.

———. "The Date of the Settlement of the Philistines in Canaan." *Tel Aviv* 23 (1995) 170–84.

———. "The Philistine Settlements: When, Where and How Many?" In *The Sea People and Their World: A Reassessment*, edited by Eliezer D. Oren, 159–80. Philadelphia: University of Pennsylvania, 2000.

Galil, Gershon. "The Administrative Division of the Shephelah." *Shnaton—An Annual for Biblical and Ancient Near Eastern Studies* 9 (1985) 55–71 (Hebrew).

Gibson, Shimon. "The Tell ej-Judeideh (Tel Goded) Excavations: A Re-appraisal Based on Archival Records in the Palestine Exploration Fund." *Tel Aviv* 21 (1994) 194–234.

Gilboa, Ayelet, et al. "Philistine Bichrome Pottery: The View from the Northern Canaanite Coast." In *"I Will Speak the Riddles of Ancient Times": Archaeological and Historical Studies in Honor of Amihai Mazar on the Occasion of His Sixtieth Birthday*, edited by Aren M. Maeir and Pierre de Miroschedji, 303–34. Winona Lake, IN: Eisenbrauns, 2006.

Givon, Shmuel. "Harasim (Tel)." In *NEAEHL* 5:1766–7.

Greenberg, Raphael. "New Light on the Early Iron Age at Tell Beit Mirsim." *BASOR* 265 (1987) 55–80.

Herzog, Zeev. "The Arad Fortresses" (in Hebrew). In *Arad*, edited by Ruth Amiran et al, 113–292. Tel-Aviv: Hakibutz Hameuchad and the Israel Exploration Society, 1997.

Katz, Hayah, and Avraham Faust. "The Assyrian Destruction Layer at Tel ʿEton." *IEJ* 62 (2012) 22–53.

———. "The Chronology of the Iron Age IIA in Judah in the Light of Tel ʿEton Tomb C3 and Other Assemblages." *BASOR* 371 (2014) 103–27.

Killebrew, Anne E., and Justin Lev-Tov. "Early Iron Age Feasting and Cuisine: An Indicator of Philistine-Aegean Connectivity?" In *DAIS—The Aegean Feast: Proceedings of the 12th International Aegean Conference, University of Melbourne, Centre for Classics and Archaeology, 25-29 March 2008*, edited by Louise A. Hitchcock et al., 339–46. Aegaeum 29. Liège: Histoire de l'art et archéologie de la Grèce antique, Université de Liège / Austin: Program in Aegean Scripts and Prehistory, University of Texas at Austin, 2008.

Lipschits, Oded, et al. "Tel Azekah 113 Years After: Preliminary Evaluation of the Renewed Excavations at the Site." *NEA* 75 (2012) 196–206.

Mazar, Amihai. "The Debate over the Chronology of the Iron Age in the Southern Levant: Its History, the Current Situation and Suggested Resolution." In *The Bible and Radiocarbon Dating: Archaeology, Text and Science*, edited by Thomas E. Levy and Thomas Higham, 15–30. London: Routledge, 2005.

———. "The Iron Age Chronology Debate: Is the Gap Narrowing? Another Viewpoint." *NEA* 74 (2011) 105–11.

de Miroschedji, Pierre. *Yarmouth I*. Paris: Recherche sur les civilizations, 1988.
———. "Yarmuth: The Dawn of City States in Southern Canaan." *NEA* 62 (1999) 2–19.
Na'aman, Nadav. "The Date of the List of Towns that Received the Spoil of Amalek (1 Sam 30: 26–31)." *Tel Aviv* 37 (2010) 175–87.
———. "The Shephelah According to the Amarna Letters." In *The Fire Signals of Lachish: Studies in the Archaeology and History of Israel in the Late Bronze Age, Iron Age, and Persian Period in Honor of David Ussishkin*, edited by Israel Finkelstein and Nadav Na'aman, 281–99. Winona Lake, IN: Eisenbrauns, 2011.
Noth, Martin. *Das Buch Josua*. Tübingen: Mohr/Siebeck, 1953.
Ofer, Avi. "The Judean Hills in the Biblical Period." *Qadmoniot* 31.115 (1998) 40–52 (Hebrew).
Rainey, Anson F. "The Administrative Division of the Shephelah." *Tel Aviv* 7 (1980) 194–201.
Sapir-Hen, Lidar, et al. "Pig Husbandry in Iron Age Israel and Judah: New Insights Regarding the Origin of the 'Taboo.'" *ZDPV* 129 (2013) 1–20.
Seger, Joe D. "Halif (Tel)." In *NEAEHL* 2:553–9.
Shai, Itzhak., et al. "The Fortifications at Tel Burna: Date, Function and Meaning." *IEJ* 62 (2012) 57–141.
Shavit, Alon. "Settlement Patterns of Philistine City-States." In *Bene Israel: Studies in the Archaeology of Israel and the Levant During the Bronze and Iron Ages in Honour of Israel Finkelstein*, edited by Alexander. Fantalkin and Assaf Yasur-Landau, 135–64, 266–78. Leiden: Brill, 2008.
Tappy, Ronald E. "East of Ashkelon: The Setting and Settling of the Judean Lowlands in the Iron Age IIA." In *Exploring the Longue Durée: Essays in Honor of Lawrence E. Stager*, edited by J. David Schloen, 449–63. Winona Lake, IN: Eisenbrauns, 2009.
———. "Zayit (Tel)." In *NEAEHL* 5:2082–3.
Ussishkin, David. "A Synopsis of the Stratigraphical, Chronological and Historical Issues." In *The Renewed Archaeological Excavations at Lachish (1973–1994)*, edited by David Ussishkin, 50–119. 5 vols. Tel-Aviv: Tel-Aviv University, 2004.
———. *Biblical Lachish: A Tale of Construction, Destruction, Excavations and Restoration*. Jerusalem: Israel Exploration Society, 2014.
Zimhoni, Orna. "The Iron Age Pottery of Tel 'Eton and Its Relations to the Lachish, Tell Beit Mirsim and Arad Assemblages." *Tel Aviv* 12 (1985) 63–90.

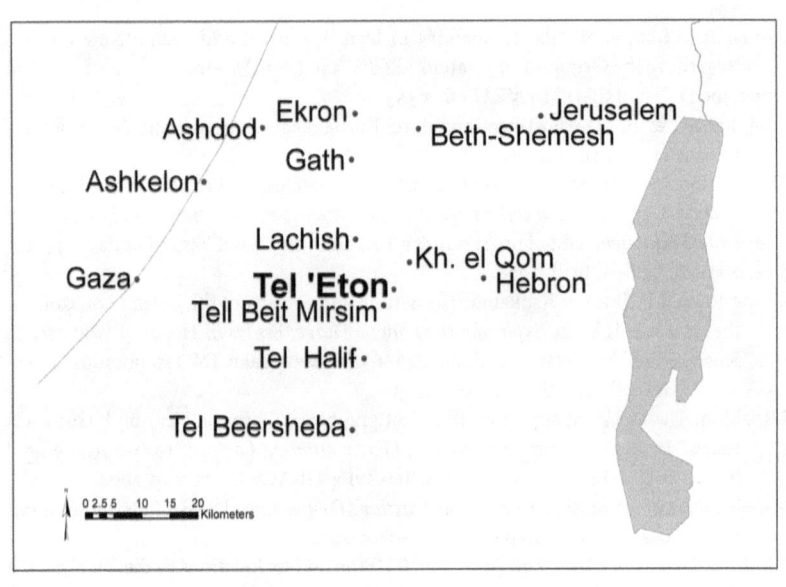

Figure 1: Location Map of Tel 'Eton (prepared by Yair Sapir)

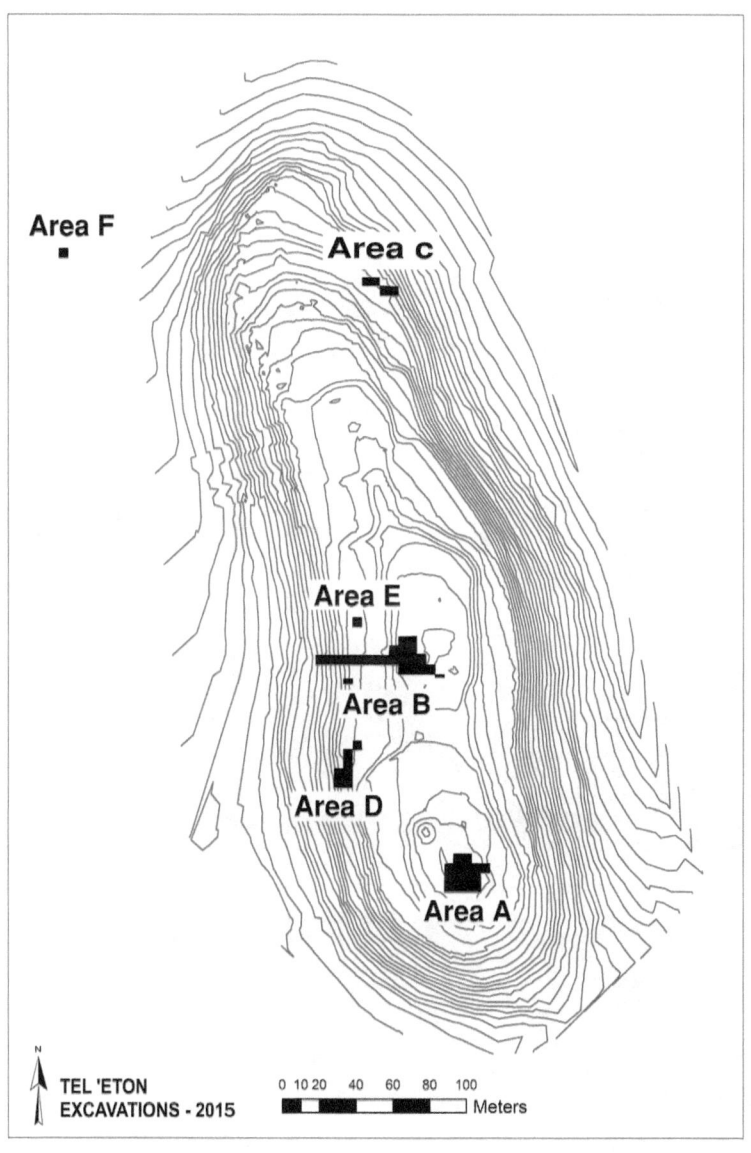

Figure 2: Excavation Areas at Tel 'Eton (prepared by Tamar Olenick)

Figure 3: The Assyrian Destruction Layer in Room 101C, Area A
(photograph by Avraham Faust)

Figure 4: The Assyrian Destruction Layer in Area B (Square S48)
(photograph by Avraham Faust)

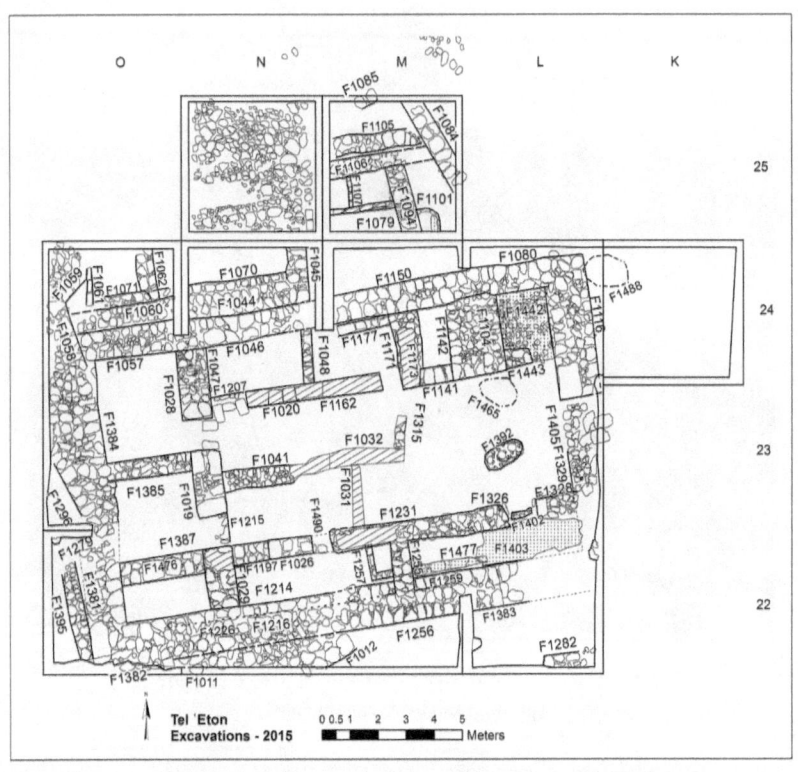

Figure 5: Area A—up-to-date plan of the excavations, reflecting the current state of the area (prepared by Segev Ramon, Yair Sapir and Tamar Olenick)

Figure 6: Part of the 8th-Century Ceramic Assemblage
(photograph by Avraham Faust)

3

Jerusalem in Rome: Moses Mendelssohn on the Arch of Titus Menorah

Steven Fine

YESHIVA UNIVERSITY

Few archaeological artifacts have elicited more modern rabbinic comment than the menorah bas relief of the Arch of Titus (figure 1). The Arch, constructed by the Emperor Domitian around 81 CE on Rome's Via Sacra, commemorates the triumphal parade awarded to Titus in the summer of 71 CE and well documented in Flavius Josephus' *Jewish War*.[1] For most of its history, rabbis showed relatively little interest in the Arch of Titus, its menorah evoking no comment by Jews—even though the reliefs of the Arch survived from antiquity to the modern period relatively unscathed and were in full views of all passers by. It was only in the late 18th century, after images of the bas reliefs of the Arch began to spread throughout Europe, that Jews seem to have taken an active interest in this menorah.[2] The best guide to this monument was a relatively small book by the Christian Hebraist Adriaan Reland,

---

1. *Jewish War* 7.119–62. See further Pfanner, *Der Titusbogen*; and Yarden, *Spoils of Jerusalem*. The present article draws upon my recently completed manuscript, *The Menorah: From the Bible to Modern Israel*, which it subsequently enhanced. Many thanks to my colleagues Joshua Karlip and Daniel Rynhold, who discussed aspects of Mendelssohn studies with me.

2. Preschel, "ha-Menorah"; and Fine, *The Menorah*.

a Dutch scholar of biblical geography who produced *De spoliis templi Hierosolymitani in arcu Titiano Romae conspicuis liber singularis: arcum ipsum & spolia templi in eo sculpta tabulae in aes incisae exhibent* (Utrecht, 1716). Classical and neo-classical trends in European culture brought greater attention to the Arch of Titus, one of the few standing artifacts of ancient Rome (figure 2)—and one of particular significance to Christianity. Europeans embarking on the "Grand Tour," eventually including Jews,[3] had first hand experience with the Arch of Titus and brought paintings and prints of this artifact northward with them, even as developing European nation states looked to Rome for models in their own republican and imperial constructions. Over the course of the 19th and 20th centuries secularizing Jews took interest in the Arch of Titus, refracting their process of modernization through the prism of its bas reliefs. Jewish reflection on the Arch of Titus and its menorah well reflects the hopes, dangers and failures of the Emancipation process, and the Arch menorah often graphically symbolized this en*light*enment. The first "rabbinic" response to this process appears in Moses Mendelssohn's commentary on Exodus 25, which appears in his *Sefer Netivot ha-Shalom* (first published in 1780–1783) or simply called the *Be'ur*, "The Commentary." In this short note, dedicated to our friend Ziony Zevit—a master of the intersection of text, artifact, and history—I will reflect on the complexities of this relationship with the Arch of Titus menorah at an early stage as refracted through Mendelssohn's commentary.

Moses Mendelssohn's *Sefer Netivot ha-Shalom* was created explicitly as an educational vehicle to ease German speaking Jewry into the body politic of modern Prussia.[4] It was a tool of Emancipation, its translation into High German printed in Hebrew script, even as its commentary, the *Be'ur*, aspired for a kind of modernized rabbinism—a bridge document of the *Haskalah*. Mendelssohn's focus upon both philology and critical use of rabbinic sources strikes one today as rather conservative. At the time, however, this was a very modern—though religiously conservative—document, adapting the best *wissenschaftliche* practices of the day to a rabbinic idiom. The readership of the *Be'ur* is well known, as subscription lists are preserved. Steven Lowenstein has discussed the subscribers in an important article,[5] showing that the first subscribers to the *Be'ur* lived mainly in northern Europe and disproportionately included the Berlin Jewish elite, of which Mendelssohn was a major presence. As an elite, increasingly committed to German classicizing educational models, *Bildung*, these Jews would have been quite aware

---

3. Biemann, *Dreaming of Michelangelo*; Wilton and Bignamini, *Grand Tour*.
4. Altmann, *Moses Mendelssohn*, 368–83; and Sorkin, *Moses Mendelssohn*, 53–91.
5. Lowenstein, "Readership."

of the Arch of Titus, an artifact that Mendelssohn viewed with considerable consternation. In a sense, the Arch stood as a bridge between western culture and Jewish culture, a fulcrum upon which to balance an increasingly complex Jewish-German identity. Its menorah was known to all as a "Jewish" artifact at the heart of Rome, a point where "Rome and Jerusalem," "Judaism and Hellenism," converge.[6]

From the late 18th century, Christian pilgrims write that Jews avoided walking under the Arch, though this practice is unmentioned in Jewish sources. This abstention likely grew after the papal reconstruction of this monument in 1821,[7] followed by the popularization of its style in triumphal arches across Europe, the most prominent being the Arc de Triomphe, commissioned by Napoleon in 1806 and completed during the reign of Louis-Phillipe in 1836. Before the reconstruction under Pius VII, the Arch of Titus was part of a regular thoroughfare—difficult to avoid, symbolically less prominent. By the mid-19th century at the very latest it became something of a Jewish pilgrimage site, which included the ritualized ambiguity of not walking beneath it. For Mendelssohn, the Arch, and particularly its menorah, was a disturbing external vantage point from which rabbinic tradition could be judged by Jews who were no longer fully committed to the authority of rabbinic interpretation—influenced by Christian negative evaluations of rabbinic literature.[8] In this sense, the Arch menorah panel was dangerous, for through it emancipating though still ostensibly traditionalist Berlin Jews could see themselves, and judge themselves against an actual historical artifact. For this reason, Mendelssohn took the unusual step of discussing an archaeological artifact in the pages of *Sefer Netivot ha-Shalom*, a book that by its title promises to be a "way of peace," teaching its readers to navigate between their ever more complex religious and social commitments.

Completing a rather long and complex philological treatment of the Tabernacle menorah, Mendelssohn's comments are tied to Exodus 25:40, וּרְאֵה וַעֲשֵׂה בְּתַבְנִיתָם אֲשֶׁר־אַתָּה מָרְאֶה בָּהָר "And see that you make them after the pattern for them, which is being shown you on the mountain" (RSV):

ודע שבעיר רומי, בתוך החרבות שנשארו מהארמוני' והטירות שהיו שם בימי קדם, נשארו עוד היום שיורים מבנין מפואר של שיש שהקימו לכבוד טיטוס ועסספאפאסיאונוס, נקרא ארק"א ד"י טיט"ו (טריומף באגגן דעם טיטוס), וניכרי' שם תמונות בולטות מכלי המקדש שהוליך הצר עמו משבי ירושלים, בשובו מלהחריב את בית אלהינו, ובתוכן צורת המנורה ניכרת היטב עד היום הזה, ואולם כפי הנראה מתוך

---

6. Rajak, "Jews and Greeks."
7. I will deal with this phenomenon in a forthcoming article on the ritualization of Arch visits by Jews in the modern period.
8. See Breuer, "Politics, Tradition, History."

Jerusalem in Rome

הספרי' אשר שם העתיקו את התמונות ההן, אין לסמוך עליהן כלל, ויתכן שהחרש המסתת לא
כוון לעשות דוגמתן בדקדוק, ובפרט שכפי הנראה לא נעשה הבנין ההוא כי אם אחרי מות טיטוס,
ואפשר שלא שם הכלים עצמם נגד עיניו, כאשר סתת אותם, ולא דקדק לעשותם כראוי, ואולם אמת
הדבר שהוליכו כלי בית אלהינו לרומי, וגנזום שם באוצרותיהם, כמו שזכרו חז"ל במעילה (דף י"ד
ע"ב), ושם ראה ר' אליעזר בר' יוסי, שהיה כמה שנים אחר החורבן, את הציץ ואת הפרוכת (כדאי'
שם במעילה ובשבת דף ס"ג ע"ב וביומא דף נ"ז ע"א ובסוכה דף ה ע"א) ובסוף פרק אחרון דאבות
דר' נתן איתא מכתשת של בית אבטינס ושולחן ומנורה ופרוכת וציץ עדיין מונחי' ברומי:

> And know that in the city of Rome, among the ruins that remain from palaces and castles there still remains to this day remains of a magnificent building of marble that they erected in honor of Titus and Vespasian called the *Arco di Tito* (*Triumph bogen dem Titus*). Recognizable there are the bas reliefs of the Temple vessels that the enemy brought with him from the capture of Jerusalem—when he returned from having destroyed the house of our God—and among them the image of the menorah is easily recognizable to this very day. However, it appears from the books in which they copied there those images, they cannot be trusted at all. It is possible that the stone carver had no intention to copy them exactly—especially as the building was apparently not constructed until after the death of Titus. It is possible that he did not place the vessels themselves before his eyes when he carved them, and was not careful to make them appropriately. It is true that they took the vessels of the house of our God to Rome, and hid them there in their treasury—as our Sages, of Blessed Memory, remember in [Babylonian Talmud tractate] Me'ilah (14b),[9] and there Rabbi Eliezer son of Rabbi Yose, who lived a few years after the destruction [of the Temple], the [priestly] frontispiece [ṣiṣ] and the curtain [parokhet] (Me'ilah, ad loc., Shabbat 63b, Yoma 47a, Sukkah 5b) and the end of the last chapter of the *Fathers According to Rabbi Nathan* [version A, chapter 41, p. 131] says that "the grinding tool of the house of Avtinas and the table and the menorah and the curtain and the frontispiece are still stored in Rome."

This text begins with a description of the Arch of Titus, an object that he points out still exists in Rome. Sight is an important theme of this discussion. It is Mendelssohn's claim that the image of the menorah on the Arch of Titus is incorrect, specifically because it does not conform with Rabbinic descriptions of the menorah. He knows this from "books" with images of the Arch panel, which were quite common in his period. Reland's volume is by far the best of these, based upon actual measurement of the Arch menorah

---

9. Vilna ed., 17b

and drawings made on location by an anonymous British scholar (figure 3). It is significant that Mendelssohn explicitly admits that he himself had not seen the Arch, and there is no evidence that he visited Rome. He relies on etchings in books. This sidepoint both connects to his general theme of "seeing" and shows just how widely this sort of image had been disseminated through the print medium by his time. The image was apparently so well known that Mendelssohn polemicized against the Arch menorah, but did not provide an image of the offending artifact—perhaps because he had no capacity for illustrations (there are none anywhere in the *Be'ur*), as a form of erasure, or just because everyone knew what the Arch menorah looked like! Mendelssohn's reliance on books also absolves him of a personal search for these artifacts in Rome itself, and so allows the claims of Rabbinic literature to stand unchallenged. Significantly, Mendelssohn never mentions or discusses the other Temple vessels that appear in the Arch bas reliefs, the Table of Showbread and the horns, even though the table does not fit rabbinic norms either. Clearly this is because this rather simple table, which appears in very low relief and is damaged, never became part of the public conversation about the Arch, and was not seen as a challenge.

Though he never describes the offending elements of the menorah—which he must assume are widely recognized—Mendelssohn's concerns seem to have been focused on the six-sided base and not with the branches, which are rather close to standard Jewish and Christian representations of the menorah. The base, however, finds no precedent in Scripture, the literature of the rabbis, nor the history of Jewish art until late in the 19th century.[10] It began to appear in European art only during the 17th century, most famously in Nicholas Poussin's much acclaimed *The Destruction and Sack of the Temple of Jerusalem* (1625–1626), now at the Israel Museum.[11] Rabbinic tradition asserts that the base of the menorah was a three-legged tripod,[12] a form of lampstand that was common in the Roman world and the most common representation in Jewish and pre-modern Christian art (figures 4–5). Though no extant literary sources discuss the base explicitly, it is worthy of note that no Jewish image of the menorah from late antiquity through modern times represented the Arch base, with its images of mythological animals—even among those from Rome. On occasion, early modern Roman Jewry portrayed a heavy base that hearkens back to the Arch in images that appeared in public places, but never with the tell-tale

---

10. The Hanukkah lamp collection of the Jewish Museum, New York well reflects the breadth of menorah images in 18th-century Europe. See Braunstein, *Five Centuries of Hanukkah Lamps*, pp. 12, 48, 65, 67, 68, 70, 105, 128–9, 233, 235–9, 255, 265, 304–7.

11. Inventory number B99.0001

12. b. Menaḥ. 28b. See Herzog, "Ṣurat ha-Menora," 97.

animals. We see this, for example on a fragment of a fountain from the Jewish ghetto of Rome, dated 1614 (figure 6).[13] At the same time, images of the menorah branches that are much like those of the Arch were quite common across Jewish visual culture, and were unquestioned. It seems likely to me that Mendelssohn falls within this interpretive tradition. If the base of the Arch of Titus menorah was the correct one, then Jewish tradition must of necessity have been in error. Mendelssohn set out to defend the rabbis, while carefully avoiding offending Gentile sensibilities.

To do this, he imagines a scenario whereby the Roman artisan made an artifact that does not represent the menorah of the Temple. In this way he creates some space between Judaism and the lamp of the Roman bas relief. Mendelssohn offers two options. He points out, first, that the artisan may not have intended to present the menorah accurately, which thus allows for both the Roman relief and the rabbis to be "correct." He immediately adds the possibility that Titus died before the artisan could see the actual menorah in his storehouse. This explanation relies upon b. Meʿil. 17b, which has it that the vessels were hidden away in the imperial *genizah*, though this text makes no mention of the menorah *per se*. It is indeed true that the Arch was built a decade after the triumphal march, and soon after Titus died in 80 CE. What Mendelssohn either elides, or did not know, was that Josephus (*Jewish War* 7.158–62) writes that the menorah and the table were displayed in the Temple of Peace, not far from the Arch of Titus. The rabbinic explanation, of course, is central to his argument, since his audience could well be aware of that text (or at least, impressed by Mendelssohn's erudition in citing it). Mendelssohn claims that the artisan worked from memory and did not intend to provide an exact image of the menorah absolves the Roman artisan from error. His goals were just different. As a member of a colonized people hoping for admission to German society, this is an attractive answer, as it avoids explicit blame of the artists of a major artifact of the Classical tradition. The discrepancy was thus not the "fault" of the rabbis, nor the "fault" of Roman culture writ large, but was based upon differing concerns. This sense of sight clearly connects the inaccurate approximation made by the Roman to the commandment to "see that you make them after the pattern for them, which is being shown you on the mountain." He did not follow the God-given "pattern," creating an object that errs in its presentation of the biblical lampstand. Mendelssohn goes still further, asserting that the Rabbis—who knew that the Temple vessels had reached Rome—had a more trustworthy knowledge of the menorah. For this reason, Mendelssohn recounts in great detail all of the rabbinic sources that were available to him. The ancient

13. Di Castro, "Jews of Rome."

rabbis, like sophisticated Germans of his own day, visited Rome, and thus were to be trusted in their depiction of the menorah. Pointedly, he even provides a date for Rabbi Eliezer son of Rabbi Yose, whom we now know as a Tanna of the fifth generation, ca. 170 CE or so, to "a few years after the destruction."[14] In so doing, Mendelssohn provides a viable historical time frame for Rabbi Eliezer's sighting of the Temple vessels. Unfortunately for Mendelssohn, *Midrash Sifre Zuṭa* was not published until 1894, nearly a century later.[15] A tradition preserved in this Tannaitic document claims that Rabbi Shimon bar Yohai went to Rome and "saw" the menorah. This text would have made his point in no uncertain terms![16]

Mendelssohn's approach to the Arch menorah reflects his larger response to what we might call the colonial gaze on Judaism, and his larger attempt to provide his Hebrew audience with a counter-narrative to the one normative among his German correspondents. It is the inverse of a discussion of the Ark of the Covenant that appears in his philosophical tract *Jerusalem*, a book directed to a largely non-Jewish audience. There he argues for deep cultural knowledge as a prerequisite for cultural judgement: "In judging the religious ideas of a nation that is otherwise unknown," Mendelssohn writes, "one must . . . take care not to regard everything from one's own *parochial* point of view, lest one should call idolatry what, in reality, is perhaps only *script*."[17] Among Mendelssohn's examples of colonizing interpretation is the cherubim of the Ark of the Covenant. These biblical artifacts have a long tradition of interpretation among both Jews and Christians, since they go against an anti-iconic strain in Biblical interpretation that goes back as far as Josephus and was particularly prevalent in Protestant thought:

> In plundering the Temple, the conquerors of Jerusalem found the cherubim on the Ark of the Covenant, and took them to be the idols of the Jews. They saw everything with the eyes of barbarians, and from their point of view. In accordance with their own customs, they took the image of the divine providence and prevailing grace for an image of the Deity, the Deity itself, and delighted in their discovery.[18]

I wonder whether Mendelssohn here avoided identifying the Babylonian destroyers of the First Temple in 586 BCE in order to quietly insinuate

14. Margalioth, *Enṣiqlopedya*, 51.

15. Koenigsberger, *Sifre Zuṭa*.

16. *Sifre Zuṭa*, *Be-Haʿalotkha* to Numbers 8:2; Fine, *Art, History and the Historiography of Judaism*, 71.

17. Mendelssohn, *Jerusalem*, 113.

18. Ibid, 114. See Leonard, *Socrates and the Jews*, 54.

the Romans as well. Many medieval and modern Christians saw the Ark of the Covenant, which they imagined was taken by Titus and illustrated on the Arch spoils panel (in fact, what they "saw" was the Showbread table). Mendelssohn's comment on the Ark might well have been said against the Roman sculptor of the Arch menorah, which he believed to have been remade by Rome in its own (idolatrous) image, and which he clearly saw as a challenge to Judaism. Maintaining Jewish aniconism against the Arch menorah base with its "illicit" images almost certainly stands behind our *Be'ur* tradition, especially when set against his general attitudes toward idolatry as exemplified in his strident interpretation of the idolatry in the *Be'ur* and in *Jerusalem*.[19] Ingrid Lohmann argues that the trope of aniconism was central to Mendelssohn's project, "a plea for an extended universalism" where Judaism and Protestantism are in agreement. Were the Arch menorah an accurate approximation of the Temple menorah, it would mitigate against this highly sought-after unanimity. Mendelssohn thus explained this artifact away, protecting both the interpretive authority of the rabbis and the proximity of their religion to that of the Protestant majority.

Mendelssohn's polemic against the Arch of Titus menorah in defense of Rabbinic tradition is the first of a series of such texts, the others of which responded to the choice of the Arch menorah as symbol of the State of Israel in 1949. These rabbinic responses—by Rabbi Isaac Halevy Herzog (1956), by Rabbi Yosef Qafiḥ (1967) and most recently by Rabbi Menachem Mendel Schneerson (1986),[20] each follow lines first charted by Moses Mendelssohn—though none of these rabbis cites Mendelssohn explicitly. Nonetheless, it is not unlikely that Herzog was aware of the comments in the *Be'ur*. Mendelssohn's comments were popularized by Brooklyn rabbi Tovia Preschel in a 1975 article, and could well have been known by Schneerson and his followers. The pathway from the unacknowledged Herzog to Qafiḥ is likely, as they were contemporaries. Schneerson explicitly cites Qafiḥ in his footnotes. In each of these cases, rabbis construct polemics against the Arch of Titus menorah in support of rabbinic interpretation. "Halakhic" interest in the Arch menorah is part and parcel of the modernization process, an attempt by rabbis to maintain their sense of traditional authority, up against one of the best known western "places of memory." Their defense, set in motion by Moses Mendelssohn, is a very modern enterprise.

---

19. Lohmann, "Motiv des Bilderverbots." This phenomenon is discussed more generally by Bland, *The Artless Jews*.

20. Herzog, "Ṣurat ha-Menora"; Qafiḥ in Maimonides, *Mišna 'im Peruš* 3: 119–20; and Schneerson, *Hilkhot Bet ha-Beḥira*, 50–51.

BIBLIOGRAPHY

Altmann, Alexander. *Moses Mendelssohn: A Biographical Study*. Tuscaloosa: University of Alabama Press, 1973.

Biemann, Asher D. *Dreaming of Michelangelo: Jewish Variations on a Modern Theme*. Stanford, CA: Stanford University Press, 2012.

Bland, Kalman P. *The Artless Jew: Medieval and Modern Affirmations and Denials of the Visual*. Princeton: Princeton University Press, 2000.

Braunstein, Susan L. *Five Centuries of Hanukkah Lamps from the Jewish Museum: A Catalogue Raisonné*. New York: Jewish Museum, 2004.

Breuer, Edward. "Politics, Tradition, History: Rabbinic Judaism and the Eighteenth-century Struggle for Civil Equality." *Harvard Theological Review* 85 (1992) 357–83.

Di Castro, Daniela. "The Jews of Rome, the Solemn Possession Ceremonies of the Popes and Fourteen Ephemeral Displays of the Seventeenth Century." In *Et Ecce Gaudium: The Roman Jews and the Investiture of the Popes*, edited by Daniela di Castro, 22–36. Translated by Lenore Rosenberg. [Rome]: Araldo de Luca, 2010.

Fine, Steven. *Art, History and the Historiography of Judaism in the Greco-Roman World*. Brill Reference Library of Judaism 34. Leiden: Brill, 2013.

———. *The Menorah: from the Bible to Modern Israel*. Cambridge: Harvard University Press, 2016.

Herzog, Yaakov Halevy. "Ṣurat ha-Menora še-be-Qešet Ṭiṭus." In *Scritti in Memoria Di Sally Mayer, 1875–1953. Saggi Sull'ebraismo Italiano*, edited by U. Nahon, 95–98. Jerusalem: Fondazione Sally Mayer / Milan: Scuola superiore di Studi Ebraici, 1956.

Koenigsberger, Bernhard. *Sifre Zuṭa . . . 'al Sefer Be-Midbar*. Frankfurt: Kaufmann, 1894.

Leonard, Miriam. *Socrates and the Jews: Hellenism and Hebraism from Moses Mendelssohn to Sigmund Freud*. Chicago: University of Chicago Press, 2012.

Lohmann, Ingrid. "Das Motiv des Bilderverbots bei Moses Mendelssohn." *Zeitschrift der Deutsche Gesellschaft für die Erforschung des 18. Jahrhunderts* 36 (2012) 33–42.

Lowenstein, Steven. "The Readership of Mendelssohn's Bible Translation." *HUCA* 53 (1982) 179–213.

Maimonides, Moses, *Mišna 'im Peruš Rabbenu Moše ben Maimun, Maqor ve-Targum*, edited by Yosef Qafiḥ. Jerusalem: Mosad Harav Kook, 1967.

Margalioth, Mordecai, with Yehudah Aizenberg. *Enṣiqlopedya le-Ḥakhme ha-Talmud ve-ha-Ge'onim*. 2nd ed. Tel-Aviv: Yavneh, 1995.

Mendelssohn, Moses. *Jerusalem, oder über religiöse Macht und Judentum*. Berlin: Mauer, 1783.

———. *Jerusalem, or, On Religious Power and Judaism*. Translated by Allan Arkush. Hanover, NH: Brandeis University Press / University Press of New England, 1983.

———. *Sefer Netivot ha-Shalom*. Berlin: Starcke, 1783.

Pfanner, Michael. *Der Titusbogen*. Beiträge zur Erschliessung hellenistischer und kaiserzeitlicher Skulptur und Architektur 2. Mainz: von Zabern, 1983.

Preschel, Tovia. "Ha-Menorah še-be-Ša'ar Ṭiṭus be-Roma." *ha-Do'ar* 53 (1975) 579–80.

Rajak, Tessa. "Jews and Greeks: The Invention and Exploitation of Polarities in the Nineteenth Century." In *The Jewish Dialogue with Greece and Rome*, 535–57. Arbeiten zur Geschichte des antiken Judentums und des Urchristentums 48. Leiden: Brill, 2001.

Reland, Adriaan. *De spoliis templi Hierosolymitani in arcu Titiano Romae conspicuis liber singularis: arcum ipsum & spolia templi in eo sculpta tabulae in aes incisae exhibent.* Trajecti ad Rhenum. [Utrecht]: Broedelet, 1716.

Schneerson, Menachem Mendel. *Hilkhot Bet ha-Beḥira.* Brooklyn: Kehot, 1986.

Sorkin, David. *Moses Mendelssohn and the Religious Enlightenment.* Berkeley: University of California Press, 1996.

Wilton, Andrew, and Ilaria Bignamini. *Grand Tour: The Lure of Italy in the Eighteenth Century.* London: Tate Gallery, 1996.

Yarden, Leon. *The Spoils of Jerusalem on the Arch of Titus: A Re-Investigation.* Skrifter utgivna av Svenska institutet i Rom 16. Stockholm: Svenska Institutet i Rom, 1991.

Figure1: Spoils of Jerusalem relief, Arch of Titus
(Courtesy of the Arch of Titus Project)

Figure 2: Menorah base of the Arch of Titus Menorah relief
(Courtesy of the Arch of Titus Project)

Figure 3: Drawing of the Menorah from Adriaan Reland,
De spoliis templi Hierosolymitani, 1716.

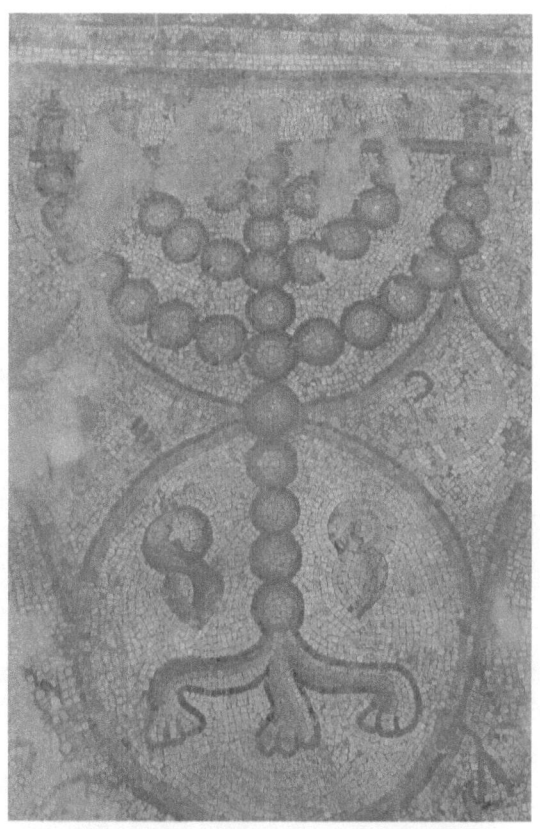

Figure 4: Mosaic Pavement from Maon (Nirim), 6th century
(Photograph by Steven Fine)

Figure 5: Raphael, *The Expulsion of Heliodorus from the Temple*, 1512, Vatican Museums (Photograph by Steven Fine)

Figure 6: Fountain from the Jewish ghetto of Rome, 1614
(Photograph by Steven Fine)

4

Ekron of the Philistines: A Response to Issues Raised in the Literature

Seymour Gitin

W. F. ALBRIGHT INSTITUTE OF
ARCHAEOLOGICAL RESEARCH

It is my pleasure to dedicate this article to Ziony Zevit, my esteemed colleague and friend, who has done much to foster a dialog on the interchange between biblical and archaeological studies. Over the years, Ziony and I have engaged in a long-term dialog on issues relating to this interchange within the context of the history and religion of ancient Israel. One example of these issues raised in the literature is the perception of the chronological, historical, and economic implications of dating the expanded city of Ekron to the 7th century BCE and its destruction to the very end of that century. The former is assigned to Stratum IC of the first three quarters of the 7th century BCE and the latter to Stratum IB, dated to 604 BCE.[1] The following

1. The fourteen excavation seasons at Tel Miqne-Ekron were directed by Professors Trude Dothan and Seymour Gitin during the years 1981–1996, under the auspices of the W. F. Albright Institute of Archaeological Research and the Hebrew University of Jerusalem. For a summary review of the excavations, see Dothan and Gitin, "Miqne, Tel (Ekron)," 1952–1958. A list of publications presenting the excavation results appears in Dothan and Gitin, *Tel Miqne-Ekron: Summary*. The three most recently published studies are Gitin, "Iron Age IIA–B: Philistia"; Gitin, "Iron Age IIC: Judah"; and Gitin, "Iron Age IIC: Philistia." Thanks go to Edna Sachar for her meticulous copy-editing of

analysis is offered in response to the arguments raised by Nadav Na'aman, Peter James, and Lawrence Stager against this dating and its implications.[2]

Na'aman maintains that Ekron Stratum IC represents an important city in the time of Sargon II, ca. 720 BCE, founded in the second half of the 8th century. He bases this on the documentary evidence provided by the Azekah inscription, which mentions a large fortified city that Na'aman identifies as Ekron. The city was "surrounded with great towers and exceedingly difficult [its ascent?]. It had a palace like a mountain."[3] If this indeed referred to Ekron, the description could only apply to the ten-acre upper city on the northeast acropolis in Stratum IIA of the 8th century. It included a city wall and a seven-meter-wide mudbrick tower with stone facing, which may be the features depicted in a relief in Sargon II's palace at Khorsabad, in which the Assyrians are shown besieging the city of *'amqar(r)ūna* (Ekron), dated either to 720 or 712 BCE.[4] The Azekah description cannot apply to Ekron's expanded lower city, with its extremely low and flat profile and its massive reoccupation in Stratum IC in the 7th century.[5] Na'aman bolsters his identification with 8th-century texts that "mention [Ekron] alongside Gaza, Ashkelon, and Ashdod—as a royal Philistine city in Amos 1:6–8 and Sennacherib's 701 inscription."[6]

Na'aman's second documentary source for an 8th-century dating is based on his interpretation of the relatively heavy tribute Ekron paid to Assyria during the reign of Sargon II as demonstrating its economic strength.[7] However, of the five tribute texts he cites, only one is definitively from the time of Sargon II. Na'aman states that another could be dated to the reign of Sargon II; a third is dated much later, to the time of Padi (699 BCE); and the date of the fourth is unknown. As for the fifth text, although Na'aman

---

the manuscript.

2. Some of the content of my response to the issues raised by Na'aman appears in Gitin, Garfinkel, and Dothan, "Occupational History." An analysis dealing with the issues raised by James and Stager appears in a different format, with additional information, in Gitin, "Temple Complex 650 at Ekron," 247–49.

3. Na'aman, "Ekron under the Assyrian and Egyptian Empires," 85.

4. Gitin, "Philistines in the Books of Kings," 340.

5. Another possible identification is suggested by Maeir ("The Tell es-Safi/Gath Archaeological Project 1996–2010," 54), who points out that even if Na'aman's 8th-century dating is accepted, "the relative position of the city in terms of the historical geography of the region is very likely to have been Gath. The city was noted as being situated on a high mountain and seems to have been in some direct proximity to Azekeh—both fitting perfectly with Tel es-Safi/Gath."

6. Na'aman, "Ekron under the Assyrian and Egyptian Empires," 85.

7. Ibid., 84.

asserts that it should be dated to Sargon II, he offers no supporting evidence.[8] Even if all of these tribute texts were related to the time of Sargon II, whether they add up to heavy tribute paid by Ekron remains questionable.[9] More important is determining when Ekron's expansion began, as this was the basis for achieving its maximum prosperity. This expansion should not be attributed to the reign of Sargon II, but rather to the period of Ekron's 'favored-nation' status in the late Assyrian Empire. Originally, Na'aman suggested that the expansion followed Sennacherib's 701 BCE campaign,[10] but he later qualified this position by questioning the impact of the *pax Assyriaca* on Ekron, pointing out that "the available sources do not suggest that Ekron enjoyed preferred status among the western vassals of Assyria, and all the conclusions to that effect rest on archaeological evidence."[11] While the documentary evidence demonstrates that preferred status was conferred by Sennacherib by transferring the towns of Judah that he had plundered to Assyria's western Philistine vassals of Ashdod, Ashkelon, Ekron, and Gaza[12]—interpreted by Bunimovitz and Lederman as part of a calculated Assyrian policy to encourage the economic growth of Philistia[13]—the question is how this status affected each of the vassals. The physical evidence indicates that Ashdod reached its peak under Sargon II, when the city expanded to include a lower city,[14] but does not offer any information on the impact of the preferred status granted by Sennacherib. As for Ashkelon, since the excavations have not yet been completed and the Iron IIB data have not yet been published, comparisons between the periods of Sargon II and Sennacherib are not possible. In Gaza, Sargon II opened a *karu*, a sealed port or harbor, in which Assyrians and Egyptians mingled and conducted trade,[15] but no evidence exists for the period of Sennacherib. Ekron is the single exception for which there is documentary and physical evidence providing sufficient information for both the period of Sargon II and of Sennacherib, and for the impact of 'favored-nation' status. In the last quarter of the 8th century, the above-mentioned relief dated either to 720 or 712 BCE depicting the siege of *'amqar(r)rūna* (Ekron) in Sargon II's palace must be related to Stratum

8. Ibid.

9. The tribute that Na'aman concludes was paid to the Assyrian kings was miniscule compared to what Holladay ("Hezekiah's Tribute," 327–28) has proposed as the wealth of Judah and Israel during the Neo-Assyrian period.

10. Na'aman, "Two Notes on Ashkelon and Ekron," 223.

11. Na'aman, "Ekron under the Assyrian and Egyptian Empires," 87.

12. *ANET*, 288; for Ashkelon in particular, see *ARAB*, 143 (312).

13. Bunimovitz and Lederman, "Final Destruction of Beth Shemesh," 22.

14. *Ashdod VI*, 6; Kogan-Zahavi, "Ashdod," 1573–74.

15. Elat, "Economic Relations," 27.

IIA in Field I on the summit of the northeast acropolis. On the other hand, the record of Sennacherib's campaign in 701 BCE provides the basis for dating Ekron's expanded city to after it was granted 'favored-nation' status. This is supported by the physical evidence, which demonstrates that this new status affected Ekron in a spectacular way and brought about its greatest period of prosperity.

If Ekron had begun to expand, as Na'aman asserts, in the 8th century, the enlarged lower city should have produced a significant assemblage of 8th-century pottery types, which is not the case. The small and limited corpus of Iron IIB 10th–8th-century pottery that does appear is represented by 317 residual forms, slightly less than 0.034 percent of the entire Field IV Lower ceramic corpus of 9,437 forms.[16] The residual forms usually consist of small fragments that come mostly from secondary sources, such as mudbricks, fills, and construction loci. They originated in the earlier Iron IIB Stratum II documented only on the summit of the upper city northeast acropolis in Field I, not represented in Field IV Lower.[17] Furthermore, no other archaeological evidence exists in the lower city to support Na'aman's art-historical interpretation that is based on questionable textual inferences.[18] Therefore, his conclusion that Stratum IC at Ekron was founded in the second half of the 8th BCE does not stand up to either a closer examination of these documents or to the archaeological evidence.

Peter James has also proposed that the date of the beginning of Ekron Stratum IC be lowered—to a date later than that proposed by Na'aman, but earlier than that suggested by Lawrence Stager (discussed below)—based on his dating of the Ekron Royal Dedicatory Inscription to 675–650 BCE, the period to which he assigns the reign of Ikausu, King of Ekron, since the date of the dedication of the Temple Complex 650 sanctuary must fall within the reign of Ikausu, who built it.[19] However, it is not known when Ikausu succeeded Padi, his father, to the throne. All that is known is that the last time Padi is documented in the Assyrian Annals is in a text dated

---

16. Gitin, "The Iron Age IIC Pottery."

17. This phenomenon is similar to the presence in the lower city of a limited corpus of residual Late Bronze Age pottery in fills and construction loci, especially in the mudbricks from Iron Age buildings. In both cases, the disposition, quantity, and types of pottery do not support the existence of occupational levels in the lower city during either the Late Bronze Age or the Iron II. This is confirmed by the stratigraphic gaps that exist in the lower city for both periods, and is part of the established pattern of expansion, when the upper and lower cities were occupied, and contraction, when only the upper city was occupied.

18. Na'aman, "Ekron under the Assyrian and Egyptian Empires," 85.

19. James, "Dating Late Iron Age Ekron," 88–89.

to 699 BCE[20] and that Ikausu is mentioned in the Annals of Esarhaddon dated to 673 BCE[21] and in the Annals of Ashurbanipal dated to 667 BCE.[22] Thus, Ikausu could have succeeded his father after 698 BCE and could have ruled for thirty-one years until 667 BCE, the last time he is mentioned in the Assyrian Annals. Alternatively, as James has suggested, he could have succeeded his father after 698 BCE and ruled for forty-eight years until 650 BCE.[23] Consequently, if the dating of Stratum IC depended solely on the date of Ikausu's reign, as James would have it, Stratum IC could be dated within a range of forty-eight years, that is, from 698 BCE to 650 BCE, and not only to 675–650, as James contends.[24] Also, even though the earliest date for Ikausu is 673 BCE based on a textual reference and even assuming he did rule for twenty-five years, that does not mean that Stratum IC had to have begun at 675 BCE. On the contrary, the large Stratum IC city occupying ca. seventy-five acres, with its well-designed town plan, was built over a number of years and should be dated to the first quarter of the 7th century.[25]

James considers this dating a "*non sequitur*, as the Assyrian references to Ikausu are from the second quarter of the 7th century."[26] However, the dating of Stratum IC to the first quarter of the 7th century BCE is based on Neo-Assyrian texts, as pointed out above, and their linkage to the archaeological data. The former provide the political and economic context and chronological time-frame for Ekron's physical expansion and the establishment of its industrial olive oil production center. The latter, the stratigraphic and ceramic data, corroborate the dating of Stratum IC.

As for the sanctuary of Temple Complex 650, an integral part of the Stratum IC city, support for dating it to the first quarter of the 7th century is provided by Esarhaddon's Succession Treaty of 672 BCE excavated at Tell Tayinat.[27] It includes a curse invoking Šarrat-Ekron, who, according to Lau-

---

20. *ANET*, 288; Fales and Postgate, *Imperial Administrative Records, Part II*, 42.
21. *ANET*, 291; Millard, "Books and Writing in Kings," 191.
22. *ANET*, 294; Millard, "Books and Writing in Kings," 191.
23. In his reconstruction of the dates of Padi and Ikausu, taking into consideration the storage jar inscription in which Padi is mentioned, James further suggests that "as we have no Ekronite king list after Ikausu, we cannot rule out that there was a second king Padi" (James, "Dating Late Iron Age Ekron," 94 n. 9). However, another king of Ekron is known after Ikausu, namely, Adon, the last king of Ekron, whose letter in Aramaic to the pharaoh of Egypt is probably dated to 604 BCE (Porten, "The Identity of King Adon," esp. pp. 36–37, 43–45).
24. James, "The Date of the Ekron Temple Inscription," 92.
25. Gitin, Dothan, and Naveh, "A Royal Dedicatory Inscription from Ekron," 16.
26. James, "Dating Late Iron Age Ekron," 88.
27. Harrison, "West Syrian *Megaron* or Neo-Assyrian *Langraum*?"

inger, "should be identified with Ptgyh, the Lady of Ekron known from the Ekron inscription."[28] If the goddess of the sanctuary of Temple Complex 650 was already so well known in 672 BCE as to be referred to in a royal Assyrian text, the Stratum IC temple structure must already have existed in the first quarter of the 7th century and could not have been constructed later.

Lowering the date of the beginning of Stratum IC, as James proposes, would not only fly in the face of the linkage of the Assyrian Royal Annals with the archaeological record, but also eliminate most of the period during which Ekron was a prosperous Assyrian vassal city-state in the first half of the 7th century, when the Neo-Assyrian Empire was at the height of its power in the west.[29] This would create a significant gap in the documented history of the city, which James has dismissed out of hand as being immaterial. He argues that if the "start of Stratum IC were lowered to c. 675–650 BC, then the gap is created only if we cling to the dates for Stratum II, guesstimated before the Inscription was found."[30] Of course, the dates of Stratum II and its absence from the lower city, as discussed above, demonstrate that they are not a "guesstimate," but based on physical data.

In his analysis, James fails to recognize the effect of the special preference or 'favored-nation' status conferred on Ekron as an Assyrian vassal, which generated Ekron's expansion in Stratum IC. According to the Annals, after Sennacherib destroyed most of the cities of Judah in 701 BCE, he gave the towns of the defeated King Hezekiah to Padi, King of Ekron. Many of these had cottage industries for olive oil production, like Gezer, Beth-Shemesh, and Tell Beit Mirsim; and thus, Ekron inherited parts of the Shephelah with its large groves of olive trees, as well as the know-how of Judean olive oil production technology.

To understand the rationale behind James's proposed dating for Stratum IC, it needs to be seen in the context of his general revision of Iron Age chronology, in which he lowers the traditional date of the end of the Late Bronze Age by 250 years,[31] moving it well into the Iron Age.[32] He also lowers the date of the end of the Iron Age in Philistia by reassigning the destruction of Ekron Stratum IB from 604 to 570 BCE, based on his revision of the dating of the Greek Archaic pottery both from this stratum at Ekron

28. Lauinger, "Esarhaddon's Succession Treaty at Tell Tayinat," 119 (line VI:47).
29. Eph'al, "Israel, Fall, and Exile," pp. 276–82, 286–8; Gitin, "Tel Miqne-Ekron in the 8th Century BCE," 61–63.
30. James, "Dating Late Iron Age Ekron," 88.
31. James, *Centuries of Darkness*, 195–203, 318–20.
32. A number of Egyptologists also do not accept this revision, for example, Ward, "Review of *Centuries of Darkness*."

and from the late Iron Age II destruction phase at Ashkelon.[33] This, in turn, he bases on a statement by Herodotus on the early history of Naukratis, James's type-site for Archaic period pottery.[34] He does not, however, succeed in establishing a convincing case that Herodotus provides an absolute date for the appearance of Archaic period pottery at Naukratis, as he himself admits—"Of course the argument from Herodotus' clipped account is far from conclusive"[35]—and he acknowledges regarding this pottery that "most archaeologists since Petrie have tended to date the earliest Greek pottery at the site to the mid or late 7th century BC."[36] One of many possible rebuttals is Möller's effective argument that Herodotus's characterization of Naukratis as a *polis* implies that a Greek port of trade already existed in the late 7th century BCE and was not established, as Herodotus states, by the Egyptian Pharaoh Amasis, whose reign forms the basis for James's dating of the Archaic pottery to 570 BCE.[37] The most recent and conclusive argument against this dating is represented by the large assemblage of East Greek pottery from Ashkelon published by Waldbaum, in which she marshals all of the available evidence for its 7th-century BCE dating not only at Ashkelon, but also at Naukratis.[38]

The assemblage of East Greek pottery at Ashkelon comes from the final occupation phase of the 7th century BCE, the destruction of which has been attributed to Neo-Babylonian King Nebuchadrezzar's 604 BCE campaign.[39] This is based on Wiseman's reading of a text in the Babylonian Chronicles,[40] which, in turn, also supports the 604 BCE date for the destruction of Ekron.[41] Although Wiseman later raised some questions concerning the Ashkelon reading,[42] it was subsequently confirmed by Irving Finkel.[43] James nevertheless continues to dispute it, stating that "there is no guar-

33. James, "Dating Late Iron Age Ekron," 93.

34. James, "Naukratis Revisited," 235.

35. Ibid., 262.

36. Ibid., 236. Although only a few pages in this publication are cited, James's analysis provides the best summary published thus far of all the evidence for dating Archaic period pottery based on Herodotus versus the archaeological data.

37. Möller, *Naukratis*, 184–88.

38. Waldbaum, "Greek Pottery," 130–40, and 139 for Naukratis specifically.

39. Ibid.

40. Wiseman, *Chronicles of Chaldaean Kings*, 85.

41. Gitin, "The Philistines in the Prophetic Text," 276 n. 2. For a more recent discussion, including reference to Na'aman's position in support of the 604 BCE date, see Fantalkin, "Meẓad Ḥashavyahu," 132.

42. Wiseman, *Nebuchadrezzar and Babylon*, 28.

43. Finkel *apud* Stager, "Ashkelon and the Archaeology of Destruction," 72* n. 1.

antee that this is the correct reading ... To hang the entire chronology of late Iron Age Philistia on a debated restoration seems perilous."[44] However, when Ran Zadok collated the Chronicle once again, he confirmed Finkel's reading and the identification with Ashkelon.[45] Thus, James's dismissal of the Babylonian Chronicle date is rejected, and the Chronicle clearly trumps Herodotus as a fixed point for Archaic period chronology in dating the destructions of Ashkelon and Ekron.[46] Consequently, James's dating for both the beginning of the Iron IIC in Philistia (Ekron Stratum IC) and its end (the destruction of Ekron Stratum IB) are not substantiated by the evidence.

James's most recent evaluation of the evidence for dating Ekron Strata IC and IB and the destruction of Stratum IB is presented within the context of his analysis of the late 7th-century dating of Meẓad Ḥashavyahu, which is contemporaneous with the final phase of the late Iron IIC at Ekron and Ashkelon. He again dismisses out of hand the confluence of the textual and archaeological evidence in support of the dating of Ekron Stratum IC to the first quarter of the 7th century,[47] including the significance of Ekron's 'favored-nation' status, once more creating a gap at Ekron in the first quarter of the 7th century, when it would have achieved its greatest growth under the Neo-Assyrian Empire.

In further support of his proposed Ekron Stratum IC chronology, while James had initially re-dated the Temple Complex 650 sanctuary to the second quarter of the 7th century, he now suggests that it could even date to the third quarter of the 7th century.[48] Ironically for one who places such an uncompromising emphasis on dated textual references, he fails to take into consideration the evidence presented in my earlier rebuttal of his position based on Esarhaddon's 672 BCE Succession Treaty cited above. To reiterate, if the goddess Šarrat-Ekron (identified with *Ptgyh*, the Lady of Ekron[49]) was already so well known in 672 BCE as to be referred to in a royal Assyrian

---

44. James, "Dating Late Iron Age Ekron," 91.

45. Zadok *apud* Fantalkin, "Why Did Nebuchadnezzar II Destroy Ashkelon," 87 n. 1.

46. Also *contra* James's Herodotus-based dating, Fantalkin ("Identity in the Making," 202 n. 81) concludes that the East Greek pottery from Ashkelon and Meẓad Ḥashavyahu overlaps with that from Naukratis, based on the linkage of this pottery to the period of Egyptian rule following the withdrawal of the Assyrians around 620 BCE: "The sudden and massive appearance of East Greek pottery on the coastal plain of Israel toward the end of the 7th century B.C.E. and its subsequent disappearance after only a few years fit the time-span during which the area fell under Egyptian rule" (ibid., 202).

47. James, "Meẓad Ḥashavyahu Reconsidered," 357 n. 35.

48. Ibid., 357.

49. Lauinger, "Esarhaddon's Succession Treaty at Tell Tayinat," 119 (line VI:47).

text, then Temple Complex 650 must already have existed in the first quarter of the 7th century BCE.

As for the Babylonian destruction of Ekron Stratum IB, James argues "against the bizarre idea that the rulers of the Neo-Babylonian Empire (unlike the Assyrians) simply laid waste to cities in the Levant and deliberately left (or kept) them deserted for decades, leaving us with a 'Babylonian Gap' in the archaeological record. This makes no sense in economic terms."[50] While James rejects Stern's explanation that the Babylonian focus was on the welfare of the city of Babylon to the exclusion of the periphery,[51] he fails to consider Dandamayev's assessment that the fall of the Assyrian Empire had significant economic consequences. Dandamayev's explanation is that Ekron's olive oil industry was destroyed in the Babylonian conquest because the well-organized Assyrian world was replaced with primitive states that did not recognize the value of retaining the well-developed Assyrian administrative institutions and economic centers.[52]

Regarding the date of the destruction of Ekron Stratum IB, which is linked to that of the Babylonian destruction at Ashkelon, James assigns it to the 6th century, ca. 570–565 BCE.[53] He suggests that a date closer to the mid-6th century would shorten the alleged century-long abandonment and go a long way toward 'closing' the consequent chronological gap between the end of the Iron Age and the beginning of the Persian period at Ashkelon.[54] This he supports by again disputing the readings of Finkel and Zadok of the Babylonian Chronicle entry for the destruction of Ashkelon in 604 BCE, and then unsuccessfully attempting to revise Ashkelon's late Iron II stratigraphy to rationalize his 6th-century date. The excavators have associated the 604 BCE destruction with Phase 7 in Grid 50 (the marketplace), the equivalent of Phase 14 in Grid 38 (the winery), representing the last settlement before the Persian city.[55] James, on the other hand, contends that the evidence published thus far does not rule out that the conquest of Ashkelon by Nebuchadrezzar II may have occurred in Phase 8 rather than in the last pre-Persian Phase 7.[56] According to the excavators, however, there is no evidence for a Phase 8 destruction (dated to the 8th century), but there is consistent and substantial evidence for a destruction at the end of Phase

---

50. James, "Meẓad Ḥashavyahu Reconsidered," 348.
51. Stern, *Archaeology of the Land of the Bible*, 303.
52. Dandamayev, "Assyrian Traditions during Achaemenid Times," 42–43.
53. James, "Meẓad Ḥashavyahu Reconsidered," 347.
54. Ibid., 348.
55. Stager, "Ashkelon and the Archaeology of Destruction," 71*.
56. James, "Meẓad Ḥashavyahu Reconsidered," 345.

7. There is also no evidence of occupation after Phase 7 and before 520 BCE (Phase 6 in Grid 50/Phase 13 in Grid 38). Furthermore, there is a massive gap between Phase 7 and Phase 6 (Grid 38 Phases 14 and 13), after which every aspect of city planning changed. This gap is the most pronounced in the history of the site from the second millennium through the Crusader period.[57]

In further support for lowering the dates of the destruction of Meẓad Ḥashavyahu into the 6th century, and with it the final Iron IIC strata at Ekron and Ashkelon, James repeats his argument against the consensus for dating the Corinthian and East Greek pottery of the Archaic period to the end of the 7th century.[58] Based on his reading of Herodotus's dating of the Greek settlement of Naukratis, he again lowers the date of this pottery by ca. thirty-five years, to 565 BCE.[59] In his analysis, however, he fails to consider Waldbaum's extensive discussion of the East Greek pottery from Ashkelon.[60] In addition, while he brings to bear a great deal of evidence from the Levant, he does not consider the Greek evidence in depth, especially the recently published material from Assesos near Miletus (destroyed by the Lydians in 608 BCE)[61] and from Miletus itself, and its implications for Greek chronology.[62] Consequently, James's arguments now are no more convincing than those in his earlier publications.

Lawrence Stager has also suggested a different dating for Stratum IC at Ekron, later than that suggested by Na'aman and later than the first quarter of the 7th century, as I have posited. He contends that the expansion of the city and "what propelled the olive oil industry at Ekron into the international sphere was not a dying Assyria but a rising Egypt, ever the greatest consumer of the Levantine olive oil," and therefore, "the expansion of Ekron and the development of its oil industry occurred after Assyrian interest and power in the West had begun to wane in the late 640s."[63] He does not agree that there were two 7th-century phases at Ekron, with a diminution in olive oil production in the second, although this diminution is demonstrated by the reuse of olive press equipment, including pressing vats and stone weights,

---

57. Written communication from Daniel Master, October 22, 2015.
58. For an overview of this pottery, see Waldbaum, "Iron Age I–II: Greek Imports," 509–11.
59. James, "Meẓad Ḥashavyahu Reconsidered," 357.
60. Waldbaum, "Greek Pottery."
61. Kalaitzoglou, *Assesos*, 63.
62. Written communication from Jane Waldbaum, November 22, 2015.
63. Stager, "Ashkelon," 70*–71*.

in the construction of Stratum IB.[64] Thus, Stager dates both Stratum IC and IB at Ekron to the period of Egyptian hegemony from 640–604 BCE.[65] What led him to this conclusion is the perception that the discarded components of olive oil production equipment in secondary use in Stratum IB do not represent a general phenomenon throughout the tell, and therefore do not provide a basis for positing two 7th-century phases.[66] Consequently, he asserts that this neither indicates the existence of an oil industry prior to Stratum IB—that is, in Stratum IC—nor a diminution in oil production in Stratum IB. But the reuse of Stratum IC olive oil production components in the rebuilding activities of Stratum IB is, in fact, a general phenomenon reflected in architectural modifications in the buildings of all of the zones of occupation of Stratum IB,[67] and an integral and characteristic aspect of Stratum IB construction activities.[68] As such, it represents one of the major indicators for two occupation phases in the 7th century. Twenty-eight components of olive oil production from the Field I Summit, Fields II and III in the industrial zone, and Field IV Lower in the elite zone were reused in Stratum IB, and another two components from Field III were discarded and sealed below Stratum IB.

64. Gitin, "Neo-Assyrian and Egyptian Hegemony," 57*–58*; Gitin, Garfinkel, and Dothan, "Occupational History."

65. Stager, "Ashkelon and the Archaeology of Destruction," 71*.

66. Stager *apud* Vanderhooft, *The Neo-Babylonian Empire*, 74.

67. Gitin, "Tel Miqne-Ekron in the 7th Century B.C.," 224. Temple Complex 650, however, is one of the few structures that did not exhibit any indication of two building phases, including the secondary use of discarded oil production equipment that could only have originated in Stratum IC. This further supports the contention that Temple Complex 650 was built in Stratum IC, during the period of Assyrian hegemony. Otherwise, like the other Stratum IB structures, it, too, would presumably have had elements of discarded olive press equipment incorporated in the construction of the walls.

68. The 7th-century stratigraphic profile at Ekron is not an isolated phenomenon; it is paralleled by similar profiles at the three other Philistine capital cities that existed at this time. At Ashdod, Stratum VII, with its industrial pottery workshops, is dated to the Assyrian period, and Stratum VI, which exhibits a reduction in industrial ceramic activity, is assigned to the Egyptian phase (*Ashdod II–III*, 89–96; *Ashdod IV*, 57). Timnah (Tel Batash), Ekron's daughter city, went through a period of regeneration at the beginning of Stratum II, during the Assyrian period (Kelm and Mazar, *Timnah*, 139–58); later, toward the end of Stratum II during the Egyptian phase in the last decades of the 7th century, there is a diminution in olive oil production at the site (Kelm and Mazar, *Timnah*, 159–60, 162; *contra* Mazar, *Timnah [Tel Batash] I*, 263). At Ashkelon, the stratigraphy of the winery also demonstrates two phases in the 7th century, the later of which, representing the Egyptian phase, shows a diminution in production (Master, "The Seaport of Ashkelon," 207). This is demonstrated in *Ashkelon 3*, 13–15, with Figs. 2.2–2.3 showing the plans of the original and remodeled 7th-century winery in Grid 38 Phase 14.

On the Field I Summit, an olive press was reused in the construction of a Stratum IB buttress in Building 761.[69] Another press from a foundation trench for a wall assigned to Stratum IIB in Building 757 was most likely intrusive, but clearly sealed below Stratum IB.[70] In the olive oil industrial zone in Field II, there are four examples of the reuse of oil production equipment in Stratum IB: a perforated stone weight blocked an installation/threshold in Area 181;[71] another was reused in a wall in Area 182;[72] and two oil presses were reused in walls in Areas 198[73] and 214.[74]

In the olive oil industrial zone in Field III, there are five examples of the reuse of olive oil press equipment in Stratum IB. Four perforated stone weights were reused in the walls of Buildings 504,[75] 506,[76] and 507,[77] and one in the surface paving of Building 504.[78] In addition, a discarded olive crushing basin and press were found in a pit sealed in Stratum IB in Building 502.[79]

In the Field IV Lower elite zone, there are seventeen examples of the reuse of olive oil production equipment in Stratum IB. Five olive presses were found in secondary use in Buildings 651,[80] 652,[81] and 653,[82] and three were reused as part of or constituting installations in Buildings 654[83] and 653.[84] An olive crushing basin was found in secondary use in Building 652,[85] and four perforated stone weights were reused in the construction of walls

---

69. Press INW.28070 in Buttress INW.28003 for Wall IVNW.28002.
70. Press in Wall INE.1028.
71. Weight blocking Installation/Threshold IISW.181009.
72. Weight in Wall IISW.182016.
73. Press IISW.198009 in Wall IISW.198010.
74. Press in Wall IISW.214001.
75. Weight in Wall IIISE.37006.
76. Weights IIINE.12045 and 2052 in Wall IIINE.12010.
77. Weights IIINE.12035 and 2048 in doorjambs of Walls IIINE.12022 and 12039.
78. Weight in Surface IIISE.37007.
79. Basin IIISE.26021 and Press IIISE.26023 in Pit IIISE.26031.
80. In Wall IVNW.25021.
81. In Wall IVNE.10007.
82. Presses IVNE.25021, 25022, and 25024 in Wall IVNE.25018.
83. Press IVNE.23009 and Vat (or Press) IVNE.24005.
84. Press IVNE.26003.
85. Basin IVNE.10005 in Wall IVNE.10016.

and socles in Buildings 651,[86] 651/655,[87] and 654.[88] Two perforated stone weights were reused in Building 651, one as a pillar base[89] and the other as part of an installation.[90] Another two were found in Building 651 in a fill below a Stratum IB layer of cobbles and a surface,[91] and another in Building 655 in debris below a Stratum IB debris/stone layer.[92] Thus, the evidence negates Stager's contention that the 7th century at Ekron is not represented by two strata.

Stager also contends that Temple Complex 650 could be dated late in the reign of Ikausu, around the mid-7th century, during Ashurbanipal's reign.[93] Given the *Sitz im Leben* of Ekron attested in the Neo-Assyrian texts and the linkage with the archaeological evidence for Stratum IC, Stager's lower dating is not possible. By implication, it would mean, as discussed above, that the Stratum IC city or at the very least the elite zone of which Temple Complex 650 is the focal point must similarly be dated to near the end of the Assyrian period. This would create a significant gap in the documented history of the city, eliminating the prosperous Assyrian vassal city-state of Ekron of the first half of the 7th century. Stager's late dating is also refuted by Esarhaddon's 672 BCE Succession Treaty mentioning Šarrat-Ekron, identified as the goddess *Ptgyh*. To reiterate the arguments presented above, this demonstrates that Temple Complex 650 must already have existed in the first quarter of the 7th century.

Some confusion has arisen regarding Stager's position with the publication of one of the Ashkelon excavation reports, in which he repeats his earlier statement that the olive oil industry at Ekron should be dated to the period of Egyptian influence in Philistia.[94] In the concluding chapter of the same publication, however, Master and Stager write that "there is no doubt that the Assyrians transformed the southern Levant at the end of the 8th century and everything that happened afterward was affected by their actions … The Assyrians did not directly determine these outcomes [referring to the economic expansions in Philistia], but they certainly created

---

86. Wall IVNW.25020.

87. Socle IVNW.42006.

88. In Socle IVNE.8011 of Wall IVNE.8004 and in Wall IVNE.24012.

89. Stone Weight IVNW.40006.

90. Stone Weight IVNW.9020A.

91. Obj. No. 4339 in Fill IVNW.10010 below Stratum IB Cobbles IVNW.10006 and Surface IVNW.10007.

92. Obj. No. 4431 in debris layer IVNW.42026 below debris/stones IVNW.42024.

93. Stager *apud* Gitin, "Neo-Assyrian and Egyptian Hegemony," 56*.

94. Stager, "Ashkelon on the Eve of Destruction," 10.

the conditions in which others changed their economic behavior to take advantage of the new situation that had been created."[95] This implies a significant change in Stager's position, namely, that Assyria was responsible, if only indirectly, for the establishment of Ekron's olive oil industry, and undercuts his proposed dating thereof to the last third or last quarter of the 7th century, when Philistia was under Egyptian influence. This change in position is further implied by a statement in the same chapter, in which Ekron's oil industry is dated to the equivalent of Stratum IC. This is apparent from Master and Stager's comparison of "the absence of late 7th-century East Greek imports in the original construction of the [Ashkelon] winery and the construction of similar production units in the nearby Philistine city of Ekron sometime in the first half of the 7th century (a date based on inscriptional evidence)."[96] This also further supports the existence of two 7th-century occupation phases at Ekron, refuting Stager's claim to the contrary.

With these responses to Na'aman, James, and Stager, it is my hope that the issues they raised have been sufficiently addressed to confirm the excavator's dating of Ekron's late Iron II strata and its economic implications.

BIBLIOGRAPHY

APIN-IH = Gitin, Seymour, ed. *The Ancient Pottery of Israel and Its Neighbors from the Iron Age through the Hellenistic Period*. Jerusalem: Israel Exploration Society, 2015.

Ashkelon 3 = Stager, Lawrence E., Daniel M. Master, and J. David Schloen. *Ashkelon 3: The Seventh Century B.C. Final Reports of the Leon Levy Expedition to Ashkelon 3*. Harvard Semitic Museum Publications. Winona Lake, IN: Eisenbrauns, 2011.

Bunimovitz, Shlomo, and Zvi Lederman. "The Final Destruction of Beth Shemesh and the *Pax Assyriaca* in the Judean Shephelah." *Tel Aviv* 30 (2003) 3–26.

Dandamayev, Muhammad. "Assyrian Traditions during Achaemenid Times." In *Assyria 1995: Proceedings of the 10th Anniversary Symposium of the Neo-Assyrian Text Corpus Project, Helsinki, September 7–11, 1995*, edited by Simo Parpola and Robert M. Whiting, 41–48. Helsinki: University of Helsinki, 1998.

Dothan, Moshe. *Ashdod II–III: The Second and Third Seasons of Excavations 1963, 1965*. 'Atiqot 9. Jerusalem: Department of Antiquities and Museums, 1971.

Dothan, Moshe, and David Ben-Shlomo. *Ashdod VI: The Excavations of Areas H and K (1968–1969)*. Israel Antiquities Authority Reports 24. Jerusalem: Israel Antiquities Authority, 2005.

---

95. Master and Stager, "Conclusion," 740. For further support for this position, see the analysis of the economic impact of the *pax Assyriaca* and its implications for the development of Ekron's olive oil industry in Younger, "The Assyrian Economic Impact," 189 n. 28.

96. Master and Stager, "Conclusion," 739.

Dothan, Moshe, and Yosef Porath. *Ashdod IV: Excavation of Area M.* 'Atiqot 15. Jerusalem: Department of Antiquities and Museums, 1982.

Dothan, Trude, and Seymour Gitin. "Miqne, Tel (Ekron)." In *NEAEHL* 5:1952–58.

———. *Tel Miqne-Ekron: Summary of Fourteen Seasons of Excavation 1981–1996 and Bibliography 1982–2012.* Jerusalem: W. F. Albright Institute of Archaeological Research and Hebrew University of Jerusalem, 2012. Available at https://academia.edu *s.v.* Seymour Gitin.

Elat, Moshe. "The Economic Relations of the Neo-Assyrian Empire with Egypt." *JAOS* 98 (1978) 20–34.

Eph'al, Israel. "Israel, Fall, and Exile: Assyrian Dominion in Palestine." In *The Age of Monarchies: Political History*, edited by Abraham Malamat, 276–90. World History of the Jewish People 4/1. Jerusalem: Massada Press, 1979.

Ekron 9/2 = Gitin, Seymour, Trude Dothan, and Yosef Garfinkel, in *Tel Miqne-Ekron Excavations 1985–1988, 1990, 1992–1995: Field IV Lower—The Elite Zone, Part 2: The Iron Age IIC Late Philistine City*. Tel Miqne-Ekron Final Report Series 9/2. Harvard Semitic Museum Publications. Winona Lake, IN: Eisenbrauns, forthcoming.

Fales, F. Mario, and J. Nicholas Postgate, eds. *Imperial Administrative Records, Part II: Provincial and Military Administration*. State Archives of Assyria 11. Helsinki: Helsinki University Press, 1995.

Fantalkin, Alexander. "Identity in the Making: Greeks in the Eastern Mediterranean during the Iron Age." In *Naukratis: Greek Diversity in Egypt: Studies on East Greek Pottery and Exchange in the Eastern Mediterranean*, edited by Alexandra Villing and Udo Schlotzhauer, 199–208. British Museum Research Publication 162. London: British Museum, 2006.

———. "Meẓad Ḥashavyahu: Its Material Culture and Historical Background." *Tel Aviv* 28 (2001) 3–166.

———. "Why Did Nebuchadnezzar II Destroy Ashkelon in Kislev 604 B.C.?" In *The Signal Fires of Lachish: Studies in the Archaeology and History of Israel in the Late Bronze Age, Iron Age, and the Persian Period in Honor of David Ussishkin*, edited by Israel Finkelstein and Nadav Na'aman, 87–111. Winona Lake, IN: Eisenbrauns, 2011.

Gitin, Seymour. "Iron Age IIA–B: Philistia." In *APIN-IH*, 257–80.

———. "Iron Age IIC: Judah." In *APIN-IH*, 345–63.

———. "Iron Age IIC: Philistia." In *APIN-IH*, 382–418.

———. "The Iron Age IIC Pottery." In *Ekron 9/2*, Chapter 4A.

———. "Neo-Assyrian and Egyptian Hegemony over Ekron in the 7th Century BCE: A Response to Lawrence Stager." *Eretz-Israel* 27 (2003) 55*–60*.

———. "Philistines in the Books of Kings." In *The Books of Kings: Sources, Composition, Historiography and Reception*, edited by Baruch Halpern and André Lemaire, 301–64. VTSup 129. Leiden: Brill, 2010.

———. "The Philistines in the Prophetic Text: An Archaeological Perspective." In *Hesed ve-Emet: Studies in Honor of Ernest S. Frerichs*, edited by Jodi Magness and Seymour Gitin, 273–90. Brown Judaic Studies 320. Atlanta: Scholars Press,1998.

———. "Tel Miqne-Ekron in the 7th Century B.C.: City Plan Development and the Oil Industry." In *Olive Oil in Antiquity (Israel and Neighboring Countries from the Neolithic to the Early Arab Period)*, edited by David Eitam and Michael Heltzer, 219–42. History of the Ancient Near East, Studies 7. Padova: Sargon, 1996.

---. "Tel Miqne-Ekron in the 8th Century BCE: The Impact of Economic Innovation and Foreign Cultural Influences on a Neo-Assyrian Vassal City State." In *Recent Excavation in Israel: A View to the West: Reports on Kabri, Nami, Miqne-Ekron, Dor and Ashkelon*, edited by Seymour Gitin, 60–80. Archaeological Institute of America Colloquia and Conference Papers 1. Dubuque, IA: Kendal/Hunt, 1995.

---. "Temple Complex 650 at Ekron: The Impact of Multi-Cultural Influences on Philistine Cult in the Late Iron Age." In *Temple Building and Temple Cult: Architecture and Cultic Paraphernalia of Temples in the Levant (2.-1. Mill. B.C.E.)*, edited by Jens Kamlah, 223–56. Abhandlungen des Deutschen Palästina-Vereins 41. Wiesbaden: Harrassowitz, 2012.

Gitin, Seymour, Trude Dothan, and Joseph Naveh. "A Royal Dedicatory Inscription from Ekron." *IEJ* 47 (1997) 1–16.

Gitin, Seymour, Yosef Garfinkel, and Trude Dothan. "Occupational History: The Stratigraphy and Architecture of Iron Age II Strata Pre-IC, IC, IB, and IA." In *Ekron* 9/2, Chapter 1.

Harrison, Timothy P. "West Syrian *Megaron* or Neo-Assyrian *Langraum*? The Shifting Form and Function of the *Tell Taʿyīnāt (Kunulua)* Temples." In *Temple Building and Temple Cult: Architecture and Cultic Paraphernalia of Temples in the Levant (2.-1. Mill. B.C.E)*, edited by Jens Kamlah, 3–21. Abhandlungen des Deutschen Palästina-Vereins 41. Wiesbaden: Harrassowitz, 2012.

Holladay, John S. "Hezekiah's Tribute, Long Distance Trade, and the Wealth of Nations ca. 1000–600 BC: A New Perspective." In *Confronting the Past: Archaeological and Historical Essays on Ancient Israel in Honor of William G. Dever*, edited by Seymour Gitin, J. Edward Wright, and J. P. Dessel, 309–32. Winona Lake, IN: Eisenbrauns, 2006.

James, Peter. "The Date of the Ekron Temple Inscription—A Note." *IEJ* 55 (2005) 90–93.

---. "Dating Late Iron Age Ekron (Tel Miqne)." *PEQ* 138 (2006) 85–97.

---. "Meẓad Ḥashavyahu Reconsidered: Saite Strategy and Archaic Greek Chronology." In *Walls of the Prince: Egyptian Interactions with Southwest Asia in Antiquity: Essays in Honour of John S. Holladay Jr.*, edited by Timothy P. Harrison, Edward B. Banning, and Stanley Klassen, 333–70. Culture and History of the Ancient Near East 77. Leiden: Brill, 2015.

---. "Naukratis Revisited." *Hyperboreus: Studia Classica* 9 (2003) 235–64.

---. *Centuries of Darkness: A Challenge to the Conventional Chronology of Old World Archaeology*. London: Cape, 1991.

Kalaitzoglou, Georg. *Assesos: Ein geschlossener Befund südionischer Keramik aus dem Heiligtum der Athena Assesia*. Milesische Forschungen 6. Mainz: von Zabern, 2008.

Kelm, George L., and Amihai Mazar. *Timnah: A Biblical City in the Sorek Valley*. Winona Lake, IN: Eisenbrauns, 1995.

Kogan-Zahavi, Elena. "Ashdod." In *NEAEHL* 5:1573–74.

Lauinger, Jacob. "Esarhaddon's Succession Treaty at Tell Tayinat: Text and Commentary." *JCS* 64 (2012) 87–123.

Maeir, Aren M. "The Tell es-Safi/Gath Archaeological Project 1996–2010: Introduction, Overview and Synopsis of Results." In *Tell es-Safi/Gath I: The 1996–2005 Seasons*, 2 vols., edited by Aren M. Maeir, 1–88. Ägypten und Altes Testament 6. Wiesbaden: Harrassowitz, 2012.

Master, Daniel M. "The Seaport of Ashkelon in the Seventh Century BCE: A Petrographic Study." PhD diss., Harvard University, 2001.

Master, Daniel M., and Lawrence E. Stager. "Conclusion." In *Ashkelon 3*, 737–40.

Mazar, Amihai. *Timnah (Tel Batash) I: Stratigraphy and Architecture: Text*. Qedem 37. Jerusalem: Hebrew University of Jerusalem, 1997.

Millard, Alan. "Books and Writing in Kings." In *The Books of Kings: Sources, Composition, Historiography and Reception*, edited by Baruch Halpern and André Lemaire, 185–202. VTSup 129. Leiden: Brill, 2010.

Möller, Astrid. *Naukratis: Trade in Archaic Greece*. Oxford Monographs on Classical Archaeology. Oxford: Oxford University Press, 2000.

Na'aman, Nadav. "Ekron under the Assyrian and Egyptian Empires." *BASOR* 332 (2003) 81–91.

———. "Two Notes on Ashkelon and Ekron." *Tel Aviv* 25 (1998) 219–27.

Porten, Bezalel. "The Identity of King Adon." *BA* 44 (1981) 36–52

Stager, Lawrence E. "Ashkelon and the Archaeology of Destruction: Kislev 604 BCE." *Eretz-Israel* 25 (1996) 61*–74*.

———. "Ashkelon on the Eve of Destruction, Kislev 604 BCE." In *Ashkelon 3*, 3–11.

Stern, Ephraim. *Archaeology of the Land of the Bible*. Vol. 2, *The Assyrian, Babylonian and Persian Periods 732–332 BCE*. Anchor Bible Reference Library. New York: Doubleday, 2001.

Vanderhooft, David S. *The Neo-Babylonian Empire and Babylon in the Latter Prophets*. Harvard Semitic Monographs 59. Atlanta: Scholars Press, 1999.

Waldbaum, Jane C. "Greek Pottery." In *Ashkelon 3*, 127–338.

———. "Iron Age I–II: Greek Imports." In *APIN-IH*, 509–32.

Ward, William A. Review of *Centuries of Darkness: A Challenge to the Conventional Chronology of Old World Archaeology*, by Peter James. *AJA* 98 (1994) 362–63.

Wiseman, Donald J. *Chronicles of Chaldaean Kings (626–556 B.C.) in the British Museum*. London: British Museum, 1956.

———. *Nebuchadrezzar and Babylon*. Oxford: Oxford University Press, 1991.

Younger, K. Lawson. "The Assyrian Economic Impact on the Southern Levant in Light of Recent Study." *IEJ* 65 (2015) 179–204.

5

Regional and Local Museums for Archaeology in the First Years of the State of Israel

Raz Kletter

University of Helsinki

The aim of this paper is to trace the history and development of regional and local museums active in archaeology in the early years of Israel (ca. 1948–1967), based on written documents.[1] I dedicate this paper to Ziony Zevit in gratitude for his original scholarship and open-minded personality, which I have enjoyed on more than one occasion.

Translations of documents from Hebrew are by the author. The transliteration of place and personal names is notoriously complex. For example, persons 'Hebraized' their names, and even the same person could use various spellings (Cimbalist, Tsori, Tzori, Zori). I have used common spellings as far as possible. Files from the National Archive, Jerusalem, are abbreviated GL (*Ginzakh Le'umi*).

---

1. The Bet-Miriam museum at Kibbutz Palmahim (officially founded 1969, origins perhaps 1950) is discussed by Guzetti, *Walk through the Past*; unavailable to me currently. Rahmani and Larsen, *Museums of Israel*, and Rosovsky and Ungerleider-Mayerson, *Museums of Israel*, are both practical guides with many pictures but few historical details.

The Ottoman and British Mandate Periods

Under growing western influence, Palestine/Israel saw its first museums in the 19th century. Important antiquities from excavations (since 1890) were taken to the Imperial Museum in Istanbul, which began in 1846 as a collection of antiquities. Other antiquities were kept in an Imperial Museum (*müze-i hümayun*) in Jerusalem, founded in 1901 with antiquities mainly from the excavations of Frederick Bliss (1859–1937). They were kept in a room in the Mamuniye School, later stored in the Citadel; opinions of western scholars of this museum were not flattering.[2]

This was not the first museum—that honor belongs to the museum of the Jerusalem Literary Society headed by James Finn (consul of Britain in Jerusalem in 1846–1863), established in late 1849. The Palestine Exploration Fund (PEF) also opened a museum in Jerusalem, which operated at several venues. In 1902–1915 it was located in one room at St. George's College. The German consulate started a museum in Jerusalem in 1876, which was active for several years, and later was reestablished by Gustav Dalman. There were also a few private collections of westerners. The most famous was that of Baron Ustinov in Jaffa; it was taken abroad and sold after World War I, but large items from the Baron's garden remained. Other collectors were Conrad Schick (1822–1901), Gustav Dalman (1885–1941), and Herbert Clark (1856–1921; Appendix 1:23). Among the Jewish community only one significant collector is known—Samuel Raffaeli (1867–1923).[3]

With the British Mandate Period (1917–1948) a new era began. A Department of Antiquities was established in 1920 and it included a Keeper of Museums (William Phythian-Adams). A museum was started in the same year, based on the antiquities left by the Ottomans. This was the nucleus for the Palestine Archaeological Museum (PAM, also known as the Rockefeller Museum), which was opened in 1938. There were several collections and museums with antiquities in Jerusalem, mainly in study and religious institutes, such as the Notre Dame Monastery or the Greek Orthodox Patriarchy. A Museum of Islam was founded in 1923 on the Temple Mount.[4] The Mandatory Period also saw the beginning of regional and local museums,

---

2. St. Laurent and Taşkömür, "Imperial Museum," 17–26.

3. Shay, "The Museums"; Shay, "Collectors and Collections"; Shay, *Museums and Collections*; Kletter, *Just Past*, 27–28.

4. Iliffe, "Palestine Archaeological Museum"; Iliffe, *Short Guide*; Sussman and Reich, "History of Rockefeller"; St. Laurent and Taşkömür, "Imperial Museum," 26–37; Cobbing and Tubb, "Before Rockefeller"; Kletter, *Just Past*, 174–92; Kletter, "Archaeology in Jerusalem," 136–39; Goren, "Scientific Organizations"; Fuchs and Herbert, "Representing Mandatory Palestine," 309–24; Gibson, "British Archaeological Institutions," 131–33.

though their number remained small. Site museums were established in a few excavated sites notably Caesarea and Megiddo, and an open air museum was established in Ashkelon.

In the pre-state Jewish *Yishuv* there were modest beginnings of museums by small groups of enthusiasts interested in "knowledge of the Land" (*yedi'at ha-aretz*).[5] They included the Bezalel Museum of Art in Jerusalem; the Tel-Aviv Museum (mainly art); Sturman House at Tel Yosef; the collection/museum of A. Roche in Haifa; the Museum of Jewish Antiquities at the Hebrew University (which was never opened to the public); Bet Sevivatenu in Tel-Aviv; the Yaskil collection in Haifa; and Ohel Sarah House at Tel Adashim.[6]

The Growth of Museums in Israel

In 1948, soon after Israel's birth, the governmental "Unit of Antiquities" (*maḥleqet 'atiqot*) was founded with thirteen workers under Shemuel Yeivin (1896–1982), affiliated at first to the Public Works Administration. The new Unit owned few antiquities and no museum, since East Jerusalem, with PAM and the Old City religious and research institutions, remained under Jordanian control. Regional and local museums were few, and some of them were damaged or looted during the war.[7]

Following the principle of continuity in government, and to keep a position for the former employee of the Mandatory Department of Antiquities Pinhas Penuel Kahane (1904–1974), he was nominated as "Supervisor of Regional Museums." Kahane started visiting museums, handing reports.[8] Yeivin mentioned a "museum unit" within the Antiquities Unit, where Kahane was supposed to work under a "treasurer" that handled newly discovered antiquities.[9] Indeed, antiquities started pouring in from new excavations, deserted places, etc.; but there was no "museum unit." Soon the Antiquities Unit opened a temporary exhibition in its offices, which developed into a permanent museum. The Supervisor of Regional Museums became Supervisor of the Museum; other curators were added to assist him,

5. Inbar, *History of Museums*; Inbar and Shiller, *Museums in Israel*, 19.

6. See Appendix 1: nos. 1, 3, 8, 11, 13, 18, 29, 39; also Inbar and Shiller, *Museums in Israel*. Add an exhibition by the Israel Exploration Society, Inbar, *History of Museums*, 145–46.

7. Kletter, *Just Past*, 19–30.

8. *Alon* 3 (1951) 64; GL1340/14, Yeivin, attachment to budget memorandum 18.11.1949; GL44864/14, general report January 1949.

9. GL44883/8, definition of positions in the Antiquities Unit, attached to letter of 29.11.1948.

at first on a temporary basis. In 1954 Ruth Amiran replaced Kahane, but she left in 1955 to excavate at Hazor,[10] and in the same year the Antiquities Unit became the Israel Department of Antiquities and Museums (henceforward, IDAM), affiliated to the Ministry of Education and Culture. Ruth Hestrin (1918–1995) replaced Amiran; in 1968–1984 the position was held by Y. L. Rahmani (1919–2013). He was Chief Curator of the State Antiquities; since the IDAM museum no longer existed (it was amalgamated in 1965 into the Israel Museum).[11]

The number of regional/local museums in Israel grew rapidly. We can chart this growth from lists in the IDAM records. In January 1949 the IDAM listed eighteen museums dealing with archaeology (including the IDAM's own), three of which were just planned. The next list of February 1949 shows twenty names, while a list from May 1954 contains twenty-nine. In 1955 Yeivin remarked that seven municipal museums were established since 1948: Haifa, Tel-Aviv, Tiberias, Akko, Beersheva, Bet-Shean, and Ashkelon. Yeivin also mentioned thirty regional/local "collections" (the lists include not just archaeological, but various other museums—for nature, art, etc.). A list from 1958 included sixty-eight museums: thirteen in Jerusalem, six in Tel-Aviv, and six in Haifa. There were eleven "urban and regional museums" (mostly in cities) and no less than thirty-two local museums, mostly in *kibbutzim*. By 1960 there were more than forty local/regional "collections" in *kibbutzim* alone.[12] Not every place was known to the IDAM, so probably more existed, especially in earlier years.[13]

In 1962 the Ministry of Education performed a survey of museums and for that aim the IDAM sent questionnaires to 125 places. In 1966 Rahmani listed 114 museums for archaeology or with archaeological collections. They included:

- One central museum (Israel Museum, Jerusalem).

- Seven municipal museums (Haifa, Tel-Aviv, Tiberias, Akko, Jaffa, Bat-Yam, Petakh Tikvah).[14]

- Ten regional museums (Bet-Shean valley; Gilboa; Gerar Region; Hulah Valley; Jezreel; Carmel; Negev; En-Gedi; Emek Hefer; Shephelah;

10. Katz, *Ruth Amiran*, 99; Kletter, *Just Past*, 221–7.

11. On Rahmani, see Kloner and Zias, "Obituaries."

12. GL44872/4, various documents and lists; Yeivin, *Archaeological Activities*, 20–21; Inbar and Shiller, *Museums in Israel*, 19–20; Bar-Or, *Our Life Requires Art*, 7.

13. Yeivin lamented about unreported *kibbutzim* collections, GL44872/4, letter 31.5.1955,

14. The same number of municipal museums was mentioned in 1955, but only four names reoccur.

Revivim), of which five belonged to municipalities or local/regional councils, four to *kibbutzim,* and one to a public company.

- Seventy-seven local museums: sixty-four of *kibbutzim,* five of Christian religious institutions, four in antiquity sites, two in schools, one in a village, and one of a local council. Further nineteen museums were "professional" (that is, dedicated to specific subjects such as underwater archeology or prehistory).

Rahmani assumed that several more *kibbutzim* collections were unknown to the IDAM. In 1967 Avraham Biran (1909–2007), then Director of IDAM, mentioned 140 museums in Israel, of them seventy-five were archaeological.[15]

Local museums grew especially in *kibbutzim,* where some sixty were established between 1935 and the 1960s—mostly after 1948 and for archaeology. There were also nature museums and a few Holocaust museums. Museums for the History of Settlement were established only since the 1960s, because earlier this subject was not considered to be worthy of exhibition.[16]

Why and how was this growth achieved? There is no doubt about the "why"—the *raison d'etré* of the new museums was Zionist ideology. The museums for archaeology were especially popular, since archaeology was the most significant science for establishing national identity. The museums should connect the modern nation with its past or, in Hestrin's words, allow "identification with the forefathers of the Jewish People."[17] Naturally, there was also the collecting desire, and peoples' interest was roused when they stumbled upon antiquities during building, ploughing fields, touring the surroundings, etc.

The traditional view about the "how" maintained that establishing a new museum was achieved by one or a few "enthusiasts," with an almost religious zeal, building everything with their bare hands.[18]

---

15. GL44874/11, list 24.1962, letter by Rahmani, 17.1966; Biran, "Museums in Israel," 3. Rahmani listed every museum with antiquities; Biran probably museums dedicated fully to archaeology. On Biran see Ilan, "In Memoriam."

16. Bar-Or, *Museums in Kibbutzim.*

17. Hestrin, "Local and Regional Museums," 34; cf. Kahane, GL 44872/4, memorandum 16.10.1948; Bar-Or, *Museums in Kibbutzim;* Inbar and Shiller, *Museums in Israel,* 20; Biran, *Museums in Israel,* 2.

18. Inbar, *Museums in Kibbutzim,* 10, 13; Inbar, *History of Museums,* 1; 167; Inbar and Shiller, *Museums in Israel,* 20. This repeats much older views, for example, Biran, *Museums in Israel,* 2–3. On settlement museums in Israel see Katriel, *Performing the Past.* On the ideological use of the 'enthusiast' figure in later times, see Azulay, "with open doors," 84–85; Bar-Or, *Our Life Requires Art,* 10–14.

Efron asked, "How can a *kibbutz*, a modest rural settlement, permit itself the luxury of a full-scale museum"? This was a rhetorical question: she gave no answer except the vague "collective nature" of *kibbutzim* and the claim that collections grew in "natural and organic" ways. She also treated only four larger museums, which were atypical. The reality saw a lot of modest, small-scale museums. As Bar-Or clarified, the enthusiasts could succeed only when they were backed up by the entire *kibbutz* or movement—with budget, free days from work, etc.[19] Financing exhibitions, rooms, furniture, guarding, etc., was far from easy. In a summary prepared for a lecture in a *kibbutzim* seminary, an IDAM author explained that some *kibbutzim* solved it by voluntarily work; others by small sums taken from the Holocaust compensation money (*shillumim*). Few received money for cultural activities. The author was in favor of convincing State bodies (other than the IDAM, of course) to support financially such museums.[20]

One may conclude that the museums did spring "from below," a spontaneous initiative of private individuals and small circles. None was established by the State and centralized planning did not exist. However, developing an "antiquities corner" into a real museum with a special building required funds and cooperation on a level higher than a few private "enthusiasts."

Types and Aims of Museums

The boundaries between various kinds of local/regional museums were not well-defined by the IDAM, and the same place could be called by various terms. The lists of museums in File GL44872/4 show considerable changes, beyond natural processes of growth and decline. They reflect a three-tier concept (excluding central museums) of local, regional, and urban museums. Regional and urban museums were larger than local museums, but this has to be concluded from the lists, as no criteria were offered. Urban/municipal museums were often defined as regional museums, probably due to their larger size.

In 1967 Hestrin defined three levels of museums. First there were local museums—however, all the given examples were in *kibbutzim*. A second level included regional museums: larger, usually "embracing" an area with several local "collections" and having at least one qualified curator (Kefar Menahem, Bet Ussishkin at Kibbutz Dan, etc.) (Fig. 1). Here Hestrin included "a number of municipal museums [which] are, in fact, regional

---

19. Efron, "Museums in Kibbutzim," 42; Bar-Or, *Museums in Kibbutzim*.

20. GL44872/4, summary for lecture, October 1960 (anonymous).

museums" (Beersheva, Bet-Shean, Akko, and Tiberias). On a third level she put recent "site museums" in excavated sites, for example, Megiddo, Bet-Shearim, and Hazor.[21] In fact, site museums existed since the Mandate Period and were local museums.

In 1968 the central bureau of statistics required data on museums. A meeting was arranged with the IDAM and the participants agreed on a definition of "museum"—the only one I found in the IDAM files concerning regional/local museums:

> The definition of museum will be adjusted to that of UNESCO, which states: "a museum is any permanent body which acts for collecting, preserving, study and especially exhibition to the public of items of cultural value: artistic, historical, scientific and technological collections and zoological and botanical gardens. In this definition are included also historical and archaeological sites, memorials, and church treasures that are officially open to the public."[22]

There was little discussion of aims of museums. Perhaps everybody took museums for granted, and had no need to discuss their obvious Zionist roles. One author referred to this question when preparing a lecture for a *kibbutzim* seminary:

> The first and historical goal of a *kibbutz* collection is to serve as a place of study and inspiration to the local and regional dwellers ... This [cultural] asset will demonstrate the rootedness and stability of the *kibbutz* and village man.[23]

The Museums and the 'Friends of Antiquities'

Many of the museum "enthusiasts" were related to a new body established by the Antiquities Unit in 1948—the "Friends of Antiquities" (henceforward, FA in short).[24] The aim of this new body was to serve as eyes and ears to the Antiquities Unit, helping supervision of sites, since the Unit was far too small to safeguard even major antiquities sites. Another aim was keeping contact between the Unit and the wider public. Typically, when there was an archaeological collection or museum, it was established and managed

---

21. Hestrin, "Local and Regional Museums," 35–37.
22. GL44872/4, summary, May 1968, no. 641.
23. GL44872/4, summary, October 1960.
24. Kletter, "Friends of Antiquities," 2–15.

by an FA.[25] Enthusiasts started collecting antiquities, often joining the FA. Naturally, they wanted to share their hobby with other members of the *kibbutz* or village, so modest "antiquities corners" sprang up in any available place, whether public or private (little property was private in a *kibbutz*). At this moment, the collection became a museum and could appear under either term in the IDAM files.

The IDAM arranged lecture days for FAs on identifying, registering, and keeping antiquities. The first was made on 22–26 June 1949 in Jerusalem for managers of regional museums and FAs. IDAM employees, including Ruth Amiran, Pinhas Penuel Kahane, Emanuel Ben-Dor and Shemuel Yeivin, lectured on typology, pottery restoration, registering, etc.[26] In 1956, honoring UNESCO International Museums' Week, the IDAM held an exhibition in Jerusalem on "how to arrange an antiquities corner," intended for managers of local collections.[27]

Creating More Museums?

Documents indicate the interest of the Antiquities Unit (later IDAM) in establishing new local/regional museums already in its early days. Ruth Amiran, at the time Supervisor of the Northern District of the IDAM, sent a short letter titled "regional museums" to Shemuel Yeivin, Director of IDAM, on September 8, 1948 (Fig. 2). Amiran stated that the IDAM sees gladly and encourages "decentralization" of antiquities, which means also establishing new regional museums. This "assists in educating the people and in furthering civilized attitude towards cultural assets." Yet this also causes (unexplained) "difficulties" to scholars.[28]

Amiran was not alone. Ben-Dor, Deputy Director of the Antiquities Unit, stated in October 1948 that "the Antiquities Unit intends to help establishing regional museums and to give them professional advice."[29] A slightly later report concluded:

25. cf. Hestrin, "Local and Regional Museums," 34.

26. GL44864/14, report for June, 4.7.1949.

27. GL1430/14, summary of 1956, 22.12.56. In 1956 the IDAM planned to issue a special guide for regional and local museums in Israel. Interested museums were asked to share expenses; but response was disappointing and nothing materialized.

28. GL 44872/4; Katz, *Ruth Amiran*, 80–82. Decentralization was an ideology adopted at the time in Israel. The population was allegedly too much concentrated in the center (notably Tel-Aviv), other regions being empty (partly, though never officially, on account of the Naqba). The government wished to "de-centralize" the country, sending new immigrants to the periphery.

29. GL44864/14, Report by Ben Dor, 14.10.48.

In recent years small museums began to be established in various places in the Land. Their aim is to collect the antiquities of their surroundings. The Antiquities Unit offers these museums help in the form of professional advice. A special supervisor [=Kahane] visits the regional museums and assists in the sorting and arranging of the antiquities.[30]

Spurred by Amiran's activity, Pinhas Kahane responded with a three-page memorandum for administration and structure of regional museums under the IDAM. Kahane suggested that establishment of regional museums, even the smallest, should be supported, since:

It shows the enthusiasm of the local people, their will to study the past remains of our land, the wish to widen their knowledge and to discover, collect and proudly present antiquities.[31]

Kahane set two minimal requirements for regional museums: 1. a room for presenting the antiquities and for meetings and lectures; 2. a manager who knows the region well, has general knowledge in history and archaeology, and is capable of organizing. The IDAM should guide regional museums, preferably by visits of the Supervisor of Regional Museums (i.e., Kahane). Kahane offered practical suggestions:

1. Occasional visits by the IDAM's Supervisor (Kahane) to advise, discuss plans, etc.
2. Setting priorities of work—touring and marking sites on maps was apparently a priority.
3. The IDAM should give study collections of sherds to museums, so they could learn how to date finds and sites (this, however, is impossible at the moment).
4. The IDAM should give museums complete vessels, since sherds are not sufficient. This may take years; meantime 'duplicates' can be exchanged with regional museums (meaning antiquities of the same type, not modern replicas). Even duplicates are at the moment unavailable; the IDAM can send drawings/photos instead.
5. Arranging meetings for museum managers.
6. Issuing a journal on "archaeological-topographic problems" and on arranging a museum. Kahane dreamt about a scientific, even if popular, journal, with an editorial board.

30. GL 44864/14, Report 15.5.48–31.12.48, page 5.
31. GL 44872/4, memorandum 14, 16.10.1948.

86   Le-maʿan Ziony

7. Cardex of objects (see more below).

8. Kahane mentioned as "examples" a large regional museum (Sturman House) and a small local one (Bet Sevivatenu)—out of place in this list of suggestions

9. Some centralization is required, but it should not become "administrative": the local nature of regional museums should be maintained.

10. Knowledge of the Land includes natural sciences, so museums for nature should be encouraged by the IDAM too.

Kahane's memorandum was passed to Emanuel Ben-Dor. He agreed in principle, but noted politely that the plan was "too big," especially in view of the lack of IDAM employees for supporting it. Points 5–6 could be made as part of the FA activity, while natural sciences (point 10) were not under the IDAM's responsibility.[32]

Encouraging growth of local/regional museums was natural in the early years of the State. The lack of museums in general and in Jerusalem in particular, and the need for nominating FAs, pushed the Antiquities Unit in this direction. FAs had to deal with discovery of antiquities in various circumstances. Not every antiquity should be taken to Jerusalem, and with the permanent shortages of workers, vehicles and budget, it was not feasible even if desired. Antiquities had to be kept locally, better by trusted FAs than by unknown collectors.

Encouraging growth of museums was often the public policy of the IDAM, for example in Yeivin's publications.[33] The growth was presented as a positive achievement, in which the IDAM had a share. We need to remember that encouraging local collections was the IDAMs way of protecting antiquities and receiving news "from the field." If parts of such collections were exhibited, not at the IDAM's expense, there was little reason to object. Or was there?

Checking the Growth of Museums?

Quite early we start to find in the documents a more skeptical view towards the growth of local/regional museums. A sign appears in Amiran's early mention of such museums as a "difficulty," but without further explanation.

On 19.1.1951 Kahane wrote a memorandum (GL44872/4) on the value of local collections (Fig. 3). In his view, such collections grow naturally and

---

32. GL 44872/4, letter, 31.10.1948.
33. Yeivin, *Archaeological Activities*, 21; Yeivin, *Decade of Archaeology*, 55–56.

the IDAM should not prevent it, only guide and ensure scientific standards. The IDAM must be notified about new collections, and demand insurance, safekeeping in locked cupboards, registration, and exhibition with proper labels. Special finds must be delivered for the IDAM central museum in Jerusalem. In theory, a "corner of antiquities" may spring up in every settlement, but Kahane believed that these demands will slow the rate and regulate a responsible growth. For the first time we find the view that the growth should be limited—and can be by simple administrative measures.

A letter by Yeivin from May 1955 shows similar concerns. It was a response to an application by Aharon Wagman of the Caesarea (Sedot Yam) Museum, c/o the Ministry of Education, about enlargement—or rather, financial support. Yeivin noted that other museums handed similar requests too. The IDAM tries to maintain balance: it supports development and growth of local/regional museums, but it "always required three necessary conditions" for opening new "collections":

1. Appropriate place—at least one room in a public building;
2. Appropriate furniture for exhibition and for safekeeping antiquities;
3. A responsible person for handling the collection.

Yeivin noted that the IDAM cannot cover expenses. It gives professional advice and in exceptional cases small sums for establishing collections. However:

> In no way do I think that the Government must allocate any sums for daily maintenance of such collections. Finally, the people who collect must realize that they cannot hold the rope from both ends. On the one hand, they want to keep any discovery found in the area of their settlements or by their members elsewhere (whether from chance finds or excavations). They protest loudly about any antiquity which the IDAM takes . . . for its central collection in Jerusalem. On the other hand, they demand governmental budget or at least donations for maintaining these local collections.[34]

In the early years, the IDAM did not have a budget for establishing and maintaining local/regional museums. In later years, there was some funding. As an example, in budget year 1971/2 572,500 Israeli lira[35] were

---

34. GL44872/4, Yeivin, letter 7781a, 31.5.1955.

35. In early 1971, this equaled ca 163,500$ (ca 1 million US$ in today's terms). It was roughly equivalent to the IDAM's yearly budget for excavations and surveys. The money came from the Ministry of Education, not from the IDAM's budget.

allocated to thirty-one museums (excluding the Israel Museum). Of these, four museums were solely archaeological (receiving 25,500 lira) and fifteen had archaeological collections (receiving 168,000 lira). Non-archaeological (supported) museums included five art museums; four history museums; two ethnographical museums, and one museum of nature.

Since the IDAM did not finance the museums, budget was not a main concern. We see it in a document from October 1960, written by an IDAM author (perhaps Kahane or Yeivin) in preparation for a lecture in a seminar of heads of cultural committees of *Ha-Shomer Ha-Tza'ir kibbutzim*. The author pointed out that the IDAM's policy towards local museums/collections followed that of the British Mandate Department of Antiquities. By law, all the antiquities belong to the State; finds must be reported to the IDAM, which can confiscate them under certain conditions. The author lamented the results when speaking about the British Mandate period:

> According to this Law, most of the beautiful finds at the time, when not hidden from the eyes of the [British] authorities, or not sold to antiquities' dealers, were moved to Rockefeller Museum and with the division of Jerusalem transferred to the authority of the Jordanian Kingdom.[36]

The author explained that in Israel a "certain compromise" was reached between the law and "daily customs." The IDAM recognizes collections of antiquities in *kibbutzim* as public collections; those handling collections were nominated as FAs, and negotiations take place in case of discovered antiquities and "their division between the various bodies."[37] Naturally, collectors want to keep rare/important antiquities locally, while the IDAM prefers taking them for its museum in Jerusalem. UNESCO recommends de-centralizing, in order to safe-keep better the antiquities; to prevent "blank areas" on the museum map; and to maintain the relations between the antiquity and its original site. So the author was quite favorable to local/regional museums. Yet the terms seem confused: "division" (or partage) meant that the antiquities not taken by the State became private property of the excavation team and could be exported. Surely this cannot serve as model for relations with local collections/museums. A Law should be followed, especially by the State body responsible for it; but the IDAM lacked the means of supervising the growing number of museums and collections.

36. GL44872/4; actually Rockefeller passed to an international Board of Trustees; it was nationalized by Jordan only in 1966; Kletter, *Just Past*, 190–92.

37. Ibid. "Division of antiquities" (partage) was a common archaeological concept at the time. At the end of an excavation or season the finds were divided between the State and the excavation team.

In 1966 Rahmani noted that lack of central planning caused several problems:

1. Jerusalem, the capital, has no city museum (Rahmani suggested to establish one, or add a building for this aim in the Israel Museum).
2. Centers of the "old Yishuv" (Rahmani included here also early Zionist settlements), such as Safed, Nahariya, and Rehovot, lack museums for their own history (except the Aharonson House at Zikhron Yaakov). There are no museums of *'Aliyot* (the 'waves' of immigration, especially before 1948).
3. New development towns and immigrant settlements lack museums (Qiryat Shemona, Lod, Ramla, etc.); as well as most rural settlements (except *kibbutzim*).
4. Ethnic minorities have no museums for their history and ethnography.[38]
5. Regional museums are unevenly spread; they are lacking in the Galilee, Carmel, Judah Mountains, Lachish Region, Philistia, Negev Highlands, and Eilat.
6. Museums about wine and oil should be established.

Rahmani believed that the minorities and the "Old Yishuv" are strong enough to take up the gauntlet themselves. However, the IDAM must help immigrant settlements by establishing "cultural centers" (library, lecture and exhibition hall, a few study rooms); also regional museums in Safed, Bet Shemesh, Qiryat Gat, Ashdod, Sede Boqer and Eilat. Biran, then Director of IDAM, answered that "as long as there is no dedicated municipal body to handle local museums, any act that we shall do shall come to naught."[39] The IDAM also lacked the budget required for such plans.

The dynamics of small museums caused headaches to the IDAM. On 14.12.1969 Rahmani reported to Biran that there once was a collection of antiquities at Kibbutz Gevim; but the lady which handled it left and the collection was dispersed, except one stone pillar and one capital (Fig. 4). Rahmani recommended closing the file and "wiping [it] off the map." To this Biran answered: "I agree to your recommendation, but what does it mean to wipe off the map, and how does one close a file which is not a file?" Rahmani explained (added in handwriting):

---

38. For later years see Kark and Perry, "Museums and Multiculturalism," 95–97; Goldstein, "On Display"; and Broshi, "Archaeological Museums in Israel."
39. GL44872/4, Rahmani, letter 17.1.1966; Biran, letter 23.1.1966.

"1. One removes a pin from the map;

2. You are right, there was no file; the file was mainly empty" [sic].⁴⁰

One cannot avoid feeling the irony here. Apparently Rahmani had a map of Israel with pins marking collections/museums. Is Biran not aware of this, has he never set foot in Rahmani's office? Does he not know that there are files of museums? That the file was empty shows that the manager of this museum never registered the antiquities; perhaps it was not much of a museum. That Biran knows so little about the procedures indicates how ephemeral the supervision of local collections/museums was to the IDAM.

Records of visits to thirty-one museums and collections (made also in order to judge if a museum deserved financial support) by Rahmani and the "Unit for Culture" in the Ministry of Education and Culture in late 1968 reveal the sad state of many places. Not just in villages and *kibbutzim*; for example, the report on the Tiberias Museum stated:

Archaeological Museum—Tiberias

1. The building is old, unfitting (an old mosque). Improvements have been made, but [the situation] is still unsatisfactory.
2. The archaeological exhibition is not of sufficient level.
3. The Manager is working hard but the municipality neglects the museum.
4. Noticeable reduction in numbers of visitors.
5. We should influence the municipality to move the museum to a more fitting building.
6. There is no basis for financial support.⁴¹

Registering Museums

Amiran suggested in August 1948 that regional museums should be required to register their objects in a unified cardex, sending one copy to the IDAM. Emanuel Ben-Tor, deputy director of IDAM, recommended the idea and suggested that the IDAM will supply the cards. Yeivin decided that cards will be given free of charge to small museums, while larger museums would pay the costs. A report from late 1948 stated:

---

40. GL44872/4, letters 14.12.1969; 21.12.1969.
41. GL44872/4, 1.12.1968.

The Unit tries to introduce a unified system of registering of all the antiquities in museums and even in private collections. For that aim a cardex which can serve as an example for all those interested was printed.[42]

The form for such a card (form "AT-5") survives (Fig. 5).[43] It occupies about half a page and is quite simple. The type was to be written first (juglet, lamp, etc.), followed by "material," "period," "origin" (=site), and measures. The field "acquired" would give the date and/or origin of acquisition. Following fields would define the museum/collection ("in the collection"), the item number, and a textual description. Place was left for a picture/figure. Museums were asked to make two copies and to send the first ten cards to the IDAM for initial check; later, by batches of fifty.[44]

In fact, registration proceeded very slowly. The IDAM lacked workers and budget while FAs and managers of local collections/museums lacked knowledge and time. Registering meant risk of removal of major antiquities to the IDAM museum. There was more to it, because it meant a change in legal status—an acknowledgment of the State's ownership. The finds could remain where they were, but as a temporal arrangement, by the grace of the IDAM. Probably in 1950s Israel, when private property was not the most sacred thing, most local museums would have gladly registered their finds if only the State would have financed it. The lack of budget prevented the progress of registering.

In December 1957 Ephrat Yeivin, who worked at Yeivin's excavation at Tell el-'Areini (then thought to be Gath), handed a plan for touring and registering museums for prehistory in winter, when the excavations halt. This was approved and done. Then Ruth Hestrin was nominated as Supervisor of Regional Museums, visiting many city museums and local collections and helping to establish a few more, including an exhibition of grain in the Dagon Silos in Haifa.[45] In 1969 Ruth Peled continued the operation;[46] but it is hard to say if the rate of registered finds was larger than the rate of their addition to local collections/museums. In 1965 Rahmani complained about the "collection habits" of some museum managers:

---

42. Various documents in GL44872/4, e.g., Kahane, memorandum 14; Ben-Dor, letter 31.10.1948. The quote is from GL44864/14, report for 15.5.48–31.12.48, page 5.

43. GL44872/4, dated 10.12.1948.

44. Yeivin, GL44872/4, letter 10.12.1948.

45. GL44883/12, report for budget year 1957–1958, page 10; GL44872/4, letters 22.12.58, 9.1.59, 20.2.59, 7.4.1969, etc.

46. See Inbar and Shiller, *Museums in Israel*, 243.

To: Director of IDAM

Subject: "Collecting" of Museum Managers

Reading now the museums' files, a sorry picture is being clarified, of "collecting" by certain managers of museums, which is not much different from private collecting, for several reasons:

1. The items are not registered in the State Treasures and sometimes they are not registered at all;

2. Some of the items come from illegal excavations, sometimes by encouragement of the museum manager;

3. There is no arrangement concerning ownership of the items even in their places, that is, exchanges, sale and anything else are possible [meaning: might occur].

Even at present these things are a transgression to the existing Law, especially paragraph 4 of the Antiquities Ordinance. I assume the situation demands discussion within the IDAM and maybe later a conference for explanation to museum managers. It is inconceivable that they will continue to do, even if innocently and intentionally, things that defy law and good order.[47]

Biran only noted on the margin that the IDAM should start registering the assets, and meantime make procedures for registering new finds.

In 1966 Dr. A.W. Kalimowski, member of the Archaeological Council, applied to Binyamin Mazar, the Chair. Visiting Santander in Spain, he saw an extensive and accurate cardex of public libraries. Why not employ such a cardex for antiquities from all the museums and collections in Israel? Mazar handed the request to Biran, Director of IDAM, who explained that it was started long ago, but delayed by lack of budget. The IDAM also started a cardex for archaeological libraries; this too was stopped for lack of budget. Now the antiquities cardex was again on the agenda and soon they will nominate a Supervisor of Local Museums to handle it (indeed, Yaacov Meshorer was nominated to this position in late 1966).[48] During the 1990s the IAA registered many collections and local museums, but also encouraged creation of more local displays, lending them antiquities (if the antiquities originate from various places, the display is not "local" anymore, unlike most of the 1950s–60s "antiquities corners").[49]

47. GL44872/4, letter 31.12.1965.

48. GL44872/4; letters by Kalimowski 7.10.1966; Biran 12.10.1966; Rahmani 5.12.1966.

49. On regional museums in Israel in recent years see Shamir, "Regional

Discussion and Conclusions

In this study we discussed regional/local museums in the first years of Israel. We did not treat central museums, which deserve a separate study.

Although a few regional/local museums existed before 1948, they became a significant phenomenon only later, when many more (ca. 120) were established. This did not happen immediately, since the first few difficult years with the austerity regime (*tzena'*) did not encourage establishment of museums. The growth was spontaneous, by initiative of "enthusiasts" who established mainly small-scale exhibitions ("antiquities corners"). Quite many places struggled and did not survive. Relatively few places grew into larger, permanent museums—that when the enthusiast/s succeeded in recruiting support of entire communities or bodies. Cities and regional councils were strong enough to found municipal/regional museums. These too were few and not immune from failure. Failures of municipal/regional museums occurred in economically-weak peripheral cities, for example, Beersheva, Bet-Shean, and Tiberias.

The IDAM sorted museums by several categories—local, urban/municipal, regional, professional, and site-museums, though clear criteria were not defined. One can perhaps differentiate two main types, based on size: a majority of small local museums (mostly in *kibbutzim*, but also a few site museums); and a limited number of larger museums (regional, municipal, and "professional," i.e., dedicated to a specific topic).[50]

Shared by almost all the museum enthusiasts was Zionist ideology with its stress on the ties of the nation to the far past. The museums, therefore, stressed "our past." In Anderson's terms, the modern nation created for itself a basis in the past, obsessively using "hard" scientific materials.[51] As Anderson says, we should not think of this in terms of fake, but of powerful creation. The 1950s–70s museums served as unofficial end-branches of the State. The feelings of belonging to the place and of contact with the distant past were genuine for the museum enthusiasts.

Why were so many of the local museums established in *kibbutzim*? Careful analysis offers an explanation. Most of the local museums were established by *kibbutzim* that existed before 1948, not in new development cities and villages. This, because the most basic requirement was enthusiasts with deep feelings for the local place. Such enthusiasts could not be

---

Archaeological Museums"; Shamir, "Archaeological Exhibits in Israel."

50. In Australia, a plethora of forms exits; two basic rural types are community museums (volunteer-managed) and regional museums (managed by local government with paid trained staff), Winkworth, "Let a Thousand Flowers," 2.

51. Anderson, *Imagined Communities*.

produced overnight. Until 1948, 177 *kibbutzim* were established; by the end of 1949 they numbered 211. Only seventeen were added between 1948 and 1961 and just three more until 1969. While young in years, pre-1948 *kibbutzim* were veteran in comparison to the multitude of other, post-1948 settlements. In addition, unlike post-1948 immigrants, veteran *kibbutzim* members bonded together in preparatory groups (*hakhsharot*) years before founding a *kibbutz*. Another factor was the fact that *kibbutzim* members originated mainly from Europe, where "museumization" already was part of culture.[52]

The IDAM encouraged—though not financially—establishment of museums. This was natural in view of the circumstances. The IDAM could not prevent private collecting of antiquities by members of settlements, *kibbutzim* and even cities. Unlike cities, *kibbutzim* cultivated and held *de facto* large tracts of land (even if legally it belonged to the State). This was one more reason why many antiquities collections/museums formed in *kibbutzim*—they held land, which was full of antiquities.[53] The IDAM needed the FAs as eyes and ears. Many museum "enthusiasts" were also FAs: people interested in archaeology and "knowledge of the land," who knew intimately the surrounding region and loved it deeply. The IDAM had to tolerate the collecting, but encouraged display, thus turning collections to museums. This made them visible and easier to monitor. Just like the *kibbutzim* lands, the antiquities collections of *kibbutzim* were State property *de jure*, *kibbutzim* property *de facto*.[54]

Is this creation of many local museums by few enthusiasts unique, as some claim?[55] Comparisons teach that it is not; consider, for example, post-WWII Australia. In 1975 a Committee on Museums in Australia discovered:

> The hundreds of small museums that had been founded in the previous 15 years. This was a 'popular and vigorous grass-roots movement' ... arising from a curiosity about everyday life in the past that was not being satisfied by the major state museums.[56]

They numbered close to 1000 in 1975 (and more than 3000 today). Most of them were formed by enthusiasts "from below":

---

52. Cf. Inbar, *History of Museums*, 10; Bar-Or, *Our Life Requires Art*, 23.

53. As noticed by Inbar, "Museums in Kibbutzim," 10.

54. Unless if registered by the IDAM. Much later, land became a treasure trove, arousing bitter debates on how it should be used, e.g., http://www.acri.org.il/he/700; http://www.court.org.il/nato/nato6.htm.

55. For example, Kol-Inbar, "In need of Long Breath"; cf. Inbar and Shiller, *Museums in Israel*, 20.

56. Condé, "Orphans of Government," 2.

> Australia has experienced an extraordinary flowering of museums and the accumulation of collections in nearly every rural town and village, in regional cities and many suburbs ... This is the most remarkable and sustained grass roots movement ever seen in Australia ... The development of community museums is a truly local initiative, forged by local enterprise, mad ambition, shared enthusiasm and millions of hours of volunteer work. Most of the museums in regional Australia were created with little or no government funding and that is how they continue to operate.[57]

As in Israel, in Australia too, such museums were based on "deep attachment to place" and expressed communities' "self-beliefs" not just about the past, but also about their own future.[58] Local/regional museums in Australia met similar problems of maintenance over the years, suffering from "decaying buildings" and "rabbit warrens of small rooms."[59] In both states, the authorities gave mainly "advisory services," though "after decades of funding of advisory services, there is no evidence that advice leads to more sustainable collections or the renewal of museums in regional Australia."[60]

Another comparison is with ethnographic museums in Italy. They appeared first in North Italy in the 1970s. Their aim was preserving traditional lifestyles, which were abandoned on a large scale due to rapid industrialization and urbanization after WWII. The museums were formed by single or small groups of youngsters spontaneously, meeting objection or ignorance by the authorities (recognition came much later). When first listed (1985) there were 150 such museums; by 1991 there were 400 and by 2009 around 1300. Often they were private or local institutions, run by volunteers. This phenomenon is relatively young and studies of it are mostly supportive.[61]

Some claim that the uniqueness of the early Israeli museums was their archaeological focus.[62] However, subjects of museums vary greatly and local/regional museums are mostly dedicated to a specific surrounding, so each one is unique. Naturally, the early museums in Israel focused on the far past, since the places where they were located were all newly established

---

57. Winkworth, "Let a Thousand Flowers," 1; cf. Maycock, "Local Museums," 5. The situation in Western Australia is somewhat different, but similar problems appear, Kimberley et al., "Drawing People Together."

58. Winkworth, "Let a Thousand Flowers," 1.

59. Ibid., 1, 5

60. Ibid., 4.

61. Bertolino, Museology and Ethnography, 290–91; Forni, "Ethnographic Museums"; Maggi, "Ecomuseums in Italy."

62. Thus Inbar, *History of Museums*, 2, 169–71.

and were not considered worthy of muzeumization. In addition, the Zionist background demanded connection with the far past, skipping periods of Islamic and Christian rule, which were not seen as a fitting model.

States are more likely to invest in large, central museums. Local museums are often created "from below" by local enthusiasts, since they have deep feelings for their own little corner of the globe. If local people were not crazy enough to establish local museums, very few of them would exist.

What remained from this world of small, local antiquities corners of the 1950s–60s? Reliable data is not easily available. Some 180–200 museums existed in Israel c. 1990, but there is no updated publication that lists them. The official body—the Association of Museums in Israel (*'iggud ha-muze'onim*) is content with a list of sixty-eight (probably recognized) museums; of them thirteen are in *kibbutzim*, but only five of them are archaeological museums. A private site lists c. 230 museums, of them thirty-two are in *kibbutzim*; but only about ten of them are archaeological museums or deal with archaeology.[63] So the *kibbutzim* still have many more museums than relative to their population size (2.2 percent in 2005); only the stress is no longer on archaeological museums. History of settlement is the dominant theme.[64] Also, with a few exceptions, the names are not the same. Most of the founders and their collections/museums are no longer with us.

Finally, we should also appreciate what was achieved (Fig. 6). The small antiquities corners and exhibits had educational value, whose fruits are seen in younger generations of "enthusiasts" for archaeology. In addition, without the dedicated museum enthusiasts and FAs in the first decades of the State, at a time when the supervision of sites by the IDAM was extremely limited, many more antiquities would have been lost and destroyed.

Acknowledgments

I wish to thank Nimrod Getzow, Zvi Gal, and Orit Shamir for reading the manuscript before publication and for making valuable comments. Orit

---

63. Inbar, *History of Museums*, 1; Inbar and Shiller, *Museums in Israel*, 17, 317; www.icom.org.il: The Shephelah Museum (closed); Bet-Miryam, Palmahim; Bet-Ussishkin, Dan (mostly nature museum); En-Dor Archaeological Museum; Prehistoric Man Museum, Ma'ayan Baruch; Yarmukian Culture Museum, Sha'ar ha-Golan; Wilfried Israel House, Hazorea; Mediterranean and Regional Archaeology Museum, Nir David; Philistine Ekron Museum, Revadim; maybe add a museum of copies of scrolls at Almog. According to Shamir, "Archaeological Exhibits in Israel," 11, there are c. 250 museums and exhibits for archaeology in Israel today.

64. Inbar and Shiller, *Museums in Israel*, 20; Bar-Or, *Our Life Requires Art*, 8.

Shamir kindly allowed me to use photos from Gevim and Ussishkin House. Karmit Romano-Hvid drew my attention to Gardi's book on the Ussishkin House Museum.

Appendix 1: Early Local/Regional Museums

The list includes museums active in the field of archaeology in the first years of the State of Israel (roughly 1948–1955). For the sake of simplicity we call all museums, though some were only collections or small-scale exhibits. The list is arranged by alphabetic order of places, divided into central, regional/municipal, and local museums. It is *not* a practical guide for present day visitors. Whenever possible, we added names of managers. In some cases we only have names of FAs (but in most cases, museum managers were also FAs).

A. Central Museums

1. Jerusalem, Bezalel Museum. Established 1906; a zoological and later an art museum. Opened to the public 1912. Manager Mordechai Narkiss. It had a large collection of coins. Closed 1929; re-opened 1935; amalgamated into the Israel Museum in 1965.[1]
2. Jerusalem, IDAM Museum. Started as a temporary exhibition in 1949. Manager P. P. Kahane. Closed 1965, antiquities transferred to the Israel Museum.
3. Tel-Aviv Museum of Art. Opened 1932 at the house of Meir Dizengoff. Manager Karl Schwartz (1933–1947). Predominantly an art museum, with occasional archaeological exhibitions/lectures.[2]

---

1. *Alon* 3, 1951:56; Katz, "Bezalel Art Museum"; Ofrat-Friedlander, "Bezalel Museum"; Inbar, *History of Museums*, 17–49.
2. Shay, "City like This," 122–32; Inbar and Shiller, *Museums in Israel*, 96; Inbar, *History of Museums*, 50–78.

B. Regional/Municipal Museums

4. Akko, Municipal Museum. Established after 1948. Manager Dr. Zeev Goldman. Planned as a museum of Arab folklore in the Crusader Castle with items from deserted villages; but the Castle was appropriated by the Ministry of Health. Since 1954 located in a Turkish Hammam. Closed in the 1980s, today there are new exhibitions in the Municipality Building and the Castle.[3]

5. Bet-Shean. Established after 1948. Sometimes called municipal museum, sometimes local collection. Manager, FA, and City Mayor Noah Mardiger. Hopes of locating it in the Crusader Castle did not materialize.[4]

6. Beer-Sheba. Municipal or Negev Museum. Established c. 1953. Manager and FA Dr. Z. Ben-Zvi.[5]

7. Caesarea—Sedot Yam, House of Hanna Senesh. Established 1950; manager and FA Aharon Wagman. Sometimes mentioned as a local museum. It had a room with antiquities, including items from the British Mandate Caesarea museum, damaged in 1948.[6]

8. En-Harod and Tel-Yosef, Sturman House. Regional Museum, established 1941; manager and FA Nehemia Cimbalist/Zori. http://www.beit-shturman.co.il/he/.[7]

9. Haifa, Fabzner House. This was a library for science (not a museum), founded in Tel-Aviv 1919, and moved to Haifa 1923.

10. Haifa, [National] Maritime Museum. Established 1953, manager Arieh Ben-Eli.[8]

11. Haifa, Municipal Museum. Founded 1949 or 1951; mainly art museum. Manager Alexander Roche/Rosh (formerly, I used the spelling Rash, but Roche/Rosh is more accurate).[9]

---

3. Inbar and Shiller, *Museums in Israel*, 158–59.

4. *Alon* 3, 1951:5; GL44866/3, Yeivin, letter 1.1.1950; Yeivin, *Archaeological Activities*, 21–22.

5. Inbar and Shiller, *Museums in Israel*, 229–30.

6. *Alon* 1, 1949:19; *Alon* 3, 1951:5; Yeivin *Archaeological Activities*, 22; Shiller, *Guide for Museums*, 86–88; Inbar and Shiller, *Museums in Israel*, 187–8; Kletter, *Just Past*, 4–7, 26–27.

7. Shiller, *Guide for Museums*, 59–60; Inbar and Shiller, *Museums in Israel*, 170–72; Inbar, *History of Museums*, 131–43.

8. Inbar and Shiller, *Museums in Israel*, 125–26.

9. Ibid., 121.

12. Hazorea. Wilfrid Israel House. Sometimes called a local museum. Founded 1951. FAs Ehud Tal and Ezra Meirhof (http://www.wilfrid.org.il/).[10]

13. Jerusalem, The Hebrew University, Museum of Jewish Antiquities. A collection never opened to the public. Based on a 1936 donation by M. Kootcscher; building ready 1940; first manager Eliezer Sukenik.[11]

14. Kefar Yehoshua, Hankin House. Founded 1950; mainly nature museum. Manager (until 1960) Menahem Zaharoni (1912–1979), teacher, collector, and leader of a circle for Knowledge of the Land: https://sites.google.com/a/merchavim.tzafonet.org.il/hankin/menachem. Zaharoni also participated in Aharoni's survey of Galilee. There was also a private collection of coins in this village, by Eliyahu Amizur (1903–2004).[12]

15. Sha'ar ha-Golan. Manager and FA Yehuda Roth. Opened 1950, first exhibition in a bomb shelter. Today the Museum for Yarmukian Culture.[13]

16. Tel-Aviv, Haaretz (later Eretz-Israel) Museum. Started from the private collection of Walther Moses, manager of the Dubek Cigarette Company. First building (the Glass Pavilion) 1958. Manager Hayim Alperin.[14]

17. Tel-Aviv Municipal Museum, Abu-Kabir (later Tel-Aviv—Jaffa Archaeological Museum). Opened 1951. First Manager Yaacov Kaplan (1911–1989), the municipal archaeologist of Tel-Aviv.[15]

18. Tel-Aviv, Bet Sevivatenu ("house of our environment"). Manager Shmuel Avitzur (1908–1999). At first (1938), a small museum of finds brought by the "Sevivatenu" circle for Knowledge of the Land. Since

---

10. Shiller, *Guide for Museums*, 70–73; Inbar and Shiller, *Museums in Israel*, 181–2; Bar-Or, *Our Life Requires Art*, 198–252.

11. Sukenik, "Twenty Five Years," 53–54; http://www.ynet.co.il/articles/ 0,7340,L-4087604,00.html#n; Inbar, *History of Museums*, 149–59.

12. Kletter, *Just Past*, 163–4; http://www.youtube.com/watch?v=mT2GiLsTh8k; Inbar and Shiller, *Museums in Israel*, 180–81; http://www.albumjezreel.co.il/pioneer_information/527.

13. *Alon* 3, 1951:5; www.myc.org.il; Shiller, *Guide for Museums*, 51–52; Inbar and Shiller, *Museums in Israel*, 165–6.

14. Shay, "City like This," 132–4; www.eretzmuseum.org.il.

15. *Alon* 3, 1951:56; *Alon* 4, 1953:14; Kempinski, "in memorial," 88–89; Gophna, "in memorial," 55; Inbar and Shiller, *Museums in Israel*, 106–7.

Early Local/Regional Museums   101

1954, the "Man and his Work" museum, affiliated to the Hayim Avshalom Institute. Later, part of the Eretz-Israel Museum.[16]

19. Tiberias, Municipal Museum. Opened c. 1953 in an abandoned mosque. Manager Tirzah Markus-Rabbani (not a FA; FAs in Tiberias were Y. Yemini and Sh. Landau).

C. Local Museums

20. Ashkelon/Majdal. The Mandatory Period open air museum was still guarded in 1949 by the same Arab family, which lived on the tell.[17] After the expulsion of the Majdal inhabitants to the Gaza Strip, an agreement was reached (ca 1952) between the IDAM, the Military Administration of Ashkelon, and the Moslem and Druze Department of the Ministry of Religious Affairs to open a "regional museum" in a deserted mosque in the city. Most of the finds of the open air museum were moved there, also other antiquities found in the city. Though called by Yeivin "municipal museum," it remained a storage place and was soon closed down.[18]

21. Alumoth, Lower Galilee (*kibbutz*). Mainly prehistoric finds. FA Yoel Fruzhinin. The *kibbutz* was dissolved in the early 1960s.

22. Bet-Alpha (*kibbutz*). This site is famous for the synagogue, found in 1928 and published by Sukenik in 1932. (The synagogue is actually located on the land of Kibbutz Hefzibah, and not on the land of Kibbutz Beth Alpha, so the geographical and terminological situation is a bit confusing). It had no FA; in 1960 a large collection of coins is mentioned as exhibited there—probably of Misha Reshef (1912–2000), who also helped Aharoni in the Galilee Survey.

23. Clark collection of Antiquities, YMCA, Jerusalem.

24. Emeq-Hefer, Rupin College. FA Gershon Tamir. Ram Gophna mentions a plan to make a museum there in the early 1950s. Exhibition started only in 1959 in a building of the College, remaining for some 20 years (http://www.liderman.co.il.)[19]

---

16. Avitzur, "Man and His Work Museum"; Avitzur, *Man and His Work Atlas*; Regev and Shiller, *Selected Papers*, 7–8; Shay, "City Like This," 135–36.

17. Kletter, *Just Past*, 119, Fig. 15.

18. *Alon* 3, 1951:4–5; Yeivin, *Archaeological Activities*, 22.

19. Inbar and Shiller, *Museums in Israel*, 193.

25. En-Gev (*kibbutz*). Opened 1949. FAs Claire Epstein and Mordechai Neustadt (later Neustadt's brother, Mendel Nun). Epstein (1911–2000), later scholar of the Golan Heights and winner of the Israel Prize, moved to Ginnosar in 1953. En-Gev now has the museum for fishing in the Sea of Galilee and an antiquities exhibition.[20]

26. En ha-Mifratz (*kibbutz*). Manager and FA Zvi Sapir (1910–1951), the *mukhtar* (head) and first teacher, an amateur archaeologist (www.rav-dori.co.il/previewpage.aspx?str=3498).[21]

27. Givat-Hayim (*kibbutz*). Planned "house for the Study of the region," manager "to be" Reuven Ha-Yisraeli (1910–1968), local FA, teacher and organizer of a circle for Knowledge of the Land.[22]

28. Ha-Hotrim (*kibbutz*); manager and FA (until c. 1953) Moshe Barak (1925–2012). The Kibbutz settled in 1948 in the abandoned German colony Neuhardhoff, moving in 1952 to its present location (http://info.palmach.org.il).

29. Haifa, Neve-Sha'anan. A collection belonging to the painter Avraham Yaskil (1894–1987); re-opened as a public collection in 1949. Yaskil established a circle of art enthusiasts and, in the 1940s, an art museum in Neve-Sha'anan's Bet ha-Am. This probably means the Tel-Amal building, which stood deserted for 10 years, becoming a cinema in 1949 and later a synagogue.

30. Hanita (*kibbutz*). Founded 1956. FA Moshe Dohovny (Yada'ayah).[23]

31. Har Tabor. The collection exhibited in the Italian church.[24]

32. Ma'ayan Baruch (*kibbutz*). FAs Amnon Asaf and Micha Livneh. Opened 1952. Presently the "Prehistoric Man Museum" with c. 140,000 items from the Hulah valley. Asaf started collecting in 1946 and for years refused to register the finds.[25]

---

20. *Alon* 2, 6; Yeivin, *Archaeological Activities*, 22; Hess, "Claire Epstein"; Shiller, *Guide for Museums*, 119–20; Inbar and Shiller, *Museums in Israel*, 246.

21. Inbar and Shiller, *Museums in Israel*, 247.

22. *Alon* 2:6; Givat Hayim Newsletter 310, 1.1.1968.

23. Yeda'aya and Gil, *Western Galilee*, 71–72; 196, Shiller, *Guide for Museums*, 37–38.

24. Inbar and Shiller, *Museums in Israel*, 242

25. Haaretz Newspaper, Tourist Tip 237, 16.5.2013; http://www.youtube.com/watch?v=OcQzcKfaueU; www.ugmp.co.il); http://www.maayan-baruch.co.il/museum; Shiller, *Guide for Museums*, 16–27.

33. Mishmar ha-Emeq (*kibbutz*). Founded 1950. Manager and FA Raphael Grunberg/Giveon (1916–1985)—Egyptologist, later Professor in Tel-Aviv University.[26]

34. Mishmar ha-Negev (*kibbutz*). FA David Alon (1926–2000), a scholar of the Neolithic and Chalcolithic periods, one of the Gilat excavators.[27]

35. Nahariya, the Cultural House (*bet ha-tarbut*). FA Otto Stiel, later joined by Menahem Glaser.[28]

36. Nazareth. Several museums in Monasteries, including the Franciscan Order, Church of the Annunciation.

37. Petah Tiqva, *Yad la-Banim*. Built 1951. This was the first "Memorial for Sons" building—cultural houses named after those fallen in wars.

38. Ramat-Gan. Bet-Zvi. Founded 1950 as a cultural and youth house, now a school for theater. FA Hanan Lernau (http://www.beit-zvi.com/?CategoryID=159).

39. Tel-Adashim, Ohel Sarah. Manager and FA Yariv Shapira. A cultural center established in 1943, named after Sarah Lishanski (1884–1924). Building built 1957; Yariv Shapira collected hundreds of items exhibited there since 1960. Since 1965 it was a school and since 1985 the Jezreel Valley College. The fate of the antiquities is unknown.[29]

40. Stela Maris Monastery, Haifa. A room with antiquities from the vicinity.[30]

41. Susita, "planned." Susita was a classical city on the Israeli side of the 1948 ceasefire border with Syria. It was used by the Army as a military post protecting En-Gev. Claire Epstein, FA at En-Gev, excavated there. The border location prevented realization of the plan. A local collection was established instead at En-Gev.[31]

---

26. Manor, "In Memoriam"; Shiller, *Guide for Museums*, 74; Inbar 1988, *Museums in Kibbutzim*, 17; Inbar and Shiller, *Museums in Israel*, 246.

27. Later closed, collections moved to the Alon Centre: Shiller, *Guide for Museums*, 119.

28. Inbar and Shiller, *Museums in Israel*, 154.

29. Tidhar, *Entsiklopedya*, 701–2; http://www.itamar-books.co.il/?mode=nl&n=92.

30. Inbar and Shiller, *Museums in Israel*, 242.

31. Ma'ariv Newspaper, 10.1.1951; *Alon* 1, 6; *Alon* 2, 6; Kletter, *Just Past*, 39, 307 Fig. 33.

Appendix 2: Other Museums

These places appear in lists from 1958–1960.[1] Some were established in those years; a few existed earlier, but were not listed. We present these places in brief.

A. Regional/Urban/Professional Museums:

42. Shrine of the Book, Jerusalem. An exhibition of scrolls (since 1957) at Giv'at Ram; the complex famous today was opened only in 1965.
43. Museum of Prehistoric Archaeology, Hebrew University, Cremieux St. (probably only "planned," an initiative of Moshe Stekelis).
44. Chief Rabbinate, Jerusalem, Hechal Shlomo; founded 1958. Antiquities related to religious customs and ritual. This exhibition preceded the founding (in 1961) of the Museum of Jewish Art called now after Sir Isaac Wolfson.[2]
45. Pontifical Biblical Institute, Botta St., Jerusalem.
46. Schocken Library, 6 Balfour St. (later Hebrew Union College). Built 1935.
47. (Kibbutz) Sa'ar, Maritime Museum. FA Baruch Safrai.[3]
48. Dagon Museum, Haifa. Director R. Hecht; dealing with grain, founded c. 1955.[4]

---

1. Yeivin, *Decade of Archaeology*, 60–61; and GL44872/4.
2. Inbar and Shiller, *Museums in Israel*, 68–69.
3. Ibid., 246.
4. Ibid., 136–7.

B. Local Museums

These museums were all located in *kibbutzim*, except Megiddo (site museum, 59).

49. Ussishkin House, Dan. Founded 1955, manager Elimelech Hurwitz.[5]
50. Ayyelet ha-Shahar, Zifroni House. Founded 1950, mainly a library (also today). FAs Avraham Aderet and Israel Shalit. In the 1960s the Hazor Museum was established at this *kibbutz*.
51. Barkai. Exhibition in a shelter. FA Hayim Burdeli.[6]
52. Beeri. FA Rina Nishri-Hevron, b. 1925, a prolific author of books on Knowledge of the Land. The collection still exists, located in a shelter.[7]
53. Gat. FA Yaacov ha-Yaari.[8]
54. Huqoq. FA Yoav Fogelson (1926–2011).
55. Kabri. Details unknown.[9]
56. Kefar Menahem. Later called the Shephelah Museum, now closed. Manager Manfred Moshe Israel, a teacher.
56. Ma'aleh ha-Hamisha. FA Shemuel Brandman (1914–1968).[10]
57. Ma'agan Mikha'el. Underwater Archaeology Museum, founded 1959. FA Elisha Linder (1924–2009), the pioneer of underwater archaeology in Israel.[11]
58. Ma'oz Hayim. Manager Avshalom Yaacobi (b. 1916), who discovered the Synagogue there in 1974.[12]
59. Megiddo site Museum.[13]
60. Megiddo Kibbutz. Further details unknown.
61. Metzer. Since c. 1954. FA (later IAA Archaeologist) Gershon Edelstein (http://www.daaton.co.il/Article.aspx?id=600).
62. Na'an. FA Shemarya Gutman.

---

5. Ibid., 142–3; Shiller, *Guide for Museums*, 23–25; Gardi, *Even Neyar*.
6. Shiller, *Guide for Museums*, 123; Inbar and Shiller, *Museums in Israel*, 244.
7. Shiller, *Guide for Museums*, 123; Inbar and Shiller, *Museums in Israel*, 244.
8. Shiller, *Guide for Museums*, 121; Inbar and Shiller, *Museums in Israel*, 245.
9. Shiller, *Guide for Museums*, 123.
10. Ibid., 98–99; Inbar and Shiller, *Museums in Israel*, 221–23.
11. Ibid., 247.
12. Ibid., 245.
13. Ibid., 248.

63. Nahshon. FAs Yehuda Shabak and Yehuda Shirai.

64. Nirim. FA Arieh Shreiber.

65. Revivim, mainly prehistoric finds. FA Yosef Feldman ("Arab Yossi"). Feldman started the first En-Gedi Field School (1959), and in 1984 founded and headed for 26 years the Society for Preservation of Heritage Sites (http://eng.shimur.org/Default.aspx). The fate of the Revivim collection is unclear.

66. Saʻasa. Founded 1959; preceding the Avram Rashkes Museum opened in 1968.[14] Manager probably Eliyahu Ilan, who helped Aharoni in his Survey.

67. Shaʻar ha-Amaqim. Not documented in the IDAM 1950s files; it was a collection housed and probably exhibited in a hut since 1955.[15]

68. Shamir. FA Hayim Kena'ani (1920–2004).[16]

69. Tirat Zvi. FA probably Uri Eliav (1919–2005) (Pers. Comm. Zvi Gal).

70. Yas'ur. FA Zeev Adir (1921–1991).

BIBLIOGRAPHY

Alon. Bulletin of the IDAM. Jerusalem: Ministry of Education. Hebrew (5 vols., I, II, III, IV, V–IV, issued respectively in 1949, 1950, 1951, 1953, and 1957; authors not mentioned).
Anderson, Benedict. *Imagined Communities*. London: Verso, 1983.
Avitzur, Shemuel. "Man and His Work Museum, Tel Aviv." *Museum* 20/1 (1967) 49–50.
———. *Man and His Work: Historical Atlas of Tools and Workshops in the Holy Land*. Jerusalem: Carta, 1976 (Hebrew).
Azulay, Ariela. "With Open Doors: Museums for History in the Israeli Public Space." *Theory and Criticism* 4 (1993) 79–95. (Hebrew)
Bar-Or, Galia. "Museums in the Kibbutzim from the 1930s to the 1960s." Not dated. http://museumeinharod.org.il/hebrew/articles/museums_in_the_kibbutz.html. (Hebrew)
———. *'Our Life Requires Art.' Art Museums in the Kibbutzim, 1930–1960*. Beersheva: Ben Gurion University of the Negev, 2010. (Hebrew)
Bertolino, M. A. "Museology and Ethnography in Italy: an Historical Perspective." In *Great Narratives of the Past. Traditions and Revisions in National Museums*, 285–96. Conference proceedings from *EuNaMus, European National Museums: Identity Politics, the Uses of the Past and the European Citizen, Paris*. Edited by Dominique Poulot, Felicity Bodenstein, and José María Lanzarote. *EuNaMus*

---

14. Ibid., 246; Shiller, *Guide for Museums*, 35–36.

15. Ibid., 68–69.

16. Ibid., 29–30.

Report 4. Linköping University Electronic Press, 2011. http://www.ep.liu.se/ecp_home/index.en.aspx?issue=078.
Biran, Avraham. "Museums in Israel." *Museum* 20/1 (1967) 2–3.
Broshi, Magen. "Archaeological Museums in Israel: Reflections on Problems of National Identity." In: *Museums and the Making of 'Ourselves': The Role of Objects in National Identity*, edited by Flora S. Kaplan, 314–29. London: Leicester University Press, 1994.
Cobbing, Felicity J., and Jonathan Tubb. "Before the Rockefeller: The First Palestine Museum in Jerusalem." *Mediterraneum* 5 (2007) 79–89.
Condé, Anne-Marie. "The Orphans of Government: The Committee of Inquiry on Museums and National Collections (The Piggot Report, 1974–1975)." In *Understanding Museums: Australian Museums and Museology*, edited by Des Griffin and Leon Paroissien. Canberra: National Museum of Australia, 2011.
Efron, Zusia. "Museums in the Kibbutzim." *Museum* 20/1 (1967) 42–45.
Forni, G. 1999. "Ethnographic Museums in Italy: A Decade of Phenomenal Growth." *Museum International* 51/4 (1999) 47–52.
Fuchs, R., and Herbert, G. "Representing Mandatory Palestine: Austen St. Barbe Harrison and the Representational Buildings of the British Mandate in Palestine, 1922–37." *Architectural History* 43 (2000) 281–333.
Gardi, T. *Even Neyar* (Rock, Paper). Tel Aviv: HaKibbutz HaMeuchad, 2011. (Hebrew)
Gibson, Shimon. "British Archaeological Institutions in Mandatory Palestine 1917–1948." *PEQ* 131 (1999) 115–43.
Goldstein, Kaylin. "On Display: The Politics of Museums in Israeli Society." PhD diss. University of Chicago, 2003.
Gophna, Ram. "In Memoriam Kaplan." *Qadmoniyot* 85–86 (1989) 55. (Hebrew)
Goren, Haim. "Scientific Organizations as Agents of Change: the Palestine Exploration Fund, the Deutsche Verein zur Erforschung Palästinas and Nineteenth-century Palestine." *Journal of Historical Geography* 27 (2001) 153–65.
Guzetti, Andrea. "A Walk through the Past. Towards the Study of Archaeological Museums in Italy, Greece, and Israel." PhD diss. Bryn Mawr College, 2012.
Hess, Orna. "Claire Epstein (1911–2000)." *Jewish Women's Archive: Encyclopedia*. http://jwa.org/encyclopedia. 2000.
Hestrin, Ruth. "Local and Regional Museums." *Museum* 20/1 (1967) 34–37.
Ilan, David. "In Memoriam Avraham Biran (1909–2007)." *BASOR* 353 (2009) 1–5.
Iliffe, J. H. "The Palestine Archaeological Museum, Jerusalem." *The Museum Journal* 38 (1938) 1–22.
———. *A Short Guide to the Exhibition Illustrating the Stone and Bronze Ages in Palestine*. Palestine Archaeological Museum Guides 1. Jerusalem: Palestine Archaeological Museum, 1949.
Inbar, Yehudit. "The History of the Museums in Palestine until the Establishment of the State of Israel, as an Expression of the Zionist Vision." MA thesis, The Hebrew University of Jerusalem, 1992. (Hebrew)
———. "Museums in Kibbutzim." In *Guide for Museums in the Kibbutzim*, edited by Ely Shiller, 9–17 [= *Ariel* 60]. Jerusalem: Ariel, 1988. (Hebrew)
Inbar, Yehudit, and Ely Shiller, eds. *Museums in Israel* [= *Ariel* 72–74]. Jerusalem: Ariel, 1995.

Kark, Ruth, and Noam Perry. "Museums and Multiculturalism in Israel." In *Themes in Israeli Geography*, edited by Jacob Maoz and Igal Charney, 88–99. Haifa: University of Haifa, 2012. [= Special Issue of *Horizons in Geography* 79–80.]

Katriel, Tamar. *Performing the Past: A Study of Israeli Settlement Museums*. Mahwah, NJ: Erlbaum, 2013.

Katz, Haya, *Ruth Amiran: A Biography*. Haifa: Pardes, 2011. (Hebrew)

Katz, Karl. "The Bezalel National Art Museum." *Museum* 20/1 (1967) 8–15.

Kempinski, Aharon. "In Memoriam Y. Kaplan." *Archeologiya* 3 (Bulletin of the Israel Association of Archaeologists) (1989) 88–89. (Hebrew)

Kimberley, Webber, et al. "Drawing People Together: The Local and Regional Museum Movement." In *Understanding Museums: Australian Museums and Museology*, edited by Des Griffin and Leon Paroissien, 1–8. Canberra: National Museum of Australia, 2011.

Kletter, Raz. "Archaeology in Israel, 1948–1967: Selected Documents." In *The Politics of Israel's Past*, edited by Emanuel Pfoh and Keith W. Whitelam, 136–51. Sheffield: Sheffield Phoenix, 2013.

———."Friends of Antiquities: The Story of an Israeli Volunteer Group and Comparative Remarks." *JHS* 8 (2008) 2–20. http://www.jhsonline.org/Articles/article_79.pdf. Printed version in *Perspectives on Hebrew Scriptures* V, edited by Ehud Ben-Zvi, 49–76. Piscataway, NJ: Gorgias, 2009.

———. *Just Past? The Making of Israeli Archaeology*. London: Equinox, 2006.

Kloner, Amos, and Joe Zias. "Obituaries: L. Y. Rahmani." *IEJ* 63 (2013) 233–34.

Kol-Inbar, Yehudit. "In Need of a Long Breath." *Panim* 10 (1999). http://www.itu.org.il/?CategoryID=570&ArticleID=1783. (Hebrew)

Maggi, Maurizio, "Ecomuseums in Italy. Concepts and Practices." *Museologia e patrimônio* 2/1 (2009) 70–78.

Manor, Giora, "In Memoriam R. Giveon." In *Geva: Archaeological Discoveries at Tel Abu Shusheh—Mishmar ha-Emeq*, edited by Benjamin Mazar, ix–xi. Tel-Aviv: HaKibbutz HaMeuchad, 1988.

Maycock, Sarah. "Local Museums—from Relic to Reinvigoration." 2014. 1–8. Paper available at: http://une-au.academia.edu/SarahMaycock.

Ofrat-Friedlander, Gideon "The Bezalel Museum (1905–1929)." In *Bezalel 1906–1929*, edited by Nurit Shiloh-Cohen, 31–116. Israel Museum Catalogue. Jerusalem: Israel Museum, 1983.

Rahmani, Levy Yitzhak, and Peter Larsen. *The Museums of Israel*. New York: Rissoli, 1976.

Regev, Yoav, and Eli Shiller. *Selected Papers in the Knowledge of the Land of Israel. Manufacturing Processes and Customs of Life*. Jerusalem, Ariel, 1988.

Rosovsky, Nitza and Joy Ungerleider-Mayerson. *Museums of Israel*. New York: Harry Abrams, 1989.

Shamir, Orit "Archaeological Exhibits in Israel." *Ariel* 194 (2011) 11–24.

———. "Regional Archaeological Museums and Exhibits in Israel." In *Regional Museums for Social Harmony*, edited by Jane Legget, 156–63. Beijing: Foreign Language Press, 2014.

Shay, Oded. "A City Like This Cannot Be without a Museum—on the First Museums and Other Collections in Tel Aviv in the Mandatory Period." *Cathedra* 138 (2011) 111–38. (Hebrew)

———. "Collectors and Collections in Palestine at the End of the Ottoman Era." *Le Muséon* 122 (2009) 449–71.
———. *Museums and Collections in Late Ottoman Palestine*. Jerusalem: Bialik, 2014. (Hebrew)
———. "The Museums and the Archaeological Collections of the British Exploration Societies in Ottoman Palestine." *New Studies on Jerusalem* 12 (2007) 165–77. (Hebrew)
Shiller, Ely, ed. *Guide for Museums in the Kibbutzim* [= *Ariel* 60]. Jerusalem: Ariel, 1988.
St. Laurent, Beatrice, and Himmet Taşkömür. "The Imperial Museum of Antiquities in Jerusalem 1890–1930: An Alternative Narrative." *Jerusalem Quarterly* 55 (2013) 6–45.
Sukenik, Eliezer L. "Twenty Five Years of Archaeology." In *Hebrew University Garland: A Silver Jubilee Symposium*, edited by Norman Bentwich, 43–57. London: Constellation, 1952.
Sussman, Varda, and Ronny Reich. "The History of the Rockefeller Museum." In *Zeev Vilnay Jubilee Volume*, edited by Ely Schiller, 83–92. Jerusalem: Ariel, 1987. (Hebrew)
Tidhar, David. *Enṣiqlopedya le-Ḥalutse ha-Yishuv u-Vonav* (= *Encyclopedia of the Founders and Builders of Israel*). 19 vols. Tel-Aviv: Sifriyat Rishonim (David Tidhar), 1947–1971. http://www.tidhar.tourolib.org/.
Winkworth, Kylie. "Let a Thousand Flowers Bloom: Museums in Regional Australia." In *Understanding Museums: Australian Museums and Museology*, edited by Des Griffin and Leon Paroissien, 2–8. Canberra: National Museum of Australia, 2011.
Yeda'aya, Moshe, and Eli Gil, eds. *Western Galilee. Collected Papers of the Regional Circle for Knowledge of the Land*. Haifa: Sulam Tsor and Ga'aton Regional Councils, 1961. (Hebrew)
Yeivin, Shemuel. *Archaeological Activities in Israel*. Jerusalem: Ministry of Education and Culture, 1955.
———. *A Decade of Archaeology in Israel, 1948–1958*. Istanbul: Nederlands Historisch-Archaeologisch Instituut in Het Nabije Oosten, 1960.

Figure 1: Dan, Ussishkin House: archaeological exhibition. Photograph by Orit Shamir. The museum was built from stones taken from the deserted village Hunin (Gardi, *Even Neyar*).

Photo courtesy of Orit Shamir, Israel Antiquities Authority.

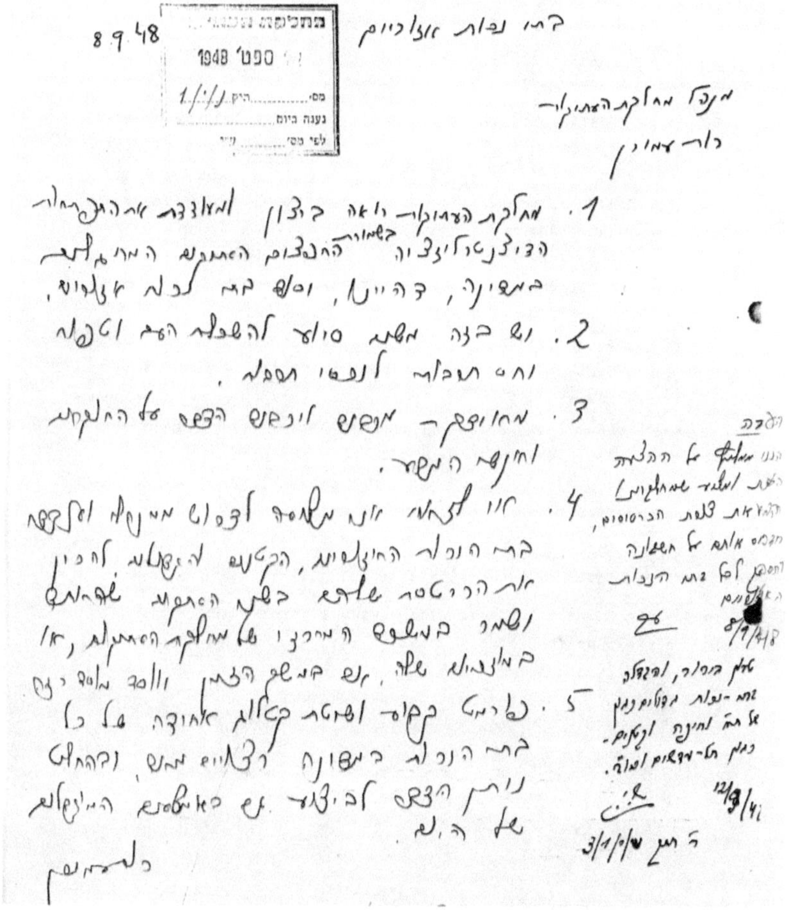

Figure 2: Letter by Amiran on museums, September 1948, GL44872/4.

Courtesy of the Israel State Archives.

תזכיר בקשר עם האוספים המקומיים

את ערכם של האוספים המקומיים אפשר להגדיר במשפטים אחדים :
א) האוסף מרכז סביבו את התעניינותם של תושבי המקום, הכפר או הקיבוץ,
או העיירה בתרבות העבר של סביבתם.   ב) הספריורתיות המקומית וחוש האספנות
מוצאים את פרקונם בטיפול באוסף המקומי.   ג) הערך החינוכי בשביל דור
הצעיר אינו דורש פירוט מיוחד כאן.

האוסף המקומי צומח, איסוא, מתוך נטיות טבעיות, ואסור על-כן, לנסות
לדכא על-ידי תחוקה נטירת כאלו. מסיבות אלו אני בעד זה שנניח לאוספים
המקומיים להתהוות ואף להתפתח מני ידוע (ראה לחלן) באופן טבעי. עלינו
כמובן, לכוון את הנטיות האלו ולתאם אותן לצרכים המדעיים שמחובת מחלקת העתי
העתיקות לחגן עליהם.   א)עלינו לדעת על כל אוסף עם התחלת קיומו.
ב) עלינו לדרוש בישוח האוסף על אחריות חוד או מזכירות המקומיים,
בטיפולם הקבוע של איש אחד או אפילו שניים. ג) עלינו לדרוש חדר מיוחד
עם ארונות נעולים.   ד) עלינו להקפיד על רישום מדויק בספר רישום ובקטלוג
עם תשומת לב מיוחדת למוצא של החפצים.   ח) עלינו לדרוש כי החפצים אחרי
סידורם הראשון יוצגו לראווה כדי שהאוסף ימלא את מטרתו העיקרית באזורו.
התצוגה צריכה לחיעשות בליווי כתובות ובאחריות מדעית.   ו) כמובן מוכנה
מחלקת העתיקות לעזור לאוספים לפי בקשותיהם.   ז) חממונים על האוספים
צריכים לדעת כי חפצים מיוחדים במינם יש למסור למחלקת העתיקות בהתאם
לצרכים המדעיים של המוזיאום המרכזי.

הדברים האלה צריכים כמובן לבוא לידיעתם של כל חובבי העתיקות.

ברצוני לחזור ולהדגיש שלדעתי אין למנוע את החפתחותם של מוסדות
כאלה, גם אם נניח כי במשך הזמן יווצר אוסף מקומי, בצורת "פינה", חדר" או
בית, בכל ישוב וישוב בארץ. יחד עם זאת יש להניח כי התנאים שתציג מחלקת
העתיקות, המפורטים לעיל, יגרמו לחאסף ידוע בהתפתחותם, או במלים אחרות,
יגרמו להתפתחות מסודרת ואחראית של המוסדות האלה.

פ.כ.

19/11/51

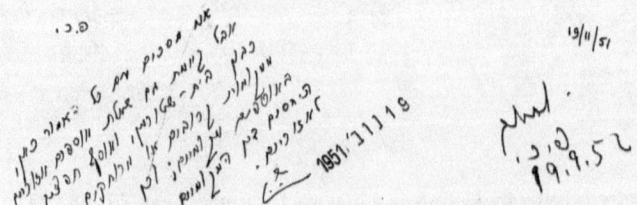

Figure 3: Memorandum by Kahane, November 1951, GL44872/4.

Courtesy of the Israel State Archives.

Figure 4: The remains of the Gevim archaeological collection
(photograph by Orit Shamir)

Photograph courtesy of Orit Shamir, Israel Antiquities Authority.

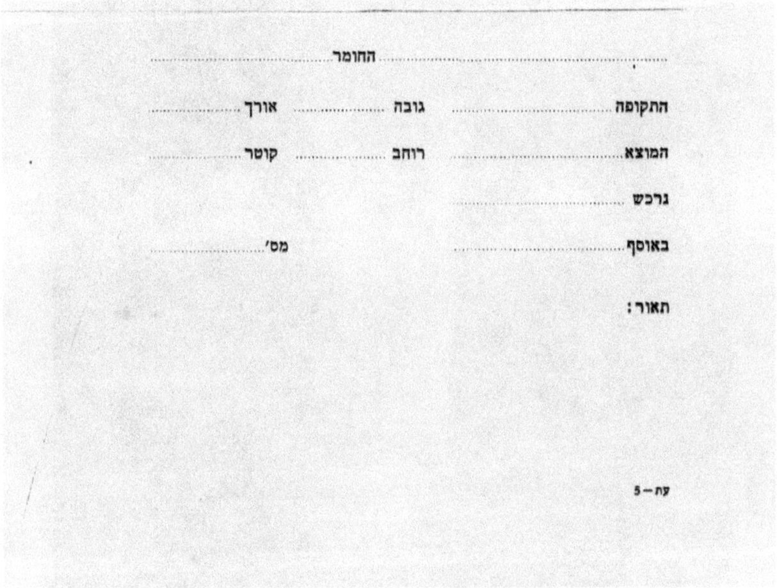

.... :	.... החומר ....
התקופה	גובה .... אורך ....
המוצא	רוחב .... קוטר ....
נרכש	
באוסף	מס' ....
תאור :	

עת – 5

Figure 5: Form for Registering Museum finds, October 1948, GL44872/4.

Courtesy of the Israel State Archives.

Figure 6: Chana Benyamini in the archaeological exhibition of underwater finds, Kibbutz Saʻar, 1962.

Courtesy of the Israel National Photo Collection, photo D267-211 (unknown photographer).

6

Disks and Deities: Images on Iron Age Terracotta Plaques

Carol Meyers

DUKE UNIVERSITY

Introduction

Small terracotta plaques depicting a female figure holding a round object or disk are among the most intriguing kinds of iconographic data that have survived in the archaeological record of the southern Levant. The figures are naked or partly naked and are adorned in various ways. Iron Age in date, they are part of the larger corpus of terracottas that Ziony Zevit—to whom I dedicate this article with great respect for his scholarship and much gratitude for his friendship—discusses in his monumental book, *The Religions of Ancient Israel*. He remarks that "plaques and [pillar] figurines representing animate beings are the most common of cultic artifacts and potentially one of the most significant sources of insight into Israelite religion."[1] It is no accident that Zevit's statement mentions both plaques and figurines, for these small terracotta anthropomorphic objects are almost always considered together.

1. Zevit, *Religions of Ancient Israel*, 267.

The sizeable corpus of small female figurines, which includes disk-holding plaque figurines and disk-holding pillar figurines, has evoked considerable scholarly attention for more than a century. Various classificatory systems have been proposed, including James Pritchard's 1943 publication, *Palestinian Figurines in Relation to Certain Goddesses Known through Literature*.[2] Pritchard's typology is still useful but nonetheless problematic, for it mixes "shape, function, representation, chronology, and manufacturing technique."[3] One example of his flawed typology is the inclusion of all disk-holding figurines in one category, even when other features of the objects are distinctly different.[4]

As Pritchard's classification indicates, the presence of a disk is typically the governing typological characteristic of both plaque and pillar figurines, irrespective of any other aspect of figurine manufacture, iconography, date, or provenance. This primacy of the disk in figurine taxonomies persists more than half a century later in two monographs, both of which discuss disk-holding plaques together with disk-holding figurines.[5] Moreover, the authors of these books, along with most other scholars, identify the disks on both artifact types as drums.

In addition to presuming that all the disks represent drums, another feature of figurine scholarship is the penchant for linking both plaque figurines and pillar figurines with one or another of the Canaanite deities known from ancient texts. To his credit, because he recognized that the iconographic features of the terracottas could not be associated with any literary references, Pritchard was unwilling to identify them with a specific goddess.[6] Most others are less reluctant; they assume that the figurines represent deities and connect them with specific goddesses. For example, in the 1930s W. F. Albright identified several Late Bronze Age plaque figurines from Tell Beit Mirsim with the goddess Astarte—hence the common designation "Astarte plaque."[7] He also referred to the Iron II pillar figurines as "pillar goddesses" representing Astarte.[8] More recently John Day linked the

---

2. Pritchard, *Palestinian Figurines*. Pilz's 1924 article, "Die weibliche Gottheiten Kanaans," was the first to classify them.

3. Zevit, *Religions of Ancient Israel*, 268.

4. Pritchard, *Palestinian Figurines*, 19–21, 54, assigns them all to Type V, "Figurine Holding Disc."

5. Paz, *Drums, Women, and Goddesses*; Sugimoto, *Female Figurines*.

6. Yet Pritchard, *Palestinian Figurines*, 87, did not completely rule out the goddess hypothesis.

7. Albright, "Astarte Plaques and Figurines."

8. Albright, *Archaeology of Palestine and the Bible*, 121.

Late Bronze Age plaques with Asherah.[9] And William Dever has asserted that the Late Bronze Age plaques were the prototype of both the plaque and pillar figurines of the Iron Age, that they represent the Egypto-Semitic deity Qudshu (probably Asherah/Athirat), and that, with their fluid iconography, they might represent any of the Great Goddesses of Canaan—Anat, Asherah, Astarte, or anyone else.[10] Many link the pillar figurines with prominent breasts to Asherah,[11] and a few suggest that they represent minor figures in the Canaanite pantheon.[12] Another possibility is that all these terracottas were intentionally made as generic females so that they might invoke any or all female supernatural powers.[13] This diversity of opinion reflects the lack of conclusive evidence, for none of the terracottas bear labels or names.

Because plaque figurines and pillar figurines are so closely linked, the Iron Age disk-holding plaque figurines that are the focus here cannot be considered apart from the pillar figurines. Thus this essay begins by analyzing iconographic and technological features of disk-holding pillar figurines and their putative relationship to the large corpus of pillar figurines known as Judean Pillar Figurines (JPFs). In doing so, I dispute the common claim that the pillar figurines represent deities. Next, the Iron Age plaque figurines and their possible Late Bronze Age precursors are examined. While agreeing with most scholarship on these objects, which supposes that the disk-holding plaque figurines represent female deities, I contest the common identification of those disks as drums—for that identification disregards important details of the disks on each kind of figurine, leads to facile assumptions about the identity of the pillar figurines, and obscures important features of the plaque figurines—and then offer an alternative understanding of the disks. Finally, the concluding section highlights an often overlooked aspect

---

9. Day, "Ashtoreth," 494.

10. Dever, *Did God Have a Wife?*, 177, 185. However, he tends to be more specific in discussing one type, Judean Pillar Figurines; he connects them with Asherah, listing seven reasons for doing so ("Judean 'Pillar-Base Figurines,'" 134–5).

11. E.g., *Did God Have a Wife?*, 194; Keel and Uehlinger, *Gods, Goddesses*, 333–35; Kletter, *Judean Pillar-Figurines*, 76–77, 81; and Engle, "Pillar Figurines." Kletter, *Judean Pillar-Figurines*, 77, admits, however, that "conclusive evidence is lacking." For a cogent critique of the Asherah identification, see Merlo, "Asherah." Sugimoto, "*Judean Pillar-Figurines*," also rejects the Asherah identification and prefers a connection with Astarte or Ishtar.

12. E.g., Cornelius, *The Many Faces of the Goddess*, 4–6. Smith, *Memoirs of God*, 86–119, comments on the different tiers of Canaanite deities and the fluidity of the Canaanite pantheon.

13. Suggested by Warsaka, "Female Figurines," 3, in reference to small nude figurines found throughout the pharaonic periods.

of religious rituals in the world of the Bible, an aspect likely reflected in the iconography of the disk-holding plaques.

Terracotta Pillar Figurines

Disk-holding pillar figurines are a small subset of a much larger group of pillar figurines, the interpretation of which has influenced the way the disk-holding examples have been understood. Hence the larger group of which they are part, at least in terms of their general pillar morphology, must first be briefly discussed.

The term "pillar figurine" denotes a corpus of many hundreds of small—most are 10–20 cm in height—terracotta objects or parts thereof.[14] These objects feature a female body with the lower half in the shape of a solid, hand-made pillar that flares slightly at its base, forming a pedestal allowing the figure to stand on its own. Thus no legs or feet or genitals can be seen, but the head and upper body are depicted. The heads are either hand-made and rather crude or mold-made with a detailed treatment of the head. The hair in most molded examples is shown as rows of curls that frame the face; the curls extend across the forehead, and the sidelocks never extend below chin length.[15] The figurines are usually covered with a white wash, and the facial features—with the eyes often exaggerated—are marked with paint on the mold-made heads. The woman's arms are bent at the elbows with her hands under her breasts, either supporting the breasts or placed slightly below them. Virtually all pillar figurines are dated to the Iron IIB-C period (8th–early 6th centuries BCE). Because most were found at Judean sites, they are commonly called Judean Pillar Figurines, or JPFs.[16]

The arm position, which draws attention to the breasts, is the characteristic feature of these artifacts in the interpretative tradition. As noted above, most scholars assume that the JPFs represent one of the Canaanite goddesses, who are presumed to be fertility goddesses, and that the prominent breasts signify fertility, hence the frequent designation "fertility figurines." They suppose that the JPFs functioned in prayers or supplications for fertility addressed to a Great Mother. This association with goddesses

---

14. The most complete catalog to date (in Kletter, *Judean Pillar-Figurines*) includes 854 items. Many, however, are fragments, making the absolute number debatable. See Dever's comments (*Did God Have a Wife?*, 180) on the quantity.

15. So Kletter, *Judean Pillar-Figurines*, 30.

16. The several examples that predate or postdate this period can probably be discounted for stratigraphic or stylistic reasons, and the same can be said for those few found outside the boundaries of Judah. See the discussion of chronology and distribution in Kletter, *Judean Pillar-Figurines*, 40–48.

has been influenced by Canaanite literature and by the possible mentions of Asherah as a goddess or cult object in the Hebrew Bible.

However, would these figurines be associated with deities if there were no documents to consult? Considering the JPFs *without* using textual information makes it less likely that they depict deities. Archaeologists working at prehistoric sites have long interpreted similar anthropomorphic figurines without the benefit of written sources and in so doing have shown that images of humans can be differentiated from images of deities by considering a range of features.[17] I have summarized in another publication their methodology for distinguishing between divine and human images.[18] Although not all of the typological attributes they list are relevant, several salient features of deity images bear mention. One is that they are more likely to be made of expensive materials such as precious metals. Another is a technical aspect, namely, the expert fashioning of details. Perhaps the most prominent feature is morphology, especially the use of iconic components: headdresses, plants, animals, jewelry, and other symbolic elements.

Taking these attributes into account means disputing the dominant view that the JPFs represent a deity. For one thing, the JPFs are made of clay, an inexpensive material. Also, many—notably those with pinched faces and handmade bodies—are rather crudely formed; and the bodies of all seem to be handmade. In addition, although those with mold-made heads have well-defined facial features, virtually all have mitten-shaped hands, without delineation of individual fingers and sometimes with no distinct wrist. Finally, perhaps most important is their lack of iconic elements. None wear headdresses or other headgear, and there is apparently no depiction of jewelry around the wrists or necks. All told, they lack features associated with representations of deities. Their identity as human females would not, however, preclude a religious function; the prominent breasts of some (but not all) examples suggest a role in the quest for fertility or successful lactation although an apotropaic function is also possible.[19]

---

17. See especially Ucko, "Interpretation of Prehistoric Anthropomorphic Figurines," 38–54; Ucko, *Anthropomorphic Figurines*; Voight, *Hajji Firuz Tepe*; and Voight, "Çatal Höyük in Context." One of the few archaeologists of the southern Levant to adopt this approach is Peter Moorey, *Idols of the People*, 2–3. Analysis of both plaque and pillar terracottas sometimes intuitively uses many of the criteria suggested by anthropologists; see, e.g., Tadmor, "Female Cult Figurines," 149, 157, 161.

18. Meyers, "Terracottas without Texts," 117–21.

19. For the fertility/lactation function, see Meyers, "Terracottas without Texts," 123–6; and Meyers, *Households and Holiness*, 27–31. Darby, *Interpreting Judean Pillar Figurines*, makes a strong argument for their use in protection and healing rituals. Other possible and even multiple functions are summarized by Schmitt, "Elements of Domestic Cult," 62–65, who also rejects identifying them with a deity.

The argument against linking the JPFs with a deity also applies to a small group—fewer than twenty in number[20]—of the pillar-figurine type: those that hold a disk in their hands, thereby leading many to connect them with the disk-holding plaque figurines. Like the JPFs, these images vary in size: some are as small as 5 cm, a few are as tall as 22 cm, and the average height is 12 cm. They have a hollow, usually wheel-made pillar base; the heads are mold-made or sometimes hand-modeled. The arms are bent at the elbow to hold the disk, with the arms, hands, and disk all formed by hand and attached to the pillar. Some are undecorated, but others have remnants of simple red and/or black painted lines depicting stripes on the woman's garment. The hair is sometimes painted black; and the simple hairstyle—shoulder-length hair, either braided or loose (the latter with rounded ends), and even bangs—represents the woman's own locks, not a wig. Except for the garment stripes, there is a marked absence of decoration: the female figures lack hats, crowns, wreaths, or headdresses; and they wear no necklaces, bracelets, earrings, or other items of personal adornment. In short, like the JPFs, they likely represent human females rather than deities.

The usual identification of the disks they hold, unlike the identification of the figures themselves, poses no problems. Their shape and size, and also the position and rendering of the hands, support the consensus that the disks represent small frame drums. They are round in shape but have no markings or other indications of adornment or accoutrements; this is typical of frame drums in representations of musicians in ancient Near Eastern art.[21] By considering the proportionality of the disks in relation to the figures holding them, the dimensions of the life-size drums they depict can be estimated as approximately 20–25 cm in diameter, which is exactly the size of most frame drums in ancient iconography.[22] The position of the disk suggests the way it was played: it is held in the middle of the chest and perpendicular to it, supported from below by the left hand with the right hand stretched across it, striking it. Portrayals in ancient art of processions

---

20. Paz's catalog (*Drums, Women, and Goddesses*, 39–44) has fourteen examples; Kletter, *Judean Pillar-Figurines*, 35, 281–2, lists nine of them along with several fragmentary pieces that are probably drum players; and Sugimoto, *Female Figurines*, 129–32, has seventeen specimens. Sugimoto also includes some rather anomalous examples—all from different areas of the Levant; many are fragmentary or possess typological features quite different from the "standard" type described here and are thus not included in my tally.

21. E.g., the depiction on a Phoenician ivory pyxis, now in the British Museum: http://www.britishmuseum.org/research/collection_online/collection_object_details/collection_image_gallery.aspx?partid=1&assetid=105331&objectid=282806.

22. Montagu, "Tambourine [Timbrel]." Present-day frame drums are also about this size.

of female musicians, with women playing similar disks along with other instruments, further support the frame-drum identification.[23] (The drums are sometimes called tambourines—frame drums with metal jingles attached to the frame—but there is no evidence that the frame drums known throughout the ancient Near Eastern had rattling elements; certainly none are depicted in the iconographic record.[24])

Although pillar figurines with drums are similar to JPFs in general size and shape and also date to the 8th to early 6th centuries BCE, they differ in important stylistic and morphological ways: the bases are wheel made rather than hand formed; all the heads are molded; the hair style is very different; the facial features are more delicate; and the arms and hands support a musical instrument, not the female's breasts. Just as significant is the divergent provenance. Virtually all are from coastal or Phoenician sites (e.g., Achzib, Tyre, Shiqmona, Kharayeb) rather than from the Judean heartland, which is the provenance of virtually all of the JPFs.[25] Moreover, hundreds of female drum-players of the same period have been recovered from excavations in Cyprus, where they continue into post-Iron II periods.[26] For all these reasons, the terracottas depicting females playing frame drums bear little significant relationship to the JPFs other than that they depict human females and may depict a cultic activity, such as performance in a religious procession or other cultic event.[27]

---

23. E.g., the procession on a silver bowl from Cyprus; see Karageorghis, "Cypriot Silver Bowl," 14, Fig. 1. A similar procession appears on the pyxis mentioned in n.21.

24. Montagu, "Tambourine [Timbrel]." Joachim Braun, *Music in Ancient Israel/Palestine*, 30, comments that the ancient frame drum—the *tōp* of Biblical Hebrew—"had no metal jingles attached to its sides."

25. For the date and provenance (where known) of the disk-holding pillar figurines, see the catalogs in Paz, *Drums, Women, and Goddesses*, 39–43, and Sugimoto, *Female Figurines*, 129–32.

26. Although most of the drum-playing terracottas come from Cyprus, this artifact type likely originated in Phoenicia and had Mesopotamian precursors; so Karageorghis, "Terracottas," 18. The Cypriot examples are part of a large assemblage of pillar figurines, many playing other musical instruments. Yet only women are shown playing the frame drum, perhaps attesting to a female performance tradition; see Meyers, "Of Drums and Damsels," 19–25. Note that the five uses of *tōp* in the Hebrew Bible in which the gender of the musician can be identified (Exod 15:20; Judg 11:34; 1 Sam 18:6; Jer 31:4) all indicate female drummers.

27. Frame drums were also used in celebratory and secular contexts; see Meyers, "Frame Drums in the Ancient Levant."

Plaque Figurines with Disks

The Iron Age plaque figurines that are the focus of this article depict adorned, naked or semi-naked female figures holding disks. It is the disk-holding feature that has led scholars to associate them with the disk-holding pillar figurines. For that link to be maintained, the Iron Age plaques would have to be considered depictions of humans, and the disks would have to be understood as portrayals of drums. Addressing the first issue—whether they represent deities or humans—must take into account their relationship with the plaque figurines of the Late Bronze Age, for they share certain morphological and stylistic features with those figurines and are probably part of the same iconographic tradition.[28] Both the Late Bronze and Iron Age examples are formed by pressing a lump of clay into a mold. The female figure in the finished artifact appears in relief against a flat background, hence the common designation "relief" figurines.

The Late Bronze Age antecedents are 12 to 20 cm in height and come from both Canaanite and Egyptian sites.[29] The breasts and genitals of the figures are often prominently depicted, leading most scholars to assume that the plaques are related to concerns about reproduction; thus, like the JPFs, they are often labeled "fertility figurines."[30] As might be expected for a type with many Egyptian examples, their elaborate hairdos or headdresses are often of the Hathor type. They are also adorned with one or more kinds of jewelry: earrings, necklaces, armlets, bracelets, anklets, and pendants. In addition, they hold objects, notably animals (snakes) or plants—but *not* disks. Several are shown standing on animals (lions or horses). According to the criteria mentioned above in the discussion of pillar figurines, it is unlikely that these figures represent humans. Although they are made of an inexpensive material, the special hairdos or headdresses, items of personal adornment, and iconic objects indicate that they depict female deities, the identity of which, as already noted, is in dispute.

---

28. Some Late Bronze examples ae unadorned and hold no objects and thus should be distinguished from the adorned object-holding figurines; see Tadmor, "Female Cult Figurines," 139–73. This distinction is valid even if Tadmor's identification of the unadorned type as mortuary figures is disputed.

29. A catalog can be found in Cornelius, *The Many Faces of the Goddess*, Cat. 5.24–5.25, 5.31–61a. These 39 items belong to the type he calls "Naked woman holding objects"; 23 other items of this type are made of other materials (e.g., limestone, metal, faience). See also Hadley, *Cult of Asherah*, 191–95; Keel and Uehlinger, *Gods, Goddesses*, 66–68.

30. However, recent research contests that designation. Like the JPFs (see n.19), these plaques may serve a protective rather than procreative function; so Creel, "Manipulating the Divine."

Similar plaques depicting nude females come from Iron Age contexts—mostly Israelite and coastal areas rather than Judean sites.[31] Dating mainly to the Iron I and early Iron II periods (12th–9th centuries BCE), they predate the disk-holding pillar figurines.[32] At 6–10 cm high, most are slightly smaller than the Late Bronze ones. Also, the molding is often shallower and the anthropomorphic depictions generally cruder. Still, many of their stylistic elements show marked continuity with the earlier types.[33] At least half have elaborate hairdos, mainly of the up-curled Hathor type, and others have feather or Uraeus headdresses. Discerning jewelry is not always possible because many specimens are fragmentary, but most appear to be adorned. Their arms are in various positions: some have one or both arms extended along their sides or across their chests, many hold lotus blossoms, and a sizeable group features the arms bent at the elbow with the hands cupping the breasts. These features strongly suggest that, like their Late Bronze precursors but unlike the pillar figurines, they represent deities. Whether they signify any or all of the Canaanite great goddesses or a more accessible minor deity cannot be determined.

The Iron Age disk-holding plaque figurines are similar to the ones just described. There are at least forty, and perhaps as many as sixty-five, examples from sites in the southern Levant.[34] They also date mainly to the Iron I and early Iron II periods and come from areas other than Judah. Some are intact, but most are fragmentary. Although they vary somewhat in style, they are similar to the other Iron Age plaques and likewise show continu-

---

31. Kletter, *Judean Pillar-Figurines*, 34–35, 270–74, nos. 5.V.2–5.V.6, lists seventy-three specimens; many are fragmentary, however, making their features uncertain.

32. Ibid., 34–35; cf. Tadmor, "Female Cult Figurines," 171–2. Some few may be slightly later, but their archaeological contexts are unclear.

33. Kletter, *Judean Pillar-Figurines*, 34, says that they are "in the tradition" of the Late Bronze types.

34. Ibid., 268–70, has forty-one examples; Paz, *Drums, Women and Goddesses*, 13–38, lists sixty-five examples, forty-seven from west of the Jordan and another eighteen from east of the Jordan; and Sugimoto, *Female Figurines*, 115–24, presents fifty-five pieces, thirty-four from west of the Jordan and another twenty-one from east of the Jordan. These diverse provenances preclude connecting them with any single ethnic, political, or religious group, although they may represent the continuation of Late Bronze Canaanite traditions among Iron Age peoples of the southern Levant, Israelites (people of the Northern Kingdom) included. Several anomalous figurines (e.g., the one in Beck, "Human Figurine with Tambourine") have male genitals and are considered hermaphroditic. Sugimoto, *Female Figurines*, 38–41, therefore relates them to the possible male-female identity of Astarte-Qemosh. In any case, these anomalous examples are not included in this discussion because they are few in number, they date to the 7th or 6th century and thus postdate the unambiguously female plaques, and they are from east of the Jordan or from Edomite sites.

ity with the Late Bronze ones. They are somewhat cruder than their Late Bronze Age precursors, but there is similar close attention to detail. The facial features tend to be coarse, with disproportionately large or protruding eyes and a large nose; the mouth is sometimes accentuated but sometimes not shown at all. Most are fully or partially naked; where visible, the sexual features—genitals (depicted as a triangle) and breasts—are prominent. The skirts or himations on the semi-naked examples are decorated with geometric designs (dots, triangles, short lines, zigzags), vertical or diagonal stripes, or both. Items of personal adornment are common, and multiple types are often depicted; they include earrings, belts, necklaces, arm bands, bracelets, and anklets. Heads have survived on about half of the examples, and the coiffures vary. Some seem to have short hair, but most have long hair that hangs on either side of the face, sometimes in braids. At least one sports a Hathor coiffure. The stylized renderings of the upper part of the hairdos on the crown of the head make it difficult to determine if there are headdresses fitted over the hair. Nonetheless, crowns and turbans can be discerned in about half the examples with intact heads.

Taken together, these characteristics of the disk-holding Iron Age plaque figurines indicate that, like the other Iron Age plaques and the earlier Late Bronze ones, they represent deities.[35] Moreover, the coarse facial features, the decorated garments, the jewelry, and the headdresses set them apart from the disk-holding pillar figurines, as does their plaque form.[36] Although some few have locks of hair hanging on either side of the face as do the pillar figurines, the hair is rendered quite differently: the locks lack the rounded bottom typical of the pillar figurines' hair.

The one feature that putatively links these two sets of artifacts is the disk held by the female figure in both. As noted above, the disks held by pillar figurines are undoubtedly frame drums. In contrast, although many scholars also identify the disks held by the plaque figurines as drums, other possibilities have been suggested, for identifying round objects in ancient art is difficult. Erwin Goodenough long ago noted this problem in his work on early Jewish iconography and listed four possibilities for identifying disks: bowl or plate, round loaf of bread, solar disk, and drum.[37] These are exactly the same as the suggestions for the plaques: their Mesopotamian

---

35. Another possibility is that they represent female cult personnel serving a fertility goddess; so Paz, *Drums, Women, and Goddesses*, 78.

36. It is thus highly unlikely, contra to the opinion of Dever (*Did God Have a Wife?*, 185) and others (e.g., Hadley, *Cult of Asherah*, 204) that the plaque figurines are antecedents of the pillar figurines; so Tadmor, "Female Cult Figurines," 172.

37. Goodenough, *Jewish Symbols*, 62–76.

antecedents have been labeled plates;[38] they have been termed sun disks;[39] they have been considered cakes or round bread loaves;[40] and, of course, they have been called drums (or, anachronistically, tambourines).[41] The first two suggestions have received little support, but stylistic elements of the last two deserve closer attention. Identification of the disks entails examining all their details: size, position (including the way they are held), shape, and decoration.[42]

- *Size.* The size of the disks calculated in relation to the size of the figure produces estimates of life-size drums that vary considerably; some would have been as small as 12 cm in diameter—improbably small for a frame drum—and others as large as 30 cm. Such variation was not a characteristic of frame drums, but ancient bread loaves—especially those of elites—varied considerably in size.

- *Position.* The position of the disk and the hands is noteworthy. In virtually all examples, the disk is parallel to the body, usually clutched to the left side of the chest. Also, the disks are usually held with both hands, which are positioned in various ways: sometimes one on either side of the disk, sometimes both below it, and sometimes with one hand on the side and the other at the bottom. In short, the hands do not appear to be striking a drum. Rather, with the disks held against the chest, the female figures are displaying them, as they might a sacral object—in this case a bread offering.

- *Shape.* The disk on the Taanach mold has a slightly cupped or convex surface. This shape would disqualify it as drum, which would have had either a flat or slightly concave surface like the disks of the drum-holding pillar figurines.[43] Instead, the convex disk is a suitable depiction of a rounded loaf. Also, several disks appear to be torus-like rings

38. Van Buren, *Clay Figurines,* 89–90, pl. 25, figs. 123, 124.

39. Amiran, "Note on Figurines."

40. E.g., Lapp, "1963 Excavation at Ta'annek," 40, fig. 21, in reference to a 10th-century-BCE plaque mold. Lapp changed his mind after Hillers published his influential analysis: "Goddess with the Tambourine." Dever, "Judean 'Pillar-Base Figurines,'" 130, more recently accepts the bread identification.

41. Ibid. More recent studies, as already indicated, support the drum interpretation. See Paz, *Drums, Women, and Goddesses,* 72–74; Sugimoto, *Female Figurines,* 24–25; Kletter, *Judean Pillar-Figurines,* 34, 35–36; and Keel and Uehlinger, *Gods, Goddesses,* 164–5. Keel and Uehlinger, however, acknowledge some uncertainty.

42. The information about ancient bread loaves that informs these points is provided below in the Discussion section.

43. Pointed out by Braun, *Music in Ancient Israel/Palestine,* 128.

rather than solid disks. This attribute similarly reduces the likelihood that the disks are drums, but it is consonant with the fact that some ancient loaves were ring shaped.

- *Decoration.* Perhaps the most salient factor is the presence of decorations, which are found on all but the crudest or most stylized examples. Decorative elements include small dots, indentations, or circles near the outer edge in one row or sometimes two; one or more circular bands around the outer edge; dots over the entire surface; zigzag or triangular patterns around the outer edge; an crossed line in the center. This use of decorations does not resonate with the way frame drums are depicted in other ancient iconographic media, where they are almost always undecorated. But elite breads in the ancient Near East were frequently decorated.

These features in the aggregate indicate that the disks on the Iron Age plaque figurines do not portray frame drums but rather depict round bread loaves or cakes.

Discussion

This study of the Iron Age disk-holding plaque figurines began by noting the importance of identifying both the female figure and the disk she holds, especially in comparison with the disk-holding pillar figurines to which they are often linked. Analyzing salient iconographic features of the female figures and then of the disks indicates that the pillars and plaques are distinct artifact types. Both are small terracotta objects depicting females, but otherwise they diverge. The pillars likely represent humans whereas the plaques depict a deity, although the identity of that deity, or deities, remains an open question. And the human pillar figures hold drums whereas the non-human plaque figures hold round loaves of bread or cakes. Those loaves, held as they are by non-humans, are thus arguably cultic objects. Indeed, two of the plaques are attached to a model shrine, further suggesting that they had a role in Iron Age rituals.[44] Also, they are found in both cultic and domestic contexts, each of which was an arena of ritual activities.[45] The loaves held by the Iron Age plaque figurines thus signify the importance of bread not only

---

44. For figurines attached to a shrine model, see Sugimoto, *Female Figurines*, 124 (T21), 151 (T21).

45. Sugimoto, *Female Figurines*, 20–21, Table 1, lists the context, where known, of the plaques. Cultic activities were not limited to designated spaces; see the essays in Albertz et al., *Family and Household Religion*.

as the major component of the daily fare of all but also as food for elites and gods in ancient religious life. Moreover, certain features of the production and use of bread shows congruencies with the disks held by the Iron Age plaque figurines, thus highlighting the role of bread in religious life.

Cereal products, mainly bread but also gruel, were the staple foods of the ancient Near Eastern diet, providing the major source of calories for ordinary folk. Bread also figured prominently in the everyday meals and even the banquets of the elites.[46] Texts recounting royal repasts emphasize the variety as well as the quantity of all sorts of victuals, bread included. As many as 300 different kinds of breads have been documented in texts from ancient Syria and Mesopotamia.[47] The same was true in ancient Egypt, where bakers produced a staggering variety of loaves according to references in texts and organic remains found in royal tombs.[48] An allusion to this variety appears in the Joseph narrative, which refers to "all sorts of baked goods" prepared by the chief baker for the Pharaoh (Gen 40:17).

The variety of elite bread types was a function of the ingredients used in their production: different types of bread depended on the fineness of the grain and the addition of an array of spices, sweeteners, fruits, and nuts to the basic flour-water combination. The variety was also a function of the wide assortment of shapes, sizes, and decorations represented in ancient art or named in texts. The Hebrew Bible mentions some ten different kinds of bread according to shape as well as mode of preparation.[49] One of them—the *ḥallâ*, a ring-shaped loaf—may correspond to the ring-shaped disks on the plaques as well as the ring-shaped loaves known from Mesopotamian sources. The size of loaves also varied, judging from iconographic depictions and also from bread molds discovered in both Mesopotamia and Egypt. The variations in the size of the disks held by the plaque figurines are somewhat reminiscent of the size differentials of Egyptian bread molds: some are as small as 5 cm in diameter (dubbed "cupcake" molds) and others are up to 20 cm across.[50] Mold-made breads were often decorated with geometric designs like dots and triangles, precisely the kinds of decorations on many

---

46. On the role and types of bread in the diets of the elites, see Meyers, "Royal Repasts," 141–44.

47. See Curtis, *Ancient Food Technology*, 205; cf. Milano, "Food and Diet," 216–7.

48. Samuel, "Bread."

49. Reed, "Bread," 778.

50. These molds were found at a 17th- to 16th-century BCE site that the excavators named Umm Mawagir, Arabic for "Mother of Bread Molds," because of the quantities of molds they discovered; see Yale Archaeological Institute in Egypt, "Introduction: Umm Mawagir."

plaque-figurine disks.[51] Indeed, the decorated disks on the plaque figurines bear remarkable similarity to depictions of bread in a 12th-century BCE Egyptian tomb painting, where a court-bakery scene shows circular loaves with two bands around the outer edge and multiple dots in the center.[52]

Offerings to the gods—including bread—reflected the comestibles and potables of the diets of the elites, which in turn were an elevated and expanded version of the diets of ordinary folk. The choicest aspects of household fare, including the fancy decorated loaves of the palace, became the sacrificial regime.[53] Or, as Mary Douglas famously put it, "a very strong analogy between table and altar stares us in the face."[54] Daily bread offerings are mentioned in Mesopotamian and Hittite texts.[55] Although often overlooked because of the extensive treatment of animal sacrifice in the Pentateuch and its frequent mention elsewhere in the Hebrew Bible, bread too was part of biblical offerings and sacrifices (in both P and other sources) and presumably of Israelite ones. For example, every mention of *ḥallâ*, including a reference to the twelve enigmatic loaves (*leḥem happānîm*) on the golden table of the tabernacle (Lev 24:5–6), is found in a cultic context.[56] The tabernacle loaves are deemed "most holy" (*qōdeš qŏdāšîm*, Lev 24:9), and certain breads are deemed "holy bread" (*leḥem qōdeš*) in contrast to "common bread" (*leḥem ḥol*) according to the narrative in 1 Sam 21:4–7 (NRSV, 1 Sam 21:3–6).[57] And that tantalizing passage in Jeremiah (7:18) about household offerings bears special mention because it refers to special sacrificial loaves (*kawwānîm*) offered to the Queen of Heaven.[58] The sequel passage (Jer 44:15–25) implies that the offering of loaves and libations was believed to help procure agricultural prosperity.

Whether construed as food for the deity, a symbolic substance to please the deity in return for divine favors (like the "cakes" in Jeremiah), a mechanism for conveying food to cultic personnel (who ate portions of the offerings and sacrifices), a mode of connecting worshipper to deity, or

---

51. On the variety of shapes (including rings) and the use of molds, see Ellison, "Methods of Food Preparation," 91; see also Curtis, *Ancient Food Technology*, 207.

52. The painting is from the tomb of Ramses III; see Samuel, "Bread," 197.

53. See Meyers "Feast Days and Food Ways," 236–7.

54. Douglas, "Deciphering a Meal," 71.

55. See the texts mentioned in Haran, *Temples and Temple Service*, 221–4.

56. All these references are in P except 2 Sam 6:19, part of a narrative in which David distributes round loaves and other foodstuffs to the people in the sacrificial event celebrating his bringing of the ark to Jerusalem.

57. The sacral uses of bread are summarized in Dommershausen, "*leḥem*," 525–29.

58. Although "Queen of Heaven" may be a catch-all term for any or all of the West Semitic goddesses, Astart/Ishtar is the most likely; so Lundbom, *Jeremiah 1–20*, 476–77.

several of these factors, bread was a component of the range of offerings in the ancient Near East in general and surely in the coastal and northern areas where the Iron Age plaques were discovered. In fact, affordable bread offerings were probably more common in everyday family religious life than were animal sacrifices.[59]

The disks on plaque figurines likely reflect the presence of bread in the sacrificial regimen of various Iron Age groups in the southern Levant, although the absence of plaque figurines with disks in Judean territory hardly implies the absence of bread as a sacred food in the southern kingdom. Perhaps the fact that the plaque figurines depicted deities precluded their use in Judean religious culture with its emerging aniconism and monolatry.[60] In any case, the plaques offer no clues about the actual rituals in which they may have been used, the identity of the deity to whom they were offered, or what using them meant to the offerer. Function is notoriously difficult to establish, and efforts to identify function in the absence of directly relevant texts may be futile. Yet we can speculate that, with sacrificial loaves clutched to their bodies, the plaque figurines embodied the hopes of worshipers that their offerings would be accepted and thus signified the desired efficacy of their ritual acts. Perhaps Zevit said it best in emphasizing that the general function of the female figures was to "invoke the numinous, to localize the general, and to assure contact and communication" between people and divine powers.[61] The Iron Age plaque figurines with disks indicate the importance of bread as a ritual substance intended to effect that connection between human and deity.

BIBLIOGRAPHY

Albertz, Rainer, et al., eds. *Family and Household Religion: Toward a Synthesis of Old Testament Studies, Archaeology, Epigraphy, and Cultural Studies.* Winona Lake, IN: Eisenbrauns, 2014.

Albright, William F. *The Archaeology of Palestine and the Bible.* 3rd ed. New York: Revell, 1935.

---

59. See Meyers "Feast Days and Food Ways," 236. Note that in ancient West Asian households, a portion of bread (*kispu*) was set aside for deceased ancestors at household meals; so van der Toorn, "Family Religion," 26.

60. Hendel, "Aniconism," among others, associates the lack of anthropomorphic figures depicting deities in the archaeological record of Iron Age Israel with biblical aniconism. He focuses on male deities and Yahwism, but the lack of goddess images in Judah in late Iron II, assuming that the JPFs depict humans, would reflect the emergence of Yahweh as sole deity in the late monarchy (see Smith, *Memoirs*, 114–23).

61. Zevit, *Religions of Ancient Israel*, 274.

———. "Astarte Plaques and Figurines from Tell Beit Mirsim." In *Mélanges Syriens offerts à monsieur René Dussaud*, 107–20. Bibliothèque archéologique et historique 30. Paris: Geuthner, 1939.

Amiran, Ruth. "A Note on Figurines with 'Disks.'" *Eretz-Israel* 8 (1967) 99–100 [Hebrew], *71 [English summary].

Beck, Pirhiya. "A Human Figurine with Tambourine." In *Imagery and Representation Studies in the Art and Iconography of Ancient Palestine: Collected Articles*, 437–46. Journal of the Institute of Archaeology of Tel Aviv University, Occasional Publications 3. Tel-Aviv: Emery and Claire Yass Publications in Archaeology, 2002.

Braun, Joachim. *Music in Ancient Israel/Palestine: Archaeological, Written, and Comparative Sources*. Translated by Douglas W. Stott. Grand Rapids: Eerdmans, 2002.

British Museum. "pyxis/box." http://www.britishmuseum.org/research/collection_online/collection_object_details/collection_image_gallery.aspx?partid=1&assetid=105331&objectid=282806.

Cornelius, Izak. *The Many Faces of the Goddess: The Iconography of the Syro-Palestinian Goddesses Anat, Astarte, Qedeshet, and Asherah c. 1500–1000 BCE*. Orbis Biblicus et Orientalis 204. Fribourg: Academic, 2004.

Creel, Andrea. "Manipulating the Divine and Late Bronze/Iron Age 'Astarte' Plaques in the Southern Levant." Paper presented at the annual meeting of the American Schools of Oriental Research, San Francisco, November 19, 2011.

Curtis, Robert I. *Ancient Food Technology*. Technology and Change in History 5. Leiden: Brill, 2001.

Darby, Erin. *Interpreting Judean Pillar Figurines: Gender and Empire in Judean Apotropaic Ritual*. FAT 2/69. Tübingen: Mohr/Siebeck, 2014.

Day, John. "Ashtoreth." In *ABD* 1:491–94.

Dever, William G. *Did God Have a Wife? Archaeology and Folk Religion in Ancient Israel* Grand Rapids: Eerdmans, 2005.

———. "The Judean 'Pillar-Base Figurines': Mothers or 'Mother-Goddesses?'" In *Family and Household Religion: Toward a Synthesis of Old Testament Studies, Archaeology, Epigraphy, and Cultural Studies*, edited by Rainer Albertz, et al., 129–41. Winona Lake, IN: Eisenbrauns, 2014.

Dommershausen, Werner. "leḥem." In *TDOT* 7:521–29.

Douglas, Mary. "Deciphering a Meal." *Daedalus* 101 (1972) 61–81.

Ellison, Rosemary. "Methods of Food Preparation in Mesopotamia (c. 3000–600 BC)." *Journal of the Economic and Social History of the Orient* 27 (1984) 89–98.

Engle, James R. "Pillar Figurines of Iron Age Israel and Asherah/Asherim." PhD diss., University of Pittsburgh, 1979.

Goodenough, Erwin R. *Jewish Symbols in the Greco-Roman Period*, vol. 5: Fish, Bread, and Wine. Bollingen Series 37. New York: Bollingen Foundation, 1956.

Hadley, Judith. *The Cult of Asherah in Ancient Israel and Judah: Evidence for a Hebrew Goddess*. Cambridge: Cambridge University Press, 2000.

Haran, Menachem. *Temples and Temple Service in Ancient Israel: An Inquiry into the Character of Cult Phenomena and the Historical Setting of the Priestly School*. Oxford: Clarendon, 1978.

Hendel, Ronald. "Aniconism and Anthropomorphism in Ancient Israel." In *The Image and the Book: Iconic Cults, Aniconism, and the Rise of Book Religion in Israel and* the Ancient Near East, edited by Karel van der Toorn, 205–28. Contributions to Biblical Exegesis and Theology 21. Leuven: Peeters, 1997.

Hillers, Delbert. "The Goddess with the Tambourine: Reflections on an Object from Taanach." *CTM* 41 (1979) 606–19.

Karageorghis, Vassos. "A Cypriot Silver Bowl Reconsidered 1. The Iconography of the Decoration." *Metropolitan Museum Journal* 34 (1999) 13–20.

———. "The Terracottas." In *La Nécropole d'Amathonte, Tombes 113-367, III.1*, edited by Vassos Karageorghis, Olivier Picard, and Christiane Tytgat, 1–52. Études Chypriotes IX. Nicosia: Service des Antiquités de Chypre, Ecole Française d'Athènes, and Fondation A. G. Leventis, 1987.

Keel, Othmar, and Christoph Uehlinger. *Gods, Goddesses, and Images of God in Ancient Israel*. Translated by Thomas H. Trapp. Minneapolis: Fortress, 1998.

Kletter, Raz. *The Judean Pillar-Figurines and the Archaeology of Asherah*. BAR International Series 636. Oxford: Archaeopress, 1996.

Lapp, Paul. "The 1963 Excavation at Ta'annek," *BASOR* 173 (1964) 4–44.

Lundbom, Jack R. *Jeremiah 1–20*. AB 21A. New York: Doubleday, 1999.

Merlo, Paolo. "Asherah." In *Iconography of Deities and Demons in the Ancient Near East*, edited by Christoph Uehlinger and Jürg Eggler. Orbis Biblicus et Orientalis, Series Archaeologica. Fribourg: Academic Press, forthcoming. Pre-print online, last updated 3 February 2010: http://www.religionswissenschaft.uzh.ch/idd/prepublications/e_idd_asherah.pdf.

Meyers, Carol. "Feast Days and Food Ways: Religious Dimensions of Household Life." In *Family and Household Religion: Toward a Synthesis of Old Testament Studies, Archaeology, Epigraphy, and Cultural Studies*, edited by Rainer Albertz et al., 225–50. Winona Lake, IN: Eisenbrauns, 2014.

———. "Frame Drums in the Ancient Levant." In *Transculturation & Organology: Frame Drums in History and Context*, edited by Richard Graham. Ohio: Kent State University Press, forthcoming.

———. *Households and Holiness: The Religious Culture of Israelite Women*. Facets. Minneapolis: Fortress, 2005.

———. "Of Drums and Damsels: Women's Performance in Ancient Israel." *BA* 54 (1991) 16–27.

———. "Royal Repasts and Social Class in Biblical Israel." In *Feasting in the Archaeology and Texts of the Hebrew Bible and Ancient Near East*, edited by Peter Altmann and Janling Fu, 129–47. Winona Lake, IN: Eisenbrauns, 2014.

———. "Terracottas without Texts: Judean Pillar Figurines in Anthropological Perspective." In *To Break Every Yoke: Essays in Honor of Marvin L. Chaney*, edited by Robert B. Coote and Norman K. Gottwald, 115–30. Social World of Biblical Antiquity 2/3. Sheffield: Sheffield Phoenix, 2007.

Milano, Lucio. "Food and Diet in Pre-Classical Syria." In *Production and Consumption in the Ancient Near East*, edited by Carlo Zaccagnini, 201–71. Budapest: University of Budapest, 1989.

Montagu, Jeremy. "Tambourine [Timbrel]." *Grove Music Online / Oxford Music Online* http://www.oxfordmusiconline.com:80/subscriber/article/grove/music/42874.

Moorey, Peter. *Idols of the People: Miniature Images of Clay in the Ancient Near East*. Schweich Lectures. Oxford: Oxford University Press, 2003.

Paz, Sarit. *Drums, Women, and Goddesses: Drumming and Gender in Iron II Israel*. Orbis Biblicus et Orientalis 232. Fribourg: Academic Press, 2007.

Pilz, Edwin. "Die weibliche Gottheiten Kanaans." *ZDPV* 47 (1924) 129–68.
Pritchard, James B. *Palestinian Figurines in Relation to Certain Goddesses Known through Literature*. American Oriental Series 24. New Haven: American Oriental Society, 1943.
Reed, Stephen A. "Bread." In *ABD* 1: 777–80.
Samuel, Delwen. "Bread." In *Oxford Encyclopedia of Ancient Egypt*, edited by Donald B. Redford, 1:196–98. Oxford: Oxford University Press, 2001.
Schmitt, Rüdiger. "Elements of Domestic Cult in Ancient Israel." In *Family and Household Religion in the Levant*, by Rainer Albertz and Rüdiger Schmitt, 57–219. Winona Lake, IN: Eisenbrauns, 2012.
Smith, Mark S. *The Memoirs of God: History, Memory, and the Experience of Israel*. Minneapolis: Fortress, 2004.
Sugimoto, David T. *Female Figurines with a Disk from the Southern Levant and the Formation of Monotheism*. Tokyo: Keio University Press, 2008.
———. "The Judean Pillar Figurines and the 'Queen of Heaven.'" In *Transformation of a Goddess: Ishtar -Astarte—Aphrodite*, edited by David T. Sugimoto, 141–65. Orbis Biblicus er Orientalis 263. Fribourg: Academic Press / Göttingen: Vandenhoeck & Ruprecht, 2014.
Tadmor, Miriam. "Female Cult Figurines in Late Canaan and Early Israel." *In Studies in the Period of David and Solomon and Other Essays*, edited by Tomoo Ishida, 139–73. Winona Lake, IN: Eisenbrauns, 1982.
Toorn, Karel van der. "Family Religion in Second Millennium West Asia (Mesopotamia, Emar, Nuzi)." In *Household and Family Religion in Antiquity*, edited by John Bodel and Saul M. Olyan, 20–36. The Ancient World: Comparative Histories. Malden, MA: Blackwell, 2008.
Ucko, Peter J. *Anthropomorphic Figurines of Predynastic Egypt and Neolithic Crete with Comparative Material from the Prehistoric Near East and Mainland Greece*. Royal Anthropological Society Occasional Paper 24. London: Andrew Szmidla, 1968.
———. "The Interpretation of Prehistoric Anthropomorphic Figurines." *Journal of the Royal Anthropological Institute* 92 (1962) 38–54.
Van Buren, E. Douglas. *Clay Figurines of Babylonia and Assyria*. Yale Oriental Series, 16. New Haven: Yale University Press, 1930.
Voight, Mary M. "Çatal Höyük in Context: Ritual at Early Neolithic Sites in Central and Eastern Turkey." In *Life in Neolithic Farming Communities: Social Organization, Identity, and Differentiation*, edited by Jan Kuijt, 253–93. New York: Kluwer Academic, 2000.
———. *Hajji Firuz Tepe, Iran: The Neolithic Settlement*. Hasanlu Excavation Reports I. University Museum Monograph 50. Philadelphia: The University of Pennsylvania Museum of Archaeology and Anthropology, 1983.
Warsaka, Elizabeth. "Female Figurines (Pharaonic Period)." In *UCLA Encyclopedia of Egyptology*, edited by Willeke Wendrich. Los Angeles: UCLA Department of Near Eastern Languages and Cultures, 2008. http://digital2.library.ucla.edu/viewItem.do?ark=21198/zz000s3mm6.
Yale Archaeological Institute in Egypt. "Introduction: Umm Mawagir in Kharga Oasis: an Industrial Landscape of the Late Middle Kingdom/Second Intermediate Period." http://www.yale.edu/egyptology/ummmawagir.html.
Zevit, Ziony. *The Religions of Ancient Israel: A Synthesis of Parallactic Approaches*. New York: Continuum, 2001.

7

An Early Iron Age Phase to Kuntillet ʿAjrud?

William M. Schniedewind

UNIVERSITY OF CALIFORNIA, LOS ANGELES

The common view that Kuntillet ʿAjrud was a single-period site relies on a narrow foundation. While the exact dating of the site of Kuntillet ʿAjrud has been the subject of some discussion,[1] some consensus has developed around the idea that the site dates to the late 9th to mid-8th century BCE. Yet, there is good reason to suspect that the site served multiple generations, and the predominance of the archaeological data simply reflects the final period that naturally had the greatest accumulation of data. It is a particular pleasure to offer this study to Ziony Zevit, whose own monumental work, *The Religions of Ancient Israel*, is a hallmark of the integration of the larger archaeological context of the site of Kuntillet ʿAjrud with the drawings and inscriptions.[2] As Zevit has emphasized, the inscriptions "have to be interpreted within the context of the site as a whole."[3] Herein, I propose a more holistic approach to the history of Kuntillet ʿAjrud, proffering epigraphic, architectural, material culture, and ^{14}C evidence, which indicate that the site should be understood

---

1. Gunneweg, Perlman, and Meshel, "Origin of the Pottery of Kuntillet ʿAjrud"; Ayalon, "Iron Age II Pottery Assemblage"; Singer-Avitz, "Date of Kuntillet ʿAjrud"; and Freud, "Date of Kuntillet ʿAjrud."

2. Zevit, *Religions of Ancient Israel*, 370–405.

3. Ibid., 371.

as a multi-generational settlement along the Darb el-Ghazza trade route that runs from the Red Sea to the Mediterranean.

Kuntillet 'Ajrud was first and foremost a way station on the Darb el-Ghazza caravan route, which runs from the Gulf of Aqaba (i.e., Ezion-Geber/Eilat) to the Mediterranean Sea (i.e., Gaza) (see map).[4] Even the final excavation report by Ze'ev Meshel, which emphasizes the religious nature of the site,[5] acknowledges that it was a perennial water source in an arid region that lay on important crossroads for trade.[6] In other words, whether or not Kuntillet 'Ajrud was at one time a religious site, its location is first of all chosen for the availability of water along the well established Darb el-Ghazza route.

Another issue that must be addressed is the proximity and relationship between Kuntillet 'Ajrud and Kadesh-Barnea, which lies 50 km to the north. It is well established that the well-watered site of Kadesh-Barnea was a multi-generational site spanning the entire Iron II period.[7] Although Kuntillet 'Ajrud did not offer the same well-watered character as Kadesh Barnea, it did provide a convenient stop along the trade route with ample water supplies for caravans. Na'aman and Lissovsky call the comparison between the two sites "misleading" and argue, "The Negev fortresses were built to withstand attack and siege by armed troops, while Building A was not constructed to face such attacks. In fact, strong fortifications were unnecessary in this remote desert region, and the building was constructed to provide security to its inhabitants and visitors against sudden local raids, rather than attacks by regular troops."[8] But this misconstrues the relationship and forces the incorrect assumption that all Negev fortress sites functioned precisely equally and the same. Yet Kadesh-Barnea was a major fortress along the route, while Kuntillet 'Ajrud served as a secondary fortress. Indeed, Kuntil-

---

4. See Meshel, "History of 'Darb el-Ghaza." Finkelstein (e.g., "Archaeology of Tell el-Kheliefeh," 108) has omitted one of the main routes from the Red Sea, namely, the route straight north up the Aravah to En-Hatzevah (= biblical Tamar). This emphasizes his proposed early Edomite kingdom, but it ignores the natural geography, especially the more than 5000-foot climb up to the Edomite plateau above the Rift Valley. In sum, roads reflect an interplay between natural topography and historical circumstances.

5. Meshel, *Kuntillet 'Ajrud* (note the term "Religious Site" in the subtitle to the volume). There is considerable debate about whether Kuntillet 'Ajrud might have been a religious and cultic site (see Hadley, "Kuntillet 'Ajrud"), but even if we concede that it was a special religious site (and I would not), the site was certainly also a station along the Darb el-Ghazza route.

6. Meshel, "The Site," in Meshel, *Kuntillet 'Ajrud*, 3.

7. See, for example, Dothan, "Fortress at Kadesh Barnea"; Cohen and Bernick-Greenberg, *Excavations at Kadesh Barnea*; and Finkelstein, "Kadesh Barnea."

8. Na'aman and Lissovsky, "Kuntillet 'Ajrud, Sacred Trees and the Asherah," 187.

let ʿAjrud could have been by-passed if caravans were well-watered. And it may not have been continuously occupied in all periods and at all times of the year. At the same time, it is difficult to believe that the site would have been completely abandoned as long as it lay along the Darb el-Ghazza route and as long as that trade route was active. Of course, the fortunes of the site of Kadesh-Barnea were likewise tied to the activity along the Darb el-Ghazza route. Finkelstein, for example, hypothesizes that Kadesh-Barnea substratum 4b covered "the entire sequence of the Iron IIA, between the late 10th and the late 9th/early 8th centuries BCE."[9] The water supplies at Kuntillet ʿAjrud would have been there during the occupation of the settlement at Kadesh Barnea. It makes little sense that the availability of water along the arid Darb el-Ghazza route would have been ignored by caravans as well as by those who built the fortresses at Kadesh Barnea. In other words, scholars should be looking for signs of occupation activity at Kuntillet ʿAjrud rather than minimizing the possibility.

Early Stone inscriptions

There are three significant corpuses of inscriptions that suggest different phases of Kuntillet ʿAjrud. First, the well-known ink inscriptions on three pithoi have received the most attention. They include abecedaries and other school exercises written in Hebrew script, which mention blessings by "Yahweh of Samaria and his *Asherah*" that have drawn considerable attention. These inscriptions are firmly dated by scholars to about 800 BCE, and they find nice parallels in the Samaria Ostraca and other early 8th-century ink inscriptions. Second, the plaster wall inscriptions written in Phoenician script that we shall discuss below. Finally, there are two stone inscriptions that are in an early alphabetic script quite unlike either the plaster wall inscriptions and/or the ink inscriptions on the pithoi.

The two large stone inscriptions pose one of the more puzzling problems for the dating of Kuntillet ʿAjrud (KA 1.1 and 1.2). The editors admit that they "seem to be early Hebrew inscriptions of the end of the 10th century or the beginning of the 9th century BCE."[10] Although paleographic dating is difficult,[11] this assessment is a fair assessment based on the paleography of the inscriptions. The authors compare the paleography primarily to the Byblos inscriptions, the Ahiram sarcophagus, and the Gezer Calendar—that is, to inscriptions usually dated to the 10th century

---

9. Finkelstein, "Kadesh Barnea," 123.
10. Aḥituv, Eshel, and Meshel, "The Inscriptions," in Meshel, *Kuntillet ʿAjrud*, 75.
11. See Schniedewind, "Problems in the Paleographic Dating of Inscriptions."

BCE. The paleography of the stone inscriptions suggests a much earlier date than the other inscriptions, particularly the ink inscriptions, from Kuntillet 'Ajrud. Nevertheless, the editors conclude, "Inscriptions 1.1–1.2 too are to be dated to the late 9th–early 8th century BCE, like the other inscriptions from the site."[12] Given that Meshel had concluded that Kuntillet 'Ajrud was a one-period site dating to the late 9th–early 8th century BCE, there was really no other conclusion that could be made. But what are the implications for the paleographic dating of inscriptions? This conclusion really makes a mockery of any attempt to date inscriptions paleographically.

One serious problem for paleographic dating arises from the differences in materials. That is, it is difficult to compare stone-incised inscriptions with the ink inscriptions that predominate the epigraphic record at Kuntillet 'Ajrud. Fortunately, we have two other stone descriptions from the site. KA 1.3 and 1.4 are also two short stone inscriptions incised with personal names on the rim of bowls. The paleography of both these inscriptions are more well-developed and fit more easily into the late 9th–early 8th-century BCE date that is preferred by the authors. In fact, as a result, the paleography of KA 1.3–1.4 warrants no discussion in the official publication. Furthermore, we may compare these stone inscriptions with a variety of other 9th-century stone inscriptions that are securely dated (e.g., Mesha Stele, Tel Dan), which also suggest that KA 1.1–1.2 are not easily downdated to the end of the 9th century BCE.

Phoenician writing

Another curious aspect of the inscriptional corpus at Kuntillet 'Ajrud are the plaster wall inscriptions that are written mostly using Phoenician script.[13] In the official publication, there are five plaster wall inscriptions written in Phoenician script (4.1–4.5), and one that is written in Hebrew script (4.6). Ziony Zevit suggests that the Phoenician characteristics of some of the plaster inscriptions point to "a transition period in Israelite scribal practices."[14] It should also be noted that most of these inscriptions are quite fragmentary and are comprised of multiple plaster wall fragments. For example, KA 4.6 is comprised of about thirty-two pieces, many of which have no legible letters on them.

---

12. Aḥituv, Eshel, and Meshel, "The Inscriptions," in Meshel, *Kuntillet 'Ajrud*, 77.

13. Ibid., 105–19.

14. Zevit, *The Religions of Ancient Israel*, 377. Mastin, "The Inscriptions Written on Plaster," likewise supports the mixed Phoenician character of these inscriptions.

The question is why were KA 4.1–4.5 written in Phoenician script and how does this comport with understanding Kuntillet ʿAjrud as a single-period site? There are several different scribal hands represented at the site representing different paleographic traditions. First of all, we can identify at least two separate scribal hands in the pithoi inscriptions. This is particularly evident in the adjacent abecedaries (see KA 3.11–3.14),[15] and most likely points to a master and an apprentice. One plaster wall inscription (4.6) is written by a Hebrew scribe. Although it seems to be a different scribal hand than the pithoi inscriptions, it still remains within the Hebrew tradition. However, most of the wall inscriptions in Phoenician script require an entirely different scribal training. The Phoenician wall inscriptions also have another scribal feature that sharply distinguishes its scribe from those of the pithoi, namely the use of a vertical dividing line " | " instead of a dot " • " as a scribal auxillary mark used for separating words. This is a feature best known from the Gezer Calendar, and it is not used in any other inscriptions from Kuntillet ʿAjrud. This further underscores that it is an entirely different scribal tradition.

The paleography of the Phoenician wall inscriptions themselves illustrate periodization. Although the inscriptions are quite fragmentary, they show clear evidence of at least three different hands in KA 4.1, 4.2, and 4.3. This is most clear when comparing the letters *he* and *taw* (see Table 1). Suffice it to say, it is quite difficult to imagine these three hands coming from a single short period at Kuntillet ʿAjrud. And then there is the additional problem that these scribal hands are quite different from the early paleography of the stone inscriptions as well as the Hebrew paleography of the pithoi. In sum, the history of writing as evidenced in the paleography is much too complex for a short one-period site.

	4.1	4.2	4.3
he			
taw			

Table 1. Phoenician Scripts (based on Meshel, *Kuntillet ʿAjrud*, 126)

---

15. All references to the inscriptions use the numbering in the official publication by Aḥituv, Eshel, and Meshel, "The Inscriptions," in Meshel, *Kuntillet ʿAjrud*.

Two Structures

One of the more odd aspects of Kuntillet ʿAjrud is the presence of two separate structures, Buildings A and B, on the site. Building A is a relatively well-preserved rectangular fortress (25x15m) whose walls were preserved to a height of 1.5 meters in some places, while Building B is a poorly preserved group of walls located about five meters to the north of the fortress that seems to impede its entrance. Building B seems to be mostly destroyed by the erosion of the hilltop (and this process may have begun even in antiquity). Although the erosion of the hill almost completely erased Building B, traces of architecture and material culture were preserved and excavated. Meshel was aware of the unique and odd nature of Building B, and he notes that there are "no parallel structures for comparison."[16] Indeed, there are no other Negev fortresses that have a secondary building like it. There are phased sites like Kadesh-Barnea that have separate buildings for different periods, but not two adjacent buildings. Meshel uses the apparent unique nature of these two buildings to advance a religious interpretation of Building B asking, "Did it serve the main function of the site which, we think, was a religious one? Was the Platform the base of a *bamah*?"[17]

The state of preservation of Building B stands in stark contrast to Building A. As Meshel notes, "many of its stones being in a fully disintegrated state even before excavations began."[18] Although the material remains were meager, there is certainly evidence that there were multiple phases. For example, in the Southern Wing Courtyard, Meshel writes that "at elevation 1.60 and some 0.20 m below the occupation level mentioned above, was a layer containing pieces of branches, straw, patches of ash, a few date pits, and a piece of rope. This is the second piece of evidence of some activity that took place here prior to, or during, the construction of Building B."[19] The other straw sample from the site was ^{14}C dated to the Iron IIA period (discussed below). The presence of ash here and elsewhere in Building B suggest that the structure could have been destroyed and then poorly rebuilt. In the Northern Wing, Meshel describes what seems to be a destruction layer, "From this elevation [1.30–1.40 m] down to the floor (at elevation 1.60–1.70) was a layer of earth and black ash, devoid of stone rubble and branches, but containing here and there small quantities of material that

---

16. Meshel and Goren, "Architecture, Plan and Phases," in Meshel, *Kuntillet ʿAjrud*, 13.
17. Ibid.
18. Ibid., 53.
19. Ibid., 58–59.

seems to be disintegrated mud bricks."[20] Moreover, the striking differences in the quality of construction and preservation between Building B and the fortress (Building A) only serve to further suggest that Kuntillet ʻAjrud was not a simple one period site. The site apparently had a more complex history.

Pottery

The archaeological remains found at Kuntillet ʻAjrud have generated some vigorous debate.[21] The problem lies in the ambiguous nature of some of the evidence that lends itself to different reconstructions. As Gabriel Barkay noted about the more general problem of dating Negev fortresses: "It is difficult to reach a conclusion concerning the fortresses, as their interpretation depends on their dating, and their dating involves serious difficulties. In many studies, the scholars appear to be caught up in a circular argument, in which the dating is based on the general interpretation given to the fortress phenomenon and is in turn used to support the proposed interpretation of the character of the fortresses."[22] The situation has not changed much, and the circular reasoning is usually tied to historical interpretations. It is difficult to assign precise dates to the site, although the evidence would allow for dates ranging from the 10th century through the end of the 8th century BCE. In the final publication of the pottery, Etan Ayalon enumerates some of the problems of dating: "a number of inherent problems must be borne in mind: scanty materials for comparison from strata dated to the end of the 9th and first half of the 8th centuries BCE; in contrast, a plethora of finds from the last third of the 8th century, resulting in a distorted chronological picture; subjective limitations in the method of typological comparison . . ."[23] The last phase of the site should be the easiest period to date chronologically, but even this has proved the subject of considerable debate at Kuntillet ʻAjrud. The beginning of the settlement is naturally even more difficult to date on the basis of the pottery typology. There are certainly hints in the pottery assemblage that the site could have been established in the Iron IIA period.

The preponderance of pottery dates to the Iron II period, mostly the Iron IIB (that is, ca. 840–701 BCE). There are several pottery forms that have parallels in the Iron IIA period (ca. 980–840 BCE), but the site has usually been interpreted as a "one-period site," which would preclude multiple phases. On the other hand, Lily Singer-Avitz has argued that the pottery

---

20. Ibid., 53.
21. See the sources cited in note 1.
22. Barkay, "Iron Age II–III," 324.
23. Ayalon, "Pottery Assemblage," in Meshel, *Kuntillet ʻAjrud*, 245.

assemblage as a whole points to the late 8th or early 7th century. She argues that the strongest parallels are to Lachish III (destroyed by Sennacherib in 701 BCE) and suggests the site be connected with the neo-Assyrian activity in the region.[24] Her analysis was then critiqued by several scholars, and she subsequently offered a reasoned defense of her position.[25] What becomes clear is that the pottery analysis is conditioned on historical connections. This point is made by Meshel in his rebuttal to Singer-Avitz's revised dating.[26] Of course, Meshel's dating of the site is also dependent on historical analysis, namely, trying to associate the site with biblical references to northern activity in Judah and the south.[27]

There are examples of pottery forms that could be placed in the Iron IIA period. One particularly interesting example are two pottery fragments from a Cypriot Biochrome II type krater.[28] These types of kraters have been in Phoenicia as well as along the southern coast of Israel. Ayalon also cites parallels from Ashdod Stratum VIII (paralleling the so-called Ashdod Ware) as well as Megiddo Stratum Va, which would date these to the late Iron IIA. Ayalon also notes a bag-shaped jar with "early parallels" in Hazor Stratum Xb, Beersheva Stratum V, and Arad Stratum XII—parallels that fit into the early Iron II period.[29] Other examples could be brought. To be sure, there are explanations for early pottery types found in later assemblages, and these examples cannot be used to isolate an earlier phase to Kuntillet 'Ajrud. Many of the pottery types are found in both Iron IIA and IIB, so it is difficult to isolate Iron IIA without destruction layers. Finkelstein and Piasetzky state the situation negatively, "Unambiguous Iron IIA pottery was not found at Kuntillet 'Ajrud."[30] Yet, there is quite a bit of ambiguity in the pottery assemblage from the site. Finkelstein wants the unambiguous example, but such pottery is naturally difficult to come by without destruction layers. Moreover, the pottery assemblages are naturally concentrated in the latest phase of the site.

---

24. Singer-Avitz, "Date of Kuntillet 'Ajrud," 197–228.

25. Finkelstein and Piasetzky, "Date of Kuntillet 'Ajrud," 175–86, Freud, "Date of Kuntillet 'Ajrud," 169–74; Singer-Avitz, "Date of Kuntillet 'Ajrud," 110–19.

26. Meshel, "Appendix B," in Meshel, *Kuntillet 'Ajrud*, 277.

27. See, for example, Meshel's chapter entitled, "The Nature of the Site and Its Biblical Background," *Kuntillet 'Ajrud*, 65–69, as well as his comments in the introductory "Summary" to the volume.

28. See the discussion in Ayalon, "The Pottery Assemblage," in Meshel, *Kuntillet 'Ajrud*, 215.

29. Ayalon, "Iron Age II Pottery Assemblage," 162.

30. Finkelstein and Piasetzky, "Date of Kuntillet 'Ajrud," 182.

One significant aspect of the pottery assemblage is a connection to Phoenicia as well as northern Israel. The connection with northern Israel is not unexpected, especially given the northern theophoric names as well as the mention of "Yahweh of Samaria" in the inscriptions. The connection with Phoenicia is perhaps more unexpected. In the pottery assemblage, Ayalon makes note of several Phoenician parallels, and petrographic analysis of the clay also points to pottery manufactured in Cyprus or the Aegean zone.[31] Such pottery types underscore the point that the site was involved in long-range trade that was likely supported by the state. They also cohere with the aforementioned point that the plaster inscriptions in the fortress were written in "Phoenician script." As the same time, Ayalon cautions, "Despite the formative Phoenician influence, there are no vessels in the assemblage which can be defined with certainty as Phoenician, except possibly a jug and additional decorated fragments."[32] The Phoenician influence raises the question of what sorts of trade items would have been passing along the Darb el-Ghazza route and what time period would fit. The Phoenician material culture, unfortunately, is inclusive and could easily fit a range of dates in the Iron IIA though IIB period.

^{14}C

The ^{14}C results from Kuntillet 'Ajrud were limited to thirteen relevant samples. And, the samples give a variety of dates, mostly clustering in the late 9th century through mid-8th century BCE. The chronological calibration after 750 BCE is "noisy and almost completely flat," as Carmi and Segal point out, and yields a "relatively wide range of possibilities."[33] But the calibrated range of the dates certainly allows for an earlier phase. Indeed, 6 of the 13 samples have calibrated dates that begin in the Iron IIA period; and, two samples actually point specifically to the Iron IIA period. Sample RT-1829 was a tamarix tree that was retested four times and yielded dates in the Iron IIA and early Iron IIB (891–886 BCE, 846–798 BCE, 895–876 BCE, 856–792 BCE). An even more interesting bit of evidence was Sample RT-2097, a piece of straw—that is, a short-lived sample—that was excavated at a depth of 2.5 meters in the Southern Storeroom (Locus 256), which would be the lowest occupation level of the fortress. This yielded calibrated dates between 991–848 BCE. This would place the earliest activity of the

---

31. Ayalon, "Pottery Assemblage," in Meshel, *Kuntillet 'Ajrud*, 243–5.

32. Ibid., 244.

33. Carmi and Segal, "^{14}C Dates from Kuntillet 'Ajrud," in Meshel, *Kuntillet 'Ajrud*, 61.

site securely in the Iron IIA period. Discussions of the ¹⁴C dating ignore this sample because it does not fit into the theory that Kuntillet ʿAjrud was a one-period site dating to the early 8th century. These two samples serve to point out that ¹⁴C data is hardly precise enough to justify the conclusion that Kuntillet ʿAjrud is a one-period site or to narrowly define the parameters of the settlement in the early 8th century BCE.

Historical interpretations have been critical for scholars using the ¹⁴C data. For example, Finkelstein and Piasetzky conclude, "The ¹⁴C determinations seem to indicate that the site was built between 820 and 795 BCE and was abandoned after 745 BCE. Historical consideration discussed in this article may narrow this time-span to ca. 795– 730/720 BCE."[34] In point of fact, all these dates are contingent on historical interpretations with the ¹⁴C data serving only as general support. To begin with, 745 BCE is the date of the Assyrian king Tiglath-Pileser III's ascension, not a radiocarbon date (which could never be that precise). In addition, 820–795 BCE contextualizes the site around the reign of Israelite king Joash who is mentioned in the Bible as capturing the Judean king Amaziah (2 Kgs 14:11–13). Amaziah in turn begins his reign somewhere around 795 BCE, depending on the chronology, and is supposed to have rebuilt the Red Sea port of Eilat (2 Kgs 14:22). Joash's successor, Jeroboam II, probably comes to the throne around 790 BCE and supposedly restores the Arabah to Israel (2 Kgs 14:25). The dates 730/720 BCE are both general dates related to the Assyrian campaigns in northern Israel. Indeed, the ¹⁴C curves become problematic in the mid-8th century BCE, and precise dating is not possible for the late 8th century. In sum, these ¹⁴C are entirely based on biblical and near eastern historical interpretations. Indeed, the ¹⁴C data actually allows for a much earlier as well as later settlement activity, but it is historical interpretation that has delimited the settlement period.

Certainly, we might expect the ¹⁴C dates to cluster around the last phase of the site; however, they do not appear precise enough to bear the weight of the narrow historical conclusions that have been offered. Indeed, the attempt to narrow the history of the site into one period seems to sweep aside some of the other evidence that would suggest Kuntillet ʿAjrud had an earlier phase in the Iron IIA period. Unfortunately, the literary sources (both biblical texts and near eastern texts) have very little to say that can definitely be applied to the settlement history of Kuntillet ʿAjrud. While it is safe to say that most of the radiocarbon, paleographic, and pottery evidence support settlement in the late 9th or early 8th century, they do not preclude occupation in earlier or later periods. Moreover, there are striking

---

34. Finkelstein and Piasetzky, "Date of Kuntillet ʿAjrud," 184.

hints of earlier activity in the epigraphy, architecture, and ¹⁴C dates. The site was clearly secondary to the more well-watered and developed site of Kadesh-Barnea that lies 50 km to the north, but both sites served the Darb el-Ghazza route from the area of modern day Eilat to Gaza.

Summary

In sum, the evidence allows for a much longer period of activity at Kuntillet 'Ajrud ranging from the late 10th century through the late 8th century BCE. There is no reason to assume that a site like Kuntillet 'Ajrud was destroyed in a multiple conflagration(s) that would yield well-stratifed archaeological layers. The material culture of a continuously occupied (and secondary) site like this is naturally concentrated on its later activity, and yet there is certainly evidence for a longer period of activity than a simple one-period 8th-century site.[35]

BIBLIOGRAPHY

Ahituv, Shmuel, Esther Eshel, and Ze'ev Meshel. "The Inscriptions." In *Kuntillet 'Ajrud: An Iron Age II Religious Site on the Judah–Sinai Border*, edited by Ze'ev Meshel, 73–142. Jerusalem: Israel Exploration Society, 2012.

Ayalon, Etan. "The Iron Age II Pottery Assemblage from Ḥorvat Teiman (Kuntillet 'Ajrud)." *Tel Aviv* 22 (1996) 141–205.

———. "The Pottery Assemblage." In *Kuntillet 'Ajrud: An Iron Age II Religious Site on the Judah–Sinai Border*, edited by Ze'ev Meshel, 205–74. Jerusalem: Israel Exploration Society, 2012.

Barkay, Gabriel. "The Iron Age II–III." In *The Archaeology of Ancient Israel*, edited by Amnon Ben-Tor, 302–73. New Haven: Yale University Press, 1992.

Carmi, Israel, and Dror Segal. "¹⁴C Dates from Kuntillet 'Ajrud." In *Kuntillet 'Ajrud: An Iron Age II Religious Site on the Judah–Sinai Border*, edited by Ze'ev Meshel, 61–64. Jerusalem: Israel Exploration Society, 2012.

Cohen, Rudolph, and Hannah Bernick-Greenberg. *Excavations at Kadesh Barnea (Tell el-Qudeirat) 1976–1982*. Israel Antiquities Authority Reports, 34. Jerusalem: Israel Antiquities Authority, 2007.

Dothan, Moshe. "The Fortress at Kadesh Barnea." *IEJ* 15 (1965) 134–51.

Finkelstein, Israel. "The Archaeology of Tell el-Kheleifeh and the History of Ezion-geber/Elath." *Semitica* 56 (2014) 105–36.

---

35. Postscript: The fine collection of essays in *Maarav* 20.1 (2013 – though published in December 2015), dedicated to *Kuntillet 'Ajrud: Iron Age Inscriptions and Iconography* (thus the official designation of this issue of the journal) arrived while the present article was in the production stage. I have not, accordingly, been able to incorporate the many interesting opinions and findings expressed in the *Maarav* essays into my article.

---. *The Forgotten Kingdom: The Archaeology and History of the Northern Israel.* Ancient Near East Monographs, 5; Atlanta: Scholars, 2013.

---. "Kadesh Barnea: A Reevaluation of Its Archaeology and History." *Tel Aviv* 37 (2010) 111–25.

Finkelstein, Israel, and Eliezer Piasetzky. "The Date of Kuntillet 'Ajrud: The ^{14}C Perspective." *Tel Aviv* 35 (2008) 175–85.

Fleming, Daniel E. *The Legacy of Israel in Judah's Bible: History, Politics, and the Reinscribing of the Tradition.* Cambridge: Cambridge University Press, 2012.

Freud, Liora. "The Date of Kuntillet 'Ajrud: A Reply to Lily Singer-Avitz." *Tel Aviv* 35 (2008) 169–74.

Gunneweg, Jan, Isadore Perlman, and Ze'ev Meshel. "The Origin of the Pottery of Kuntillet 'Ajrud." *IEJ* 35 (1985) 270–83.

Hadley, Judith M. "Kuntillet 'Ajrud: Religious Centre or Desert Way Station?" *PEQ* 125 (1993) 115–24.

Mastin, B. A. "The Inscriptions Written on Plaster at Kuntillet 'Ajrud." *VT* 59 (2009) 99–115.

Meshel, Ze'ev. "The History of 'Darb el-Ghaza'—The Ancient Road to Eilat and Southern Sinai," *Eretz-Israel* 15 (1981) 361–62 (Hebrew).

---. *Kuntillet 'Ajrud: An Iron Age II Religious Site on the Judah-Sinai Border* Jerusalem: Israel Exploration Society, 2012.

---. "The Nature of the Site and Its Biblical Background." In *Kuntillet 'Ajrud: An Iron Age II Religious Site on the Judah-Sinai Border*, edited by Ze'ev Meshel, 65–69. Jerusalem: Israel Exploration Society, 2012.

---. "The Site: Location, Environment and Exploration." In *Kuntillet 'Ajrud: An Iron Age II Religious Site on the Judah-Sinai Border*, edited by Ze'ev Meshel, 3–9. Jerusalem: Israel Exploration Society, 2012.

---. "Summary," in *Kuntillet 'Ajrud: An Iron Age II Religious Site on the Judah-Sinai Border*, edited by Ze'ev Meshel, xxi–xxii. Jerusalem: Israel Exploration Society, 2012.

Meshel, Ze'ev, and Avner Goren. "Architecture, Plan and Phases." In *Kuntillet 'Ajrud: An Iron Age II Religious Site on the Judah-Sinai Border*, edited by Ze'ev Meshel, 11–60. Jerusalem: Israel Exploration Society, 2012.

Na'aman, Nadav, and Nurit Lissovsky. "Kuntillet 'Ajrud, Sacred Trees and the Asherah." *Tel Aviv* 35 (2008) 186–208.

Schniedewind, William M. "Problems in the Paleographic Dating of Inscriptions." In *The Bible and Radiocarbon Dating: Archaeology, Text and Science*, edited by Thomas E. Levy and Thomas Higham, 405–12. London: Equinox, 2005.

Singer-Avitz, Lily. "The Date of Kuntillet 'Ajrud." *Tel Aviv* 33 (2006) 196–228.

---. "The Date of Kuntillet 'Ajrud: A Rejoinder." *Tel Aviv* 36 (2009), 110–19.

Zevit, Ziony. *The Religions of Ancient Israel: A Synthesis of Parallactic Approaches.* New York: Continuum, 2001.

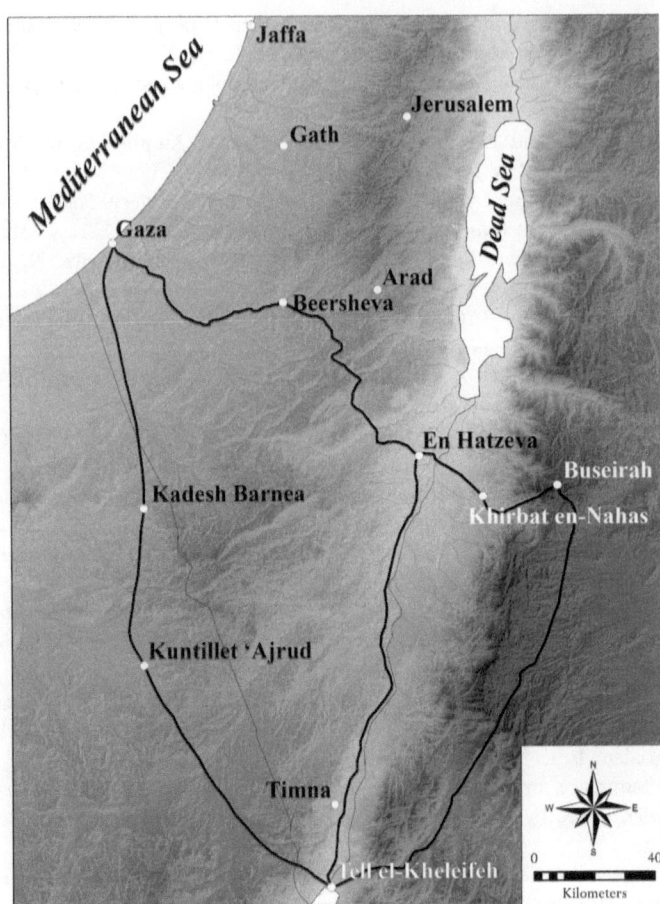

Map by Amy Karoll based on data publically available via the United States Geological Survey.

Part 2: Bible

8

Psalm 122: The Idealized Jerusalem

Adele Berlin

UNIVERSITY OF MARYLAND

It is a pleasure to contribute to a volume honoring my friend and colleague, Ziony Zevit. I share many of his interests in biblical studies, most of all poetry, so I dedicate this study of Psalm 122 to him.

First, a few preliminary observations about the nature of psalms, and poetry in general. The speaking voice in the psalm, whether it be first person or third person, should not be confused with the author. We are not so naïve as to conflate the narrator of a modern novel with its author, and neither should we conflate an ancient poet with the speaker in the poem. A poet can create any speaking voice he likes—a king, a poor man, an exiled Judean. Similarly, the intensity of a description in no way proves that the author actually experienced what he describes, or was even a witness to the events. The intense descriptions in the book of Lamentations have led some to conclude that they must be eye-witness accounts, but this is to misunderstand the nature of literature. The problem is more acute in Psalms, because form critics have been so insistent on finding the place in life (*Sitz im Leben*) of psalms. But generally the only evidence such scholars have is the information from within the psalm itself, so they easily mistake the speaking persona and the scenario in which he speaks for the actual author and the setting in which the psalm was written. For example, it is widely believed that a Judean exile wrote Psalm 137, "By the canals of Babylon," but there is no external support for this conclusion. Anyone could have written a poem about a Judean in exile. Likewise in the case of Psalm 122; we should not assume that a pilgrim wrote or sang this psalm, although most commentaries do.

The text of Psalm 122 presented here is from the St Petersburg (Leningrad) Codex. The text in the Aleppo Codex is the same, save for one difference in orthography, to be noted below. The translation is my own.

1 שִׁיר הַמַּעֲלוֹת לְדָוִד שָׂמַחְתִּי בְּאֹמְרִים לִי בֵּית יְהוָה נֵלֵךְ׃
2 עֹמְדוֹת הָיוּ רַגְלֵינוּ בִּשְׁעָרַיִךְ יְרוּשָׁלָ͏ִם׃
3 יְרוּשָׁלַ͏ִם הַבְּנוּיָה כְּעִיר שֶׁחֻבְּרָה־לָּהּ יַחְדָּו׃
4 שֶׁשָּׁם עָלוּ שְׁבָטִים שִׁבְטֵי־יָהּ עֵדוּת לְיִשְׂרָאֵל לְהֹדוֹת לְשֵׁם יְהוָה׃
5 כִּי שָׁמָּה ׀ יָשְׁבוּ כִסְאוֹת לְמִשְׁפָּט כִּסְאוֹת לְבֵית דָּוִיד׃
6 שַׁאֲלוּ שְׁלוֹם יְרוּשָׁלָ͏ִם יִשְׁלָיוּ אֹהֲבָיִךְ׃
7 יְהִי־שָׁלוֹם בְּחֵילֵךְ שַׁלְוָה בְּאַרְמְנוֹתָיִךְ׃
8 לְמַעַן אַחַי וְרֵעָי אֲדַבְּרָה־נָּא שָׁלוֹם בָּךְ׃
9 לְמַעַן בֵּית־יְהוָה אֱלֹהֵינוּ אֲבַקְשָׁה טוֹב לָךְ׃

1. A Song of Ascents. Of David. I rejoiced that they say to me "We are going to the House of the Lord."

2. Our feet used to stand within your gates, Jerusalem.

3. Jerusalem, the built up one, indeed, a city that was bound up all together.

4. Where the tribes ascended, the tribes of Yah; a decree to Israel to give thanks to the name of the Lord.

5. For there sat the thrones of justice, the thrones of the house of David.

6. Ask for peace for Jerusalem, may those who love you be tranquil,

7. May peace be within your ramparts, tranquility within your citadels.

8. For the sake of my brothers and friends let me speak for peace for you.

9. For the sake of the House of the Lord our God let me seek good for you.

The psalm is about Jerusalem. The name "Jerusalem" echoes throughout the psalm, in the triple repetition of the name and in the sounds of the letters of the name, שׁ, ל, מ, especially in vv. 6–8. More emphasis on the city is provided by the apostrophe to Jerusalem; the speaker addresses Jerusalem in vv. 2, 7–9. The Temple, בֵּית ה', frames the poem, with the addition of אֱלֹהֵינוּ in the last verse that strengthens and personalizes the speaker's connection with the Temple. Verbs of motion, "to go, to stand, to ascend, to sit," provide movement to and within the city (cf. Ps 1:1: "go, stand, sit").

The psalm dates from the Persian period. This dating may find confirmation in the spelling of *David* with a *yod* in v. 5 in the Leningrad Codex (although the Aleppo Codex lacks this *yod*).[1] It would seem from verses 1, 7, and 9 that the Second Temple was standing. If in v. 1 the speaker is a Second Temple figure being told about a pilgrimage, that pilgrimage must be to the Second Temple. At the end of the psalm, the hope for the well-being of the Temple suggests even more strongly that the Second Temple exists. "For the sake of the Temple" does not sound like a prayer for a non-existing Temple, any more than "for the sake of my brothers and friends" is for friends who do not yet exist. It is the Second Temple, and the possibility of a pilgrimage to it, that, in my interpretation, prompts the speaker's "virtual pilgrimage" to the First Temple.

Most commentaries understand Psalm 122 as recording a first-person eye-witness account by a pilgrim on a pilgrimage to Jerusalem, to the Second Temple. They see him joining a group of pilgrims and then standing in Jerusalem, on the Temple Mount, pointing out where pilgrims from earlier times came and where the Davidic court was held. They disagree about whether the pilgrim is speaking while still at the Temple, giving a play-by-play description, or looking back on his pilgrimage after he has arrived home. The argument is based largely on the interpretation of the verbal tenses, especially the verb form in v. 2. עֹמְדוֹת הָיוּ רַגְלֵינוּ בִּשְׁעָרַיִךְ יְרוּשָׁלָ͏ִם : Many see the action in the present: "Our feet now stand/are standing within your gates, Jerusalem" (NRSV, NIV, NASB, Hossfeld and Zenger, 332). Others opt for the past tense: "Our feet stood/ were standing" (NJPS, van Wieringen, deClaissé-Walford, et al.). To my mind, all these translations, and the arguments they are meant to support, miss the mark because the translators are trying to fit the verbal form into their judgment that this is an account of a pilgrimage to the Second Temple. They think this because the first verse mentions a pilgrimage and because, as one of the Songs of Ascents, the psalm is assumed to be a pilgrim song, that is, a song that was actually sung by pilgrims going to Jerusalem.

The verbal form in v. 2, היה plus participle, may be past progressive, future progressive, or jussive progressive, depending on the context. It often has a durative sense. In later books, the construction may be influenced

---

1. This "full" spelling is found in late biblical books like Chronicles. It is anomalous in Psalms, where it is apparently the only case even though a number of psalms are dated to the Persian period, and the superscriptions, also considered late, all have the shorter spelling of "David." See Freedman, "Spelling of the Name 'David.'"

by Aramaic usage, and is similar to Rabbinic Hebrew.[2] The phrase עֹמְדוֹת הָיוּ רַגְלֵינוּ is best rendered "our feet would stand," "our feet would be standing," or "our feet used to stand." Comparable examples are Jer 26:18: "Micah used to prophecy"; Neh 6:19: "they would say . . . they would bring forth"; 2 Sam 3:6: "Abner would be supporting the house of Saul"; 2 Kgs 18:4: "the Israelites had been offering sacrifices." While it is possible that the meaning is "our feet used to stand and are still standing now," the next three verses (3–5) emphasize how things were in the past, not how they are now. Therefore, I do not read this psalm as a description of a current pilgrimage to the Second Temple. The speaker is not acting as a tour guide pointing out the historical sites on the Temple Mount of the Persian period, as some commentaries would have it. I would add that "our feet" need not be the feet of the people planning a pilgrimage in v. 1. More likely, they are the feet of the speaker as he joins himself with all others in past pilgrimages.

My analysis of v. 2 and the psalm as a whole leads me to the following understanding of its scenario. The psalm is a Second Temple psalm with a Second Temple speaker, but it is not describing a Second Temple pilgrimage. The speaker is told that people plan to go to the (Second) Temple, and this brings him joy (v. 1).[3] Suddenly he pictures himself in Jerusalem. The commentaries bridge this gap by assuming that the speaker joined the other pilgrims and that they have now arrived at Jerusalem.[4] But it is not stated that the speaker joined the other pilgrims (as most scholars assume); perhaps it was simply the thought of a pilgrimage that stirred his imagination about pilgrimages in the past. In either case, he imagines being a pilgrim to the First Temple. He recalls how Jerusalem used to be (vv. 2–5).[5] Actually, as we shall see, he recalls an idealized picture of Jerusalem. Then at the end of the psalm he steps back into the present, the time of the Second Temple, to ask for the well-being of Jerusalem (vv. 6–7).

---

2. Waltke and O'Connor, *Introduction*, 628–9; see also Joüon and Muraoka, *Grammar*, 411–2; Sáenz-Badillos, *History*, 121.

3. Many translations read "I rejoiced when they said to me" (NRSV, NJPS), as if בְּאֹמְרִים were the infinitive. But there is no manuscript evidence for this reading. Better to recognize that the preposition ב regularly follows the verb שמח to indicate its object, as reflected in my translation and several others (NIV, Allen, Goldingay, deClaissé-Walford, et al.).

4. Some say that the "feet are standing at the entrance to Jerusalem, but בִּשְׁעָרַיִךְ means "within your gates," that is, inside the city (see, e.g., Exod 20:10; Deut 5:14).

5. The First Temple imagery has led van Wieringen, "Psalm 122," 753, n. 28, to suggest that the speaker is in exile; so also the medieval exegete David Qimḥi. The apostrophe to Jerusalem in v. 2 does not resolve the issue, as in this figure of speech the entity addressed may be in the speaker's presence or far removed, as in Psalm 137.

Verses 3–5 describe the idealized Jerusalem of old. This is not Second Temple Jerusalem. It is an idealized First Temple Jerusalem. The city was הַבְּנוּיָה, built up, the way it was before it was destroyed. "Built" is a term that, when used of Jerusalem, generally means "rebuilt," as in various passages in Ezra and especially in Jer 30:18 (which bears a striking resemblance to our psalm); Jer 31:38; Isa 44:28. Some commentaries translate "rebuilt," but they take it as referring to Nehemiah's Jerusalem. I think that the speaker is describing pre-destruction Jerusalem but is using postexilic terminology. He does this again in v. 4, "the tribes of Yah" (see below). In fact, this type of terminological anachronism is not uncommon and may often be a clue to dating a psalm.

The phrase כְּעִיר שֶׁחֻבְּרָה־לָּהּ יַחְדָּו is a crux since the word חֻבְּרָה occurs only here. The *kaf* is best taken as the *kaf veritatis*, "in truth," rather than the comparative "like." The translations "a city knit together" (NJPS); "bound together" (cf. RSV, Hossfeld and Zenger, deClaissé-Walford); "compacted together" (KJV) do not clarify the meaning. It may refer to the city's architectural features, echoing "built up," or to its unifying focal point for the gathering of all the tribes, as the capital of the county, foreshadowing the following verse. LXX reads "shared in common," which seems to favor the second interpretation.

Most important for my discussion are verses 4 and 5:

שֶׁשָּׁם עָלוּ שְׁבָטִים שִׁבְטֵי־יָהּ . . . כִּי שָׁמָּה | יָשְׁבוּ כִסְאוֹת לְמִשְׁפָּט כִּסְאוֹת לְבֵית דָּוִיד

Jerusalem is the place to which, in the past, all the tribes of the LORD ascended, and it was the royal seat of the Davidic dynasty. "Tribes of Yah" is an unusual expression meaning the tribes who are the LORD's possession, i.e., the tribes of Israel. A similar designation for Israel or Judah is found in other exilic or postexilic writings: "Your allotted tribe" (Jer 10:16; 51:19; Ps 74:2; see Deut 32:8–9). Isaiah 63:17 has the plural "tribes." See also Isa 49:6: "to raise up the tribes of Jacob and to restore the survivors of Israel." In Psalm 122 the reference is to the tribes at the time of the monarchy, but the terminology is postexilic (another terminological anachronism, like "built" in v. 3). In historical reality, Jerusalem was the pilgrimage site for all the tribes for only the briefest time, during the reign of Solomon, and the Bible has no record of pilgrimages then. But this psalm is not about pilgrimages; it is about Jerusalem and what it symbolized. In this verse Jerusalem symbolizes the capital of the united kingdom.

The second symbolic idea is Jerusalem as the seat of the Davidic monarchy. It is there that the thrones of judgment sat, the thrones of the house of David. *Thrones of judgment.* An important function of the king was to dispense justice—see 2 Sam 15:2, 6 where Absalom takes this role for himself, signifying that he is king; 1 Kgs 3:16–28 where Solomon adjudicates between the two mothers. Justice is associated with the Davidic monarchy in 2 Sam 8:15 (= 1 Chr 18:14), where David ruled over all Israel and executed righteous justice; and also in Isa 9:6; 16:5; Jer 21:12. *The thrones of the house of David. Thrones* (plural): the seat of the kings of the Davidic dynasty. The emphasis here is on the royal administration rather than on the Temple and cultic matters.

One would expect that in an account of a pilgrimage more attention would be given to the Temple itself and the ceremonies within it. But, as I have been suggesting, this psalm is not about a pilgrimage to the Temple. The description of Jerusalem encapsulates two major themes of postexilic thought: the re-establishment of the united kingdom and the restoration of the Davidic monarchy. Despite the rebuilding of Jerusalem and the Temple, these two hopes had not yet been realized, and they never would be.

At the end of the psalm, the speaker steps out of the past and into the present, with his prayer for the well-being of Jerusalem, the rebuilt Jerusalem of his own day. It was a fragile city; according to Nehemiah its rebuilding was slow and beset by problems. But its welfare was vital for the safety of the people of Judah and for the Temple, that is, for the national-religious community of the restoration. In v. 7 Jerusalem's ramparts and citadels are mentioned. These are visual symbols of the city's strength and glory in Ps 48:13–14 and the structures that were destroyed in Lam 2:5, 7, 8. They represent the rebuilt Jerusalem, making it equivalent to the un-destroyed Jerusalem—more of an ideal than a reality in Nehemiah's time. They are a bridge between the idealized past and the (hoped for) present. Who are the "brothers and friends" of the speaker in v. 8? Presumably those with whom the speaker associates himself are those who love Jerusalem (v. 6), perhaps one faction within the Judean community (see also Isa 66:10), as opposed to "those who hate Zion" in Ps 129:5. They would seem to be people who would plan a pilgrimage to Jerusalem (v. 1).

What did this psalm mean to a Second Temple audience? They are not being given a vicarious experience of pilgrimage to the Second Temple, or "a look back at the 'history of the beginnings' of Jerusalem."[6] The pilgrimage is a literary scenario through which the psalm expresses the hopes for the complete restoration, still unfulfilled, that anticipates the re-unified kingdom of Israel with a Davidic king on its throne. Jerusalem stands at the center of these hopes for the future, as it does for the rebuilt Temple and the Temple community of the psalm's present.

---

6. Hossfeld and Zenger, *Psalms 3*, 335.

BIBLIOGRAPHY

Allen, Leslie C. *Psalms 101–150*. 2nd ed. Word Biblical Commentary 21. Waco, TX: Nelson, 2002.
deClaissé-Walford, Nancy, Rolf A. Jacobson, and Beth LaNeel Tanner. *The Book of Psalms*. NICOT. Grand Rapids: Eerdmans, 2014.
Donner, Herbert T. "Psalm 122." In *Text and Context; Old Testament and Semitic Studies for F. C. Fensham*, edited by W. Claassen, 81–91. JSOTSup 48. Sheffield: JSOT Press, 1988.
Freedman, David N. "The Spelling of the Name 'David' in the Hebrew Bible." *HAR* 7 (1983) 89–104.
Gerstenberger, Erhard S. *Psalms, Part 1: with an Introduction to Cultic Poetry*. Forms of the Old Testament Literature 14. Grand Rapids: Eerdmans, 1988.
———. *Psalms, Part 2 and Lamentations*. Forms of the Old Testament Literature 15. Grand Rapids: Eerdmans, 2001.
Goldingay, John. *Psalms 90–150*. Grand Rapids: Baker, 2008.
Hossfeld, Frank Lothar, and Erich Zenger. *Psalms 3*. Translated by Linda M. Maloney. Hermeneia. Minneapolis: Fortress, 2011.
Joüon, Paul. *A Grammar of Biblical Hebrew*. Translated and revised by T. Muraoka. Rome: Pontifical Biblical Institute, 1993.
Kraus, Hans-Joachim. *Psalms 60–150: A Commentary*. Translated by Hilton C. Oswald. Continental Commentaries. Minneapolis: Augsburg, 1989.
Sáenz-Badillos, Angel. *A History of the Hebrew Language*. Translated by John Elwolde. Cambridge: Cambridge University Press, 1996.
Waltke, Bruce, and M. O'Connor. *An Introduction to Biblical Hebrew Syntax*. Winona Lake, IN: Eisenbrauns, 1990.
Weiss, Meir. אמונות ודעות במזמורי תהילים. Jerusalem: Mosad Bialik, 2001. Pp. 164–70.
van Wieringen, Archibald. "Psalm 122: Syntax and the Position of the I-Figure and the Text-Immanent Reader." In *The Composition of the Book of Psalms*, edited by Erich Zenger, 745–54. Proceedings of the 57th Colloquium Biblicum Lovaniense, held Aug. 5–7, 2008, Maria-Theresia Kolleg and Papst Adrian VI. Kolleg, Katholische Universitat Leuven. Bibliotheca Ephemeridum Theologicarum Lovaniensium 238. Leuven: Peeters, 2010.

9

The *Qeré* in the Context of the Masorah Parva

Michael V. Fox

UNIVERSITY OF WISCONSIN, MADISON

Explaining the *Qeré*

The *ketiv* is simply the written text in any manuscript, though the term is usually used only of words paired with a *qeré*. It is more difficult to determine the origin and original function of the *qeré*. While the *qeré* is always studied in conjunction with the *ketiv* (as it must be), little attention has been paid to its form and function in the Masorah Parva (Mp).

What, then, are the *qerayin*? I came to this question from the standpoint of a text critic, because I had undertaken to write an eclectic edition of Proverbs, along with a text-critical commentary, as my contribution to the major enterprise entitled "The Hebrew Bible: A Critical Edition" (HBCE).[1] To that end, I had to decide how to approach the *ketiv-qeré* pairs, because only one member could be selected for the eclectic text. The original working assumption of the project was that the *qeré* and *ketiv* are to be treated as textual variants with equal *a priori* claims to validity (though a critic could choose either). But is this accurate?

---

1. Fox, *Proverbs*.

To better understand the nature of the *qerayin*, I examined them in the light of the Masorah Parva (Mp), of which they are an integral part. As a trial probe (and to assemble a manageable data-base), I limited my examination to the Mp of three books, Psalms, Job, and Proverbs. My data comes from three manuscripts, the Aleppo Codex (dated to the early 10th century CE), the Leningradensis (dated to 1008–1009 CE), and a Yemenite codex, Cambridge University, Add. Ms. 1753 (dated to 1577 CE).[2] For comparative purposes I also looked at the Second Rabbinic Bible (RB²) (1524–25 CE) and BHS (1977) but do not give a full accounting of these editions.

In the present essay, I consider verses with a *qeré* or a *qeré* equivalent to see how the manuscripts annotate the word in question. I set aside cases where all three have a full *qeré*, with the entire word and the marker ק׳, for this situation is typical and gives no further information. (They are appended to the tables.) The Mp differs from manuscript to manuscript. The manuscripts I examined agree on the phenomena, though sometimes they describe them in different ways. These differences hold clues to the nature and history of the *qerayin*.

Theories of the Origins and Functions of the *Ketiv-Qeré* Readings

The *ketiv-qeré* variants have been explained in various ways. They are surveyed for the entire Bible and evaluated by Robert Gordis[3] and for the Pentateuch and Former Prophets, by Maimon Cohen.[4] I regard their explanations as partly valid, but I will suggest a more effective and economical way of explaining the system. What, then, are the *qerayin*?

A Variety of Types?

Robert Gordis argued that the *qeré* system includes different types of annotations. He hypothesized three phases in the development of the *qeré* system: (1) the substitution of readings for the Tetragrammaton and the use of euphemisms for terms considered indecent; (2) the addition of readings to disambiguate the base text (this must have happened, he notes, before the addition of vowel signs); and (3) the collation of worthwhile readings from

---

2. Inscribed by Sa'adia ibn Yehoshua ibn Sa'adia in Yemen in 1577, used in microfilm at the Hebrew University.

3. Gordis, *Biblical Text*, 7–28.

4. Cohen, *The Ketiv*, 2–7.

other manuscripts.⁵ The first two explanations are uncontested; the third is open to question. Mordecai Breuer distinguishes different types of *qerayin*: (1) honorifics and euphemisms; (2) words resulting from development of the language; (3) variants. He adds an exceptional case, לֹא/לוֹ, on which see below, §3.1.

Qeré as Correction?

The idea that the *qeré* readings are corrections of a faulty text was first proposed by Abravanel in the introduction to his commentary on Jeremiah and later accepted by several Reformation scholars.⁶ Against this theory, various scholars have objected that the Masoretes were conservators of a tradition for whom correction would have run contrary to "the spirit of the Masorah."⁷ Moreover, many cases of *qeré* are faulty and can hardly be considered corrections. In addition, the *qeré* is "superior" to the *ketiv* (in terms of grammatical and semantic appropriateness) in only a minority of cases, some 200 in Gordis's calculation.⁸ Hence textual correction does not seem to be the motive.

Collation: Ketiv-Qeré as Manuscript Variants?

Observing that many *qerayin* are inferior to the *ketiv*, sometimes even meaningless or contrary to grammar, Harry Orlinsky argued that they cannot be corrections, from which he generalized to all *qerayin*.⁹ Instead he proposed that both the *ketiv* and the *qeré* derive from mechanical collation of three manuscripts. The majority reading became the *ketiv*, the minority one the *qeré*. Orlinsky conjectures that when there were three variants, the collators (now exercising judgment) dismissed the least likely one.¹⁰

Orlinsky's theory is pure conjecture, and the Qumran Bible manuscripts have not supported it. Moreover, if the purpose of the system were to preserve variants, the Masoretes could have listed two marginal variants as well as one, and it is unlikely that their mss always agreed on at least two forms. Another objection is that the *qeré* is very often an expansion of the

---

5. Gordis, *Biblical Text*.
6. See Gordis, *Biblical Text*, 12.
7. Gordis, *Biblical Text*, 24.
8. Ibid., 23–24.
9. Orlinsky, "The Origin."
10. Ibid., 191–2.

defectiva writing of the third masculine plural suffix (ו → יו), the one in which there is the most frequent ambiguity in consonantal writing.[11] The emphasis on disambiguation for this morpheme (found in other types of *qerayin* as well) suggests a motive other than mechanical collation. Moreover, there is no reason to think that the *plene* writing, rather than the *defectiva*, would be the predominant spelling in the manuscript that supplied the variants for the *qeré* notations. Also, some Mp notes, like ק׳ איו in 24:1 and others (see the tables) are not a means of preserving variants and belong entirely to the realm of scribal, not editorial, practice.

Orlinsky says, puzzlingly, that there was no attempt to mark *plene-defectiva* issues as would be expected if the *qeré* were a correction.[12] But, in fact, *plene* writings are common and well-exemplified among the *qerayin*.[13] For further considerations weighing against the collation theory see Albrektson, "Reflections."[14]

Two Traditions

In a thorough study of all the *ketiv-qeré* pairs in the Aleppo Codex of the Pentateuch and Former Prophets, Cohen argues that the system of *qerayin* originated in the oral reading tradition.[15] (This was earlier suggested, briefly, by James Barr,[16] and then developed further by Saul Levin.[17]) Cohen seeks to provide a single, inclusive explanation that can account for every detail of the system.[18] He argues that the *ketiv* represents the written tradition and the *qeré* the oral reading tradition. These are equally valid traditions that (he conjectures) go back to the biblical authors and transmitted equally valid variants.[19] Cohen affirms his adherence to "the philological approach, the approach that accepts the text as it is written, as it is set before us today."[20] In practice he precludes explanations that posit textual errors, though he does not deny the possibility of their existence.

11. See Gordis, *Biblical Text*, 87–92.
12. Orlinsky, "The Origin," 189.
13. Gordis, *Biblical Text*, 86–92.
14. Albrektson, "Reflections."
15. Cohen, *The Ketiv*.
16. Barr, "A New Look," 36.
17. Levin, "'Qeri' as the Primary Text."
18. Cohen, *The Ketiv*, 9.
19. Ibid., 310.
20. Ibid., 9.

Certain objections may be raised to Cohen's approach, including the oral-written dichotomy he posits:

1. A monocausal explanation may be reductionist and force diverse phenomena into a single mold.[21]

2. There are certainly textual errors in the *ketiv-qeré* systems (examples in Proverbs are 1:27; 19:19; 20:21; 23:6, 26; and 26:2). They do not disappear even under the efforts of a "philological" explanation. Sometimes both forms are wrong, from a literary-philological point of view.[22] (Of course an error of this sort may be the *earlier* reading, but Cohen is arguing for the philological validity of both variants.)

3. Likewise, while one may claim that the two systems, *qeré* and *ketiv*, are, in some way, "equally valid," this is not true of individual variants. Some are simply wrong, and when this is the case, it is almost always the *qeré* that makes more sense. In Proverbs, I consider the *ketiv* preferable to the *qeré* only in 17:27, 20:16, and 26:2, but these are my literary judgments and in the Commentary in my HBCE Proverbs, I explain how a scribe could have considered the *qeré* better and produced it as a cue to the meaning of the verse.[23]

Cohen strains credulity when he rationalizes far-fetched usages such as עשר *ketiv* (supposedly meaning "made ten times as much" = "made a lot")[24] for עָשָׂה *qeré* (1 Kgs 22:49),[25] כלבו *ketiv* (supposedly meaning that Caleb looked "like his heart") for *qeré* 1 Sam 25:3),[26] וידא *ketiv* (supposedly meaning "made distant") for וַיֵּדַד *qeré* (2 Kgs 17:21),[27] or חי *ketiv* (with איש חי supposedly meaning an "animal-like man," hence a swift soldier) for חַיִל *qeré* (2 Sam 23:20).[28] The midrash-like logic of these explanations weakens Cohen's theory. However, it does suggest ways the early readers could impose sense on an erroneous *ketiv* without considering it *wrong*.[29]

---

21. By way of analogy—a strong one—consider that modern footnotes serve several different functions (citation of source; addition of information; statement of tangential thoughts or data; interaction with others' ideas). What they share is an attempt to clarify something in the body of the text.

22. See Gordis, *Biblical Text*, 155.

23. Fox, *Proverbs*.

24. Cohen, *The Ketiv*, 278–79.

25. Ibid., 268–72.

26. Ibid., 285–6.

27. Ibid., 279–81.

28. Ibid., 296.

29. An example is the midrashic treatment of the *ketiv* in Midrash Proverbs to Prov 23:31: "Woe to him who sets his eyes on the cup (כוס), because the seller is setting *his*

4. We might also question whether the *qerayin* consistently represent an oral tradition. Most of the *qeré* readings are clarifications of an ambiguous writing, such as ברגלו/בְּרַגְלָיו and make no difference to pronunciation. A scribe may have heard the word pronounced, and that pronunciation may have derived from a tradition, which is to say an older reading, but it is also possible that the scribe chose the plural rendering because that made sense to him. A great many times, the *defectiva* plural is vocalized as /āw/ with no comment. Why was the "tradition" ignored there? Also, the frequent agreements of the *qeré* with ancient translations may show only that a translator and a Masorete came to the same conclusion. There are hundreds of *plene/defectiva* variants in the Kennicott and de Rossi (KR) collections and even in the better controlled group of Masoretic manuscripts listed in Breuer 2003, so we need not assign the *plene* writings in *qerayin* to a tradition. Also, some *qerayin* are relevant to the way one thinks of a word but not to its audible pronunciation. At Ps 10:10, L has ק׳ כָּאִים חֵיל and A has כתב מלה חדה וקרי תרת׳ מלין ("It is written as one word and read as two words"). Even as one word (K חלכאים), the pronunciation is the same. Likewise in Ps 55:16, A's כת מלה חדה וקרי תרת׳ is a *qeré* that does not affect the pronunciation; similarly Ps 123:4.

5. In any case, there is no evidence for a single, continuous oral tradition parallel to the textual transmission. There were undoubtedly reading practices that maintained one or another pronunciation. These are evidenced in the Naḥal Ḥever Minor Prophets manuscript, which adjusts the Greek translation toward what would become M, including its vocalization.[30] But this is not evidence for a single tradition stream extending from authors to the *qerayin*. Moreover, the books not meant for public reading, such as Proverbs, Job, Ezra-Nehemiah, and Chronicles, could not have supported a precise and unchanging oral tradition.

---

eyes on [the buyer's] כיס (pocket)."

30. Barthélemy, *Les devanciers d'Aquila*, 169–98. Examples from 8Ḥev XIIgr ("R"): Hab 1:5, ἐκδιηγήται is changed to ἐκδιηγ]ήθη = M's passive יְסֻפָּר; Hab 1:16, ἐλίπανεν is changed to ἐλίπανθη = M's G-stem שָׁמֵן. The following statistics (taken from Tov, *Greek Minor Prophets*, 147–53) show how the sources align with regard to vocalization: (a) R = M ≠ G: 15x (+ 5x in reconstruction); (b) R = G ≠ M: 21x; (c) G = M ≠ R: 2x; (d) R ≠ M, G 6x. The group (a) is where R probably shows a dependence on an oral practice similar to M's. Overall, R moves closer to M's vocalization but not in a radical fashion that might show a fully developed reading tradition at this time. None of the above cases have *qerayin*. There are no cases extant of R correcting toward a *qeré*.

6. Cohen is right that the *qerayin* readings are not corrections, for, as he says, the nature of the Masoretic enterprise was to preserve texts, not to correct them.[31] And, if the Masoretes were correctors, why did they leave numerous flawed variants in the written text untouched?[32] But to speak, as many do, of "corrections" is a biased formulation, for whatever the *qerayin* do, they *do not correct* the body text as modern emendations do. They leave it untouched. They sit in the Mp along with numerous other annotations without tampering with the text proper.

Emanuel Tov supports the oral tradition theory in his 2008 study of the Qumran biblical texts. He observes that the *qerayin* are not reflected in these manuscripts, neither in the body of the texts nor the margins. Given the frequency of the Masoretic *qerayin* and the large number of biblical manuscripts from Qumran, it is fair to infer that the *qerayin* are neither ancient textual variants nor marginalia. Tov concludes that "the *ketiv/qere* variants reflect an oral tradition, which only at a late stage was put into writing in the Masoretic tradition."[33] He notes that several *qerayin* are mentioned in rabbinic sources, as in b. ʿErub. 26a, "It is written [in 2 Kgs 20:4], 'the city' [העיר] but we read [קרינן] 'court' [חצר]."

Such Talmudic references do show that some rabbis considered that the text was sometimes to be pronounced differently from the way it is written and hence that the practice of *qerayin* (using the term קרינן "we read") is pre-Medieval. They do not, however, prove that the *qeré-ketiv* pairs were consistently older than the work of the Masoretes or even that they constituted a single and continuous tradition. Rather, the *qerayin* record a variety of reading practices and interpretations (as to whether a noun was singular or plural, for example). And neither the rabbinic "we read" formula nor the absence of written *qerayin* at Qumran prove that they were all transmitted orally. Some of the *qerayin* mentioned below demonstrably were not.

The Treatment of Qerayin in Three Manuscripts

Dark shading: orthographic description; light shading: apocopation; no shading = no note in Mp; ? = uncertain; . . . = not preserved

---

31. Cohen, *The Ketiv*, 6.

32. "Flawed," it should be emphasized, is an evaluation from the viewpoint of the modern understanding of grammar and semantic appropriateness.

33. Tov, "*Ketiv/*Qere Variations," 205.

The Qeré in the Context of the Masorah Parva   163

Table 1: PSALMS verse	ketiv	MpA	MpL	MpY
10:5	דרכו	דְּרָכָיו ק׳	כָּיו ק׳	כָּיו ק׳
10:10	חלכאים	כתב מלה חדה וקרי תלת מלין	חֵיל כָּאִים ק׳	חֵיל כָּאִים ק׳
10:12	עניים	עֲנָוִים ק׳	עֲנָוִים ק׳	?
17:11	סבבוני	...	סְבָבוּנוּ ק׳	ו׳ ק׳
17:14	וצפינך	...	וּצְפוּנְךָ ק׳	וּצְפוּנְךָ ק׳
18:51	מגדל	...	מַגְדִּיל ק׳	ל׳ חס׳
24:6	דרשו	...	דֹּרְשָׁיו ק׳	דֹּרְשָׁיו ק׳
26:2	צרופה	יתיר ו	צָרְפָה ק׳	יתיר ו׳
30:4	מיורדי	יתיר ו	מִיָּרְדִי־ ק׳	יתיר ו׳
38:21	רדופי	יתיר ו [unclear]	רָדְפִי־ ק׳	יתיר ו׳
42:9	שירה	ב׳ חד כתב רה וחד כת רו	שִׁירוֹ ק׳	null
54:7	ישוב	יָשִׁיב ק׳	יָשִׁיב ק׳	null
55:16	ישימות	כתב מלה חדה וקרי תרת׳	יַשִּׁי מָוֶת ק׳	כתיב מלה חדה וק׳ תרתין מלין
71:20	תחיינו (L) תחינו (A)	תְּחַיֵּנִי ק׳	תְּחַיֵּנִי ק׳	תְּחַיֵּנִי ק׳
71:20	תַּעֲלֵנִי (L, A) תעלנו (Y)	null	null	תַּעֲלֵנִי ק׳
74:11	חוקך	חֵיקְךָ קרי	חֵיקְךָ ק׳	null
77:20	ושביליך	יתיר י	וּשְׁבִילְךָ ק׳	יתיר י׳
79:10	בגיים	וים ק׳	בַּגּוֹיִם ק׳	בַּגּוֹיִם ק׳
89:29	אשמור	ל׳ מל	אֶשְׁמָר־ ק׳	ל׳ מל׳
101:5	מלושני	יתיר ו׳	מְלָשְׁנִי ק׳	יתיר ו׳
105:40	שלו	שָׁלָיו ק׳	null	שָׁלָיו ק׳
119:147	לדבריך	יתיר י	לִדְבָרְךָ ק׳	יתיר יוד
119:161	ומדבריך	יתיר י	וּמִדְבָרְךָ ק׳	null
123:4	לגאיונים	כתב מלה חדה וקרי תרת׳ מלין	null	כתב מלה
129:3	למענותם	לְמַעֲנִיתָם ק׳	לְמַעֲנִיתָם ק׳	י׳ ק׳
139:6	פלאיה	פְּלִיאָה ק׳	פְּלִיאָה ק׳	פְּלִיאָה ק׳ [unclear]
140:10	יכסומו	יְכַסֵּימוֹ ק׳	יְכַסֵּמוֹ ק׳	יְכַסֵּימוֹ ק׳
Notes	18:51, MpL: Second hand. 18:51, MpY: מַגְדִּל is written defectiva only in Ps 18:55. In 2 Sam. 22:51 it is written מַגְדִּיל. 54:7, MpY: The omission must be an error, because the ketiv יָשׁוּב is impossible.			

(27 occurrences of non-agreement)

Qerayin in Psalms on which the three manuscripts agree: 5:9 (K הושר / Q הִיְשָׁר); 6:4 (K ואת / Q וְאַתָּה); 9:13 (K ענוים / Q עֲנָוִים); 9:19 (K ענוים / Q עֲנִיִּים); 10:10 (K ודכה / Q יִדְכֶּה / עֲנִיִּים); 11:11 (K נודו / Q נוּדִי); 39:1 (K לידיתון / Q לִידוּתוּן); 41:3 (K יאשר / Q וְאָשֵׁר); 49:15 (K וצירם / Q וְצוּרָם); 51:4 (K הרבה / לִידוּתוּן); 56:7 (K יצפינו / Q יִצְפּוֹנוּ); 58:8 (K חצו / Q חִצָּיו); 59:11 (K חסדו / הֶרֶב); 59:16 (K ינועון / Q יְנִיעוּן); 60:7 (K וענגו / Q וַעֲנֵנִי); 66:7 (K ירימו / Q יָרוּמוּ); 71:12 (K חישה / Q חוּשָׁה); 71:20 (K הראיתנו / Q הִרְאִיתַנִי); 72:17 (K חַסְדֵי); 73:2 (K נטוי / Q נָטָיו); 73:2 (K שפכה / Q שֻׁפְּכוּ); 73:10 (K ינין / Q יָנוּן); 73:16 (K היא / Q הוּא); 74:6 (K ועת / Q וְעַתָּה); 77:1 (K ידיתון / Q יְדוּתוּן); 77:12 (K אזכיר / Q אֶזְכּוֹר); 85:2 (K שבות / Q שְׁבִית); 89:18 (K ישיב / Q יָשׁוּב); 90:8 (K שת / Q שַׁתָּה); 92:16 (K עלתה / Q עוֹלָתָה); 100:3 (K ולא / Q וְלוֹ); 102:4 (K כחו / Q כֹּחִי); 105:18 (K רגליו / Q רַגְלוֹ); 105:28 (K תרים / Q תָּרוּם); 106:45 (K חסדו / Q חֲסָדָיו); 119:79 (K וידעו / Q וְיֹדְעֵי); [34] דבריו / Q דְּבָרוֹ; 126:4 (K שבותנו / Q שְׁבִיתֵנוּ); 139:16 (K ולא / Q וְלוֹ); 140:11 (K ימיטו / Q יִמּוֹטוּ); 140:13 (K ידעת / Q יָדַעְתִּי); 145:6 (K וגדולתיך / Q וּגְדֻלָּתְךָ); 147:19 (K דברו / Q דְּבָרָיו); 148:2 (K צבאו / Q צְבָאָיו). (43 occurrences of A = L = Y.)

Table 2

JOB verse	*ketiv*	MpA	MpL	MpY
1:21	יצתי	חס	יָצָאתִי ק׳	חס׳
6:2	והיתי	ו׳ ק׳	וְהַוָּתִי ק׳	
6:21	לא	null	לוֹ ק׳	null
9:13	תחתו	ד חס׳	תַּחְתָּיו ק׳	null
14:5	חקו	ל חס׳	חֻקָּיו ק׳	חֻקָּיו ק׳
15:15	בקדשו	ל חס׳	בִּקְדֹשָׁיו ק׳	בִּקְדֹשָׁיו ק׳
15:31	בשו	ל, חס א׳	בַּשָּׁיו ק׳	חס׳
20:11	עלומו	מי ק	עֲלוּמָיו ק׳	עֲלוּמָיו ק׳
21:13	יבלו	יְכַלּוּ קרי	יְכַלּוּ ק׳	not visible
26:14	דרכו	ח׳ חס	דְּרָכָיו ק׳	דְּרָכָיו ק׳
30:11	יתרו	ב׳	יִתְרִי ק׳	יִתְרִי ק׳
31:20	חלצו	ציו ק	חֲלָצָיו ק׳	חֲלָצָיו ק׳
37:12	בתחבולתו	תיו ק	תיו ק׳	

34. L has דברוו, which is a copyist's error.

38:1	מנ|הסערה	מִן הַסְּעָרָה ק'	מִן הַסְעָרָה ק'	מִן ׀ הַסְעָרָה ק' כתב מלה חדה וקרי תרתין מלין
38:12	ידעתה שחר	יְדַעְתָּ הַשַּׁחַר ק' כת א	יְדַעְתָּה הַשַּׁחַר קרי	יְדַעְתָּה הַשַּׁחַר קרי
39:30	ואפרחו	ל' חס'	only caret ל	
40:6	מנ|סערה	מִן סְעָרָה קרי	מִן סְעָרָה קרי	מִן ׀ הַסְעָרָה ק' כתב מלה חדה וקרי תרתין מלין
42:11	אחיתיו	ל'	אֲחִיוֹתָיו ק'	ל'
Notes	15:31, MpA: I.e., the word is written *defectiva*; the usual writing is with א. This is a virtual *qeré*. 30:11, MpA: The *ketiv* is vocalized יְתָר. There is no *qeré*. 38:12, MpA: Note divided between right and left margins.			

(18 occurrences of non-agreement)

Qerayin in Job on which the three manuscripts agree: 1:10 (K את / Q אַתָּה); 2:7(K עד / Q וְעַד); 5:18 (K וידו / Q וְיָדָיו); 6:29 (K ושבי / Q וְשֻׁבִי); 7:1(K על / Q עֲלֵי־); 7:5 (K וגיש / Q וְגוּשׁ); 9:30(K במו / Q בְּמֵי־); וּבוֹ); 10:20 (K יחדל / Q וַחֲדָל); 10:20 (K ישית / Q וְשִׁית); 13:15 (K לא / Q לוֹ); 15:22 (K וצפו / Q וְצָפוּי); 16:16 (K חמרמרה / Q חֳמַרְמְרוּ); 19:29 (K שדין / Q שַׁדּוּן); 21:20(K עינו / Q עֵינָיו); 24:1(K וידעו / Q וְיֹדְעָיו); 24:6(K יקצירו / Q יִקְצוֹרוּ); 26:12(K ובתובנתו / Q וּבִתְבוּנָתוֹ); 26:14 (K גבורותו / Q גְּבוּרוֹתָיו); 27:15 (K שרידו / Q שְׂרִידָיו); 30:22 (K תשוה / Q תּוּשִׁיָּה); 31:11 (K הוא / Q הִיא); 31:11(K והיא / Q וְהוּא); 33:19 (K וריב / Q וְרוֹב); 33:21 (K ושפי / Q וְשֻׁפּוּ); 33:28(K נפשי / Q נַפְשׁוֹ); 33:28 (K וחיתי / Q וְחַיָּתוֹ); 38:41 (K ילדו / Q יְלָדָיו); 39:12(K ישיב / Q יָשׁוּב); 39:26 (K כנפו / Q כְּנָפָיו); 40:17 (K פחדו / Q פַּחֲדָיו); 41:4 (K לא / Q לוֹ); 42:2 (K ידעת / Q יָדַעְתִּי); 42:10 (K שבית / Q שְׁבוּת); 42:16 (K וירא / Q וַיִּרְאֶה). (34 occurrences of A = L = Y.)

Table 3: PROVERBS				
verse	*ketiv*	MpA	MpL	MpY
2:8	חסידו	ב' חס'	חֲסִידָיו ק'	חֲסִידָיו ק'
3:27	ידיך	יתיר י	יָדְךָ ק'	יָדְךָ ק'?
3:28	לרעיך	יתיר י	לְרֵעֲךָ ק'	לְרֵעֲךָ ק'?

6:13	בעינו	בְּעֵינָיו ק׳	null	בְּעֵינָיו ק׳
6:13	ברגלו	בְּרַגְלָיו ק׳	ח׳ חס׳	בְּרַגְלָיו ק׳
6:16	תועבות	יתיר ו׳	יתיר ו׳	יתיר ו׳
8:35	מצאי¹	מָצָא ק׳	יתיר י׳	מָצָא ק׳
22:8	יקצור	ג׳ מל׳	יתיר ו׳	null
22:11	טהור	ל׳ ומל׳	טְהָר־ ק׳	null
22:25	ארחתו	תיו ק׳	אָרְחֹתָיו ק׳	אָרְחֹתָיו ק׳
23:6	תתאו	null	אִיו ק׳	null
23:31	בכיס	ו׳ ק׳	בַּכּוֹס ק׳	בַּכּוֹס ק׳
24:1	תתאו	null	אִיו ק׳	null
24:17	איביד	אוֹיִבְךָ ק׳	יתיר י׳	יתיר י׳
26:21	מדונים	ל׳ ק׳	מִדְיָנִים ק׳	מִדְיָנִים ק׳
27:20	ואבדה	null	וַאֲבַדּוֹ ק׳	וַאֲבַדּוֹ ק׳
31:27 M^L M^Y	הליכות	—	null	null
31:27 M^A	הליכות	הֲלִיכוֹת	—	—
Notes	24:17: RB² and *BHS* make this a *qeré*, אוֹיִבְךָ.			

(18 occurrences of non-agreement)

Qerayin in Proverbs on which the three manuscripts agree: 1:27 (K כשאוה / Q כְּשׁוֹאָה); 2:7 (K וצפן / Q יִצְפֹּן); 3:15 (K מפניים / Q מִפְּנִינִים); 3:30 (K יכשולו / Q יַכְשִׁילוּ); 3:34 (K תריב / Q תָּרִיב); 4:16 (K ולעניים / Q וְלָעֲנָוִים); 6:14 (K מדנים / Q מִדְיָנִים); 8:17 (K אהביה / Q אֹהֲבַי); 11:3 (K ושדם / Q וְשָׁדְּדֵם); 12:14 (K ישוב / Q יָשִׁיב); 13:20 (K הלוך / Q הוֹלֵךְ); 13:20 (K וחכם / Q יֶחְכָּם); 14:21 (K עניים / Q עֲנָוִים); 15:14 (K ופי / Q וּפִי); 16:19 (K עניים / Q עֲנָוִים); 16:27 (K שפתיו / Q שְׂפָתוֹ); 17:13 (K תמיש / Q תָּמוּשׁ); 17:27 (K וקר / Q יְקַר); 18:17 (K יבא / Q בָּא); 18:19 (K ומדונים / Q וּמִדְיָנִים); 19:7 (K ישאל / Q וְשָׁאַל); 19:16 (K יומת / Q יָמוּת); 19:19 (K גרל / Q גְּדָל); 20:4 (K לא / Q לוֹ); 20:16 (K נכרים / Q נָכְרִיָּה); 20:21 (K באישון / Q בְּאֱשׁוּן); 20:21 (K מבחלת / Q מְבֹהֶלֶת); 20:30 (K תמריק / Q תַּמְרוּק); 21:19 (K מדונים / Q מִדְיָנִים); 21:29 (K דרכיו / Q דַּרְכּוֹ)³⁵; 22:3 (K ויסתר / Q וְנִסְתָּר); 22:20 (K שלשום / Q שָׁלִישִׁים); 23:5 (K התעוף / Q הֲתָעִיף); 23:5 (K יעוף / Q וָעוּף); 23:24 (K גול / Q גִּיל); 23:24 (K יגול / Q יָגִיל); 23:24³⁶ (K יולד / Q וְיוֹלֵד); 23:29 (K תרצנה / Q תִּצָּרְנָה)³⁷; 23:26 (K וישמח / Q יִשְׂמַח); 25:24 (K מדונים / Q מִדְיָנִים); 26:2 (K לא / Q לוֹ); 26:21 (K מדונים / Q מִדְיָנִים)

35. יָבִין and דַּרְכּוֹ are treated as a single *qeré* in M^L.
36. M^A treats the second two *qerayin* in this verse as a single *qeré*.
37. M^A seems to vocalize this as תִּצָּרְנָה.

Q / ורעה (K 27:10 (בְּשִׁפָתָיו / Q בשפתו (K 26:24 ;(מְדִיָנִים / Q מדונים (K
וּבְתַרבִית (K 28:8 ;(וְדוֹר / Q דור (K 27:24 ;(מְדִיָנִים / Q מדונים (K 27:15 ;(וָרֵעַ
K) 30:18 ;(אֲדֹנָיו / Q אדנו (K 30:10 ;(שֹׂנֵא / Q שנאי (K 28:16 ;(וְתַרְבִּית / Q
54 ;(בַּלַיְלָה / Q בליל (K 31:18 ;(נְטָעָה / Q נטע (K 31:16 ;(וְאַרְבָּעָה / Q וארבע
occurrences of A = L = Y.)

The *Qerayin* as Cues

Many *qerayin* are susceptible to various explanations. Numerous variants are equally valid grammatically and hardly alter the meaning of the text, for example וצפן / יצפן; ענוים / עניים; ויסתר / ונסתר; דור / ודור (see the tables). These could be written variants or they could be oral variants, though this does not explain their origin *as qerayin*. While allowing for these possible backgrounds and media of transmission, I want to propose that the *qerayin*, except for the euphemisms, are essentially scribal annotations meant to protect the precise consonantal orthography of words, in preparation for the addition of vocalization by specialists.

A clue to the function of the *qeré* readings is the way they actually appear in the Mp. They can differ considerably from manuscript to manuscript.

The *ketiv* is always an unvocalized consonantal form. In the codices and many editions the *ketiv* is used as a prop for the *qeré*'s vowels.[38] In the present essay the vowels are attached to the *qeré*, to which they belong. There are four main types of *qerayin* or *qerayin*-equivalents, that is to say, notes that give essentially the same information as the *qeré*:

1. The standard format, e.g., בשפתיו 'ק (Prov 26:24). The great majority of entries take this form. These are listed after the table for each book. This essay will consider the less common forms.

2. Apocopations: For example, in Prov 23:6 M[L], איו 'ק stands for תֵּאָו 'ק, and in 22:25, תֵּאָיו. In Prov 22:25, תיו 'ק stands for אָרְחֹתָיו 'ק. An even more severe abbreviation is in 23:31, 'ו 'ק, for בַּכּוֹס. In Job 20:11, מיו 'ק is short for עלומיו 'ק, hence עֲלוּמָיו. These seem to be too intricate a way to inform a reader on the proper pronunciation, since he would have to combine the *qeré* and *ketiv* to know what to say. In Job 6:2, the *ketiv* is וחיתי; Mp[A] has just קרי 'ו. This note is not oriented to an oral reader

---

38. Breuer explains that the vowels had to be in the *ketiv* to support the accents, which must be in the context of their accentual unit (Breuer, "Ketiv," 13).

but to a scribe who knows that והותי is a possibility but should not be written here.

3. *Orthographic annotations*: The Mp very often describes the spelling of a word (or, occasionally, a word-pair). However, I take note only of the cases where another manuscript has an explicit *qeré* for the same word or where the implied pronunciation of the notes is very different from that of the *ketiv*. Such annotations are of several types.

   a. Descriptions and counts. A notation of the frequency of occurrences of the form of the *ketiv* reminds the copyist not to impose a more common spelling. There are of course a great many frequency counts in the Mp. I am concerned with those that specify the orthography in a way that corresponds to a *qeré* that appears in another manuscript.

   b. *Defectiva*: In Job 1:21, for יצתי M^Y has simply 'חס "*defectiva*." There is only one way this word can be *defectiva*, namely by the absence of the 'aleph. The copyist is thus reminded to write it that way. On טהור in Prov 22:11, M^L has: ל' ומל', "this is the only case of this spelling, and it is *plene*." The note does not really affect pronunciation; it is primarily directed to the copyist. Mp^A gives it a full *qeré*. In Ps 18:55, Mp^Y notes that מַגְדִּל is *defectiva* only here. In M^L, a second hand has inserted a full *qeré*: מַגְדִּיל ק'. In Job 15:15, marking בקדשו as 'חס in M^A is enough to show that the suffix is singular, for otherwise the *ketiv* would not be *defectiva*. The scribe is thus reminded to write בִּקְדֹשָׁו. It is helpful, though unnecessary, when this item is provided with a *qeré*, 'בִּקְדֹשָׁיו ק, as it is in the other two manuscripts.

   c. *Plene*: In Prov 22:8 on יקצור, M^A has ג' מל' "three times *plene*." It is not the count but the description "*plene*" that tells the scribe how to write the word. M^L achieves the same thing by noting that this is a case of a superfluous *waw*. None of the mss has a *qeré*—יִקְצָר.—but it gets one in BHS. An interesting case is מִן | הַסְּעָרָה ק in both Job 38:21 and 40:6, where the Mp of M^A and M^L have the *qeré* in the usual form while M^Y gives the information in full: כתב מלה חדה וקרי תרתין מלין, "it is written as one word but read as two words." Somewhat puzzling is the note on ידעתה שחר in M^A at Job 38:12: כת א', "it is written as one (word)." Apparently this means that ידעתה is written with the *he* attached, as one word, whereas the letter actually belongs with the next word. The note יְדַעְתָּה הַשַּׁחַר קרי in the other two manuscripts is clearer.

d. Superfluous letters, marked by *yattir*. In Prov 24:17, on the *ketiv* איביך, M^A and M^Y have יתיר י, "a superfluous *yod*." By noting that the *yod* is superfluous, the Mp indicates that the *yod* does not belong to the word as it should be read and understood, which is a singular. This is a way of affirming that the writing איביך is the *correct* one. A *qeré* is not necessary, though M^L gives it one. In Prov 6:16 at תועבות, all three manuscripts have יתיר ו. Two factors eliminate the ambiguity: the fact that the first syllable of תועבה is always written with a *waw*, and the vocalization placed on the *ketiv*: תּוֹעֲבוֹת. The Mp note plus the vocalization constitutes a virtual *qeré*. RB² and BHS (among others) make it explicit.

e. Other descriptions, such as "written as two words."

4. Null. Sometimes a manuscript lacks a parva note where there is a *qeré* in one or two of the other manuscripts. In most cases, the absence causes no real ambiguity, since the *ketiv* has the vocalization that a *qeré* would have. In Prov 23:6, M^L has תִּתְאָו and does not really need a *ketiv*, except to remind the scribe *not* to write it with a *yod*. Twice, however, the null makes a difference. In Job 6:21, for the *ketiv* לא, M^L has לו ק but M^A and M^Y have nothing, making לא the default. (In fact, neither "no" nor "for him" makes good sense here. The correct reading is probably לי, "to me," which was miscopied as לו.) In Job 30:11, for the *ketiv* יתרו, M^L and M^Y have יתרי ק, while M^A has null, leaving the reader with יתרו ("*his* bowstring," which is what the context requires)—but vocalized יִתְרוֹ (which is impossible). The absence of a note must be an error.

The Mp annotations that parallel *qerayin* in other mss show several things.

(1) The *qerayin* are not primarily a record of textual variants. One does not preserve a variant by specifying one letter in it (ק י for כוס, for example) or the last three letters (as in ק ציו for חלציו). Nor do abbreviated annotations show the kind of precision that was dedicated to the preservation of the *ketiv*. Nor do counts of *plene* and *defectiva* writings preserve variants, though they do help accuracy in the replication of a word.

In some cases, a reading may have arisen as a written variant and known to a copyist in that form, but it was made a *qeré* not to preserve it but to guard the *ketiv* from change by someone who may know that variant and be inclined to embed it in the text. Sometimes the *ketiv* is a graphic error while the *qeré* offers a more comprehensible and expected form, as in Prov 20:21: M^K מבחלת, M^Q מבהלת. If there is a preservationist motive here, it is directed at the *ketiv*. *Qerayin* of the sort קרי ולא כתיב, "it is read but not written," must have arisen in a text or in a reading tradition or there would have been no motive for the Masorete to preserve them in the Mp.[39]

Occasionally there is evidence for a written variant. A rather strange case is in Ps 105:18, where the *ketiv* is רגליו and the *qeré* is רַגְלוֹ. This is the opposite of the usual practice, in which the *ketiv* of the 3 m. sg. suffix is written *defectiva -w* and disambiguated as *-yw* in the *qeré*. In this verse, the idiom calls for the plural: "they tortured his *feet* in iron"). Someone must have been aware of a *vocalized* variant רַגְלוֹ (if it were unvocalized, the *ketiv* would provide all the necessary information) and added the *qeré* to show that the *plene* writing be maintained in the text, though it is unclear why anyone would prefer the singular. G and S too have the plural.

(2) The apocopated *qerayin* and most of the orthographic annotations do not offer much help in oral reading. A reader would have to make use of a fully Masoretic codex and reconstruct the *qerayin* from hints in the Mp. In any case, partial words and orthographical annotations are not really needed for pronouncing a text that is already vocalized, and the Masoretes must have been working with a vocalized text when undertaking orthographic counts. The only clear function of such notes is the preservation of the written text.

Many *qerayin* make no difference to pronunciation and could not have been preserved by oral transmission. When the ending is the third masculine singular pronominal suffix on a plural noun and the *qeré* has it *plene*, the reader gets no information from the *qeré* that he would not learn from the *ketiv* supplied with the standard vocalization, and, in fact, some manuscripts lack this type of *qeré* while others have it. To the scribe, the *qeré* with *yod-waw* shows that the suffix is *not* written with a *yod*.

This is true also לו/לא, in which the *qeré* sounds exactly like the *ketiv* and cannot be grounded in oral tradition. Breuer explains that the Masoretes counted all the places where the writing differs from the usual form, including the places where לא was written for לו or לו for לא.[40] Such annotations are in fact found in early manuscripts. Later, these annotations were reversed: instead of counting the places

---

39. Some *qerayin* appear as in KR *ketivin* manuscripts. But it is unlikely that manuscripts holding them were maintaining an ancient writing that emerged only in the late medieval KR manuscripts. More likely, *qerayin* were incorporated into the body of the texts of these (often faulty) manuscripts.

40. Breuer, "*Ketiv*," 12–13.

in which לא was written in place of לו, "they counted the places where they read לא in place of לו. And this formulation naturally led to *qeré* notations in all these places," and the reverse happened where לו was written for לא.[41] Breuer calls this a קרי מדומה, an "imaginary *qeré*." It is not clear in what sense one of these words was "read" for the other, since their sound is identical. Rather, the *qeré* must be a cue to the way to understand the word in context. Still, Breuer's description of how a graphic note can become a *qeré* is relevant to the types of transformations I discuss here, in which a *qeré* arises from a scribal notation, not from oral practice.

(3) There are many *yattir* notations, mostly unaccompanied by a *qeré*. These clearly have to do with the written form, and no oral tradition would have transmitted them. It is unlikely that *qerayin* that give expression to the form indicated by the *yattir* were transmitted by a process entirely separate from the *yattir* notations that lack a *qeré* and for different motives, especially when some manuscripts lack the *qeré* while others have it.

There Is a Typological Development Leading into Qerayin

(1) A *defectiva* notation could be turned into a *qeré* with a *plene* spelling.

(2) A partial writing could be expanded into a full writing based on the apocopated form.

(3) An orthographic clue such as יתיר could be made into a *qeré* by leaving out the superfluous letter. It is unlikely that a copyist or Masorete would go in the other direction in any of these modifications, for example by taking a note such as יצאתי ק' in Job 1:21 and reducing it to חס'; or by reducing the explicit יָדַעְתָּה הַשַּׁחַר קרי in Job 38:12 to a rather enigmatic כת' א' ("it is written as a single word").

(4) New *qerayin* are added over time.[42] Since none of the three manuscripts examined derives directly from another, a later manuscript (e.g., Y) could hold an Mp that is prior in some regards to the one in an earlier manuscript.[43]

---

41. Ibid., 12–13.
42. See Dotan, "Masorah," 16.1419–20 (1st edition) = 13.615–16 (2nd edition).
43. M^Y is chronologically somewhat later than RB^2 (1524–1525), though the form of the Yemenite manuscript is very close to its Mp and belongs to an earlier stage of development than the does the eclectic Mp of RB^2.

A new *qeré* appears in M^A at Prov 31:21, in which an anomalous *ketiv* הילכות is provided with a new *qeré*, הֲלִיכוֹת, the correct form, which is elsewhere an unremarked *ketiv*. This is a notional correction, not a scribal one.

An interesting new *qeré* appears in M^Y, in Ps 71:20[44]: *qeré* תַּעֲלֵנִי, *ketiv* תעלנו. This *qeré* arose to preserve its *ketiv* from the incursion of the form תעלני, which is the *ketiv* in the other manuscripts. In M^A and M^L, the verbs in the *ketiv* are "showed us," "revive us," and "raise me up." The suffix of the third verb is incongruous. The *qerayin* are "showed me" and "revive me," which are consistent with the third verb, "raise me up," which then does not require a *qeré*. In M^Y, the verbs in the *ketiv* are "showed us," "revive us," and "raise us up," which are consistent. The *qeré* "raise me up" tells the reader that he can use the first person singular suffix with the third verb, as in the other manuscripts, but tells the copyist to write the last verb with a plural suffix, at the cost of consistency.

Qerayin are added even in modern times. RB² has some additional *qerayin*. G. E. Weil's Mp in BHS[45] and even Dotan's meticulous edition of the Leningradensis show this process still at work.[46]

If the *qeré*'s primary role *in the Mp* is to help the copyist, the question arises why a *qeré* would be a different but equally meaningful form; for example, יָצְפֹּן for וצפן in Prov 2:7?[47] or even a form that seems worse?[48] Such *qerayin* do seem to reflect a different text form or oral usage. Possibly the copyist would be inclined to introduce these forms and is being cautioned against doing so. The existence of such variants need not arise from a desire to preserve a variant reading, because they are not being preserved *as text*. They are not even being preserved as marginal variants.[49] The *qerayin* belong to the Mp, along with a large number of other scribal annotations.

---

44. I say "new" with respect to the manuscripts I examined. Possibly they appear earlier as well.

45. To the *qerayin* actually found in his base text, the Leningradensis, Weil adds *qerayin* at Prov 6:14, 16; 8:35; 22:8; and 24:17; Ps 119:161; and more.

46. Dotan describes his policy in the treatment of the *qerayin* thus: "Therefore, though keeping exactly to the text of the Leningrad manuscript, we were occasionally obliged to deviate from it for the sake of the customs and conventions that have become rooted since the manuscript was written" (A. Dotan, *Leningradensis*, x–xi).

47. See Gordis's List 81 "Q equal in value to K" (*Biblical Text*, 151–2).

48. I do not find any clear examples in the books I examined, but there are a fair number in Gordis's List 80 ("K preferable to Q"). These are almost all graphic variants and thus seem to reflect a different text. However, the preferability of the *ketiv* is an exegetical judgment and not necessarily in accord with the Masoretes'.

49. Tov, "*Ketiv/Qere* Variations," 201.

The *qerayin* were not corrections or words to be incorporated in the body of the text by the next copyist, as is the case with interlinear and marginal variants in the Qumran scrolls (esp. 1QIsa[a] and Mur XII)[50] and medieval Ben Sira manuscripts from the Cairo Geniza. Like most Mp annotations, the *qerayin* are a device to preserve the exact form of the consonantal base text, the *ketiv*, in preparation for the addition of vocalization by a specialist. The *qerayin* functioned much like the *sebirin* in protecting the written text from the copyist's expectations, except that the *sebirin* were not to be pronounced.

Full *qerayin* can serve as a cue to the oral reader as well, which is their primary use today. They do not appear in the scrolls used for ritual lections, but manuscripts and editions can be used in preparation for that function.

The sample of texts examined in this essay supports the hypotheses that the *qerayin*, like the other notes in the Mp, serve as guides to copyists on the proper form of the written text, and further that they developed over time and were not a unified tradition. In the light of this conclusion, I decided that the *qeré* is not the Masoretic text, even if it is correct from the standpoint of text-critical judgment and may be preferred to the *ketiv* as an emendation.[51]

BIBLIOGRAPHY

Albrektson, Bertil. "Reflections on the Emergence of a Standard Text of the Hebrew Bible." In *Congress Volume, Göttingen 1977*, 49–65. VTSup 29. Leiden: Brill, 1978.

Barr, James. "A New Look at Kethibh-Qere." *Oudtestamentische Studiën* 21 (1981) 19–37.

Breuer, Mordecai. *The Biblical Text in the Jerusalem Crown Edition and its Sources in the Masora and Manuscripts*. Jerusalem: Keren Ha-Masora, 2003.

———. "Ketiv ve-Qeré." In *Peraqim be-'Ivrit li-Tqufoteha. 'Asufat Zikkaron le-Šošana Bahat*, edited by Moshe Ben-Asher. 'Asufot u-Mevu'ot be-Lašon 2. Jerusalem: The Academy for the Hebrew Language, 1997. (Hebrew)

Cohen, Maimon. הכתיב והקרי שבמקרא [*The Ketiv and the Qeré in the Biblical Text*]. Jerusalem: Magnes, 2007.

Dotan, Aron. *Biblia Hebraica Leningradensia*. Peabody, MA: Hendrickson, 2001.

———. "Masorah." In *EncJud*, 1st ed. (1971) 16.1419–20 = *EncJud*, 2nd ed. (2007), 13.603–56.

Fox, Michael V. *Proverbs: A Critical Edition with Introduction and Textual Commentary*. The Hebrew Bible: A Critical Edition. Edited by Ronald Hendel et al. Atlanta: SBL Press, 2014.

---

50. Ibid., 201.

51. I thank my assistant Catherine Bonesho for working through the Mp texts with me, discussing the sometimes difficult readings, and endlessly checking the details.

Gordis, Robert. *The Biblical Text in the Making: A Study of the Kethib–Qere*. 2nd ed. New York: Ktav, 1971.

Levin, Saul. "The 'Qeri' as the Primary Text of the Hebrew Bible." *General Linguistics* 36 (1999) 182–233.

Orlinsky, Harry M. "The Origin of the Kethib–Qere System: A New Approach." In *Congress Volume, Oxford 1959*, 184–92. VTSup 17. Leiden: Brill, 1960.

Tov, Emanuel. *The Greek Minor Prophets Scroll from Naḥal Ḥever (ḤevXIIgr)*. DJD VIII. Oxford: Clarendon, 1991.

———. 2008. "The *Ketiv/Qere* Variations in the Light of the Manuscripts from the Judean Desert." In *Hebrew Bible, Greek Bible, and Qumran: Collected Essays*, 198–205. Texts and Studies in Ancient Judaism 121. Tübingen: Mohr/Siebeck, 2008.

Weil, Gerhard E., ed. "Masorah Parvah." In *Biblia Hebraica Stuttgartensia*, passim. Stuttgart: Deutsche Bibelgesellschaft, 1997.

10

The Odd Prophet Out and In

Zev Garber and Bruce Zuckerman

LOS ANGELES VALLEY COLLEGE / UNIVERSITY OF
SOUTHERN CALIFORNIA

The Jonah Problem

Among those to whom God has consigned the task of speaking on His behalf in the *Tanakh*, Jonah might best be deemed the odd prophet out. As Jonah's actions and interactions with the Deity and others are related to us in this brief biblical book, we are often made to feel as though we have been transported to the other side of the Looking Glass. That is, judged by the conventions established elsewhere in the Latter Prophets, as laid out in its fourteen other books, just when we look for things that *should* be on the left, we find them instead on the right and vice versa. To be more specific, just when we expect Jonah to fulfill a set of standard prophetic expectations, he starts to do things that appear to be distinctly un-prophetic. And then, when he finally does something you might expect a prophet normally to do, this either gets twisted the wrong way around or is seemingly portrayed in the "right" way for all the wrong reasons. Jonah just leaves you scratching your head and asking the question: why is he *doing* that? Or perhaps, more to the point, why is God directing the action in such a manner that Jonah ends up doing the things he does?

The Twisted Prophet

It is easy to highlight some of the more salient aspects of this topsy-turvy world of Jonah. To begin with, one's conventional expectation for any book in the Latter Prophets is that the divine message is and ought to be the central focus. Granted, on occasion, a given prophetic book may segue into a bit of narrative, but such an account is always meant to be a stage-setter, whose primary function is to put God's message in the appropriate context (compare, for example, the short narrative of Amos 7:10–15, which sets up the immediately following, scathing prophecy of verses 16ff.). Still, this kind of third-person narrative is never meant to over-shadow the First-Person divine declaration that the prophet conveys at the behest of the biblical Deity.

Except in the case of Jonah. There, the prophetic message (Jonah 3:4) is short, blunt, and almost seemingly beside the point. Instead, it is the story—with the divinely designated prophet-turned-fugitive making a dramatic run-for-it in an attempt to evade God's prophetic commission; then a bizarre, stormy sea voyage, capped off with one whale of a fish story, accompanied by a Psalmic interlude; and finally all the unexpected events that then ensue in Nineveh—that holds the reader's attention from start to finish. Things are entirely flip-flopped: instead of the narrative setting the context for the all-important prophetic message, the divine message seems to serve merely as the pretext for a story that, as it progresses, just gets curiouser and curiouser.

The elements of this story also seem to be turned inside-out, when judged against prophetic conventions. Every aspect of the prophetic experience, as portrayed in the Latter Prophets, makes it *clear* that prophecy is not an optional choice that the divinely chosen messenger can take or leave as he may desire; rather, it is an irrepressible compulsion, not to be denied for even a moment. Except in the case of Jonah. Even though YHWH's double command to Jonah—*qūm lēk*, "Arise! Go!" (Jonah 1:2)—indicates that immediate action on the prophet's part was called for, when Jonah heard God's command, he decided that this might be a good time to take it on the lam for Tarshish (Jonah 1:3). The Bible never makes it quite clear precisely where Tarshish would have been located; still, it would seem that Jonah decided to head across the ocean in a vain attempt to get about as far away from the biblical God's normal jurisdiction as one could possibly imagine.

This puts him at odds with the rest of the Latter Prophets, who never had the choice of flight. Compare Amos, who used a telling proverb to make the point that prophecy was for him a knee-jerk reaction and that he had no other option than to declare *with all deliberate speed* the divine message he had been given—"The lion has roared, who can but fear? The Lord YHWH has spoken, who can but prophesy?" (Amos 3:8)—or Jeremiah, who characterized prophecy as a divinely coerced necessity that could not be resisted even for a moment—

> I said to myself, I will not mention Him or speak anymore in His Name,
> But it has become in my heart just like a burning fire shut up in my bones, And I try to hold it in, but cannot. (Jer 20:9)

Then there is the matter of the people of Nineveh, against whom YHWH instructed Jonah to deliver His prophetic condemnation "because their evilness has come to My attention" (*ki 'āltāh rā'ātām lĕpanay*; 1:2). Here, at least, Jonah seems to have been following standard prophetic procedure by delivering a divine oracle against the capital of a foreign, enemy nation. In doing so, he stood in good company—compare Amos 1:3—2:3 or Ezek 26:1—28:19, to cite just two other examples out of many. But just when you might think we have *at last* encountered something conventional, this also skews off in a rather strange direction.

Consider: when an Amos or an Ezekiel was instructed to deliver their oracles against various foreign villains, they were allowed to do so from a safe distance. The message of God's wrath against the nations was solely confided to Israel/Judah rather than to the heathens God had chosen to condemn. After all, why give this kind of useful, inside-information to the opponents of YHWH's Chosen People? Who knows what they might try to do to counteract it? Better for disaster to sneak up upon them unawares, while they remained ignorant of its *true* source. This too falls in line with convention, since elsewhere in the Latter Prophets the biblical God only sent prophetic messages to the Israelites/Judahites. This point is well made, for example, in Amos where YHWH declared:

> You alone have I singled out
> Of all the families of the earth—
> That is why I will call you to account
> For all your iniquities. (Amos 3:2, NJV)

Except in the case of Jonah. Only Jonah was instructed to go into the heart of enemy territory to deliver God's message *directly* to a pagan people.[1] There can be little wonder that this unprecedented divine commandment led Jonah to consider that this might be an opportune time to take a long sea voyage.

Most especially, there is the little matter of the message *itself*—the divine condemnation which Jonah was apparently told to deliver, up-close-and-personal, once he had expended a day's worth of effort, walking into town, presumably in order to get as close to Nineveh's civic center as possible (Jonah 3:3-4). We note that this message was "apparently told" to Jonah because the narrative never makes it entirely clear just when precise instructions were conveyed to this reluctant prophet. To be sure, in Jonah 3:2 God mentioned "the message which I plan to tell you," and then in verse four Jonah relayed the message: "Just 40 days and Nineveh will be overturned"; so in the intervening time we might logically assume that the biblical God imparted the wording of His condemnation of Nineveh to Jonah in more specific and precise terms.

And, in fairness, we can further note that this is hardly the only time that biblical narratives have jumped from point "a" to point "c" without specifically mentioning the implicit, intervening point "b." For example, in Gen 22:2, God instructed Abraham to prepare to sacrifice Isaac "on one of the mountains that I will indicate to you," which, we are told, was somewhere in the land of Moriah. Still, just when God gave Abraham more detailed directions as to which of the Morian heights he and his son Isaac should scale is not noted elsewhere in this narrative. Similarly, when Amos imparted a divine condemnation to the priest Amaziah and his family in YHWH's name (Amos 7:17), it is a little unclear just when the prophet received this oracle.[2] Still, even taking all this into account, it strikes one as a bit odd that the Jonah-narrative never clarifies how and when Jonah was told exactly what to say. One might almost imagine that Jonah decided to ad-lib the message, figuring that he had already been told by YHWH to condemn Nineveh in

---

1. There is, of course, the case of the foreign prophet Balaam, who was commissioned to prophesy against Israel on behalf of the foreign nation of Moab, according to the book of Numbers (22:2ff.). But this too seems a bit odd and ends up with its own set of reversals. Since, thanks to the discovery of the Deir 'Alla Inscription, we now know that Balaam had considerable credibility in the Trans-Jordan region, one suspects that his role in the Numbers narrative has some parallel with the role of Jonah in terms of the original intention of this biblical tradition.

2. For further discussion of this point, Garber and Zuckerman, "Rabin Assassination," 91–92. Page citations here and below are from the revised version (see the Bibliography).

broadest terms and that it was therefore up to him to fill in, however briefly, the gory details.

Still, compared to other considerations *vis-à-vis* Jonah's prophetic message, this may seem a minor point. The substance of the message itself also strikes one as way out-of-kilter—when measured against other prophetic messages in the Latter Prophets—not so much for what it said, but more for what it left unsaid. To begin with, this prophecy was never explicitly labeled as a divine message from YHWH. Most irregular. Indeed, it would not be very easy to find another instance in the Latter Prophets where a divine message is not explicitly ascribed to the One who sent it. Virtually all such communications are qualified by "Thus says YHWH," "Utterance of YHWH," or some similar phraseology. Prophets were understandably very careful to make sure that everyone to whom they spoke *knew* that this was a *divine* message they were imparting and was not to be construed as representing a given prophet's own personal idea or opinion whatsoever. No need to kill the messengers, since they were only following orders straight from the Top. This is always made abundantly clear—except in the case of Jonah.

This lack of divine-qualification for a prophetic message seems particularly strange in consideration that it was meant to be conveyed to Nineveh, laconically described as an *'îr gĕdōlāh lē'lōhîm* (Jonah 3:3)—all of which, one must grant, was technically true. Nineveh was certainly known to be a "big city" (*'îr gĕdōlāh*) by the standards of the day, a point reiterated in Jonah several times (cf. also Jonah 1:2, 3:2, 4:11). Maybe, as verse 3 goes on to add, there was a bit of an exaggeration regarding the claim that it would take someone three days to traverse Nineveh; but this hyperbole may have been meant to underscore that, compared to the hamlets with which Jonah's intended audience was most familiar, Nineveh must have been *some* metropolis.

Moreover, no doubt, it would have been common knowledge that Nineveh was in the possession of (more literally, "owned by") a wide variety of gods (the referenced *'ĕlōhîm*[3]) to whom the Ninevite population owed and did obeisance. So what is the likelihood that they would grasp that *this time* it was the great-and-powerful (but largely unknown) YHWH who was sending them a divine threat not only worthy of being grasped but also worthy of being taken seriously? Consider in this respect that, when Moses conveyed a similar, sharply-worded message from the biblical God to the Egyptians—a people who certainly worshipped as many gods as the inhab-

---

3. We should note in passing that we have taken the phrase *'îr gĕdōlāh lē'lōhim* fairly literally rather than as some sort of superlative—"a god-awful big city"—as it is often interpreted. For various objections to this latter approach, see, for example, the discussion in Sasson, *Jonah*, 228.

itants of Nineveh ever did, if not more—Pharaoh responded (to his and all the Egyptians' detriment, as it turned out), "Who is YHWH, that I should pay him any attention?" (Exod 5:2). This leads one to expect a similar response from the Ninevites, especially since, as we are later informed, they appeared to have been not too terribly sophisticated about such religious and moral matters and were better characterized as a people so ignorant that they could not "distinguish their right from their left"—especially in regard to such issues (Jonah 4:11). Indeed, one might even wonder whether they would have been likely to understand Jonah's message in the first place, considering that he was apparently speaking in Hebrew. In contrast to the dialect of the eastern Semitic language of Akkadian that was spoken in Nineveh, Jonah's northwest Semitic vernacular was not terribly close from a linguistic standpoint. [4]

It is also a little disconcerting that the many easily justifiable reasons why God would seek to condemn Nineveh were also left unspecified. After all, besides being a great metropolis, Nineveh also happened to be the capital of the Assyrian Empire—one of the most dreadful and implacable enemies that the biblical peoples would ever encounter. The Assyrians were the kind of opponents invoked in the Bible as the ultimate bogey-men—as in "The Assyrians are gonna getcha, if you don't watch out!" Consider this description of Nineveh found in the prophetic book of Nahum:

> Ah, city of crime,
> Utterly treacherous,
> Full of violence,
> Where killing never stops!
> Crack of whip
> And rattle of wheel,
> Galloping steed and bounding chariot!
> Charging horsemen
> Flashing swords,
> And glittering spears!
> Host of slain
> And heaps of corpses,
> Dead bodies without number—
> They stumble over the bodies.
> (Nah 3:1–4 NJV)

---

4. It is possible, one may suppose, that Jonah spoke to them in Aramaic, a language with which at least the Ninevites scribes would more likely have been familiar. Of course, the text does not indicate this—the quoted statement is ostensibly in Hebrew. Even granting that Jonah *might* have spoken in Aramaic, one can only wonder whether the Ninevite man-on-the-street would have grasped what he was saying.

No wonder that, when Isaiah invoked the Assyrians as the rod of the biblical God's anger (Isa 10:5), the image was designed to depict the most fearsome retribution that could ever befall the pitiful Israelites.

Of course, one might well argue that the narrative did not need to belabor the obvious in its description of Nineveh. Perhaps the impressive dimensions of its metropolitan borders were deemed to be a lesser-known bit of information worthy of more particular mention. It is just that elsewhere in the Latter Prophets, when such an utterly evil enemy of Israel was targeted in this fashion—or for that matter, when Israel and Judah were themselves the targets of prophetic condemnation—there was never any hesitation by YHWH to tick off in great detail the rationale for punishment. Indeed, the need to justify punishment by elaborately laying out all the sins of a wayward people is what you should expect to find in the Latter Prophets—and so you do indeed find, except here in the book of Jonah.

At this point in the Jonah story it looks like the prospects for his prophecy—let alone for Jonah himself—were not auspicious: We have here a city infamous for its pursuit of evil, day-in and day-out; confronted by an unknown, locally non-credentialed prophet; speaking a foreign language, representing a foreign, probably unfamiliar God; who briefly reported on behalf of this alien, unnamed deity that the city was going to be destroyed in short order for reasons left unspecified. So what should have happened? At minimum, one might have expected something akin to the reaction that Amos received when he condemned Israel and its then king Jeroboam II at Bethel (cf. Amos 7:12-13): expulsion of an unofficial, unauthorized, and unrecognized "seer" by the municipal and religious authorities[5] and, even more likely, recourse to punishment a good deal harsher than that. Even if Jonah had managed to extricate himself from Nineveh without harm, one would hardly expect that the message he delivered from YHWH would have made any significant impact on the Ninevites.

That at least would fall in line with what normally happened in the Latter Prophets. A prophet delivered YHWH's message of warning and urged all and sundry to repent and seek forgiveness before it was too late. For the most part, no one ever listened before-the-fact to such messages, nor did the targets of prophecy ever take concerted, across-the-board actions to divert and mitigate the oncoming divine wrath. Except in the case of Jonah. Jonah 3:5ff. chronicles this miraculous transformation. It begins with a simple— but no less amazing—understatement. Upon hearing Jonah's fateful words of condemnation, immediately—indeed in the very next verse—we are told, "But the people of Nineveh put their faith in God" (cf. Jonah 3:4-5). To

---

5. See Garber and Zuckerman, "Rabin Assassination," 93-94.

begin with, what makes this statement so extraordinary is not only the sudden conversion of the Ninevites into believers in the credibility of Jonah's message, but also that they seemed immediately to grasp instinctively that this previously unmentioned Instigator of Jonah's prophetic condemnation must be none other than that Hebrew-speaking *'Ĕlōhīm par excellence*, the God of the Israelites and the Judahites Himself. They must have reasoned it out: Who among all the *'ĕlōhīm* is always sending prophets out to condemn everyone in sight if not the one and only *'Ĕlōhīm*—even called *the God* (*Hā'Ĕlōhīm*) by them in Jonah 3:9 (cf. verse 10), as if to emphasize this point?

In any case, the news of Jonah's prophetic message went straight up the chain of command with a swiftness that seems especially designed to make the reader's head spin. From the highest to the lowest, from commoner to king, all the Ninevites suddenly acted in stunning unity and with remarkable efficiency to assuage God's anger through fasting, dressing in sackcloth, sitting on ash heaps, and even festooning their cattle with sackcloth—the whole *megillah* (Jonah 3:5–8). Not only that, but without further prompting the citizens of Nineveh instinctively seemed to recognize that, in order to counter and allay the message Jonah was told to "call out against" (*qĕrā' 'al*) the Great City (Jonah 1:2), they needed to "call unto God" (*wayyiqrĕ'u 'el-'Ĕlōhīm*; cf. Jonah 1:14) that from *now on* they intended—each and every one—to turn back from the practice of the evil (*hārā'āh*) they normally did and that they would further cease and desist from committing all the violence that had previously stained their hands on an everyday basis (Jonah 3:8).

The Ninevites, we are told, reasoned it out as a simple, moralistic tit-for-tat: if we make a U-turn, maybe then He will do likewise: "Who knows?" as they are recorded as saying, "Maybe the God will turn back and relent and turn back from His wrath so we do not have to perish" (Jonah 3:9)— which seems just the sort of naïve rationale you might expect from an ignorant people who couldn't tell left from right. But for any more experienced reader of the Bible, in general, and the Latter Prophets, in particular, this would seem at best a tortured logic, unsophisticated in its characterization of the standard operating procedures for YHWH. To be sure, the biblical God could and often did show mercy. But never before had He shown mercy to such an arch-enemy of the Israelite/Judahite people as the Assyrians; and, even when He had forgiven His own Chosen People, He had typically exacted a significant punishment before doing so.

On the other hand, a clever lawyer might argue that the Ninevites had some reasonable grounds for their appeal to YHWH, based upon their unique set of special circumstances. It might well have been plea-bargained on their behalf that, up until the very moment they heard Jonah's all-too-brief prophecy, no one, nowhere had ever measured up to YHWH's standard of justice necessary for repentance and forgiveness, as characterized in the Latter Prophets; indeed, even His very own Chosen People had always fallen far short of divine expectations on numerous occasions. As YHWH articulated these requirements throughout the Latter Prophets, divine justice was expected to be scrupulously pursued by an entire community, because God judged a given people as a unit, while taking far less account of the relative merits of the individuals who made up that community. From YHWH's perspective righteous action had to involve an *entire* society from top-to-bottom in order to be credible and efficacious. For example, Israel was compared to a wall measured by God for moral straightness in Amos, and if this wall, taken as a whole, turned out to be crooked, it had to be destroyed—even if this meant the destruction of some of the bricks that composed the wall, which were true and properly formed (Amos 7:7–9).[6] Unfortunately, imperfect humankind (cf. Gen 8:21) has never been able to form such a wholly righteous community—and this especially includes the Israelites and Judahites—that could be deemed to have come even remotely close to measuring up to this standard of societal justice—except, of course, the Ninevites, as described here in Jonah.

Moreover, when the Israelites/Judahites are compared to the inhabitants of Nineveh, there is even further grounds for giving the latter special consideration. After all, God's Chosen People *should have known better*; unlike the Ninevites, they had been repeatedly warned by the prophets about all this and duly punished for not listening: Compared to the Assyrians, they were well drilled in sorting out their moral right from left. In contrast, the Ninevites were given just a *single* threat from YHWH; and as soon as they heard it, they promptly took appropriate action. In this respect it is arguable that their ignorance served as their shield. How were they expected to know how to act if No One from on High had ever previously informed them about this?

There is some irony here; for it turns out that, when seen in this light, Jonah's prophecy actually may be deemed to have been fulfilled—and promptly too. Note, in this respect, that the operative verb employed in Jonah's divine message, "Just 40 days and Nineveh will be overturned" (*nehpāket*), could just as easily be read, "turned over," or perhaps even better in this context, "turned upside down."[7] From a moral standpoint, that

---

6. For further discussion of this point, see Garber and Zuckerman, "Rabin Assassination," 86–89.

7. For a discussion of this term, see, e.g., Sasson, *Jonah*, 234–6.

would seem to be exactly what occurred in Nineveh according to the book of Jonah: An inveterately wicked people, upon receiving their first prophetic message from God as imparted by Jonah, made a sudden and abrupt moral pirouette, prompting the immediate discontinuation of their normal unjust and evil practices and—presto, change-o—they transformed themselves into moral paragons. Moreover, this turn-around apparently did not take some 40 days to accomplish but rather just the seemingly brief time period encompassed by the space between two biblical verses.

And, while we are at it, we might further note that the laconic description of Nineveh in 4:3 as an *'îr gĕdōlāh lē'lōhîm* also needs to be rethought in light of Nineveh's dramatic conversion. To be sure, prior to Jonah's prophecy this was indeed a city owned by a wide variety of gods (*lē'lōhîm*), but after YHWH's message was not only proclaimed by Jonah but also instantly heeded by *all* the inhabitants of Nineveh—two-legged and four-legged alike—it became a big city owned by God (*lÊ'lōhîm*)—arguably the most Godly city the Bible has ever documented.[8] Perhaps, then, it is not so surprising that YHWH decided, in light of this unprecedented set of circumstances, to make an exception in this one case. Which further leads one to the inevitable conclusion that, among the Latter Prophets, Jonah is the *only one* who was ever completely successful, in that he delivered a divine message of doom before-the-fact that actually changed an entire people from being wicked into being righteous. Perhaps, then, it is not so unreasonable that, when YHWH noted the singular, concerted actions of the Ninevites, "when they turned around from their evil ways, God decided to forego the evil (*hārā'āh*) which He said He would do to them and did not do so" (Jonah 3:10).

Nonetheless, one has to admit that this phrasing in Jonah 3:10 sits a bit uncomfortably in a biblical text. After all, if read simply and directly, this would seem to imply that had God actually decided to punish Nineveh as originally planned, His actions might have been characterized as some sort of manifestation of evil. Translators rush to God's defense by assigning to this term in context a mitigating sense such as "punishment" (NJV), "calamity" (NRSV), "disaster" (NEB), based, one suspects, less on context and more out of a sense that *nothing* God could ever do should ever be translated, as

---

8. A good deal, of course, depends on how the text employs *'ĕlōhîm*—should it be understood as a grammatical plural, "gods," or as the Bible normally employs it, as an all encompassing plurality as singularity, "God"? Even in 3:5 (cf. verse 8) it might be argued that the Ninevites put their faith in "gods," that is, the local *'ĕlōhîm* of their Great City. It is only in 3:9, when *'ĕlōhîm* is employed with singular verbs that all ambiguity as to whether "gods" or "God" is meant can be certainly resolved. Here and above we have tried to indicate this distinction by using lower-case *'ĕlōhim* when "gods" is meant and upper-case *'Ĕlōhîm* when "God" is meant.

the text would seem to suggest here—"the evil"—even though it is qualified with the definite article, apparently to give it added emphasis—not just any old "evil" but "*the* Evil" and thus worthy of capitalization in translation, just as is the case for "*the* God."

Perhaps so. Nonetheless, the situation only seems to get murkier when Jonah 3:10 is juxtaposed to the immediately following verse (Jonah 4:1), which reads, *wayyēraʿ ʾel-yōnāh rāʿāh gĕdōlāh*. When translated in the plainest, most obvious fashion, this phrase would seem to mean, "But it was taken to be a great evil by Jonah." One might think that Jonah would have been thrilled to learn that his prophecy actually had a decisive impact and might even have transformed a dangerous enemy of his own people into the very model of a just society, devoutly respectful of his patron God YHWH and thus no longer a threat to his homeland. Not on your life. In fact, Jonah 4:1 would seem not only to belie such an assumption, but also to reiterate the view that, potentially, God and Evil are not necessarily mutually exclusive.

But there's more—the Jonah-narrative is not quite done with its use of the term "Evil" in juxtaposition with the biblical God. While in the midst of displaying a flash of anger, upon learning of the Ninevites' reformation, Jonah began what might be best described as rant in the guise of a prayer (Jonah 4:2): "See here, YHWH, is this not exactly what I predicted when I was still on my home ground? That is why I made to flee to Tarshish, since I knew You are a God 'compassionate and gracious, slow to anger and full of mercy and foregoing of Evil' (*hārāʿāh*)." First of all, the narrative seems ostensibly to be alluding to yet another instance where a point "b" has been apparently hurdled over in the narrative's mad dash to get from point "a" to "c." After all, what Jonah claimed to be a recollection is new information for the reader that, nonetheless, is presented as old news, or at least so Jonah would have us believe. Still, we almost seem to be invited to speculate: If we might have had a little suspicion in Jonah 3:4 that Jonah ad-libbed the precise wording of his short prophecy, then, might a similar sort of thing be happening here again? Could it be that Jonah was extemporaneously making up a rationale after-the-fact for his reluctance to prophesy, while trying to palm it off as something he had long before said (or at least thought)?

It should be noted that, in translating the rationale for Jonah's "I-knew-it-all-along" explanation in Jonah 4:2, we have placed Jonah's description of God in quotation marks. We have done so because this specific series of divine rubrics almost certainly reflects a well-known and clichéd phraseology found in other divine descriptions scattered throughout various biblical texts.[9] A passage in the book of Joel (cf. 2:12–14), in particular, comes so close to the wording in Jonah that one might be tempted to propose a direct dependency of the latter on the former. But more likely, both Joel and Jonah were simply relying on a common store of well-known, prayerful boilerplate that one invoked when trying to urge YHWH to show a bit of mercy. In particular, Joel's wording in 2:13, where the biblical God is described as "foregoing of Evil" (*niḥām ʿal hārāʿāh*) nearly matches the phrasing in Jonah 4:2; yet one cannot help but wonder whether the emphasis in both texts should be taken in much the same way. Surely, it would have been a lesser evil to up-end the Ninevites, who had committed well-documented atrocities on an international scale, than would have been the case to do so to YHWH's Chosen People. Granted, the Israelites and Judahites had done many bad things in their day, but nothing even close to the magnitude of what the Assyrians had done. One begins to wonder, when considering divine action (or inaction) in Joel versus Jonah, just how evil is Evil, anyway?

Finally, one further point. Just as Jonah was concluding his rant, he decided to make his own plaintive appeal to God: "Look, YHWH, why don't You just put an end to my existence, for I would be better dead than alive" (Jonah 4:3). This has the ring of something familiar; in fact, it *almost* seems right. Prophets, not to mention other aggrieved parties, on occasion seemed to appeal to the biblical God for help in arranging for them to pack it in. For example, Jeremiah not only wished to die, but cursed the day he was born (Jer 20:14–18; cf. 15:10); and using somewhat similar sentiments, so likewise did Job (3:1–24), who repeated this desire on a number of occasions throughout his book.[10] Elijah also asked God to kill him off (1 Kgs 19:2–4), as did Moses (Num 11:15).[11] So, when Jonah asked YHWH to end his life, he seemed to be fulfilling the prophetic stereotype of a despairing prophet who asks God to help him put an end to it all. But once more, when you look at this more closely, you come to realize that Jonah's desire to die does not make much sense, because he had become depressed and despairing of his life for all the wrong reasons. Jeremiah, Job, Elijah, and Moses each had plenty of good reasons for wanting to go into a divinely assisted death spiral. They all wished that God would end their respective lives because in each case their divinely orchestrated existence seemed to be failing.

The exception is Jonah. He was in despair because he had succeeded where every other prophet had failed. Thanks to the short and pithy message, which he had delivered on behalf of God, Jonah had saved Nineveh

---

9. For a convenient chart and accompanying commentary, tracking the use of the phrases that compose this stereotypical divine description, see Sasson, *Jonah*, 280–83.

10. See further the discussion in Zuckerman, *Job the Silent*, 118–35.

11. See, conveniently, the discussion in Sasson, *Jonah*, 283–6.

from impending doom and abetted God in reforming the ultimate epitome of a wicked people. If God now owned the Great City, one would have thought that not only would Jonah have been pleased with this miraculous turn-of-affairs, but he would have looked forward to being celebrated by the grateful Ninevites as the toast of the town. But instead he rejected any local adulation he might have been expected to receive, exiled himself to the city's outskirts, despaired of his life, and wished for a divinely delivered death. The only cold comfort he could manage in the heat of the day was thanks to the shade of a soon to wither plant, for which he claimed to have felt more pity, so the story concludes, than he did for the 120,000 ignorant Ninevites, not even taking into account their even dumber, sackcloth-attired cattle (Jonah 4:5–10).

When all these issues are considered, it must be admitted that Jonah is a *very strange* story to wander into the Latter Prophets, indeed. One can only wonder: How and why should an account of such an unbiblical turn-of-events get into the Bible? Of course, we shall never know the answer for sure, since the process that led to the canonization of any part of the *Tanakh*—let alone Jonah—is, by-and-large a closed book to us; and we hardly have any specific historical clues to aid us in opening it up. But perhaps, in order to address this question, we should first focus upon what might have been the intent of the book of Jonah *before* it entered the canon; or even more basically, why such a strange little book was written in the first place.

The Incredibility of Jonah

Certain points can be established with reasonable certainty. First and most probably, the Jonah narrative was never originally intended to record and reflect actual, historical events or portray the genuine message and career of a prophet after the manner of the other books of the Latter Prophets. More likely, it is better characterized as a fabulous fable. To be sure, there seems to have been a genuine prophet named Jonah ben Amittai (with the same patronymic as we find for Jonah in the Latter Prophets), who gets passing mention in 2 Kgs 14:25. Presumably, he was a prophet of some considerable clout, too, since he apparently served as part of the entourage of Jeroboam II, the then king of Israel (8th century BCE)—the same king to whom we alluded above who appeared in a cameo role in the book of Amos. In fact, Jeroboam's ability to restore the borders of Israelite territory to near their original Solomonic dimensions apparently was encouraged by a prophetic message delivered by none other than this genuine Jonah. And one may further well imagine that this historical Jonah delivered a number of telling oracles against the foreign nations from whom Jeroboam wrested back these originally Israelite lands.

Still, what we know about the history of that time and place makes any further connection of this legitimate Jonah to his namesake in the Latter Prophets seem pretty tenuous. First there is the matter of prophetic reluctance. The Kings narrative never once hints that this historical Jonah ever felt any need to go to sea in order to avoid prophesying. In fact, he is further characterized in the Kings narrative as being YHWH's "servant," indicating that he was likely a model prophet in every sense of the word. Even his patronymic, with its implicit invocation of faithfulness, implies that he was a steadfast and truthful adherent of YHWH.[12]

More to the point, there is the matter of Nineveh. There is no suggestion in any other biblical text, let alone other historical records, including the vast store of cuneiform tablets that have been recovered by excavators from Nineveh itself, that Jonah actually went there, that any sudden moral conversion of the Great City ever took place, or that the Ninevites ever paid the slightest heed to the authority of the biblical God YHWH. Quite to the contrary. The Assyrians invested considerable effort into destroying both YHWH and His people. Both the Former and the Latter Prophets track the grim progress of the Assyrian conquest of Israel in the 8th century BCE, followed by the Northern Kingdom's destruction and subjugation and then the ensuing exile of its principal leaders—evil actions so effective that, as far as the rest of the Bible is concerned, these Israelites were wiped off the face of the map and expunged from further memory. They are not known as the Ten Lost Tribes (in later legend) for nothing. As for Judah, it barely escaped a similar fate.

Furthermore, there is never any indication elsewhere in the Bible or in any other ancient record that the people of Nineveh ever had even the slightest second thoughts about the adverse actions they committed against the Israelites and Judahites. Their extensive written annals clearly boast to the contrary. To be sure, while it is a well-documented historical fact that the Assyrian Empire ultimately collapsed, one might wish to give the lion's share of the credit more to the Babylonians and their patron god Marduk rather than to YHWH. Even granting that YHWH was somehow pulling the strings somewhere in the background (as the Bible claims He did in abetting the rise of the Persian king Cyrus [cf., e.g., Isa 45:1–3]), this is never associated elsewhere in any manner, shape, or form to anything that the actual Jonah ben Amittai ever did.

---

12. See, for example, the discussion in Sasson, *Jonah*, 69.

So to reiterate, there seems to be absolutely no historical validity to the claims made in the book of Jonah. Nineveh never reformed, Jonah never took a long sea voyage or ever intoned a hymn while lodged in the belly of a big fish, nor did he actually do any of the other bizarre things this narrative claims that he did. All these elements serve notice that the book of Jonah was made up out of a string of imagined, fabulous events that were meant to be the elements of an entertaining, clever, and often even comical tall tale. Indeed, it is highly probable that its original target audience would have quickly recognized that the Jonah-narrative was patently absurd—and this, most likely, was precisely its author's intention.

Jonah in the Mirror

If the first intention of the book of Jonah was not to convey the same kind of serious, legitimate prophetic message found elsewhere in the Latter Prophets, then what was its intention? A clue indicating what the author of Jonah may have had in mind can best be found, perhaps, in the major theme that we have highlighted throughout this discussion—the constant emphasis placed on reversal. As noted above in some detail, not only was Nineveh turned upside-down, but just about every prophetic convention one encounters elsewhere in the Latter Prophets was likewise up-ended. There is one literary genre that can most easily be associated with the construction of this type of Looking Glass world where left is on the right and right is on the left: the satire and, more specifically, the satire as parody.

Not surprisingly, a number of exegetes have suggested that this is the best way to classify the book of Jonah,[13] and it may be further noted that parodic elements are not infrequently found elsewhere in the Bible and other ancient Near Eastern literature as well. In regard to this, one of us (Zuckerman) has argued, for example, that the original intention of the author of the Joban Dialogue was to use the folk-tradition centered on Job, which depicts him as a long-suffering but patient paragon (cf., e.g., Jas 5:11), as the object of a satire that turns this stereotype of the silent, God-fearing sufferer on its head for purposes of parody. In doing so, the following description of parody was suggested:

> Parody takes the common values and normal conventions of the tradition that are its object and twists them, usually turning them inside out—thereby making them look ridiculous and absurd. The surprise, even shock, of this effect compels readers to

---

13. See, for example, the discussion in Sasson, *Jonah*, 335–7.

take a closer look at these traditional values that previously they had unquestioningly accepted as normal. Because the parody displays these values from a completely different perspective, readers see them with fresh eyes and begin to grasp what is abnormal in the "normal," what is unconventional about the conventional. Usually this counterpoint is amusing because the effect of seeing traditional values in an untraditional manner is almost inevitably comic. Yet beneath the comedy there can also be something a good deal darker: at the base of parody one commonly encounters anger playing a bass harmony against the comic melody.[14]

Such a characterization works rather well when applied to the book of Jonah. Like most parodic works, it might be best described as a "literary chameleon, taking on the coloration of one thing, then another,"[15] in this particular case, the various prophetic stereotypes that it then proceeds to twist and subvert. There are a number of comic scenes presented through a text that bristles with word-plays, clever allusions, and impossible scenarios that end up, nonetheless, being presented in a matter-of-fact manner, as though they were as deadpan as Buster Keaton's face when this master comic was in the throes of his most antic stunts.

Nonetheless, it would be incorrect to assume that whoever penned the book of Jonah only desired to entertain his readers with a superficial burlesque or farce. As noted above, great satire (and in our opinion Jonah should be properly placed in that category) has a serious purpose always lurking beneath the jokes. As suggested in the description of parody cited above, its aim is to refocus the reader's attention so that the subject matter—in this case a close examination of the protocols of biblical prophecy—is viewed from a different and opposite perspective. In every other book in the Latter Prophets this focus is largely centered on three concerns: the prophet, the message the prophet delivered, and the people who received it. But we would like to suggest that the author of Jonah wished to break the reader's fixation on these issues by turning the tables, as it were, and compelling the reader to consider an aspect of prophecy she or he might otherwise have taken for granted: the nature and the motive of the One who sent these divine messengers out in the first place—YHWH Himself.[16]

Consider in this respect a genuine prophetic message, the inaugural instructions that YHWH directed Isaiah to deliver to the Judahites:

---

14. Zuckerman, *Job the Silent*, 44–45.
15. Ibid., 136.
16. For a similar argument regarding Job, see ibid., 48–49.

> Go and say to this people:
> Listen hard, but do not understand;
> Look hard, but do not grasp.
> Deaden this people's mind—
> Clog up its ears,
> And its eyes seal up,
> Lest it perceive through its eyes,
> And by its ears comprehend,
> So its mind will grasp,
> And turn and heal itself.
> (Isa 6:9–10)

When seen from the conventional perspective, this is certainly a harrowing message—all the more so because it correctly predicted the course of the original Isaiah's entire career. He did deliver hard prophetic messages, which the Judahites duly heard and saw but which they never came close to comprehending, let alone obeying. Thus, Isaiah's prophecy was vindicated, and his actions fulfilled divine intentions: His generation never really took it to heart, and as a result they received no respite. Like the wall in Amos' prophecy mentioned above, they were all but pulverized, brick-by-brick.

However, if we turn our focus away from the prophet, the message he delivered, and the people who heedlessly received it, and refocus instead—as the book of Jonah suggests that we ought to do—on the Deity who sent this message, a serious question arises. What was God's aim in orchestrating this futile and foredoomed exercise in the first place? Why send a prophet on such a pointless and self-defeating errand? Even worse, why demand that a prophet deliver the truth in so unvarnished a fashion that this only enhanced the people's tendency to turn away from such dreadful news and therefore hastened their destruction? Was this not as absurd as sending Jonah off to condemn Nineveh? Granted, the visions of Isaiah were canonized because they were both divinely inspired and correctly predicted what was to come; moreover, from a biblical standpoint, this message was ultimately mitigated by the comforting divine words delivered by his successor, Second Isaiah, beginning some 34 chapters later, to a later generation seemingly hopelessly exiled in Babylon. Nonetheless, the question remains: why did YHWH opt for such a perverse, yet for Him standard operating procedure? If He always planned to forgive His people double for their sins (Isa 40:2), why not just do so in Isaiah 6 and on behalf of an earlier generation instead of waiting and allowing His people to suffer in the interim?

In the Jonah-narrative, as we have discussed above, God is depicted as *almost* having done Evil (*hārāʿāh*) against Nineveh. He ultimately did not do so, as the text goes out of its way to state clearly (Jonah 3:10), but perhaps we may wish to show more sympathy to Jonah's reaction to God's inaction, which the prophet takes to be a great Evil, in and of itself. After all the *real* Nineveh never showed anyone any mercy, as would have been painfully common knowledge to Jonah's original ancient audience. Why then could YHWH *ever* forgive them and forego punishment while continuing to inflict *hārāʿāh* on His own Chosen People? These are the questions that flash beneath the surface of the book of Jonah, and its author's intention is to compel his ancient readers to consider them in the guise of an ostensibly amusing, even ridiculous fable that, nonetheless, has a very serious, parodic agenda.

There is no certain evidence that allows us to date the book of Jonah; conceivably it could be dated to the pre-exilic, exilic or post-exilic periods, although the latter two time-frames seem far more likely than the former.[17] Nor do we know enough about the actual Jonah ben Amittai to propose a rationale why the author of the Bible's Jonah-narrative singled-out and expropriated this figure to be the butt of his satire. Still, we can guess that the author of Jonah and the target audience, at whom he originally aimed his satire, still had the bitter taste of defeat and humiliation in their collective mouths due to the heavy toll that Assyrians and/or their conquering successors in Babylon had exacted on Israel and Judah. Like Jonah awaiting the destruction of Nineveh that never came, they shared a deep and abiding anger bordering on despair, as they sat by the rivers of Babylon (Ps 137:1) or other places of exile and remembered what used to be. And they must have wondered when they read the book of Jonah: why would God forego doing Evil to the Ninevites and yet let so much Evil befall those He claimed to love more than all the other nations on the earth? Like Jonah, whose plant God made to grow and then just as quickly caused to perish (Jonah 4:6ff), they must have wished to question why God's seemingly whimsical actions gave and then all too quickly withdrew[18] the shelter His pitiable people needed to survive? To such as these, perhaps Jonah might well have served as an exasperated spokesman—not so much a prophet sent from

---

17. For a survey of the issues, see conveniently the discussion in Sasson, *Jonah*, 26–28.

18. That the agent of the destruction of the plant is a worm suggests its own irony. The Assyrians were God's agents in the destruction of Israel: How appropriate that the true contempt that the author of Jonah held for Nineveh should be revealed by this writer in implicitly comparing them to this lowest form of life.

God but—appropriately—the reverse: an advocate of the people delivering an all too human message back to YHWH.

Double Reverse: From Out to In

So such a rationale may help us explain how Jonah became the odd prophet out, but clearly, as his presence deep in the heart of the Former Prophets well attests, he did not stay that way for very long. So this leads us to the next question we may wish to address: How did Jonah become the odd prophet *in*? In order for us to start to consider this, it may be helpful to take into account the unintended consequences that sometimes occur when an unsophisticated audience reads or hears a particularly clever parody. One such consequence is what may be termed the "Ozymandias Effect" after the sonnet by Percy Shelley. This poem ironically depicts a shattered, long neglected statue of the self-styled "king of kings" Ozymandias, whose inscription urged its readers to "Look on my works . . . and despair!" Shelley went on to note, employing one of the finer alliterative phrases in English literature, "Nothing besides remains: Round the decay / Of that colossal wreck, boundless and bare, / The lone and level sands stretch far away." Of interest to us, however, is an earlier line in which Shelley described the subtle relationship between the sculptor and the haughty despot who was his patron. In the sculptor's depiction of Ozymandias with "frown / And wrinkled lip and sneer of cold command," the poet noted that the artist deeply understood the "passions" of this long-dead king, which Shelley characterized by the trenchant phrase: "The hand that mock'd them and the heart that fed."

The suggestion of mockery here indicates that the sculptor deliberately desired to create an image less for the purposes of aggrandizement and praise and more for the purpose of satire. That is, the artist used all his talent and skill to distort and twist the physical characteristics which he "stamp'd on these lifeless things" in order to create a parody of the *real* king's features that would make manifest to any clever viewer all the shallow pretensions of Ozymandias. Yet it was these very distortions that appealed to the king's vanity. Ozymandias' heart fed deeply when he beheld the super-real image, and he saw in it the very essence of who he *really* was, while being completely blind to the irony that motivated the artist's actual intentions.[19]

This is a case of what may be termed "shorn-away satire" or, perhaps better, "pared-down parody," in which two elements come into play. On the one hand, the consummate skill invested by the artist in such a clever, ironic

---

19. For an earlier discussion of the "Ozymandias Effect" as applied in the book of Job, see Zuckerman, *Job the Silent*, 60–61.

work is what attracts the attention of an audience in the first place. But some members of this audience—perhaps even most of them—are blind and deaf when it comes to grasping the finer points of the underlying joke. Instead, they strip away all the irony and take the absurd, super-reality as the genuine article. They are like those who dress-up in mock-Victorian finery in order to celebrate an "Authentic Charles Dickens Christmas," but who tune out the serious underpinnings of Dickens' *A Christmas Carol*, whose justifiably famous but intentionally horrific features attracted their attention in the first place.

Still, the Ozymandias Effect does not usually come into play unless there are further powerful factors that motivate a given audience to refuse to see what otherwise should be plain for them to see. Such a motivation in the aftermath of the destruction of Israel and the exile of Judah is not hard to find, especially in light of the predominantly harsh messages sent by YHWH to his Chosen People in the Latter Prophets. God made it all too abundantly clear: He demanded and continues to demand communal justice—which was and remains an impossible standard for the exilic and post-exilic Jews or, for that matter, any other human society ever to fulfill. Like Amos' wall, they were and will always remain seriously awry. For this reason, they merited and received appropriate punishment from their angry and disappointed God. And logically there should be no respite in the future since they were no better than they had been in the past. From the standpoint of divinely measured justice, nothing had really changed or was ever likely to change. They had been doomed in the past and should be foredoomed in the present and future.

Fortunately, the prophets and their audience ultimately recognized that the biblical God offered an avenue of escape from this conundrum: What the people could not do for themselves God was willing to do on their behalf by forgiving their inveterate injustices and forbearing from exacting well-deserved punishment. So there was a faint glimmer of hope, especially in consideration of YHWH's enduring promise, first made to the patriarchs, that He would never completely abandon them or their descendants, no matter what they did. Thus, for example, appended to the end of the otherwise unremittingly harsh and negative pre-exilic prophecy of Amos there is a later oracle of reassurance, restoration and forgiveness (Amos 9:14–15);[20] likewise, a usually despairing book of Jeremiah records the vision of a day to come when a divinely transformed covenant will be ingrained into the very make-up of the people (Jer 31:13–34) or where the former things

---

20. See Garber and Zuckerman, "Rabin Assassination," 96–97.

communicated to the original Isaiah will be superseded by the latter things God revealed to his successor in the Babylonian Exile (e.g., Isa 43:18–19).

Perhaps it is not all that surprising that the various later arbiters of what was sacred enough ultimately to be included in the *Tanakh* looked for a further precedent that showed that YHWH was truly capable of offering forgiveness and could further forego punishment—even if that forgiveness might seem totally unmerited and this punishment was all too richly deserved. For them, the book of Jonah, especially when shorn of any hint of irony, could serve an invaluable role. For when read in a simple, but superficial manner, it seemed to give both hope and reassurance through a telling comparison: If a people as wicked and as ignorant as the Ninevites could find a way to be completely and utterly reformed when they heard the biblical God's message and if God could forego punishment even to *them*, not to mention their pitiful cattle, then surely there may be a chance for *us*.

When the other Latter Prophets delivered messages of assurance that God would forget His people's many transgressions and forgive them, these divine messengers were speaking about a promise that would be fulfilled sometime in the unspecified future. But the great thing about the book of Jonah, when read as a shorn-satire taken as a record of something that *really happened*, is that it documented an extreme case of divine forgiveness that had *already* occurred and was *already* on the record. It could therefore be employed as a kind of reminder of this, not only to the people but to YHWH: You did this once before, so it would appear that You are quite capable of doing so again.

It is not without significance that in the much later rabbinic discussion of the book of Jonah, there is little, if any, investment in its interpretation as a satire. A good deal of interpretive energy is spent on a wide range of matters, to be sure, but the emphasis is consistently placed on viewing Jonah as a genuine prophet who participated in real events. For example, as noted above, he is equated without the slightest hesitation with the "real" Jonah ben Amittai, who prophesied during the reign of Jeroboam II. The rabbinical spin on why this otherwise exemplary prophet tried to escape the divine mission was that he ran off, not out personal reluctance, but rather for reasons of piety. Jonah, it was noted, was understandably concerned lest the Ninevites, whom he divined were on the point of repenting (*qĕrôbê tĕšûbâh*), might therefore undermine God's credibility and thus suggest that God is a false God or that His Shekinah (that is, His Holy Presence) could or should not be found outside of the Holy Land (Pirqe de-Rabbi Eliezer, 10). These are significant theological issues upon which the early rabbis brooded, but they *only* made credible sense if the story was taken at face value.

Perhaps the most significant indication of the importance the story of Jonah ultimately has developed in Judaism is the decision to include a recitation of the book as the *Haftarah* at the *Minḥah* (afternoon) service in the traditional Yom Kippur liturgy, due to its story serving as proof of God's willingness to forgive those who repent. We may have no way of knowing who decided on this or when the decision was made, but the overall rabbinic motivation would seem clear enough. The time of *Minḥah* is very conducive of prayers to be heard as day is coming to an end. B. Meg. 31a reflects the view that *Maftir Yona* depicts the concept of repentance so starkly and completely that it can stir hearers to repent of their ways and even modify their conduct.[21]

Like the Ninevites once did, the entire Jewish community annually gathers as a unit, from highest to lowest, on the Day of Atonement to acknowledge all their missteps and confess to the rampant injustice that inevitably continues to persist within their community. And like the Ninevites, they also fast, but they go a step further than the inhabitants of the Great City ever did. Where the latter only tore their garments and put on sackcloth and similarly, but with absurd ignorance, dressed their cattle in like fashion, the Jewish community at Yom Kippur heeds the plea found in Joel to "rend your hearts and not your garments" (Joel 2:8). It is in this context that the book of Jonah is read as a two-way reminder of the precedent it has established—all the more important because it is a precedent sanctioned by the sacredness and authority of a canonized scripture embedded in the center of the Latter Prophets. On the one hand, Jonah reminds the Jewish community of God's enduring commitment to forgiveness, and on the other it further serves as a renewal of the appeal to YHWH, so the biblical Deity will not forget His people but will continue to show mercy unto them even as He did, for far less reason, on behalf of the Ninevites. To drive this point home, directly upon the conclusion of the reading of Jonah, the text of Mic 7:18–20 is quoted, which praises the biblical God as incomparable to the other *'ĕlōhīm* due to His capacity to be "forgiving of iniquity and remitting transgression." Like Pharaoh's horses and riders, God will hurl the people's sins into the depths of the sea and turn back from His anger in order to comfort them.

And there may be a final implication. If one takes the book of Jonah as pared-down parody that therefore presents a *genuine* account of the actions of the Ninevites, it would seem clear that their repentance must have been

---

21. M. Ta'an. 2:1 relates that on fast days the elder of the congregation used to address the worshippers in the words of admonition: "Brethren, it is not written of the men of Nineveh that God saw their sackcloth and their fasting, but that *God saw what they were doing and how they turned from their evil way*" (Jonah 3:10).

short-lived. In fact, as the biblical accounts elsewhere further attest, the Assyrians must have soon gone right back to their ways of evil, forgot about their promises to YHWH and for this reason were duly punished thereafter. But if the Ninevites soon forgot, the annual recitation of the book of Jonah at Yom Kippur serves notice that the Jewish community will never forget. They may still be as imperfect and as unjust as they have always been, but they are at least self-aware and capable of recognizing right from left. Should they ever waver in this, they can always turn back to the book of Jonah, which serves as an enduring reminder of the miraculous and merciful things God is always capable of doing.

In like manner, the interpretation of Jonah as a pared-away parody apparently made a smooth transition from the Jewish to the Christian canon. Indeed, if anything, the story-line of Jonah, when taken without a hint of irony, arguably served to address Christian concerns even better than it did the concerns of Jews. This is due to the early Christian Church's capability of identifying far more easily with the Ninevites, as presented in the book of Jonah, than Jews were ever capable of doing. This is already indicated in the gospel of Matthew with the attributed comment of Jesus regarding the "sign of Jonah" (Matt 12:38–41). When Pharisaic members of his contemporary Jewish community challenged Jesus by asking for a "sign" that would serve to confirm his credibility, Jesus responded contemptuously by branding them "a wicked and adulterous generation." In doing so, he implicitly took the traditional prophetic stance that the measure of the entire Jewish community of his time and place remained deeply out of whack, as it has always been flawed, due to its tolerance of injustice, day-after-day, and its adulterous pursuit of other gods. Besides this, Jesus seems to have reserved a special place in Hell for the Pharisees, due to what he took to be their obsessions with practice over focus on the basics necessary for a proper relationship with God.

Of course, one may note that the Ninevites, owned, as they originally were, by many 'ĕlōhîm, were hardly better than the Jews and indeed ought to have been considered a good deal worse. Still, Christians had an opportunity to put a different spin on the comparison between the Ninevites and the Jews—one that the Jewish community could and would never allow. Jesus declared, "The men of Nineveh will stand up at the judgment with this generation and condemn it; for they repented at the preaching of Jonah, and now something greater than Jonah is here" (Matt 12:41 RSV). Jesus wished to reaffirm the prophetic standards, noted above, and that the Jewish community *should have known and heeded* God's message but never managed to do so, despite repeated warnings and punishments. But the ignorant Ninevites needed only one "sign" to recognize the truth and to act accordingly in their naïve ignorance with repentance and thus to become a people truly owned by the singular 'Ĕlōhīm. The implication to early Christians was obvious. They were the first century equivalents of the simple-minded but sincere Ninevites. Because most Christians were non-Jewish converts, they too were unschooled in the arcane practices and customs followed by the more sophisticated Pharisees and their ilk. They freely accepted the proposition that they had hardly begun to distinguish their left from their right. But like the Ninevite pagans, at first owned by many gods, they just ignored the past and its tangle of rabbinic customs and requirements and embraced a new sign which pointed out the way for them: All they really needed to do was to accept the one 'Ĕlōhīm as their Lord and Master through the intercession of His Son. Ignorant they might be, but at the time of final reckoning it would be these simple-minded Christians who would be redeemed, while the Jews, mired in the past and focused more on form rather than substance, would be condemned. The "Ozymandias Effect" could thus act with full force on such Christians, anxious to carve out their own sacred space at the expense of the Jews, using the book of Jonah as their guide. It gave them a rationale for deeming themselves the *genuine* chosen ones. After all, if God could save such great and ignorant sinners as the Ninevites, He could certainly do that much and more for them as well.

Odd Theology In and Out

We have taken the position in this study that the most "obvious" approach to the reading of Jonah is to view it as a parodic satire that makes mockery of standard prophetic conventions in order to raise serious questions about the intentions of the biblical God as the Instigator of these divine messages. Yet, as we have further noted, from a theological perspective, both Jews and Christians have willfully refused to accept the satirical intent of Jonah's author and, by moving the book into the sacred context of the Bible, have employed it instead to address concerns focused on divine forgiveness. First Jews and then Christians have used the book as a means of comparing themselves to the Ninevites in order to advance each of their respective standings before God and in each instance to make a case for their special relationship to the Deity.[22]

But there is a final point to consider. If the satirical interpretation is the "obvious" approach, how come it took so long for anyone to notice this?[23]

---

22. For a similar argument regarding the book of Job, see Zuckerman, *Job the Silent*, 175–9.

23. One of the earliest modern thinkers to designate Jonah as a satirical work was

Almost certainly, part of the reason this proves to be so is due to the aura of sacredness that comes to any piece of literature once it has been subsumed into the Bible. On being granted this unique status, such a book will soon attract interpretive hedges,[24] intended to justify its presence within the Holy Canon. One sees this in Jonah, for example, in the way that commentators and translators handle "Evil" (*hārā'āh*) in provocative association with YHWH, as discussed above, to connote any sort of punishment or disaster, but to avoid at all costs the "obvious" sense of the term.

Of course, this is not the only instance of an odd biblical book being rethought and hedged once it has been granted canonical status. Thus, Song of Songs became a metaphorical depiction of God's love for His Chosen People (or Christ's love for the Church) rather than what it obviously is: a series of lyrics celebrating passionate and carnal love; and Job was perceived as a model of patience, even though a reading beyond chapter two well demonstrates that he was obviously the most impatient of men due to the divine attack (even though mitigated by the buffer of Satan) that destroyed everything except his life;[25] and Ecclesiastes was depicted as being the slightly cynical collected thoughts of a wise but aging Solomon—sentiments worthy of being read as an academic exercise and out of respect for so wise a man, but not to be taken to heart since their obvious interpretation is to depict a Deity who could care less about the Jews or anyone else for that matter. In all these instances, the obvious intent of the original authors has been stripped off and hedged around—yet at the same time these challenging themes are still there to be tacitly engaged. Thus, if one wishes to consider the premise that the biblical God is indifferent, one may do so in Qoheleth;[26] if one wishes to consider divinely inflicted suffering without moral justification, one may turn to Job; if one wishes to celebrate the erotic aspects of love, one may indulge in Song of Songs[27]—and if one wishes to ponder what is the point of delivering futile prophetic messages, Jonah is there as the book that turns the tables on YHWH. Granted, the concepts emphasized in these books challenge more traditional biblical theology, but they can nonetheless be more safely engaged because this is being done in a sacred context. An interpreter can thus seriously consider a theologically

---

Thomas Paine (1795) in his treatise *The Age of Reason*. See *Selected Writings of Thomas Paine*, 466ff.

24. See Garber and Zuckerman, "Rabin Assasination," 79–80.
25. As discussed in Zuckerman, *Job the Silent*, esp. 13–15.
26. See the discussion in ibid., 81–84.
27. Ibid., 53–58.

outlying concept simply because it has been transported through a sacred Looking Glass.

Nonetheless, we should not forget that all of these "strange" biblical books were composed well before their aura of sacredness could skew and blur the perceptions of their intended audiences. By the same token, in this increasingly secularized modern world, the aura of biblical sacredness has dramatically dimmed, allowing us with greater freedom to apply analytical modes of criticism that make it far easier for us to see the "obvious" that was always there. Moreover, the events that have shaped the modern world in the twentieth and twenty-first centuries have further served to sharpen a modern critic's vision—especially when one begins to measure a biblical book like Jonah against them.

Indeed, when we begin to make modern analogies to the correspondences in the book of Jonah, the recent Evil most obviously comparable to the Ninevites is manifest in the Nazis and their regime. From a modern perspective, they are the Assyrian Empire on steroids. It does not take too much effort to imagine a hypothetical satirical scenario—if anything, even more absurd than sending Jonah to Nineveh: Suppose God had sent a prophetic messenger to Berlin at the height of the Nazi Evil, as embodied in the Shoah, warning the Third Reich of dire consequences if this erstwhile Master Race did not cease and desist its evil practices at once? And suppose the Nazis had actually listened, festooned not only themselves but their Tiger Tanks with sackcloth, and sat upon the ash heaps from their gas chambers and furnaces and appealed to God to forego the Evil that He had planned for them? And finally, imagine that God, as He did with Nineveh, decided to recognize this change in attitude so that they were forgiven and did not perish.

Despite being absurd, the theological ramifications of this notion are troubling. No rational person would benignly accept forgiveness as a righteous, divine action in such a case; indeed, we might well despair and consider the foregoing of Nazi punishment a great Evil just as Jonah did at Nineveh and, like him, we might prefer to die rather than witness it taking place. Such a cutting-edge was probably behind the writing of Jonah in the first place—when the Assyrians were a recent reality rather than a distant memory, just as the Nazis are for us today. When one replaces the Ninevites with storm-troopers, a modern eye can see more clearly what the author of Jonah may have originally intended.

Jewish tradition has a way of addressing such an extreme case of forgiveness. From the rabbincal perspective this is more a human-to-human issue than it is a concern between God and humankind. Thus, the Sages interpret "atonement for you . . . that you may be clean from all your sins before [meaning toward] the Lord" (Lev 16:30) to mean that God can only grant forgiveness of sins which are directed against Heaven but does not have the power to forgive sins committed towards one's neighbor. In this respect, Yom Kippur atones for sins "between man and God" only. For the sins "between man and his fellow," one must satisfy one's fellow-human first and then request forgiveness.[28] The process is an intricate direct encounter between perpetrator and victim. Genuine remorse, abstention from further offending action, and total restitution on the side of the guilty are prerequisites; and the injured is obligated to provide forgiveness no later than the third request.[29] God cannot intervene between perpetrator and victim. Only the injured party can forgive. But there is a dramatic exception to this if the victim is murdered and hence is no longer there to grant forgiveness. The only way to forgive murder in Judaism is not to murder.[30] On such grounds, God would seem to have overextended His authority in Jonah, and also on such grounds it must follow that there never should be complete forgiveness from God for those who perpetrated the murder of millions. The Nuremburg trials and later the trial of Adolf Eichmann serve as modern testimonies that simply underscore this point.

Imagining the Nazis as morally reformed Ninevites is an utter fantasy, of course, just as was the case for the original Ninevites when they were trivialized in the book of Jonah. But in the pre- and post-Shoah modern world, there have been—and there will continue to be—atrocities that rise to the same level and that don't ever seem to go away in Armenia, Rwanda, Iraq, Syria, and Pakistan, just to name a few examples that easily spring to mind—not to mention places far closer to home, wherever home may be. The horrors committed by the perpetrators of violence against their fellow humans never seem to cease nor are they something that can be ignored. But can they ever be forgivable? Desmond Tutu, in his attempt to bring together South Africa in a post-Apartheid era, has made a case for forgiveness—not for the sake of the agents of violence but rather for the peace-of-mind of the victims. In leading and establishing his "Truth and Reconciliation Commission" he argued:

> To forgive is not just to be altruistic. It is the best form of self-interest. It is also a process that does not exclude hatred and anger. These emotions are all part of being human. You should never hate yourself for hating others who do terrible things: the

---

28. b.Yoma 85b.
29. Shulḥan ʿArukh, ʾOraḥ Ḥayyim 606:1.
30. Explicitly stated in the Decalogue, *lōʾ tirṣaḥ*, "you shall not murder." See Exod 20:13 and Deut 5:17.

depth of your love is shown by the extent of your anger. However, when I talk of forgiveness I mean the belief that you can come out the other side a better person. A better person than the one being consumed by anger and hatred. Remaining in that state locks you in a state of victimhood, making you almost dependent on the perpetrator. If you can find it in yourself to forgive then you are no longer chained to the perpetrator. You can move on, and you can even help the perpetrator to become a better person too.[31]

One wishes to agree, and yet it is undoubtedly an insurmountable task for some to follow this heart-felt advice. The late Elie Wiesel, as spokesman for the Holocaust generation, found the only meaningful response to this kind of unforgivable sin is silence.[32]

Such issues remain at the core of Jonah, which, as we have noted from the outset, is a book that places an emphasis on reversals. In this respect it also serves as a modern mirror that flips past and present, and always makes one wonder the extent to which divine and human forgiveness is ever possible and, if possible, even appropriate.

BIBLIOGRAPHY

Garber, Zev, and Bruce Zuckerman. "The Rabin Assassination in the Long View and the Short View: Biblical Radicalism in a Modern Context." *Hakirah, A Journal of Jewish & Ethnic Studies* 1 (2003) 69–88. Revised in Zev Garber and Bruce Zuckerman. *Double Takes: Rethinking Issues of Modern Judaism in Ancient Contexts*, 79–104. Studies in the Shoah 26. Lanham, MD: University Press of America, 2004.

———. "Why Do We Call the Holocaust 'The Holocaust'? An Inquiry into the Psychology of Labels." In *Double Takes: Rethinking Issues of Modern Judaism in Ancient Contexts*, 3–30. Studies in the Shoah 26. Lanham, MD: University Press of America, 2004.

Paine, Thomas, *The Age of Reason* (1795). In *Selected Writings of Thomas Paine*. Edited by Ian Shapiro and Jane E. Calvert. New Haven: Yale University Press, 2014.

Sasson, Jack M. *Jonah*. AB 24B. New York: Doubleday, 1990.

Zuckerman, Bruce. *Job the Silent: A Study in Biblical Counterpoint*. New York: Oxford University Press, 1991.

---

31. http://theforgivenessproject.com/stories/desmond-tutu-south-africa/. We are grateful to our colleague Donald Miller for drawing this to our attention.

32. See Garber and Zuckerman, "Why Do We Call," 11.

11

Canon, Codex, and the Printing Press

Frederick E. Greenspahn

FLORIDA ATLANTIC UNIVERSITY

Several recent books bear titles that include the words "How the Bible Became..."[1] Although these books focus on different topics, ranging from the commitment of Israelite traditions to writing to the contents of individual biblical books and their ascription of authority, their titles all presume that the Bible itself was a product of antiquity, whether the Persian period or the years when Christianity and rabbinic Judaism took shape under Greco-Roman domination.[2] That assumption has led not only to various descriptions of the history of canonization, but also to more recent descriptions of Judaism and Christianity as resting on or, more colorfully, being divided by a "common Scripture."[3] For example, the "Statement on Christians and Christianity" issued by a group of prominent Jewish figures in the year 2000 stated that "Jews and Christians seek authority from the same book—the

---

1. E.g., Hall, *How the Bible Became A Book*; Isbell, *God's Scribes: How the Bible Became the Bible*; Schniedewind, *How the Bible Became a Book, The Textualization of Ancient Israel*; Satlow, *How the Bible Became Holy*. Cf. Miller, *How the Bible Came to Be: Exploring the Narrative and Message*; Smith, *How the Bible Was Built*; Berman, *Created Equal, How the Bible Broke with Ancient Political Thought*; Shinan and Zakovitch, *From Gods to God, How the Bible Suppressed or Changed Ancient Myths and Legends*.

2. Cf. Lemche, "The Old Testament—A Hellenistic Book?"

3. Biale, *Blood and Belief*, 3; Kugel, *The Bible as It Was*, 47.

Bible (what Jews call 'Tanakh' and Christians call the 'Old Testament')."[4] That sentiment echoed Abraham Lincoln's second inaugural address, which sought to bring the Northern and Southern states together by observing that "Both read the same Bible and pray to the same God."[5]

Lincoln's words may have been appropriate for the overwhelmingly Protestant America of 1865, but they overlook the fact that the Roman Catholic Old Testament includes books that are not accepted by Protestants, not to mention the canons of various Eastern churches which recognize still more.[6] Taking Jewish tradition into account makes matters even more complex.

The basis for this diversity is that, like many cultural phenomena, "the Bible" as we know it today was not created at any one time or place—not Yavneh, not Nicaea, not Trent—but over centuries.[7] Even the process of defining its contents was not entirely straightforward, as the evidence from Qumran alongside the New Testament's quotation of Enoch and the rabbis' occasional citations from Ben Sira and *Megillat Ta'anit* makes clear.[8] So, too, the establishment of an authoritative text, whether Jews' masoretic text or the Greek and Latin editions used by Christians, was a matter of evolution rather than election. And, as we shall see, determining definitive arrangements, which are often cited as the distinguishing features of Christian and Jewish editions, actually took far longer than is usually recognized.

To be sure, the structure of Jewish and Christian editions seems to convey meaning. Thus, the second and the third sections of the Jewish Bible refer to *torah* in their opening chapters,[9] and the book of Chronicles closes with the report of Cyrus' decree permitting the Judeans to return to their homeland (2 Chr 36:22–23), an arrangement sometimes thought to be reflected in the gospels' reference to the deaths of Cain and Zechariah (Matt 23:35 and Luke 11:51).[10] Analogously, modern Christian Old Testaments

---

4. "Dabru Emet," *The New York Times*, September 10, 2000.

5. Basler, *Collected Writings of Abraham Lincoln*, 8:333.

6. Cf. Rüger, "Extent of the Old Testament Canon," 303–6; McDonald, *Forgotten Scriptures*, 95–96 and 224 nn.6–9; and Cowley, "Biblical Canon of the Ethiopian Orthodox Church," 318–23.

7. Cf. Gould, "Creation Myths of Cooperstown," 14–24.

8. Cf. Jude 14–15; m. Ta'an. 2:8; m. 'Abot 4:4; y. Ber. 7:2, 11b; y. Naz. 5:5, 54b; b. Nid. 16b; b. Šabb. 11a; b. 'Erub. 54a, b. Ḥag. 13a; b. Yebam. 63b; b. Ketub. 110b; b. B. Qam. 92b; b. B. Bat. 98b; b. Sanh. 100b; Kallah Rab. 3:4 and 7.

9. Josh 1:7–8 and Ps 1:2; the Pentateuch might be included, since rabbinic tradition connects the word rēʾšît in Gen 1:1 with Torah (Gen. Rab. 1:1). It is a pleasure to ackowledge Michael Carasik for having directed me to Alexander Rofé, "Devotion to Torah-Study," 625–6.

10. Cf. Peels, "Blood 'from Abel to Zechariah,'" 586–94. The reference to Zechariah

close with Malachi's statement that Elijah will herald the future Day of the Lord (3:23, ET 4:5), which seems to prepare readers for the New Testament's presentation of Jesus as the fulfillment of ancient prophecy. However, these contemporary facts need not be ancient nor, therefore, necessarily evidence of the history of the canonization process.

In fact, among Christian communions, only Protestant and Catholic editions of the Old Testament end with Malachi.[11] Moreover, the 4th-century Codex Vaticanus places the Minor Prophets ahead of Isaiah, Jeremiah, and Ezekiel.[12] On the Jewish side, both the 10th-century Aleppo Codex and the 11th-century Leningrad Codex put Chronicles at the beginning of the Writings, while the Babylonian Talmud opens that section with Ruth rather than Psalms.[13] Medieval Jewish manuscripts are equally diverse; some begin the Writings with Chronicles and others with Psalms. Likewise, Esther sometimes appears at the end of the Writings, a position elsewhere given to Lamentations, with great variety as to the intermediate sequence of books in that section.[14] Still other manuscripts place the Five Scrolls after the Pentateuch, presumably because of their liturgical use on major holidays.[15]

Early Christian editions are no more uniform than their Jewish counterparts. Neither Alexandrinus nor Sinaiticus ends its Old Testament with the prophets, but with the poetic and didactic books, albeit while placing Ruth, Chronicles, Ezra, and Nehemiah alongside related books in the Former Prophets.

The order of the Latter Prophets is also subject to significant variation. Although Isaiah appears first in the Leningrad and Aleppo codices (as in all three ancient Greek codices),[16] the Babylonian Talmud lists it after Jeremiah and Ezekiel. Even the Minor Prophets, though often identified collectively as "the twelve,"[17] are not uniformly arranged. Hosea routinely appears first;

---

is widely taken as an allusion to 2 Chr 24:20–22.

11. E.g., the Ethiopian Church put Ben Sira, Pseudo-Josephus, Jubilees, and 1 Enoch after the prophetic corpus; cf. McDonald, *Origin of the Bible*, 117–8.

12. Beckwith, *The Old Testament of the New Testament Church*, 193–4.

13. b. B. Bat. 14b. Jerome lists Job first, followed by Psalms, Proverbs, Qohelet, Canticles, Daniel, Chronicles, Ezra, and Esther (Preface to Samuel-Kings, *PL* 28:599). 'Adat Devorim cites this as a distinguishing feature between Palestinian and Babylonian editions, cf. Ginsburg, *Introduction to the Massoretic-Critical Edition*, 3, n. 1.

14. Cf. Beckwith, *The Old Testament of the New Testament Church*, 452–64.

15. Ginsburg, *Introduction to the Massoretico-Critical Edition*, 4.

16. Elliott, "Manuscripts, The Codex and the Canon," 116, speculates that, like the Pauline epistles, they may be arranged according to length.

17. The first explicit reference is Melito's statement "the 12 in 1 book" (*ton dōdeka en monobiblō*, Eusebius, *Ecclesiastical History* 4.xxvi.4 (LCL 1:392–3); cf. Jerome, "Duodecim Prophetae in unius voluminis" (Epistle 53:8, *PL* 22:546 and "Preface to the XII,"

however, Hebrew texts (and modern Christian editions, though widely said to reflect the Greek arrangement) follow it with Joel, Amos, Obadiah, Jonah, and then Micah, while Vaticanus and Alexandrinus put Amos and Micah ahead of the others.[18] It has even been suggested that one Qumran manuscript (4QXII[a], mid-2nd century BCE) places Jonah at the end.[19]

In sum, the so-called "normative" Jewish sequence of both the Prophets and the Writings isn't attested until the late 15th- and early 16th-century printed Bibles, while today's "standard" Christian arrangement differs from all three of the oldest Greek codices, even in the placement of the prophetic books and the order of the Minor Prophets. There is simply no basis for the claim that contemporary arrangements—whether Christian or Jewish—are ancient, much less theologically necessary.

That shouldn't be surprising. As has been widely noted, the idea of a proper order would have been meaningless for most of Jewish and Christian history, during which "the Bible" was, as James Barr put it, "not a volume one could hold in the hand, but a cupboard or chest with pigeonholes, or a room or cave with a lot of individual scrolls."[20] Indeed, the various terms with which Jewish tradition identifies these works—*tôrâ, miqrā', sĕpārîm,* and *kitbê qĕdeš*—describe genres more than collections.[21] Even the discrete groups into which these books are divided, such as *nĕbî'îm* and *kĕtûbîm*, are categories, not fixed corpora, much less ordered arrangements.[22]

To be sure, the evidence from Qumran does show that several books, most often the Pentateuch and the Minor Prophets, were sometimes combined.[23] However, it was the adoption of the codex that made it practical to

---

PL 28:1071), though Theodore of Mopsuestia describes them as separate books written together (at Ps 39:8b, Devreesse, *Le Commentaire de Théodore de Mopsueste sur les Psaumes [I–LXXX]*, 248). Sir 49:10 and Acts 7:42–43 refer to prophetic figures, not necessarily their books.

18. So too, presumably, Codex Sinaiticus, which is lacking Amos and Micah; this is continued in Orthodox Bibles; cf. McDonald, *The Origin of the Bible*, 117–8. This order is first attested in ḤevXIIgr (mid-1st-century BCE), while the masoretic sequence is first found at Murabba'at (2nd-century CE); cf. Jones, *Formation of the Book of the Twelve*, 4–5.

19. Fuller, "The Twelve," 221; but see Guillaume, "The Unlikely Malachi-Jonah Sequence."

20. Barr, *Holy Scripture*, 57. Cf. Sarna, "Order of the Books," 408; and Smith, *Palestinian Parties and Politics*, 173 n. 284.

21. Leiman, *Canonization of Hebrew Scripture*, 57; cf. Aristeas 155 (*graphēs*, but *nomos* in §168).

22. Cf. Beecher, "Alleged Triple Canon," 127–8.

23. According to Tov, *Revised Lists of the Texts from the Judaean Desert*, 113–7, 4Q365 includes all 5 books of the Pentateuch; 4Q364 includes all but Leviticus; 4Q366 includes Exodus, Numbers, and Deuteronomy; 4Q1, 4Q11, and 4Q158 include Genesis

include the entire panoply of sacred writings in a single volume.[24] Although Christians adopted that format long before it was accepted by Jews, it took several centuries before codices could accommodate the entire corpus of scriptural works.[25] Even then, it is not clear that these codices, or their 10th- and 11th-century Jewish successors, were what we understand a Bible to be—namely, complete and exhaustive collections of divinely inspired writings. The great Christian codices of the 4th and 5th centuries included works, such as the Epistle of Barnabas, Clement, and the Shepherd of Hermas, that were not part of the eventual Christian canon, while sometimes omitting accepted books like Maccabees that were.[26] Rather, they appear to have been anthologies of sacred works or possibly scribal *tours de force*. Thus the references to *ta biblia*, *bibliotheca*, or, in Jewish communities, *ěśrîm w'arba'* ("the 24"), all of which suggest collections rather than a single book as *the* Bible is often considered today.[27]

The fact that ancient writers compiled lists of sacred works does not undermine that point, nor does their following standard patterns reflect a

---

and Exodus; 4Q17 includes Exodus and Leviticus; 1Q3 includes Leviticus and Numbers. Kraft, "What is 'Bible'?," 107–8, n. 10, identifies early Greek codices with multiple Old Testament books as P. Baden 56 (late 2nd-century CE—Exodus and Deuteronomy), P. Beatty 6 (early 3rd—Numbers and Deuteronomy), P. Beatty 9 (early 3rd—Ezekiel, Daniel, and Esther), P. Freer (late 3rd—Minor Prophets), and P. Bodmer 46 (3rd-4th, Daniel, Susannah, and Thucydides). Cf. Jerome's Preface to the Twelve (Minor) Prophets (*PL* 28:1072). But Aristeas 310 may be referring to the Torah as 5 separate scrolls of Torah. The rabbinic sources y. Meg. 3:1, 73d–74a; b. B. Bat. 13b; and b. Meg. 19ab, discuss the (hypothetical) possibility of separate scrolls.

24. As acknowledged by Schniedewind, *How the Bible Became a Book*, 167. The first reference to an edition within one cover (pandect) is by Cassiodorus (d. 580; *Institutiones* 1:12.3, ed. Mynors, 37). According to McDonald, *Origin of the Bible*, 44 and 105, the first Christian manuscript to contain the entire New Testament and nothing else is from ca. 1000. The oldest complete Vulgate manuscript (Codex Amiatinus) is from the 8th century, and the first individually owned one-volume modest format Bible is from the 13th; cf. Light, "New Thirteenth-Century Bible," 276; Rouse and Rouse, "*Statim invenire*," 221. However, Smith, *What is Scripture?*, 268 n. 28, observes that the format did not become common until early in the 13th century.

25. According to Roberts and Skeat, *Birth of the Codex*, 48, it was not until the 3rd-century that codices could accommodate more than 150 leaves. Augustine mentions Jewish codices ("De Fide Rerum" 1.6, *PL* 40:179). There is no basis for the reference by Silver, *Story of Scripture*, 174, to a one-volume Tanakh in the 6th century.

26. According to Jerome, Barnabas "inter apocryphas scripturas legitur" ("De Viris Illustribus" 6 [*PL* 23:650]). Cavallo, "Between Volume and Codex," 87, notes that early codices typically included several works.

27. Cf. de Hamel, *Glossed Books of the Bible*, 12, Stern, "Rabbinic Bible," 254, n. 7. See also the colophon to the Leningrad Codex, though its introduction refers to *miqra' šālēm*, accessible in Freedman et al, *Leningrad Codex*, 3 and 994. Isaac Leeser still titled his 1853 translation *The twenty-four books of the Holy Scriptures*.

fixed order, but only the convention of presenting them in logical groups and sequences. How else would one arrange Genesis-Kings?[28] Even the Major and Minor Prophets are presented in the chronological order of the rulers in whose time their superscriptions say they were active.[29]

The only explicit pre-modern references to an order are found in Jerome, the Decretum Gelasianum, the Babylonian Talmud, and the *Dialogue of Timothy and Aquila*.[30] Significantly, these differ both from each other and from the modern Jewish and Christian arrangements. Moreover, the words used by these texts (Hebrew *sēder*, Greek *taxis*, and Latin *ordo*) can all mean "collection" as well as "sequence."[31]

As has occasionally been noted, though most often only in passing, it took a second technological development—the printing press—before the idea of a fixed order could take hold.[32] By enabling the mass production of inexpensive editions, that made it possible for one previously existing sequence of scriptural works to prevail.[33] In other words, it was not until the late Middle Ages or the early modern period that Christians and Jews came

---

28. Melito's reversal of Leviticus and Numbers (Eusebius, *Ecclesiastical History* 4:26.14 [LCL 1.392]) is presumably a mistake, though he also places the Minor Prophets after Jeremiah and before Daniel and Ezekiel.

29. This includes Jonah (according to 2 Kgs 14:25), though not Obadiah (if identified with the figure mentioned in 1 Kgs 18:3); cf. Cassuto, "Sequence and Arrangement," 5. The assumption that the arrangement was chronological underlies the discussion of Isaiah's position in b. B. Bat. 14b. Elliott, "Manuscripts, The Codex and the Canon," 116, regards the arrangement of the major prophets as based on length). Cf. Nogalski, *Literary Precursors*, 85–87, for a discussion of the history of the compilation of the minor prophets.

30. B. B. Bat. 14b; Jerome, "Preface to Samuel and Kings" (*PL* 28:598–600); Varner, *Ancient Jewish-Christian Dialogues*, 144–5; "Decretum Gelasianum" (*PL* 59:157–9). Although Melito claims to have been asked for the number and order (*ton arithmon kai opoia tēn taxin*) of "ancient writings," he provides only their names (Eusebius, *Ecclesiastical History* 4:26.13 LCL 1:392). Jerome puts the Writings, including Daniel, at the end, albeit starting with Job and ending with Esther, while the *Dialogue of Timothy and Aquila* places Chronicles ahead of Samuel-Kings and puts most of the Writings ahead of the Prophets, followed by Esdras, Judith, and Esther.

31. E.g., m. Sukkah. 4:4; b. Ketub. 103b; b. Šabb. 31a (hence the Mishna's six *sĕdārîm*); Herodotus 8:86 (LCL 4.82); Thucydides 4:72.2, 5:68.3, and 7:5 (LCL 2.334, 3.130, 4.12); Plato *Laws* VII 809D (LCL 10.72); Aristotle *Rhetoric* III:xii.6 (LCL 22.424); Aeschylus, *The Persians* 298 (LCL 1.135); Sophocles, *Oedipus at Colonus* 1311 (LCL 1.266); Cicero, *De Officiis* 1:xl.143/2 (LCL 144); but cf. *De Divinatione* I:lv,125 [LCL 10.72]); Vulgate 3 Kgs 6:36; Caesar, *Gallic War* 5:51 (LCL 22.424); Juvenal 6:502; Virgil, *Aeneid* V:120 (LCL 1.480); Pliny, *Natural History* VII.v.3 and lvi.208 (LCL 2.646 and 4.12); and Suetonius, *Lives of the Caesars* II (Augustus) xliv.1 (LCL 1.220).

32. E.g., Posner and Ta–Shema, *Hebrew Book*, 86; and McDonald, *Forgotten Scriptures*, 120.

33. Cf. Goshen-Gottstein, "Foundations of Biblical Philology," 83.

to see the Bible as a single book rather than a collection, albeit a theologically cohesive one.[34]

The beginnings of that conceptual shift can be seen in the 12th-century transformation of the word "Bible" from being understood as a Greek (neuter) plural (*ta biblia*) of *to biblion* (the diminutive of *biblos*) to a Latin (feminine) singular.[35] Something similar happened with the Hebrew *Tanakh*, which was originally an acronym, but has in recent centuries come to be perceived as an actual word.[36]

The idea of a fixed order, which is now taken for granted and then cited in support of theological conclusions, is, therefore, a late medieval or early modern construct, as is our tendency to think of *the Bible* as a single work rather than a collection of books with common ideas. The process of canonization owes as much to technology as to theology. As a result, it is a mistake to think of it as having been completed in the fullest sense until the 15th or 16th centuries. Nor should we assume that this process has come to an end and that the form we take for granted will survive another five hundred years. Following Marshall McLuhan's dictum that "the medium is the message," changing technology, most conspicuously the development of digital media, is likely to spawn new understandings of Scripture, rendering our notion of a fixed sequence meaningless.[37]

BIBLIOGRAPHY

Barr, James. *Holy Scripture, Canon, Authority, Criticism*. Philadelphia: Westminster Press, 1983.

Basler, Roy P., ed. *The Collected Writings of Abraham Lincoln*. New Brunswick, NJ: Rutgers University Press, 1953.

Beckwith, Roger. *The Old Testament of the New Testament Church and Its Background in Early Judaism*. Grand Rapids: Eerdmans, 1985.

---

34. Cf. rabbinic citation of prooftexts from each of the three sections (e.g., b. Meg. 31a; b. 'Abod. Zar. 19b; b. Sanh. 90b; and b. B. Qam. 92b (albeit citing Sir 13:15 as Writings and contrary to m. Kelim. 12:2). Swanson, *Closing of the Collection*, 320–21, points out that all of these are amoraic sources.

35. Kraft, "What is 'Bible'?" 110, cites the 11th-century Lindisfarne Latin library catalog: "unam bibliam in duobus voluminibus" then "bibliotheca, id est vetus et novum testamentum in duobus libris." For Latin singular usage, cf. H. Höpfl, "Écriture Sainte," 2:461.

36. Cf. Ben-Yehuda, *Millon ha-Lashon ha-'Ivrit*, 8:7825; and Sperling, *Students of the Covenant*, 12, n. 36. See also Shabbatai Cohen on Shulḥan 'Arukh Yoreh De'ah 245:5, as cited by Zimmels, *Ashkenazim and Sephardim*, 146 n.6.

37. Cf. Simon, "Can the People of the Book," 51; and O'Leary, "In the Beginning Was the Word."

Beecher, Willis J. "The Alleged Triple Canon of the Old Testament." *JBL* 15 (1896) 118–28.
Ben-Yehuda, Eliezer, *Millon ha-Lashon ha-'Ivrit ha-Yeshana ve-ha-Ḥadasha*, vol. 8, edited by N. H. Tur-Sinai. New York: Yoseloff, 1960.
Berman, Joshua. *Created Equal: How the Bible Broke with Ancient Political Thought*. New York: Oxford University Press, 2008.
Biale, David. *Blood and Belief: The Circulation of a Symbol between Jews and Christians* Berkeley: University of California Press, 2007.
Cassiodorus. *Institutiones*. Edited by R. A. B. Mynors. Oxford: Clarendon, 1937.
Cassuto, Umberto. "The Sequence and Arrangement of the Biblical Sections." In *Biblical and Oriental Studies*, 1.1–6. Jerusalem: Magnes, 1973.
Cavallo, Guglielmo. "Between Volume and Codex: Reading in the Roman World." In *A History of Reading in the West*, edited by Guglielmo Cavallo and Roger Chartier, 64–89. Amherst: University of Massachusetts Press, 1999.
Cowley, Roger W. "The Biblical Canon of the Ethiopian Orthodox Church Today." *Ostkirchliche Studien* 23 (1974) 318–23.
Devreesse, Robert. *Le Commentaire de Théodore de Mopsueste sur les Psaumes (I–LXXX)*. Vatican City: Biblioteca Apostolica Vaticana, 1939.
Elliott, James K. "Manuscripts, The Codex and the Canon." *JSNT* 63 (1996) 105–23.
Finsterbusch, Karin, and Armin Lange, eds. *What Is Bible?* Contributions to Biblical Exegesis & Theology 67. Leuven: Peeters, 2012.
Freedman, David Noel, et al., eds., *The Leningrad Codex: A Facsimile Edition*. Grand Rapids: Eerdmans / Leiden: Brill, 1998.
Fuller, Russell E. "The Twelve." In *Qumran Cave 4/X*, 221–318. DJD XV. Oxford: Clarendon, 1997.
Ginsburg, Christian D. *Introduction to the Massoretico-Critical Edition of the Hebrew Bible*. New York: Ktav, 1966.
Goshen-Gottstein, Moshe. "Foundations of Biblical Philology in the Seventeenth Century, Christian and Jewish Dimensions." In *Jewish Thought in the Seventeenth Century*, edited by Isadore Twersky and Bernard Septimus, 77–94. Cambridge: Harvard University Press, 1987.
Gould, Stephen Jay. "The Creation Myths of Cooperstown." *Natural History* 98:11 (November, 1989) 14–24. Reprinted in Stephen Jay Gould, *Bully for Brontosaurus: Reflections in Natural History*, 42–58. New York: Norton, 1991.
Guillaume, Philippe. "The Unlikely Malachi–Jonah Sequence (4QXII[a])." *JHS* 7 (2007) article 15. http://www.jhsonline.org/Articles/article_76.pdf.
Hall, Terry. *How the Bible Became a Book*. Wheaton, IL: Victor, 1990.
de Hamel, Christopher. *Glossed Books of the Bible and the Origins of the Paris Booktrade*. Wolfeboro, NH: Brewer, 1987.
Höpfl, Hildebrand. "Écriture Sainte." In *Dictionnaire de la Bible, Supplément*, edited by Louis Pirot, et al., 2:457–87. Paris: Letouzey & Ané, 1928–1992.
Isbell, Charles David. *God's Scribes: How the Bible Became the Bible*. Warren Center, PA: Shangri-La, 1999.
Jones, Barry Alan. *The Formation of the Book of the Twelve*. Atlanta: Scholars, 1995.
Kraft, Robert A. "What Is 'Bible'?—From the Perspective of 'Text': The Christian Connections." In *What Is Bible?* edited by Karin Finsterbusch and Armin Lange, 105–11. Contributions to Biblical Exegesis & Theology 67. Leuven: Peeters, 2012.
Kugel, James. *The Bible as It Was*. Cambridge: Harvard University Press, 1997.

Leiman, Sid Z. *The Canonization of Hebrew Scripture*. Hamden, CT: Archon, 1976.
Lemche, Niels Peter. "The Old Testament—A Hellenistic Book?" *SJOT* 7 (1993) 163–93.
Light, Laura. "The New Thirteenth-Century Bible and the Challenge of Heresy." *Viator* 18 (1987) 275–88.
McDonald, Lee Martin. *Forgotten Scriptures, The Selection and Rejection of Early Religious Writings*. Louisville: Westminster John Knox, 2009.
———. *The Origin of the Bible: A Guide for the Perplexed*. London: T. & T. Clark, 2011.
Miller, John. *How the Bible Came to Be: Exploring the Narrative and Message*. New York: Paulist, 2004.
Nogalski, James. *Literary Precursors to the Book of the Twelve*. BZAW 217. New York: de Gruyter, 1993.
O'Leary, Amy. "In the Beginning Was the Word; Now the Word Is on an App." *New York Times*, July 26, 2013.
Peels, Hendrik G. L., "The Blood 'from Abel to Zechariah' (Matthew 23,35; Luke 11,50f.) and the Canon of the Old Testament." *ZAW* 113 (2001) 583–601.
Posner, Raphael, and Israel Ta-Shema, eds. *The Hebrew Book: An Historical Survey*. Jerusalem: Keter, 1975.
Roberts, Colin H., and T. C. Skeat. *The Birth of the Codex*. London: British Academy, 1983.
Rofé, Alexander. "The Devotion to Torah-Study at the End of the Biblical Period: Joshua 1:8; Psalms 1:2; Isaiah 59:21." In *The Bible in the Light of Its Interpreters: Sarah Kamin Memorial Volume*, edited by Sara Japhet, 622–28. Jerusalem: Magnes Press, 1994 (Hebrew).
Rouse, Richard H., and Mary A. Rouse. "*Statim invenire*: Schools, Preachers, and New Attitudes to the Page." In *Renaissance and Renewal in the Twelfth Century*, edited by Robert L. Benson and Giles Constable with Carol D. Lanham, 201–28. Cambridge: Harvard University Press, 1982.
Rüger, Hans Peter. "The Extent of the Old Testament Canon." *The Bible Translator* 40 (1989) 301–8.
Sarna, Nahum M. "The Order of the Books." In *Studies in Jewish Bibliography, History and Literature in Honor of I. Edward Kiev*, edited by Charles Berlin, 407–13. New York: Ktav, 1971.
Satlow, Michael L. *How the Bible Became Holy*. New Haven: Yale University Press, 2014.
Schniedewind, William M. *How the Bible Became a Book: The Textualization of Ancient Israel*. Cambridge: Cambridge University Press, 2004.
Shinan, Avigdor, and Yair Zakovitch. *From Gods to God, How the Bible Suppressed or Changed Ancient Myths and Legends*. Philadelphia: Jewish Publication Society, 2012.
Silver, Daniel Jeremy. *The Story of Scripture, From Oral Tradition to the Written Word*. New York: Basic Books, 1990.
Smith, Charles M. *How the Bible Was Built*. Grand Rapids: Eerdmans, 2005.
Simon, Charles. "Can the People of the Book Become the People of the iPad?" *CJ – Voices of Conservative/Masorti Judaism* 6:2 (2012–2013) 10, 51.
Smith, Morton. *Palestinian Parties and Politics that Shaped the Old Testament*. London: SCM, 1987.
Smith, Wilfred Cantwell. *What Is Scripture? A Comparative Approach*. Minneapolis: Fortress, 1993.

Sperling, S. David. *Students of the Covenant: A History of Jewish Biblical Scholarship in North America*. Confessional Perspectives Series. Atlanta: Scholars, 1992.

Stern, David. "The Rabbinic Bible in Its Sixteenth-Century Context." In *The Hebrew Book in Early Modern Italy*, edited by Joseph R. Hacker and Adam Shear, 76–108. Phladelphia: University of Pennsylvania Press, 2011.

Swanson, Theodore Norman. "The Closing of the Collection of Holy Scriptures: A Study in the History of the Canonization of the Old Testament." PhD diss., Vanderbilt University, 1970.

Tov, Emanuel. *Revised Lists of the Texts from the Judaean Desert*. Leiden: Brill, 2010.

Varner, William. *Ancient Jewish-Christian Dialogues*. Lewiston, NY: Mellen, 2004.

Zimmels, Hirsch J. *Ashkenazim and Sephardim: Their Relations, Differences, and Problems as Reflected in the Rabbinical Responsa*. London: Oxford University Press, 1958.

12

Piercing God's Name: A Mythological Subtext of Deicide Underlying Blasphemy in Leviticus 24[1]

Theodore J. Lewis

JOHNS HOPKINS UNIVERSITY

Abstract

This study looks at the severity of blasphemy by examining the curious blasphemous expression of "*piercing* (√*nqb*) God's name" that one finds three times in the book of Leviticus (Lev 24:11,16 [2x]). It suggests that the choice of the word "piercing" is telling, that the mythological subtext of this blasphemy is nothing short of deicide. To blaspheme is to wield effectual words against God with the intention of doing lethal harm. Such an understanding solves why blasphemy (deserving of capital punishment) was positioned within the context of *lex talionis* laws of commensurate retribution with respect to killing (Lev 24:15–22).

---

1. Few scholars in our field possess the breadth and expertise of Ziony Zevit. Even fewer are as perceptive, engaging, and gracious. Thus it is with delight that I join many colleagues in celebrating Ziony's accomplishments and humanity.

Introductory Matters, Part 1: "Piercing" God's Name and Its Legal Context

The English word "blasphemy" covers a wide range of verbal actions wherein a person uses the power of words to speak contemptuously, impiously or irreverently in order to abuse, curse, reproach, revile, show contempt, cause injury ("injurious" words), slander, speak evil of, or even despise someone, typically God. I have no intention of wading into the nuances of such a large topic. The goal of this paper is narrow, to look at the curious blasphemous expression of *"piercing* (√*nqb*) God's name" that occurs on three occasions in Leviticus 24 (24:11, 16 [2x]). In addition, the current treatment highlights but does not fully explore the considerable (and conspicuous) social dimensions of the passage, a subject for another time.[2]

Over the years, interpreters have focused on the subtle and nuanced notions of blasphemy in Leviticus 24 though without adequately probing the expression itself. Why was the idiom of "piercing God's name" coined? What might have informed such a turn of a phrase? The relevant text in Leviticus 24 reads as follows:

11 וַיִּקֹּב בֶּן־הָאִשָּׁה הַיִּשְׂרְאֵלִית אֶת־הַשֵּׁם וַיְקַלֵּל וַיָּבִיאוּ אֹתוֹ אֶל־מֹשֶׁה . . .

12 וַיַּנִּיחֻהוּ בַּמִּשְׁמָר לִפְרֹשׁ לָהֶם עַל־פִּי יְהוָה: . . .

15 לֵאמֹר אִישׁ אִישׁ כִּי־יְקַלֵּל אֱלֹהָיו וְנָשָׂא חֶטְאוֹ:

16 וְנֹקֵב שֵׁם־יְהוָה מוֹת יוּמָת רָגוֹם יִרְגְּמוּ־בוֹ כָּל־הָעֵדָה כַּגֵּר כָּאֶזְרָח בְּנָקְבוֹ־שֵׁם יוּמָת:

---

2. The social dimensions of our passage (Lev 24:10–23) are on full display. The narrative involves a person of mixed ethnicity who came out "among the Israelites" (*wayyēṣēʾ . . . bĕtôk bĕnê yiśrāʾēl*). His mother's name and Israelite tribal lineage are marked ("Shelomit, the daughter of Dibri, of the tribe of Dan") in contrast to the briefest mention that his father was an Egyptian. The quarrel (that leads to the blasphemy by the half-Israelite) is described with an additional ethnic marker: the offender's mixed lineage stands in contrast with the non-mixed lineage of his contender ("the [full] Israelite," *ʾîš hayyiśrĕʾēlî*). We know not the nature of the quarrel, but the setting ("within the camp," *bammaḥăneh*) and the resulting blasphemy suggest ethnic and theological conflict.

Hierarchically, Moses is the socially validated leader who relays the divine verdict of guilt and the sentence of death by stoning. The social space of execution changes as the maledictor is then brought "outside the camp" (*ʾel miḥûṣ lammaḥăneh*) from his temporary imprisonment (*mišmār*) within the camp while he awaits adjudication. Society at large has a stake in the matter (with blasphemy injuring the social fabric of this theocentric community). All who heard (i.e. those who had witnessed and were thus soiled by) the offense must physically touch the offender (laying their hands on his head) as an act of transference, transmitting the social stain back to its source (cf. Kitz, *Cursed*, 163). The entire assembly (*kol hāʿēdâ*) must carry out the execution and they do so—with the narrative underscoring that the punishment was divinely ordained, communicated through Moses, and with the legal ruling applicable to stranger and native alike (*kaggēr kāʾezrāḥ*).

And the Israelite woman's son *blasphemed (lit. pierced) the name (of YHWH)* and cursed; and so they brought him to Moses ... Then they put him in custody, that the mind of YHWH might be shown to them ... 'Whoever curses his God shall bear his sin. And whoever *blasphemes (lit. pierces) the name of YHWH* shall surely be put to death. All the congregation shall certainly stone him, the stranger as well as him who is born in the land. When *he blasphemes (lit. pierces) the name (of YHWH)*, he shall be put to death. (Lev 24:11–12, 15–16)

There is no doubt in our passage that the expression √*nqb* + *šēm* refers to blasphemy of the divine name YHWH, especially with its juxtaposition with the verb *qll* "to curse" that occurs twice in the passage.[3] That the Hebrew root *nqb* is used to designate effectual (injurious) words (e.g. cursing, hexing) is known elsewhere, as in Prov 11:26 and Job 3:8.[4]

מֹנֵעַ בָּר יִקְּבֻהוּ לְאוֹם וּבְרָכָה לְרֹאשׁ מַשְׁבִּיר׃

He who withholds grain—the nation will curse him,
While there are blessings on the head of a distributor.
(Prov 11:26)

יִקְּבֻהוּ אֹרְרֵי־יוֹם הָעֲתִידִים עֹרֵר לִוְיָתָן׃

May those who cast spells on the day (*yām*? Sea?) hex it,[5]
Those prepared to arouse Leviathan.
(Job 3:8)

---

3. The debate about whether the use of two verbs here constitutes two actions or one does not impact our interpretation. For example, Fishbane prefers seeing these two verbs as a hendiadys as opposed to Brichto who sees a distinction. See Fishbane, "Jeremiah," 163 n. 2, and Brichto, *The Problem*, 143–7. Brichto's assertion that "not a single occurrence of *qillel* has proven to mean 'curse'" is quite strained and is not embraced by any modern lexica.

4. Though the verb in these two passages (*yiqqĕbuhû*) presents as a I-N verb (thus from √*nqb*), it could be analyzed from the related root (by-form?) *qbb*. The overlapping notions of "blasphemy" (< *to pierce [*nqb*] a divine name) and "cursing" (*qbb*) certainly facilitated the mixing of the root types. Morphologically, the mixing of I-N roots and geminate roots is known from Hebrew where some prefixal geminate verbs present as if they were from I-N roots (e.g. *yissōb*; but contrast *yāsōb*), and especially from Aramaic where geminate prefixal verbs regularly follow I-N inflection (e.g. *yibbōz*). Our passage in Leviticus 24 has to be using the root *nqb* and not *qbb* due to the participle in Lev 24:16 (*nōqēb* not *qōbēb*) as well as the infinitive construct *bĕnoqbô*.

5. Though not necessary, many scholars would repoint *'ōrĕrê-yôm* to *'ōrĕrê-yām*, "those who curse Yam," to form a more precise synonymous parallel. It is not surprising, as first noted by Fishbane ("Jeremiah," 153), that we find such material being used in later Aramaic incantation texts such as this one from Nippur:

Yet much more frequently, the root *nqb* is used to refer to piercing, a meaning well attested in the Hebrew Bible, epigraphic Hebrew, and in various cognate languages (e.g., Aramaic, Syriac, Arabic, Ugaritic). The Siloam Tunnel Inscription (*KAI* 189) that dates to ca. 700 BCE presents four occurrences of the root *nqb* designating the act of boring through rock (*KAI* 189:1 [2x], 2, 4). Mention is made of "the manner of the breakthrough" (*dbr hnqbh*) and "the day of the breakthrough" (*bym hnqbh*) as well as in mid-process "while there were still three cubits to be breached" (*wbʻwd šlš ʼmt lhnqb[h]*).[6] Second Kings 12:10 (Eng 12:9) describes the priest Jehoida *boring* a hole in the lid of a chest (*wayyiqqōb ḥōr bĕdaltô*). Second Kings 18:21// Isa 36:6 depicts a broken reed *piercing* (*nĕqābâ*) a hand. Hag 1:6 depicts a leaky purse pierced with holes (*ṣĕrôr nāqûb*). Even more relevant to our subject at hand are occurrences of the root *nqb* in mythological contexts that will be addressed below on pages 223–27.

In addition to being struck by the strangeness of the idiom (how could one and why would one "pierce" a name?), the positioning of blasphemy here in the context of *lex talionis* law having to do with killing is equally perplexing. In general, to find a legal setting for cursing is not surprising, for as Anne Marie Kitz has underscored, "curses petition the deities for rulings in the heavenly court," and as such "frequently they are wrapped in legal terminology."[7] Yet why would blasphemy incur the severity of capital punishment (Lev 24:16, 23)? And why is it listed among *lex talionis* law whose immediate context articulates the commensurate retribution of killing a man who murdered another (Lev 24:17, 21b), the making of "life for life" (*nepeš taḥat nepeš*) restitution for the killing of an animal (Lev 24:18, 21a), and the penalty in kind and degree for physical disfigurement (fracture for fracture, eye for eye, tooth for tooth) (Lev 24:19–20)?

ʼšpnʼ lkwn bʼyšpʼ dymʼ
wʼyšpʼ dlwytn tnynʼ
I enchant you with the adjuration of Yam,
And the spell of Leviathan the serpent.

For the MT's *ʼōrĕrê-yôm*, see Noegel ("Job iii 5," 556–62) who argues that *mĕrîrê yôm* refers to "day demons."

6. The form *hnqbh* has been taken either as a feminine noun "boring, tunneling" (*nĕqābāh*) or as a Niphal infinitive with a 3 m sg suffix "its being bored/tunneled through" (*hinnāqibō*).

7. Kitz, *Cursed*, 4, 68–74.

Introductory Matters, Part 2: Name = Identity

As insightful and poetic as they are, we need not the fields of semiotics, socio-linguistics, and ethnography nor Shakespeare's "a rose by any other name would smell as sweet" to remind us of the obvious: our names are tied to our essence and identity. Names are integral to one's sense of self and family, and central to identity formation as we navigate our place in society. How we use and treat the names of others is equally telling about social perception and negotiation. The significance of names was not lost on the ancients and their use of names is a constant field of study, with the latest being the social analysis by Rainer Albertz.[8] Theologically, the ubiquitous presence of theophoric elements in personal names attests to the symbiotic relationship of deity and identity.

Due to such significance, the obliteration of one's name is a profound act, that of a deity even more so. Ideally, one's name was preserved through one's offspring (cf. Deut 25:6; Judg 21:17; 2 Sam 14:7; Ruth 4:10), and even after death with commemoration rituals binding ancestors to the living (2 Sam 18:18). Invoking the names of the deceased (and thereby, in part, their essence) endowed "the living with a family identity that is anchored in the past."[9] The importance of one's enduring name finds physical expression in funerary stelae where we read of curses invoking the wrath of the gods should one efface a person's name.[10]

Given such cultural weight, only extreme situations occasion individuals to employ the severe rhetoric of blotting out (*mḥh*), cutting off (*krt*), or destroying (*'bd, šmd*) a person's or a people's name—and with it their identity, essence, and memory. Cases in point are the levels of wickedness that prompt God to blot out his human creation via the flood (Gen 6:7; 7:4, 23), the desire to see the cessation of enemy nations (Exod 17:14; Deut 25:19; Isa 14:22) or the psalmist's celebration of the eternal eradication of his enemies' names (Ps 9:6-7 [Eng 9:5-6]). With a reciprocity reminiscent of *lex talionis* law, another psalmist curses the enemies cursing him (Ps 109:17-19), and with invective seeks the blotting out the name of those who sought the death

---

8. See Albertz and Schmitt, *Family and Household Religion*, 245-386. In addition to his social analysis, Albertz includes a massive amount of data in the tables listed in §5.1-5.16.

9. Van der Toorn, *Family Religion*, 48, 52; Lewis, "How Far Can Texts Take Us?," 194-96.

10. See, for example, the Karatepe (Azatiwada) inscription (*KAI* 26 A iii 13-14,18-19, iv 1; C iv, 15ff.) where Azatiwada curses the person who effaces his name by invoking the gods to efface the person and his kingdom.

of the poor, needy, and brokenhearted (Ps 109:2–3,9,13,15,16–18,31; cf. Ps 69:5,15–16, 23–29 [Eng 69:4,14–15, 22–28]; Jer 18:23).

There is no explicit reference in the Hebrew Bible to the blotting out of a god's name, though implicit references say as much. Deut 12:3 commands the destruction of divine images representing illicit gods such that their names are destroyed. Zech 13:2 has YHWH declaring that he will cut off the names of the foreign gods (lit. the names of their *'ăṣābbîm* "effigies") such that they will no longer be remembered (cf. Zeph 1:4). To blot out a name, then, is identity *de*formation, including effacing one's very existence and future memory.

There are no references to YHWH's name having ever been destroyed, though performative speech acts of cursing and blasphemy (to be treated immediately below) are attempts at doing just such serious injury. In addition, there are examples of doing actual injury to YHWH's name of a "lesser" degree that do not involve speech. Ezekiel repeatedly describes how YHWH must act "for the sake of His Name" that his people profaned (*ḥll*) through their depravity resulting in the exile (e.g. Ezek 20:9,14,22,39; 36:20–23; 39:7).[11] There is also an implicit example of "despising" (*bzh*) and "scorning, reviling" (*n'ṣ*) YHWH's name in the original text of the David narrative in 2 Sam 12.[12] In even these "lesser" cases, the seriousness of the offense is underscored. In Ezekiel, YHWH acts at great cost to vindicate the holiness of his Name and reputation (Ezek 36:21). In the David narrative, the son born of David and Bathsheba's illicit relations will die due to David

---

11. See Greenberg, *Ezekiel*, 729.

12. 2 Samuel 12 describes how David's actions as an adulterer (with Bathsheba) and murderer (killing her husband Uriah) constituted acts of despising (*bzh*) YHWH. YHWH says explicitly so to David ("you despised me" *bĕzitānî*) while adding that this despising will cause the sword never to depart from his house (2 Sam 12:10). The context of this accusation twice more refers to the desecration, yet with the MT's euphemistic expressions aimed at safeguarding the name YHWH. The MT of 2 Sam 12:9 has YHWH asking David "Why have you despised *the word of* YHWH" (*madûaʻ bāzîtā 'et-dĕbar yhwh*), and 2 Sam 12:14 notes that the son born of David and Bathsheba's illicit relations will die because David "utterly scorned *the enemies of* YHWH" (*niʼēṣ niʼaṣtā 'et-ōyĕbê yhwh*).

The former is a simple circumvention similar to the Aramaic Targums' use of paraphrases and/or substitutes such as the *Memra* ("command, word"), the *Yeqara* ("majesty, honor"), and the *Shekinta* ("residing presence") of God to avoid expressing the corporeality of God. In contrast, the latter is an explicit euphemism that attracts attention to itself. The resulting meaning in the current context is nonsensical. To scorn the enemies of God should be a good thing.

For the text critical reasoning for reconstructing the original text of 2 Sam 12:9, 14 that in each case refers to desecrating YHWH directly (*madûaʻ bāzîtā* <> *yhwh*; *niʼēṣ niʼaṣtā* <> *yhwh*), see McCarter, *II Samuel*, 295–6. On similar euphemisms, see below n. 19 and n. 55.

"utterly scorning YHWH" (*niʾēṣ niʾaṣtā* <> *yhwh*), and the sword will never depart from his house (2 Sam 12:10, 14).

Introductory Matters, Part 3: Blasphemy and Effectual Words

That words are powerful is self-evident. There is a reason why people are inspired by the power of poetry or persuaded by the power of rhetoric. In ancient Near Eastern rituals, words were also used in an effective manner, such as when ritual specialists would employ incantations for their apotropaic power to avert evil.[13] Multiple literary genres were used for their effective power in the ancient Near East. In the Hebrew Bible one finds imprecations (e.g. Ps 17:13-14; Ps 35:1-8; Ps 55:10,16 [Eng 55:9,15]; Ps 69:23-29 [Eng Ps 69:22-28]; Ps 79:10b-12; Ps 109; Ps 137:7-9; Ps 140:10-12 [Eng 140:9-11]; Obad 15-16), curses (cf. 1 Sam 14:24; 2 Sam 16:7; Job 2:9), curse rituals (Deut 27:11-26; Num 5:11-31), curse neutralization (Judg 17:2), sympathetic magic (Jer 51:59-64), execration texts (cf. Jer 19:1-11; Amos 1:2—2:16), effective prayer requests (e.g. Num 11:2; 1 Sam 1:20; Dan 10:12), apotropaic intercession,[14] and perhaps, Ziony Zevit would suggest, even an exorcistic formula (cf. Isa 30:22).[15]

---

13. Concentrating here on effectual words used in ritual contexts is not to minimize the equally "active" way in which such words were used literarily. Consider, for example, the animated curse (*ʾālâ*) that is given flight in Zech 5:1-4 (as a *mĕgillâ ʿāpâ* "flying scroll") as it then enters and consumes the homes of the thief and the perjurer who swears falsely by YHWH's name (*hannišbāʿ bišmî*). Compare the Arslan Tash incantations (*lḥšt*) that have their own *ʾlt*-curses, *ʿpt*-"fliers" and incantation scroll (*mnty kmglt*) together with spells against "house entering." For the text edition, see Pardee, "Les documents," 15-54.

Another "active" literary usage can be found in Deut 29:19 (Eng 29:20) where the curse (*ʾālâ*) "lies in wait (to pounce) upon" (*rābĕṣâ bô*) the violator of the covenant—followed by YHWH blotting out his name from under heaven. On such "lurking to pounce," cf. Gen 4:7 where sin lurks (*ḥaṭṭāʾt rōbēṣ*) as well as the use of cognate terms in Akkadian (*rābiṣu, rabāṣu*) for lurking demons.

14. For the category of apotropaic intercession (with examples from the Hebrew Bible, Mesopotamia, and Anatolia) as seen through the lens of speech-act theory, see Broida, *Forestalling Doom*.

15. So Zevit (*The Religions of Ancient Israel*, 521) who suggests that Isaiah 30:22 may actually be employing "an exorcistic formula" to rid one of impurity with the words *kĕmô dāwāh ṣēʾ* which he translates "Like illness, go out!" As for the explicit use of incantations in ancient Israel, see Lewis ("Job 19 in the Light of the Ketef Hinnom Inscriptions and Amulets") where I argue that Job 19 (with its choice of the words *sēper, ṣûr*, and *ʿēṭ-barzel*) contains imagery of an engraved (*ḥqq, ḥṣb*) apotropaic scroll and burial inscription.

In other words, when used as performative speech, certain words (when used correctly[16]) were thought to have power and efficacy.[17] That the degree of perceived power and efficacy attributed to such words could be maximal is evidenced by capital punishment being assigned to cursing God and king.[18] For example, the Covenant Code contains legislation against

16. There are occasional indications that the way in which such speech was performed was essential to perceived efficacy. See Fishbane's ("Jeremiah," 164) remarks about the "paranomastic assonance" that "typif[ies] the rhythm and force of incantations" "just as puns and *Wortspielen* are characteristic of the magical words found in omens and oracles." See too the comments by Farber ("Associative Magic") and Greaves ("Wordplay," 165) on the way in which puns in magical texts are not merely expressions of literary wit, but "part of the actual mechanism by which some incantations were to have their effect." As already pointed out by Greaves ("Wordplay," 166–7), a clear example of such is found in *KTU* 1.100.65b–67a, one of the snake incantations from Late Bronze Age Ugarit. The text reads (with my tentative vocalization):

'arʿarama yanaʿʿirannaha
sissinnama yassiyannaha
'idatama yaʿddiyannaha
yābilatama yabilannaha
With a tamarask he expels it (the venom),
With a date palm he makes it fall into utter oblivion,
With a *'adattu*-cluster he makes it pass away,
With a carrier he carries it away.

For the Hebrew Bible, in addition to Fishbane's examples, see Jer 10:11 (translated below in n. 18).

17. See Broida's (*Forestalling Doom*) analysis that unpacks the nuances of "causative speech" in light of speech-act theory, from John L. Austin's notion of "performativity" to John R. Searle's taxonomy of "illocution" and "perlocution" to Jørgen Podemann Sørensen's notions of "magical agency" and his questioning of the illocutionary force of supernatural speech acts. We follow Broida (*Forestalling Doom*, 37) in asserting that such "causative speech acts were understood by the cultures using them to have real transformative power, and thus can be justifiably said to have illocutionary force" due to their theistic worldview that embraced "supernatural empowerment."

For older treatments that interacted with the work of Austin, see Thistleton, "The Supposed Power of Words," 293–6, and Mitchell ("The Meaning of BRK," 173–6) whose work concentrates on the theological rather than the sociological and anthropological. For Northwest Semitic scholars working on performative speech, see especially Sanders ("Performative Utterances," 161–81) and Dobbs-Allsopp, "(More) on Performative Utterances in Semitic," 36–81. For a detailed history of recent research on curses, see Kitz, *Cursed*, 9–31.

18. In addition, see Blank ("The Curse," 83) who argues that "the fear of the effective power of the spoken word best explains the total absence of [explicit] blasphemy in the Bible." Blank goes on to note that the fact that "the Bible nowhere contains the curse formula directed against God, i.e. blasphemy . . . is all the more remarkable because the Bible is by no means lacking in passages referring to the *possibility* of a curse directed against God" (Blank's emphasis). Blank's point is very well taken. And yet, if the verb *yēʾbadû* of Jeremiah 10:11 is translated as a jussive (thus the understanding of the LXX), the following curse would result:

cursing God and *nāśî'*-ruler (Exod 22:27 [Eng 22:28]) that Dtr fleshes out with Jezebel's trumped-up accusation against Naboth (that he had cursed God and king) for which he is stoned to death (1 Kgs 21:10,13).[19] The blasphemer of God and king in Isa 8:21-22 (even if motivated by hunger) is thrust into utter darkness. The blasphemy by Eli's sons against God[20] is such a severe offense that YHWH swears that it will never be expiated by sacrifice or offering (1 Sam 3:13-14; cf. Exod 20:7; Deut 5:11). Shimei's curse against David (2 Sam 16:5-13) resonated with the king throughout his life such that (according to Dtr's portrayal) he nullifies his initial reprieve (2 Sam 19:21-23) by giving explicit instructions to have Shimei executed by Solomon (1 Kgs 2:8-9, 44-46). To a lesser (sociological) degree we read of cursing one's father and mother, yet the severity of such an utterance remains the same with capital punishment still assigned (Exod 21:17).

The Underlying Empowerment

Such verbal enactment was envisioned as tapping into an underlying power source (divine or demonic) beyond human capability.[21] For our interests, consider especially the way in which the divine name was used effectively, such as Jacob swearing by "The Fear (*paḥad*) of his father Isaac" (Gen

---

"The gods who did not make (*'ăbadû*) the heavens and the earth—May these perish (*yē'badû*) from the earth and from under the heavens."

It is of interest that this verse is written in Aramaic, the only Aramaic to appear in the book of Jeremiah. Lundbom (*Jeremiah*, 593) remarks that the "elaborate chiasmus and wordplay point to a pithy saying" (cf. the pun on *'ăbadû* "make" and *yē'badû* "perish"; *'ĕlāhayyā'* "gods" and *'ēlleh* "these"; *'arqā'* "earth" and *'ar'ā'* "earth"). Yet such constructions and the use of Aramaic could likely be due to its magical content (see n. 16 above).

19. As widely recognized, in each of these verses, *brk* is used euphemistically for cursing. Cf. above, n. 12 and below, n. 55.

20. Reading *'ĕlōhîm* here for MT's *lāhem* in line with the LXX, the *tiqqûnê sôpĕrîm*, and almost all commentators (e.g., McCarter, *I Samuel*, 96) who recognize how the original text was changed for pious reasons.

21. Note how it was customary for incantation specialists to give credit to the gods for the effectual power underlying their words. Such *šiptu ul yuttun (yattun)*, "the incantation is not mine," phrasing is an expression of "legitimation" often used as a closing formula in incantations. See Lenzi, "*šiptu ul yuttun*," 131–66; *Reading Akkadian Prayers and Hymns*, 19–20; and Lewis, "The Identity and Function of Ugaritic Sha'tiqatu," 19 n.62.

This is not to deny à la Bourdieu the sociological aspects of performative speech and how it can be used as a medium of power by which a speaker promotes self-interest. See Bourdieu, *Language and Symbolic Power*.

31:53),[22] priests putting the Name YHWH onto the people (Num 6:27),[23] and Elijah cursing the 42 boys "in the name of YHWH" (*běšēm yhwh*, 2 Kgs 2:24). In epigraphic Hebrew, our best examples are the Ketef Hinnom amulet inscriptions where we have clear Iron Age evidence of the power of the divine name YHWH being used for apotropaic purposes.[24]

In this light, it is easy to see how blasphemy is a serious affront in that it not only seeks injury to a name, and hence the name holder's essence and memory (see pp. 217–19 above); it also constitutes the use of supernatural power to bring about said injury. Though the power of demons and genii (beneficent and malevolent) is well documented in the ancient Near East and appears in the archaeological record of ancient Israel, the conceptual world of the author of Leviticus 24 would be envisioning YHWH as the

22. The occasion of Gen 31:53 is a treaty between Jacob and Laban. Treaties customarily contained sections of conditioned self-curses for failure to keep the stated stipulations. Here Jacob swears by the deity named "Fear (*paḥad*) of his father Isaac." While this epithet could refer to the deity whom his father revered, in the context of treaty curses, it likely refers to "Fear" as a hypostatic expression designating "He who occasions fear for covenant violators" (cf. *paḥad yhwh* who rises to terrify [*běqûmô laʿărōṣ*] in Isa 2:19, 21). Note how Jacob swearing by the name "Fear" [= "the god who instills fear"] would be satisfying for the current nonaggression pact where Laban has concerns about Jacob ill-treating his daughters (*tĕʿanneh* mentioned in Gen. 31:50) and doing him harm (*rāʿāh* mentioned in Gen 31:52).

Note too how Mal 1:14 curses (*ʾārûr*) a cheater of proper cult, mentions the name YHWH *ṣĕbāʾôt* plus epithets (*melek gādôl*), and then remarks that YHWH's name is "feared among the nations" (*šĕmî nôrāʾ baggôyim*).

Returning to Jacob, note how subsequent tradition invokes the "Name of the God of Jacob" (parallel to YHWH) for protection (*yĕśaggebkā*) in a "day of trouble" (*bĕyôm ṣārâ*) (Ps. 20:2 [Eng 20:1]).

23. Cf. McBride ("The Deuteronomic Name Theology," 110) who comments: "Here *šēm* connotes the hypostatic (cult) presence of YHWH himself dynamistically activated, 'set' upon the people to affect their welfare when the priests invoke the name with the blessings." Propp also sees the wording of Num 6:27 as using "the image of an amulet apropos of the blessing." Personal communication to Dolansky, *Now You See It, Now You Don't*, 90 n. 279.

It occasions little surprise that the blessings that precede Num 6:27 (i.e. Num 6:22–26) were inscribed for apotropaic purposes on the Ketef Hinnom amulets and on incantations from later Jewish Antiquity (see Lewis, "Job 19 in the Light of the Ketef Hinnom Inscriptions and Amulets"). The exegetical midrash Sifre Numbers 40 (I, 191) [~ mid-3rd-century] understands the blessing "May YHWH keep you" to refer to keeping one from the demons. Similarly, Targum Pseudo-Jonathan Numbers [~ 7th/8th century] translates the first part of the blessing: "May the Lord bless you and guard you in all your endeavors from (the demons of) darkness (*lyly*) and from frightening demons (*mzyyʿy*) and midday demons (*bny ṭyhrry*) and morning demons (*bny ṣpryry*) and destroyers (*mzyqy*) and night demons (*ṭlny*)."

24. It is occasionally overlooked that the two Ketef Hinnom inscriptions were written on amulets that were to be worn as talismans around one's neck. See Lewis, "Job 19 in the Light of the Ketef Hinnom Inscriptions and Amulets."

inherent power behind effectual speech.[25] That the name being potentially injured is divine raises the stakes to the highest degree, and even more so in that the power of God (i.e. the power behind the effectual words) is being employed against God.

Mythological Subtext: Part A

Returning to the passage at hand, when our author describes the injurious actions of the blasphemer toward YHWH's name, he does not use the more common vocabulary of blotting out (*mḥh*), cutting off (*krt*), or destroying (*'bd, šmd*) a name. Instead we find the curious notion of "*piercing*" (√*nqb*) God's name" (Lev 24:11,16 [2x]). In addition to the mundane use of the root *nqb* for piercing documented above, we also find a cosmic use of the verb in *Chaoskampf* traditions where YHWH pierces the negative protagonist (the sea monster Yam, the dragon Leviathan).

Hab 3:8–15 contains an archaic or archaizing poem that is seen as a structural unit based on its repetitive water vocabulary. It portrays YHWH as a charioteer armed for battle with bow and arrows as well as with a spear (3:8–9,11,13) with which he *pierces* (*nqb*) the enemy. We enter the story mid-stream. One can only guess at the plotline that led our poet to cry out:

> Were you angry with the rivers (*nĕhārîm*), O YHWH,
> Was your wrath against the rivers (*nĕhārîm*),
> Did you rage against the sea (*bayyām*),
> When you drove your steeds,
> Your victorious chariots?
> You laid bare your bow,
> ... (your) shafts ...[26]

---

25. The subject of demonology, biblical and otherwise, is beyond the scope of this study. See the helpful taxonomy by Walton ("Demons in Mesopotamia and Israel") and additional bibliography in Lewis, "The Identity and Function of Ugaritic Shaʿtiqatu," 22 n. 69.

As to the archaeological record, see Zevit's (*The Religions of Ancient Israel*, 344) synthesis of Herrmann's database (attesting to the widespread presence of amulets, mostly Egyptian in nature) arguing that they comprised "a type of insurance" "in Israelite comprehension and interpretation." See too the fragmentary Neo-Assyrian stone plaque-amulet of the Lamashtu class published by Mordechai Cogan and the presence of Pazuzu pendants from Beth-Shean, Megiddo, and Horvat Qitmit. See Cogan, "A Lamashtu Plaque," 155–61; Ornan, "An Amulet of the Demon Pazuzu," 517–9; Amiran, "Two Luristan Fibulae," 88–91 Pl. XVIII, Fig. 1 a–d; and Beit-Arieh et al. *Ḥorvat Qitmit*, 270–71, Fig. 6.2.

26. The textual complexities of Hab 3:9b are well known and gave rise, according

> Torrents of water (*zerem mayim*) swept by,
> The abyss (*tĕhôm*) gave forth its voice . . .
> At the brilliance of your flying arrows,
> At the radiance of your lightning-like spear . . .
> You smote the head of the wicked one[27]
> slashing, head to foot.
>
> . . . . .
>
> With his own spear you pierced (*nāqabtā*) (his) head,
> When his warriors stormed out to scatter us . . .
> You trampled the sea (*bayyām*) with your horses,
> You parched the many waters (*mayim rabbîm*).[28]
>
> (Hab 3:8–11, 13b–15)

Francis I. Andersen notes "the fusion of the mythological and the historical" with "the historical focus on the crossing of the Reed Sea."[29] The hostile "nations" mentioned within the poem (3:12–14,16) are for Andersen "universal, potentially eschatological" whereas for John Day they point toward the Babylonians.[30] Where Andersen sees "only an echo" of the original

---

to Hiebert (*God of My Victory*, 26) and Andersen (*Habakkuk*, 321), to more than 100 interpretations already by the mid-1850s. There is no point to sifting them here. Readers are directed to Hiebert and Andersen for a synthesis of the competing proposals, none of which has gained wide acceptance.

The word for "shafts" (*maṭṭôt*) seems clear enough at first glance, but one would expect "arrows" (*ḥiṣṣîm*) to parallel "bow" (*qešet*) in Hab 3:9a. Yet compare our poet's artistry in Hab 3:11 where "the brilliance of (YHWH's) flying *arrows*" (*'ôr ḥiṣṣêkā yĕhallēkû*) parallels "the radiance of (his) lightning-like *spear*" (*nōgah bĕraq ḥănîtekā*).

27. The text here is difficult. The translation here follows Andersen (*Habakkuk*, 337) in seeing MT's *mibbêt* as a later insertion rather than the interpretation of Hiebert (*God of My Victory*, 36–40) and others who (using Ugaritic parallels) see a metathesis (*bmt*) referring to the "back" of the enemy. That the text has suffered from textual confusion is also seen in LXX's understanding that YHWH brings death (*thanatos* = Hebrew *māwet*) on the heads of the wicked. In the following line, *'ārôt* is equally difficult and here too we follow Andersen's understanding (*Habakkuk*, 337–38).

28. Pointing MT's *ḥōmer* as a D inf absolute (*ḥammēr*) as a substitute for a finite verb (so Andersen, *Habakkuk*, 339). On the root *ḥmr* designating "to be hot, parched, dried up," see the cognate evidence (Ugr, MHeb, Arm, Arb), and esp. *KTU* 1.83.13 (so Pitard, "The Binding," 279, and Lewis, "'Athtartu's Incantations," 217–8) as well as the bitumen pits (*be'ĕrōt ḥēmār*) in Gen 14:10. For additional references to YHWH drying up the sea, cf. Nah 1:4 and Ps 106:9.

Note how *yām* and *mayim rabbîm* are parallel terms here and elsewhere (Ps 93:4). Smith ("The Baal Cycle," 168 n. 67 following Caquot, Sznycer and Herdner) notes how Yammu's epithet "the great god" (*'il rbm*) in *KTU* 1.3.III.39 could be "elliptical for *mym rbm*, 'mighty waters' referring to the cosmic waters."

29. Andersen, *Habakkuk*, 316.

30. Ibid., 334; Day, *God's Conflict*, 105.

mythological tale behind Hab 3:8, Theodore Hiebert asserts that the formulaic pair (*yām//nāhār*—that he renders as singular plus enclitic-*m* following Albright) constitutes "the waters of chaos, YHWH's cosmic foe, . . . an enduring reflection of the ancient name of the dragon of chaos."[31] Indeed, for Hiebert, "the enemy is a cosmic one. It is the ancient dragon of chaos, River//Sea." Nonetheless, Hiebert too agrees that we have a "blending of the cosmic and historical realms" where the "cosmic battle is recited to celebrate God's victory in earthly wars."[32]

Two additional occurrences of the verb *nqb* in a mythological context are found in the divine speeches in the book of Job. Job 40:24–26 [Eng 40:24—41:2] reads:

> Can one take (the behemoth-beast) with . . .[33]
> Can one pierce (*yinqob*) (his) nose with hooks?
> Can you drag out Leviathan with a fishhook?
> Can you bind down his tongue by a rope?
> Can you put a rope through his nose?
> Can you pierce (*tiqqôb*) his jaw with a hook?

These three occurrences of the root *nqb* in mythological contexts are even more provocative when set against other such combat myths in the Hebrew Bible that feature YHWH piercing cosmic foes, though using the synonymous verb *ḥll*.

> By his power, (YHWH) quelled the Sea (*yām*),
> By his skill, he smote Rahab (*rāhab*).
> By his wind, the heavens . . . ,
> His hand pierced (*ḥōlălâ*) the Fleeing Serpent (*nāḥāš bārîaḥ*).[34]
> (Job 26:12–13)

---

31. Andersen, *Habakkuk*, 317; Hiebert, *God of My Victory*, 6–7, 23.

32. Hiebert, *God of My Victory*, 108.

33. The MT's reading "with his eyes" (*bĕʿênāyw*) is difficult to interpret and has occasioned a range of emendations (for a list, cf. Clines, *Job 38–42*, 1157) none of which is compelling.

34. To interpret Job 26:12–13 one must wrestle with substantive problems that cannot be solved with certainty. Yet certain solutions seem likely. It seems likely that this passage forms a part of Bildad's speech and not Job's reply as 26:1 implies. Such is the consensus of scholars. See, for example, Dhorme, *A Commentary on the Book of Job*, xlviii, 368; Pope, *Job*, xx; and Habel, *The Book of Job*, 366.

The verb *rāgaʿ* (26:12) is translated in one of three ways (see representative translations listed below). The root occurs in the G transitive stem only here and in Isaiah 51:15 = Jer 31:35 where it refers to YHWH as "the one who stirs up (*rōgaʿ*) the sea so its waves roar." On *rgʿ* as "stirring up," cf. NEB's translation of Job 26:12 and the LXX to Isaiah 51:15 (*ho tarassōn tēn thalassan*). Dhorme (*A Commentary on the Book of*

> Awake, awake, clothe yourself with strength,
> O arm of YHWH!
> Awake, as in days of old,
> As in the distant past!
> Was it not you who hewed Rahab in pieces,[35]
> who pierced (*měḥôlelet*) the Dragon (*tannîn*)?
> Was it not you who dried up the Sea (*yām*),
> the waters of the great deep (*těhôm rabbâ*)?
> (Isa 51:9–10a)

Such piercing of a mythological seven-headed dragon by a warrior deity is known elsewhere in the ancient Near East as depicted in the iconography of Figure 1 that comes from Tell Asmar.[36]

Job, 374) argues for the "dividing" of the sea (cf. NEB and Tg *gzr*). Finally, a case can be made for *rgʻ* designating the "quelling, stilling," of the sea (cf. LXX *katepausev*; see, for example, RSV, NRSV, NJPS, Pope, *Job*, 185; Habel, *The Book of Job*, 365; Day, *God's Conflict*, 38). As Pope points out, *Chaoskampf* myths universally describe the quelling, not the agitating of Sea, and such an understanding is fitting for Job 26:12.

The MT of 26:13 is straightforward ("By his wind the heavens are luminous/fair") yet hardly fitting the context of 26:12–13 that has the motif of combat repeating in every other line. The varying treatments in the versions (see Dhorme, *A Commentary on the Book of Job*, 375) attest to the long-standing confusion regarding the verse in general and *šiprâ* in particular. Recovering the author's original understanding is impossible. Yet Pope's (*Job*, 185–6) remark about the Akkadian word used for the net (*sapāru*; Enuma Elish IV, 41) in which Tiamat is ensnared is tantalizing (and beyond coincidence for our *šiprâ*?). While Pope's redivision of the MT's *šāmayim* ("By his wind he put Sea [*śm ym*] in a bag") seems drastic, his speculative analysis may very well approximate the original.

Lastly, the mention of *nāḥāš bārîaḥ* in 26:13 recalls the Fleeing Serpent (*bṯn brḥ*) that Baʻlu was said to vanquish in *KTU* 1.5.I.1–3 and *KTU* 1.82.38.

35. Scholars note how 1QIsaᵃ has *mōḥeṣet*, "smiting," (cf. Job 26:12) rather than MT's *maḥṣebet*, "hewing," and prefer the latter as *lectio difficilior*. Be that as it may, *mōḥeṣet* functioned as a variant reading.

36. For futher analysis of the Tell Asmar seal, see Rendsburg, "UT 68 and the Tell Asmar Seal."

Figure 1: A warrior deity piercing a seven-headed dragon from Tell Asmar. From: Henri Frankfort, *Iraq Excavations of the Oriental Institute 1932/33. Third Preliminary Report of the Iraq Expedition*. Oriental Institute Communications, No. 17. Chicago: The Oriental Institute of the University of Chicago / The University of Chicago Press, 1934. Page 49, Figure 43. Seal Impression As. 32.738. (Courtesy of the Oriental Institute of the University of Chicago)

In sum, we are suggesting that the curious idiom of "piercing" (*nqb*) the name of YHWH hearkens back to a mythic tradition whereby vanquished gods and/or preternatural foes were "pierced" by a warrior god. Such traditions are quite old in their origin, as evidenced by similar motifs from Late Bronze Age Ugarit and elsewhere.[37] These aged *Chaoskampf* traditions are attested in the Hebrew Bible's archaic poetry (Exod 15:1-12; Ps 29; Hab 3:8-15), yet even more so in the exilic and post-exilic periods (Ps 74:12-17; Ps 77:17-21 [Eng 77:16-20]; Ps 93:1-4; Isa 51:9-11; Job 26:12-13; Isa 27:1) where a "cosmic renaissance" tapped them for their mythic power. Thus there is no problem with these traditions being available for the author of Leviticus 24 no matter how one dates the Holiness Code (Lev 17-26).

One last link in our chain of evidence needs to be unpacked. To this point we have demonstrated that: (a) names are tied to identity and thus YHWH'S name was thought to be tied to His essence; (b) to blot out or to destroy a name was a profoundly serious act, even more so if directed toward divinity; (c) words of blasphemy are best understood as effectual words, i.e. words understood to have real efficacy as they were inherently empowered by the divine; and (d) the vocabulary of "piercing" was used of cosmic battles, that is, battles revealing ultimate supremacy whereby a

37. The well-known Babylonian creation story of Enuma Elish (with Marduk battling Tiamat) readily comes to mind, though even earlier we find similar stories of the warrior god Tishpak, the chief god of Eshnunna (Lewis, "CT 13.33-34 and Ezekiel 32"). From the Levant we have references to Adad of Aleppo defeating Tiamat and Ba'lu of Ugarit fighting Yammu, the Litanu and *tunnanu*-dragons, and Môtu, the god of Death.

victorious deity vanquishes divine or preternatural foes. What is left to flesh out for our idiom ("to pierce a name") is how names might appear in such a battle context.

Mythological Subtext, Part B: Divine Names in War Contexts

I have documented elsewhere how royal and divine names were used as weapons as they could constitute the very presence of the monarch or deity on the battlefield. Ramses III's inscriptions from Medinet Habu curse the Sea Peoples by having his name consume them in their land. Thutmosis IV employs iconography that depicts his name as a fighting cartouche wielding a mace as it subdues enemies in a battle.[38] In Mesopotamian lore, we read of heaven and earth trembling at the mere thought of Ishtar's name, a preeminent name that awed the gods and to which humans paid homage. Biblical tradition similarly called out to the gods (or heavenly beings) (běnê 'ēlîm) to ascribe to YHWH "the radiance and strength" of his Name (kābôd wāʿ ōz . . . kĕbôd šĕmô; Ps 29:1–2).

YHWH's Name, explicitly equated with YHWH himself in Deut 28:58, is radiantly powerful (nikbād) and terrifying (nôrāʾ). The manifestation of YHWH's presence in battle via his Name is well documented from its ritual invocation in the "Song of the Ark" (Num 10:35–36) to its invocation over his Ark as a war palladium (2 Sam 6:1–2) to the hypostatic tradition found in Isa 30:27–33.[39]

> The Name of YHWH (šēm yhwh) comes from afar,
> In blazing wrath…
> His tongue like a devouring fire,
> His breath like a raging torrent…
> YHWH sounds the radiance of his thunder,
> Reveals the descending blow of his arm
> In raging wrath, in a devouring blaze of fire,
> In tempest, rainstorm, and hailstones.
> At the thunder of YHWH Assyria will be terrified
> When he smites with his rod…
> (Isa 30:27–28a, 30–31)

---

38. See Lewis, "Athtartu's Incantations," 219–20.

39. The hypostatic use of a divine name in battle also occurs in one of the plaster inscriptions from Kuntillet ʿAjrud mentioning "The Name of El on the day of wa[r]" (šm ʾl bym mlḥ[mh]). See Meshel (Kuntillet ʿAjrud, 110); Lewis, "Athtartu's Incantations," 221.

Similarly, Psalm 20, that "as a whole refers to a military event,"[40] contains a series of invocations that look to the protective power inherent in the Name of YHWH:

> May YHWH answer you in the day of trouble!
> May the Name of the God of Jacob protect you!
>
> May we shout for joy over your victory,
> arrayed by (military) standards in the Name of our God!
>
> They [call] on chariots, they [call] on horses;
> but we invoke the Name of YHWH our God:
>
> "O YHWH, grant victory!"
>
> May the King answer us in the day of our invocation.
> (Ps 20:2, 6, 8, 10 [= Eng 20:1, 5, 7, 9])

Especially noteworthy is the way in which YHWH's Name is employed as a weapon *per se* in the story of David battling Goliath:

> Then David said to the Philistine, "You come against me with sword, spear and scimitar; but I come against you with the Name of YHWH of Armies (*běšēm yhwh ṣěbā'ôt*), the God of the ranks of Israel, whom you have defied."
> (1 Sam 17:45)

Here the Name of YHWH is made parallel to tangible weapons that are wielded in battle. Note how the Name is then followed by two fitting military epithets, YHWH *Ṣěbā'ôt*, literally "YHWH of Armies" and "the God of the (military) ranks of Israel" (*'ělōhê ma'arkôt yiśrā'ēl*). Elsewhere YHWH confers power on David his chosen warrior by the power of his Name to such a degree that David too is imagined as conquering the cosmic deity Sea (*yām* // *něhārôt*) (Ps 89:20b–25).[41]

The Blasphemer's Logic, Part 1: The Possibility of Deicide

The blasphemer's logic would run something like this. (If this sounds heretical, remember, he's a blasphemer!) If then the Name of God (as a manifestation of divine presence) can go to battle, then, logically, combatants can attack and even defeat the Name of God in battle. As YHWH can blot out

---

40. So Kraus, *Psalms 1–59*, 281.

41. This echo of cosmic battle is reminiscent of Adad letting King Zimri-Lim use his divine weapons, the very weapons Adad used to defeat Tiamat. For a convenient text and translation, see Nissinen et al., *Prophets and Prophecy*, 21–22 with additional bibliography.

the name of his enemies, so, logically, could his name be blotted out by a stronger entity. Just as YHWH can pierce and kill Yam or Leviathan, so too can He be pierced and killed. (From a Canaanite perspective, though Ba'lu can indeed defeat the god Death [Môtu], so Death [Môtu] can indeed *pierce* and kill Ba'lu.[42])

Despite romantic notions about the inherent immortality of the gods in the ancient Near East, we see clear indications that gods can and do die.[43] There are the well-known stories of the deaths of Osiris in Egypt and Ba'lu at Ugarit, yet their emergence later in the myths erases the fear that they remained dead. Dumuzi's descent into the underworld evokes ritual mourning reflected in Mesopotamian literature and in the Bible (Ezek 8:14). Occasionally we can point to religious iconography of one deity killing another (e.g., Figure 2) which comes as no surprise to anyone familiar with the creation myth Enuma Elish (where Ea kills Apsu and Mummu, Marduk kills Tiamat, etc.).

Figure 2: A god cuts the throat of another god. From a cylinder seal of the Akkadian period. From: Jeremy Black and Anthony Green, *Gods, Demons and Symbols of Ancient Mesopotamia: An Illustrated Dictionary*. Illustrations by Tessa Rickards. Austin: University of Texas Press, 1992. Copyright ©1992
(Courtesy of the University of Texas Press,
the Trustees of the British Museum, and the British Museum Press)

---

42. The full narrative is found in *KTU* 1.5.I.1–1.5.VI.10. The specific reference to Môtu "piercing" (*ṭ'n*) Ba'lu occurs in *KTU* 1.5.I.26 (cf. Isa 14:19).

43. Dead gods, like dead humans, can even have ghosts. See Moran, "The Creation of Man," 54–56.

Other tales, both East and West Semitic, that tell of the death of the gods include those in the *Chaoskampf* tradition, those dealing with rebellious gods, and the killing of those who were deemed guilty of some offense (cf. Qingu in Enuma Elish VI). Compare especially the tale of Atrahasis (1.4.223–26) that tells of the slaughter of the rebel god Ilawela (formerly read as Geshtu-e and We-ila) whose flesh, blood, "spirit" (*eṭemmu*), and "intelligence" (*ṭēmu*) are then used as ingredients for making humans.

Yet the musings found in Ugarit's Kirta Epic may be more telling. It is hard not to feel the uncertainty voiced as Kirta's son weeps for his ailing father and wonders: *'u'ilm tmtn* "Do gods die after all?" (*KTU* 1.16.I.22 // *KTU* 1.16.II.43). Perhaps there was enough instability in the Levant regarding the permanence of the divine that it would have been appealing for the ancient Israelites to name their deity YHWH "the (permanently) existing one." Is it just a coincidence that YHWH (a divine name written with a prefixal verbal form that can designate past durative as well as future durative) comes to bear the *ʿôlām* epithet of El (Gen 21:33; Isa 40:28; Jer 40:10) who exists "from everlasting to everlasting" (Ps 90:2 *mēʿôlām ʿad ʿôlām ʾattâ ʾēl*)? Similarly, what prompted Israelite authors to describe YHWH as "the living god" (Pss 42:3; 84:3)[44] if all gods were by definition immortal? One advantage of understanding Exod 3:14's etymological puzzle as dealing with eternal existence is that it would be in concert with the following verse. Together the two verses would underscore that "the god who is" bears a name that reflects the permanency of his character.

> YHWH has sent me.
> This shall be my name *forever*,   *zeh šĕmî lĕʿôlām*
> This is my appellation *for all eternity*.   *zeh zikrî lĕdōr dōr*
> (Exod 3:15)

Back to our blasphemer and his logic (i.e., faulty logic according to the tenets of normative Yahwism). Due to the ubiquitous presence of theophoric elements in personal names, one could posit that ancient Near Eastern peoples were rarely atheists. Thus one of the underlying reasons for blaspheming could be the blasphemer's belief in other gods (whom biblical writers term *ʾĕlōhîm ʾăḥērîm*), that is, a god or gods whom the blasphemer would deem more powerful.[45] In the identity politics of Lev 24:10, the blas-

---

44. Cf. Mettinger, *In Search of God*, 82–91.

45. To judge from the Hebrew Bible's own witness, as well as extra-biblical epigraphic and archaeological data, the worship of gods other than YHWH in ancient Israel was ongoing. The very laws that command one not to worship *ʾĕlōhîm ʾăḥērîm* (Exod 20:3; 23:13; Deut 5:7; 6:14) imply such practices.

Alternatively, the blasphemer could indeed be an atheist, such as described in Psalm

phemer in question is half-Egyptian on his father's side (*wĕhû' ben-'îš miṣrî*) who quarrels with "a man of Israel," presumably designating a person of 100% Israelite lineage.[46] Could the quarrel have been about divinity as much as it was about ethnicity? (Or, another way to frame the question, *why* is it that the author of Leviticus 24 highlights the part Egyptian bloodline of the blasphemer who "goes out among the people of Israel"?)

If the blasphemer does indeed worship another god, then it stands to reason that he believes that YHWH is weaker than his god. Thus, in his conceptual world, YHWH is indeed able to be defeated. If our blasphemer were retelling Dtr's tale of the capture of the Ark of YHWH by the Philistines (i.e. the Ark which bear's YHWH's Name and is referred to as *'ĕlōhîm* in 1 Sam 4:7), he would underscore that *YHWH can indeed be captured*, and then, in contrast to Dtr's resolution of the story, spin a tale of YHWH's defeat.

The Blasphemer's Logic, Part 2: Hubris and Pragmatics of Deicide (via the Employment of Blasphemous Words)

Yet the blasphemer is not content to let another deity do his battle. His passion, mixed with hubris, clouds his thinking allowing him to take matters into his own hands. He fails to consider a key problematic detail: that the tales of deicide noted above were of gods battling gods. Like the Prince of Tyre in Ezekiel 28, known for his pride and corrupted wisdom, the blasphemer too considers himself on par with *'ĕlōhîm* (Ezek 28:2,6,9).

Yet what deicidal strategy could a mortal (even a hubristic mortal) employ? There are no legendary ancient Near Eastern traditions of mere humans, spear in hand, successfully defeating the gods. That a god can be killed does not imply that a human can do it in and of himself. Thus the blasphemer turns to the only power (effectual words) and logic he knows will work, illogical though it may be for such a supposed non-believer. He employs a curse (empowered by YHWH) against YHWH. Once again we

---

10 where "a wicked person ... curses and renounces YHWH" (*rāšā'* ... *bērek* [used euphemistically] *ni'ēṣ yhwh*) due to his pride (*gōbah 'appô*) that asserts that "there is no God" (*'ên 'ĕlōhîm*). In such a case, he feels he can blaspheme without any fear of repercussion, for the recipient of his words does not exist. The logical difficulty (why then bother to curse such a non-existent entity?) would have escaped such speakers unless their desire was not to curse God per se, but rather to use such rhetoric against theists.

46. See the remarks above (n. 2) regarding the social dimensions of our passage. Levine (*The JPS Torah Commentary Leviticus*, 166) further underscores that the blasphemer's genealogy is "certainly significant" by noting that his mother was from the tribe of Dan (Lev 24:11), whose northern cult practices were considered illegitimate by the Jerusalemite priesthood and hence the authors of Leviticus 24.

must consider the underlying psychology of effectual words that allows a person of lesser power to bring about a desired result (by tapping into divine power) against a much greater enemy.[47] This is perfectly illustrated by effectual words (e.g. curses, imprecations) that are used at a distance against a much greater force—indeed, even against nation states (Ps 137:7-9; Ps 79:10b-12; Obad 15-16).[48] Alternatively, one could posit that the blasphemer is invoking a hypostatic entity that represents YHWH (and can access His power) but at the same time can act independently—and importantly for the blasphemer's thinking and purpose—out of accord with YHWH's wishes similar to the "Anger of YHWH" in 2 Sam 24.[49]

As already surmised in the Talmud (b. Sanh. 56a), the blasphemer is invoking YHWH to curse YHWH.[50] Or, better nuanced, the blasphemer, with malevolent hubris, invokes a God-empowered imprecation that proclaims the hex: "May YHWH pierce the Name of YHWH!" Just as only YHWH is able to pierce (nqb) a cosmic deity such as Yam (Hab 3:14) and preternatural beasts such as Behemoth and Leviathan (Job 40:24-26 [Eng 40:24—41:2])—where no human would stand a chance—so only YHWH (or an independent YHWH-istic hypostatic entity[51]) would be able to bring about the blasphemer's desire to pierce/kill the Name (and hence essence) of YHWH.

---

47. Though farther afield, consider how Pharaoh Pepi I—though a believer—can nonetheless appeal to magic to threaten any god who does not assist him in his ascent to the sky. See Pyramid Text 539, §1322-1324; Allen, *The Ancient Egyptian Pyramid Texts*, 174; *ANET* 137a.

48. Though the blasphemer in Leviticus 24 is charged with an oral crime, at times effectual words were ritualized. See, for example Num 5:11-31; Jer 19:1-11; 51:59-64.

49. See 2 Sam 24:1ff // 1 Chr 21:1ff, and the exposition by McCarter, "When Gods Lose Their Temper," 90-91. See too Kitz (*Cursed*, 162 n. 18) who frames this as the blasphemer trying to access YHWH's "evil" side, a position that is "untenable" and would thus have a "boomerang effect" on the blasphemer. See also Blank's ("The Curse," 85) remarks about such cursing "backfiring."

50. The Talmud's insight was advocated already in Livingston, "The Crime of Leviticus," 352-3. See too a different line of thinking by Milgrom (*Leviticus 23-27*, 2109; *Leviticus*, 292) following D. N. Freedman who suggests that the reciprocal logic of humans and God blessing one another (and "feeding" one another) suggests the same reciprocity could apply to the efficacy of curses. Milgrom does presume that the name of God would be used in cursing God.

51. See above, n. 49.

Conclusion: The Adjudication of Deicide

The blasphemer's performative cursing in Leviticus 24 is severely serious, entirely different in degree from Job's use of caustic words to challenge God and His nature (Job 16:6–14).[52] The maledictor in Leviticus 24 is deadly serious. Raymond Westbrook and Bruce Wells state succinctly: "Blasphemy was essentially the act of putting a curse—or attempting to put a curse—upon a deity. It was the ultimate act of rebellion."[53] It is argued above that (a) the content of the blasphemous curse in Leviticus 24—using the language of "piercing" (*nqb*) YHWH's Name—was that of deicide, and (b) the illicit means—the attempted appropriation of YHWH's power for this most extreme act—constituted an additional act of rebellion.[54] Due to such an act of killing, *lex talionis* law would require capital punishment.[55] Thus it is that the blasphemy narrative of Lev 24:10–14,23, and the resulting punishment (Lev 24:13,23), were positioned within the context of *lex talionis* laws of commensurate retribution with respect to killing (Lev 24:15–22).[56]

One could argue that the blasphemer's act was an act of *attempted* killing, for God was indeed not killed due to the man's words. Yet effectual words were perceived to be powerful and even lethal. Thus, to write anachronistically, the man had discharged what he considered to be a lethal weapon in committing his crime. In criminal law, his intention to kill and his overt actions using a lethal means make him guilty of an indictable offense that carries a maximum penalty.

---

52. Note that there is no indication of Job's harsh words constituting an accusation of blasphemy deserving of capital punishment.

53. Westbrook and Wells, *Everyday Law*, 71.

54. Is it just a coincidence that Zech 5:3–4 juxtaposes the crimes of theft (*gnb*) and swearing falsely by the name of YHWH (*hannišbāʿ bišmî laššāqer*) as two offenses that are placed under a severe curse that destroys both violators' homes down to the last timber and stone? Could it be that swearing falsely using YHWH's name was thought of as an act of theft (i.e. stealing/appropriating the godly name for ungodly purposes)? Cf. Jer 7:9.

55. In our opinion, the same act of (attempted) cursing of the divine with (potential) lethal ramifications is reflected in Job 2:9. Here too we have *brk* used euphemistically for cursing the deity (cf. above n. 12 and n. 19). Had Job actually followed his wife's advice and cursed God, he would have died as a result though the means by which (human or divine) are not stated. Thus we agree with the Peshitta translators who see this as an act of blasphemy ($\sqrt{sh}$'). For many other interpretations, see Seow, *Job 1–21*, 305.

56. Raymond Westbrook ("Biblical and Cuneiform Law Codes" 3–20), my late colleague and expert in ancient law, had previously argued how our passage, and the Covenant Code overall, fit within the context of ancient Near Eastern law codes and their practical application. The argument here provides a "link" that makes his case even stronger. See Westbrook ("Biblical and Cuneiform Law Codes" 20).

Addendum:

In light of the double meaning of *nqb* documented above (to pierce; to pierce a name → to commit blasphemy, to curse), it may be just a likely coincidence that Hebrew also has two homonymous *ḥll* roots: (a) *ḥll* I "to be defiled; to profane," and (b) *ḥll* II "to pierce." (4Q560 even uses the root for "piercing demons.") Though actual pronunciations are unknown, cognate languages and historical linguistics allow us to reconstruct that the former originated as *ḥll with the initial ḥ consonant conventionally thought to represent a voiceless pharyngeal fricative, while the latter originated as *ḫll with the initial consonant ḫ conventionally thought to represent a voiceless velar fricative. These two originally distinct ḥ and ḫ phonemes (cf. Arabic, Ugaritic, Ethiopic) were of such similarity that they merged in Hebrew with the polyphonous letter ח being used to mark both phonemes.[57]

Though distinct in their historical, etymological origin, together these two *ḥll* homonyms somewhat track the dual meanings of *nqb*—being used of literal piercing (of Sea, Behemoth, and Leviathan) and profaning (i.e. piercing God's name). As noted in our discussion above, *ḥll* II is used of piercing the cosmic Sea and sea dragon (Job 26:12-13; Isa 51:9-10a). Repeatedly H and Ezekiel use *ḥll* I for the profaning of YHWH's name by various means (Lev 18:21; 19:12; 21:6; 22:2, 32; Ezek 20:39; 36:20, 22-23; 39:7).

Such tracking can be just a philological coincidence. And yet the author of the book of Ezekiel (who statistically uses both *ḥll* I and *ḥll* II far more than any other author) does play off of *ḥll* I and *ḥll* II. In looking again at Ezekiel 28, we find the Prince of Tyre (who asserted that he was *'ĕlōhîm*), repeatedly being "pierced" and/or "defiled" (28:7,8,9,16,23; cf. 26:15)—even "deadly pierced" in the heart of the seas (*yammîm*) in 28:8. Notably, he is pierced/profaned by YHWH (28:16), and in part because he was known for "profaning" sanctuaries (Ezek 28:18).[58]

ḥll II in the sense of "pierced" often designates slain corpses, and death is indeed most defiling. Thus this could be the obvious reason for why Ezekiel could play off the two *ḥll* homonyms. Yet perhaps, especially in the case of the profaning (*ḥll* I) "*'ĕlōhîm*-Prince" of Tyre who was pierced (*ḥll* II), Ezekiel also echoed H's profaning/piercing-a-god double entendre of *nqb*. Note especially Ezekiel's close association with H.

---

57. Cf. Blau, *Phonology and Morphology*, 75.
58. Cf. Ezek 13:18-19 that mentions the profaning (*ḥll* I) of YHWH through illicit cultic hunting (*lĕṣôdēd nĕpāšôt*) and killing (*lĕhāmît nĕpāšôt*).

BIBLIOGRAPHY

Albertz, Rainer, and Rüdiger Schmitt. *Family and Household Religion in Ancient Israel and the Levant*. Winona Lake, IN: Eisenbrauns, 2012.

Allen, James P. *The Ancient Egyptian Pyramid Texts*. 2nd ed. SBLWAW 23. Atlanta: Society of Biblical Literature, 2015.

Amiran, Ruth. "Two Luristan Fibulae and an Urartian Ladle from Old Excavations in Palestine." *Iranica Antiqua* 6 (1966) 88–91 Pl. XVIII, Fig. 1 a–d.

Andersen, Francis I. *Habakkuk*. AB 25. New York: Doubleday, 2001.

Beit-Arieh, Itzhaq et al. *Ḥorvat Qitmit: An Edomite Shrine in the Biblical Negev*. Tel Aviv: Institute of Archaeology of Tel Aviv University, 1995.

Blank, Sheldon H. "The Curse, Blasphemy, the Spell and the Oath." *HUCA* 23 (1950–1951) 73–95.

Blau, Joshua. *Phonology and Morphology of Biblical Hebrew: An Introduction*. Winona Lake, IN: Eisenbrauns, 2010.

Bourdieu, Pierre. *Language and Symbolic Power*. Cambridge, MA: Polity, 1992.

Brichto, Herbert Chanan. *The Problem of Curse in the Hebrew Bible*. Journal of Biblical Literature Monograph Series 13. Philadelphia: Society of Biblical Literature and Exegesis, 1963.

Broida, Marian W. *Forestalling Doom. "Apotropaic Intercession" in the Hebrew Bible and the Ancient Near East*. AOAT 417. Münster: Ugarit-Verlag, 2014.

Clines, David J. A. *Job 38–42*. Nashville: Nelson, 2011.

Cogan, Mordechai. "A Lamashtu Plaque from the Judaean Shephelah." *IEJ* (1995) 155–61.

Day, John. *God's Conflict with the Dragon and the Sea: Echoes of a Canaanite Myth in the Old Testament*. Cambridge: Cambridge University Press, 1985.

Dhorme, Édouard. *A Commentary on the Book of Job*. Nashville: Nelson, 1967.

Dobbs-Allsopp, F. W. "(More) On Performatives in Semitic." *Zeitschrift für Althebraistik* 17–20 (2004–2007) 36–81.

Dolansky, Shawna. *Now You See It, Now You Don't: Biblical Perspectives on the Relationship between Magic and Religion*. Winona Lake, IN: Eisenbrauns, 2008.

Farber, Walter. "Associative Magic: Some Rituals, Wordplays, and Philology." *JAOS* 106 (1986) 447–49.

Fishbane, Michael. "Jeremiah IV 23–26 and Job III 3–13: A Recovered Use of the Creation Pattern." *VT* 21 (1971) 151–67.

Greaves, Sheldon W. "Wordplay and Associative Magic in the Ugaritic Snake-bite Incantation RS 24.244." *UF* 26 (1995) 165–67.

Greenberg, Moshe. *Ezekiel 21–37*. AB 22A. New York: Doubleday, 1997.

Habel, Norman C. *The Book of Job*. Philadelphia: Westminster, 1985.

Hiebert, Theodore. *God of My Victory: The Ancient Hymn in Habakkuk 3*. Harvard Semitic Monographs 38. Atlanta: Scholars, 1986.

Kitz, Anne Marie. *Cursed Are You! The Phenomenology of Cursing in Cuneiform and Hebrew Texts*. Winona Lake, IN: Eisenbrauns, 2014.

Kraus, Hans-Joachim. *Psalms 1–59: A Commentary*. Translated by Hilton C. Oswald. Continental Commentaries. Minneapolis: Augsburg, 1988.

Lenzi, Alan. *Reading Akkadian Prayers and Hymns: An Introduction*. SBL Ancient Near East Monographs 3. Atlanta: Society of Biblical Literature, 2011.

———. "*šiptu ul yuttun*: Some Reflections on a Closing Formula in Akkadian Incantations." In *Gazing on the Deep: Ancient Near Eastern and Other Studies in Honor of Tzvi Abusch*, edited by Jeffrey Stackert, Barbara N. Porter, and David P. Wright, 131–66. Bethesda, MD: CDL, 2010.

Levine, Baruch A. *Leviticus*. JPS Torah Commentary. Philadelphia: Jewish Publication Society, 1989.

Lewis, Theodore J. "'Athtartu's Incantations and the Use of Divine Names as Weapons." *JNES* 71 (2011) 207–27.

———. "CT 13.33–34 and Ezekiel 32: Lion-Dragon Myths." *JAOS* 116 (1996) 28–47.

———. "How Far Can Texts Take Us? Evaluating Textual Sources for Reconstructing Ancient Israelite Beliefs about the Dead." In *Sacred Time, Sacred Place: Archaeology and the Religion of Israel*, edited by Barry M. Gittlen, 169–217. Winona Lake, IN: Eisenbrauns, 2002.

———. "The Identity and Function of Ugaritic Sha'tiqatu: A Divinely Made Apotropaic Figure." *JANER* 14 (2014) 1–28.

———. "Job 19 in the Light of the Ketef Hinnom Inscriptions and Amulets." In *Puzzling Out the Past: Studies in the Northwest Semitic Languages and Literatures in Honor of Bruce Zuckerman*, edited by Marilyn Lundberg, Steven Fine and Wayne T. Pitard, 99–113, 319–20. Culture and History of the Ancient Near East 55. Leiden: Brill, 2012.

Livingston, Dennis H. "The Crime of Leviticus XXIV 11." *VT* 36 (1986) 352–53.

Lundbom, Jack R. *Jeremiah 1–20*. AB 21A. New York: Doubleday, 1999.

McBride, S. Dean. "The Deuteronomic Name Theology." PhD diss., Harvard University, 1969.

McCarter, P. Kyle. *I Samuel*. AB 8. Garden City, NY: Doubleday, 1980.

———. *II Samuel*. AB 9. Garden City, NY: Doubleday, 1984.

———. "When Gods Lose Their Temper: Divine Rage in Ugaritic Myth and the Hypostasis of Anger in Iron Age Religion." In *Divine Wrath and Divine Mercy in the World of Antiquity*, edited by Reinhard G. Kratz and Hermann Spieckermann, 78–91. FAT 33. Tübingen: Mohr/Siebeck, 2008.

Meshel, Ze'ev. *Kuntillet 'Ajrud (Ḥorvat Teman) An Iron Age II Religious Site on the Judah-Sinai Border*. Jerusalem: Israel Exploration Society, 2012.

Mettinger, Tryggve N. D. *In Search of God: The Meaning and Message of the Everlasting Names*. Philadelphia: Fortress, 1988.

Milgrom, Jacob. *Leviticus: A Book of Ritual and Ethics*. Continental Commentaries. Minneapolis: Fortress, 2004.

———. *Leviticus 23–27*. AB 3B. New York: Doubleday, 2001.

Mitchell, Christopher Wright. *The Meaning of BRK "To Bless" in the Old Testament*. SBL Dissertation Series 95. Atlanta: Scholars, 1987.

Moran, William L. "The Creation of Man in Atrahasis I 192–248." *BASOR* 200 (1970) 48–56.

Nissinen, Martti et al. *Prophets and Prophecy in the Ancient Near East*. SBLWAW 12. Atlanta: Society of Biblical Literature, 2003.

Noegel, Scott B. "Job iii 5 in the Light of Mesopotamian Demons of Time." *VT* 57 (2007) 556–62.

Ornan, Tallay. "An Amulet of the Demon Pazuzu." In *Excavations at Tel Beth-Shean 1989–1996, Volume 1*, edited by Amihai Mazar, 517–19. Jerusalem: Israel Exploration Society, 2006.

Pardee, Dennis. "Les documents d'Arslan Tash: Authentique ou faux?" *Syria* 75 (1998) 15–54.

Pitard, Wayne T. "The Binding of Yamm: A New Edition of the Ugaritic Text KTU 1.83." *JNES* 57 (1998) 261–80.

Pope, Marvin H. *Job*. AB 15. Garden City, NY: Doubleday, 1965.

Rendsburg, Gary A. "UT 68 and the Tell Asmar Seal." *Orientalia* 53 (1984) 448–53.

Sanders, Seth L. "Performative Utterances and Divine Language in Ugaritic." *JNES* 63 (2004) 161–81.

Seow, Choon Leong. *Job 1–21*. Illuminations. Grand Rapids: Eerdmans, 2013.

Smith, Mark S. "The Baal Cycle." In *Ugaritic Narrative Poetry*, edited by Simon B. Parker, 81–176. SBLWAW 9. Atlanta: Society of Biblical Literature, 1997.

Thistleton, Anthony C. "The Supposed Power of Words in the Biblical Writings." *JTS* 25 (1974) 283–99.

Toorn, Karel van der. *Family Religion in Babylonia, Syria and Israel*. Studies in the History and Culture of the Ancient Near East 7. Leiden: Brill, 1996.

Walton, John H. "Demons in Mesopotamia and Israel: Exploring the Category of Non-Divine but Supernatural Entities." In *Windows to the Ancient World of the Hebrew Bible: Essays in Honor of Samuel Greengus*, edited by Bill T. Arnold, Nancy L. Erickson, and John H. Walton, 229–46. Winona Lake, IN: Eisenbrauns, 2014.

Westbrook, Raymond. "Biblical and Cuneiform Law Codes." *RB* 92 (1985) 247–65. Reprinted in *Law from the Tigris to the Tiber: The Writings of Raymond Westbrook*, edited by Bruce Wells and Rachel Magdalene, 3–20. Winona Lake, IN: Eisenbrauns, 2009.

Westbrook, Raymond, and Bruce Wells. *Everyday Law in Biblical Israel: An Introduction*. Louisville: Westminster John Knox, 2009.

Zevit, Ziony. *The Religions of Ancient Israel: A Synthesis of Parallactic Approaches*. London: Continuum, 2001.

13

Varia on Crowns and Diadems in the Bible and Mesopotamia[1]

Shalom M. Paul

THE HEBREW UNIVERSITY OF JERUSALEM

In a recent article, Shawn Zelig Aster shed new light on Psalm 21 as a royal psalm describing an enthronement ritual and the accompanying acts of divine favor and benificences which the deity bestows upon the king, sharing with him the attributes of כבוד, הוד, and הדר, which reflect the Mesopotamian concept of *melammu*.[2] By these divine grants the king henceforth possesses those unique attributes reserved for the deity himself.

Here I would like to call attention to yet another gift granted to the king which was not elaborated upon by Aster. In v. 4b the text reads תָּשִׁית לְרֹאשׁוֹ עֲטֶרֶת פָּז "You have set upon his head a crown of fine gold." In the ancient Near East gods are portrayed as wearing crowns as insignia of their god-head.[3] The Akkadian interdialectic semantic equivalent of the Hebrew expression for a "crown of fine gold" (עֲטֶרֶת פָּז) is *agû ḫurāṣu*, which appears several times in descriptions of deities. See, for example, the citation in an

---

1. To Ziony, a dear friend and colleague on his "crowning" academic career.

2. Aster, "On the Place of Psalm 21," 307–20. For a comprehensive study of these terms, see Aster, *Unbeatable Light*.

3. On crowns and diadems in Mesopotamia, see Unger, "Diadem und Krone," 201–11; Calmeyer, "Mauerkrone," 595–6.

inscription of Agum II Kakrime, a Kassite king of Babylon: *agê ... ḫurāṣi ina qaqqidšu lu aškunuma*, "I indeed placed upon his (Marduk's) head a crown ... of gold."[4] Similarly in an inscription of Nabonidus, the last king of Babylon: *agâ ḫurāṣi simat ilūtišu ša apru rašuššu*, "the golden crown befitting his (Šamaš's) divinity with which his head was covered."[5] Compare likewise the following statement of Nabonidus: *agê ḫurāṣi kīma labīrimma ... eššīš abni ... maḫar Šamaš bēlija ukīn*, "I made anew the golden crown like the old one ... and placed it before Šamaš, my lord."[6] Thus it can be seen that yet another divine gift, along with the attributes of כבוד, הוד, and הדר, with which the king is invested metaphorically in this psalm, is the "golden crown," which thereby relates him intimately with the God of Israel.

Another expression for a "golden crown" in Akkadian is *kilīlu ḫurāṣi*.[7] Hebrew equivalents are עֲטֶרֶת זָהָב,[8] which was bestowed upon Mordechai (Esth 8:15), and עֲטֶרֶת פָּז, which adorned the head of the High Priest Aaron (Sir 45:12).[9] In the book of Esther mention is also made of כֶּתֶר מַלְכוּת, "a

---

4. Oshima, "Another Attempt," 235–6, II:50–III:3.

5. Schaudig, *Die Inschriften Nabonids*, 379, I:43; see also line 47.

6. Ibid., 380, II:34–38.

7. Parpola, *Correspondence*, 34, 11: rev. 5. For its Hebrew etymological and semantic equivalent, כְּלִיל, see Tawil, "Two Biblical Architectural Images," 39–40. See also *CAD* K, 358, where at the end of the entry on *kilīlu* there is mention of a GILIM KÙ.GI with the same meaning.

For a very rare term, *mammû ḫurāṣu*, appearing in a broken context, see Ambos, *Mesopotamische Baurituale*, 120: rev. 50 (*ma-an-me-e ḫurāṣi*). Another reference may be found in Ebeling, *Tod und Leben*, 128:30 (*ma-am-mi ḫurāṣi*).

8. It is interesting to note that such a crown is also mentioned in a Phoenician inscription, לעטר ... עטרת חרץ, "to crown ... with a golden crown," but this is not related to the crown of a deity (Donner and Röllig, *KAI*, 1:13, 60.1–3).

9. Two other possible references to a golden crown may also be cited: (1) In Exod 28:36 and Lev 8:9 mention is made of a priestly golden head ornament (צִיץ [ה]זָהָב) worn by Aaron. Since the word appears coupled with נֵזֶר (Exod 39:30; Lev 8:9), which designates a crown (see 2 Sam 1:10; 2 Kgs 11:2; Ps 89:40; cf. Ps 132:18), many commentators have interpreted it also to mean a crown. See, e.g., Elliger, *Leviticus*, 112: "die goldene Blume ist eine relative junge Form des Diadems"; Milgrom, *Leviticus 1–16*, 512: "*nēzer* ... is a synonym of the previously mentioned *ṣîṣ*"; 513: "*nēzer* and *ṣîṣ* are synonyms"; Propp, *Exodus 19–40*, 446: "Whatever its precise definition, *ṣîṣ* connotes a head ornament, equivalent to a crown (*nēzer*)." He then compares this to "the golden diadem worn by the high priest of Hierapolis." See Attridge and Oden, *Syrian Goddess*, para. 42: "He (the High Priest) alone wears purple and is crowned with a golden tiara" (καὶ τιάρῃ χρυσέῃ ἀναδέεται); (2) Based on the reconstruction of the "Self-Glorification Hymn" from a Qumran scroll (1QH[a] XXVI:8) describing a rejected and despised individual who reckons himself as being elevated to the rank of divine beings, the reading לוא בפז (א)כת[יר] לי, "I will not crown myself with pure gold," has been plausibly suggested. For the text, see Stegemann and Schuller, *Qumran Cave 1:III*, 298. For the reconstruction, see Eshel, "The Self-Glorification Hymn," 428 (text), 430 (note).

royal crown," first in connection with Vashti (1:11) and then with Esther (6:8). This term is the interdialectal equivalent of *agû šarrūti*, mentioned many times in Mesopotamian royal inscriptions.[10]

Another descriptive term is כְּלִיל תִּפְאֶרֶת, "a glorious crown," first mentioned in Sir 45:8, on the head of Aaron,[11] and subsequently found in the liturgy of the Sabbath morning service, where it is stated that God bestowed such a crown on Moses at the time of the giving of the Torah.[12] A synonymous term, עֲטֶרֶת תִּפְאֶרֶת, is cited in the coronation of Jerusalem (Ezek 16:12). This expression, which also appears in Jer 13:18, Ezek 23:42, Prov 4:9, 16:31 (and compare in parallel stichs, Prov 17:6), complements Isa 28:5: "On that day the LORD of Hosts shall become a crown of beauty (עֲטֶרֶת צְבִי) and a diadem of splendor (צְפִירַת תִּפְאָרָה) for the remnant of His people." This may be compared to its Akkadian cognates, *agû ṣīru*,[13] "a majestic/splendid crown," and *agû tašriḫtu*, "crown of splendor."[14]

The motif of a city serving as a crown for its patron deity is documented in a prayer addressed to Bel (Marduk) during the Mesopotamian New Year festival: ᵈ*Bēl šubtaku Bābilu*ᵏⁱ *Borsip*ᵏⁱ *agûku*, "Bel, your dwelling is the city of Babylon, your crown is the city of Borsippa."[15] This, in turn, may be compared to Isa 62:3, "You (Jerusalem) shall be a glorious crown (עֲטֶרֶת תִּפְאֶרֶת)[16] in the hand of the Lord and a royal diadem (K צנוף, Q צָנִיף) in the palm of God's hand," where Jerusalem serves as the ornamental insignia of God's kingship. For the anomaly of "in the hand/palm of God" rather than on His head, see the comment of Luzzato on this verse: "In reverence to God, he did not say, 'on the Lord's head,' but rather 'in the hand of' and 'in the palm of,' since because of His affection for you, you shall always be in His hands . . . and the reason for the metaphor of a crown is that the Lord shall find glory in you, as in Prov 12: 4: אֵשֶׁת-חַיִל עֲטֶרֶת בַּעְלָהּ, 'A capable wife

---

10. See *CAD* A1, 155.

11. This expression was misunderstood by the Septuagint, where it is translated "sublime magnificence" (Skehan and Di Lella, *Wisdom of Ben Sira*, 506), understanding Heb. כְּלִיל as "perfection."

12. It first appears in the liturgy of the 9th century, in the Siddur Amran Gaon. See Goldschmidt, *Seder Rav Amran Gaon*, 72, line 36.

13. For an example, see *CAD* A1, 115.

14. For citations, see *CAD* T, 296, all of which, however, refer to the splendor of the new moon.

15. Thureau-Dangin, *Rituels Accadiens*, 129:15–16.

16. Note the rhyming couplet.

is the crown of her husband.'"[17] In Rabbinic literature, Jerusalem also served as a "golden city" crown (עִיר שֶׁל זָהָב = יְרוּשָׁלַיִם שֶׁל זָהָב).[18]

BIBLIOGRAPHY

Ambos, Claus. *Mesopotamische Baurituale aus der 1. Jahrtausend v. Chr.* Dresden: Islet, 2004.

Aster, Shawn Z. "On the Place of Psalm 21 in Israelite Royal Ideology." In *Mishneh Todah: Studies in Deuteronomy and Its Cultural Environment in Honor of Jeffrey H. Tigay*, edited by Nili S. Fox, David A. Glatt-Gilad, and Michael J. Williams, 307–20. Winona Lake, IN: Eisenbrauns, 2009.

———. *The Unbeatable Light: Melammu and Its Biblical Parallels.* AOAT 384. Münster: Ugarit, 2012.

Attridge, Harold W., and Robert A. Oden. *The Syrian Goddess (De Dea Syria) Attributed to Lucian.* Texts and Translations 9. Greco-Roman Religious Series 1. Missoula, MT: Scholars, 1976.

Calmeyer, Peter. "Mauerkrone." In *Reallexikon der Assyriologie und vorderasiatischen Archäologie* 7, edited by Dietz-Otto Edzard, 595–6. Berlin: de Gruyter, 1987–1990.

Donner, Herbert, and Wolfgang Röllig. *Kanaanäische und aramäische Inschriften (= KAI)*, 3 vols. Wiesbaden: Harrassowitz, 1962–1964.

Ebeling, Erich. *Tod und Leben nach den Vorstellungen der Babylonier.* Berlin: de Gruyter, 1931.

Elliger Karl. *Leviticus.* Handbuch zum Alten Testament 4. Tübingen: Mohr, 1966.

Eshel, Esther. "The Self-Glorification Hymn." In *Qumran Cave 4:XX: Poetical and Liturgical Texts*, Part 2, 421–32. DJD 29. Oxford: Clarendon, 1999.

Goldschmidt, Daniel, ed. *Seder Rav Amram Gaon.* Jerusalem: HaRav Kook Institute, 1971 (Hebrew).

Luzzato, Samuel David. *Il Profeta Isaia* (ספר ישעיה). Padua: Bianchi, 1855 (Hebrew).

Milgrom, Jacob. *Leviticus 1–16.* AB 3. New York: Doubleday, 1991.

Oshima, Takayoshi. "Another Attempt at Two Kassite Royal Inscriptions: Agum-Kakrime Inscription and the Inscription of Kurigalzu the Son of Kadashmanharbe." In *Babel und Bibel* 6, edited by Leonid Kogan, 225–68. Orientalia et Classica 43. Winona Lake, IN: Eisenbrauns, 2012.

Parpola, Simo, ed. *The Correspondence of Sargon II, Part 1: Letters from Assyria and the West.* State Archives of Assyria 2. Helsinki: Helsinki University Press, 1987.

Paul, Shalom M. *Isaiah 40–66: Translation and Commentary.* Grand Rapids: Eerdmans, 2012.

———. "Jerusalem of Gold—Revisited." In *Divrei Shalom: Collected Studies of Shalom M. Paul on the Bible and the Ancient Near East, 1967–2005*, edited by Shalom M. Paul, 333–42. Culture and History of the Ancient Near East 23. Leiden: Brill, 2005.

Propp, William H. C. *Exodus 19–40.* AB 2A. New York: Doubleday, 2006.

Schaudig, Hanspeter. *Die Inschriften Nabonids von Babylon und Kyros' des Grossen samt den ihrem Umfeld Enstandenen Tendenzschriften: Textausgabe und Grammatik.* AOAT 256. Münster: Ugarit, 2001.

---

17. Luzzato, *Il Profeta Isaia*, 609–10. See Paul, *Isaiah 40–66*, 552–3.

18. See Paul, "Jerusalem of Gold—Revisited," 338–42.

Skehan, Patrick W., and Alexander A. Di Lella. *The Wisdom of Ben Sira: A New Translation with Notes.* AB 39. New York: Doubleday, 1987.
Stegemann, Hartmut, and Eileen Schuller. *Qumran Cave 1:III: 1QHodayot^a.* DJD 40. Oxford: Clarendon, 2009.
Tawil, Hayim. "Two Biblical Architectural Images in Light of Cuneiform Sources (Lexicographical Note x)." *BASOR* 341 (2006) 37–52.
Thureau-Dangin, François. *Rituels Accadiens.* Paris: Leroux, 1921.
Unger, Eckhard. "Diadem und Krone." In *Reallexikon der Assyriologie und vorderasiatischen Archäologie* 2, edited by Erich Ebeling and Bruno Meissner, 201–11. Berlin: de Gruyter, 1938.

14

Psalm 20 and Amherst Papyrus 63, XII, 11–19: A Case Study of a Text in Transit

Karel van der Toorn

UNIVERSITY OF AMSTERDAM

It is an honor and a joy to contribute to a Festschrift that celebrates Ziony Zevit, the man and his work. I have chosen to present a study of a text that Ziony has worked on in the past and which is surely still dear to him. As might be expected, there is agreement (very much) and some disagreement (less). That is the way it goes when friends sit together and discuss.

There are not many cases where scholars of the Bible have access to the text behind the text, the text as it was before the editors of the Hebrew Bible transformed it into the received text as we know it from our *Biblia Hebraica*. The rare cases where we can actually compare the pre-biblical shape of a text with its biblical form deserve special attention. Historical-critical studies of the Bible have demonstrated that most books of the Bible have gone through various stages before they reached their present—canonical—form. However, the textual archaeology required to discover earlier textual strands is forced to find its evidence on the surface of the final text. By submitting that text to a close reading, we try discover inner contradictions and tensions—indications of the distance that separates the earlier from the later textual strand. Obviously, reconstructions of an earlier text on the basis solely of that text in the final stage of its transmission are open to the dangers of circular reasoning and idiosyncratic presuppositions. So in the interest of methodical rigor of text-historical criticism, the documented cases of textual development must be used to establish a set of rules—rules in the sense of tendencies, patterns, probabilities, observed regularities—that help us understand the logic that commands the scribal editing of texts from the stream of tradition. The two versions of the Book of Jeremiah constitute an outstanding and very helpful instance of documented text revision; the comparison between Psalm 20 and an Aramaic hymn from the Amherst papyrus is another one—not widely known and beset with difficulties of its own, but very illuminating for our understanding of the scribal practice of deliberate text revision.

Since the publication of the Aramaic hymn in the 1980s, there has been general agreement that the correspondences with the biblical Psalm 20 are so striking that we must assume a correlation between the two texts.[1] Their structure is identical, and the similarities of terminology and thought are numerous. In order to grasp the parallels at a glance, it suffices to put the two texts side by side; to facilitate the synopsis, I shall present the Aramaic text in Aramaic characters. I follow, moreover, the poetic structure of the two hymns; on the left side is the Hebrew text, on the right side the Aramaic one; corresponding lines face each other; those parts of the Hebrew text that have no correspondence in the Aramaic one face a blank; the same is true the other way around.

---

1. The discovery of the parallel between Amherst papyrus 63 XII 11–19 and (parts of) Psalm 20 was made by Richard Steiner and, independently one year later, by Jan Willem Wesselius. Their discovery appeared in print at almost the same time, see Nims and Steiner, "Paganized Version"; and Vleeming and Wesselius, "Aramaic Hymn."

A		2 יַֽעַנְךָ֣ יְ֭הוָה בְּי֣וֹם צָרָ֑ה יְ֝שַׂגֶּבְךָ֗ שֵׁ֤ם ׀ אֱלֹהֵ֬י יַעֲקֹֽב׃	יעננא יהו במצורינא עננאי אדני במצורינא היכשת בשמין סהרא
B		3 יִשְׁלַֽח־עֶזְרְךָ֥ מִקֹּ֑דֶשׁ וּ֝מִצִּיּ֗וֹן יִסְעָדֶֽךָּ׃	שלח עזירך מן כל רש ומן צפאנא יהו יסעדנא
C		4 יִזְכֹּ֥ר כָּל־מִנְחֹתֶ֑ךָ וְעוֹלָתְךָ֖ יְדַשְּׁנֶ֣ה [סֶֽלָה׃]	
D		5 יִֽתֶּן־לְךָ֥ כִלְבָבֶ֑ךָ וְֽכָל־עֲצָתְךָ֥ יְמַלֵּֽא׃	ימתן אלנא מרי כבלבן כל יעצת יהו יהמלי
E		6 נְרַנְּנָ֤ה ׀ בִּ֘ישׁ֤וּעָתֶ֗ךָ וּבְשֵֽׁם־אֱלֹהֵ֥ינוּ נִדְגֹּ֑ל	
D'		יְמַלֵּ֥א יְ֝הוָ֗ה כָּל־מִשְׁאֲלוֹתֶֽיךָ׃	יהמלי יהו כל משאל לבנא
F		7 עַתָּ֤ה יָדַ֗עְתִּי כִּ֤י הוֹשִׁ֥יעַ ׀ יְהוָ֗ה מְשִׁ֫יח֥וֹ יַ֭עֲנֵהוּ מִשְּׁמֵ֣י קָדְשׁ֑וֹ בִּ֝גְבֻר֗וֹת יֵ֣שַׁע יְמִינֽוֹ׃	
G		8 אֵ֣לֶּה בָ֭רֶכֶב וְאֵ֣לֶּה בַסּוּסִ֑ים וַאֲנַ֓חְנוּ ׀ בְּשֵׁם־יְהוָ֖ה אֱלֹהֵ֣ינוּ נַזְכִּֽיר׃	אל בכשת אל בחנת מרי אלהנא יהו (יהו) תרנא עמננא אר אנחנא
H		9 הֵ֭מָּה כָּרְע֣וּ וְנָפָ֑לוּ וַאֲנַ֥חְנוּ קַּ֝֗מְנוּ וַנִּתְעוֹדָֽד׃	
I		10 יְהוָ֥ה הוֹשִׁ֑יעָה	
J		הַ֝מֶּ֗לֶךְ יַעֲנֵ֥נוּ בְיוֹם־קָרְאֵֽנוּ׃	יען מחר אלביתאל
K			בעל שמין מרי יברך לחסידיך ברכתך

Presented this way, the parallels in structure and terminology are obvious. In their beginning, middle, and end the two texts echo each other. Even when translated into English, the similarities are clear. "May the LORD answer you in the day of trouble"// "May Yahu answer us in our anxiety"; "May He give to you according to your heart, and may He fulfill all your wishes"// "May Yahu give to us according to what is in our heart (. . .) may Yahu fulfill all desire"; "Some by chariots, some by horses—but as for us, we will call upon the name of the LORD our God"// "Some by the bow, others by the spear—but as for us, Yahu our Bull is with us"// "The LORD . . . will answer us the day we call"// "The god Bethel will answer us tomorrow." There can be no doubt that we are in the presence of two versions of what is basically the same text.

Two versions of basically the same text—putting it that way begs a number of questions. How can two texts that are different nevertheless be qualified as basically the same, and when does one text become a version of another one? I recognize the legitimacy of such questions and will try to answer them. But before I launch into a close analysis of the similarities and dissimilarities between our two texts, it is necessary to say a few words about the background and the context of the Amherst papyrus.[2] The scroll owes its name to Lord Amherst of Hackney, a private collector with money to spend and an infatuation for things Egyptian. He acquired papyrus 63—our text—as part of a lot found in an earthen jar in the vicinity of Thebes (Luxor).[3] That lot had papyri written in Greek and in Demotic; for paleographic reasons, papyrus 63 is generally dated to the 4th century BCE. The language of the Demotic papyri is Egyptian—except for number 63. As accurately established by Noel Aimé-Giron in 1923 and—independently— by Bowman in the early 1940s, the script is Demotic but the language is Aramaic.[4] Important sections of the text have been published, transliterated, and translated; a preliminary translation of the entire papyrus into English is available since 1993; but so far there is no scholarly edition of the complete text.[5] Richard C. Steiner has been preparing one for a number of years; Tawny Holm (Pennsylvania State University) is preparing a transliteration and translation for the SBL Writings from the Ancient World series;

---

2. For an excellent introduction to the Amherst papyrus, see Kottsieper, "Aramaic Literature," 426–9. Our papyrus is twice referred to erroneously as papyrus Amherst "23."

3. Newberry, *The Amherst Papyri*, 55.

4. See Nims and Steiner, "Paganized Version," 261.

5. For treatments of other sections of the manuscript, see Steiner and Nims, "You Can't Offer your Sacrifice and Eat it Too"; and Steiner and Nims, "Ashurbanipal and Shamash-shum-ukin."

in the meantime, scholars interested in the text must work on the basis of photographs or the actual text itself. Nearly all of the text is now in the Pierpont Morgan Library in New York; fragments are kept in the Michigan University library at Ann Arbor; the Oriental Institute of the University of Chicago possesses a batch of photographs, taken in 1901, of nearly the complete text.[6]

The Demotic script of the papyrus may seem baffling to Semitic scholars, but is not exceedingly difficult. The scribe has used some 40 consonant signs; some 30 multi-consonantal signs; plus about 5 determinatives as word-dividers. The difficulty is not in the complexity of the script but in the relation between the Demotic graphemes and the Aramaic phonemes, on the one hand, and in establishing the correct reading of those signs that can render related yet distinct consonants. The transposition of the Demotic script into the Aramaic may easily convey the impression of a one-to-one correspondence between the two; such is not the case; in fact, presenting the hymn in the Aramaic script is to a high degree a matter of interpretation.

The relation between Demotic signs as used in the Amherst papyrus and Aramaic sounds is complex because the Demotic makes no distinction between certain voiced and unvoiced consonants. Since not all native speakers of Egyptian heard the difference between *d*, *t*, and *ṭ*, the Demotic uses one sign where the Aramaic alphabet has three; the same is true for the distinction between *g*, *k*, and *q*; between *z* and *s*; and there is one sign that can be used to render Aramaic *l* and *r*. Where these Demotic signs occur, the correct Aramaic reading involves choices of interpretation. A second difficulty has to do with the multi-consonantal signs. The reading of most of them has been established on the basis of Demotic usage and the context in which they occur in the papyrus. The reading of some signs, however, is still contested. This is especially true of the sign that has here been rendered as Yahu,[7] but which Richard Steiner reads as Horus[8] and Ingo Kottsieper as El.[9] What's in a name? In this case, it matters quite a bit. So much for the

---

6. My own work on papyrus Amherst 63 is based on the Chicago photographs of 1901, a copy of which was kindly provided to me by John A. Larson Jr. During a visit at the Pierpont Morgan, John Vincler, Head of Reader Services, gave me access to more recent photographs of the text (2012 or 2013).

7. For the reading of the sign as Yahu see Zauzich, "Der Gott"; Vleeming and Wesselius, *Studies in Papyrus Amherst 63*, 39–42; and Rösel, "Israel's Psalmen in Ägypten?" 97–98.

8. Nims and Steiner, "Paganized Version," 265, 271–2.

9. Kottsieper, "Papyrus Amherst 63," 70; Kottsieper, "Anmerkungen zu Pap. Amherst 63," 385–90; Kottsieper, "El—ferner oder naher Gott," 37–41.

difficulties of rendering the Demotic into Aramaic; there is much that might be added, but this suffices for the present purpose.

One word about the nature of papyrus Amherst 63. It is a scroll of considerable size, written in 23 columns, most of which have close to 20 lines. It is not one text but a collection of texts; those texts are separated from each other by a sign that has to be read as *sôph*, "end"; it is a device that allows the scribe to continue on the same line with another composition; in only two instances texts—or text blocks—are demarcated by leaving a space empty (between columns XV and XVI) or by a vertical line of dots (between columns XVII and XVIII). Literary devices such as the refrain confirm the coherence of the single units. It is a matter of debate whether these separate units are part of a coherent whole. Steiner has made a case for interpreting the papyrus as the liturgy of a New Year festival; the arguments he advances are not compelling, however. It is especially difficult to see how the Tale of Two Brothers—which I would prefer to call the Story of the Fall of Babylon—at the end of the text would fit in with an assumed liturgy. The papyrus is more likely to be taken as a selection of individual texts that had significance for the community behind the scroll; the scroll is a container rather than a libretto; it may be compared to a box into which the scribe has piled a number of compositions. In view of the language, the community originally consisted of speakers of Aramaic; in view of the deities that play a role in the papyrus (Bethel, Anat, Yahu, Herem-Bethel, Eshem-Bethel, Baal-Shamayin, Nabu, Nanaya) the community must historically be related to the Arameans and Judeans at Syene and Elephantine whom we know about from papyri and potsherds from the 5th century BCE. As a working hypothesis, I would suggest that the community of papyrus Amherst 63 consisted of the descendants of the Aramean and Judean soldiers who had been forced to leave Syene and Elephantine after the Persians lost their hold on Egypt c. 400 BCE.

The Aramaic hymn that has such a close correspondence to Psalm 20 is part of a section in the papyrus that contains two other hymns that seem to have biblical connections. Column XII 12–19 is the hymn we will be considering; XIII 1–10 and 11–17 are hymns of comparable length and tenor.[10] This is the only section of the papyrus in which the name Yahu occurs, and the same is true for the occurrences of the honorific term Adonay (written as '*dny*); only in VIII 7 do we find another mention of Yahu (possibly with Ashera as his consort), but that is in the context of a hymn that seeks to address all the gods known in the community. The concentration of references

---

10. For a transliteration, translation and commentary see Vleeming and Wesselius, *Studies in Papyrus Amherst 63*, 61–79.

to Yahu in precisely this section is in fact an argument for reading the Demotic sign or sign group as Yahu; Horus makes no sense, and El seems out of place—also in view of the parallelism with Adonay. The three Yahwistic hymns of papyrus Amherst 63 most likely come from the literary legacy of the Elephantine community. That community is called "Judean" in the Elephantine papyri; yet there can be no doubt that it contained an important Israelite component—important and probably older. The North-Israelite origins of a significant part of the military settlement at Elephantine have long been acknowledged by scholars. As we shall see, the analysis of the Aramaic hymn points to the same conclusion.

Let us now pass to the comparative analysis of the two hymns. When Richard Steiner and Charles Nims, on the one side of the Atlantic, and Jan Willem Wesselius and Sven Vleeming, on the other, started their work on the Amherst papyrus in the early 1980s, the Aramaic hymn of XII 11–19 was one of the first texts they chose to publish. And for a good reason; it was relatively unproblematic and the parallel with the Biblical psalm signaled the relevance of their discovery. "Ancient Papyrus a Riddle No More," claimed *The New York Times* on October 11, 1982; the article was full of quotes by Richard Steiner, several of which were about the "paganized version" of Psalm 20. All subsequent studies of the Aramaic hymn and the Biblical psalm agree about the fact that they entertain a relationship of dependence. Disagreement focuses on the issue of historical priority. Steiner assumes that Psalm 20 is the earlier text and that the Aramaic hymn is an adaptation designed to suit the needs of a pagan audience; only few scholars have followed this view.[11] Most researchers have reversed the proposition; they claim anteriority for the Aramaic hymn and see the biblical Psalm as an adaptation.[12] Most authors choose a position in the middle and speculate about an older hymn—presumably Canaanite—to which both Psalm 20 and pAmh XII 11–19 are indebted.[13] But even if we follow the latter suggestion, we are still faced with the question about historical priority, though it may be formulated in a slightly different way: which one of the two compositions stands closest to the presumed original?

How do we steer clear of private preconceptions in establishing historical priority? The documented cases of texts from antiquity that are extant

---

11. See Nims and Steiner, "Paganized Version"; for a reasoning along the same lines see Segert, "Preliminary Notes," 272.

12. Kottsieper, "Anmerkungen zu Pap. Amherst 63." In the same vein, see Saur, *Die Königspsalmen*, 86.

13. See Weinfeld, "Pagan Version"; Zevit, "Common Origin"; Delcor, "Remarques sur la datation du Ps. 20"; Rösel, "Israel's Psalmen in Ägypten?" 97; and Heckl, "Inside the Canon and Out."

in copies from different periods demonstrate the existence of a pattern. The different versions of the Gilgamesh Epic or the Book of Jeremiah show that the longer text is the later text. In the process of transmission and edition, the tendency of scribes is to respect what has been received; adaptation to new circumstances and different tastes takes the form, normally, of textual expansion; scribes find it easier to add a line than to suppress one. If we want to formulate this as a rule of text-historical investigation, we might coin the formula *textus brevior anterior*; or alternatively, and a little less highbrow, brevity is a sign of antiquity in the history of a text; the natural tendency for scribes is to expand the text they are working on.

Going by the principle of *brevior anterior*, the Aramaic hymn is older than the biblical psalm—older, that is, in terms of the editorial history of the text. The synopsis of the two texts show that verses 4, 6a, 7, and 9 of Psalm 20 have no equivalent in the Aramaic hymn; conversely, only the last line of the Aramaic hymn ("May Baal Shamayin speak your blessings on account of your acts of generosity") is without a parallel in the biblical text. By the rule of thumb of text-historical investigation, then, the Aramaic hymn represents an earlier layer of the tradition. We will use this as our working hypothesis and see if the detailed study of the correspondences—or the absence of correspondences—points to the same conclusion. I will endeavor to use this exercise in close reading at the same time to establish a number of corollary principles that can help us as guidelines in text-historical research—also where the older text is no longer extant and, therefore, accessible only through the text-critical scrutiny of the text in its canonical shape.

Let us begin by looking at the evident parallels; they are evident but not for that matter perfect. Every parallel exhibits differences—some of them subtle, others less so. "May the LORD answer you in the day of trouble" is not exactly the same thing as "May Yahu answer us in our anxiety." Where the Aramaic is a prayer for the community, the Hebrew text is a prayer for an individual; a single "you" whom the remainder of the text identifies as "the king." Another difference is the absence of the parallel line in the Hebrew text; the Aramaic repeats the opening line, substituting Adonay for Yahu: "May Yahu answer us in our anxiety, may Adonay answer us in our anxiety." The Hebrew only has the variant version of the first part and skips the parallel line. As a matter of fact, on this point the Hebrew text is the briefer one. At first sight, this would seem to run against the *brevior anterior* principle formulated in the previous paragraph. But upon reflection, there is an excellent reason for the scribal editor of Psalm 20 to reduce the parallelism to a single phrase. At the time he was editing the Psalm, the religious taboo against speaking the name of God meant that the four consonants with which the divine name was written (*yhwh*)—originally pronounced as Yahua or Yahweh—had come to be read as Adonay, "My Lord." The later Masoretic vocalization follows that reading. Most English translations of the Hebrew Bible render it as "LORD," printed in small caps. So the audience of Psalm 20 would hear the first line of the prayer as "May Adonay answer you in the day of need"—which would make the repetition of the line with Adonay completely redundant.

The absence of repetition in A is an exceptional instance where the biblical psalm is shorter than the Aramaic hymn. In this case, however, that does not point to anteriority; quite the contrary; it is easy to explain why a biblical scribe would turn two phrases into one; for the putative redactor of the Aramaic hymn there would be no reason to elaborate a single line into a parallelism; he would not have added anything of significance to his text. So the one place at which the Hebrew editor of the text actually suppresses a line from the text that he is working from actually supports the hypothesis of the priority of the Aramaic text.

Nearly all the other scribal interventions in the text can be classified as either changes or additions. The additions are obvious; I have pointed them out and will return to their significance shortly. From the perspective of text-historical research the changes made by the scribe are in a sense more interesting than the additions; the changes do show a particular form of respect for the text as the scribe had received it; as he altered the text, he attempted to somehow preserve its original form. A futile attempt in a way, since by changing a text the scribe does in fact depart from what to him was the original. Yet to stay as close to the original as possible, he tried to retain at least the sound of the earlier text. Let me quote a few instances, all from the first lines of the prayer. Aramaic במצורינא becomes Hebrew בְּיוֹם צָרָה; מן כל רש is transformed into מִקְדֶּשׁ; and ומן צפאנא is replaced by וּמְצִיּוֹן. The change in meaning is obvious; the change in sound is subtle. If you speak the words fast enough, the change is almost imperceptible to the ear; but the eye of the reader spots it at once.

While trying to preserve the sound of the original, then, the scribe was changing its meaning. What kind of changes did he perform? There are, first of all, the innocent changes; innocent meaning that they do not imply a complete change of perspective. The innocent changes usually tend to give a more general meaning to the text in order to make it fit a greater variety of situations. "The day of need" is more open as a category than "our anxiety"—especially when we take into consideration that the Aramaic can also refer more specifically to a siege.[14] Toward the end of the Aramaic hymn, there is an expression of hope in the swift deliverance of the community. "May the god Bethel answer us tomorrow." The Hebrew parallel reads: "May He [i.e., the Lord] answer us the day we call." "The day we call" takes away the urgency of "tomorrow" and allows the prayer to be recited on any number of occasions.

---

14. Kottsieper, "Anmerkungen zu Pap. Amherst 63," 241.

Most changes are not so innocent. The disappearance of Resh and Zaphon as places from which Yahu will send his power and lend support to his people has a theological motive; these are place names associated in the mind of the Hebrew scribe with foreign deities; Zaphon is the holy mount of Baal, and Resh of Bethel.[15] The Aramaic text identifies Bethel with Yahu, as is clear from the finale of the hymn; so it sees no objection against the idea that Yahu comes to the rescue of the believers from the mountains where he has his abode. To the Hebrew scribe this notion is unacceptable; he has changed *kol reš*, "all of Resh," into the very general word *qōdeš*, "sanctuary," and Zaphon has become Zion—the common designation of the temple mount in Jerusalem.[16] The wholesale erasure of the god Bethel from the Hebrew text is in line with the theological revision of the editor.

There is one other change I wish to highlight. It is an intriguing one because it throws into relief one of the characteristics of the poetic methods employed in the composition of the psalms. In the middle of the hymn the text opposes those who put their trust in bow and spear to those who put their confidence in Yahu. "Some by the bow, others by the spear—but as for us, the Lord our God, Yahu our Bull is with us." Bow and spear have disappeared in the Hebrew text, but the thought the poet advances is very much the same. "Some in chariots, others in horses—but as to us, we shall be strong in the name of Yahu our God."[17] The reference to Yahu as a bull (*tr* < *ṯār*, cf. the Ugaritic expression *ṯr il*, "Bull El") has been suppressed for theological reasons; but the choice to put chariots and horses in the place of bow and spear is more in the nature of a free variant. Steiner has nicely drawn attention to the parallel with Psalm 46:10 "He shatters the bow and chops up the spear," followed in verse 12 by the expression "The LORD of Hosts is with us."[18] It demonstrates that "bow and spear" was just as conventional a pair as "chariots and horses."[19] It is possible that the Hebrew scribe preferred "chariots and horses" because of their repeated occurrence in the

---

15. The connection between Baal and Zaphon is very strong; so strong, in fact, that Baal is often referred to as Baal-Zaphon, also in places that are far from Syria. Note the place Baal-Zaphon in the Nile delta, see Eissfeldt, *Baal Zaphon*. It is less known that the combination Baal-Zaphon also occurs as a designation of Mt Zaphon, see, e.g., Lie, *The Inscriptions of Sargon II*, 38, line 230, kur[superscript kur]*ba-'i-il-ṣa-pu-na šadû rabû*. See also Niehr, "Zaphon צפון."

16. Though see Ps 48:3, where the poet simply equated Zaphon and Zion.

17. Read *nagbîr* instead of *nazkîr*, in view of LXX and Syr.

18. Steiner and Nims, "You Can't Offer your Sacrifice and Eat it Too," 113.

19. For the pair "bow and spear" elsewhere see Jer 50:42. Compare the more frequent pairing of "bow and sword," as in Ps 44:7 "For I do not put my trust in my bow, nor will my sword save me."

books of the prophets.[20] That explanation, however, is not necessary. The use of standard formulas is common procedure in the Psalms; it reflects their origin in an oral culture.[21] So the choice of a variant expression may have been without ulterior motive.

The most obvious interventions of the Hebrew poet are extant in the expansion of the text through additions. Most of these additions are part of the editorial strategy to put an existing text in a new frame. Two aspects of this reframing stand out: the new perspective is Judean, and the new focus is on the king. The transformation of Zaphon into Zion (and of Resh into the more neutral "sanctuary") produces a Jerusalem perspective on the text; the transformation of the "we" into the singular "you" puts the king in the center of the text. The earlier text had no reference to the king; it was a prayer for and by the community. The singular "you" of Psalm 20 refers to the king throughout the text. The Lord will "answer you," "exalt you," "send your help," "support you," etc. It is only at the end that the word *melek*, "king" falls; but *mašiaḥ*, "the anointed one," mentioned in verse 7 is another indication of the identity of the "you" who is addressed throughout the Psalm. Verse 4 is an addition stressing the king's generous performance of his cultic duties; verse 7 expresses confidence in the divine salvation of the king; a similar idea, this time formulated as a prayer, is interpolated in the last verse.

With the exception of verse 9, which reads like a commentary on the "chariots and horses" statement of the preceding verse, all the additions serve to emphasize the pivotal role of the king in the salvation that will accrue to the community. The mere fact that the royal focus derives primarily from additions proves that it is secondary. Because of the new focus the scribal editor had to adapt the earlier text by substituting "you" for "us" and "we." But the substitution has not been complete. The last line of Psalm 20 remains very close to the finale of the Aramaic hymn, disregarding for a moment the change of "tomorrow" into "the day we call." "He shall answer us"—"us" rather than "you"; it is striking precisely because of the poetic technique of the *inclusio*—the end rhymes with the beginning. It does rhyme in the Aramaic hymn; it does not rhyme exactly in the Hebrew text. This, it seems to me, is one of the tensions a close reading of Psalm 20 without knowledge of the Amherst papyrus 63 would be able to spot. We now know that the tension is the result of an imperfect adaptation of a traditional text to a new perspective.

20. See, e.g., Isa 31:1; Jer 17:25; 46:9. See also Ps 76:6.
21. See van der Toorn, *Scribal Culture*, esp. 110–15; and, with a focus on the book of Psalms, Culley, *Oral Formulaic Language*.

All the evidence we have passed in review proves to corroborate the hypothesis we formulated at the outset: since the Aramaic hymn is the shorter text, it is indeed likely to be earlier than Psalm 20; the so-called *brevior anterior* principle. It is true that the Aramaic text has one repetition that has vanished from the Hebrew; but the only viable explanation for its disappearance actually proves the developmental order earlier assumed. There is one single exception, though. The very last line of the Amherst papyrus hymn has no corresponding part in the biblical Psalm. "May Baal Shamayin pronounce your blessings on account of your acts of kindness." Kottsieper thinks this is addressed to an unnamed human being; it falls out of line with the general structure of the hymn and must therefore be considered an addition.[22] I agree that the line has all the appearances of an addition; not because it addresses a human being, though, for the "you" (singular) who is the object of the blessing could be Bethel/Yahu; after all, gods do bless one another—not only humans. But the request for a divine answer in the preceding line serves as a poetical form of closure of the prayer: it opens and ends with the hope for an answer. Psalm 20 has preserved this stylistic device. So I would assume that the reference to Baal Shamayin has been added. Why? I can only guess. Let us be content by observing that this addition makes the hymn more inclusive and therefore better suited to a community that was ethnically and religiously mixed.

If we do assume that the last line of the Aramaic hymn is a later addition, we must conclude that neither the Aramaic nor the Hebrew text is the original one—whatever is actually meant by the word "original" in this context. At the same time, though, there is no denying the fact that the Aramaic version represents a stage in the literary transmission of the prayer that precedes the version as we know it from Psalm 20. The biblical poem is a Judahite revision of an existing text, reframing it in such a way that it focuses on the figure of the king. The prayer thus became a document of the royalist Zion theology. Since the Aramaic hymn stands closer to the text as it was in the initial stages of the tradition, we may peruse it for evidence of the time and the milieu in which the prayer did earlier circulate.

On the assumption that Yahu is the correct reading of the multi-consonantal sign Steiner reads as Horus and Kottsieper as El, the Aramaic hymn is a document of a religion in which Yahu and Bethel are identified. So much can be deduced from the fact that the invocation addressed to Yahu at the beginning corresponds with a similar invocation addressed to Bethel at the end; the stylistic device implies that Bethel is used as another name of Yahu. The mention of Resh as the place from where Yahu comes in action has

---

22. Kottsieper, "Anmerkungen zu Pap. Amherst 63," 240.

similar implications. Throughout Amherst papyrus 63, Resh is the abode of Bethel; Bethel, moreover, is also associated with such mountains or mountain ranges as the Lebanon, Siryon, and Zaphon. So if Yahu is pictured as acting from Resh and Zaphon, the implication is that Yahu and Bethel are different names of one God. Now the identification of Bethel and Yahu is not unique to the Amherst papyrus. We also find it in the papyri of the Judean community at Elephantine. The goddess Anat-Bethel (*TAD* C3.15:123–125) occurs also under the name Anat-Yahu (*TAD* B7.3:3); there are references to Herem-Bethel (*TAD* B7.2:7–8) and Eshem-Bethel (*TAD* C3.15:123–125) but never to Bethel as such—except as an element in theophoric personal names. The most likely explanation of the phenomenon is to suppose that Yahu had taken the place of Bethel through identification. The fact that Anat-Bethel and Eshem-Bethel shared in the contributions to the temple of Yahu (*TAD* C3.15:123–125) points to the same conclusion. On the strength of this evidence I suggest that the Aramaic hymn we have been looking at was brought to Egypt by Israelite migrants who ended up—or whose offspring ended up—serving in the Persian army.

I assume, then, that the Aramaic hymn has its origins in the religion that was practiced in the northern kingdom of Israel. That Bethel was venerated as a god in the north is clear from Jeremiah 48:13 ("And Moab shall be shamed because of Chemosh, as the House of Israel were shamed because of Bethel, on whom they relied"). After the Assyrians resettled the populations of conquered territories in Samaria, we also find people from the northern region of Syria who stay loyal to the worship of their gods; inhabitants of Babylonia bring their gods with them. Most of the gods we encounter in Amherst papyrus 63 are known from biblical description of the religious situation in Samaria under the impact of the Assyrian empire (2 Kgs 17:24–33); Yahu is venerated as the god of the land; but his worship took place in a context of religious pluralism. The identification of Yahu and Bethel is one of the northern characteristics of our hymn. Another one is the reference to Yahu as "our Bull"; the worship of Yahu in the shape of a calf (1 Kings 12) is hard to understand if there were a general aversion to bull imagery for Yahu.[23]

After the fall of Samaria (722 BCE), groups of inhabitants from the north sought refuge in the south. Cult personnel from such places as Bethel and Samaria brought the pre-biblical version of Psalm 20 to Judah; there it found its way to the scriptorium of the Jerusalem temple where a scribe edited it to bring it in line with the tenets of the Judean theology; hence the focus on Zion and the royal dynasty. Other northerners found a safe haven

---

23. For the bull imagery, see Wyatt, "Calf עגל."

in Egypt; they too had the pre-biblical psalm as part of their religious tradition. With its explicit references to battles and armed encounters, the hymn would have a natural place in the cult performed in the temple of Yahu in Elephantine; this was a military colony. When the community was forced to leave Elephantine, the Persians no longer being around to offer their protection, some members of the colony moved up north, probably in the company of Aramean colleagues from Syene. The forced migration reinforced the hybrid nature of the community; these were descendants of Arameans and Israelites, possibly of Judeans as well, but it is unclear whether they observed strict ethnic boundaries among them. It seems unlikely—to say the least. Papyrus Amherst 63 is a selection of the traditional texts that had importance to them; as such, it is a statement of identity of sorts. That identity is hybrid; each group added elements of their tradition to the whole. The Israelites from the former northern kingdom brought in three Aramaic hymns to Yahu, parts of which are very close, in either spirit or phraseology or both, to the Hebrew Bible. They can be considered as a legacy of the Elephantine soldiers of the 5th century BCE.

The title of this contribution promises a case study of a text in transit. The discovery of papyrus Amherst 63, in the first place, and no less important the solution to the riddle of the language, in the second, has added another documented case of textual correction and expansion. As argued above, these cases offer precious data that can help us in the historical analysis of texts for which we have no physical evidence of any forerunners; and yet we know that at one time they existed. The comparison between Psalm 20 and the Aramaic hymn has yielded evidence of patterns in the process of scribal editing and revision that may illuminate, too, the many cases of scribal expansion of texts for which we have no hard evidence. To summarize: there is the *brevior anterior* principle: shorter means older; the rule that changes in the text will tend to respect the acoustic image of the earlier text: it sounds almost the same but means something different; the tendency to change the text in order to make it applicable to a wider variety of situations: the general displaces the particular; and the attempt to put another perspective on an existing text: revision is reframing.

BIBLIOGRAPHY

Culley, Robert C. *Oral Formulaic Language in the Biblical Psalms*. Near and Middle East Series 4. Toronto: University of Toronto Press, 1967.

Delcor, Mathias, "Remarques sur la datation du Ps. 20 comparée à celle du psaume araméen apparenté dans le papyrus Amhrst 63." In *Mesopotamica—Ugaritica— Biblica. Festschrift für Kurt Bergerhof zur Vollendung seines 70. Lebensjahres am 7. Mai 1992*, edited by Manfred Dietrich and Oswald Loretz, 25–43. AOAT 232. Neukirchen-Vluyn: Neukirchener, 1993.

Eissfeldt, Otto. *Baal Zaphon, Zeus Kasios und der Durchzug der Israeliten durchs Meer*. Beiträge zur Religionsgeschichte des Altertums 1. Halle/Saale: Niemeyer, 1932.

Heckl, Raik. "Inside the Canon and Out: The Relationship between Psalm 20 and Papyrus Amherst 63." *Semitica* 56 (2014) 359–79.

Kottsieper, Ingo. "Anmerkungen zu Pap. Amherst 63, I: 12,11–19—Eine aramäische Version von Ps 20." *ZAW* 100 (1988) 217–44.

———. "Aramaic Literature." In *From an Antique Land: An Introduction to Ancient Near Eastern Literature*, edited by Carl S. Ehrlich, 393–444. Lanham, MD: Rowman & Littlefield, 2009.

———. "El—ferner oder naher Gott." In *Religion und Gesellschaft*, edited by Rainer Albertz, 25–74. AOAT 248. Münster: Ugarit-Verlag, 1997.

———. "Papyrus Amherst 63—Einführung, Text und Übersetzung von 12,11–19." In Oswald Loretz, *Die Königspsalmen: Die altorientalisch-kanaanäische Königstradition in jüdischer Sicht. Teil 1. Ps 20, 21, 72, 101 und 144. Mit einem Beitrag von I. Kottsieper zu Papyrus Amherst*, 55–75. Ugaritisch-biblische Literatur 6. Münster: Ugarit-Verlag, 1988.

Lie, Arthur Godfred. *The Inscriptions of Sargon II, King of Assyria. Part I: The Annals*. Paris: Geuthner, 1929.

Newberry, Percy E. *The Amherst Papyri, Being an Account of The Egyptian Papyri in the Collection of the Right Hon. Lord Amherst of Hackney F.S.A., at Didlington Hall, Norfolk*. London: Quaritch, 1899.

Niehr, Herbert. "Zaphon צפן." In *DDD*² 927–29.

Nims, Charles F., and Richard C. Steiner. "A Paganized Version of Psalm 20:2–6 from the Aramaic Text in Demotic Script." *JAOS* 103 (1983) 261–74.

Rösel, Martin. "Israel's Psalmen in Ägypten? Papyrus Amherst 63 und die Psalmen xx und lxxv." *VT* 50 (2000) 81–99.

Saur, Markus. *Die Königspsalmen: Studien zur Entstehung und Theologie*. BZAW 340. Berlin: de Gruyter, 2004.

Segert, Stanislav. "Preliminary Notes on the Structure of the Aramaic Poems in the Papyrus Amherst 63." *UF* 18 (1986) 271–99.

Steiner, Richard C., and Charles F. Nims. "You Can't Offer Your Sacrifice and Eat It Too: A Polemical Poem from the Aramaic Text in Demotic Script." *JNES* 43 (1984) 89–114.

———. "Ashurbanipal and Shamash-shum-ukin: A Tale of Two Brothers from the Aramaic Text in Demotic Script." *RB* 92 (1985) 60–81 & pls I–IV.

Toorn, Karel van der. *Scribal Culture and the Making of the Hebrew Bible*. Cambridge: Harvard University Press, 2007.

Vleeming, Sven P., and Jan W. Wesselius. "An Aramaic Hymn from the Fourth Century B.C." *BO* 39 (1982) 501–9. [N.B. The issue actually appeared Spring 1983.]

———. *Studies in Papyrus Amherst 63. Essays on the Aramaic Texts in Aramaic/Demotic Papyrus Amherst 63*, vol. 1. Amsterdam: Juda Palache Instituut, 1985.

Weinfeld, Moshe. "The Pagan Version of Psalm 20:2–8: Vicissitudes of a Psalmodic Creation in Israel and Its Neighbors." *Eretz Israel* 18 (1985) 130–40 (Hebrew) 70* (English summary).

Wyatt, Nicholas, "Calf עגל." In *DDD*², 180–82.

Zauzich, Karl-Theodor. "Der Gott des aramäisch-demotischen Papyrus Amherst 63." *Göttinger Miszellen* 85 (1985) 89–90.

Zevit, Ziony. "The Common Origin of the Aramaicized Prayer to Horus and of Psalm 20." *JAOS* 110 (1990) 213–28.

Part 3: Hebrew (and Aramaic) Language

15

Two *Maskilic* Explanations of the Difference between the Causative *Piʿel* and the *Hiphʿil* in Biblical Hebrew

Steven E. Fassberg

THE HEBREW UNIVERSITY OF JERUSALEM

Introduction

The stems (בִּנְיָנִים) of the Biblical Hebrew verbal system have primary and secondary functions. Sometimes these functions appear in more than one stem. The grammars state that *qal* verbs may be transitive (שָׁלַח "send"), intransitive (רָץ "run"), stative (זָקֵן 'be old'), or ambitransitive (אָכַל "eat");[1] *niphʿal* verbs may be reciprocal (נוֹעַץ "take counsel"), reflexive (נִשְׁמַר "guard oneself"), or occasionally passive (נוֹלַד "be born"); *piʿel* verbs may mark plurality of actions or arguments (שִׁבֵּר "smash"), be 'causative' (חִזַּק

---

*It is a honor to dedicate this essay to Ziony Zevit, a modern-day *Maskil*, whose wide-ranging interests include archaeology, history, literature, and language. I thank W. Randall Garr for his comments on a previous version of this paper.

1. Sometimes a dichotomy between transitive and intransitive is expressed by the terms fientive/dynamic/active vs. stative/neuter/middle.

"strengthen"),[2] or denominative (דִּבֶּר "speak") with the related functions of declarative-estimative (צִדֵּק "declare innocent") and privative (דִּשֵּׁן "remove ashes"); *hiphʿil* verbs may be causative (הֶאֱכִיל "feed"), denominative (הֶאֱזִין "give ear"), declarative-estimative (הִצְדִּיק "declare just"), or stative (הֶאֱדִים "be red");[3] *puʿal* and *hophʿal* verbs are passive (הֻלַּל "be praised," הֻשְׁלַךְ "be thrown"), and *hitpaʿel* verbs may be reflexive (הִתְאַזֵּר "gird oneself"), reciprocal (הִתְרָאָה "look upon one another"), or infrequently passive (הִשְׁתַּכַּח "be forgotten"). Often it is impossible to discern why a given verb has been assigned to a particular stem. The reasons for the overlapping of functions between the different stems are phonological, morphological, semantic, and chronological.[4]

As noted, *hiphʿil* is causative and *piʿel* sometimes also designates causative. Medieval Hebrew grammarians already mention this overlap in function and its explanation continues to intrigue scholars today. Two interesting interpretations from the period of the Hebrew Enlightenment, the *Haskalah*, however, have been overlooked in modern research. The first analysis was put forward in 1794 by Joel Bril, the second by Salomon Löwisohn in 1810–1811.

Views of Grammarians on the Overlapping Causative Use of *Piʿel* and the *Hiphʿil*

Medieval Hebrew grammarians pointed out that *piʿel* and *hiphʿil* infrequently overlap with causative meaning. Abraham Ibn Ezra (1089–1167), for example, implied in a few passages in his biblical commentaries that both *piʿel* and *hiphʿil* are causative and verbs that occur with causative meaning in both stems are at times synonymous.[5] He commented on the *hiphʿil* verb יַחֲלִיץ "give strength" in the verse וְנָחֲךָ יְהוָה תָּמִיד וְהִשְׂבִּיעַ בְּצַחְצָחוֹת נַפְשֶׁךָ וְעַצְמֹתֶיךָ יַחֲלִיץ וְהָיִיתָ כְּגַן רָוֶה וּכְמוֹצָא מַיִם אֲשֶׁר לֹא־יְכַזְּבוּ מֵימָיו׃ "The LORD will

---

2. Technically, the *piʿel* is not causative, but rather converts an intransitive verb into one that is transitive.

3. On "tolerative/permissive" uses of the *hiphʿil*, see in this volume the article of Jeffrey H. Tigay, "On the Tolerative/Permissive *Hiphʿil*," pp. 397–414.

4. See Ben-Ḥayyim, 65–60, לשון עתיקה במציאות חדשה [= Ben-Ḥayyim, *Struggle for a Language*, 67–70]; Ben-Ḥayyim, *Grammar*, §§2.1.1.0.1–2.1.1.0.4; 2.15; Joosten, "Semitic D Stem," 225–9.

5. Bacher, *Ibn Esra*, 101–2. The greatest of Bible commentators, Rashi (1040–1105), also noted this in his explanation of מְיַלְּדֹת "midwives" (Exod 1:15): הוא לשון מולידות "It is the אלא שיש לשון קל ויש לשון כבד, כמו שובר ומשבר, דובר ומדבר, כך מוליד ומיילד language of מולידות [*hiphʿil*], but there is the (same) linguistic usage in *qal* and in the derived stems such as שובר [*qal*] and משבר [*piʿel*], דובר [*qal*] and מדבר [*piʿel*], and such is מוליד [*hiphʿil*] and מיילד [*piʿel*]" (Gamliel, *Rashi*, 67).

Difference between Causative *Piʿel* and *Hiphʿil* in Biblical Hebrew

guide you always. He will slake your thirst in parched places and strengthen your bones. You shall be like a watered garden, like a spring whose waters do not fail" (Isa 58:11):

ויש אומרים שיחליץ כמו יחלץ (איוב ל"ו ט"ו) כאשר מצאנו ישליח (שמות ח, יז) ישלח (תהלים ע"ח מ"ה), ישמיח (שם פ"ט מ"ג) ישמח (איכה ב י"ז), וזהו הנכון, כי הנה הוא כמו שומר כל עצמותיו (תהלים ל"ד כ"א), והנה יחלצם משבר.

And some say that יחליץ is like יחלץ (Job 36:15 [*piʿel*]) as we found ישליח ("send"; Exod 8:17 [*hiphʿil*]), ישלח (Ps 78:45 [*piʿel*]), ישמיח ("make happy"; Ps 89:43 [*hiphʿil*]), ישמח (Lam 2:17 [*piʿel*]), and this is correct, because, behold, it is like "He guards all his bones" (Ps 34:21), and, behold, he will strengthen them from breaking.

In describing *piʿel*, Moses Qimḥi (1127?–1190?) wrote:

ולפעמים הוא משמש שימוש ההפעיל וזה במלה הנמצאת בו ובקל כמו למד למד ידע ידע שהוא כמו הלמיד והודיע אמנם זה נמצא מעט

and sometimes it (*piʿel*) occurs with the function of the *hiphʿil*, and this is (the case) with a word that is found in it (*piʿel*) and in *qal* such as למד (*qal*), למד (*piʿel*), ידע (*qal*), ידע (*piʿel*), which is like הלמיד and הודיע, though it is found infrequently.[6]

His brother Radaq (R. David Qimḥi. 1160–1235) declared that *piʿel* and *hiphʿil* can transitivize intransitive *qal* verbs as well as make transitive *qal* verbs causative (ספר מכלול, 20):

שהוא בנין הקל פעמים שהוא עומד בעצמו ופעמים שהוא יוצא לזולתו. וכאשר יהיה עומד הטור הזה שהוא בנין בקל כמו עָמַד הָלַךְ וחביריהם שהם פעלים עומדים תוציא פעל הדגש או הפעיל מהם לשני ותאמר מן עמד הֶעֱמִיד יוצא לשני כמו וְהַעֲמִיד אֶת הבהמה (ויקרא כ"ז). ומן הלך הֵלֵךְ כמו ערום הָלְכוּ בלי לבוש (איוב כ"ד). וכאשר יהיה בנין הקל יוצא כמו אָכַל פָּעַל וחביריהם שהם פועלים יוצאים תוציא פועל הדגש או הפעיל מהם גם לשלישי תאמר ראובן הֶאֱכִיל אֶת שמעון לחם והוא יוצא לשלישי כי הנה ראובן מאכיל ושמעון אוכל והלחם אכול. הנה מקרה האכילה יוצא אל שלושה.

The *qal* stem sometimes is itself intransitive and sometimes it is transitive. And when the *qal* stem is intransitive like עָמַד "he stood" הָלַךְ "he went" and related intransitive verbs, then

---

6. Qimḥi, מהלך שבילי הדעת, 45.

piʿel or the *hiphʿil* makes it transitive and you say from עָמֹד ("stand") the transitive הֶעֱמִיד ("raise up") as in "and he shall set the beast" (Lev 27:11). And from הלך ("go") הִלֵּךְ like "they made them go about naked without clothing" (Job 24:10).[7] And when the *qal* stem is transitive like אָכַל "ate," פָּעַל "did" and related transitive verbs, you make the *piʿel* or the *hiphʿil* govern a third (argument)[8] when you say "'Reuben (הֶאֱכִיל) (fed) Simeon bread' and it governs a third because, behold, Reuben feeds and Simeon eats and the bread is eaten. Behold, in the notions of feeding it governs three.

In the first half of the 20th century the standard reference grammars and dictionaries of Biblical Hebrew concurred that *piʿel* and *hiphʿil* infrequently overlap in transitivizing: sometimes they assigned subtle distinctions in meaning to *piʿel* and *hiphʿil* verbs that are stative or intransitive in *qal*, while other times they presented them as synonyms.[9] Following Albrecht Goetze's proposal for the cognate Akkadian stems (*purrusum* and *šuprusum*),[10] more recent treatments of the subject distinguish between the transitivizing ("causative") meanings of *piʿel* and *hiphʿil*. The first to do so was Ernst Jenni in a highly influential book from 1968 in which he argued that *piʿel* is factitive, i.e., it brings about a state or condition of an adjective or a stative *qal* stem verb, whereas *hiphʿil* is causative, i.e., it causes an event or process of an adjective or stative *qal* stem verb.[11] Contrast, for example, Jenni's interpretation of the factitive חִיָּה "cause to be alive" from the adjective חַי as opposed to the causative הֶחֱיָה "cause to live" from the verb חָיָה.[12] His view has been widely adopted with the acknowledgement that other languages often have difficulty in expressing the nuances.[13] Aspectually,

---

7. Radaq explicitly stated that הלכו is transitive on p. בא, where he discusses how verbs in *piʿel* and *hiphʿil* can be transitive or intransitive: קודר הלכתי (איוב ל׳) עומד, ערום הִלְּכוּ בלי לבוש (איוב כ״ד) יוצא "'I walk about in sunless gloom' (Job 30:28) intransitive, 'they made them go around naked, without clothing' (Job 24:10) transitive." Modern scholarship, however, takes הלכו to be intransitive in this verse.

8. The grammatical use of the *hiphʿil* הוציא is "make a verb יצא (transitive)," i.e., "transitivize." The expression יצא לשלישי means "transitive to a third" and indicates that there is a third argument, thus the verb is causative. In some contexts the meaning 'causative' for הוציא also seems appropriate.

9. BDB, e.g., קדש, פשט, כבד, אבד; GKC §52g; Bauer and Leander, *Historische Grammatik*, §38v"; Bergsträsser, *Grammatik*, vol. 2, §17a–b, §19a–b.

10. Goetze, "So-Called Intensive." See also Ryder, *D-Stem*.

11. Jenni, *Piʿel*.

12. Jenni, *Piʿel*, 61–65.

13. Lambdin, "Review"; Waltke and O'Connor, *Introduction*, §§24.1–2; 27.1; Van der Merwe et al., *Grammar*, §§16.4, 16.7; Williams, *Syntax*, §§141–142; Blau, *Phonology*

Jenni sees the factitive *pi'el* as indicating punctuality as opposed to *hiph'il*, which he considers durative.[14] In a later formulation, he described *pi'el* as expressing the *Aktionsart* of achievement as opposed to *hiph'il*, whose *Aktionsart* is one of accomplishment.[15]

Haskalah—the Hebrew Enlightenment

The Hebrew Enlightenment (הַשְׂכָּלָה—*Haskalah*) from ca. 1780 to 1880 was a period in which Jewish writers and educators sought to educate their co-religionists in secular and scientific subjects in order to enable them to participate in mainstream European culture. Until then Jews mainly studied Talmud and related religious texts. Advocates and supporters of the Hebrew Enlightenment, the *Maskilim*, sought to educate the Jewish masses through the publication of essays, belles-lettres, and scientific literature, which they composed in Hebrew or translated into it works written in European languages (German, Russian, French, and English). Biblical Hebrew was the medium generally chosen, as opposed to Mishnaic Hebrew or Medieval Hebrew, since the *Maskilim* considered it the most pristine and prestigious form of Hebrew; moreover, it evoked the period in which the Jews were an independent people in their homeland. The beginning of the *Haskalah* is commonly associated with the later years of Moses Mendelssohn (1729–1786), and the conclusion, with the initial stage of Zionist immigration to Palestine.[16]

The typical *Maskilic* explanation of the difference between the *pi'el* and *hiph'il* can be seen in the popular grammar by Judah Leib Ben-Zeev (1764–1811)[17]:

וזה עקר הוראתו לסבב גוף אחר להיות פועל. וזה ההבדל בינו לבין
יוצא לשלישי בפיעל כי שם יש שנים פעולים ופועל אחד, ובהפעיל הגוף
האמצעי פועל מצד ופעול מצד, והראשון רק פועל סבה, והשלישי רק
פעול, וגם בו יש במקו' אחד עומד ובמקו' אחר יוצא כי יַעֲשִׁיר אִישׁ
עומד, אנכי הֶעֱשַׁרְתִּי אֶת אַבְרָם יוצא.

---

and *Morphology*, §4.3.5.4.1. Joüon and Muraoka (*Grammar*, §52d) are not convinced that there is a discernible difference in meaning or nuance between verbs that occur in both *pi'el* and *hiph'il*.

14. Jenni, *Pi'el*, 55–65.
15. Jenni, "Aktionsarten."
16. Kahn, "Maskilic Hebrew."
17. Ben-Zeev, ר"מ§ , תלמוד לשון עברי.

And this (hiph'il) is its main meaning: to cause another person to be the agent. And this is the difference between it and between one that governs a third (argument) in the pi'el because there there are two objects and one agent, and in hiph'il the intermediate body is an agent, on the one hand, and an object, on the other, and the first is only an agent of cause, and the third is only the object, and also in one place it is intransitive and another place transitive: "when a man becomes wealthy (וְעָשִׁיר)" is intransitive[18]; "I made Abram wealthy (הֶעֱשַׁרְתִּי)" is transitive.

Joel Bril on the Overlapping Causative Use of *Pi'el* and the *Hiph'il*

Joel Bril (1760–1802) was the nom de plume of Judah ben Löwe (= ברי״ל בן רבי יהודה לווה), a German-Jewish grammarian, commentator, translator, and editor, who also published fables, essays, and poems. Bril served as co-editor with Aaron Wolfsohn of the periodical המאסף (*ha-Me'assef*) and was a friend and colleague of some of the first *Maskilim*: Moses Mendelssohn, Isaac Satanow, and Isaac Abraham Euchel. Bril published in 1794 a Hebrew grammar, עמודי הלשון, written in Judeo-German, which was revised and expanded in a second edition in 1803. He repeated in the grammar (§§ קה-קיב)[19] the well-known general functions of *pi'el* and *hiph'il*; however, he adds the following passage (§קיג), which mentions, among other things, verbs that show up in both *pi'el* and *hiph'il* with similar transitive meaning:

איזט דיא האנדלונג אים קל עוֹמֵד אונד אים פְּעֵל יוֹצֵא, זא איזט דער
הפָּעִיל (1) ענטוועדר יוֹצֵא לִשְׁלִישִׁי,[20] אלס בָּעַר ער האט געברענט
(עומד), בֶּעַר ער האט ברעננן מאבן, אנגצינדעט דאס פייער (יוצא
לשני), הבְעִיר ער האט דאס פייער עטוואס אנדערט ברעננן לאסן, ער
האט פרברענט (יוצא לשלישי). אדר (2) דער הפָּעִיל איזט אויך נור
יוֹצֵא לִשְׁנִי אבר מיט איינה אנדרן נעבן בשטיטטונג אלס דער פְּעֵל. צ״ב
שִׁכֵּן רוהן מאבן, אים שטאנד דער רוהע אימר פארט ערהאלטן (חזק
הפעולה, פרעקווענטאטיפום), הַשְׁכֵּן רוהן מאבן, אָרט אונד שטעללע
אנוויזן, פלאסירן, קִיֵּם, איינע ערריבטעטע זאכע אויפרעכט ערהאלטן,
בשטעטיגן, הָקִים איינע זאכע אין איינן אויפרעכטן שטאנד ברינגן.

---

18. More precisely, it is inchoative.

19. Bril, עמודי לשון, 1st ed., pp. 36–37; 2nd ed., pp. 86–87. There are minor differences between the editions and the later edition has been followed above. A modified so-called Rashi script is employed in the two editions, as is standard in works published in German by Jews before World War II. The vocalized words appear in Bril's work in normal square script.

20. The *dagesh* in in the *shin* is an error.

Difference between Causative *Pi'el* and *Hiph'il* in Biblical Hebrew 269

אויפֿריכטן. אדר (3) די בדייטונג זעלבסט ווייבֿט אים פֿעל אונד הִפְעִיל
פֿאן איינאנדר אבֿ' וויאואהל ביידע אויס דער גרונדבדייטונג אים קל
ענטשטעהן: אלס צ"ב בִּשֵׁל קאבֿן (דאס עסן גאאר מאבֿן) אונד הִבְשֵׁל
רייפֿן אדר צור רייפֿע ברינגן (די פֿריבֿטע גאאר מאבֿן), חַזֵק בֿפֿעסטיגן,
אונד הֶחֱזִיק אנפֿאסן, ערגרייפֿן, זיך פֿעסטע האלטן.

אנמערקונג

מאן פֿינדט אינדעסן פֿעללע, וואדער פֿעל אונד הִפְעִיל איינע גאנץ גלייבֿע
בדייטונג צו האבן שיינן, אלס, קוֹמֵם וועלבֿס זאואהל די בדייטונג
פֿאן קַיֵּם אלס די פֿאן הָקֵם האט, אונד מוֹתֵת וועלבֿס מיט הָמֵת גלייך
בדייטענד איזט. דאך מאג איך הירֿאיבר נאך ניבֿט גוויס ענטשיידן.

If the action is an intransitive *qal* and a transitive *pi'el*, the *hiph'il* either (1) governs a third (argument), such as בָּעַר "it burned" (intransitive), בִּעֵר "he burnt," "he lit the fire" (governs a second [argument]), הִבְעִיר "he had something else light the fire, he had it burnt" (governs a third [argument]); or (2) The *hiph'il* is also only transitive but with a different by-meaning than the *pi'el*. For example, שִׁכֵּן "make rest" is to maintain something in the state of rest (strength of the action; *frequentativum*). הִשְׁכֵּן "make rest" is to show the place and position, to place. קַיֵּם, to maintain something in a stable condition. הָקִים to bring a thing into an upright position, to establish; or (3) the meaning itself fluctuates between *pi'el* and *hiph'il*, although both arise out of the basic meaning of the *qal*: as, for example, בִּשֵׁל "cook" (to make the food sufficiently done) and הִבְשֵׁל "to ripen" or "make ripe" (to make the fruit sufficiently done), חִזֵק "to fasten," and הֶחֱזִיק "to take hold of, grasp, hold firm."

Remark

One finds, nevertheless, cases where the *pi'el* and *hiph'il* appear to have a quite similar meaning, like קוֹמֵם "raise up" which has the same meaning as קַיֵּם, like הָקֵם, and מוֹתֵת "put to death," which is similar to הָמֵת; however, I am not not yet able to decide with certainty.

In this passage Bril explained that (1) the *pi'el* and the *hiph'il* differ with some verbs in that the former is transitive and the *hiph'il* is causative (it governs three arguments); (2) with some other verbs the *pi'el* marks durativity, the preservation of an object in a state, whereas the *hiph'il* indicates the action that leads to the state; (3) and yet with other verbs the two stems have different meanings. He appended a remark that in some cases there appears to be no discernible difference in meaning. His second observation is germane to the topic under discussion here.

Salomon Löwisohn on the Overlapping 'Causative' Use of *Pi'el* and the *Hiph'il*

Salomon Löwisohn (שלמה לעוויזאהן; né Salomon Mór) was born in Mór, Hungary in 1788. He received a traditional yeshiva education in Prague, where he died in 1821. He is best remembered as a poet and the author of the 1816 monograph מליצת ישורון (*Melizas Jeschurun*). Löwisohn was also a grammarian of repute. In 1811 he published his first book, שיחה בעולם הנשמות, an investigation of grammatical phenomena presented through the popular genre of fictional historical dialogues between dead personalities ("dialogues of the dead"[21]) in which Radaq, perhaps the best known and most influential of medieval Jewish grammarians, discusses points of grammar with Joel Bril. Most of this dialogue was also published in installments in the Maskilic journal המאסף *ha-Me'assef* during 1810–1811.[22] Among the introductory remarks that Löwisohn put in Radaq's mouth is the following[23]:

כי לשוא עמלו כל המדקדקים אשר היו עד היום הזה למצוא כללים נכונים אשר יפרידו הוראת כל בנין מחבירו, ואשר יגבילו גבול נכון בעד שמוש כל בנין. יען כי מצאנו ערבוב ובלבול גדול בשמושי הבנינים בספרי הקודש. כי כן מצאנו בהרבה פעלים בנין הפעיל לבדו מוציא את בנין הקל, ובמקצת הפעלים משפט ההוצאה הוא על בנין פָּעֵל לבדו, ובפעלים אחרים רבים ישתתפו שניהם יחד להוציא את בנין הקל.

> For in vain all the grammarians until now have striven to find correct rules that would separate the meaning of each stem from the other, and which would establish a correct border for the use of each stem since we have found great mixture and confusion in the use of the stems in the Holy Books. We have indeed found that with many verbs only the *hiph'il* stem makes the *qal* stem

---

21. Pelli, *Genre*, 213–44.

22. Löwisohn published in 1812 *Beth Haossef*, a work on linguistic phenomena in Hebrew, which included for the first time an introduction to the grammar and the lexicon of Mishnaic Hebrew. It was subsequently reprinted in 1815 in a new edition of *Mishnayot* edited by Anton Schmid in Vienna. שיחה בעולם המתים [*Sicha Beolam Hanschamoth*] and *Beth Haossef* were republished together in 1849 under the title *Investigationes Linguae* [מחקרי לשון] (Löwisohn, *Investigationes*) and more recently in 1957 (Löwisohn, מחקרי לשון).

23. Cited according to the 1811 book (Löwisohn, שיחה בארץ החיים, p. ג).

Difference between Causative *Pi'el* and *Hiph'il* in Biblical Hebrew

transitive, but with some verbs only the *pi'el* stem makes (the *qal* stem) transitive, and with many other verbs both of them (*pi'el* and *hiph'il*) make the *qal* stem transitive.

Löwisohn appropriated Radaq's name in order to lend credence to the views that he wished to put across. Radaq, however, did not write in his grammar ספר מכלול [24] that the use of the stems was confused, though he does give examples of overlapping functions: he wrote that intransitive verbs occur in both *qal* and *pi'el*, on the one hand, and in *qal* and *hiph'il*, on the other. In the first case, Radaq explained that the *pi'el* verb indicates plurality, and in the second, that the *hiph'il* verb expresses intensivity:

ובמקומת מעוטים ימצאו בנין פעל הדגש ובנין הפעיל פעלים עומדים. וכשהם עומדים באים לחזק הפעולה לפיכך באו בזה הבנין. וזה ההפרש בין בנין הקל העומד ובין בנין פִּעֵל או הפעיל עומד כמו ושער שחור צָמַח בו (ויקרא כ"ג). שהוא עומד מן הקל וכן ושערך צָמֵּחַ (יחזקאל י"ו). מן הדגש עומד אלה שזה מורה על רוב הצמיחה ועל מהירתה לפיכך נשתמשו בו בבנין הדגש. וכן אָדְמוּ עצם מפנינים (איכה ד'). קל עומד וכן אם יַאֲדִימוּ כתולע (ישעי' א'). הפעיל עומד אלא שזה יותר אדום.

> And in a few places intransitive verbs are found in the *pi'el* stem and the *hiph'il* stem. And when they are intransitive they serve to strengthen the action, therefore they come in this stem. And this is the difference between the intransitive *qal* stem and the intransitive *pi'el* or *hiph'il* stems like "and black hair grew (צָמַח) in it" (Leviticus 13), which is intransitive *qal* and "and your hair grew (צָמֵּחַ)" (Ezekiel 16), which is intransitive *pi'el*. This indicates the luxuriance of the growth and its speed; therefore, they used it in the *pi'el* stem. And so "they were redder (אָדְמוּ) than pearls" (Lamentations 4) is an intransitive *qal* and also "if they be red (יַאֲדִימוּ) like crimson" (Isa 1) is an intransitive *hiph'il* except that it is redder.

For Radaq's comment on the overlapping of *pi'el* and *hiph'il* in transitivizing *qal* verbs, see above p. 265.

Unlike Radaq in ספר מכלול, Löwisohn searched for a difference between the *pi'el* and the *hiph'il* in marking causativity. He has Bril pose three questions to Radaq, two of which are related to the overlap between *pi'el* and *hiph'il*.[25] The first question Bril asked Radaq is

---

24. Qimḥi, ספר מכלול, p. ב. Chomsky, *Kimḥi's Hebrew Grammar*, ignored this passage and did not include it in his edition of Qimḥi's grammar.

25. The questions and answers can be found on pp. ה-ח.

מדוע מצאנו במקצת הפעלים בנין פִּעֵל מוציא לבדו את בנין הקל. כמו
מן כָּבָה לָמוֹד תאמר כִּבָּה לִמֵּד בהוצאת בנין הקל, לא הַכְבָּה הַלְמֵד,
ובפעלים אחרים רבים יוצא בנין הפעיל לבדו את בנין הקל, כמו מן
נָפוֹל לא תאמר בהוצאת בנין הקל רק הִפִּיל, וכן מן אָכוֹל הַאֲכִיל? הכי
יש הבדל בין פעלת העצם המוציא אשר יבוא עליה בנין פִּעֵל לפעלת
העצם המוציא אשר יבוא עליה בנין הפעיל? ומה הוא זה ההבדל?

Why have we found with some verbs that the *piʿel* stem alone transitivizes the *qal* stem, such as from כָּבָה (and) לָמוֹד you say כִּבָּה (and) לִמֵּד when you transitivize the *qal* stem? But with many other verbs, such as from נָפוֹל, do you not say when you transitivize the *qal* stem only הִפִּיל, and similarly from אָכוֹל (you say) הַאֲכִיל? Is there a difference between the action of the object that transitivizes in the *piʿel* stem and the *hiphʿil* stem? And what is the difference?

The second question Bril posed to Radaq is

אם נאמר כי פעלת העצם המוציא אשר יבוא עליה בנין פִּעֵל אחרת
היא בעניינה מפעלת העצם המוציא אשר יבוא עליה בנין הפעיל, ויש
הבדל עצמותי ביניהם. מדוע מצאנו כמה פעלים אשר ישתתפו בהם
הפִּעֵל וההפעיל כאחד להוציא את בנין הקל? כמו מן בָּעוֹר תאמר בִּעֵר
את האש. או הִבְעִיר את האש, וכן מן נָחוֹל תאמר בהוצאת בנין הקל
נִחֵל או הִנְחִיל? וכאלה הרבה מאד?

If we say that the action of the object that transitivizes in the *piʿel* stem is different in its essence from the action of an object that transitivizes in the *hiphʿil* stem, and there is a difference in the type of object between them, why have we found several verbs in which both the *piʿel* and the *hiphʿil* participate in transitivizing the *qal* stem, such as from בָּעוֹר "kindle" you say בִּעֵר את האש or הִבְעִיר את האש ("kindle the fire"), and similarly from נָחוֹל "inherit" you say in transitivizing the *qal* stem נִחֵל and הִנְחִיל ("cause to inherit")?

Löwisohn has Radaq answer both questions in considerable detail:

בתשובת השאלה הראשונה. והוא. דע כי הפעלה היוצאת מעצם
הנושא למען הוציא פעלה אחרת בעצם אחר, תפעל על אחד משני
הדרכים. או (1) כי פעלת העצם המוציא, היא חלה על העצם האחר,
כל זמן עשות זה את פעלתו, ובכלות פעלת העצם המוציא תכלה גם
כן פעלת העצם האחר, ועל דרך זה העצם המוציא הוא גומר בפעלתו
האחת את פעלת העצם האחר. או (2) כי העצם המוציא הוא רק
מעורר על ידי פעלתו את כח העצם האחר לפעול פעלה מה, אשר לא
תכלה עדן בסור מעליו פעלת העצם המוציא, רק היא נגמרת אחרי

אשר כלתה כבר פעלת העצם המוציא הזאת אשר עוררה את כחו לפעול — ועל דרך זה העצם המוציא הוא גורם בפעלתו את פעלת העצם האחר —

And in response to the first question: know that an action that originates with a subject in order to cause another action on another object works in one of two ways, either (1) that the action of the object that is causative operates on the other object as long as it performs its action, and when the action of the object that is causative ends, the action of the other object also ends, and in this way, the object that is causative finishes in one action the action of the other object, or (2) that the object that is causative stimulates by its action the power of the other object to perform some action, which does not end when the action of the object that is causative leaves off; it is only finished after the action of the causative object which stimulated its working is already finished—and in this way the object that is causative is the reason of its working on the action of the other object—

והנה מניחי לשון עבר הניחו שני בנינים, בנין פִּעֵל ובנין הִפְעִיל להוציא את בנין הקל כפי אשר תהיה פעלת העצם המוציא על אחד משני הדרכים האלה אשר הזכרתי. כי אם תהיה פעלתו על הדרך הראשון אשר הזכרתי אז תבוא תמיד בבנין פִּעֵל, כמו בפעל כָּבָה שהבאת בשאלתך. הנה האיש אשר יוציא על ידי פעלתו את הכביה בנר או בגחלת, כאשר כלתה פעלתו כלתה גם כן פעלת הכביה בעצמים האלה, לכן יקרא הוא הַמְכַבֶּה לא הַמַכְבֶּה. וכן התלמיד הלומד מרבו לא ילמד תורת רבו רק בעוד אשר יְלַמְּדֵהוּ זה, וכאשר תכלה פעלת הרב הַמְלַמֵּד תכלה גם כן פעלת התלמיד הַלּוֹמֵד. וכן הוא הדין בפעל אָלֵף אשר אחד הוא בעניניו עם הפעל לָמֹד – ואם אמנם תהיה פעלת העצם המוציא על הדרך השני אשר הזכרתי אז תבוא תמיד בבנין הפעיל, כמו בפעל נָפֹל; הנה האיש אשר ידחה איש אחר העומד על גג הבית עד כי יפֹּל לארץ נאמר כי הוא הִפִּילוֹ לארץ, כי הנפילה לארץ היא נגמרת אחרי אשר כלתה כבר פעלת הדחיה, וכן הנותן לרעב לחם לאכול הוא מַאֲכִיל את הרעב, כי הרעב אוכל את הלחם אחרי הפסק פעלת הנתינה.

And behold those who laid the foundations of the Hebrew language established two stems, the *piʿel* stem and the *hiphʿil* stem, in order to transitivize the *qal* stem so that the action of the object is transitive in one of these two ways, which I mentioned. For if its action is the first way I mentioned, then it always occurs in the *piʿel* stem, as in *piʿel* כבה, which you cited in your question. Behold, the man who causes the action of extinguishing the candle or burning coal, when his action has ended, the action of extinguishing these objects has also ended, therefore, he is called הַמְכַבֶּה and not הַמִּכְבֶּה. Similarly, the student who learns from his master will only learn the teaching of his master if he teaches him, and when the action of the master ends, so too ends the action of the student who learns. And this is the case with the verb אָלַף whose meaning is the same as the verb לָמַד—and if the action of the object that is transitive is really according to the second method I mentioned, then it always occurs in the *hiphʿil* stem, like the verb נָפַל; behold, concerning the man who pushes another man standing on the roof of a house so that he falls to the ground, it is said that the fall to the ground finishes after the action of the pushing has ended, and similarly one who gives the hungry bread to eat, feeds (מַאֲכִיל) the hungry because the hungry person eats the bread after the action of giving has ceased.

ובתשובת השאלה השניה אשר שאלת, הנני אומר לך. דע כי תמצא לפעמים בנין הקל הכולל לפי הנראה בהוראתו רק פעולה אחת. וכאשר תשכיל היטב תמצא. כי התחלת הפעלה אשר יורה אותה בה״ק זה. היא כמו פעלה בפני עצמה הקודמת תמיד אל המשכת הפעלה הנחשבת גם כן לפעלה אחרת בפני עצמה, ובלשונות העמים הניחו עליהם שני פעלים למען סַמֵּן כל אחת בפעל מיוחד, והעברי יכניס את שתיהן בבנין קל אחד אשר ישתמש בו פעם על הוראה זאת ופעם על הוראה אחרת, כמו בנין קל קוּם הוראתו לפעמים על התחלת הקימה אחרי הישיבה (אויף שטעהאן) כמו וִישִׁישִׁים קָמוּ עָמָדוּ (איוב, ד״ט[26]) ולפעמים על המשכת הקימה (שטעהען, בעשטעהאן) כמו וְעַתָּה מַמְלַכְתְּךָ לֹא תָקוּם (שמואל א׳ י״ג[27]) — בנין קל חָיָה הוראתו לפעמים על התחיה אשר המות (אויף לעבען), כמו יִחְיוּ מֵתֶיךָ נְבֵלָתִי יְקוּמוּן (ישעיה ד״ו[28]) ולפעמים על המשך החיים אשר יחיה החי בטרם ימות (לעבען), כמו לֹא אָמוּת כִּי אֶחְיֶה (תהלים קי״ח) וכן בנין קל יָדֹעַ הוראתו לפעמים התחלת ידיעת דבר מה אשר לא ידענו עד הנה (ערפאהרען), כמו וַיֵּדַע דָּוִד כִּי עָלָיו שָׁאוּל מַחֲרִישׁ הָרָעָה (שמואל א ד״ג[29]) ולפעמים הוראתו המשכת ידיעת דבר מה אשר לא שכחנו עוד (וויססען) כמו יָדְעוּ כִּי רְעֵבִים אֲנָחְנוּ (מלכים ב׳ ז׳).

And in response to the second question that you asked, behold I say to you: know that sometimes you find the *qal* stem, which

---

26. כ״ט =.

27. The 1811 edition erroneously reads י״ד. The version in *Ha-Me'assef* has the correct chapter י״ג.

28. כ״ו =.

29. כ״ג =.

Difference between Causative *Pi'el* and *Hiph'il* in Biblical Hebrew

includes in its meaning ostensibly only one action. And when you discern carefully, you find that the beginning of the action which this *qal* stem indicates is similar to an action in itself that always precedes the continuation of the action, which is also considered a different action in itself. And in other languages speakers have coined two verbs so that each one marked a special verb, but the Hebrew (speaker) includes them both in one *qal* stem, which at times he uses it for this meaning and at other times for another meaning, such as the *qal* stem קוּם: its meaning sometimes is the beginning of rising up after sitting (*aufstehen*) such as "and the aged rose up (קָמוּ) and stood" (Job 29) and sometimes is the continuation of rising up (*stehen, bestehen*) such as "but now your kingdom will not continue (תָקוּם)" (1 Samuel 13). The meaning of the *qal* stem חָיָה is sometimes resurrection after death (*aufleben*) like "your dead will live (יִחְיוּ), (with) my dead body they will arise" (Isaiah 26), and sometimes the continuation of the life which the living will live before he dies (*leben*) like "I shall not die, but live (אֶחְיֶה)" (Psalm 118); similarly, in the *qal* stem, יָדַע whose meaning is sometimes the beginning of knowledge of a thing that we did not know up until now (*erfahren*) like "and David knew (וַיֵּדַע) that Saul was devising mischief against him" (1 Samuel 23) and sometimes its meaning is the continuation of knowing the thing that we have not yet forgotten (*wissen*) such as "they know (יָדְעוּ) that we are hungry" (2 Kings 7).

והנה כאשר ירצה העברי להוציא בנין קל כזה אזי יוכל להשתמש בכל אחד בשני הבנינים המוציאים אשר ירצה מבלי הבדל מאום ביניהם. בבנין פִּעֵל בבחינת הוראת הקל על התחלת הפעולה הַנִּגְמֶרֶת מיד בכלות פעולת העצם המוציא, ובנין הפעיל בבחינת הוראת הקל על המשכת הפעולה הַנִּגְרֶמֶת מפעולת העצם המוציא — על דרך משל המגביה את האיש השוכב על הארץ ומעמידו על רגליו הנה הוא גומר בפעולתו מיד את התחלת הקימה (דאז אויפשטעהען) ומסבב את המשכת הקימה (דאז שטעהען) לכן נאמר על צד השאלה, וחרבותיה אֲקוֹמֵם (ישעיהו מ"ד) אָקִים את סכת דוד הנופלת (עמוס ט') וכן המביא רוח חיים בפגר מת, הוא גומר בפעולתו מיד את פעולת התחיה (דאז אויף לעבען) ומסבב את המשך הקיים אשר יהיה החי הזה אחרי כן בטרם ישוב למות. (דאז לעבען) לכן נאמר ה' ממית וּמְחַיֶּה (ש"א ב') אשר הֶחֱיָה את בנה (מלכים ב' ח') וכן המגיד לנו דבר חדש אשר לא ידענו עוד הנה הוא גומר בפעולתו מיד את פעולת התחלת הידיעה (דיא ערפֿאהרונג) מסבב את המשך הידיעה אשר נדע הדבר הזה אחרי כן ימים רבים (דאז וויסען) לכן נאמר יְדַעְתָּ שחר מקומו (איוב נ"ח) הוֹדִיעֵנִי ה' קִצִּי (תהלים ל"ט).

And now when a Hebrew (speaker) wants to make such a *qal* verb transitive, then he can use whichever of the two transitive stems that he wants without any difference between them. The *piʿel* stem with regard to the meaning of the *qal* indicates the beginning of the action that is finished from the transitive action of the object, and in the *hiphʿil* stem with regard to the meaning of the *qal* indicates the continuation of the action, which is caused by the action of the object that is transitive—for example, who raises (הַמַּגְבִּיהַ) a man lying on the ground and sets him up on his feet, behold, he finishes with his action immediately the beginning of the standing up (*das Aufstehen*) and causes the continuation of the standing up (*das Stehen*). Therefore it is said figuratively, "and I will restore (אֲקוֹמֵם) her ruins" (Isaiah 44), "I will set up (אָקִים) the fallen booth of David" (Amos 9) and thus who brings spirit of life to a corpse, he finishes with his action immediately the action of resurrection (*das Aufleben*) and causes the continuation which the living will live afterwards before he again dies (*das Leben*). Therefore, it is said "The LORD deals death and gives life (וּמְחַיֶּה)" (1 Samuel 2), "whose son he revived (הֶחֱיָה)" (2 Kings 8), and similarly who tells us a new thing which we did not already know while he finishes with his action the beginning of the piece of news (*die Erfahrung*) and causes the continution of the piece of news which we will know this thing many days afterwards (*das Wissen*). Therefore, it is said "and caused the dawn to know (יִדַּעְתָּ) its place" (Job 38), "make known to me (הוֹדִיעֵנִי), O LORD, my end" (Psalm 39).

והדין הזה נוהג בכל פעלי מקרה, יען כי כל בנין קל מפעלי מקרה יורה, כן על תלות המקרה בעצם, כן על התמדת המקרה בו, כמו חָכָם גָּדוֹל שָׁכּוֹר (וויזע, גראס, ראוישוג וועדעון-זיין) לכן כאשר תרצה להוציא את בנין הקל תאמר חִכֵּם או הֶחְכִּים גִּדֵּל או הִגְדִּיל, שִׁכֵּר גם הִשְׁכִּיר.

And this is the case with all verbs of accidence[30] since all verbs in the *qal* stem are of accidence, thus the dependence of the accidence on an object and on the perpetuation of the accidence on it, such as חָכָם גָּדוֹל שָׁכּוֹר (*weise* 'wise,' *gross* 'large,' *rauschig werden sein* 'to become intoxicated'). Therefore, when you want to transitivize the *qal* you say חִכֵּם or הֶחְכִּים, גִּדֵּל or הִגְדִּיל, שִׁכֵּר or הִשְׁכִּיר

---

30. On the use of the Aristotelian term "accidence" among Hebrew grammarians, see, e.g., Maman, "Ibn Janāḥ," 115–9.

Difference between Causative *Pi'el* and *Hiph'il* in Biblical Hebrew

ומבלעדי אלה יתכן עוד שיבואו שניהם בנין פִּעֵל ובנין הפעיל להוציא
בנין קל אחד, אבל כל אחד נבדל בהוראתו מחבירו ע"פ החק אשר
בררתי לך, בתשובתי על שאלתך הראשונה, כמו מפעל מות תאמר
בהוצאת בנין הקל מוֹתֵת או הָמִית, וההבדל ביניהם הוא, כי זה אשר
יכה את האיש הבריא והשלם בגופו מכת מות, עד כי ימות מהמכה
הזאת אחרי זמן מה, יהיה אחרי רגעים מעטים, הוא יקרא מֵמִית (כי
לעולם לא ימות איש בריא ושלם בגופו תחת יד המכו מכת מות, אף
אם יוסר את ראשו בפעם אחת) אבל האיש אשר הכה מכת חרב והרג
ואך ניצוץ חיות אחד הוא נשאר תקוע בלבו, הנה זה אשר יוסיף להכותו
עוד ויכבה את שביב הניצוץ החלש הזה הוא יקרא מְמוֹתֵת, כי מיד
אחרי פגעו בו הוא מת ובטלו כל חושיו. והוא כאבן דומם. וכן העולל
הטמון ברחם אמו אשר לא חי עוד חיים שלמים ואך נצני החיות החלו
לפרוח בו. הנה זה אשר יפרוץ את בנין גופו כרגע ברחם אמו נאמר
עליו כי הוא מוֹתְתָהוּ — ועל דרך זה הוא ההבדל בין בנין פִּעֵל לבנין
הפעיל משרש יָלוֹד. כי האיש אשר ישכב את האשה ומסבב שתלד את
הילד לאחר מספר איזה חדשים הוא הַמּוֹלִיד (א), אבל החיה העוזרת
וגומרת את פעלת הלידה היא הַמְיַלֶּדֶת — וכן תבדיל על דרך זה בין
בנין פִּעֵל לבנין הפעיל משרש נָחוֹל כאשר תדוק היטב בכתובים.

And, besides these, others (verbs) may also occur in the *pi'el* stem and the *hiph'il* stem in order to make the *qal* stem transitive, but each one is distinguished in its meaning by the rule which I made clear for you, concerning my answer to your first question, such as from the verb מוֹת you say in making a transitive from the *qal* stem מוֹתֵת or הָמִית. And the difference between them is when he beats to death a completely healthy man so that he dies after a while from this beating, after a few moments, he will be called מֵמִית (because a completely healthy man never dies from a strong blow, unless he is beheaded in one fell swoop), but the man who was already beaten greviously with a sword, and yet one spark of vitality remains embedded in his (the beaten man's) heart, he who continues to beat him and extinguishes this weak spark, he is called מְמוֹתֵת, since after he (the beater) hurts him, he (the beaten man) dies and all his senses cease, and he is like an inanimate stone. And so, too, is the infant hidden in his mother's womb who has not yet lived a full life but the sparks of vitality began to blossom in him. When he breaks out all at once from his mother's womb, it is said about him that מוֹתְתָהוּ 'he killed him,' and in this way is the difference between the *pi'el* stem and the *hiph'il* stem of the root יָלוֹד. Because the man who sleeps with a woman and causes her to give birth to a child after a number of months is הַמּוֹלִיד, but the live one who helps and finishes the birthing activity is called הַמְיַלֶּדֶת—and thus, when you check carefully in the written texts, you distinguish between the *pi'el* stem and the *hiph'il* stem from the root נָחוֹל.

The gist of Löwisohn's view on the difference between *pi'el* and *hiph'il* is that the effect of the former (*pi'el*) ends with the cessation of the action of the *pi'el* verb, whereas the effect of the latter (*hiph'il*) continues after the cessation of the *hiph'il* verb's action. Löwisohn's view of the continuing effect of the action of the verb is strikingly like that of Bril, but in a different stem. For Bril it is the *pi'el*, but for Löwisohn it is the *hiph'il*.

Conclusion

The overlap in use of *pi'el* and *hiph'il* is a phenomenon which is recognized already by medieval Jewish grammarians. They did not, however, assign separate meanings to verbs that occurred in both stems. In contrast, two *Maskilic* grammarians, Joel Bril and Salomon Löwisohn, assumed that the use of different stems marks different meanings, though they disagreed over which stem denoted what meaning. Bril, who published his theory first, advanced the idea that the *pi'el* stem signifies the preservation and lasting effect of an action, whereas the *hiph'il* marks an action leading up to the state induced by the action. Löwisohn, who admired Bril greatly, as evidenced by his inclusion in the dialogue of the dead together with Radaq, expressed, in the guise of Radaq, a different view from that of Bril. For Löwisohn it was the *hiph'il* stem that implied an ongoing and enduring state while the *pi'el* denoted telicity. Bril presented his understanding of the use of the stems without any textual examples; Löwisohn buttressed his analysis with biblical verses. The distinction between the two *Maskilim* is highlighted by their discussion of the *hiph'il* of the verb קום: for Bril it signified the continuation of the object in a raised state but for Löwisohn, it was the action of raising the object.

It is of historical interest that two *Maskilim* at the turn of the 18th century both felt that one stem marked a state resulting from a verbal action, and no less curious that the two contemporaries disagreed as to which stem it was. Bril's 1794 interpretation of the *pi'el* as denoting the continuation of a state or condition of an action related to an intransitive verb in the *qal* stem reminds one of the factitive notion assigned to *pi'el* by Jenni in his pathbreaking 1968 book. Löwisohn in 1811 reached a similar result, but with the *hiph'il*. Reading these *Maskilic* analyses of the verbal stems inevitably recalls Qohelet's eternal truth: וְאֵין כָּל־חָדָשׁ תַּחַת הַשָּׁמֶשׁ "And there is nothing new under the sun" (Qoh 1:9).

BIBLIOGRAPHY

Bacher, Wilhelm. *Abraham Ibn Esra als Grammatiker*. Strassburg: Trübner, 1882.

Bauer, Hans, and Pontus Leander. *Historische Grammatik der hebräischen Sprache des Alten Testamentes*. Halle/Saale: Niemeyer, 1922.

Ben-Ḥayyim, Zeʾev. *A Grammar of Samaritan Hebrew Based on the Recitation of the Law in Comparison with the Tiberian and Other Jewish Traditions*, with assistance from Abraham Tal. Jerusalem: Magnes / Winona Lake, IN: Eisenbrauns, 2000.

———. "לשון עתיקה במציאות חדשה." *Leshonenu Laʿam* 4 (1953), fascicles 3–5, 8–9. Reprinted in במלחמתה של לשון (*The Struggle for a Language*), 36–85. Jerusalem: Academy of the Hebrew Language, 1992.

Ben-Zeev, Judah Leib. ספר תלמוד לשון עברי כולל יסודות דקדק הלשון מן התנועות השמות הפעלים והמלות ועם שמוש הלשון והרכבת המאמרים. 3rd ed. Vienna: Schmid, 1811.

Bergsträsser, Gotthelf. *Hebräische Grammatik*. 2 vols. Leipzig: Hinrichs, 1918–1929.

Blau, Joshua. *Phonology and Morphology of Biblical Hebrew*. Linguistic Studies in Ancient West Semitic 2. Winona Lake, IN: Eisenbrauns, 2010.

Bril, Joel. עמודי לשון המיוסדים על אדני ההגיון לתועלת התלמידים החפצים ללמוד שפת עבר שפה ברורה להבין במקרא מפורש ושום שכל / דיא עלעמנטע דער עברישן שפראבכע נאך לאגישן פרינציפן ענטוויקקלט איין האנדבוך פיר לעהרער חברת חנוך. 1st ed. – Berlin: נערים, 1794; 2nd ed. Prague: Die Gebrüder, Stiasny, 1803.

Chomsky, William. *David Ḳimḥi's Hebrew Grammar (Mikhlol) Systematically Presented and Critically Annotated*. Philadelphia: Dropsie College for Hebrew and Cognate Learning, 1933.

Gamliel, Chanoch. רש״י כפרשן ובכלשן: תפיסות תחביריות בפירוש רש״י לתורה [*Linguistics in Rashi's Commentary*]. Jerusalem: Bialik Institute, 2010.

Goetze, Albrecht. "The So-Called Intensive of the Semitic Languages." *JAOS* 62 (1942) 1–8.

Jenni, Ernst. *Das hebräische Piʿel*. Zurich: EVZ, 1968.

———. "Aktionsarten und Stammformen in Althebräischen: Das Piʿel in verbesserter Sicht." *ZAH* 113 (2000) 75–90.

Joosten, Jan. "The Functions of the Semitic D Stem: Biblical Hebrew Materials for a Comparative-Historical Approach." *Orientalia* 67 (1998) 202–30.

Joüon, Paul, and T. Muraoka. *A Grammar of Biblical Hebrew*. Second reprint of the second edition, with corrections. Rome: Gregorian & Biblical Press, 2009.

Kahn, Lily. "Maskilic Hebrew." In *EHLL*, 2:581–5.

Lambdin, Thomas O. "Review of Ernst Jenni, *Das hebräische Piʿel*." *CBQ* 31 (1969) 435–7.

Löwisohn, Salomon. "שיחה בעולם הנשמות," המאסף ט' 3 (ניסן ה'תק״ע) י״ב – י״ט; (אייר ה'תק״ע) ל״ו – מ״ב; (סיון ה'תק״ע) ס״ט – ע״ב; (ה'תק״ע) ט' 4 (אב, התק״ע) ס״ט-ע״ט; י' 2 (טבת, ה'תקע״א) כ״א – כ״ז; (אדר, ה'תקע״א) צ״ה – ק.

———. שיחה בעולם הנשמות בין הרב ר' דוד קמחי, ובין החכם ר' יואל ברי״ל כוללת שלשה. מאמרים בחקירות עיוניות נשגבות בדקדוק לשון עבר. Prague: Sommer, 1811.

———. בית האוסף כולל כמה חקירות בדקדוק לשון עבר בחקירות עיוניות נשגבות בדקדוק. לשון עבר [*Beth Haossef enthaltend verschiedene gramatikalische und philologische Untersuchungen in der hebräischen Sprache*]. Prague: Sommer, 1812.

———. מליצת ישורון: ספר כולל למודי המליצה העברית, מבוארים במשלים רבים ממליצות ספרי הקודש [*Melizas Jeschurun*]. Vienna: Schmid, 1816.

———. *Investigationes Linguae sive Due Opera Celebris Docti Pragensis* Salomonis Lewisohn sub. tit. *Sicha Beolam Hanschamoth et Beth Haosef illustrata et aucta a poeta judaico A. B. Lebensohn cum multis utilibus annotationibus ab editore Judeio Behak*= מחקרי לשון כולל שני ספרים שיחה בעולם הנשמות, ובית האסף להרב החכם הנעלה מוה' שלמה לעוויזאהן מפראג עם הערות תוספות הרבה מאת הרב המשורר החכם מוה' אד"ם הכהן לעבענזאהן נ"י גם הרבה הערות מועילות מאת המוציא לאור. Vilna: Rom, 1849.

———. מחקרי לשון, with an introduction by Israel Zmora. Tel-Aviv: Maḥbaroth LeSifruth, 1957.

Maman, Aharon. "Ibn Janāḥ: Between Logic and Grammar and His Classification of the Parts of Speech." In *Judaeo-Arabic Culture in al-Andalus: Proceedings of the 13th Conference of the Society for Judaeo-Arabic Studies Cordoba 2007*, edited by Amir Ashur, 111–20. Cordoba: Oriens Academics, 2013.

Pelli, Moshe. *In Search of Genre: Hebrew Enlightenment and Modernity*. Lanham, MD: University Press of America, 2005.

Qimḥi, David. ספר מכלול. Lyck: Fetzall, 1842.

Qimḥi, Moshe. מהלך שבילי הדעת. Mantua: Meir ben Ephraim, 1563.

Ryder, Stuart A. *The D-Stem in Western Semitic*. The Hauge: Mouton, 1974.

Van der Merwe, Christo H. J., Jackie A. Naudé, and Jan H. Kroetze. *A Biblical Hebrew Reference Grammar*. Biblical Languages: Hebrew 3. Sheffield: Sheffield Academic, 1999.

Waltke, Bruce K., and M. O'Connor. *An Introduction to Biblical Hebrew Syntax*. Winona Lake, IN: Eisenbrauns, 1990.

Williams, Ronald J. *Williams' Hebrew Syntax*. 3rd ed. Revised and expanded by John C. Beckman. Toronto: University of Toronto Press, 2007.

16

Kissing through a Veil: Translating the Emphatic in Biblical Hebrew

Richard Elliott Friedman

UNIVERSITY OF GEORGIA

I am sitting next to Ziony Zevit in a session at an international conference. The speaker is going on about chiasms, impressing on us that these literary forms keep appearing throughout several books of the Bible. Ziony, who knows that chiasm is so ubiquitous that it appears in almost any text ever written, leans over to me and says, "This would work on a phone book." (Actually, a phone book, going from A to Z, is one of the few texts that are not in fact chiasmic, but I take his point.)

He raises his hand and asks the speaker, "Have you ever found a text in the Bible on which this *doesn't* work?"

The speaker, not realizing that this is an unsympathetic question, answers enthusiastically, "No! I've never found a single text on which this doesn't work!"

Zevit says, "Then what do we learn from it?"

The speaker, still not perceiving what is happening, says, "I think I see what your problem is," and goes into a lengthy explanation.

But my story ends here. Ziony Zevit is a fine scholar. He sees the point and goes right to it. And, on the evidence of this one episode, he has little patience for uninsightful scholarship.

I am lecturing to a group of laypersons, undergraduate students, and rabbinical students at a mountain retreat in Georgia. I want to explain a rather technical point of Biblical Hebrew grammar, a fairly recently identified form, that makes a great deal of difference in our understanding of many biblical passages. I say that we now know that if the subject precedes a perfect verb then this is how we get the past perfect in Biblical Hebrew. Thus, for example, when the Bible begins with the notice וְהָאָרֶץ הָיְתָה תֹהוּ וָבֹהוּ, this does not mean "the earth was shapeless and formless" (or "unformed and void"), as it has usually been understood. It means, rather, "the earth *had been* shapeless and formless." I explain that this point of grammar may answer the old theological question of whether Genesis 1 understands there to have been anything prior to the moment of creation. This opens the door to all kinds of questions about what may or may not have preceded this world. I am there hoping to have conveyed fairly simply the function and significance of this technical grammatical observation.

And then three graduate students in the audience say, "Oh, you mean it's the Anterior Construction," as if this is the most obvious thing in the world. I stop, look at them, and say, "You're from Los Angeles, aren't you?" No doubt about it: students of Zevit. Ziony Zevit is not only a fine scholar. He is a fine teacher.

I am honored to know him and to contribute something to this book in his honor.

Already as a child I heard the old line that studying the Bible in translation is like kissing through a veil. At that point I had not gotten in enough kissing to appreciate that this meant an even bigger difference than I realized. My concern now is that through the veils of our Hebrew Bible translations we produce an English that no one ever spoke or wrote. For example, when trying to capture the Hebrew construct, we lose the English possessive. So a Bible translator never goes over to his friend Doug's house; he tells his wife, "I'm going to the house of Doug." She answers, "Great. Can you pick up my stockings at the Secret of Victoria?" I mean more than just the standard issue of literal versus idiomatic here. I mean cases involving the *structure* of the two languages, so that each language has a different mechanism for conveying something. English uses possessives or the word "of" to convey what Hebrew conveys with constructs. The resulting problem is not only one of capturing what the original said. It is also a problem of sheer clumsiness in the translation wherever this mechanism occurs. Likewise, as I pointed out in the "Notes on the Translation" in my *Commentary on the Torah*, English translators, for some unarticulated reason, have been averse to using contractions, even when translating dialog in common speech.[1] In normal spoken English, one almost never speaks for as much as five minutes without using a contraction. But in Bible translations contractions are so taboo that filmmakers avoid them even in scenes in which the actors are audibly and visibly talking. The result is that practically every conversation in the Bible sounds artificial in translation. Pharaoh answers Moses' famous "Thus says Yahweh: Let my people go" with a strong, sharp: "I don't know Yahweh, and I won't let your people go." But in *The Prince of Egypt*, Ralph Fiennes as the Pharaoh says: "I do not know the LORD. Neither will I let your people go." Instead of "I won't" it has "Neither will I." Does anyone speak that way? (I was a consultant on that film, so I share any blame for not pointing it out at the time.)

There may be no more persistent case of these phenomena of *clumsiness perpetuum* than the problem of translating Biblical Hebrew's emphatic into an English emphatic. Emphatics are hard enough to capture anyway, let alone in a language that has no punctuation to provide a signal of which words are to be emphasized. As far as I am able to determine, none of the five existing manuscripts of the Gettysburg Address includes italics to indicate which words were emphasized. So some claim that he did not say, "Government *of* the people, *by* the people, and *for* the people," but rather "Government of the *people*, by the *people*, and for the *people*." And similarly, practically every actor who has ever played Hamlet has read its most famous line as: "To be or *not* to be. That is the *question*," when it seems to me that the logic of the play would rather suggest the emphasis: "To *be* or not to *be*. *That* is the question."

Now how do we express the emphatic on the written page in English? We use italics, underlining, boldface, or exclamation points. Biblical Hebrew, in the absence of all four of these visual tools, had to express emphasis not graphically but in mechanisms that were contained in the words. Let us consider some of those mechanisms.

The first is the infinitive absolute, used as an infinitival emphatic. It is placed before (or, occasionally, after) a finite verb. My teacher Thomas Lambdin wrote in his grammar that the English translation often requires the use of adverbs such as "surely, certainly, indeed."[2] And that is in fact what most translators have done:

מוֹת יוּמָת "He will surely be put to death." (Gen 26:11 + 23 additional times in the Bible)

---

1. Friedman, *Commentary on the Torah*, xiii.
2. Lambdin, *Introduction to Biblical Hebrew*, 158.

שָׁמוֹר תִּשְׁמְרוּן אֶת־מִצְוֺת יְהוָה אֱלֹהֵיכֶם "You shall certainly observe the commandments of YHWH your God" (Deut 6:17)

אִם־רָאֹה תִרְאֶה "If you will indeed see." (1 Sam 1:11)

But in Gen 18:10, when God tells Abraham that He will come back in nine months and Sarah will have given birth to a son, if we translate the Hebrew שׁוֹב אָשׁוּב as "I shall surely return" or "Indeed I shall return," it sounds awkward in its context. In fact, following perfectly normal English conversation up to this point between Abraham and his three visitors, this sudden "I shall surely come back" sounds just plain silly. Verily. It is as if in this paper I would suddenly say whither I am going. (It is like in the film *The Ten Commandments*, where Charlton Heston as Moses speaks in fairly normal English, but then suddenly he says to Pharaoh Yul Brynner, "With our wives and our cattle will we go.") Even if we would translate שׁוֹב אָשׁוּב as "I'll definitely come back," we would achieve a less awkward wording, but we might be overtranslating the Hebrew infinitive absolute, giving it a specificity of meaning that it does not really possess. And in Gen 20:18, where we read that God holds back the wombs of Abimelek's kingdom, the Hebrew phrase עָצֹר עָצַר does not work well with any of these adverbs. So the King James and Speiser and others make it "He closed fast." And most other translations simply give up and do not convey the presence of the infinitive at all. The primary, underlying function of the infinitive absolute is not to convey definiteness or certainty nor to express what we mean in English by "indeed" or "surely." Its function is to emphasize the verb, *whatever* verb it structures.

Adding a negative complicates things further. In Exod 5:23, when Moses complains to God that וְהַצֵּל לֹא־הִצַּלְתָּ, most English translations since the King James make it some variation of "and you have not saved *at all*." NJV makes it "and *still* you have not delivered." But, again, "at all" goes beyond what the Hebrew infinitive expresses, and "still" is still worse. The complication of the negative is especially visible when we look at a case in which we get the same infinitival emphatic with and without the negative element. In Gen 2:17, God tells the human not to eat from the tree of knowledge of good and bad because "in the day you eat from it: you'll die!"—Hebrew מוֹת תָּמוּת. But twelve verses later, the snake denies this and says, "you won't die!"—Hebrew לֹא־מוֹת תְּמֻתוּן (Gen 3:4). The only difference (outside of the pluralization) is the word לֹא. But what do the translations do with these two verses: The NEB makes the first one "you will certainly die" and the second one "Of course you will not die." The REB corrected the first to "you are surely doomed to die," but left the second one as "Of course you will not die." Speiser, similarly, made the first "you shall be doomed to death" but made the second one "you are not going to die." The King James and its clones translated the two consistently, making the first "thou shalt surely die" and the second "Ye shall not surely die." But what it gains in consistency it loses in meaning because the formulation "Ye shall not surely die" is unclear. It can mean that you definitely will not die, but it can also mean that it is not certain whether you will die or not. The bottom line is: none of the standard renderings of the infinitive absolute works on the same form with a negative element.

Put two infinitival emphatics in the same verse, and it gets even more complicated. In Deut 8:19, there are two infinitive absolutes in parallel to each other. Moses tells the people that if they forget, שָׁכֹחַ תִּשְׁכַּח, then they will perish, אָבֹד תֹּאבֵדוּן. None of the usual translations works well for both phrases, so the translators are forced to choose two for the same sentence. "If you do at all forget, then you shall surely perish." And in Gen 22:17, when God promises Abraham emphatically both to bless him and to multiply his seed, saying בָרֵךְ אֲבָרֶכְךָ וְהַרְבָּה אַרְבֶּה, few translations can find a comfortable way to handle both phrases in a row. The RSV has "I will indeed bless you, and I will multiply." The translator thus chose to use the adverb for the first phrase but not for the second even though the two phrases are structurally the same in the Hebrew. The King James has "in blessing I will bless thee, and in multiplying I will multiply thee," which is lovely, but in order to get there the translator had to change from the way the infinitive absolutes are handled elsewhere in the same work. The NEB gave up altogether when it made it "I will bless you abundantly and greatly multiply," which is not lovely and not representative of what is going on in the Hebrew. Speiser, too, shifted from his usual way of handling the infinitive absolute and dropped the adverbs in this verse. Again, none of the standard renderings of the infinitive absolute works when the form occurs twice in the same verse.

Now, on certain models of translation, this does not matter. For example, a translation that is intended not to achieve a felicitous English but rather to reproduce what is going on in the Hebrew, such as Everett Fox's translation of the Torah, and in some cases my colleague William Propp's translation of Exodus, never has to face these choices of English adverbs. Propp repeats the verb. Thus he translates God's words to Moses רָאֹה רָאִיתִי אֶת־עֳנִי עַמִּי as "I have seen, seen the humiliation of my people" (Exod 3:7). Fox would do שׁוֹב אָשׁוּב as "I will return, yes, return." The phrase שָׁמוֹר תִּשְׁמְרוּן אֶת־מִצְוֺת יְהוָה אֱלֹהֵיכֶם is "keep, yes, keep the commandment of YHWH your God" (Deut 6:17). He does מוֹת יוּמָת as "He must be put to death, yes, death!" in one text (Gen 26:11) and "is to be put-to-death, yes, death" in others (Exod 21:12, 15, 17; Lev 20:2). That last one is tricky because, to be consistent with the other cases, it should be "is to be put-to-death, yes, is to be put-to-death." And, where there is a negative element, Fox is forced to do the whole thing differently, because how do you add the word "yes" when one is trying to convey "no"?! So he translated וְהַצֵּל לֹא־הִצַּלְתָּ as "and rescued—you have not rescued your people!" Propp used the exact same wording in his Exodus commentary in the Anchor Bible, but since he does not add the word "yes" to his positives, he did not have to be inconsistent in his rendering of this negative. And where there are two infinitive absolutes in the same verse, Fox chose, as the "traditional" translators did, to use two different mechanisms to translate the same Hebrew structure. So he translated the parallel of שָׁכֹחַ תִּשְׁכַּח and אָבֹד תֹּאבֵדוּן as "if you forget, yes, forget . . . perish, you will perish." My point is that what such a translator is trying to do is to imitate the Hebrew, as much as possible, not to produce nice English. When one reads such a translation the English feels wrong, but that is just the point: to convey the notion that Hebrew does not work the same as English. One has to read only one page of Fox's *The Five Books of Moses* to get it. That is a perfectly legitimate aim for a translation, and there should be translations of this sort out there to make this essential point known. Propp especially clarifies and justifies the aims of such translation, noting that it preserves ambiguities, conveys to some extent the experience of reading the original, and "maintains a necessary sense of temporal and cultural distance between reader and text."[3]

But, meanwhile, back at the translations that are walking the traditional tightrope between conveying the Hebrew meaning and being good English, what is the best way to convey the infinitival emphatic? Let me give one more example to help set up my answer. When God tells Moses in Deut 31:18 הַסְתֵּר אַסְתִּיר פָּנַי, should we understand that as "I shall *surely* hide my face"? or as "I shall *utterly* hide my face"? Those are two different things. Either makes sense. And if we use adverbs for translating the Hebrew infinitival emphatic, we are forced to choose one or the other. The problem, again, is that the choice of the English mechanism of adverbs for conveying the Hebrew mechanism of the infinitive absolute calls for overtranslating: adding a degree of specificity that an adverb contains and an infinitive does *not* contain.

So what English mechanism would work better? Let's consider the other cases of Hebrew mechanisms of emphasis first.

The second such mechanism that I wish to consider is the explicit use of a pronoun together with a verb. In Genesis 14, Abram tells the King of Sodom that he will not take so much as a thread or a shoelace in return for having helped the king. Abram says that this is so that the king will not ever be able to claim אֲנִי הֶעֱשַׁרְתִּי אֶת־אַבְרָם

---

3. Propp, *Exodus 1–18*, 40.

"I made Abram rich" (v. 23). But the pronoun *'ănî* is not necessary to express this. We would have understood this if the text had read simply הֶעֱשַׁ֖רְתִּי אֶת־אַבְרָֽם. The pronoun is not extraneous, though. The verse does not mean "I made Abram rich." It means "*I* made Abram rich." This is further indicated by the structure of the next verse. Though Abram has refused any compensation, he says:

בִּלְעָדַ֗י רַ֚ק אֲשֶׁ֣ר אָֽכְל֣וּ הַנְּעָרִ֔ים וְחֵ֙לֶק֙ הָֽאֲנָשִׁ֔ים אֲשֶׁ֥ר הָֽלְכ֖וּ אִתִּ֑י עָנֵר֙ אֶשְׁכֹּ֣ל וּמַמְרֵ֔א הֵ֖ם יִקְח֥וּ חֶלְקָֽם׃

"Except only what the boys have eaten and the share of the people who went with me: Aner, Eshcol, and Mamre. *They* will take their share." (Or, if you read the verb as a jussive: "Let them take their share.")

Without the pronoun *hēm*, we could have understood the verse to mean "Aner, Eshcol, and Mamre will take their share." The addition of the pronoun introduces emphasis: "*They* will take their share." I, Abram, will not take anything, but *they* will take their share." Thus the two otherwise extraneous pronouns convey the emphases that are vital to the points that Abram is making to the king. What do the English translations do to convey this emphasis? Nothing. It is simply lost in translation. NJV comes the closest by translating אֲנִ֥י הֶעֱשַׁ֖רְתִּי אֶת־אַבְרָֽם as "It is I who made Abram rich." That is not quite emphasis, but at least it is close.

Likewise, when God tells Moses at the burning bush that He will have Aaron speak for Moses in Egypt, the text is: וְדִבֶּר־ה֥וּא לְךָ֖ "He will speak for you" (Exod 4:16). Even though the words וְדִבֶּר לְךָ֖ alone would have conveyed "He will speak for you," the pronoun *hû'* is not extraneous. It provides the emphasis: "*He* will speak for you." And, stronger still, a few verses earlier, the text combines both of the mechanisms that we have observed so far: the infinitive absolute and the pronoun with verb. It reads: דַּבֵּ֥ר יְדַבֵּ֖ר הֽוּא. This phrase does not translate as "Indeed he will speak." It means "*He* will *speak*!"

Likewise in Deut 31:23, where Moses tells Joshua: אַתָּ֗ה תָּבִיא֙ אֶת־בְּנֵ֣י יִשְׂרָאֵ֔ל אֶל־הָאָ֖רֶץ, the verb *tābî'* alone would mean "you will bring." *'attâ tābî'* here means "*You* will bring the people to the land." In this source, Moses has just been informed that he will die and that he is to appoint Joshua to lead the people. He then tells Joshua, "*You*—and not *I*—will take them to the land."

And likewise in Deut 29:15, when Moses admonishes the people who are assembled in front of him, and he says: אַתֶּ֣ם יְדַעְתֶּ֔ם. The verb *yəda'tem* would have been enough to convey the idea "you know." But, in context,

Moses is specifically making a point about his audience. *'attem yədaʿtem.* "*You* know what it was like in Egypt."

This was first pointed out to me by my colleague David Noel Freedman, of blessed memory, when I was sending him the pages of my translation of the Torah, and I believe he pointed it out to all of his Anchor Bible authors and Eerdmans authors. He said that he had not found a case of pronoun-plus-verb in the Hebrew Bible in which this understanding does not apply. I resisted it at first under the influence of contemporary Hebrew, in which the added pronoun seems to come and go almost at random. But, first of all, Biblical Hebrew is a written language, not spoken, and there is great care taken by the authors in the use of language. And, second, I am not so sure that the modern Hebrew pronoun-plus-verb is entirely random in any case (but that is a subject for another day).

Pronoun-plus-verb yields emphasis. And though it is consistent through the Hebrew Bible and acknowledged in a standard grammar like Lambdin's,[4] the English translations almost never represent it. (The main exception is one that we owe to Ziony Zevit for pointing out, namely: when the pronoun-plus-verb occurs in the anterior construction and serves to convey a past perfect tense rather than emphasis. Thus when the text reads וְהוּא עָבַר אֶת־הַפְּסִילִים (Judg 3:26), it means "and he [sc. Ehud] had passed the quarries," and not "he [emphatically, as opposed to someone else] passed the quarries."[5]

A third mechanism of emphasis is word order.[6] In Lev 25:42, God gives the Israelites a law: if a fellow Israelite is sold to you as a slave, you may not treat him as a slave. Why not? כִּי־עֲבָדַי הֵם. Because they are *my* slaves. They are God's slaves, not yours. If this were oral, it could say either *kî ʿăbāday hēm* or *kî hēm ʿăbāday.* The speaker could simply stress the word *ʿăbāday* with his or her voice. On the written parchment, however, the way to make the point was to use the atypical word order. But almost none of the English translations renders this line any differently than they would had the order been standard. Only Fox conveys the reversed order in his English: "For my servants are they." That captures the Hebrew order better, which is what he is trying to do, but it actually conveys the meaning worse,

---

4. Lambdin, *Introduction to Biblical Hebrew*, 83, notes the distinction between when translations may or may not need to convey the emphasis present in the Hebrew: "[They] may stand before the verb in a verbal sentence to give emphasis to the subject. This emphasis need not be strong; it may be merely that the discourse has had a shift in subject, which would not entail any special emphasis in the English translation."

5. Zevit, *Anterior Construction in Classical Hebrew*, 21.

6. Bandstra, "Word Order and Emphasis in Biblical Hebrew Narrative"; Kelley, et al., *Handbook to Biblical Hebrew*, 56, n. a.

because the patterns of English would lead a reader away from emphasizing the key word. We would naturally read it: "For my *servants* are *they*." No one would read it "For *my* servants are they"—which is what that word order means in the Hebrew.

Likewise in Deut 23:8, the law is that an Israelite cannot abhor an Edomite. The reason: כִּי אָחִיךָ הוּא "because he is your brother." Orally, one could say *kî 'āḥîkā hû'* or one could say *kî hû' 'āḥîkā*. Again, one could put the stress where one chooses. But in writing, it is the word order that tells the reader that the word *'āḥîkā*, "your brother," is the point not to be missed. Again, however, the English translations do not generally reveal that anything is going on in the Hebrew. Even Fox could not render this line consistently with the way he did the other case. There he said: "For my servants are they." But here he could not say "For your brother is he," because that would have made the whole line awkward and unclear: "You are not to abominate an Edomite, for your brother is he." *Who* is *what*?! Fox wisely chose to leave that one alone.

A fourth mechanism of emphasis is repetition. Perhaps this should be obvious, but it has not always been so. When the famous text states *ṣedeq ṣedeq tirdōp* "Justice, justice you shall pursue" (Deut 16:20), Ramban interprets the passage to mean that judges should pursue justice only by just means. Biblical scholarship being what it is, there are also surely those who will say that this is a scribal dittography. The scribe just wrote the word *ṣedeq* twice by accident (though the Septuagint and Qumran scrolls provide no support for such a claim.) On the face of it, though, the repetition of the word *ṣedeq* is best explained as emphasis. Somebody is trying to make a point, and it involves a noun. And for emphasizing a noun, *a noun*, there is nothing, *nothing*, like saying it twice.

In Num 8:16, God says about the Levites: נְתֻנִים נְתֻנִים הֵמָּה לִי. This can mean "they are given to me, every single one of them." Thus the King James renders it "They are *wholly* given to me." NJV makes it "They are formally assigned to me," which is awful. Even if *nətûnîm* correctly means "assigned," stretching the repetition of the word to arrive at "formally" is to achieve new heights of the introduction of specificity beyond what the Hebrew structural mechanism expresses. The NEB makes it "They are given and dedicated to me," which is still worse. In a polar opposite to the approach of Fox or Propp, it *hides* the repetition in the Hebrew by using two different words in English. Again, there is no Septuagint or Qumran basis for imagining a dittography here. The repetition appears rather to be a blatant way of emphasizing a point. The verse informs us that the Levites have a special task at the Tabernacle because: "They are given, *given*, to me from among the children of Israel."

I should add the caution here that repetition can mean other things as well besides emphasis, just as italics can mean things other than emphasis in English. אִישׁ אִישׁ in Hebrew does not emphasize the word "man." It means "any man." And שְׁנַיִם שְׁנַיִם in the flood story (Gen 7:9,15) means "two of each" or "by twos" (and not "two by two"![7]). It does not come to emphasize the number "two." But in cases such as the ones I treated above, it is a mechanism for conveying emphasis.

There are other cases that we might count as mechanisms of emphasis as well. These include strings of synonyms or parallels. For example, in Deut 5:3 Moses tells the people, לֹא אֶת־אֲבֹתֵינוּ כָּרַת יְהוָה אֶת־הַבְּרִית הַזֹּאת כִּי אִתָּנוּ אֲנַחְנוּ אֵלֶּה פֹה הַיּוֹם כֻּלָּנוּ חַיִּים "YHWH did not make this covenant with our fathers, but with us! We! These! Here! Today! All of us! Living!" Or in Exod 1:7 we read וּבְנֵי יִשְׂרָאֵל פָּרוּ וַיִּשְׁרְצוּ וַיִּרְבּוּ וַיַּעַצְמוּ "and the children of Israel were fruitful and teemed and multiplied and became powerful." These cases are more properly identified as stylistic rather than structural mechanisms of the language, but they still raise the question of how best to translate the emphasis that they convey into English.

The question applies as well to less definable cases, in which the translator feels that emphasis is called for by the context. If one's sense of the text is that an emphatic is contained in the verse, how should one let the readers know it? For example, in Exod 1:19, where the midwives of the Israelites tell the Pharaoh why they have failed to follow his command to kill the male newborns, my sense of the text is that they are being depicted as speaking emphatically. They say, "The Hebrew women are ḥayyôt. Before the midwife comes to them, they have given birth!" The line implies: "Wow! Unbelievable! Those Israelite women are incredible!" Though there are no structural mechanisms in the text to signal emphasis, one would not take this verse as dispassionately as, say, "Behold, my brother Esau is an hairy man and I am a smooth man."

Similarly, but with more impact on the way we understand a text, I recall the way my teacher Frank Cross would read the Eden story in Genesis to his undergraduate introductory class in Hebrew Bible. When God asks the human, "Who told you that you were naked? Have you eaten from the tree from which I commanded you not to eat?" Professor Cross read:

---

7. The translation "two by two" was a product of the merger of the J text, which had seven pairs of the "pure" animals and one pair of the "impure," with the P text which had just two of each kind, without regard to purity. In order to reconcile the Hebrew šenayim šenayim with the fact of there being fourteen of some animals, the Hebrew repetition was taken to refer to the order in which the animals board the ark, which has governed artistic representations of the flood ever since. Friedman, *Who Wrote the Bible?*, 55, 56, 59.

And the man said, "The *woman,* whom *you* placed with me, *she* gave me from the tree, and I ate."

And YHWH God said to the woman, "What is this that you have done?"

And the woman said, "The *snake* tricked me, and I ate."

Now, none of this emphasis is on the page, either in the grammar or in the wording. It derives from the translator's sense of the text. One may say that this is a case that applies specifically to an oral reading of the text to an audience. That is true, but what if this text was in fact meant for oral reading when it was composed? If so, then the author knew that the reader would have the option to choose emphases, conveyed by pauses and changes of loudness, and even by facial expressions and body gestures. And so the author bequeathed the matter of emphasis to the oral reader. But then is not the translator in a position similar to that of the oral reader? The translator cannot help but make decisions that affect the readers' perceptions of the emphases in the text.[8]

And so we come back to the first question: how is one to convey what is going on in the Hebrew in a translation that is good English? I contend that if we understand the several structures we have observed here to be mechanisms of emphasis of Biblical Hebrew, then we should use the standard mechanisms of emphasis of English to express them. In English, the standard ways to show emphasis on a printed page are italics and exclamation points. As I said at the beginning, the reason that Biblical Hebrew used mechanisms that are based on wording is that words were all that Biblical Hebrew had: no italics, no underlining, no boldface, no punctuation marks. But we have these inventions. And so it seems to me that the best way to translate Hebrew's mechanisms of emphasis is to use our mechanisms of emphasis.

מוֹת יוּמָת is "He will be put to *death!*"

שָׁמוֹר תִּשְׁמְרוּן is "You *shall* observe"

---

8. Muraoka, *Emphatic Words and Structures in Biblical Hebrew,* includes several of the categories that I have raised here—word order, personal pronoun with verb, infinitive absolute—not with an eye to translation but as matters of syntactic and lexical means of emphasis in Biblical Hebrew itself. With regard to oral reading, Muraoka says, "Undoubtedly the classical Hebrew as spoken and read by the ancient Israelites must have possessed a variety of intonations and stress accents . . . " (p. xiii). Niccacci, "Types and Functions of the Nominal Sentence," 217–18 n.11, cites Hebraists who reject the phenomenon of emphasis. Garr, however, uses the term in *Dialect Geography of Syria-Palestine,* 189–91.

אִם־רָאֹה תִרְאֶה is "If you'll *see*."

וְהַצֵּל לֹא־הִצַּלְתָּ is "and you *haven't* saved."

מוֹת תָּמוּת is "you'll *die!*"

לֹא־מוֹת תְּמֻתוּן is "you *won't* die!"

אָבֹד תֹּאבֵדוּן plus שָׁכֹחַ תִּשְׁכָּח are "If you *forget*, then you'll *perish!*"

When Abraham tells Abimelek that he does not want Abimelek to be able to say: אֲנִי הֶעֱשַׁרְתִּי אֶת־אַבְרָם, it is that he does not want him saying, "*I* made Abram rich," (Gen 14:23).

When Abraham tells Abimelek: הֵם יִקְחוּ חֶלְקָם, the point is "*They* will take their share," (Ge 14:24). *They* will, Abraham will not.

When Moses tells Joshua: אַתָּה תָּבִיא אֶת־בְּנֵי יִשְׂרָאֵל אֶל־הָאָרֶץ, his point is that "*You* will bring the people to the land," (Deut 31:23).

When God tells Moses, כִּי־עֲבָדַי הֵם, when we translate it with the English word "my" in italics, we convey the point of the Hebrew: you can't treat Israelites like slaves, "because they are *my* slaves," (Lev 25:42).

When God says about the Levites: נְתֻנִים נְתֻנִים הֵמָּה לִי, it would be, "They are *given* to me." (Num 8:15).

And where Moses says, אִתָּנוּ אֲנַחְנוּ אֵלֶּה פֹה הַיּוֹם כֻּלָּנוּ חַיִּים, the translation would best convey this with an exclamation point at the end, or else with an exclamation point after each word: us! We! These! Here! Today! All of us! Living!" (Deut 5:3).

Any given passage might best be served by italics or an exclamation point or a combination of both. That much leeway remains with the translator. By using these mechanisms in my own translation of the Torah, I sought to produce a particularly literal rendering of the Hebrew while arriving at an English that sounds like English.[9] Availing oneself of these mechanisms expands the translator's available tools, and hopefully it expands the reader's path into the text.

BIBLIOGRAPHY

Bandstra, Barry L., "Word Order and Emphasis in Biblical Hebrew Narrative: Syntactic Observations on Genesis 22 from a Discourse Perspective." In *Linguistics and Biblical Hebrew*, edited by Walter R. Bodine, 109–23. Winona Lake, IN: Eisenbrauns, 1992.

Fox, Everett. *The Five Books of Moses*. New York: Schocken, 1995.

Friedman, Richard Elliott. *The Bible with Sources Revealed*. San Francisco: HarperSanFrancisco, 2004.

---

9. Friedman, *Commentary on the Torah*, see the comment on emphasis on p. xv. This translation also appears in Friedman, *The Bible with Sources Revealed*.

———. *Commentary on the Torah*. San Francisco: HarperCollins, 2001.
———. *Who Wrote the Bible?* 2nd ed. San Francisco: HarperOne, 1987.
Garr, W. Randall. *Dialect Geography of Syria-Palestine 1000–586 B.C.E.* Philadelphia: University of Pennsylvania Press, 1985.
Kelley, Page H., Terry L. Burden, and Timothy G. Crawford. *A Handbook to Biblical Hebrew: An Introductory Grammar*. Grand Rapids: Eerdmans, 1994.
Lambdin, Thomas. *Introduction to Biblical Hebrew*. New York: Scribner, 1971.
Muraoka, T. *Emphatic Words and Structures in Biblical Hebrew*. Jerusalem: Magnes / Leiden: Brill, 1985.
Niccacci, Alviero, "Types and Functions of the Nominal Sentence." In *The Verbless Clause in Biblical Hebrew: Linguistic Approaches*, edited by Cynthia L. Miller, 215–48. Winona Lake, IN: Eisenbrauns, 1999.
Propp, William H. C. *Exodus 1–18*. AB 2. New York: Doubleday, 1999.
Zevit, Ziony. *The Anterior Construction in Classical Hebrew*. SBL Monograph Series 50. Atlanta: Scholars, 1998.

17

H. H. Rowley's *Aramaic of the Old Testament* after (Almost) a Century

Lester L. Grabbe

UNIVERSITY OF HULL

It was not much less than a century ago, in 1929, that H. H. Rowley's well-known monograph appeared.[1] This was clearly a substantial work although, as several others of Rowley's works, it had primarily an anti-fundamentalist

---

1. Rowley, *Aramaic of the Old Testament*. Throughout this article, reference is often made to original sources and to several secondary sources. To save space, I shall refer to these frequent sources by the following abbreviations in the text (followed by page number):
BL = Bauer and Leander, *Grammatik des Biblisch-Aramäischen*
MF = Folmer, *Achaemenid Aramaic*
HHR = Rowley, *Aramaic of the Old Testament*
KAK = Kitchen, "The Aramaic of Daniel"
TAD = Porten/Yardeni, *Textbook of Aramaic Documents from Ancient Egypt*
TMBP = Muraoka/Porten, *A Grammar of Egyptian Aramaic*
The following abbreviations are used for references to the various sorts of Aramaic:
AchAram = Achaemenid Aramaic (c. 700 to 300 BCE, even though the Achaemenid empire did not actually begin so early; roughly equivalent to what has often been called "Imperial Aramaic" or "Official Aramaic")
BAram = Biblical Aramaic (Aramaic of Daniel and Ezra)
EAram = Early Aramaic (Old Aramaic and Achaemenid Aramaic)
OAram = Old Aramaic (before 700 BCE)
QAram = Qumran Aramaic (to about 300 BCE, a subdivision of *Middle Aramaic*, which encompassed Qumran, the targums, and other rabbinic writings)

aim.² It was as thorough a study of the subject as the then current documentation allowed, despite being in part a response to an earlier study by Robert Dick Wilson, who had argued that the Aramaic of the book of Daniel belonged in the Persian period.³ The purpose of Rowley's discussion about Aramaic language was to refute that position and demonstrate that the language of Daniel was of an Aramaic later than Achaemenid Aramaic. A number of responses were forthcoming over the years⁴; the last explicit review was by K. A. Kitchen in 1964. As far as I am aware, the debate has been silent since Kitchen wrote, though the recent short monograph by Zdravko Stefanovic seems to have the implicit aim of responding to Rowley.

Yet in the meantime many new texts have been published, and a significant number of new grammatical and lexical studies have appeared.⁵ Now, after the better part of a century has passed, it seems a good time to evaluate where we stand with regard to the Aramaic of Daniel, in the context in which Rowley was addressing the question. In a short article such as this, I do not propose to go over old ground. Kitchen's study, for example, often had nothing new to say under several of the headings used by Rowley. I propose to treat cursorily those sections where there is nothing to be added to Rowley's discussion and, instead, concentrate on areas where determination of the type of Aramaic in Daniel seems best exemplified (the Aramaic of Ezra will be mostly ignored⁶). I shall also generally ignore later Aramaic (Nabatean, Palmyrene, targumic, etc.), which Rowley frequently cited.

Survey of Rowley's Arguments

Essentially, Rowley concluded that the Aramaic of the Old Testament was later, as dated by purely linguistic criteria, than the Aramaic of the 5th-century papyri. In particular the Aramaic of Daniel could not possibly be dated to the 6th century and occasionally could be shown as later than even that of Ezra. Rowley's investigation can be summarized as follows, according to his own major headings:

Orthography (pp. 16–39). Rowley speaks of BAram in terms of phonology at times when he is actually referring only to orthography. Thus,

---

2. One of his major anti-fundamentalist works was *Darius the Mede*. I use the term "fundamentalist" in the sense of one committed to the inerrancy of the Bible.

3. Robert D. Wilson, "The Aramaic of Daniel." Rowley was also able to make use of the study by Walter Baumgartner, "Das Aramäische im Buche Daniel."

4. See Part 2 for a survey of some of these.

5. Footnote 1 lists some of the more important of these.

6. For discussion and references to the Aramaic of Ezra, see Grabbe, "Persian Documents."

Rowley can say, "we shall recognize that the evidence clearly suggets, to use no stronger word, that Biblical Aramaic is phonetically later than that of the Papyri" (HHR 39). Rowley put considerable weight on difference between the orthography of EAram and that of BAram to show that the latter was late.

Use of h (ה) *versus* ' (א) *at the end of words* (pp. 39–50). Although Rowley states here as he often does that the "balance of the evidence" would put BAram later than the papyri, he would be "very cautious" in drawing any conclusions.

Pronouns (pp. 51–65). Of Rowley's sixteen points, he notes that in fourteen of them Daniel differs from the papyri and agrees in only two; on the other hand, Daniel agrees with the later targums in nine of these points. Ezra in this case is closer to AchAram than is Daniel.

Substantives (pp. 65–67); *Adverbs* (pp. 67–71); *Prepositions and Conjunctions* (pp. 71–73); *Interjections and Particles* (pp. 73–76). Rowley basically seems to agree that there is little conclusive to be gained from his investigation of these.

Verbs (pp. 76–98). Rowley examines twenty-two separate points. Of these he finds only eight of some significance.

Syntax (pp. 98–108). Although there are "few differences which are important," Rowley does find seven different features which he feels "would again indicate for Biblical Aramaic a place intermediate between that of the Papyri and that of the later dialects" (HHR 106). He does not, however, place equal weight on all these since "several of the points, taken by themselves, would give little clear guidance" (HHR 106). He seems to single out three of his points as being perhaps more incisive.

Vocabulary and Loanwords (pp. 108–28; 129–53). Apart from loanwords Rowley seems to have found little of significance in vocabulary: "We have found some indications pointing to a period for Biblical Aramaic intermediate between that of the Papyri and that of the Targums, but taken by themselves they could not bear much weight, and most of the evidence that comes under the heading of Vocabulary must be pronounced quite neutral" (HHR 128). Most of his energy is concentrated on loanwords, primarily Greek. Greek words in Daniel are very significant to Rowley who reiterates Driver's well-known conclusion: "the Greek words demand . . . a date after the conquest of Palestine by Alexander the Great."[7]

General Conclusions (pp. 153–6). In his general conclusion (pp. 153–6) Rowley emphasizes that the orthography is of most significance since our information is fullest here. In matters of accidence, BAram seems to occupy

---

7. Driver, *Introduction*, 508, italics in the original.

a position intermediate between that of the papyri and the targums, while the study of syntax "has but confirmed this conclusion." Vocabulary is mostly neutral except for the Greek loanwords "in Daniel which mark that book as being almost certainly not of Babylonian origin in the sixth century B.C." On the whole, there is little to distinguish the language of Ezra from that of Daniel, but what there is tends to put Ezra closer to the papyri in time.

Reactions to Rowley

The standard view of Rowley's work seems to have been well summarized by Franz Rosenthal who referred to it as "a very industrious and detailed work filled with data, but one which was not always incisive enough and thus considered much which was irrelevant for the subject in question."[8] H. H. Schaeder,[9] though he evidently did not know of Rowley's book, critiqued the earlier study by Walter Baumgartner[10] that contained several of the arguments used by Rowley. A number of Schaeder's criticisms were later picked up by one of Rowley's major critics, K. A. Kitchen (see below).

K. A. Kitchen

It was more than thirty-five years after Rowley published his study that the first major critique of it appeared (KAK). Although Kitchen's article was clearly apologetic, it has nevertheless been frequently cited in bibliographical references and quoted with approval by so eminent an Aramaist as E. Y. Kutscher (see below). Kitchen's essay was ostensibly a full study of the question but was in fact primarily a review of Rowley, as Rowley himself noted in his own review of the publication.[11]

Kitchen emphasized what others had noted before him, that much of the detailed work in Rowley's study led to negative results—when all was said and done, the data simply were insufficient to give any certain indication of a date for the language. Unfortunately, Kitchen often felt compelled to argue with a rather strident tone and not infrequently gave an unfair impression about Rowley's claims. It is true, as already pointed out, that Rowley often felt compelled to refer to a "balance of evidence" or "cumulative evidence"

8. Rosenthal, *Die aramaistische Forschung*, 67 n. 3: "ein sehr fleissiges, ausführliches und materialreiches Werk, das aber nicht immer scharf genug sichtete und darum vieles berücksichtigte, was für die Fragestellung belanglos ist."
9. Schaeder, *Iranische Beiträge I*.
10. Baumgartner, "Das Aramäische im Buche Daniel."
11. Rowley, "Review of *Notes on Some Problems in the Book of Daniel*," 113.

which put BAram late when actually he admitted the arguments were weak. But despite this tendency toward overstatement, Rowley was by and large quite fair about which aspects of his argument were weak and which were stronger. Yet if one reads Kitchen without having read Rowley carefully, one is left with the impression that Kitchen discovered a great deal which Rowley overlooked. On the contrary, in most cases Kitchen is simply arguing from Rowley's own data—evidently having nothing to add to it—and does not really come to any conclusion different from Rowley's own.

Thus, Kitchen devotes much space to demolishing strawmen. He gives the impression of tearing down Rowley's arguments when in fact Rowley either did not advance such arguments or gave only slight weight to them. A good example is the following statement by Kitchen: "Items like X:13 are wholly indecisive; if assimilation and non-assimilation of initial radical *n* are both attested both 'early' and 'late', they prove nothing because they could as easily be considered a residual archaism" (KAK 70). This sounds as if Kitchen has completely pulled the rug out from under Rowley at this point; in fact, Rowley himself stated that this particular item "cannot be stressed, in view of the agreement of the Zenjirli inscriptions with the Biblical usage" (HHR 96).

Another example is put by Kitchen under the headings, "Apparently Late Criteria. (a) Illusory lexical and phonetic examples": "Under X:16 the verb *slq* in Daniel is observed to assimilate the *l* as in Palmyrene, once having a 'compensatory' *n*. The assimilation already occurs in Old Aramaic in the 8th century BC, while for *n*, probably compare P. Brooklyn 6:10" (KAK 71). Again it appears as if Kitchen has exposed a fallacious argumentation; Rowley, however, makes no use of this example in his actual discussion but dismisses it along with several other examples as irrelevant because of lack of comparative data (HHR 95). Most of what Kitchen says in regard to morphology and syntax does not go beyond Rowley's data nor really differ from Rowley's own statements (KAK 68–75).

Yet Kitchen does deal with most of the arguments which Rowley himself considered substantial. They will be cataloged under "Discussion" below.

E. Y. Kutscher[12]

As probably the greatest living authority on Aramaic until his death in 1971, the opinion of Kutscher on the question naturally carries considerable weight. Kutscher did not discuss Rowley's work in detail but did cite

---

12. See especially Kutscher's two articles with the title, "Aramaic."

Kitchen's review as "clearly an apologetic attempt, but well done. . . . He has marshalled all the evidence pertaining to the problem and handled it carefully." His actual criticisms, though brief, are the following:

> 1. Rowley's belief that BAram has not been modernized runs into trouble when the Hermopolis papyri (unknown when Rowley wrote) are considered. For example, final /a/ is always written with *h* rather than ' which is characteristic of the other papyri from this period. Also Rowley makes no attempt to explain the archaizing spelling of, e.g., the Nabatean inscriptions (*z* instead *d*) even though these are long after Daniel by any account. Further, the language of the *Genesis Apocryphon* from the 1st-century BCE is quite different from BAram even though only a century younger by Rowley's reckoning. "Therefore, the only answer seems to be either the assumption of modernization" or the assumption that BAram represents an aberrant form of Imperial Aramaic like the Hermopolis papyri.

> 2. Rowley's arguments from Greek are unconvincing because there was Greek influence before Alexander, though this influence would have been from the dialects of Asia Minor. Since these dialects are not well recorded, it is possible that the terms for musical instruments unknown in Attic could have entered from the Asian dialects. On the other hand, the absence of Greek influence in areas in which one would have expected them (e.g., names of officials) cannot be explained away.

Kutscher's critique is in certain ways rather surprising (apart from his rather generous assessment of Kitchen, in the light of criticisms made below). Of course, Rowley could not have benefited from the Hermopolis papyri as Kutscher himself observes; nevertheless, he put little weight on the question of orthography with *h* versus ' for the final long /a/. Also, archaizing is always possible in a late text, as in the Nabatean inscriptions, but this does not explain the lack of early orthography in a text said to be early unless one postulates later scribal modernizing, while to postulate such is not to prove it (further on this point below).

Peter Coxon[13]

Although he did not write a monograph nor even a long article, laying out his view of the Aramaic of Daniel (as far as I know), Coxon did write several

---

13. Coxon, "Greek Loan Words"; "Syntax"; "Problem of Consonantal Mutations."

articles that presented a conservative view of BAram. What he did publish represents a critique of Rowley; his articles certainly also give the impression of his believing that Daniel was written in the 6th century BCE.

Zdravko Stefanovic[14]

This seems to be the only recent study to address the question. Although it is not laid out as a critique of Rowley, this seems to be at least part of Stefanovic's aim. His essential argument is that the language of Daniel has a great deal in common with Old Aramaic. He is right about this, but is it really relevant to the question? Most reviewers have pointed out that this is methodologically very flawed.[15] By the same arguments, we could show that modern English was not different from the language of Chaucer, since the heritage of modern English from Middle English is very large.

Discussion

This section evaluates Rowley's arguments and the counter-arguments of Kitchen and others. For convenience, this section is organized according to Rowley's subject divisions.

Orthography (pp. 16–39)

Rowley put considerable weight on the difference between the orthography of Early Aramaic and that of Biblical Aramaic to show that the latter was late. At the time when Aramaic adopted the palaeo-Hebrew alphabet it contained phonemes which had not yet merged as they had in the Canaanite dialects. These phonemes were represented by certain graphemes in early inscriptions but by different graphemes in later documents because of phonological changes:

Phoneme	Old Aramaic	Middle Aramaic
/ḏ/	z (ז)	d (ד)
/ṯ/	š (שׁ)	t (ת)
/ẓ/	ṣ (צ)	ṭ (ט)
/ḍ/	q (ק)	ʻ (ע)

---

14. Stefanovic, *The Aramaic of Daniel in the Light of Old Aramaic*.

15. E.g., Collins, "Review of Stefanovic, *Aramaic of Daniel*." One has to confess some astonishment that Sheffield Academic Press accepted the monograph for publication.

In inscriptions up to about 700 BCE the earlier graphemes are used consistently; after about 200 BCE the latter were used with few exceptions. The period in between is a period of transition with both spellings, though usage is often complicated. According to Rowley's investigations the following data emerged:

- /ḏ/: in AchAram texts *z* predominates overall. A few words, mostly nouns, are consistent in having *d*, while pronouns are almost always with *z*, except for a handful of examples with *d*.[16] Many of these are found in the texts written by the scribe Haggai bar Shemaiah and may represent a special case (MF 55, 698–9). BAram, on the other hand, consistently has *d*, and Rowley is quite right to argue that this fits with post-Achaemenid usage (much less post-6th century).

- /ḍ/: although AchAram texts have a mixture of *q* and ʿ, *q* predominates; BAram agrees with later Aramaic in using ʿ (MF 63–70; MTBP 8–9). Rowley's conclusions fit more recent study.

- /ṭ/ and /ẓ/: BAram seems to have much the same usage as AchAram, which was also Rowley's general verdict (cf. MTBP 7–8, 9).

As Kitchen correctly notes (KAK 53 n. 123), Rowley at times speaks of BAram in terms of phonology at times when he is actually referring only to orthography. Thus, Rowley can say, "we shall recognize that the evidence clearly suggests, to use no stronger word, that Biblical Aramaic is phonetically later than that of the Papyri" (p. 39). But contrary to Kitchen's confident assertion that the sound changes reflected in the later orthography had already occurred before the 6th century, the question of when the actual sound shift of /ḏ/ to /d/ came about is currently debated (MF 60–63). Furthermore, in spite of his confusing expression, Rowley has still made a point: the transitional period of orthography suggested by AchAram texts is already complete before the writing of BAram. In the Bible we find consistently the later orthography, in Daniel in particular. (For Kitchen's response to this key point, see the next several paragraphs.)

What is Kitchen's response to this argument? Although Kitchen expends a good deal of polemical verbiage over the issue, he ultimately concedes that Rowley has a point. This is clear in that he does not attempt to refute Rowley but rather advances a theory to explain the situation. Of course, Kitchen does not admit that he is theorizing to explain away the data

---

16. Examples at Elephantine where /ḏ/ is represented by *d* are דה *TAD* A2.5:7; ודי *TAD* B3.12:30, 31; די *TAD* B3.4:12; דילך *TAD* D5.3:2; B3.10:14; דילכי *TAD* B2.7:7, 11, 16; דך *TAD* D7.48:1; B3.10:10; דכא *TAD* B2.8:6; דכי *TAD* B2.8:9; לדכם *TAD* B3.8:2; דנה *TAD* D23.1.XVIC.6; A5.2:8, 9; ודנה *TAD* B3.11:3; דהב *TAD* B3.1:9.

but instead speaks of Rowley's "assumption." To summarize briefly, Kitchen argues that in the process of copying, the orthography of the biblical text was updated to reflect the conventions of a later age. In other words, most of the Aramaic evidence we have is from first-hand texts (original inscriptions and manuscripts) or from copies made at a time very proximate to the original. Literature which is copied and recopied over the generations as was the biblical text, however, may well be updated by later scribes and thus made to look later than it really is. This theory is evidently important to Kitchen because he spends a good deal of space developing it and also invokes it in the case of morphology and syntax later on.

Kitchen's support for his theory takes two forms. The first is the analogy with other ancient Near Eastern literature. Using Egyptian examples specifically, as those best known from his own specialty, he shows that very early literature in some cases has been revised at a later period to remove the original archaic language and modernize it. The examples Kitchen gives are well taken and could, as he says, be multiplied many times over. However, at this point Kitchen ceases to follow logical argument and falls back into his apologetic stance:

> In the light of the comparative evidence briefly sampled above, it should be obvious that orthographic change (sometimes 're-vision', sometimes more gradual) is normal—and the onus of proof lies on those who would maintain that the Aramaic text of Daniel or Ezra could not or did not fare similarly in similar circumstances. [KAK 66]

This is an absurd statement. To give a few examples of orthographic change does not prove that such was normal; on the contrary, he also gives examples to show that texts could be copied with little or no change. And, further, as any scholar knows, the "onus of proof" is on the one who advances a theory. Kitchen has argued that the texts of Daniel and Ezra were altered by later scribes. He has *not proved* this; he has only *theorized* it; therefore, it is his responsibility to prove that such in fact took place. In the case of Ezra, we have some indications that some of the supposed "documents" have been updated, because alongside younger linguistic usage (which characterizes most of these documents) are some examples of Achaemenid grammatical usage and orthography.[17] But the Aramaic of Daniel consistently represents post-Achaemenid orthography (and grammar, as discussed below).

Of course, if Daniel was updated at a later time, as Kitchen theorizes, what does this say about its historical veracity? The volume to which he contributes assumes a high degree of textual and historical integrity for the

---

17. For a further discussion, see Grabbe, "Persian Documents."

book. But if the language can be updated, what is to prevent other changes to the text: additions, subtractions, substantial revisions? This consideration has considerable consequences for the believability of the book, while those who argue that the book is early almost always are concerned that the book also be fully trustworthy.

Use of h (ה) versus ' (א) at the end of words (pp. 39–50)

As noted earlier, Rowley states here that the balance of the evidence would put BAram later than the papyri, though he would be very cautious in drawing any conclusions.

Pronouns (pp. 51–65)

Of Rowley's sixteen points, he notes that in fourteen of them Daniel differs from the papyri and agrees in only two (#7; #12); on the other hand, Daniel agrees with the later targums in nine of these points. Ezra in this case is closer to the papyri than is Daniel, in his opinion.

Achaemenid Aramaic Personal Pronouns	Aramaic of Daniel Personal Pronouns
1. אנת	1. אנתה
2. הו	2. הוא
3. הי	3. היא
4. אנחנה, אנחן	4. אנחנא
5. אנתם	5. אנתון
6. המו, הם	6. אנון, המון
Pronominal Suffixes	Pronominal Suffixes
8. ־ך	8. ־נא
9. ־כם	9. ־כון
10. ־הם	10. ־הון
Other Pronouns	Other Pronouns
11. זך, זכי	11. דך, דכי
13. זנה	13. דנה
14. אז	14. דא
15. אל, אלה	15. אלון, אלין
16. די	16. די

- #1: 'nth "you (ms)" occurs about a dozen times in Daniel as the *ketiv*, agreeing with later orthography, but in the approximately fifty occurrences in the Elephantine papyri it is always 'nt (TMBP 43–44).

- ##2–3: The *hwʾ/hyʾ* of Daniel contrasts with the exceptionless *hw/hy* of AchAram (MF 102–3).
- ##4, 8: early AchAr independent pronominal forms are *ʾnḥnh* or *ʾnḥn*; likewise, Daniel has the form *ʾnḥnh* or *ʾnḥn*. However, except for two or possibly three examples in Egypt the pronominal suffix *-nʾ* of Daniel does not occur until late (the Hellenistic period and the Samarian papyri right at the end of the Persian period [MF 155–8]). As the verbal afformative, *-nʾ* does not occur in Egypt, only in the late Samarian papyri (MF 159–61).
- ##5–6, 9–10: These pronominal suffixes are very important, because almost all have *-m* (*-tm*, *-km*), while only a few late AchAr examples have *-n*; none has the *-wn* that is consistently used by Daniel.
- ##11, 13, 14, 16 have really already been covered above (under orthography, in connection with *z*- rather than *d*-).
- #15: Although *ʾln* apparently occurs in OAram, as well as Daniel, it is not found in the Egyptian papyri which have almost entirely *ʾlh* (TMBP 56, n. 270).

Kitchen's response is that this is all "mere orthography," but he ignores that most of these represent important morphological differences. Also, the orthography cannot be dismissed, because it was clear that scribes respected the orthographical tradition. For example, the contrast of the *hwʾ/hyʾ* of Daniel with the *hw/hy* of the papyri might seem trivial, but the consistent orthography shows that this was important to the scribes and cannot be dismissed lightly. When changes start to come about in the Achaemenid period, they are generally introduced gradually. In some cases, there were no exceptions; in others, changes had started to be made, but the extent of change was gradual and could be measured in dated texts.

Other Non-Verbal Forms (pp. 65–76)

Substantives (pp. 65–67); *Adverbs* (pp. 67–71); *Prepositions and Conjunctions* (pp. 71–73); *Interjections and Particles* (pp. 73–76). Rowley basically seems to agree that there is little conclusive to be gained from his investigation of these.

Verbs (pp. 76–98)

Rowley examines twenty-two separate points, of which he finds twelve of some significance (though these can be reduced to nine):

Achaemenid Aramaic	Aramaic of Daniel
1. Termination of pf 2 mpl usually תם־.	1. Termination of pf 2 mpl in ־תון.
2. Termination of pf 1 cpl always ־ן.	2. Termination of pf 1cpl in ־נא.
7. With only a couple of exceptions, perfect of reflexive stems in EAram is את־.	7. Perfect of reflexive stems with הת־.
13. Nonassimilation of first radical of פ״ן verbs in imperfect and infinitive.	13. Assimilation of first radical of פ״ן verbs in imperfect and infinitive.
15. No נ in the *peal* imperfect of ידע.	15. Insertion of נ in the *peal* imperfect of ידע.
19. Frequent retention of weak radical in *peal* pf 3fs of 3rd weak radical verbs.	19. Frequent omission of weak radical in *peal* pf 3fs of 3rd weak radical verbs.
20. Frequent retention of י and א in ל״י and ל״א verbs.	20. Usually י before final inflection in ל״י and ל״א verbs.
21. Preformative י used on *peal* imperfect, 3ms, 3mpl, and 3fpl of הוה.	21. Use of ל preformative in *peal* imperfect 3ms, 3mpl, and 3fpl of verb הוה.
22. Present participle of ע״ו verbs with י or nothing for 2nd radical.	22. Present participle of ע״ו verbs with א.

- #1 BAram has the later *-twn* for the perfect 2 mpl, whereas the AchAram texts have mainly the earlier *-tm*.
- #2 BAram has *-n'* for 1 mpl while the papyri have the older *-n* (MF).
- #7 AchAram always has *'it-* (with perhaps one exception), whereas BAram frequently has *hit-* (cf. TMBP 16–19).
- #13 and #15 continue with the assimilation, nonassimilation, or dissimilation of *n* discussed earlier. This applies to the first radical of initial *n* verbs in imperfect and infinitive, where the Hellenistic tendency is to assimilate the *n*, in contrast to the Achaemenid tendency to preserve it (MF 88–90; cf. TMBP 10–12). On the other hand, Daniel has a non-etymological *n* inserted into several forms of *yd'*; however, with

possibly one exception (in the broken text, D4.25.1) the Elephantine papyri have no examples of *n* in more than twenty-five occurrences.

- #19 BAram regularly drops the 3rd radical in final *h* (= final *y*) and final ʾ verbs, whereas AchAram texts generally retain it (TMBP 124).
- #20 BAram almost without exception has *y* for both final ʾ and final *y* verbs, whereas AchAram generally distinguishes between the two types of verbs (MF 222–36).
- #21 BAram (more than twenty examples) uses the preformative *l* in *peal* imperfect 3ms, 3mpl, and 3fpl of verb *hwh*, whereas preformative *y* is normal in AchAram (no examples with *l* occur in the many occurrences at Elephantine).
- #22 BAram present participle of middle *w* verbs has ʾ for the 2nd radical (BL pp. 51, 214 [§13j, §58d]), while AchAram texts have *y* or nothing (TMBP 131).

Syntax (pp. 98–108)

Although there are "few differences which are important," Rowley does find seven different features which he feels "would again indicate for Biblical Aramaic a place intermediate between that of the Papyri and that of the later dialects." He does not, however, place equal weight on all these since "several of the points, taken by themselves, would give little clear guidance." He seems to single out three of his points as being perhaps more incisive:

Achaemenid Aramaic	Aramaic of Daniel
3. ל only occasionally used for accusative.	3. ל frequent marker for the direct object.
4. No preposition is used with the name of the king in dates.	4. ל precedes name of king in dates.
7. Verbs of wish, command, purpose and the like (such as כהל and יכל) tend to be complemented by a prefix conjugation form.	7. ל plus infinitive complements verbs of wish, command, purpose and the like, such as כהל and יכל.

- #3 Contrary to Rowley, more recent study has not seen a major difference between AchAram and BAram in the use of *l-* to mark the accusative. Folmer has argued that the difference in different text collections is likely to be defined by its syntactic environment (MF 362–65).

- #4 Rowley argued that in dates in Achaemenid documents, with one exception, either no preposition or *b-* is used before the name of the king (in the phrase "year x of PN the king" or something similar), whereas Daniel (7:1; cf. 2:1) agrees with later usage in making *l-* precede the name of the king. Kitchen added another couple of examples to the one given by Rowley, and at least one more can be found (*TAD* B1.1:1; B3.2:1; B5.1:1; B7.1:1), thus taking away much of the force of Rowley's argument.

- #7 Rowley's argument here is trickier to evaluate. He notes that Daniel uses *l-* plus the infinitive to complement verbs of wish, permission, purpose, and the like, such as *khl* and *ykl*; on the other hand, the earlier papyri tend to be complemented by a prefix conjugation form. Although a number of examples of the infinitive complementing such verbs are found in AchAram texts (MTBP 259–60), Daniel appears to be different (cf. MF 371–6; 634–40). For example, no Achaemenid text has *ykl* complemented by an infinitive, but Daniel has many examples (2:10, 27, 47; 3:17, 29; 4:15, 34; 5:16 (*bis*); 6:5, 21). It looks as if Rowley has a point here.

In this instance, of Rowley's three primary examples more recent finds have tended to undermine two of them. However, although the third one is dismissed by Kitchen (KAK 74), Rowley's comments still appear to be relevant with the third (#7).

Vocabulary (pp. 108–28)

Apart from loanwords Rowley seems to have found little of significance. Although he concludes that "Biblical Aramaic once more stands very much nearer to the Targums than do the Papyri" (HHR 139), in his general summary he notes that apart "from the significant Greek terms, we have insufficient data to confine within very narrow limits the possible date of the Aramaic sections of Ezra or of Daniel" (HHR 155). Kitchen for some reason feels it necessary to go back over the entire ground again with much the same results as Rowley except for the Greek and Persian loans.

However, it would be worth noting at this point three items which differ between Daniel and AchAram, which do not occur in Rowley as far as I am aware.[18] Yet they seem to offer support to his position:

---

18. These were pointed out by MF (211–2, 422–3, 711–2, 754). On the plural ending of '*ab* in BAram, compare BL (p. 201 [§53 i–j]).

Achaemenid Aramaic	Biblical Aramaic
אגור "temple"	בית "temple"
אחר (may introduce main clause of conditional sentence)	(ב)אדין (may introduce main clause of conditional sentence)
אבהין (*abahîn*) plural of "father"	*אבהן (*abahān) plural of father, as indicated by such plural forms as אבהתי.

Loanwords (pp. 129–53)

For the most part borrowing from other languages—Hebrew, Akkadian, Persian, etc.—is of little assistance in dating the Aramaic of the OT. The one exception to this, Greek words in Daniel, is very significant to Rowley who reiterates Driver's well-known conclusion: "the Greek words demand . . . a date after the conquest of Palestine by Alexander the Great."[19] (He said little about Persian loanwords, though this is important to Kitchen, as we shall see below.)

Daniel 3:5, 7, 10, 15

LXX and Theodotion	MT[20]
σάλπιγγος	קַרְנָא
σύριγγος	מַשְׁרוֹקִיתָא
κίθαρος	קִיתָרֹס
σαμβύκησης	שַׂבְּכָא / סַבְּכָא
ψαλτηρίον	פְּסַנְטֵרִין
συμφωνία (not Theodotion)	סוּמְפֹּנְיָה
παντὸς γένους μουσικῶν	וְכֹל זְנֵי זְמָרָא

    Three Greek names of musical instruments have been identified in the Aramaic text of Dan 3:5, 7, 10, 15: *kitharos, psaltērios, sumphōnia*. No one seems to question this, though there is a debate about the meaning of *sumphōnia*. In Polybius (26.1.4; 30.26.8) it seems to mean "band of musicians." Yet most commentators on Daniel see it as the name of an instrument.[20]

    19. Driver, *Introduction*, 508, italics in the original.
    20. See the discussion in Collins, *Commentary on the Book of Daniel*, 20, 183–4. Grelot ("L'orchestre de Daniel III 5, 7, 10, 15," 36–38) argues that it is name of an

Those who defend the 6th-century BCE date for Daniel long ago developed a thesis to counter Driver's argument.[21] This has two parts: the first is essentially that Greek words were borrowed into the ancient Near East long before the time of Alexander, because the Greeks had contact with the ancient Near East from an early period. A complementary aspect to this hypothesis is the assertion that one should find many more Greek words in Daniel if it was written in the 2nd-century BCE (the text of Daniel should be "swarming" with Greek words). For example, Kutscher argues that if Daniel 3 was written during the Greek period, we would expect Greek terms for the administrative officials listed in 3:2–3.

That might seem like a logical conclusion, but it is only a guess. What does the *evidence* from actual Aramaic texts show. First, are there Greek words in EAram texts, as some have postulated? The best way to check this is to survey the Aramaic vocabulary in Hoftijzer and Jongeling's *Dictionary of the North-West Semitic Inscriptions*. Although there are many Greek borrowings into the Aramaic vocabulary, they are almost all late, primarily into Palmyrene, Nabatean, or Jewish Aramaic. A handful of Greek etymologies have been suggested for words in AchAram, but about the only one for which there seems any consensus is στατήρ *statēr*, a coin worth about two silver sheqels. The reason for borrowing the Greek name would be obvious.

A second check is whether Jewish Aramaic documents from the post-Alexander period have many Greek words in them, as the hypothesis has postulated. The fact is that although we find some Greek words in Aramaic documents from shortly after the Hellenistic conquest,[22] few Greek words were borrowed into Jewish Aramaic in the pre-Roman Greek period. We can see this by looking at the vocabulary list in the *Handbook of Palestinian Aramaic Texts*, edited by Joseph Fitzmyer and Daniel Harrington, and by an examination of the Aramaic texts from Qumran via Edward Cook's *Dictionary of Qumran Aramaic*. These two sources contain practically all the Aramaic vocabulary in Jewish documents and literature known from about 300 BCE to about 150 CE. In all this Aramaic Jewish literature, what we find are a dozen Greek words (at least two considered doubtful) and two Latin words. The Jewish texts during this period are far from "swarming" with borrowed Greek words, much less the Aramaic of the Achaemenid period.

As for Kutscher's argument that we should find Greek terms for the administrators in Dan 3:2–3, a good check would be Syriac which borrowed

---

instrument not only in Daniel 3 but also in Polybius 26.1.4.

21. See the references in HHR 129–53; also KAK 44–50; Coxon, "Greek Loan-Words," to name a few.

22. See, e.g., examples given in Cross, "Aramaic Ostracon."

a good deal of Greek, including the terms of official administrators. Yet we find that the Peshitta translation of Daniel into the Syriac Aramaic dialect uses only Aramaic terms in this list of administrators:

LXX	Theodotion	Peshitta	MT
σατράπαι	ὕπατοι	רבי חילא	אֲחַשְׁדַּרְפְּנַיָּא
στρατηγοί	στρατηγοί	מרותא	סִגְנַיָּא
τοπάρχαι	τοπάρχαι	שליטנא	פַּחֲוָתָא
ὕπατοι	ἡγούμενοι	ארגדיא	אֲדַרְגָּזְרַיָּא
διοικηταί	τύραννοι	גרבדיא	גְדָבְרַיָּא
		תרבדיא	דְּתָבְרַיָּא
		תפתיא	תִּפְתָּיֵא
τοὺς ἐπ' ἐξουσιῶν κατὰ χώραν	τοὺς ἐπ' ἐξουσιῶν καὶ πάντας τοὺς ἄρχοντας τῶν χωρῶν	ולכל שולטן מדינתא	וְכֹל שִׁלְטֹנֵי מְדִינָתָא

As the parallel list of administrators in the Greek translations indicates, there were plenty of Greek terms that could have been used, but apparently the translators found Semitic terms more satisfactory. Kutscher's hypothesis—for it was only a hypothesis—is not supported by the actual linguistic data.

In reviewing Kitchen's study, Rowley concentrated on the Greek question. He noted that he had actually answered Kitchen's objection in his earlier book, that the word *sumphōnia* "is unknown in Greek as the name of a musical instrument before the second century B.C. . . . Here Mr Kitchen notes that West Semitic words appear in Egyptian texts long before they are attested in West Semitic texts. But West Semitic texts are scarce compared with Egyptian texts, whereas classical Greek literature is abundant compared with the scanty volume of Aramaic texts of the period at issue."[23] Rowley went on to reiterate his argument that the lack of Greek words in Daniel, except for the three in question, was due to the deliberate anti-Hellenistic policy of the writer who used Greek names of musical instruments to caricature the Greeks in the guise of the Chaldeans.

---

23. Rowley, "Review of D. J. Wiseman, et al., eds., *Notes on Some Problems in the Book of Daniel*," 115.

Although Rowley was mostly silent about loanwords from Iranian, Kitchen spends considerable time on the Persian loanwords. Although basically concluding that the data are insufficient to draw any conclusions, on two points he proposes that there is some argument for an early dating of Daniel: (1) For certain Persian technical terms for government officials, "the Old Greek (and later) renderings are hopelessly inexact—mere guesswork" (p. 43), thus suggesting that Daniel was written long before the Greek period. (2) The loanwords in Daniel and Ezra are all specifically Old Persian whereas the Persian of the 2nd-century was already Middle Persian. The first point is a moot one: did the translators really not understand the terms in the text, which were mainly general terms for administrators?[24] It is not at all clear that there is a gap between the Aramaic text and the Greek translation.

Kitchen's second point has no force, however, since the bulk of all Persian loanwords entered Aramaic during the Persian period. That is, after the Greek conquest it seems that few if any Persian words entered the permanent lexical stock. Rather, there was a rapid loss of Persian words not well integrated into Aramaic until a stable core of adopted Persian elements was reached. Thus, the majority of Persian loanwords in any stage of Aramaic in the west are likely to have entered during the Old Persian period, since there was no longer contact with Iranian speakers. The situation was different in the east, of course, and we find that Middle Persian and Parthian words entered Syriac, Mandaic, and Jewish Babylonian Aramaic, especially during the Sassanian period. But there was also a core of Iranian words in Syriac that had been borrowed from Old Persian, which parallels the Aramaic used among the Jews of Palestine and the west.[25]

Rowley's Conclusion (pp. 153–6)

In his general conclusion (pp. 153–6) Rowley emphasizes that the orthography is of most significance since our information is fullest here. In matters of accidence, BAram seems to occupy a position intermediate between that of the papyri and the targums, while the study of syntax "has but confirmed this conclusion." Vocabulary is mostly neutral except for the Greek loanwords "in Daniel which mark that book as being almost certainly not of Babylonian origin in the sixth century B.C." On the whole, there is little to distinguish the language of Ezra from that of Daniel, but what there is tends to put Ezra closer to the papyri in time.

24. On this subject, cf. Grabbe, "Terminology."
25. On this, see further Ciancaglini, *Iranian Loanwords*.

Conclusions

We can now summarize some of the main points from this study, including some of the main objections to Rowley's study (especially those of Kitchen) and the result of recent studies:

1. Rowley's purpose was to show that the language of Daniel should be dated to the Hellenistic period, specifically the 2nd-century BCE. He considered his strongest arguments to lie under the category of orthography (though some of these would be more correctly labeled morphology). In his discussion of the interchange between certain graphemes (e.g., *z* and *d*) in AchAram, Rowley evidently understood this as a sign of the actual phonology of Aramaic of this period. Others think that what we see is a transitional period in which the orthography is changing from the older historical spelling to a spelling which reflects the current pronunciation; however, the time and process of the change of phonology remains controversial. In any case, we see a period of transition in orthographic practice between the early Achaemend period and the Hellenistic period.

2. Despite his rhetoric, on the question of orthography Kitchen ultimately admits that Rowley has a point. That is, he concedes that the language of Daniel *looks* later than the papyri—*looks* as if it were written much later than the 6th century BCE *from a linguistic point of view*: "in the transmission of Ezra and Daniel the later forms of current speech and of everyday writing (i.e., of the 3rd-century BCE and later) have begun to make an impact on Ezra, and have replaced wholly the older form in Daniel, giving Old Testament scholars the superficial impression that the Aramaic of Daniel is 'younger' than that of Ezra" (KAK 72).

3. Rowley had quite a long discussion on pronouns. The forms of pronouns and pronominal prefixes and suffixes (including verbal preformatives and afformatives) in AchAram are often quite different from BAram. These are not "mere orthography" (as Kitchen dismisses them) but important features of the linguistic grammar that fit particular chronological periods.

4. Similarly, nine points relating to verbs either indicated a break between AchAram and BAram, or there was significant difference in quantity relationships.

5. With regard to syntax, Rowley focused on three points (out of seven). In this case, two of his points lose cogency in light of more recent discoveries (the use of the preposition *l-* before the name of the king in

dates and the use of *l-* to mark the accusative), but the third (the form of the complement to verbs of wish, command, purpose and the like) appears to remain valid.

6. On the matter of Greek loanwords, Kitchen correctly sees this as one of Rowley's major points of proof for the lateness of Daniel. While recognizing that the matter could not be settled beyond all doubt (because it is an argument from silence), he failed to acknowledge that Rowley in this case had a valid "balance of evidence," that it was unlikely that the word *sumphōnia* as the name of an instrument was borrowed into Aramaic before the 2nd-century BCE. The three Greek words in Daniel 3 still constitute a strong argument for dating the passage to the Greek period.

7. On the question of Persian loanwords, Rowley's exact conclusions are unclear, but it is plain that he put little stress on them. Kitchen makes a rather large issue of the matter, especially stressing that the Persian words in BAram are from Old Persian. He overlooks the fact that many loanwords in any stage of early Jewish Aramaic, whether Daniel or the rabbinic targums, are likely to have entered during the Old Persian period.

8. As Kitchen recognizes, Rowley did overpress his arguments at times when they were very weak. That is, Rowley recognized they were weak but was still willing to speak of a "balance of evidence" when he should have simply drawn no conclusions. Yet much of what Kitchen says gives the wrong impression; Rowley was generally quite fair about the strength or weakness of his argument so that much of what Kitchen says is only a strawman attack. This applies especially to his sections on morphology and syntax.

9. To turn the critical spotlight on Kitchen for this last point, it has to be said that Kitchen's overriding apologetic interest has made him focus atomistically on the question. Since he is unable to prove a 6th-century date for the language of Daniel, he seems determined to say it "could" be anywhere between the sixth and second centuries. He makes no attempt to give a holistic view of the whole question and fit BAram into the historical framework of the developing Aramaic dialects. Again, whatever his failings, Rowley at least tried always to keep this perspective in the forefront of his study. The fact is that as the text of Daniel presently stands, it *could not* be from the Achaemenid period in the light of the AchAram texts currently known. No text from the Achaemenid period has language overall comparable to that of Daniel.

Kitchen in fact concedes this point, since he is forced to hypothesize that the language of Daniel was updated at a later period.

H. H. Rowley's *Aramaic of the Old Testament* has stood the test of time. In spite of several weaknesses and the undermining of the occasional argument by more recent discoveries, it is remarkable how the main points and arguments of a study almost a century old still demonstrate that the Aramaic of Daniel did not come from the 6th century BCE or even the Achaemenid period. As it exists *in its present form*, the Aramaic of Daniel dates from the post-Achaemenid period. That conclusion stands as a monument to Rowley's work so long ago.

It is a pleasure to dedicate this work to Ziony, who has devoted a good deal of his scholarly career to looking at biblical language. Long may he continue to enlighten us in this important area!

BIBLIOGRAPHY

Bauer, Hans, and Pontus Leander. *Grammatik des Biblisch-Aramäischen*. Halle/Saale: Niemeyer, 1927. Reprinted, Hildesheim: Olms, 1995.

Baumgartner, Walter. "Das Aramäische im Buche Daniel." *ZAW* 45 (1927) 81–133. Reprinted (with 'Nachträge') in *Zum Alten Testament und seiner Umwelt: Ausgewahlte Aufsätze*, 68–123. Leiden: Brill, 1959.

Brockelmann, Carl. "Review of H. H. Rowley, *The Aramaic of the Old Testament*." *MGWJ* 76 (1932) 84–87.

Ciancaglini, Claudia A. *Iranian Loanwords in Syriac*. Beiträge zur Iranistik 28. Wiesbaden: Reichert, 2008.

Collins, John J. *Daniel: A Commentary on the Book of Daniel*. Hermeneia. Minneapolis: Fortress, 1993.

———. "Review of Z. Stefanovic, *The Aramaic of Daniel in the Light of Old Aramaic*." *JBL* 112 (1993) 710–12.

Cook, Edward M. *Dictionary of Qumran Aramaic*. Winona Lake, IN: Eisenbrauns, 2015.

Coxon, Peter W. "Greek Loan Words and Alleged Greek Loan Translations in the Book of Daniel." *Transactions of the Glasgow University Oriental Society* 25 (1973–1974) 24–40.

———. "The Problem of Consonantal Mutations in Biblical Aramaic." *ZDMG* 129 (1979) 8–22.

———. "The Syntax of the Aramaic of *Daniel*: A Dialectal Study." *HUCA* 48 (1977) 107–22.

Cross, Frank M. "An Aramaic Ostracon of the Third Century B.C.E. from Excavations in Jerusalem." *Eretz Israel* 15 (1981) *67–*69.

Driver, G. R. "The Aramaic of the Book of Daniel." *JBL* 45 (1926) 110–19, 323–25.

Driver, S. R. *An Introduction to the Literature of the Old Testament*. 6th ed. Edinburgh: T. & T. Clark, 1913.

Folmer, M. L. *The Aramaic Language in the Achaemenid Period: A Study in Linguistic Variation*. Orientalia Lovaniensia Analecta 68. Leuven: Peeters, 1995.

Grabbe, Lester L. "The 'Persian Documents' in the Book of Ezra: Are They Authentic?" In *Judah and the Judeans in the Persian Period*, edited by Oded Lipschits and Manfred Oeming, 531–70. Winona Lake, IN: Eisenbrauns, 2006.

———. "The Terminology of Government in the Septuagint—in Comparison with Hebrew, Aramaic, and Other Languages." In *Jewish Perspectives on Hellenistic Rulers*, edited by Tessa Rajak, Sarah Pearce, James Aitken, and Jennifer Dines, 225–37. Berkeley: University of California Press, 2007.

Grelot, Pierre. "L'orchestre de Daniel III 5, 7, 10, 15." *VT* 29 (1979) 23–38.

Hoftijzer, Jacob, and K. Jongeling. *Dictionary of the North-West Semitic Inscriptions*. With appendices by R. C. Steiner, et al. 2 vols. HdO I.21.1–2. Leiden: Brill, 1995.

Kitchen, K. A. "The Aramaic of Daniel." In *Notes on Some Problems in the Book of Daniel*, edited by D. J. Wiseman, et al., 31–79. London: Tyndale, 1965.

Kutscher, E. Y. "Aramaic." In *Current Trends in Linguistics*. Vol. 6, *Linguistics in South West Asia and North Africa*, edited by Thomas A. Sebeok, 347–417. The Hague: Mouton, 1970.

———. "Aramaic." In *EncJud*, 1st ed. (1971) 3.259–87 = *EncJud*, 2nd ed. (2007) 2.342–59.

Muraoka, Takamitsu, and Bezalel Porten. *A Grammar of Egyptian Aramaic*. HdO I/32. Leiden: Brill, 1998.

Rosenthal, Franz. *Die aramaistische Forschung seit Th. Nöldeke's Veröffentlichungen*. 1939. Reprinted, Leiden: Brill, 1964.

Rowley, H. H. *The Aramaic of the Old Testament*. Oxford University Press, 1929.

———. *Darius the Mede and the Four World Empires in the Book of Daniel*. Cardiff: University of Wales Press, 1934. Reprinted, Eugene, OR: Wipf & Stock, 2006.

———. "Review of D. J. Wiseman, et al., eds., *Notes on Some Problems in the Book of Daniel*." *JSS* 11 (1966) 112–6.

Schaeder, H. H. *Iranische Beiträge I*. Schriften der Königsberger Gelehrten Gesellschaft, 6. Jahr: Geisteswissenschaftliche Kl., Heft 5. Halle/Saale: Niemeyer, 1930.

Stefanovic, Zdravko. *The Aramaic of Daniel in the Light of Old Aramaic*. JSOTSup 129. Sheffield Academic, 1992.

Wilson, Robert Dick. "The Aramaic of Daniel." In *Biblical and Theological Studies by the Faculty of Princeton Theological Seminary Published in Commemoration of the One Hundredth Anniversary of the Founding of the Seminary*, 261–306. New York: Scribner, 1912.

Wiseman, Donald J. et al., eds. *Notes on Some Problems in the Book of Daniel*. London: Tyndale, 1965.

18

Visual Grammar: An Eye-Tracking Perspective on Cognitive Complexity in Biblical Hebrew Pronunciation[1]

Cynthia L. Miller-Naudé, Jacobus A. Naudé,
Tanya Beelders, and Luna Bergh
UNIVERSITY OF THE FREE STATE
(BLOEMFONTEIN, SOUTH AFRICA)

1. Introduction

It is a pleasure for us to dedicate this chapter to Ziony Zevit, whose first book—*Matres Lectionis in Ancient Hebrew Epigraphs*—dealt with the question of spelling (and thus reading) of Hebrew at its earliest attestations in epigraphic sources. In this article we examine how contemporary students

---

[1]. An earlier version of this article was presented in the Applied Linguistics for Biblical Languages Section of the Society of Biblical Literature, 24 November 2014. We are grateful for the questions and comments of participants at the section. This work is based on research supported in part by the National Research Foundation of South Africa (Jacobus A. Naudé UID 85902 and Cynthia L. Miller-Naudé UID 95926). The grantholders acknowledge that opinions, findings and conclusions or recommendations expressed in any publication generated by the NRF supported research are those of the authors, and that the NRF accepts no liability whatsoever in this regard.

learn to read Biblical Hebrew, including the *matres lectionis*. We are interested in gaining insight into the processing of Biblical Hebrew in light of the cognitive complexity of the Hebrew writing system. In particular, we want to know how adult learners of Biblical Hebrew decode and interpret the orthography of Biblical Hebrew as compared to the orthography of their home language.

In order to understand precisely what students are focusing on when they read Biblical Hebrew, we have employed eye-tracking technology. Eye-tracking technology allows researchers to see exactly what students are focusing on when they read Biblical Hebrew—for example, how long they look at an orthographic feature or whether their eyes regress to a previous feature. It is therefore possible to ascertain the eye movements that fluent speakers of Biblical Hebrew use to interpret the orthography as opposed to the eye movements used by beginning students. It is also possible to compare the eye movements used by students in reading the orthography of their home language as opposed to the orthography of Biblical Hebrew.

Writing represents a form of visual communication[2] and is therefore suitable for an eye-tracking experiment. Ware describes verbal language, written language, and sign language as socially designed tools for communication, whose symbols and grammars are shared by the respective language users and which use the same specialized areas of the brain for processing information.[3] In contrast and complementary to this, visual representations of information are processed by the visual system–"an extremely powerful pattern finding system which is very good at finding structure in diagrams."[4] Its logic differs from that of verbal logic and consists mostly of structural relationships such as those revealed by voweled Biblical Hebrew, where vowel diacritics surround consonantal letters spatially and especially vertically and horizontally.[5] Biblical Hebrew thus presents a very strong form of visual communication. The word *grammar* is derived from the Greek *grammatike*, with the meanings "the art of reading and writing," "grammar," or "alphabet."[6] The first phrase of our title, Visual Grammar, emphasizes these focal points in our research.

Behavioral studies have shown that the visual characteristics of words, such as the direction in which they are written or read, word length, and their orthographic and morphological structure, affect the way in which

---

2. Kress and Van Leeuwen, *Reading Images*, 17.
3. Ware, *Visual Thinking for Design*, 133.
4. Ibid.
5. Ware, *Visual Thinking for Design*, 57, 133.
6. Kress and Van Leeuwen, *Reading Images*, 22.

words are perceived.[7] Research investigating the possible sources of slowness in both reading acquisition and skilled reading of another Semitic language, Arabic, compared to other languages has focused on the relationship between the specific characteristics of the Arabic orthographic system and cognitive processes that might be involved during word recognition and the acquisition of reading.[8] Abdelhadi et al. point out that there are two separate aspects of this relationship that might be related, namely orthographic depth (the "distance" between the graphic system and the lexical items it represents) and the visual complexity of the letters themselves.[9] With regard to Arabic for beginning readers, Abu-Rabia et al. emphasize the following points:

> Recognizing the nature of these letters and their diverse writing rules in different positions, and recognizing the different short vowels under, in, and above the letters is critical for readers' word pronunciation, which may demand considerable cognitive attention. Furthermore, short-vowel diacritics are located above, and/or in, and/or below the letters for letter-sound pronunciation. Thus, reading a fully voweled text is likely to be cognitively demanding for a beginning reader, who simultaneously must process many rules in order to extract meaning from print or read out loud accurately. A minor error can lead to a mistaken decoding through confusion of letters of the same shape.[10]

Linguistic complexity has been a research focus area in terms of fluency for some time, and it has been found that stuttering tends to occur in utterances that are linguistically more complex.[11] Packman explains that if a person uses a fluency enhancing technique, such as prolonged speech, "an increase in arousal may result in them paying more attention to it, hence increasing their control over their stuttering."[12] Our linguistics framework is that of Cognitive Linguistics. Andrews points out that one of the noteworthy contributions of Cognitive Linguistics to the study of language and brain is

---

7. Abdelhadi et al. "Perceptual Load in the Reading of Arabic: Effects of Orthographic Visual Complexity on Detection," 117.

8. See the summary of this research in Abdelhadi et al., "Perceptual Load in the Reading of Arabic."

9. Abdelhadi et al., "Perceptual Load in the Reading of Arabic," 118.

10. Abu-Rabia et al., "Word Recognition and Basic Cognitive Processes among Read-Disabled and Normal Readers in Arabic," 425.

11. See Packman, "Theory and Therapy in Stuttering: A Complex Relationship."

12. Ibid., 228.

its emphasis on combining cognitive theory-based models with reliable data sets of linguistic forms; these data sets are both pragmatically and semantically viable within their corresponding languages, speech communities, and communities of practice. CL [Cognitive Linguistics] is interested in the study of not only *imagery*, but also *perception (visual and non-visual)*.[13]

This view of Cognitive Linguistics relates to neuroscientific research on mental imagery, specifically viewer-oriented and object-oriented mental representations. Our notion of cognitive complexity invoked in this article involves cognitive attention and processing, and visuo-spatial, verbal, linguistic, and orthographic considerations.

The organization of the chapter is as follows: In section 2, we discuss notions of reading in Biblical Hebrew and difficulties in reading the Biblical Hebrew orthography, especially as compared to Modern Hebrew. Section 3 provides an overview of the theoretical aspects of the cognitive processes of reading, specifically cognitive neuroscience, active vision, cognitive linguistics, active memory, and eye movements. Section 4 describes the present eye-tracking experiment, Section 5 describes its results, and Section 6 discusses the significance of those results. Section 7 provides the conclusions.

2. Reading Biblical Hebrew

2.1 Notions of Reading Biblical Hebrew

Reading can be defined generally as "the process of decoding and comprehending written language."[14] However, because Biblical Hebrew is both a second language and a written language for students, the definition of Nassaji concerning learning to read a second language is more appropriate: "learning to read becomes less about comprehension or getting information from text than a tool for developing basic language skills."[15]

The various notions of "reading" with respect to Biblical Hebrew can be identified.[16] These notions can be summarized as follows: (1) reading involves the pronunciation of the Hebrew letters without understanding or

---

13. Andrews, "Language and Brain: Recasting Meaning in the Definition of Human Language," 22.

14. Perfetti, "Reading," 699.

15. Nassaji, "Issues in Second-Language Reading: Implications for Acquisition and Instruction," 175.

16. See Miller-Naudé and Naudé, "A Typological, Complex Systems Approach to the Teaching of Biblical Hebrew Reading."

with only limited understanding of what is being communicated; (2) reading involves the visual processing of letter-strings for word identification; in other words, reading involves "a match between the graphic input and the corresponding word representation";[17] (3) reading involves the identification of discourse-level features such as compound sentences, the embedding of direct and indirect speech, and genre specific features such as poetic lineation and poetic word pairs; (4) academic reading comprehension of Biblical Hebrew includes culturally relevant information for processing the pragmatic inferences of biblical texts. In this paper, we concentrate on the first level of reading—reading Hebrew orthography for pronunciation.

2.2 Biblical Hebrew Orthography

The orthography of Hebrew differs significantly from the orthography of the Latin alphabet. First, it is written from right to left, rather than from left to right. Second, the Latin alphabet is linear, with consonants and vowels having equivalent representational space on the line. The Hebrew alphabet differentiates consonants, which are large letters, from vowels which are superimposed as small marks below, above, or to the left of the consonants. These two features mean that the eye movements required to read Biblical Hebrew differ significantly from those used in reading a language written in the Latin alphabet.

Furthermore, the Hebrew alphabet requires the reader to interpret the orthography in a variety of ways in order to read correctly. First, the consonants that may function as *matres lectionis* must be interpreted within the context of the word as either consonants or composite vowel letters. Second, the *shewa* vowel point must be interpreted within the syllable structure of the word as either silent (ending a syllable boundary) or vocal. Third, the *qameṣ* must be interpreted within the syllable structure as either representing /o/ in closed, unaccented syllables or /ā/ elsewhere. Fourth, *dageš* may signal either a doubled consonant (*dageš forte*) or a plosive rather than a fricative consonant (*dageš lene*); readers must interpret its function within the context of the word in order to read correctly. Additional hurdles for reading the biblical text involve, first, the accentual system that is superimposed upon the text. Beginning readers must differentiate accents from vowels. Second, the *ketiv-qere* variants indicated in the biblical text require readers to consult the *masora parva* in the margin in order to properly pronounce the word. Reading Hebrew thus requires the reader to be able to

---

17. Perfetti, "Reading," 700.

interpret a dramatically different orthography in exceedingly sophisticated ways.

The process of learning to read Biblical Hebrew as a second language also differs in dramatic ways from immigrants to Israel learning to read (and speak) Israeli Hebrew. First, the orthography of Modern Hebrew is a "deep" alphabetic orthography in the sense that "the letters represent phonemes, but the mapping of graphemes-to-phonemes is not entirely transparent."[18] Because vowels are not usually indicated, Modern Hebrew orthography "cannot specify a unique phonological unit, and a printed consonant string is phonologically ambiguous, often representing more than one word."[19] As described by Frost, reading in Modern Hebrew involves two processes. First, the recognition of single letters as providing consonantal information; this process may be sufficient to read the word.[20] Second, a complete phonological representation must be provided by the reader drawing upon morphological information from the word pattern (the missing vowels).[21] Word recognition in Modern Hebrew requires that words be decomposed into their roots and then into their constituent morphemes.[22]

By contrast, the orthography of Biblical Hebrew is a shallow orthography in the sense that consonants and vowels are indicated. But this advantage is offset by the fact that Biblical Hebrew is *over*-differentiated. By this we mean that Biblical Hebrew does not offer a purely phonemic orthographic representation of the language, but rather also represents phonetic and prosodic features. As one example of phonetic representation, the *dageš lene* represents the difference between a stop and a fricative in approximately the same point of articulation (e.g. [t] vs. [θ]). The occurrence of the stop and the fricative, however, are in complementary distribution and completely predictable (i.e., the stop occurs in two positions—word initially and syllable initially after a closed syllable—whereas the fricative occurs elsewhere). There is therefore no need for these two phonetic sounds

---

18. Frost, "Reading in Hebrew vs. Reading in English: Is There a Qualitative Difference?" 236.

19. Ibid., 237.

20. Frost, "Prelexical and Postlexical Strategies in Reading: Evidence from a Deep and Shallow Orthography"; Frost, "Phonological Computation and Missing Vowels: Mapping Lexical Involvement in Reading."

21. Frost, "Becoming Literate in Hebrew: The Grain-Size Hypothesis and Semitic Orthographic Systems."

22. See Frost, "Reading in Hebrew"; Frost et al., "Decomposing Complex Words in a Nonlinear Morphology"; Frost et al., "Morphological Priming: Dissociation of Phonological, Semantic, and Morphological Factors"; Frost et al., "What Can We Learn from the Morphology of Hebrew: A Masked Priming Investigation of Morphological Representation."

to be indicated orthographically. If the *dageš* in a consonant was used purely to indicate a doubled consonant (the *dageš forte*) the task of learning to read Biblical Hebrew would be greatly simplified. The same is true of the use of one symbol—the *shewa*—to represent both the end of a syllable and an audible half-vowel. As an example of prosodic representation, we can mention the use of conjunctive *dageš* (across word boundaries).

Second, learning to read Modern Hebrew occurs concomitantly with learning to speak Hebrew. This means that learners have an oral component in their cognitive processes of learning as well a visual component. Efforts to include oral speaking in the learning of Biblical Hebrew are attempts to close this gap between the learning of Modern and Biblical Hebrew.[23]

3. Reading and Cognitive Processes

3.1 Cognitive Neuroscience of Reading

How do students actually learn to recognize the letters on the page and pronounce the words? In other words, how is the visual image on the page (letters configured as words) transformed into phonemes and words in the brain? Recent research concerning the science of reading sheds important light on the reading process. Especially significant in this regard is the work by Stanislas Dehaene and his colleagues in France.[24]

Recognising and processing the written image begins when a specialised portion of the retina, the fovea, receives photos reflected off of the written page.[25] Because the fovea occupies only 15 degrees of the visual field, a person's eyes must be in constant motion during reading in order to bring the fovea in contact with the written words. The eyes' movements are in small jerky steps called saccades. In a single fixation, the gaze can perceive about 7–9 letters.[26] There is an important asymmetry based on the direction of reading—persons who read an orthography that is arranged from left to right have a visual span greater towards the right side of the visual field, whereas persons who read a right-to-left orthography have a greater visual span towards the left.[27] This culturally determined difference in reading also

---

23. Buth, *Living Biblical Hebrew: Part One*; Buth, *Living Biblical Hebrew: Part Two*; and Overland, *Learning Biblical Hebrew Interactively*.

24. This research is summarized in Dehaene, *Reading in the Brain: The New Science of How We Read*. For a summary of the science of reading from the viewpoint of a reading specialist, see Smith, *Understanding Reading*, 65–103.

25. Dehaene, *Reading in the Brain*, 13.

26. Ibid., 14–15.

27. Ibid., 17.

relates to other writing systems; for example, readers of Chinese (which has greater character density in the visual field) will have shorter saccades and reduced visual span.

There are two major processing paths which coexist in the brain and which supplement one another during the process of reading.[28] One is the phonological path which converts a string of letters into sounds (pronunciation) and then attempts to access the meaning of the sound pattern. The second path is the lexical path, in which the brain attempts first to access the word in the mental lexicon in order to recover the identity and meaning of the word and then to recover its pronunciation.

These paths relate to the brain's neurophysical features. Magnetic imaging has demonstrated that the left occipito-temporal region is the visual word form area.[29] This area of the brain performs the visual analysis of letter and word shapes (letter strings) and transmits the information to two areas of the brain in the temporal and frontal lobes which encode sound pattern and meaning. It is important to note that the visual word form area is not identical to the area of the brain which recognizes faces, objects, etc.[30] Nor is the visual word form area identical to the area where hearing and speech perception is processed in the brain.[31] In all literate cultures, writing is processed by the same brain circuits in spite of differences of language and differences in surface forms; there are therefore neurological limits on cultural diversity in reading.[32]

Acquiring the ability to read as a child involves three major phases:[33] First, there is a brief "pictorial stage" in which children's brains "photograph" a few words. Second, there is the phonological stage in which children learn how to decode graphemes into phonemes. Third, there is the orthographic stage in which word recognition becomes fast and automatic. Brain imaging has shown that in the process of learning how to read, the brain is altered, especially in the left occipito-temporal lobe, so that the neural activity evoked by written words increases and becomes selective based upon the specific visual characteristics of the writing system. These changes in the brain occur even when illiterate adults learn how to read. For this reason, learning to read a second orthography has significant "carry-over" effects from the initial experience of the brain's learning to read.

28. Ibid., 38–39.
29. Ibid., 62, 68, 75.
30. Ibid., 74.
31. Ibid., 68.
32. Ibid., 97, 119.
33. Ibid., 195.

3.2 Active Vision

The notion of Active Vision provides an integrated account of seeing and looking, taking into consideration the role of eye-movements.[34] Active Vision emphasizes visual attention, which in turn ties in with other cognitive phenomena in our study, such as working memory (see section 3.4 below).

Active Vision is "all about understanding perception as a dynamic process" where, by means of directing the eyes, "the brain grabs just those fragments that are needed to execute the current mental activity."[35] The basis of visual thinking is "pattern perception," which is partly innate and partly learned through visual interaction with the world. Visual designs are almost always combinations in that they have aspects that support visual thinking through pattern finding and aspects that are conventional and processed through language systems. More broadly and in a unifying way, in cognitive neuroscience every piece of stored information can be thought of as a pattern, which entails that complex patterns are patterns of patterns.[36] This would be the case for the Modern Hebrew root and word patterns described by Frost et al.[37] as well as the metaphorical patterns surrounding Biblical Hebrew described below in section 3.3. It is in the inferotemporal cortex that neurons respond to particular meaningful patterns such as faces, hands, and letters of the alphabet, although in slightly different areas.[38]

Five points about Active Vision are relevant here. First of all, visual thinking is based on pattern perception, as was pointed out above. Secondly, Ware points out that almost all seeing involves "visual search," although we are not constantly aware of it.[39] Thirdly, efficient visual search can be achieved through the use of "pop-out properties."[40] The strongest pop-out effects occur when a single target object differs in some feature from all other objects. Pop-out contrast is defined in terms of the basic features that are processed in the primary visual cortex, namely color (including hue and lightness), orientation, size, motion, and stereoscopic depth as well as elongation, spatial layout, and form.[41] The features that pop out are hardwired

---

34. Findley and Gilchrist, *Active Vision: The Psychology of Looking and Seeing*. See also Bergh and Beelders, "An Eye-Tracking Account of Reference Points, Cognitive Affordance and Multimodal Metaphors."
35. Ware, *Visual Thinking for Design*, ix.
36. Ibid., 63.
37. Frost et al., "Decomposing Complex Words in Nonlinear Morphology."
38. Ware, *Visual Thinking for Design*, 168.
39. Ibid., 41.
40. Ibid., 42.
41. Ibid., 29, 42.

in the brain, not learned,[42] and can be seen in a single fixation—as opposed to elements that do not pop out and require several eye movements to find.[43]

Visual thinking is, fourthly, based on a "hierarchy of skills," which means that sophisticated cognitive skills build on simpler ones. Although human mental models of space perception are grounded in real-world interaction, the neural architecture and the most basic human capabilities (such as seeing closed shapes bound by contours as "objects") are innate.[44]

Lastly, Ware explains that when we see patterns in graphic designs, we are mostly relying on the same neural machinery that is used to interpret our everyday environment. There is, however, a "layer of meaning"—"a kind of natural semantics"[45]—that is built on top of this. For example, we use a big graphical shape to represent a large quantity in a bar chart.

3.3 Cognitive Linguistics

The exposition in the previous section ties in with two tenets of cognitive semantics; namely, that "cognitive models are mainly perceptually determined" and that "semantic elements are based on spatial or topological objects."[46] Gärdenfors proposes the notion of a conceptual space as a framework for geometric structure in cognitive semantics.[47] A conceptual space comprises a number of quality dimensions such as color, pitch, temperature, weight, and the three ordinary spatial dimensions, and corresponds closely with the domains of Langacker.[48] Also, within this framework a linguistic symbol is bipolar in that it consists of a semantic pole, a phonological pole, and the link between them.[49] Langacker defines a unit as "any cognitive or cognitively derived activity."[50] What should be kept in mind in this regard is that not only should linguistic units be seen on a continuum with non-linguistic units, but that the same applies to traditional divisions such as phonology, syntax, and morphology.

42. Ibid., 32.
43. Ibid., 29.
44. Ibid., 103.
45. Ibid., 62.
46. Gärdenfors, "Some Tenets of Cognitive Semantics," 22.
47. Ibid.
48. Langacker, *Foundations of Cognitive Grammar*, 147.
49. Ibid., 76.
50. Ibid., 60.

The natural semantics discussed above permeate our spoken language, as well as the language of design.[51] In this regard, Lakoff and Johnson argue that spatial metaphors are not just ways of making language more vivid, but that they are fundamental to the way language works in communication and reasoning.[52] Spatial metaphors occur even in an expression such as *vowels are superimposed as small marks below, above, or to the left of the consonants* that is so general in the Biblical Hebrew context that we do not necessarily even consider it to be metaphoric. To Lakoff and Johnson metaphors represent the way in which we make sense of the world, and follow the pattern-seeking of Active Vision. This aspect will be elaborated on in our forthcoming article dealing with the conceptual metaphorical patterns related to this experiment.

In a study on Arabic, researchers Ibrahim, Eviatar, and Aharon-Peretz established that specific features of Arabic orthography (such as vocalization marks) produce a visual load in respect of visual word recognition and that the effect is slower orthographic recognition as compared with other orthographies.[53] Taha postulates that the complexity of the visual information that each written Arabic word carries (such as different shapes of different letters, dots, and the vocalization marks) forces the reader to rely heavily on visual processing in addition to phonological processing.[54] In respect of the present study, it should be kept in mind, however, that phonology may have a reduced role in lexical decision tasks or silent reading compared to oral reading.[55] Oral reading may also involve more attention to phonological analysis than orthographic units or meaning relative to silent reading.[56]

Ibrahim indicates that, traditionally, oral reading accuracy and fluency are assessed by reading aloud a list of words (or pseudo-words) that are graded for length, "difficulty," and frequency of occurrence.[57] Furthermore, although measures of accuracy seem to be good predictors of variability in literary acquisition of less transparent scripts, measures of speed may be better predictors of variability in more transparent scripts. These observations

---

51. Ware, *Visual Thinking for Design*, 62.

52. Lakoff and Johnson, *Metaphors We Live By*.

53. Ibrahim et al., "The Characters of the Arabic Orthography Slow its Cognitive Processing."

54. Taha, "Reading and Spelling in Arabic: Linguistic and Orthographic Complexity."

55. See Share, "On the Anglocentrics of Current Reading Research and Practice: The Perils of Overreliance on an 'Outlier' Orthography."

56. Corcos and Willows, "The Processing of Orthographic Information."

57. Ibrahim, "Reading in Arabic: New Evidence for the Role of Vowel Signs," 249.

are also applicable to the voweled Biblical Hebrew passages in our study, which also provide morpho-syntactic information.

In the study by Ibrahim et al. as well as that of Eviatar et al., it was found that Arab-Israeli participants were slower in processing Arabic letters than Hebrew letters, despite Arabic being the participants' first language.[58] The researchers concluded that this difference was due to the greater degree of visual/graphic complexity of Arabic script compared to Hebrew. Other studies have shown, though, that decoding of both Arabic and Hebrew demands more visuo-spatial awareness or visual attention than decoding in English,[59] while Geva and Siegel established that English-Hebrew bilingual children made more visual letter recognition errors in Hebrew than in English.[60] In addition, Shimron and Sivan found that adult Hebrew-English bilinguals read text more quickly in English than in unvoweled Hebrew, but not more quickly than in Hebrew texts with vowel diacritics.[61] From this research it can be inferred that even though the addition of vowels results in a more complex visual form of the text, it still facilitated the speed of reading among that particular bilingual group.

3.4 Working Memory

A person can process limited information in working memory at a specific point in time.[62] At a cognitive level, "we allocate scarce working memory resources to briefly retain in focal attention only those pieces of information most likely to be useful."[63] As Lee, Lin, and Robertson point out, every task has a cognitive cost, and as a person becomes more used to performing a specific task, that activity requires less cognitive energy.[64] They provide the example of how a new bicycle rider must concentrate fully to learn the skills involved, which, with practice, become more automated, although a certain amount of attention is always necessary for this activity. Related to this, the

---

58. Ibrahim et al., "The Characteristics of the Arabic Orthography Slow its Cognitive Processing"; and Eviatar et al., "Orthography and the Hemispheres: Visual and Linguistics Aspects of Letter Processing."

59. Share and Levin, "Learning to Read and Write in Hebrew"; and Shatil and Share, "Cognitive Antecedents of Early Reading Ability."

60. Geva and Siegel, "Orthographic Factors in the concurrent Development of Basic Reading Skills in Two Languages."

61. Shimron and Sivan, "Reading Proficiency and Orthography: Evidence from Hebrew and English."

62. Archer, "Digital Distractions," 50.

63. Ware, *Visual Thinking for Design*, 3.

64. Lee et al., "The Impact of Media Multitasking on Learning."

concept of executive attention refers to "our ability, within the context of working memory, to prioritize information and to focus on accomplishing a specific goal without distraction from irrelevant stimuli."[65]

In this chapter, the term *language* refers to "a variety of neurological functions that serve as the basis for a wide range of actions and behaviors."[66] This implies that it is assumed that the various forms of language, such as speech, comprehension, reading and writing, are not represented in the same way neurologically. Given that the focus of this study is on pronunciation and not reading for comprehension as such, it is furthermore assumed that cognitive load was not increased in the experiment by way of language task-shifting or multitasking, which would increase demand on working memory.[67] The primary verbal-visual task for participants was pronunciation of the lines of Biblical Hebrew orthography in a right-to-left direction.

Visual working memory refers to "the temporary activation of visual objects" and has a capacity of between one and three objects, depending on their complexity.[68] A similar number of objects can be held in verbal working memory, and often the two kinds of objects are bound together. Furthermore, some objects are constructed and held only for the duration of a single fixation. A few objects are held from fixation to fixation, but retaining objects reduces what can be picked up in the next fixation.

Ware explains that "visual working memory capacity is something that critically influences how well a design works. When we are thinking with the aid of a graphic image we are constantly picking up a chunk of information, holding it in working memory, formulating queries, and then relating what is held to a new information chunk coming in from the display."[69] Ware adds that this implies that when a visual comparison is required between two graphic objects, it would be to the advantage of the viewer if the images are on the same page, for "in each case visual working memory capacity is the same, but we can pick up a chunk or two, then navigate to a new point of comparison at least ten times faster with eye movements than we can switch pages (either web pages or book pages), so side-by-side comparisons can be hugely more efficient."[70]

Visual chunks may trigger eye-movement plans and cognitive action plans needed to execute the next few mental operations.[71] Ware explains

65. Archer, "Digital Distractions," 50.

66. Andrews, "Language and Brain" Recasting Meaning in the Definition of Human Language," 26.

67. Archer, "Digital Distractions," 50.

68. Ware, *Visual Thinking for Design*, 126.

69. Ibid.

70. Ibid., 127.

71. Ibid., 115.

these temporary bindings as "acts of attention, the shifting focus of the mind."[72] As Ware points out, the prefrontal cortex has long been considered critical to the temporary bindings that occur as part of more complex plans.[73] The neuroscientists Miller and Cohen explain this as follows:

> [C]ognitive control stems from the active maintenance of patterns of activity in the prefrontal cortex that represent goals and the means to achieve them. They provide bias signals to other brain structures whose net effect is to guide the flow of activity along neural pathways that establish the proper mappings between inputs, internal states, and outputs needed to perform a given task.[74]

In Active Vision, attention is the essence of human perception and also of eye-movement control, "because looking is a prerequisite for attending."[75] The sequence of eye fixations is therefore linked to the thread of visual thinking. Ware explains that cognitive thread shifts back and forth between visual processing and language processing modalities and also that we cannot perform more than one visual or verbal task simultaneously, although we can perform a visual and a verbal task at the same time—if one of the two cognitive tasks represents a highly learned skill.[76] Thirdly, when visual and language modalities are combined, the brain is most effective. In terms of the last point, the task of pronouncing orthography is facilitated cognitively. Furthermore, in visual thinking, perception is a cognitive action sequence.[77] This also means that any images that we see and process to some extent prime the visual pathways involved in their processing and will be processed faster the next time.

3.5 Eye Movements and Cognitive Processing

The eye movements of interest in eye-tracking are saccades and fixations. As mentioned above in section 3.1, saccades are high-velocity ballistic movements which are used to reposition the eye over an area or object of interest.[78] Visual acuity is suppressed during saccades,[79] which means that

72. Ibid.
73. Ibid., 116.
74. Miller and Cohen, "An Integrative Theory of Prefrontal Cortex Function," 167.
75. Ware, *Visual Thinking for Design*, 179.
76. Ibid., 180.
77. Ibid., 118.
78. Gregory, *The Eye and the Brain: The Psychology of Seeing*.
79. Rayner, "Eye Movements in Reading and Information Processing: Twenty

while people are moving their eyes they are unable to "see." In order to "see" an object, the eye must be held still over the object. These periods of relative stability are called fixations.[80] Even during fixations, the eye is subject to small involuntary movements, referred to as fixational movements.[81] Fixational movements are not relevant to the current study and will therefore not be discussed further.

Fixations during scene perception typically last between 260 and 300 milliseconds,[82] but vary in length while reading from 100–500 milliseconds,[83] depending on whether the reading is silent or verbal.[84] Both the home language and the Hebrew passage were read aloud in this study, which may influence the fixation length. However, since both passages were read aloud, the effect would be present in both readings and is therefore implicitly controlled for.

Eye movements are good indicators of whether a person is experiencing any difficulty with reading material. The duration of a fixation, or the length of time the eye remains stable on a word, can give an indication of the cognitive processing that is occurring at that moment.[85] This can be indicative of the amount of resources required to assimilate and understand the word.

Furthermore, three types of saccades are generally present during reading.[86] The first of these are forward progressive saccades in the direction of the text. Secondly, line sweeps are saccades which move in the opposite direction and slightly downwards and serve to connect the end of a line with the start of the next line. Finally, regressive saccades are also saccades which move in a direction opposite to the direction of the text but are performed in order to re-examine a word or words which were not clearly understood.[87] Regressive saccades are dependent on the same characteristics as fixations[88]

Years of Research."

80. Ibid.

81. Martinez-Conde and Macknik, "Fixational Eye Movements across Vertebrates: Comparative Dynamics, Physiology, and Perception."

82. Rayner and Castelhano, "Eye Movements."

83. Hyrskykari, "Eye in Attentive Interfaces: Experiences from Creationg iDict, a Gaze-Aware Reading Aid."

84. Rayner and Castelhano, "Eye Movements."

85. Rayner and Pollastek, *The Psychology of Reading*.

86. Siegenthaler et al., "Comparing Reading Processes on e-ink Displays and Print."

87. Morrison and Inhoff, "Visual Factors and Eye Movements in Reading."

88. Siegenthaler et al., "Comparing Reading Processes on e-ink Displays and Print."

and give an indication of the difficulty experienced while reading.[89] The features of the reading material, such as the contrast and font characteristics, can also impact the fixation duration as well the number of fixations performed during reading. Since the font and contrast were consistent between texts in the current study, they should not unduly influence the results. Linguistic factors also influence the fixation duration while reading, amongst them the familiarity of the word, the semantic relationships between the word and the previous words, and how many meanings the fixated word has.[90]

4. The Present Study

4.1 Overview of the Experiment

Each participant was requested to read a passage aloud in English, Afrikaans, or Sesotho. These languages were chosen as they were the first languages for the sample.[91] Each participant could choose the language they were most comfortable reading for the first passage. Following this, the participant was requested to read a Hebrew passage aloud.

The text chosen for analysis was Deut 31:24–28. A text (rather than isolated words) was selected so that the analysis could better utilize the capabilities of the eye-tracking equipment to examine saccades and regressions. A biblical text was chosen which students had not read in class and which they would not be likely to recognize from their knowledge of the Bible. The text chosen also has a good selection of the phonological and orthographical features for analysis. In retrospect, it seems that the text was a bit too long for many of the students, especially those in the first year of study. This is indicated by the fact that they began to fatigue before they had completed reading the text and tended to make more errors in reading. In future research, a shorter text will be selected.

The Hebrew text was prepared for the eye-tracking experiment as follows: All verse numbers were removed from the passage so that the passage was presented as a continuous text. Since Biblical Hebrew does not use the

---

89. Rayner and Castelhano, "Eye Movements."

90. Ibid.

91. It is possible that there are significant differences in the rate of reading in Sesotho as opposed to English or Afrikaans, because Sesotho is an agglutinative language. In an eye-tracking study comparing reading in English and isiZulu (a related Bantu language), the rates of reading in isiZulu were considerably slower than those in English even though the isiZulu orthography is more transparent than that of English; see van Rooy and Pretorius, "Is Reading in an Agglutinative Language Different from an Analytic Language?"

punctuation marks of European languages (such as the period, comma, or colon), the *sof pasuq* (literally 'end of verse') mark was retained to assist students in segmenting the text into readable units. The other Masoretic accents were removed from the text, but a simple accent mark was placed over words in which the accent is not final to assist students in reading correctly. The *qere perpetuum* of the divine name (YHWH) as written by the Masoretes was retained, because this is how students learned to read the name in class.

Equivalent texts were prepared of the translation of Deut 31:24–28 into the three languages that are represented as "home languages" among the students—Afrikaans, English, Sesotho. The texts were prepared without verse numbers and in paragraph format, but all normal punctuation marks that are found in the translations were retained.

4.2 Participants

Participants were all students at the University of the Free State and were enrolled for a Biblical Hebrew class at the time the test was conducted. Participants were all undergraduate students, but varied in study year from first year to third year. Since the University of the Free State is a bilingual university, students must be fluent in at least one of the instructional languages (English and Afrikaans). Each session was therefore conducted in either English or Afrikaans based on the preference of the participant.

In total, 27 participants were tested. The data of four participants had to be discarded for the purposes of analysis as they all had a very low accuracy rate for the duration of the test. Additionally, since the analysis was conducted on only the first two lines of each passage, another four participants had to be excluded as there was no gaze data present for them for the first two lines. The analysis was therefore conducted with the participants as follows:

	English	Afrikaans	Sesotho	TOTAL
1st year	1	10		11
2nd year		6		6
3rd year		1	1	2
TOTAL	1	17	1	

Table 1. Participants in the eye-tracking study

Since the Sesotho and English groups only have one participant each, the analysis will be conducted by distinguishing between reading in a home language (the first passage in the language of choice of the participant) and Biblical Hebrew. Due to the small number of participants in each year, the analysis will not be conducted per year group.

4.3 Eye-tracking Methodology

Eye movements were recorded using an eye-tracker, which is a piece of hardware that is used to measure eye movements.[92] The texts (one in the participant's home language and one in Biblical Hebrew) were shown to each participant using a Tobii T120 eye-tracker. The frequency of this eye-tracker is 120Hz (a relatively low frequency), which means that the gaze position is sampled once every 8.3 milliseconds. For reading research, it is advisable to use a high frequency eye-tracker[93] in order to accurately measure fixation progress on words.[94] Unfortunately, a high resolution eye-tracker was not available for use in the study. As a result, the lower frequency eye-tracker was used, with the limitations thereof being recognized for the analysis of reading behavior. However, previous studies have analyzed gaze metrics during reading with low frequency eye-trackers,[95] some even as low as 60Hz.[96]

The resolution of the eye-tracking screen was set to 1280×1024. All texts used for the tests fit on a single screen so there was no need for paging or scrolling. Font size was consistent between texts, implying that the visual angle should be approximately the same for each text. Video recordings were captured of each participant reading aloud. Analysis of the eye-tracking data was primarily conducted using Tobii Studio 3.2.1. Where necessary, adjustments were uniformly made to the position of the fixations using a custom built software application. Adjustments were only made when the calibration was found to lack accuracy and was verified through the video of the participant reading aloud.

The Tobii Studio software allows various metrics to be extracted and analyzed. Applicable metrics for this study are as follows:

---

92. Duchowski, *Eye-Tracking Methodology: Theory and Practice*.
93. Biedert et al., "A Robust Realtime Reading-Skimming Classifier."
94. Hyrskykari, *Eye in Attentive Interfaces*.
95. Sharmin et al., "The Effect of Different Text Presentation Formats on Eye Movement Metrics in Reading."
96. Cf. Luegi et al., "Using Eye-Tracking to Detect Reading Difficulties."

- Number of fixations—this value indicates the total number of fixations for each participant while they were reading the passage.
- Fixation duration—this is the length, in milliseconds, of each fixation. This can then be interpreted as a total for all fixations, or the average fixation length can be analyzed.

Qualitatively, analysis can be performed using heat maps and gaze plots. A heat map indicates gaze intensity for a stimulus by superimposing a color overlay of the aggregated fixations on the stimulus. The warmer the color, the more participants looked at that location and the longer the period of the gaze. The cooler the color, the less participants looked at that location.[97] As previously mentioned in section 3.5, both fixations and saccades are of interest to eye-tracking. Because eye gaze alternates between saccades and fixations, a scan path can be constructed. Fixations are represented as circles, where the fixations of each participant is shown using a different color. The size of each individual circle is indicative of the fixation duration. The lines between the fixations are representative of saccades (drawn as straight lines even though saccades are not actually straight). Each circle has a number in it, illustrating the index of the fixation within the scan path from the start of the viewing time. Gaze plots show the scan paths of all participants while viewing the selected stimulus. Regressive saccades were detected for each participant by inspecting their respective gaze plot.

5. Results and Analysis

5.1 Average Fixation Length

The average fixation length for Afrikaans readers was 192.4 milliseconds when reading the first two lines of the Afrikaans passage; for English readers, it was 167.0 milliseconds when reading the first two lines of the English passage, and 110.0 milliseconds for Sesotho speakers while reading the first two lines of the Sesotho passage. In contrast, the mean fixation length, for all participants, when reading the first two lines of the Hebrew text was 418.3 milliseconds, markedly longer than while reading the first language text.

Suppose the following null hypothesis was tested:

> $H_0,1$: There is no difference between the mean fixation length of a reader when reading in their home language and when reading in Hebrew.

[97] Tobii, "An Introduction to Eye Tracking and the Tobii Eye Trackers."

A paired t-test confirmed that the null hypothesis could be rejected since p < 0 (t=5.79, df=18). Therefore, there is a significant difference between the mean fixation length when reading in the home language and when reading in Hebrew—average fixation length is much higher when reading Hebrew than when reading in one's home language. Therefore, cognitive processing was higher when reading Hebrew than when reading a home language passage.

The images below show a gaze plot for an English, Afrikaans, and Sesotho participant reading in their home language. Directly next to each of these is the same participant's gaze plot when reading in Hebrew. In the case of the English and Sesotho images, these were the images of the only participant in those groups. The images for the Afrikaans speaking participant were chosen as being representative of the group.

Figure 1: Gaze plot for English reader reading (a) English and (b) Hebrew passages

Figure 2: Gaze plot for Afrikaans readers reading (a) Afrikaans and (b) Hebrew passages

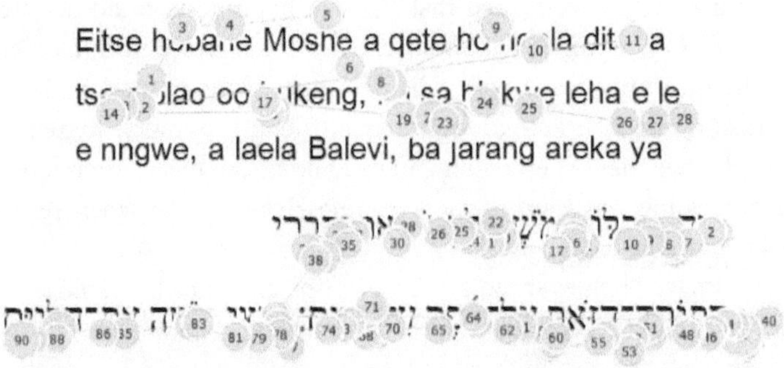

Eitse h..ba..e Moshe a qete h..., ir...la dit a tsr...lao oo...lkeng,...sa h...k..e leha e le e nngwe, a laela Balevi, ba jarang areka ya

הַֽכְּהֲנִ֖ים הַֽלְוִיִּ֑ם ...

Figure 3: Gaze plot for Sesotho reader reading (a) Sesotho and (b) Hebrew passages

Inspection of the gaze plots clearly shows more and longer fixations for the Hebrew than for the home language, specifically in the case of the English and Afrikaans groups. However, since there was only one participant in the English group, this is not a conclusive observation. Similarly, the Sesotho speaking participant exhibited much the same gaze pattern in his home language and Hebrew. The study should then be extended to include larger groups of each home language in order to determine whether this behavior is representative or unique to the participant.

5.2 Number of Fixations

The number of fixations was calculated for the first two lines of each passage. The average number of fixations for the home language is 19.95, whilst for the Hebrew passage the average number of fixations is 125.79. The English and Sesotho passages both consisted of 18 words and 67 and 68 characters respectively. The Afrikaans passage consisted of 17 words and 69 characters, while the Hebrew passage consisted of 12 words and 98 characters. The table below summarises the number of words, number of characters and average fixations per word for home language, taking the various languages into account, and Hebrew:

	Average number of fixations	Average fixations per word	Average fixations per characters
Home language	19.95	1.16	0.29
Hebrew	125.79	10.48	1.28
	$t(18) = 5.79$, $p < 0.05$	$t(18) = 6.16$, $p < 0.05$	$t(18) = 6.45$, $p < 0.05$

Table 2. Fixations in home language and in Biblical Hebrew

Paired t-tests for each of these metrics show that there is a significant difference between the average number of fixations, the average number of fixations per word, and the average number of fixations per character. Therefore, the participants struggled significantly more to read the Hebrew passage than the passage in their home language.

Regressive saccades

The mean number of regressive saccades when reading the home language passage ($\bar{x} = 1.6$) is slightly less than the mean number of regressive saccades when reading a Hebrew passage ($\bar{x} = 2.5$). A paired-test was used to test the following null hypothesis:

> $H_{o,1}$: *There is no difference between the mean number of regressive saccades of a reader when reading in their home language and when reading in Hebrew.*

Since $p < 0.05$ (t=2.66, df=18), the null hypothesis could be rejected, indicating that the number of regressive saccades is significantly more for Hebrew reading than for home language reading. Since readers fixate on each word and for longer periods, they concentrate on each separate word and read it before moving on. Because of this, one might expect that there may be less need for regressive saccades than when reading more fluently, as with the home language. However, this was not found to be the case as the Hebrew reading had significantly more regressive saccades.

6. Discussion

6.1 Eye-Tracking Metrics

With all the eye-tracking metrics analyzed, it was shown that the participants struggled significantly more whilst reading the Hebrew passage than while reading the passage in their home language. Fixation lengths were significantly longer, indicating that the participants expended more cognitive resources while reading in Hebrew. Furthermore, participants required more fixations per word and per character in order to read the Hebrew. This directly relates to the perceptual span of the reader, as readers can generally see more characters than those they are fixating on.[98] However, the perceptual span is dependent on the orientation of the text,[99] and since

98. Hyrskykari, *Eye in Attentive Interfaces*.
99. Ibid.

participants were all accustomed to reading left-to-right, their perceptual span would have been attuned to extend towards the right of their fixation. Therefore, they required more fixations in order to perceive the entire word when reading right-to-left. Increased regressive saccades also indicate that participants had to return to prior words or characters in order to successfully read the passage. In conclusion, there was increased difficulty when reading Hebrew, which is not entirely unexpected as the majority of the participants had very little experience in reading Hebrew.

6.2 Reading ability

Although our focus is on speed rather than accuracy (as discussed in sections 5.1 and 5.2), the following brief points are worth mentioning regarding pronunciation accuracy, especially in interpreting ambiguities in vowel orthography.

One question that we were particularly interested in is that of the interpretation of vocal versus silent *shewa*. Since fixation time relates to cognitive processing time, we were interested to know whether all *shewa*s are, on average, equally difficult to process or whether *shewa*s in some positions in the word are more difficult. Our findings can be summarised as follows:

First, when students encountered a known word and an unknown word with the same morphological structure and approximately the same phonological shape, they found it more difficult to process the *shewa* in the unknown word. In our text, the word דִּבְרֵי has a *shewa* in the middle of the word which must be interpreted by students as a silent *shewa*. The word was known by students and had relatively shorter fixations. By contrast, in pronouncing the word שִׁבְטֵיכֶם, which was not known to students, students required long fixations to cognitively process the silent *shewa* in the middle of the word, although the length (and thus greater phonological complexity) of the word may have also been a factor. The unknown word זִקְנֵי, which is precisely identical to דִּבְרֵי in shape, would have made an excellent word for comparison, except that it appeared too late in the text and the fatigue of the students may have contributed to the long fixation times. A similar example with almost identical words involved the word וַיְהִי, which has been learned by students and which most students were able to pronounce without excessive fixation, and the word וַיֵּצֵא, which was not known by students at the time they read the text and which resulted in very long fixations. We therefore conclude as a first working hypothesis that words which students have encountered previously require less cognitive processing to pronounce.

Second, we examined instances of vocal *shewa* appearing in the initial syllable of a word. We found that students had relatively shorter fixation times for the initial syllable of the words וְשָׂמְחֶם, וְאֶת, וְהָיָה, all of which involve a morphologically distinct first syllable—the conjunction *waw*. We also found relatively short response times which were comparable to those with conjunctive *waw* for the *shewa* in the initial syllable of the words כְּכֹלוֹת, בְּךָ, בְּעוֹדֶנִּי. We hypothesise that in these environments the fact that the individual syllable is a separate morpheme (an inseparable preposition) assists with the phonological processing of the word. Evidence from Modern Hebrew has demonstrated that readers process the orthographic structure of the word and the morphological structure of the word separately. The congruence of these two types of structure appears to aid in pronunciation. Less clear results were obtained concerning the word בְּרִית. The fact that the processing time for the initial syllable was roughly comparable even though the word is only one morpheme might be used as counter-evidence against our hypothesis that morphological information is significant for cognitive processing. However, because students knew this word, this fact could also result in decreased processing time. In future research, we wish to test this hypothesis further.

6.3 General overview

The perspective presented in this exposition is not a causal model, but rather a framework for understanding cognitive complexity related to the lack of fluency in Biblical Hebrew pronunciation among participants who were still inexperienced in this skill. Similarly, by viewing the findings regarding pronunciation through the lens of complexity (non-linear dynamics) one opens up the potential for a holistic view of the results,[100] which then includes neural occurrences, which could lead to changes in the mind and body, and in turn influence and be influenced by the communication context, situation, purpose of the task, attitudes, anxiety, and fear of negative evaluation.

In accordance with the exposition in 3.5 and the cognitive action sequences described and discussed above, the Biblical Hebrew letters and morphemes that were seen and processed prime the visual pathways involved in their processing and should be processed faster subsequently.

Our research adds to the body of literature affirming the cognitive complexity of Biblical Hebrew. It strengthens the findings in the literature mentioned that especially the visuo-spatial and orthographic complexity

---

100. See Packman and Kuhn, "Looking at Stuttering through the Lens of Complexity"; and Packman, *Theory and Therapy in Stuttering*, 228, 230.

of written Semitic languages slows down reading. The novel contribution of our findings lies especially in the eye-tracking results that show a high level of regressive saccades in the Biblical Hebrew texts, which reveal that in addition to being slowed down by complex orthography, even for pronunciation, some participants were slowed down because of their reliance on sentence context and morpho-syntactic information for problem-solving.

7. Conclusions

The initial explorations in an analysis of Biblical Hebrew reading using eye-tracking technology as reported here have a number of implications for the teaching of Biblical Hebrew:

First, it seems that the overall direction of Hebrew script from right-to-left presents some difficulty for students whose home language is written in a left-to-right script. This fact probably accounts for the increased regressive saccades in reading Hebrew as compared with reading in the home language.

Second, in interpreting the orthographically ambiguous *shewa*, students found a *shewa* in the initial syllable of a word easier to process than a *shewa* in the middle of the word. There are three possible explanations: (a) word initial position is an unambiguously vocal *shewa* and therefore easier to process; (b) word initial *shewa* often has a morphologically distinct item, such as the conjunction *waw* or the clitic preposition *beth*. The morphological boundary assisted students in identifying and correctly pronouncing the morpheme. (c) The word in the sample that does not involve a morpheme boundary was known to the students and thus required less orthographic processing to pronounce. We hope to explore the issue of orthographic ambiguities and their cognitive processing in future research.

Third, recall that acquiring the ability to read as a child involves three major phases: First, there is a brief "pictorial stage" in which children's brains "photograph" a few words. Second, there is the phonological stage in which children learn how to decode graphemes into phonemes. Third, there is the orthographic stage in which word recognition becomes fast and automatic. The reading skills of the Hebrew students are mostly in the phonological stage in which they learn how to decode graphemes into phonemes. Before they can reach the third phase in which recognition becomes fast and automatic, they have to internalize at least enough vocabulary. This gives support to teaching methods where the teaching of the alphabet and reading is postponed or where at least the focus is initially on spoken communication rather than reading.[101]

Finally, we wish to return to an observation made in Zevit concerning the study of Biblical Hebrew:

> The grammatical study of biblical Hebrew, which has continued more or less unabated since the eighth century of the common era, has traditionally been broadly focused, responding not only to "How and why does a text mean?" but also to "What does it mean?" In other words, it has never severed the nexus between exegesis and eisegesis, between text hermeneutics and the grammatical triad of phonology, morphology and syntax. This situation prevails, on the one hand, owing to the unique position of the Bible in Western civilization and its compartmentalization as an object of study primarily in university departments of religion and in denominational seminaries; on the other, it prevails because, apart from the Bible, we possess no significant, extended text in Judahite or Israelite Hebrew from the tenth through the fourth centuries B.C.E. on which we can perform our analysis uninfluenced by a 2000-year tradition of reading. Because the study of grammar, narrowly defined, has presupposed an understanding of the text, grammar has been pressed into the service of semantics. It is a rare and, I believe, a relatively modern phenomenon when an insight into grammar has led to a new appreciation of "meaning" on the semantic level.[102]

It may just be that a visual grammar based on an eye-tracking perspective of cognitive complexity in Biblical Hebrew pronunciation provides such a novel, yet anticipated, appreciation of meaning.

BIBLIOGRAPHY

Abdelhadi, Souad, et al. "Perceptual Load in the Reading of Arabic: Effects of Orthographic Visual Complexity on Detection." *Writing Systems Research* 3 (2011) 117–27.

Abu-Rabia, Salim, et al. "Word Recognition and Basic Cognitive Processes among Reading-Disabled and Normal Readers in Arabic." *Reading and Writing: An Interdisciplinary Journal* 16 (2003) 423–42.

Andrews, Edna. "Language and Brain: Recasting Meaning in the Definition of Human Language." *Semiotica* 184 (2011) 11–32.

Archer, Shirley. "Digital Distractions." *IDEA Fitness Journal* (June 2013) 46–54.

---

101. See, e.g. Buth, *Living Biblical Hebrew*; Overland, *Learning Biblical Hebrew Interactively*.

102. Zevit, "Talking Funny in Biblical Henglish," 25.

Bergh, Luna, and Tanya Beelders. "An Eye-Tracking Account of Reference Points, Cognitive Affordance and Multimodal Metaphors." In *Multimodal Epistemologies: Towards an Integrated Framework,* edited by Arianna Maiorani and Christine Christie, 13–27. London: Routledge, 2014.

Biedert, Ralf, et al. "A Robust Realtime Reading-Skimming Classifier." In *Proceedings of ETRA 2012,* Santa Barbara (2012) 123–30.

Buth, Randall. *Living Biblical Hebrew: Introduction. Part One.* Jerusalem: Biblical Language Center, 2006.

Buth, Randall. *Living Biblical Hebrew. Part Two.* Jerusalem: Biblical Language Center, 2006.

Corcos, Evelyne, and Dale. M. Willows, "The Processing of Orthographic Information." In *Visual Processes in Reading and Reading Disabilities,* edited by Dale. M. Willows et al., 163–88. Dordrecht: Kluwer Academic, 2012.

Dehaene, Stanislas. *Reading in the Brain: The New Science of How We Read.* New York: Penguin, 2009.

Duchowski, Andrew T. *Eye Tracking Methodology: Theory and Practice.* 2nd ed. London: Springer, 2007.

Eviatar, Zohar, et al. "Orthography and the Hemispheres: Visual and Linguistic Aspects of Letter Processing." *Neuropsychology* 18 (2004) 174–84.

Findlay, John M., and Iain M. Gilchrist. *Active Vision: The Psychology of Looking and Seeing.* Oxford: Oxford University Press, 2003.

Frost, Ram. "Becoming Literate in Hebrew: The Grain-Size Hypothesis and Semitic Orthographic Systems." *Developmental Science* 9 (2006) 439–44.

———. "Phonological Computation and Missing Vowels: Mapping Lexical Involvement in Reading." *Journal of Experimental Psychology: Learning, Memory, and Cognition* 21 (1995) 398–408.

———. "Prelexical and Postlexical Strategies in Reading: Evidence from a Deep and a Shallow Orthography." *Journal of Experimental Psychology: Learning, Memory, and Cognition* 20 (1994) 116–29.

———. "Reading in Hebrew vs. Reading in English: Is There a Qualitative Difference?" In *How Children Learn To Read: Current Issues and New Directions in the Integration of Cognition, Neurobiology and Genetics of Reading and Dyslexia Research and Practice,* edited by Ken Pugh and Peggy McCradle, 235–54. New York: Psychology Press, 2009.

Frost, Ram, et al. "Decomposing Complex Words in a Nonlinear Morphology." *Journal of Experimental Psychology: Learning, Memory, and Cognition* 26 (2000) 751–65.

———. "Morphological Priming: Dissociation of Phonological, Semantic, and Morphological Factors." *Memory and Cognition* 28 (2000) 1277–88.

———. "What Can We Learn from the Morphology of Hebrew: A Masked Priming Investigation of Morphological Representation." *Journal of Experimental Psychology: Learning, Memory, and Cognition* 23 (1997) 829–56.

Gärdenfors, Peter. "Some Tenets of Cognitive Semantics." In *Cognitive Semantics: Meaning and Cognition,* edited by Jens Allwood and Peter Gärdenfors, 19–37. Amsterdam: Benjamins, 1999.

Geva, Esther, and Linda Siegel. "Orthographic Factors in the Concurrent Development of Basic Reading Skills in Two Languages." *Reading and Writing* 12 (2000) 1–30.

Gregory, Richard L. *The Eye and the Brain: The Psychology of Seeing.* London: World University Library, 1966.

Hyrskykari, Aulikki. "Eye in Attentive Interfaces: Experiences from Creating iDict, a Gaze-Aware Reading Aid." Dissertations in Interactive Technology, 4. University of Tampere, 2006.
Ibrahim, Raphiq. "Reading in Arabic: New Evidence for the Role of Vowel Signs." *Creative Education* 4 (2013) 248–53.
Ibrahim, Raphiq, et al. "The Characteristics of the Arabic Orthography Slow its Cognitive Processing." *Neuropsychology* 16 (2002) 322–26.
Kress, Gunther, and Theo Van Leeuwen. *Reading Images*. 2nd ed. London: Routledge, 2006.
Lakoff, George, and Mark Johnson. *Metaphors We Live By*. Chicago: University of Chicago Press, 1980/2003.
Langacker, Ronald W. *Foundations of Cognitive Grammar*. Vol. I. Stanford: Stanford University Press, 1987.
Lee, Jennifer, et al. "The Impact of Media Multitasking on Learning." *Learning, Media and Technology* 9 (2009) 1–11.
Luegi, Paula, et al. "Using Eye-Tracking to Detect Reading Difficulties." *Journal of Eye Tracking, Visual Cognition and Emotion* 1 (2011) 41–49.
Martinez-Conde, Susana, and Stephen L. Macknik. "Fixational Eye Movements across Vertebrates: Comparative Dynamics, Physiology, and Perception." *Journal of Vision* 8 (2008) 1–16.
Miller, Earl K., and Jonathan D. Cohen. "An Integrative Theory of Prefrontal Cortex Function." *Annual Review of Neuroscience* 24 (2001) 167–202.
Miller-Naudé, Cynthia L., and Jacobus A. Naudé. "A Typological, Complex Systems Approach to the Teaching of Biblical Hebrew Reading." In *Discourse, Dialogue, and Debate in the Bible: Essays in Honour of Frank H. Polak*, edited by Athalya Brenner-Idan, 92–106. Hebrew Bible Monographs 63. Sheffield: Sheffield Phoenix, 2014.
Morrison, Robert E., and Albrecht-Werner Inhoff. "Visual Factors and Eye Movements in Reading." *Visible Language* 15 (1981) 129–46.
Nassaji, Hossein. "Issues in Second-language Reading: Implications for Acquisition and Instruction." *Reading Research Quarterly* 46 (2009) 173–84.
Overland, Paul. *Learning Biblical Hebrew Interactively*. 2 vols. Sheffield: Sheffield Phoenix, 2014.
Packman, Ann. "Theory and Therapy in Stuttering: A Complex Relationship." *Journal of Fluency Disorders* 37 (2012) 225–33.
Packman, Ann, and Lesley Kuhn. "Looking at Stuttering through the Lens of Complexity." *International Journal of Speech-Language Pathology* 11 (2009) 77–82.
Perfetti, Charles. "Reading." In *The Cambridge Encyclopedia of the Language Sciences*, edited by Patrick Colm Hogan, 699–702. Cambridge: Cambridge University Press, 2011.
Rayner, Keith. "Eye Movements in Reading and Information Processing: 20 Years of Research." *Psychological Bulletin* 124 (1998) 372–422.
Rayner, Keith, and Monica Castelhano. "Eye Movements." *Scholarpedia* 2 (2007) 3649. http://www.scholarpedia.org/article/Eye_movements.
Rayner, Keith, and Alexander Pollastek. *The Psychology of Reading*. Englewood Cliffs, NJ: Prentice-Hall, 1989.
Share, David. L. "On the Anglocentricities of Current Reading Research and Practice: The Perils of Overreliance on an 'Outlier' Orthography." *Psychological Bulletin* 134 (2008) 584–615.

Share, David L., and Iris Levin. "Learning to Read and Write in Hebrew." In *Learning to Read and Write: A Cross-Linguistic Perspective*, edited by Margaret Harris and Giyoo Hatano, 98–111. New York: Cambridge University Press, 1999.

Shatil, Evelyn, and David Share. "Cognitive Antecedents of Early Reading Ability: A Test of the Modularity Hypothesis." *Journal of Experimental Child Psychology* 86 (2003) 1–31.

Sharmin, Selina, et al. "The Effect of Different Text Presentation Formats on Eye Movement Metrics in Reading." *Journal of Eye Movement Research* 5 (2012) 1–9.

Shimron, Joseph, and Tamar Sivan. "Reading Proficiency and Orthography: Evidence from Hebrew and English." *Language Learning* 44 (1994) 5–27.

Siegenthaler, Eva, et al. "Comparing Reading Processes on E-ink Displays and Print." *Displays* 32 (2011) 268–73.

Smith, Frank. *Understanding Reading: A Psycholinguistic Analysis of Reading and Learning to Read*. 5th ed. Hillsdale, NJ: Erlbaum, 1994.

Taha, Haitham Y. "Reading and Spelling in Arabic: Linguistic and Orthographic Complexity." *Theory and Practice in Language Studies* 3 (2013) 721–27.

Tobii. "An Introduction to Eye Tracking and Tobii Eye Trackers." http://www.tobii.com/en/eye-tracking-research/global/library/white-papers/tobii-eye-tracking-white-paper.

Van Rooy, Bertus, and Elizabeth Pretorius. "Is Reading in an Agglutinative Language Different from an Analytic Language? An Analysis of isiZulu and English Reading Based on Eye Movements." *Southern African Linguistics and Applied Language Studies* 31 (2013) 281–97.

Ware, Colin. *Visual Thinking for Design*. Amsterdam: Elsevier, 2008.

Zevit, Ziony. *Matres Lectionis in Ancient Hebrew Epigraphs*. ASOR Monograph Series, 2. Cambridge, MA: American Schools of Oriental Research, 1980.

———. "Talking Funny in Biblical Henglish and Solving a Problem of the *YAQTUL* Past Tense." *HS* 29 (1988) 25–33.

19

Syntactic-Stylistic Aspects of the So-Called "Priestly" Work in the *Torah*

Frank H. Polak

TEL-AVIV UNIVERSITY

The vexed question of the dating of the pentateuchal texts that have been attributed, since Graf, Nöldeke, Kuenen and Wellhausen, to the diverse strata of the so-called "Priestly" "source" or "document," has led to severe differences of opinion that have persisted to haunt scholarship until the present day. In this study I wish to present the picture as I view it in light of large scale syntactic-stylistic analysis. The picture is far from simple. On the one hand, several text groups reveal a mixture of two styles. A number of sections in these groups are characterized by syntactic-stylistic patterns that are close to spontaneous spoken language and thus suggest oral roots or close contacts with the oral arena, such as, in narrative, Gen 1; 9; 17; Lev 9–10; Num 4; and in the parenetic-cultic-legal realm, Lev 11–13; 18–21; 25–27. However, these groups also include large sections in an intricate, elaborate style that is characteristic of the scribal desk: in narrative Gen 6–8; 28:1–9; Exod 6–7; and in the parenetic-cultic-legal sphere: Exod 12; Lev 14–15; 17; 22–24.

Other groups of texts are strongly dominated by the intricate style, but nevertheless reveal certain signs of underlying orality. I find these features in the cultic precepts (Lev 1–4; 16) and the instructions for the *miškān* (such as Exod 25; 28; 29).

These considerations raise the question how to view this particular mixture of scribal style and features that are close to orality. This question is to be discussed in the concluding section of this study. I do so in honor of Ziony Zevit's contributions to this issue, and in particular his emphasis on the need of converging lines of evidence from different domains, including exegesis, archaeology, and language study.[1] Hence this study is to honor Ziony, of old a comrade in arms and ideas, from the days of Menahem Haran's Ezekiel seminar at the Hebrew University in Jerusalem, until various panels at the SBL annual meetings concerning the dating, and in particular the linguistic dating, of biblical texts. In various conversations he has tried persuading me to discuss the linguistic profile of "P." The present study is dedicated to this subject and, of course, to Ziony.

1. P-Work and P-strata

As Norbert Lohfink has shown, the P-work is defined by the integration of narrative, legal and cultic themes in an overarching "story" in which history and legislation is embedded within a cosmological picture.[2] Hence in spite of the overwhelming diversity of the texts assembled here, it seems possible to recognize a multi-layered P-work with its various different subsections (including the alleged main and supplementary strata: P^G/P^S): the narrative pericopes; the section of the *miškān* (the "tabernacle," Exod 25–31; 35–40); the sacrificial precepts (P^O, Lev 1–5; 6–7; with the different subsections); the Purity Code (Lev 11–15); the Holiness Code (H, Lev 17; 18–26; 27), with its redaction (H^R, with traces in other P-strata), and the Priestly Redaction (P^R, in complex relationship with H^R). In spite of this diversity, the majority view ascribes the P-work in its entirety to the exilic/postexilic period, in particular in view of the fact that these strata present one single sanctuary, in accordance with the Deuteronomic call for centralization of the cult. True, this position has been problematized by a number of weighty problems: the status of profane slaughter (and thereby the eating of meat in non-ritual context), allowed by Deut 12 but forbidden by Lev 17; the Passover

---

1. The relevant essays, in chronological order, are: Zevit, "Converging Lines of Evidence"; Zevit, "Philology, Archeology and P's Legislation"; Zevit, *Religions of Ancient Israel*, 267–343, 613–90; Zevit, "What a Difference"; Zevit, "Not-So-Random Thoughts"; and Zevit, "Dating Torah Documents," 281–91.

2. Lohfink, "Priestly Narrative and History," 149, envisions a "re-translation of history into myth."

ritual that demands the smearing of blood on the doorpost of the house in order to protect it from the "destroyer" (Exod 12), whereas Deuteronomy demands the slaughter at the central sanctuary (as still performed by the Samaritans);[3] and the gifts to the priests consisting of the tenths of the gifts received by the Levites (Num 18:21–32), whereas in the postexilic period the latter class was a small minority.[4] However, in the exegetical discussion these problems are solved by the notion that the P-work includes older texts, in a multi-generational framework.[5] In this connection it is important to note the position of August Klostermann, followed by, for instance, Jan Joosten—who set out to prove that Ezekiel's prophecy presupposes the Holiness Code, and in particular the series of blessings and curses in Lev 26.[6]

However, the analysis of language usage fails to confirm the assumption of exilic/postexilic origin of these strata. Avi Hurvitz has shown that the lexical register of the P-work consistently uses Classical Biblical Hebrew (CBH) terms where the legislation of Ezekiel contains Late Biblical Hebrew (LBH) features,[7] while Robert Polzin proves that the syntactic usage of the P-work does not fit LBH, although some LBH features are found in some parts of the corpus, which often have been set apart from the main corpus (P^G) as a supplement (P^S).[8]

Two additional issues demand some attention. First, Meir Paran pointed to the widespread use of parallelism in the P-work, in P-narrative, in the ritual sections and in "H."[9] Although Paran dismissed the possibility of any

---

3. This issue is not mentioned by Blenkinsopp, "Alleged Pre-Exilic Date," for which see Milgrom, "Antiquity of the Priestly Source"; and Hurvitz, "Once Again: Linguistic Profile."

4. This question is analyzed by Zevit, "Converging Lines of Evidence," 485–93.

5. Blenkinsopp, "Alleged Pre-Exilic Date," 511.

6. Klostermann, "Beiträge," 409–17, 431–2, 443–4; Joosten, *People and Land*, 203–7.

7. Hurvitz, *Linguistic Study of the Relationship*; Hurvitz, "Dating the Priestly Source"; Milgrom, *Leviticus* 1.2–7. Qimron, "Review," 237, counters that the cultic-legal sections of Ezekiel 40–48 may postdate the prophetic book. But this argument disregards the evidence from the preceding sections of Ezekiel. In the view of our honoree (Zevit, "Converging Lines of Evidence," 494) the language usage of Ezekiel is sufficiently explained by his situation as an exile living in Babylonia, and thus does not bear on the lack of LBH features in the P-work. See also Mizrahi, "Two Hebrew Titles for the High Priest." Mizrahi, "Go Figure," shows that the form עַשְׁתֵּי־עֶשְׂרֵה, "eleven," which in Tanakh is only found in "P" and in exilic/post-exilic texts, cannot be explained as a borrowing from Aramaic or Babylonian, but must reflect an ancient numeral, עשתי, "one," also attested in Ugaritic, Epigraphic (and new) South Arabic, and (without ʿayin) in Akkadian (*ištēn*); so already Brockelmann, *Grundriss*, 1.490.

8. Polzin, *Late Biblical Hebrew*; reviewed by Rendsburg, "Late Biblical Hebrew"; and commented upon by Hurvitz, *Linguistic Study of the Relationship*, 164–70.

9. Paran, *Forms of the Priestly Style*, 98–134, X–XI.

connection between this use of parallelism and the epic tradition,[10] one may note that one of the features that has served to characterize the narrative in the P-work, the congruence of command and execution,[11] is characteristic of all ancient Near Eastern epic compositions, such as Atram-hasis, Enuma Elish, and the epic texts from Ugarit, and actually is also found in, for example, the David narrative (2 Sam 3:21, 23; 14:24).[12] Here, then, one might nevertheless sense a continuity that links certain strata of the P-work to the oral-epic roots of the biblical literary tradition.

And second, in this connection I have to point to the views of Klaus Koch, whose analysis of the instructions for the building of the Ark (Exod 25:10–16) indicates long sequences of "short clauses consisting of three or four elements (*drei- bis viergliedrichen Kurzsätzen*), all starting with a we-qatal, in series of three, four, five, ten, twelve, and even thirty clauses (*Gliedern*)."[13] His term for this syntactic-stylistic constellation is the "formulaic style" (*Formularstil*), whereas he describes the normal, more elaborate style of the P-work as the "periodic (command-)style" (*Gefügter [Befehls-] Stil*). Since he was able to show that the "periodic style" also appears in technical precepts in the same context (Exod 26), he concluded that the "formulaic style" is not context conditioned, but harks back to a preceding, ancient Vorlage, originating in the oral tradition, whereas the "periodic style" represents a later revision, during which the ancient formulaic language is transformed into a scribal style ("*zerschrieben*").[14] Thus Koch explains the transition from the oral to the written in the field of ritual instructions and

---

10. Ibid., 134–6.

11. McEvenue, *Narrative Style of the Priestly Writer*, 28–33. McEvenue's thesis concerning the similarity of the style of the P-work to children's literature and the fairy tale is entirely spurious, since fairy tales originally were not addressing "children and household"; as shown by the great scholar of ethnopoetics, Dégh, "Grimm's Household Tales," and admitted by McEvenue himself (*Narrative Style of the Priestly Writer*, 127–31).

12. Polak, *Biblical Narrative*, 60, 73; see also Houtman, *Exodus*, 3.309; and Hurowitz, "Priestly Account," 26 –28; and for Sumerian: Berlin, *Enmerkar and Ensuḫkešdanna*, 18–25; Berlin, "Shared Rhetorical Figures"; and Vanstiphout, "Repetition and Structure." Actually, so much is admitted by McEvenue, *Narrative Style of the Priestly Writer*, 28.

13. Koch, *Priesterschrift*, 7–8. Unfortunately, a striking lack of precision in terminology and analysis prevented Koch from perceiving the difference between the language of orality and this style, which in the end is still very much "scribal" in its use of noun groups. Koch perceives a strong distinction between Exod 25:1–9 and the following stretches, but syntactic analysis shows that this difference is limited to the long list in 25:4–7, whereas the sequences of short clauses are limited to vv. 10–12. Long clauses and noun groups prevail likewise in vv. 23–31.

14. Koch, *Priesterschrift*, 7–9, 96–99.

priestly *tōrōt*.[15] However, Koch's short discussion remains imprecise and does not establish firm criteria for the distinction between the two styles. What is needed is a systematic analysis of the syntactic-stylistic character of the diverse P-strata.

2. Syntactic-Stylistic Analysis and Literary Stratification

a. The Syntactic-Stylistic Characterization of Biblical Prose

In previous studies I have used a number of parameters for the syntactic-stylistic characterization of biblical narrative:

    a. the number of syntactic constituents dependent on the predicate,

    b. the number of subordinate clauses, and

    c. the number of grouped nouns, appearing in complex noun phrases.[16]

Analysis by this method indicates a distinction between two main groups. The first group is characterized by the predominance of extremely short paratactic clauses, consisting of predicate with implicit subject (and/or object suffix), or predicate with one additional slot, such as explicit subject, object or indication of place/time; subordinate clauses are rare and so are noun groups. An example for some clauses in this style:[17]

וַיֹּאמֶר יַעֲקֹב אֶל־לָבָן / הָבָה אֶת־אִשְׁתִּי / כִּי מָלְאוּ יָמָי / וְאָבוֹאָה אֵלֶיהָ:

וַיֶּאֱסֹף לָבָן אֶת־כָּל־אַנְשֵׁי הַמָּקוֹם / וַיַּעַשׂ מִשְׁתֶּה:

וַיְהִי בָעֶרֶב / וַיִּקַּח אֶת־לֵאָה בִתּוֹ / וַיָּבֵא אֹתָהּ אֵלָיו / וַיָּבֹא אֵלֶיהָ:

> Thus Jacob said to Laban, "Give me my wife, for my days are fulfilled, and let me cohabit with her." So Laban gathered all the people of the place and made a feast. And evening came, and he took his daughter Leah and brought her to him, and he cohabited with her. (Gen 29:21–23)

---

15. Rendtorff, *Die Gesetze in der Priesterschrift*, 5–22, describes "ritual" as a particular Gattung in Lev 1–3, aimed at the fixation of the rite.

16. Polak, "Sociolinguistics," 127–51; Polak, "Oral and Written," 76–100; and Polak, "Language Variation and Sociocultural Background," 310–24. The linguistic basis for this method is indicated in n.19 below.

17. The slash indicates the clause boundary. The English translations usually follow NJPSV, sometimes with slight modifications, in particular with regard to the tetragrammaton.

In this sequence we note a large number of short paratactic clauses: the entire third line (v. 23) and further הָבָה אֶת־אִשְׁתִּי, כִּי מָלְאוּ יָמָי, וְאָבוֹאָה אֵלֶיהָ. This sequence includes two short noun groups: כָּל־אַנְשֵׁי הַמָּקוֹם and לֵאָה בִתּוֹ. Two clauses include explicit subject and object/addressee: וַיֶּאֱסֹף לָבָן אֶת־כָּל־אַנְשֵׁי הַמָּקוֹם and וַיֹּאמֶר יַעֲקֹב אֶל־לָבָן. A large number of clauses include implicit subjects: in Jacob's request: וְאָבוֹאָה אֵלֶיהָ; in the description of Laban's response וַיִּקַּח אֶת־לֵאָה בִתּוֹ / וַיָּבֵא אֹתָהּ אֵלָיו and וַיַּעַשׂ מִשְׁתֶּה; and finally, with unmarked shift to Jacob: וַיָּבֹא אֵלֶיהָ. There are no subordinate clauses. The indication of time is presented in a paratactic *wayhi* clause (וַיְהִי בָעֶרֶב).[18]

This passage exemplifies the voiced, lean, brisk style (VoLB), which presents the information in short chunks and thus is close to the syntax of spontaneous spoken discourse, as analyzed in many cross-linguistic and cross-cultural discussions.[19] I distinguish between the type-1 style (48–60% short clauses), and the type-2 style (39–47% short clauses). The VoLB style prevails in the narratives of the patriarchs; the exodus-Sinai narrative; Judges 3–9, 12–19; the Samuel-Saul-David tales and the stories of Elijah, Elisha and contemporary prophets, comprising, in short, the oral-written corpus.

Quite a different style is revealed in the corpus of narratives that represents the Deuteronomic school and congeners. These texts are characterized by the low frequency of short paratactic clauses (around 25–35% of the text) and the high frequency of subordinate clauses and long noun groups, such as the following parenetic narrative:[20]

וָאוֹלֵךְ אֶתְכֶם אַרְבָּעִים שָׁנָה בַּמִּדְבָּר / לֹא־בָלוּ שַׂלְמֹתֵיכֶם מֵעֲלֵיכֶם /

וְנַעַלְךָ לֹא־בָלְתָה מֵעַל רַגְלֶךָ: / לֶחֶם לֹא אֲכַלְתֶּם / וְיַיִן וְשֵׁכָר לֹא שְׁתִיתֶם /

-לְמַעַן תֵּדְעוּ כִּי אֲנִי יְהוָה אֱלֹהֵיכֶם:

---

18. See Joosten, "Diachronic Aspects of Narrative *Wayhi*," 50–61. In modern English translations a clause of this type is often rendered as a subordinate time clause (NJPSV: "When evening came"), or is integrated in the next clause (NRSV: "But in the evening he took his daughter Leah"). These renderings obscure the strongly paratactic structure of the classical Hebrew narrative style.

19. I refer to the cross-cultural, cross-linguistic distinctions between the oral and the written style established by such eminent linguists as Wallace Chafe, Michael Halliday, Regina Weinert and Jim Miller (followed by Douglas Biber and Susan Conrad), for which see Polak, "Orality," 932; Polak, "Sociolinguistics," 132–33, 139, 149; and Polak, "Oral and Written," 60, n. 9, 101–2, nn. 57–62, 68.

20. The hyphen indicates a subordinate clause, and the equal sign a clause that is dependent on a hypotactic clause (complex hypotaxis).

I have led you forty years in the wilderness. The clothes on your back have not worn out, and the sandals on your feet have not worn out; you have not eaten bread, and you have not drunk wine or strong drink, in order that you may know, that I am YHWH your God (Deut 29:4–5).

וּשְׁמַרְתֶּם אֶת־דִּבְרֵי הַבְּרִית הַזֹּאת

וַעֲשִׂיתֶם אֹתָם־לְמַעַן תַּשְׂכִּילוּ אֵת כָּל־אֲשֶׁר תַּעֲשׂוּן:

Therefore observe faithfully all the terms of this covenant, in order that you may succeed in all that you undertake (Deut 29:8; following the NJPSV with slight variation).

This sequence includes two short clauses:
לֶחֶם לֹא אֲכַלְתֶּם and וְיַיִן וְשֵׁכָר לֹא שְׁתִיתֶם
three noun groups:
אַרְבָּעִים שָׁנָה, וְיַיִן וְשֵׁכָר, דִּבְרֵי הַבְּרִית הַזֹּאת, and
and two final clauses with embedded object clause:
לְמַעַן תֵּדְעוּ כִּי אֲנִי יְהוָה אֱלֹהֵיכֶם,
or relative clause:
לְמַעַן תַּשְׂכִּילוּ אֵת כָּל־אֲשֶׁר תַּעֲשׂוּן.

One notes two clauses with two explicit constituents (subject and indirect object: וְנַעַלְךָ לֹא־בָלְתָה מֵעַל רַגְלֶךָ / לֹא־בָלוּ שַׂלְמֹתֵיכֶם מֵעֲלֵיכֶם). An apparently simple clause includes indication of time and place, in addition to the direct object: וָאוֹלֵךְ אֶתְכֶם אַרְבָּעִים שָׁנָה בַּמִּדְבָּר. This quote exemplifies the intricate elaborate style (IES), which is prevalent in Deut 1–3; 9–10; 34; almost the entire book of Joshua (apart from Josh 2; 10); 1 Kgs 3–16; 2 Kgs 12–25; Jer 26; 36–43, comprising, in short, the Judean corpus. The IES is also in use in the texts originating in the Persian era, often with extremely high values for the complexities of syntactic subordination and long noun groups. This tendency is very strong in the Ezra chronicle and Chronicles, but less so in the Nehemiah memoirs and the scroll of Esther (the Achaemenid corpus, generally characterized by the many features borrowed from Aramaic).

b. *The Sociocultural Background of the Syntactic-Stylistic Distinctions*

One could assume that the differences between the IES and the VoLB are merely a matter of free stylistic formulation and rhetorical choice. However, careful analysis of almost ninety tales in all three corpora, centering on four different themes, indicates that the distinction between these corpora crosses theme and literary genre:[21]

a. When we look at the three corpora, the variation between the four thematic groups within these corpora is not great, in spite of the thematic and rhetorical differences; and

b. When we look at the various corpora within each of the four thematic groups, one notes significant differences between the corpora within each group, in spite of the common theme.

Thus the distinctive syntactic-stylistic profile of the three corpora is not to be explained in terms of free stylistic-rhetorical choice. An alternative explanation is called for. In this regard the linguistic characteristics of the IES provide an important cue.

The linguistic character of the elaborate style indicates a specific sociocultural background. The intricacies of the IES represent the cross-cultural, cross-linguistic characteristics of writing, which enables planning, rereading and correction, and thus is the product of a long period of training and education. Consequently, the use of this style indicates a scribal education imparting the required expertise. The use of the IES, and the largely uniform orthography,[22] in the epigraphic remains of ancient Hebrew shows that the professional scribes were educated in the norms of the official chancery.[23] The stylistic sophistication implies that this *locus* is to be identified with the royal Judean chancery.[24] The archeology of writing places this *locus* in the second half of the 8th and the 7th century.[25] It is highly unlikely that

---

21. See Polak, "Sociolinguistics," 132–6, 141–8; Polak, "Book of Samuel and Deuteronomist," 58–61, 69–73; and Polak, "Language Variation and Sociocultural Background," 310–11, 317. The four thematic groups are: battle tales, tales of anointment or public honor, festive/cultive meals, and religious discourse (prayer or prophecy).

22. The qualifier "largely" is necessitated by the honoree's investigations into the deviations from the orthographic rules, such as the graph איש in the ostraca from Lachish (3:9–10) and Arad (40:7–8); see Zevit, *Matres Lectionis*.

23. I am not entering into the question of the existence of a "school," since even formal classes probably largely represented the personal activity of the teacher-scribe, as demonstrated by the Ahiqar narrative and the "class room" found at Nippur.

24. Contacts with the official chancery are implied by the administrative data in the book of Kings, such as the age of the king when ascending to the throne, for this datum implies that the date of the birth of the king was recorded and known to the redactor of the dynastic-chronological framework; see also Leuchter, "Sociolinguistic and Rhetorical Implications," 122–4.

25. For the remains of writing, in bullae and seals, from 7th-century Judea see, for convenience, Millard, "Corpus of West-Semitic Stamp Seals"; Millard, "Books and Writing in Kings"; Lemaire, "Levantine Literacy," 29–34; Na'aman, "Literacy in the Negev"; and Na'aman, "The Distribution of Messages." The social background of

this style was created under the Babylonian and Persian domination by the scribes of the by now provincial chancery of Jerusalem when the language of the administration was official Aramaic.

By contrast, in its close resemblance to spoken language, in particular in the frequency of sequences of short paratactic clauses,[26] the VoLB shows its affinity to oral narrative. Narrators using this style, then, adhere to the habitus of the oral arena. Their fluency in and preference for this habitus indicates a sociocultural context in which the oral performance was a respected, prestigeous, and thus, in a sense, authoritative institution in society, as the bard/*aoidos* was in the Homeric context, the court minstrel in the European Middle Ages, and the guslar in pre-modern Serbo-Croatia and Bosnia. When one considers the large "Ceremonial Hall" 611 of the MB II palace at Tel Kabri,[27] one can easily imagine the role of the Singer of Tales in the Middle and Late Bronze Age, as indeed indicated by the appearance of the singer in the famous banquet scene in the Baʻal myth (*CAT* 1.3 I, lines 18–22).[28] This background entails a sociohistorical context which precedes the emergence of the well-developed royal bureaucracy in the 8th century.

So where does the P-work stand?

3. The Syntactic-Stylistic Profile of the P-Work

In view of the diversity of the various strata in the P-work it seems preferable to distinguish between different genres. Different subchapters, then, will serve to review the data for the narrative sections, the Purity and Holiness Codes (Lev 11–15; 17; 18–26; 27), and the cultic precepts.

a. The P-Narratives

Most narrative sections attributed to the P-work reveal the intricate, elaborate style.[29] In patriarchal narrative one notes the tales on the Cave of Mach-

---

ancient Israelite writing is discussed by Niditch, *Oral World*, 45–77, 95–105; and by Schniedewind, *How the Bible became a Book*, 66–75, 93–106.

26. Such as, e.g., Gen 19:1b–3; 32:26–30; 2 Sam 1:6–10a; and see Polak, "Book of Samuel and Deuteronomist," 51–52.

27. See Yasur-Landau et al., " MB II Orthostat Building at Tel Kabri," 22; Koh et al., "Middle Bronze Palatial Wine."

28. However, Smith and Pitard, *Ugaritic Baal Cycle*, 91–97, 113–5, argue that this banquet, which did not involve the mention/presence of other gods, was private; see also Smith, "Baal Cycle," 106.

29. This analysis has not been applied to single verses, in which anything is

pelah (23:1–20), Abraham's burial (Gen 25:1, 5–11), and Jacob's blessing of Isaac (28:1–9). In the narrative of the Exodus and the revelation at Mount Sinai this stratum includes the second tale of Moses' call (6:2–13; 6:26—7:6); the sign of the serpents (7:8–13); the plague of the boils (9:8–12); the section on the radiant face of Moses (34:29–35); the opening sections of the building of the tabernacle (35:1–36:7); and parts of the tales of the splitting of the Sea (14:1–4, 8–10*, 15–18, 22–23, 27*–29);[30] and the manna (16:1–3, 6–12, 15b–21a, 22–26, 32–33).[31] Similar data are found for the tales concerning the wanderings in the desert (Num 13–14;[32] 16–17;[33] 20; 31). For comparison I offer the data for the tale of Moses' death, parts of which have been attributed to "P." In the following tables the abbreviation ELC indicates an "explicit lexical constituent" (or, in other words, a part of speech) dependent immediately on the predicate, such as subject, direct/indirect object or temporal/local/final modifier (not including the suffixed pronouns). The sign "0–1 ELC" indicates short clauses (predicate with implied subject only, or predicate with one ELC), whereas the graph "2+ ELC" refers to all clauses with at least two 2 ELC's. The term Mean Noun Phrase (MNP) indicates the number of grouped nouns, divided by two (and thus expressed as noun pairs). The term "Complex Hypotaxis," a particular subset of "All Hypotaxis," refers to clauses that are dependent on subordinate clauses, or include a noun group or at least two ELC's. Another special subset includes the clauses that contain at least three ELC's (3+ ELC). These particular subcategories, if large enough, are indicative of particular scribal expertise.[34]

---

possible.

30. Here and below, the asterisk (*) indicates that only a portion of the verse or chapter listed is ascribed to the stratum at hand.

31. For the manna tale many different analyses have been proposed. If one adopts the present analysis (partly following Baentsch, *Exodus - Leviticus - Numeri*, 144–9; partly Holzinger, *Exodus*, 53–54; and partly Dillmann, *Exodus und Leviticus*, 180–81), the "non-P" section (4–5, 13–15a, 21b, 27–28 Dtr? 29–30 31, 35a) reveals a VoLB (type 2) profile (44.44% short clauses; 20.00% subordination, 45.46% grouped nouns).

32. Gray, *Numbers*, 130–32, attributes to non-P: 13:17b, 18–20, 21 (וַיַּעֲלוּ), 22–24, 26b; 14:1*, 3–4, 8–9, 11–24, 25, 26*, 39–45; and to P: 13:1–17a, 21, 25, 26*; 14:1 (וַתִּשָּׂא כָּל־הָעֵדָה), 2, 5–7, 10.

33. The P section of Num 16 includes, following Gray, *Numbers*, 188–9: 1*–2*, 3–11, 16–23, 26a, 27a*, 35. The non-P ("J") section (vv. 1*–2*, 12–15, 25, 26b, 27–32a, 33*, 34) likewise reveals a IES profile, much unlike the VoLB (types 1–2) of patriarchal narrative, for which see Polak, "Oral Substratum," 229–33.

34. Entries such as "Exod 14P," etc., refer to only those verses in the chapter ascribed to P. This table, like most other tables, is ordered from the highest figure for short clauses (Gen 9; 25) to the lowest figure, with Deut 34 as additional example.

Table 1. P-Narrative (IES)

Class / Unit	Number Clauses	0–1 ELC	2+ ELC	All Hypotaxis	Mean Noun Phrase	Complex Hypotaxis	3+ ELC
Gen 25:1, 5–11	19	42.11	42.11	15.79	121.05	5.26	26.32
Gen 9:1–26	51	41.18	37.25	21.57	104.90	13.73	13.73
Num 17	97	38.14	40.21	21.65	65.46	10.31	13.40
Num 16P	65	36.92	41.54	21.54	76.47	7.69	13.85
Exod 7:8–13	22	36.36	40.91	22.73	43.18	9.09	13.64
Exod 14P	50	34.00	54.00	12.00	70.00	4.00	8.00
Exod 16P	109	33.03	33.94	33.03	41.28	17.43	12.84
Gen 7:6, 11, 13, 14, 16a, 17a, 18–21, 24 8:1, 2a, 3b, 4b, 5, 13a, 14–19	41	31.71	51.22	17.07	158.54	---	14.63
Num 20	47	29.79	44.68	25.53	60.34	12.77	23.4
Exod 6:2—7:6	78	29.49	44.87	25.64	62.18	18.46	10.26
Exod 9:8–12	17	29.41	47.06	23.53	88.24	5.88	23.53
Num 13–14P	36	27.78	41.67	30.56	118.06	19.44	16.67
Gen 23:1–16, 19–20	56	26.79	50.00	23.21	83.04	7.14	21.43
Gen 28:1–9	31	22.58	41.94	35.48	83.88	35.48	9.68
Num 31	46	19.57	54.35	26.09	163.04	15.22	17.39
Exod 35	93	15.05	35.48	49.46	113.44	38.71	13.98
Exod 34:29–35	31	12.90	45.16	41.94	50.00	25.81	9.68
Deut 34:1–10	25	28.57	46.43	25.00	114.29	21.49	28.57

In spite of the diversity of these data, all these sections fit the IES profile. The figures for short clauses range mostly from 27 to 36% (so also Deut 34), with some lower values (12–19% in Exod 34:29–35; 35; Num 31). An exceptional case is presented by the tales of the flood (Gen 9) and Abraham's burial (Gen 25:1, 5–11) in which the high number of short clauses (41 and 42% respectively) would fit the VoLB profile (type 2). However, in both narratives the extremely high values for the frequency of grouped nouns indicate an IES profile.

The figures for hypotaxis (including complex subordination) range for the most part from 20 to 30% (Gen 9; 23; Exod 6–7; 7:8–13; 9:8–12; Num 13–14P; 16P; 17; 20; 31; similarly Deut 34), with a few narratives in the 10–20% range (Gen 6; 7–8), the 30–40% range (Gen 28:1–9; Exod 16P), or the 40–50% range (Exod 34:29–35; 35).

The percentage of grouped nouns ranges mostly from 60 to 80% (Exod 6:2—7:6; 14P; Num16P; 17; 20), with a few tales in the 40–50% range (Exod 7:8–13; 16P; 34:29–35). Higher values are found for Gen 6; 23; 28:1–9; Exod 9:8–12 (all in the 80–90% range). In five passages the values found are larger than 100%, indicating that grouped nouns are in the mean found in each and every clause, with many clauses containing more than one noun pair (Gen 7–8; 9; 25:1, 5–11; Exod 35; Num 13–14P; 31; similarly Deut 34).

This is not the only way in which P-narratives suggest diversity. A number of passages reveal the lean, brisk style of the oral-written corpus: the tales of Nadab and Abihu (Lev 10), the inauguration of the altar (Lev 9), and the scene of Abraham's blessing (Gen 17:1–8, 15–22):

Table 2. P-Narrative (VoLB)

Class \ Unit	Number Clauses	0–1 ELC	2+ ELC	All Hypotaxis	Mean Noun Phrase	Complex Hypotaxis	3+ ELC
Gen 17:1–8, 15–22	55	58.18	34.55	7.27	63.64	10.91	3.64
Lev 9:1–24	76	43.42	44.74	11.84	66.45	2.63	11.84
Gen 1:1–19	65	43.08	33.84	23.08	55.38	10.77	12.31
Lev 10:1–10	41	41.46	39.02	19.51	63.41	7.32	12.20
Gen 1:20—2:3	71	38.03	32.39	29.58	71.13	9.86	8.45

The figures for the two consecutive tales concerning the inauguration of the altar and the encroachment by Aaron's sons, Nadab and Abihu (Lev 9:1–24; 10:1–10),[35] suggest a close association with the VoLB (type 2) style, representing a subsection of the oral-written corpus. The profile of these units is a far cry from the intricate style of most narratives in the P-work. A surprising, and rather complex constellation is found in the tale of the blessing of Abraham and Sarah (Gen 17). The sections concerning the blessing and the name change (17:1–8, 15–22) reveal a style that is quite close to the VoLB (type 1) style of the oral-written corpus. The implication is that this narra-

---

35. The connection between Lev 9 and 10, by antithesis, is discussed by Nihan, *From Priestly Torah to Pentateuch*, 91–93.

tive did not arise at the scribal desk, but is rather based on, or adheres to the style of, an oral performance. Actually, the poetic style of the introduction, including the parallelism of the short clauses of the opening blessing, has already drawn the attention of Peter Weimar, who found here residues of an early stratum.[36] A style that dovetails with the IES of most narrative (and cultic instruction) in the P-work is found in the precepts concerning the circumcision (vv. 9–14, 23–27).[37]

These findings raise a severe problem. The blessing of Abraham in Genesis 17 is the first of a series of texts that invoke the divine name "El Shadday," much like Isaac's blessing of Jacob (28:3; so also 35:11; 43:14; 48:3). According to the second tale of Moses' call (Exod 6:3) this is the name by which the deity made Himself known to the patriarchs. Hence the scholarly consensus that this name is characteristic of "P."[38] However, the stylistic profile of the Abraham tale suggests that this appellation originates in an oral-epic substratum. This possibility is in keeping with the use of the name "Shadday" in the poetic tradition as embodied by Balaam's blessings (Num 24:4, 16; so also Ps 91:1, and often in Job). Notably, in the Deir 'Alla inscription the term *šdyn* indicates the deities. Hence the hypothesis that the term Shadday represents ancient tradition rather than particular "P" preferences is in accordance with the philological data.

b. P-Narrative and Orality

These findings could suggest the conclusion that the narrative parts of the P-work ultimately originate in the oral-written arena, rather than in scribal scholarship. This conclusion derives support from the particular stylistic configuration of the creation narrative. The first section of this tale is close to the VoLB (type 2) profile with its relatively high figures for short clauses (43%) and the low figures for noun phrases (55%). Hence it is important to note that this narrative includes a large number of features that are characteristic of the poetic register, such as the lexemes ברא and רְקִיעַ,[39] and the

36. Weimar, "Gen 17," 36–37.

37. Gen 17:9–14, 23–27 (23 clauses, too small for analysis): 0–1 ELC 21.74; all hypotaxis 26.09; Mean Noun Phrase 197.83.

38. One notes the use of "Shadday" in Ezek 1:21; and of "El Shadday" in Ezek 10:5, both in collocation with sound produced in the divine sphere.

39. On ברא see Gunkel, *Genesis*, 120, and cf. Ps 51:12; Ezek 28:13; in allusions to the creation theme: Am 4:13 (paralleled by יצר and עשה); Ps 89:13, 48; Isa 45:7–8, 12, 18; and as a reminder of divine majesty: Isa 40:26, 28; 41:20; 42:5; see also: Isa 4:5; 43:1, 7, 15; 48:7; 54:16; 57:19; Jer 31:22; Ezek 28:15; Mal 2:10; Ps 102:19; 148:5. In the post-Isaian allusions of Isa 65:17–18 the creation theme is applied to the announcement of the coming salvation.

phrases בְּצַלְמֵנוּ כִּדְמוּתֵנוּ (v. 21), עוֹף כָּנָף (vv. 11–12), דֶּשֶׁא עֵשֶׂב (v. 2), תֹהוּ וָבֹהוּ (v. 26) and the morphology of חַיְתוֹ־אֶרֶץ (v.24).[40] Parallelism is found in the tricolon וַיְהִי־עֶרֶב / וַיְהִי־בֹקֶר / יוֹם אֶחָד (v. 5 and further), in perfect rhythmic balance.[41] Hence the present prosaic, narrative text is to be viewed as a palimpsest, written over a poetic, hymnic prototype celebrating the creation.[42] The prosaic overwriting makes itself felt in the elaborate syntax (such as 1:9–10, 17, 26) and the expansions of the noun phrases, for instance:

אֶת־הַתַּנִּינִם הַגְּדֹלִים וְאֵת כָּל־נֶפֶשׁ הַחַיָּה ׀ הָרֹמֶשֶׂת אֲשֶׁר שָׁרְצוּ הַמַּיִם
לְמִינֵהֶם וְאֵת כָּל־עוֹף כָּנָף לְמִינֵהוּ

The great sea monsters, and all the living creatures of every kind that creep, which the waters brought forth in swarms, and all the winged birds of every kind (1:21).

אֶת־חַיַּת הָאָרֶץ לְמִינָהּ וְאֶת־הַבְּהֵמָה לְמִינָהּ וְאֵת כָּל־רֶמֶשׂ הָאֲדָמָה לְמִינֵהוּ

Wild beasts of every kind and cattle of every kind, and all kinds of creeping things of the earth (1:25).[43]

Residues of a poetic formulation have also been found in the tale of the flood (7:11; 8:2),[44] which is, after all, rooted in ancient Near Eastern epic texts.[45] The particular interaction between oral roots and scribal formulation is likewise revealed by the tales of Abraham's burial (Gen 25:1, 5–11) and the divine blessings that close the flood narrative (9:1–26). As noted above (section a), in these sections the figures for short clauses and hypotaxis fit the VoLB (type 2) style, whereas the extremely high frequency of noun groups (100–125%) is indicative of the IES.

It seems probable, then, that the narrative parts of the P-work reflect a long process of textual growth which has its roots in oral narrative and

40. See my study, "Poetic Style and Parallelism," 6–15, with references to previous literature.

41. One notes the pair עֶרֶב / בֹקֶר in Ps 30:6; Gen 49:27; Isa 17:14; Zeph 3:3; Ps 55:18; 65:9; 90:6. The phrase יוֹם אֶחָד represents gapping with ballast variant. Notably, the use of the cardinal (אֶחָד) as ordinal (the first day) is matched by Ugaritic *mk bšb' ym* ("behold, on the seventh day"), for which see Loewenstamm, "Development of the Term 'First.'"

42. So already Cross, *Canaanite Myth and Hebrew Epic*, 301. A hesitant approach is advocated by Smith, *The Priestly Vision of Genesis 1*, 175–7.

43. So also, e.g., 1:11, 26, 29–30; 2:2–3.

44. On the parallelism in the recast of 8:2b in Jub. 5:29 see Loewenstamm, "Flood," 112–3, 115; and already Gunkel, *Genesis*, 144–5. The expression תְּהוֹם רַבָּה, "the great deep" (Gen 7:11), also appears in Amos 7:4; Ps 36:7; Isa 51:10 ("Tehom, the Lady").

45. See in particular Weinfeld, "Gen. 7.11; 8.1–2."

poetry, although the lion's share of these sections reveal the intricate style of the scribal chancery. The presence of residues of oral roots seems unexpected, but is not entirely surprising. After all, a number of scholars have found signs of an oral style in the Holiness Code.

c. *The So-Called Holiness Code (Lev 17; 18–26; 27)*

The parenetic, legal and cultic section in Leviticus 18–26 (including also ch. 17; 27) contains a significant number of passages in the lean, brisk style in tandem with a number of passages in the intricate style, and thus reveals much variation.[46] The VoLB style prevails in the following sections:

Table 3. Lev 18–26; 27: The Voiced, Lean, Brisk Style

Class Unit	Number Clauses	0–1 ELC	2+ ELC	All Hypotaxis	Mean Noun Phrase	Complex Hypotaxis	3+ ELC
Type 1							
19:2–18	57	61.40	31.58	7.02	46.49	3.51	3.51
27:1–33	107	53.27	30.84	15.89	68.22	9.35	13.08
21:1–24	68	51.47	22.06	26.47	76.47	10.29	1.47
18:1–30	90	51.11	22.22	26.67	51.67	8.89	7.78
Type 2							
20:16–27	61	48.18	18.03	32.78	46.72	29.51	3.28
26:14–33	69	44.93	42.03	13.04	28.99	5.80	7.25
25:1–34	106	44.44	37.61	17.59	60.19	3.70	11.11
20:1–15	60	43.33	21.67	35.00	44.17	23.33	8.33
26:1–13	44	43.18	50.00	6.82	22.73	4.55	9.09
25:35–55	64	40.63	40.63	18.75	68.75	7.81	6.25

The syntactic-stylistic profile of chapters 18; 19; 21; and 27 is close to the type-1 style, although in Lev 21 the figures for grouped nouns and hypotaxis

---

46. Notably, Ewald, *Einleitung in die Geschichte*, 117, n. 1, has singled out Lev 18–20 for their particular language usage which "darauf hinweist dass der Verfasser hier stärker als sonst irgendwo ältere Quellen benutzt hat"; similarly Nöldeke, *Untersuchungen*, 63–64.

are on the high side,[47] with high figures for subordinate clauses in ch. 18, and for grouped nouns in ch. 27.

In chapters 20 and 25 the discourse profile represents the type-2 style.[48] Notably, the syntactic-stylistic profile of the section of the covenant blessings (26:1–13) stands midway between the two types: the frequency of short clauses fits the type-2 style, but the figures for hypotaxis and grouped nouns suit the type-1 style. A similar constellation presents itself for the first part of the covenant curses (26:14–33).

However, the final section of the covenant curses, which describes the conditions of the exile reveals, an intricate style, like many other units in this subcorpus:

Table 4: Lev 17; 22–26; Num 15: The Intricate Style

Class \ Unit	Number Clauses	0–1 ELC	2+ ELC	All Hypotaxis	MNP	Complex hypotaxis	3+ ELC
Lev 23:1–8, 24–37	53	35.85	45.28	18.87	133.96	15.09	13.21
Lev 24:1–23	73	35.62	43.84	20.55	76.03	4.11	15.07
Lev 22:2–16	57	35.09	38.60	26.32	62.28	12.28	7.02
Lev 23:10–22, 39–44	57	31.58	47.37	21.05	149.12	5.26	15.79
Lev 17	62	30.65	30.65	38.71	75.81	24.19	12.90
Lev 26:34–45	50	30.00	36.00	34.00	47.00	16.00	12.00
Num 15:2–26	58	25.86	39.66	34.48	131.03	18.97	29.31

In some of these passages the discourse profile is still somewhat close to the VoLB, with the relatively low figures for grouped nouns in Lev 26:34–45,

---

47. A similar constellation presents itself in 16:29–34, which sometimes is included in H; 22 clauses, with short clauses: 50.00%, but hypotaxis 31.82%, MNP 93.18%, and high figures for complex hypotaxis (22.73%).

48. This is not the place to discuss the relationship between the slave laws in Deut 15:12–18 and Lev 25:39–46, 47–54. But it is to be stressed that in spite of the categorical rejection of Israelite slavehood (Levinson, "Manumission of Hermeneutics," 305–9, 316–7), the date for release is tied to the Jubilee (Lev 25:40), which hardly suits the status of a "resident hireling." This term, then, seems hardly more than a white-wash for what amounts to slavehood, but differs from it in the implication that the Israelite slave cannot be sold. The legal formulation of Lev 25 includes much intricate rhetoric (for example, vv. 38, 42). The exhortation to acquire slaves from the neighboring ethnic groups (vv. 44–46) reveals an intricate, and slightly anacolouthic, syntactic structure. Here one could sense traces of a parenetic revision, possibly influenced by Deut 15.

and for hypotaxis in ch. 24. However, the figures for chapters 17 and 22 place these units firmly in the Judean corpus.[49] Even stronger data are found for the two sections of the festival calendar (Lev 23:1–8, 24–37; and vv. 10–22, 29–34). The high incidence of grouped nouns (133 and 149%) is reminiscent of the data for Numbers 15 (131%).[50] One also notes the high figures for complex hypotaxis in 23:1–8, 24–37.

Consequently, in terms of orality and scribalism the sections ascribed to H represent three different strata. The parenetic-legal sections of Lev 18; 19; 21; and 27 represent the activity of scribes who cling to the style of the oral formulation and proclamation.[51] A similar style dominates the sections of ch. 20; 25. The covenant blessings and curses (26:1–33) represent the continuation of this textualization process along the same lines, but with less clear-cut oral features.

The distinction between ch. 20 and ch. 18 is not unexpected since the section concerning forbidden intercourse in 20:11–21 is significantly variant from the series of prohibitions in 18:6–20.[52] The characterization of ch. 27, often considered an addition after the conclusion of the code with ch. 26,[53] may suggest a traditional document that was anchored in the oral tradition, and was added to H without fundamental adaptation to the IES.[54]

By contrast, the final section of the covenantal curses (26:34–45), with its announcement/description of the conditions in captivity, clearly represents the scribal style of the IES.[55] One detects a similar style in ch. 17; 22; and 24.

---

49. The attribution of Lev 17 to H is firmly rejected by Feucht, *Heiligkeitsgesetz*, 11–14, 63–64, whereas Milgrom, *Leviticus*, 2.1332, ascribes this periscope to the redaction stratum in H (H^R). Feucht, *Heiligkeitsgesetz*, 44, also notes the problems with the language usage of ch. 22. A connection between ch. 17 and 22, by the similarity of the introductory formulae, and the *inclusio* (sacrificial legislation in 22:26–30) is proposed by Nihan, *From Priestly Torah to Pentateuch*, 98–99, 397.

50. The data for Num 15 are representative of a large class in the ritual legislation of Numbers, as discussed in n. 56 below; see also Feucht, *Heiligkeitsgesetz*, 55–56.

51. See Polak, "Oral Substratum," 235–36.

52. One also notes the distinction between the ban on the offering to "Molech" (18:21) and the extended prohibition in the opening of ch. 20:2–5, with its long series of threats. See also Feucht, *Heiligkeitsgesetz*, 37.

53. Milgrom, *Leviticus*, 3.2401–2, notes the doubling of the colophon in 27:34 in comparison with 26:46.

54. See Milgrom, *Leviticus*, 3.2409.

55. The opening of this section, v. 34, was set in view of the description of the conditions in exile, concomitant with a slight change in syntactic complexity. In any case, the syntactic-stylistic variation refutes the theory that 26:3–45 form a single unit, as argued by Kuenen, *Historic-Critical Inquiry*, 283; Feucht, *Heiligkeitsgesetz*, 51. In view of the discussion of Stackert, "Sabbath of the Land," 248, one could envision a certain break in the representation of the desolation (vv. 32–33) and the idea of "making up"

Even more outspoken representatives of the scribal style are found in the two sections of Lev 23, and in Num 15, all characterized by the high incidence of long noun groups (more than 130%); in Num 15 one also notes the frequency of subordinate clauses.[56]

These findings suggest that parts of H belong to the most ancient stratum of the P-work (ch. 18; 19; 21; 27),[57] whereas other parts are slightly later (25:1–26:33). A second group (ch. 17; 22; 24) represents a style that is similar to the IES of Deuteronomy/Dtr, and thus is attributable to the late Judean monarchy. This date would fit the rebuttal (Lev 17: 3–4, 7) of the Deuteronomic permission of profane slaughter (Deut 12:20–25).[58] The content of the conclusion of the covenant curses (Lev 26:34–45) fits the exilic period. The intricate style of Lev 23 (similar to Num 15) resembles the

---

for the Sabbath years (vv. 34–35); see already Dillmann, *Exodus und Leviticus*, 620; and Graf, *Die Geschichtlichen Bücher*, 80. Levine, *Leviticus,* 275–6, who dates this text to the exilic period (*Leviticus*, 277–80), views vv. 3–33a, 37b–38 as the primary epilogue to H, with a first "postcatastrophic" addition in vv. 39b, 44–45, and a second addition, largely motivated by despair, in vv. 33b–37a, 40b–43. Attributing the base text to the Hezekian period Milgrom, *Leviticus*, 3.2273–4, 2329–37, 2362–5, likewise singles out vv. 3–33a as core text, but finds its continuation in vv. 36–42, 45 with vv. 33b–35, 43–44 as expansion.

56. The IES profile of Num 15 represents an extensive stratum in the legal sections of Numbers: ch. 1–3; 8:16–26; 10:11–28; 18:17–32; 36:1–12 (all with MNP equal to or above 100%); and 6:2–21; 9:1–14; 19 (with MNP 80–90%). Particularly noteworthy is the profile of Num 28:1–31 with 159.38% MNP, and almost 22% long clauses (including 7 ELC's in v. 13). Thus, adoption of the view of Knohl, *Sanctuary of Silence*, 8–14; and Milgrom, *Leviticus*, 2.1350–51; 3.1964, 1969–92, 2054 (and *passim*), who regard this chapter as the redactional *Vorlage* for "H" in Lev 23, entails the thesis that this *Vorlage* represents a pristine version of the list of festivals rather than the present text in Numbers.

57. Pointing to the term מִקְדָּשׁ (Lev 21:23; LXX 19:30; 26:2), Feucht, *Heiligkeitsgesetz*, 167–70, places the first stratum of H, comprising, in his view, Lev 18–23*, in the 8th century, before D, much like Joosten, *People and Land*, 203–7, and Knohl, *Sanctuary of Silence*, 206–9.

58. See Nihan, *From Priestly Torah to Pentateuch*, 411–2; but his assertion that Exod 12:6 entails profane slaughter is irrelevant, since the Passover sacrifice in Egypt precedes the establishment of the sanctuary.

profile of texts from the Persian era,[59] with the extremely high figures for noun groups.[60]

d. The Transition from Oral to Written in the Laws of Purity, Impurity and Purification (Lev 11–15)

The syntactic-stylistic profile of the section on purity and impurity is in a sense similar to the profile of the Holiness Code. Like H this code contains sections in a clear VoLB style, together with obvious IES sections.

Table 5: Lev 11–15 - VoLB and IES

Class / Unit	Number Clauses	0–1 ECL	2+ ECL	All Hypotaxis	Mean Noun Phrase	Complex Hypotaxis	3+ ECL
VoLB - type 1							
13:1–22	80	61.25	35.00	3.75	55.63	3.75	6.25
13:23–37	63	61.90	36.51	1.59	59.52	---	7.94
11:2–8	31	51.62	25.81	22.58	40.32	6.45	---
13:38–59	74	51.35	32.43	16.22	81.08	2.70	2.70
IES							
12:2–8	30	40.00	36.67	23.33	93.33	10.00	3.33
15:16–33	68	38.24	30.88	30.88	55.88	14.71	7.35
11:9–23, 39–42	42	38.10	23.81	38.10	77.38	19.05	---
15:2–15	67	37.31	28.36	34.33	27.61	23.88	5.97
11:24–38, 43, 46–47	67	31.34	10.45	43.28	56.72	25.37	---
14:2–19	61	26.23	50.82	22.95	114.75	3.28	11.48
14:20–38	58	25.86	37.93	36.21	82.76	12.07	22.41
14:39–57	53	35.85	39.62	24.53	89.62	5.66	15.09

59. The data for these sections, then, would fit the thesis of Knohl, *Sanctuary of Silence*, concerning H following P. But the data for Lev 17; 22; 24 are similar to the figures for the cultic corpus and the *miškān* pericope, whereas the figures for ch. 18–21; 26:1–33 fit the theory of Ewald (see n. 46); Klostermann, "Beiträge"; and Joosten, *People and Land*, 203–7. With regard to the description of חֻקַּת עוֹלָם לְדֹרֹתֵיכֶם as characteristic for H, as proposed by Knohl, *Sanctuary of Silence*, 46–55, it is to be noted that this phrase does not appear in Lev 18–22, and is frequent only in Lev 23 (vv. 14, 21, 31, 41; and in addition in "H:" 17:7; 24:3).

60. Let me mention Ezra 3:8–13; 1 Chr 28:1–11; 29:1–25; 2 Chr 28:5–14; 30:1–27; Jer 39:1–10; 52:4–11 (//2 Kgs 25); as well as 2 Kgs 22–23; 24. However, in most examples of Persian era narrative we do not encounter figures that high.

One encounters a clear VoLB (type 1) style in the entire chapter concerning ṣāraʿat ("scale disease"; Lev 13). In this chapter the frequency of short clauses is consistently high or very high (more than 60% in vv. 1–37), whereas the incidence of subordinate clauses is low (in these verses less than 5%). In the last part of this chapter (vv. 38–59) one notes the high incidence of noun groups (80%), a clear IES feature,[61] although the frequency of subordinate clauses (16%), is still within the characteristics of VoLB-1.

The chapter presenting the dietary laws harbors two different sections. The opening sections (11:2–8) reveal a clear VoLB style.[62] By contrast, the continuation (vv. 9–23, 39–42) is characterized by the IES, with a high frequency of noun groups (77%) and subordinate clauses (no less than 38%; almost 20% in complex hypothesis).[63]

In Lev 14; 15 one notes the IES, with the high figures for hypotaxis in ch. 15, and the high frequency of noun groups in ch. 14.

A certain transition is indicated in ch. 12, concerning the purification of women after giving birth. Some verses reveal a clear VoLB style with typical bi-clausal patterns:

אִשָּׁה כִּי תַזְרִיעַ / וְיָלְדָה זָכָר / וְטָמְאָה שִׁבְעַת יָמִים / כִּימֵי נִדַּת דְּוֺתָהּ תִּטְמָא:

If a woman conceives, and bears a male, she shall be impure seven days; she shall be impure as at the time of her menstruation (Lev 12:2).

וְהִקְרִיבוֹ לִפְנֵי יְהוָה / וְכִפֶּר עָלֶיהָ / וְטָהֲרָה מִמְּקֹר דָּמֶיהָ

זֹאת תּוֹרַת הַיֹּלֶדֶת לַזָּכָר אוֹ לַנְּקֵבָה:

He shall offer it before YHWH, and make atonement on her behalf; then she shall be pure from her flow of blood. This is the law for the one who bears a male or a female (Lev 12:7).

---

61. Baentsch, *Exodus - Leviticus - Numeri*, 369–70; Elliger, *Leviticus*, 161–2; and Milgrom, *Leviticus*, 1.808, 815, discern a supplementary stratum in 13:47–59, since it interrupts the flow from ch. 13 to ch. 14.

62. Carpenter and Harford-Battersby, *Hexateuch*, 2.155, note that the section of 11:2–8 differs from the next section (11:9–23) in its focus on domesticated/non-domesticated land animals, reflecting the immediate experience of daily life in the Israelite lands, and the non-use of the root šqṣ, in contrast with vv. 10–13, 20, 41–43; Levine, *Leviticus*, 246, connects this pericope to the mentality that regards domesticated livestock as part of the family; see also Elliger, *Leviticus*, 143.

63. The partition proposed by Milgrom, *Leviticus* 1.691–4: 2–23, 41, 42, 46, would produce a VoLB (type 2) style; with short clauses: 45.45%; hypotaxis: 31.82%; MNP 68.94%, and 13.64% complex hypotaxis.

Here, then, the basic syntactic-stylistic patterns adhere to the VoLB, whereas the further development of the instructions passes over into the intricate style of the cultic P-strata. One detects a similar pattern in the dietary precepts: the instructions concerning certain animals, and mainly the domesticated livestock, are couched in the VoLB (11:2–8), but the additional instructions, in which the entire animal world is subjected to the purity distinctions, reveal the IES (vv. 9–47). This transition is representative for the entire corpus of the Purity precepts and instructions: the basic instructions are kept in the VoLB of the oral-written corpus (ch. 11:2–8; 13), whereas the further development is dominated by the IES.

The syntactic-stylistic profile of the precepts for the cult likewise indicates a mixture of oral vestiges and scribal textualization, although scribalism is the main factor.

e. The Cultic Sub-Corpus

The cultic sub-corpus is dominated by the IES, which characterizes the pericope of the *miškān* and the precepts for the sacrifices. In these sections one notes only few features that would fit the VoLB: [64]

---

64. In Table 6 the sections are ordered from low to high, according to the figures for "All Hypotaxis," although the subgroups are defined by the frequency of short clauses. For Lev 8; 16; and Exod 12 the canonical order is adhered to.

Table 6: The Cultic Precepts

Class \ Unit	Number Clauses	0–1 ELC	2+ ELC	All Hypotaxis	Mean Noun Phrase	Complex Hypotaxis	3+ ELC
Sacrifices							
20–30% short							
Lev 1	45	26.67	68.89	4.44	91.11	---	26.67
Lev 2	44	27.27	54.55	18.18	95.45	---	15.91
4:1–21	54	20.37	61.11	18.52	136.11	5.56	27.78
4:22–35	49	20.41	57.14	22.45	78.57	10.20	24.49
7:1–34	95	28.42	35.79	35.79	101.50	12.63	14.74
30–40% short							
3:1–17	36	36.11	50.00	8.33	145.83	---	33.33
6:1–23	78	33.33	42.31	24.36	67.31	7.69	19.23
5:14–26	50	36.00	34.00	30.00	35.00	10.00	18.00
5:1–13	62	37.09	30.65	32.26	43.55	9.68	12.90
Yom HaKippurim							
16:1–17	58	37.93	41.38	20.69	97.41	17.24	22.41
16:18–28	39	33.33	48.72	17.99	79.49	15.38	12.82
Consecration							
8:1–15	47	19.15	61.70	19.15	59.57	10.64	10.64
8:16–30	39	28.21	64.10	7.69	130.77	7.69	28.21
Passover							
Exod 12:1–14 P	47	29.79	48.94	21.28	81.91	6.38	17.02
Exod 12:15–20	20	30.00	55.00	15.00	137.5	10.00	30.00

However, one notes important distinctions. The section concerning the sacrifices (so-called P⁰, Lev 1–7), includes a number of chapters with a small minority of short clauses (all less than a third of the text: Lev 1–2; 4; 7; similarly Exod 12), whereas the figures for other sections hover around a third of all clauses (Lev 3; 5; 6; similarly Lev 16). In most chapters the number of noun groups is high (more than 90% of the text: Lev 1–2; 7; similarly 16:1–17), or extremely high (more than 100%: Lev 3; 4:1–21; so likewise 8:16–30; Exod 12:15–20). Only in chapters 5–6 and 4:22–35 do we encounter lower figures (so likewise 8:1–15; and around 80%: 16:18–28; Exod 12:1–14).

In this context some findings for syntactic subordination are exceptional. As against the high figures for hypotaxis in Lev 4:22–35; 6 (20–30%) and in ch. 5; 7 (above 30%), we note low values (less than 20%) in the opening sections of the instructions for the sacrifices (Lev 1:1—4:21), and in the sections concerning the priestly consecration (Lev 8), Yom HaKippurim (Lev 16), and the Passover sacrifice (Exod 12). In these sections the figures for syntactic subordination would fit the VoLB style (type 1). These figures, then, suggest a notable exception to the heavy predominance of the IES in the cultic subcorpus. This could be a mere fluke in the evidence, but the role of the VoLB strata in Lev 9–10, the Holiness Code and the Purity Code suggest the possibility of residues of the lean, brisk style.

Some indications of such residues are revealed by the instructions concerning the *miškān*.

Table 7: The *Miškān*

Class / Unit	Number Clauses	0–1 ELC	2+ ELC	All Hypotaxis	Mean Noun Phrase	Complex Hypotaxis	3+ ELC
Exod 29:1–24	63	44.44	44.44	11.11	123.81	4.76	11.11
Lev 9:1–24	76	43.42	44.74	11.84	66.45	2.63	11.84
Lev 10:1–10	41	41.46	39.02	19.51	63.41	7.32	12.20
Exod 28	102	38.24	47.06	14.70	124.51	5.66	15.69
Exod 25:10–30	56	32.14	57.14	10.71	81.25	3.57	23.21
Exod 30:1–9, 18–22	43	30.23	51.16	18.61	75.58	11.63	18.61
Exod 37:25—38:8	34	20.59	64.70	14.71	107.35	2.94	20.59
Exod 26:31—27:5	35	20.00	62.86	17.14	108.57	---	28.57

Let me note first that in all pericopes analyzed the figures for hypotaxis fit the VoLB. Nevertheless, the dominant style in most pericopes in this section is the IES, which characterizes the prescriptions for the building of the Ark and the table (Exod 25:10–30);[65] the *pārōket* curtain and the altar (26:31—27:5); the prescriptions for the priest's clothes (Exod 28); the building of the incense altar and the bronze basin (Exod 30:1–9, 18–22); and the construction of the incense altar and the altar for the burnt offering (37:25—38:8). It is important to note the stylistic similarity since Exod 30 is mostly attributed to a supplementary stratum (P^S).[66]

One exception stands out. The instructions for the consecration of the priests (Exod 29:1–24) reveal characteristic VoLB features, such as the high figures for short clauses, and the low figures for hypotaxis. If these features resemble the data for Lev 9–10, the extremely high figures for noun groups point strongly to the IES. This mixture of oral and scribal style, which is similar to the constellation noted in Gen 9:1–26; 25:1, 5–11, is surprising since the narrative of the consecration itself (Lev 8) reveals a clear preference for long clauses.

How, then, to account for the particular nature of the precepts for the consecration of the priests? If this would be a singular phenomenon, it could be nothing more than an exceptional case. But a different conclusion is suggested by the similarity to other sections in the P-work (Lev 9–10) and the contrast with the section concerning the ceremony of the consecration itself. It appears that these chapters harbor residues of cultic legislation in the lean, brisk style of oral proclamation.

f. Stylistic Patterns in the Cultic Sub-Corpus

These findings are extremely relevant for the thesis of Klaus Koch concerning the residues of an oral tradition in Exod 25–29.[67] A telltale indication of an oral residue is the use of biclausal patterns, such as in Exod 25:11:

וְצִפִּיתָ אֹתוֹ זָהָב טָהוֹר / מִבַּיִת וּמִחוּץ תְּצַפֶּנּוּ / וְעָשִׂיתָ עָלָיו זֵר זָהָב סָבִיב:

---

65. The diction of the prescriptions for the construction of the *miškān* itself and the altar (Exod 26–27) is similar to the style of ch. 25.

66. Holzinger, *Exodus*, 144; Baentsch, *Exodus - Leviticus - Numeri*, 258–9; Noth, *Exodus*, 234–5. It is to be admitted that a fuller analysis should take the LXX into account. Koch, *Priesterschrift*, 32–33, attributes the prescriptions concerning the incense altar (30:1–10) to Jerusalemite P^G, whereas in his view the chapters 25–29 represent the ancient, non-Jerusalemite, *Vorlage*. Baentsch, *Exodus - Leviticus - Numeri*, 238, suggests (with a question mark) that ch. 28 was likewise supplementary, but Holzinger and Noth do not support this possibility.

67. Koch, *Priesterschrift*, 7–11. The value of Koch's analysis, rejected by Elliger, *Leviticus*, 8–9, has been recognized by Milgrom, "Consecration of the Priests," 273, in his discussion of Exod 29 in comparison with Lev 8.

Overlay it with pure gold, overlay it inside and outside, and
make upon it a gold molding round about.

In this pattern the first clause indicates the material by which the ark is to be covered, whereas the second clause specifies where to apply the covering.[68] One notes the chiastic order of both clauses, as well as the *qatal-yiqtol* repetition. The third clause presents an additional instruction. In the view of Klaus Koch, patterns of this type suggest composition for oral proclamation.[69] Similar biclausal patterns are found in vv. 12, 13, 15, 18–19, 24–26, 28, 31, 37. In the concluding verse one notes the preclause:

וּרְאֵה / וַעֲשֵׂה בְּתַבְנִיתָם אֲשֶׁר־אַתָּה מָרְאֶה בָּהָר׃

Look, then, and follow the patterns for them that are being shown you on the mountain (25:40).

By contrast, in the matching stretches in the section concerning the construction of the tabernacle (ch. 35–39) biclausal patterns are less frequent. For instance, one notes the elaborate pattern in the description of the covering of the ark (37:2):

וַיְצַפֵּהוּ זָהָב טָהוֹר מִבַּיִת וּמִחוּץ / וַיַּעַשׂ לוֹ זֵר זָהָב סָבִיב׃

He overlaid it with pure gold, inside and outside; and he made a gold molding for it round about.

In this verse both the indication of the material and the place where it is to be applied are presented in one single, elaborate clause, with two noun groups, where the corresponding verse (25:11) has three short clauses with one noun group each. Elaborate patterns are also found in 37:3 (matching 25:12).[70]

Biclausal structuring is very much in evidence in Exod 29.[71] Thus one notes the description of the anointment and its continuation:

וְלָקַחְתָּ אֶת־שֶׁמֶן הַמִּשְׁחָה / וְיָצַקְתָּ עַל־רֹאשׁוֹ / וּמָשַׁחְתָּ אֹתוֹ׃

---

68. See Polak, "Verbs of Motion," 166–7, 187–96; and Polak, "Orality," 933–34.

69. Koch, *Priesterschrift*, 97, 99–101.

70. But we also encounter biclausal patterns. The structuration characterizing 37:4, 7, 11–13, 15, 17 matches the patterning of 25:13, 18, 24–26, 28. However, none of these clauses is limited to a single predicate, or predicate with one additional constituent. The specification in 37:8a does not contain a predicate, unlike 25:19.

71. One notes the instructions for the offering of the first ram in 29:15–18, and the precepts for the offering of the second ram (vv. 19–21), although v. 20 contains an extensive noun group, much like vv. 22–23 (v. 24 consists of two elaborate clauses).

Take the anointing oil, pour it on his head, and anoint him. (29:7)

וְאֶת־בָּנָיו תַּקְרִיב / וְהִלְבַּשְׁתָּם כֻּתֳּנֹת׃ / וְחָגַרְתָּ אֹתָם אַבְנֵט

Then bring his sons forward, clothe them with tunics, and gird them with sashes. (29:8–9a)[72]

Notably, the terms of the description of the anointing (v. 7) are identical with those of the anointing of the masseba in Bethel by Jacob (Gen 28:18), and the anointing of Saul by Samuel (1 Sam 10:1).[73] All these passages use the verb לקח in the pre-clause, with the oil as direct object, to be continued by a second clause with יצק and the head (רֹאשׁ) as locative, in a structure that is quite similar to a corresponding phrase in Ugaritic.[74]

On the other hand, the description of the inauguration ritual (Lev 8) condenses the bi-clausal pattern into one elaborate clause:[75]

וַיִּצֹק מִשֶּׁמֶן הַמִּשְׁחָה עַל רֹאשׁ אַהֲרֹן / וַיִּמְשַׁח אֹתוֹ לְקַדְּשׁוֹ׃

He poured some of the anointing oil upon Aaron's head, and anointed him, to consecrate him. (Lev 8:12)

The opening clause is followed by a second clause that is rounded off by an infinitive clause (לְקַדְּשׁוֹ), corresponding with the statement of Exod 29:1 (לְקַדֵּשׁ אֹתָם).[76]

As a result we see that the syntactic-stylistic profile of Lev 8 is far more complex than the profile of Exod 29:1–24.[77]

---

72. The following phrase אַהֲרֹן וּבָנָיו, lacking representation in the LXX, is better viewed as a gloss.

73. See also 2 Kgs 9:3, 6.

74. Polak "Epic Formulas," 440; Pardee, "New Letter," 14–17.

75. So also Lev 8:19b (single clause) / Exod 29:16b (biclausal). By contrast, in Lev 8:26 one encounters a separate clause, whereas the instructions in Exod 29:22–23 form one single clause.

76. Unlike the divine instructions, the description of the consecration ceremony contains many extensive noun groups, notably in Lev 8:8, 9, 22.

77. This finding is not affected by the possibility of secondary expansions in Lev 8 and Exod 29 as discussed by Nihan, *From Priestly Torah to Pentateuch*, 129–47, who argues that the differences remaining after removal of the expansionary stretches are mainly stylistic. However, the stylistic data are far from neutral. The present findings support the view of Milgrom, *Leviticus*, 1.545–49, who ascribes the differentiation to adaptations and secondary interpolations in Lev 8; and note, for instance, Nihan, *From Priestly Torah to Pentateuch*, 151–52, on the correspondence between Lev 1:3–6, 8–9; and 8:18–21.

In this connection one may point to the particular use of the נתן-לקח formula, rooted in the Akkadian legal formulary as used in Ugarit, and frequent in biblical narrative.[78] In the P-work this formula is frequent in ritual context, mostly with locative meaning of נתן.[79] Its legal usage is still reflected by the explanations concerning the status of the "breast of elevation offering and the thigh of gift offering" that were taken (לָקַחְתִּי) from the Israelites and transferred (וָאֶתֵּן אֹתָם) to the Aaronide priests (Lev 7:34), the transfer of the redemption price for the first-born (Num 3:47–51), and the metaphor of the dedication of the Levites (Num 8:18–19). This formula is also used to indicate the appointment to official functions (Num 27:18–20; Deut 1:1–15). Notably, outside the P-work its ritual usage is found in texts that belong to the oral-written corpus (1 Sam 6:8), or reflect archaic ceremonies (Deut 15:17).[80]

These considerations suggest a partial justification of Koch's thesis of an oral background for the cultic sub-corpus and the instructions for the *miškān*. However, in my view this background is mainly suggested by residues of orality rather than by a full-fledged VoLB style of which we find remainders in the P-narrative (including Lev 9–10), the Purity Code and the Holiness Code. The question, then, is, how to view the socio-cultural background of these vestiges.

4. Discourse Profile and the Growth of the P-Work

The variety of syntactic-stylistic findings indicates a series of different processes behind the textualization and composition of the P-work. Thus I

---

78. Polak, "Epic Formulas," 440, 450; Greenfield, "Našû-Nadānu."

79. Exod 12:7; 16:33; 29:12–13, 20; 30:16, 34–36; 40:20; Lev 8:15, 23, 26–27; 10:1; 14:14, 15–17, 24–25; 15:14; 16:5–8, 12–13, 18; 20:14–15; 24:5–7; Num 4:9–10, 12; 5:17; 6:18,19; 7:5, 6; 16: 6–7, 17, 18; 17:11,12; 18:6–7, 26, 28; 19:2–3, 17; 20:8; 31:29, 30, 47.

80. According to Bertholet, *Deuteronomium*, 47, the law on the freeing of the slaves, like the law on the debt release, is inserted here in the wake of the precepts for the treatment of the poor in Deut 14. Lohfink, "Fortschreibung?" 158–59, views the law of Deut 15:10–18 as *Fortschreibung* of the law of Exod 21:2–11, but justly rejects the assumption that the inclusion of Deut 15:16–17 is due to the Deuteronomic rejection of the ritual implications of the mention of אֱלֹהִים, whether referring to a local sanctuary, or to family gods. It seems to me that we are dealing with Deuteronomic excerpts from a preexisting legal system dealing with debt release (15:1–2), indenture, the release of the debt slaves (15:12) and the case of voluntary non-release (vv. 16–17). Some features of this pericope seem parenetic (15:13, repeating וְכִי of the main case; and in v. 16b the motivation). Importantly, in v. 17b the case of the *'āmā* is no exception: she is to remain a slave, and is not entitled to release by the simple fact that she is not taken into marriage, as ordained in Exod 21:11. However, this issue does not bear on the use of the legal-ritual לקח-נתן formula.

will suggest different processes and trajectories for (a) the P-narrative, (b) the Holiness and Purity Codes, (c) the *miškan* pericope, and (d) the cultic sub-corpus.

a. Oral Derived Text in the P-Narrative

For the P-narrative the way from the oral performance to the scribal desk would hardly be different from the trajectory passed by other narrative sections. Thus I envision writing narrators who were well acquainted with the style of the oral narrator (the "Singer of Tales"), however without any dependence on the oral performance properly speaking. Their "oral-derived" work, though less close to the oral arena than, for example, the core of the Abraham-Jacob narrative, reflects the oral habitus, and thus is to be dated in a period in which the bureaucratic apparatus had not yet developed into a main institution in the Judahite society, that is to say before the second half of the 8th-century.[81]

These "oral-derived" narratives were taken up, revised, expanded, and continued by scribal authors who adhered to the stylistic norms of the administrative chancery rather than to the ways of the oral performance. The focus of social prestige, and thereby the socio-cultural background, is the scribal chancery and thus the well-developed royal or municipal bureaucracy of the late 8th and 7th century.

b. The Holiness and Purity Codes

Both H and the Purity Code include significant VoLB sections, both in the type-1 style (Lev 11:2–8; 13; 18–19; 21; 27) and the type-2 style (ch. 20; 25; 26:1–33). Other passages are dominated by the intricate style: ch. 11:9–47; 12; 14–15; 17; 22–24; 26:34–45. These passages, then, reflect the stylistic norms of the scribal chancery. Their probably sociohistorical background may be determined as the developed bureaucracy of the late Judean monarchy. An exilic origin may be postulated for the prediction/description of the conditions of the exile in the conclusion of the covenant curses (26:34–45), and in particular for the allusion to the possibility of future salvation (vv. 44–45). This assumption, however, seems less likely for the prohibition of profane slaughter (ch. 17), which is rather to be explained as a conservative reaction against the Deuteronomic license of such actions (Deut 12:20–25),

---

81. See §2e and n. 25 above; and more in detail, Polak, "Sociolinguistics," 116–25, 149–61; and Polak, "Language Variation and Sociocultural Background," 315–26.

and would fit the late 7th century. This periodization is likewise indicated by the stylistic profile of this pericope, which is very similar to the syntactic-stylistic character of the Deuteronomic compositions.[82] Even stronger scribal tendencies are revealed by the festal calendar of Lev 23 (in both sections) and Num 15. The extremely high figures for noun groups are reminiscent of various narrative sections from the Babylonian/Persian period.[83]

By contrast, the passages in the lean, brisk style stand out by their adherence to the stylistics of orality, and thus suggest the oral enunciation by a priestly expert.

Thus the oral arena supplies the point of departure for the formulation of the legislation in Lev 18–21; 25–27.[84] By contrast, the authority of the written text is evidenced by such sections as Lev 1–8; 17; 22:2–16; 23. In my view the best interpretation for these data is provided by the assumption that with the textualization of the norms for sacrifice, purity, and social behavior, the written text was invested with authority. In this context particular attention is due to the *Fortschreibung* in the Purity Code, where the basic descriptions in the VoLB in 11:2–8; 13 are complemented by more detailed systems in the IES. In H the elaboration of the VoLB proclamations is couched in the IES. Some cases of further elaboration are likewise found in Numbers. In the presentation of the revenues of the priests and the Levites (Num 18) one notes some VoLB features in the basic account (vv. 1–16), whereas the elaboration manifests clear IES features (vv. 17–32). A similar configuration sets VoLB vestiges in the regulation of the real estate inheritance of the women (Num 27:1–11), apart from the extreme IES features in the subsequent restrictive adapation in Num 36.

---

82. The high values for hypotaxis and the MNP are comparable to, e.g., Deut 19:1–9 (short clauses: 30.30%; hypotaxis 36.36%; MNP 75.76%). Of course, this is an indication of stylistic similarity and sociocultural background; I do not contend that both sections represent one and the same literary stratum.

83. Let me mention Ezra 3:8–13; 1 Chr 28:1–11; 29:1–25; 2 Chr 28:5–14; 30:1–27; Jer 39:1–10; 52:4–11; as well as 2 Kgs 22–23; 24. However, in most examples of Persian era narrative we do not encounter such high values; see Polak, "Sociolinguistics," 132–6.

84. This context fits the "provincial"/rural outlook of H, as described by Joosten, *People and Land*, 154–7. One also notes the importance of such concepts as עדה, which describes the assembly as a basic social and political institution, figuring high in the Rehoboam tale (1 Kgs 12:20); see Milgrom, "Priestly Terminology," 66–74, 77; Hurvitz, *Linguistic Study of the Relationship*, 65–67; Fleming, *Legacy of Israel*, 110–11.

c. The Miškān Pericopes

The residues of orality found in the pericope of the *miškān* are less obvious than the vestiges in H and the Purity Code. Nevertheless, as noted above (§3e), two factors demand our attention: the low incidence of hypotaxis; and the high figures for short clauses in the section concerning the consecration of the priests (Exod 29). The particular position of Exod 29 is of importance, for one of the differences between this pericope and the description of the consecration of the priests in Lev 8 is the adaptation of the latter pericope to the *ḥaṭṭā'ṭ* ritual as described in Lev 4; 7. It seems, then, that the textualization of the instructions in Exod 29 precedes the inclusion of Lev 8 and the ritual prescriptions of Lev 4; 7 in one and the same text complex. Another issue to be taken into account is the VoLB profile of the description of the arrangements for the travel of the Ark, the *miškān* and the entire *maḥănek* in Num 4. With its relatively high figure for short clauses, the profile of this pericope is radically different from the highly developed form of the IES in Num 1-3; 5-6; 8.[85] It seems, then, that Exod 29 and Num 4 contain vestiges of an earlier version of the *miškān* pericope that was close to the oral arena. The present text(s) of this pericope, then, represent(s) a later version that was largely adapted to the norms of the scribal chancery.

d. The Cultic Sub-Corpus

Like the pericope of the *miškān* the cultic subcorpus is heavily dominated by the IES, with high figures for noun groups and subordinated clauses in most sections. Low figures for hypotaxis were found in a number of chapters (Lev 1:1—4:21; 8; 16; Exod 12). One could contemplate a connection between these data and the findings of Rendtorff concerning the "ritual" genre in the sacrificial sections. True, Rendtorff rejected the possibility of an oral background, since in his view the schematic character of the formulary suggests a late, exilic date.[86] However, the style of oral proclamation often tends exactly to the schematics of strict patterning,[87] which we also encounter in the ancient Near Eastern and Homeric epic. Hence, like the pericope of the *miškān*, the cultic subcorpus seems to reveal a substratum of oral proclama-

---

85. Num 4:1-20 (58 clauses); short clauses 41.38%; hypotaxis 22.41%; MNP 125.00%; complex hypotaxis 12.07%; elaborate clauses 6.90%. The high figures for grouped nouns are also found in Num 1-3; 8:16-26; 15; 18:17-32 (all ≥ 100%; in ch. 6; 19 the figures are in the 80% range). In these chapters the figures for hypotaxis mostly are larger than 30%.

86. Rendtorff, *Gesetze in der Priesterschrift*, 22-23.

87. Rubin, *Memory in Oral Traditions*, 101-8, 116-21, 161-71, 299-307.

tion by the priestly expert. Notably, the description of the consecration of the priests (Lev 8) looks like an amplification and adaptation of a *Vorlage* that was close to the prescription (Exod 29), in which we found VoLB traces pointing to an oral background. One may also note that the mini-legislation of Ezekiel contains both oral and scribal elements. The scribal affiliation is obvious in the sections concerning the Levites (Ezek 44:1–14),[88] and the sacrifices (Ezek 46:1–15).[89] Some VoLB traces may be discerned in the sections concerning the altar (43:18–27),[90] the proposals for priestly clothing and behavior (44:16–31),[91] and the legislation concerning the landed property of the *nāśî'* and the cooking boils (46:16–24).[92] Still, in view of the figures for grouped nouns, elaborate clauses and hypotaxis (particularly complex hypotaxis), the profile of these sections fits the IES, and thus the Judean corpus.

According to these considerations, the cultic subcorpus ultimately originates in the oral proclamation by a priestly expert in matters of sacrifice and ritual. In the present text(s) some VoLB traces still preserve aspects of the oral enunciation. In this style the paratactic clause sequence provides a step by step development of the diverse stages of the ritual. At the same time, the scribal expansion and adaptation of the long noun groups make it possible to specify additional technical detail. In the oral proclamation an important function is fulfilled by the closure of legal and cultic prescripts by a summary statement, such as חַטַּאת הַקָּהָל הִוא – "It is the purifying offering of the congregation" (Lev 4:21);[93] זֹאת תּוֹרַת הַיֹּלֶדֶת לַזָּכָר אוֹ לַנְּקֵבָה – "This is the instruction for one who bears a male or a female" (Lev 12:7).[94] This pattern is of importance for the oral proclamation since it contributes to the clarity of the staging of the instructions. One could compare such closures

---

88. Ezek 44:1–14 (59 clauses); short clauses 25.44%; hypotaxis 35.59%; MNP 82.20%; complex hypotaxis 22.03%; elaborate clauses 16.96%.

89. Ezek 46:1–15 (53 clauses); short clauses 32.08%; hypotaxis 28.30%; MNP 114.15%; complex hypotaxis 11.32%; elaborate clauses 11.32%.

90. Ezek 43:18–27 (35 clauses); short clauses 40.00%; hypotaxis 22.86%; MNP 91.53%; complex hypotaxis 14.29%; elaborate clauses 14.29%.

91. Ezek 44:16–31 (50 clauses); short clauses 40.00%; hypotaxis 24.00%; MNP 77.00%; complex hypotaxis 14.00%; elaborate clauses 18.00%.

92. Ezek 46:16–24 (37 clauses); short clauses 56.76%; hypotaxis 24.32%; MNP 72.97%; complex hypotaxis 18.92%; elaborate clauses 8.11%.

93. Similarly, for example, Lev 5:19; 7:37 (paralleling 7:35).

94. Similarly Lev 11:46; 13:59; 14:32, 57; 15:32; Num 5:29; 6:13, 21; Num 10:28; Rendtorff, *Gesetze in der Priesterschrift*, 70–72, attributes these closing formulas, like the similar opening phraseology, to a redactional stage that preceded the present text form.

as "That's the BBC News," following the opening "This is the world news from the BBC."[95]

e. The Socio-Cultural Context of Priestly Orality

In my view these data warrant the conclusion that the P-work is ultimately rooted in an oral context. Koch has already pointed to the importance of the concept "tent" in *miškān* and *'ōhel mō'ēd*;[96] and our honoree has indicated the archeological roots of the concept of the "base" of the altar.[97] But how to assess the sociocultural background of this profile? With regard to narrative the obvious point of reference is the oral performance by the "Singer of Tales." But such context does not fit the parenetic-cultic-legal content of the sections in H and the Purity Code. In my view, in those prescriptions and legislations the VoLB is modeled on the style of the oral proclamation/exposition by the authoritative priestly expert on these matters. This context is significantly different from the arena of the oral narration, for the authority of the priest exceeds the prestige of the "Singer of Tales" by far. The proclamation of the priestly expert could hardly be less institutional than the desk of the priestly scribe, and thus the prestige of the oral proclamation would not be inferior to that of the written instructions. Hence it stands to reason that in the context of the priestly culture the authority of the oral proclamation would outlast the prestige of oral narrative or poetry. Accordingly, the VoLB could have remained in use in, for example, the 7th-century. However, the official context of priestly activity would also permit the assumption that priestly writing preceded the penning down of patriarchal and "historical" narrative. These considerations suggest placing the roots of the P-work in narrative, ritual ordinance and parenetic-legal prescription somewhere in the 9th, or at latest the 8th-century. Here, then, one could look for the antecedents of the Purity and the Holiness Code, as well as the "rituals" and prescriptions now textualized in, for example, Exod 12; 25–29; Lev 1–4.

---

95. In a certain sense the extended colophons of Lev 26:46; 27:34; Num 36:13 and Deut 28:69 are expanded forms of this basic closing formula. A rhetorical parallel is found in Deut 26:16–19, matching Deut 5:1.

96. Koch, *Priesterschrift*, 15–16; and see in particular Milgrom, *Leviticus*, 1.30. Like Hebrew *miškān* (2 Sam 7:6; Isa 54:2; Song 1:8), Latin *tabernaculum* means "tent." The reminiscence of "the *miškān* of Shiloh, the *'ōhel* he had set among men" (Ps 78:60) indicates that the idea of a tent was part and parcel of biblical cultural memory in the Judean kingdom.

97. Zevit, "Philology, Archeology and P's legislation."

However, indications of the oral roots of the P-work are only rarely preserved in their entirety. The main sections of this corpus reveal an elaborate, intricate style that fits the Judean corpus, and points to a period that is roughly coeval with the Deuteronomic legislation. In this connection one notes in particular the use of the לקח-נתן formula, since the frequency of the verb לקח greatly decreases in the Persian era, a process that is foreshadowed in the prophetic code in Ezek 43–46.[98] Thus the formative period of most of the P-work was the late Judean monarchy.

This is not to deny that some of the parts of the P-work may be exilic. Some texts could have been formulated in the Babylonian era by students of priestly scribes who were active in the Temple service by the end of the Judean monarchy. Some sections in Numbers,[99] with the high figures for both hypotaxis and grouped nouns could well fit this period.[100] However, this could hardly be the formative period. The roots of the P-work and its conception as an overarching "story," which provides a cosmological framework for legislation and history as charter myth, are to be posited in the 9th to 8th-century,[101] whereas the main strata are at home in the Judean monarchy of the 7th-century. Have I returned to Baudissin?[102] I have.

BIBLIOGRAPHY

Baentsch, Bruno. *Exodus - Leviticus - Numeri*. Handkommentar zum Alten Testament, I/2. Göttingen: Vandenhoeck & Ruprecht, 1903.
Baudissin, Wolf W. *Einleitung in die Bücher des Alten Testaments*. Leipzig: Hirzel, 1901.
Begrich, Joachim. "Die priesterliche Tora." In Joachim Begrich, *Gesammelte Studien zum Alten Testament*, edited by Walther Zimmerli, 232–60. Munich: Kaiser, 1964.
Berlin, Adele. *Enmerkar and Ensuḫkešdanna: A Sumerian Narrative Poem*. Philadelphia: University Museum, 1979.

98. Hurvitz, "Evidence of Language," 43–44; Hurvitz, "Once Again: Linguistic Profile," 181–5; Polak, "Verbs of Motion," 168–73.

99. However, this dictum cannot include the texts concerning the status of the Levites, which still preserves memory of the dedication of Temple oblates as נתונים, like the lad Samuel (LXX 1 Sam 1:11, the plus δοτόν).

100. See n. 56 above. In this respect I tend to accept the views of Achenbach and Nihan, "Priestly Laws." Levine, *Numbers 1-20*, 443-4, finds traces of late Babylonian *mišiḫtu* (and Aramaic משחתא in the letters from Elephantine) in the use of the term מִשְׁחָה / מָשְׁחָה as "portion" (Lev 7:35; Num 18:8), but Milgrom, *Leviticus*, 1.433–4, does not accept these details as proof for a late origin of these verses. In my view, the semantic distinction between "portion" and "measure" indicates that more is involved than postexilic lexical borrowing.

101. This periodization fits the chronology proposed for the use of the horned altar with *yĕsōd*, as in the *ḥaṭṭā't* ritual, by Zevit, "Philology, Archaeology and P," 38.

102. Baudissin, *Einleitung*, 162–70, 184–208.

———. "Shared Rhetorical Figures in Biblical and Sumerian Literature." *JANES* 10 (1978) 35–42.
Bertholet, Alfred. *Deuteronomium*. Kurzer Hand-Commentar zum Alten Testament, 5. Freiburg i. B.: J. C. B. Mohr (Paul Siebeck), 1899.
Blenkinsopp, Joseph. "The Alleged Pre-Exilic Date of the Priestly Material in the Pentateuch." *ZAW* 108 (1996) 495–518.
Brockelmann, Carl. *Grundriss der vergleichenden Grammatik der semitischen Sprachen*. 2 vols. Berlin: Reuther & Reichard.
Carpenter, J. Estlin, and George Harford-Battersby. *The Hexateuch according to the Revised Version Arranged in its Constituent Documents*, 2 vols. London: Longmans-Green, 1900.
Cross, Frank M. *Canaanite Myth and Hebrew Epic: Essays in the History of the Religion of Israel*. Cambridge, MA: Harvard University Press, 1973.
Dégh, Linda. "Grimm's 'Household Tales' and Its Place in the Household: The Social Relevance of a Controversial Classic Author." *Western Folklore* 38 (1979) 83–103.
Dillmann, August. *Die Bücher Exodus und Leviticus*, 2nd edition. Kurzgefasstes exegetisches Handbuch zum Alten Testament, 12. Leipzig; Hirzel, 1880.
Elliger, Karl. *Leviticus*. Handbuch zum Alten Testament, I/4. Tübingen: Mohr/ Siebeck, 1966.
Ewald, Heinrich G. A. *Einleitung in die Geschichte des Volkes Israel*. Geschichte des Volkes Israel bis Christus, 1; 2nd edition. Göttingen: Dieterichschen Buchhandlung, 1851.
Feucht, Christian. *Untersuchungen zum Heiligkeitsgesetz*. Theologische Arbeiten 20. Berlin: Evangelische Verlagsanstalt, 1964.
Fleming, Daniel E. *The Legacy of Israel in Judah's Bible: History, Politics and the Reinscribing of Tradition*. Cambridge: Cambridge University Press, 2012.
Graf, Karl-Heinrich. *Die Geschichtlichen Bücher des Alten Testaments: Zwei Historisch-Kritische Untersuchungen*. Leipzig: Weigel, 1866.
Gray, George Buchanan, *A Critical and Exegetical Commentary on Numbers*. ICC. Edinburgh: T. & T. Clark, 1903.
Greenfield, Jonah C. "Našû-Nadānu and its Congeners." In *'Al Kanfei Yonah: Collected Studies of Jonas C. Greenfield on Semitic Philology*, edited by Shalom M. Paul, et al., 2 vols., 2.720–24. Jerusalem: Magnes Press / Leiden: Brill, 2001.
Gunkel, Hermann. *Genesis*, 3rd edition. Handkommentar zum Alten Testament, I/1. Göttingen: Vandenhoeck & Ruprecht, 1910.
Haran, Menahem. "The Law-code of Ezekiel XL–XLVIII and its Relation to the Priestly School." *HUCA* 50 (1979) 45–71.
Holzinger, Heinrich. *Exodus*. Kurzer Hand-Commentar zum Alten Testament, 2. Freiburg: Mohr/Siebeck, 1902.
Houtman, Cornelis. *Exodus*. 4 vols. Historical Commentary on the Old Testament 2. Kampen: Kok / Leuven: Peeters, 1993–2002.
Hurowitz, Victor A. "The Priestly Account of the Building of the Tabernacle." *JAOS* 105 (1985) 21–30.
Hurvitz, Avi. "Dating the Priestly Source in Light of the Historical Study of Biblical Hebrew. A Century after Wellhausen." *ZAW* 100 (1988) 88–100.
———. "The Evidence of Language in Dating the Priestly Code." *RB* 81 (1974) 24–56.
———. *A Linguistic Study of the Relationship between the Priestly Source and the Book of Ezekiel*. Cahiers de la Revue Biblique 20. Paris: Gabalda, 1982.

———. "Once Again: The Linguistic Profile of the Priestly Material in the Pentateuch and its Historical Age – A Response to J. Blenkinsopp." *ZAW* 112 (2000) 180–91.

Joosten, Jan. "Diachronic Aspects of Narrative *Wayhi* in Biblical Hebrew." *JNSL* 35 (2009) 45–64.

———. *People and Land in the Holiness Code: An Exegetical Study of the Ideational Framework of the Law in Leviticus 17—26*. VTSup 67. Leiden: Brill, 1996.

Klostermann, August. "Beiträge zur Entstehungsgeschichte des Pentateuchs." *Zeitschrift für die gesammte lutherische Theologie und Kirche* 38 (1877) 401–45.

Knohl, Israel. *The Sanctuary of Silence: The Priestly Torah and the Holiness School*. Minneapolis: Fortress, 1995.

Koch, Klaus. *Die Priesterschrift von Exodus 25 bis Leviticus 16: Eine überlieferungsgeschichtliche und literarkritische Untersuchung*. Forschungen zur Religion und Literatur des Alten und Neuen Testaments, 71. Göttingen: Vandenhoeck & Ruprecht, 1959.

Koh, A. J., et al. "Characterizing a Middle Bronze Palatial Wine Cellar from Tel Kabri, Israel." *Plos One* 9,8 (2014). No pages. On line: http//:www.plosone.org/e106406 (accessed 28 August 2015).

Kuenen, Abraham. *An Historico-Critical Inquiry into the Origin and Composition of the Hexateuch*, translated by Philip H. Wicksteed. London: MacMillan, 1886.

Lemaire, André. " Levantine Literacy (ca. 1000–750 BCE)." In *Contextualizing Israel's Sacred Writings: Ancient Literacy, Orality, and Literary Production*, edited by Brian B. Schmidt, 11–45. Ancient Israel and Its Literature 22. Atlanta: Society of Biblical Literature, 2015.

Leuchter, Mark. "Sociolinguistic and Rhetorical Implications of the Source Citations in Kings." In *Soundings in Kings: Perspectives and Methods in Contemporary Scholarship*, edited by Mark Leuchter and Klaus-Peter Adam, 119–34. Minneapolis: Fortress, 2010.

Levine, Baruch A. *Leviticus: The JPS Torah Commentary*. Philadelphia: Jewish Publication Society, 1989.

Levinson, Bernard M. "The Manumission of Hermeneutics: The Slave Laws of the Pentateuch as a Challenge to Contemporary Pentateuchal Theory." In *Congress Volume, Leiden 2004*, edited by André Lemaire, 281–324. VTSup 109. Leiden: Brill, 2006.

Loewenstamm, Samuel, E. *Comparative Studies in Biblical and Ancient Oriental Literatures*. AOAT 204. Kevelaer: Butzon & Bercker / Neukirchen-Vluyn: Neukirchener, 1980.

———. "The Development of the Term 'First' in the Semitic Languages." In Loewenstamm, *Comparative Studies*, 13–16.

———. "The Flood." In Loewenstamm, *Comparative Studies*, 93–121.

Lohfink, Norbert. "Fortschreibung? Zur Technik vom Rechtsrevisionen im deuteronomischen Bereich, erörtert an Deuteronomium 12, Ex 21,2–11 und Dtn 15,12–18." In *Das Deuteronomium und seine Querbeziehungen*, edited by Timo Veijola, 133–81. Schriften der Finnischen Exegetischen Gesellschaft 62. Göttingen: Vandenhoeck & Ruprecht, 1996.

———. "The Priestly Narrative and History." In Norbert Lohfink, *Theology of the Pentateuch: Themes of the Priestly Narrative and Deuteronomy*, translated by Linda M. Maloney, 136–72. Edinburgh: T. & T. Clark, 1994.

McEvenue, Sean E. *The Narrative Style of the Priestly Writer*. Analecta Biblica 50. Rome: Biblical Institute Press, 1971.

Milgrom, Jacob. "The Antiquity of the Priestly Source: A Reply to Joseph Blenkinsopp." *ZAW* 111 (1999), 10–22.

———. "The Consecration of the Priests: A Literary Comparison of Leviticus 8 and Exodus 29." In *Ernten was man säht. Festschrift für Klaus Koch zu seinem 65. Geburtstag*, edited by Dwight R. Daniels et al., 273–86. Neukirchen-Vluyn: Neukirchener Verlag, 1991.

———. *Leviticus*, 3 vols. AB 3, 3A, 3B. New York: Doubleday, 1991–2000.

———. "Priestly Terminology and the Political and Social Structure of Pre-Monarchic Israel." *JQR* 69 (1978) 65–81.

Millard, Alan R. "Books and Writing in Kings." In *The Books of Kings: Sources, Composition and Reception*, edited by André Lemaire et al., 155–62. VTSup 129. Leiden: Brill, 2010.

———. "The Corpus of West-Semitic Stamp Seals: Review Article." *IEJ* 51 (2001) 76–87.

Miller-Naudé, Cynthia L., and Ziony Zevit, eds. *Diachrony in Biblical Hebrew*. Winona Lake, IN: Eisenbrauns, 2012.

Mizrahi, Noam. "Go Figure! The Linguistic History of the Numeral '11' in Biblical Hebrew as a Case Study for Some Pitfalls of the Linguistic Dating of P." Paper presented at the conference "Convergence and Divergence in Pentateuchal Studies: Bridging the Academic Cultures of Israel, Europe, and North America." Jerusalem, 12 May 2013.

———. "The History and Linguistic Background of Two Hebrew Titles for the High Priest." *JBL* 130 (2011) 687–705.

Na'aman, Nadav. "The Distribution of Messages in the Kingdom of Judah in Light of the Lachish Ostraca," *VT* 53 (2003) 169–80.

———. "Literacy in the Negev of the Late Monarchical Period." In *Contextualizing Israel's Sacred Writings: Ancient Literacy, Orality, and Literary Production*, edited by Brian B. Schmidt, 47–70. Ancient Israel and Its Literature 22. Atlanta: Society of Biblical Literature, 2015.

Niditch, Susan. *Oral World and Written Word: Ancient Israelite Literature*. Louisville: John Knox Press, 1996.

Nihan, Christophe. *From Priestly Torah to Pentateuch: A Study in the Composition of Leviticus*. FAT 25. Tübingen: Mohr/Siebeck, 2007.

———. "The Priestly Laws of Numbers, the Holiness Legislation, and the Pentateuch." In *Torah and the Book of Numbers*, edited by Christian Frevel et al., 109–37. FAT 62. Tübingen: Mohr/Siebeck, 2013.

Nöldeke, Theodor. *Untersuchungen zur Kritik des Alten Testaments*. Kiel: Schwers'sche Buchhandlung, 1869.

Noth, Martin. *Exodus. A Commentary*. Translated by John S. Bowden. London: SCM Press, 1962.

Paran, Meir. *Forms of the Priestly Style in the Pentateuch: Patterns, Linguistic Usages, Syntactic Structures* (in Hebrew, with English summary). Jerusalem: Magnes, 1989.

Pardee, Dennis G. "A New Letter from Ugarit." *BO* 44 (1977) 3–20.

Polak, Frank H. *Biblical Narrative: Aspects of Art and Design* (in Hebrew), 2nd edition. Jerusalem: Bialik, 1999.

———. "The Book of Samuel and the Deuteronomist: A Syntactic-Stylistic Analysis." In *Die Samuelbücher und die Deuteronomisten*, edited by Christa Schäfer-Lichtenberger, 34–73. Beiträge zur Wissenschaft vom Alten und Neuen Testament, 188. Stuttgart: Kohlhammer, 2010.

———. "Epic Formulas in Biblical Narrative: Frequency and Distribution." In *Actes du second colloque internationale Bible et Informatique: mèthodes, outils, résultats (Jerusalem, 9–13 Juin 1988)*, 435–88. Genève: Champion-Slatkine, 1989.

———. "Language Variation, Discourse Typology, and the Socio-Cultural Background of Biblical Narrative." In *Diachrony in Biblical Hebrew*, edited by Cynthia L. Miller-Naudé and Ziony Zevit, 301–38. Winona Lake, IN: Eisenbrauns, 2012.

———. "The Oral and the Written: Syntax, Stylistics and the Development of Biblical Prose Narrative." *JANES* 26 (1998) 59–104.

———. "Oral Substratum, Stylistic-Syntactic Profile and Thematic Flow in the Abraham-Jacob Narrative." In *Contextualizing Israel's Sacred Writings: Ancient Literacy, Orality, and Literary Production*, edited by Brian B. Schmidt, 217–38. Ancient Israel and Its Literature 22. Atlanta: Society of Biblical Literature, 2015.

———. "Orality: Biblical Hebrew." In *EHLL* 2.930–37.

———. "Poetic Style and Parallelism in the Creation Account (Gen. 1.1–2.3)." In *Creation in Jewish and Christian Tradition*, edited by Henning Reventlow and Yair Hoffman, 2–31. JSOTSup 319. Sheffield: Sheffield Academic Press, 2002.

———. "Sociolinguistics, a Key to the Typology and the Social Background of Biblical Hebrew." *HS* 47 (2006) 115–62.

———. "Verbs of Motion in Biblical Hebrew: Lexical Shifts and Syntactic Structure." in *A Palimpsest: Rhetoric, Ideology, Stylistics, and Language Relating to Persian Israel*, edited by Ehud Ben-Zvi et al., 161–97. Piscataway, NJ: Gorgias, 2009.

Polzin, Robert. *Late Biblical Hebrew: Toward an Historical Typology of Biblical Hebrew Prose*. Harvard Semitic Museum 12. Missoula, MT: Scholars, 1976.

Qimron, Elisha. "Review of Avi Hurvitz, *A Linguistic Study of the Relationship between the Priestly Source and the Book of Ezekiel* (1982)" (in Hebrew). *Leshonenu* 51 (1987–1988) 235–9.

Rendsburg, Gary. "Late Biblical Hebrew and the Date of P." *JANES* 12 (1982) 65–80.

Rendtorff, Rolf. *Die Gesetze in der Priesterschrift*. Forschungen zur Religion und Literatur des Alten und Neuen Testaments, 62. 2nd ed. Göttingen: Vandenhoeck & Ruprecht, 1963.

Rubin, David C. *Memory in Oral Traditions. The Cognitive Psychology of Epics, Ballads and Counting-Out Rhymes*. New York: Oxford University Press, 1995.

Schmidt, Brian B., ed. *Contextualizing Israel's Sacred Writings: Ancient Literacy, Orality, and Literary Production*. Ancient Israel and Its Literature 22. Atlanta: Society of Biblical Literature, 2015.

Schniedewind, William M. *How the Bible Became a Book: The Textualization of Ancient Israel*. Cambridge, UK: Cambridge University Press, 2004.

Smith, Mark S. "The Baal Cycle." In *Ugaritic Narrative Poetry*, edited by S. B. Parker, 81–180. SBLWAW 9. Atlanta: Scholars, 1997.

———. *The Priestly Vision of Genesis 1*. Minneapolis: Fortress, 2010.

Smith, Mark S. and Wayne T. Pitard, *The Ugaritic Baal Cycle*: vol. 2: *Introduction with Text, Translation and Commentary of KTU/CAT 1.3–1.4*. VTSup 114. Leiden: Brill, 2009.

Stackert, Jeffrey. "The Sabbath of the Land in the Holiness Legislation: Combining Priestly and Non-Priestly Perspectives." *CBQ* 73 (2011) 239–50.

Vanstiphout, Herman L. J. "Repetition and Structure in The Aratta Cycle: Their Relevance for the Orality Debate." In *Mesopotamian Epic Literature: Oral or Aural?*, edited by Marianna E. Vogelzang and H. L. J. Vanstiphout, 247–64. Lewiston: Mellen, 1992.

Weinfeld, Moshe, "Gen. 7.11, 8.1–2 against the Background of the Ancient Near Eastern Tradition." *Die Welt des Orients* 9 (1977) 242–48.

Weimar, Peter. "Gen 17 und die priesterschriftliche Abrahamgeschichte." *ZAW* 100 (1988) 22–60.

Yasur-Landau, Asaf et al. "An MB II Orthostat Building at Tel Kabri, Israel." *BASOR* 367 (2012) 1–29.

Zevit, Ziony. "Converging Lines of Evidence Bearing on the Date of P." *ZAW* 94 (1982) 481–511.

———. "Dating Torah Documents: From Wellhausen to Polak." In *Discourse, Dialogue and Debate in the Bible. Essays in Honor of Frank Polak*, edited by Athalya Brenner-Idan, 258–91. Hebrew Bible Monographs 63; Amsterdam Studies in Bible and Religion 7. Sheffield: Sheffield Phoenix Press, 2014.

———. *Matres Lectionis in Ancient Hebrew Epigraphs*. ASOR Monograph Series 2. Cambridge, MA: American Schools of Oriental Research, 1980.

———. "Not-So-Random Thoughts on Linguistic Dating and Diachrony in Biblical Hebrew." In *Diachrony in Biblical Hebrew*, edited by Cynthia L. Miller-Naudé and Ziony Zevit, 455–89. Winona Lake, IN: Eisenbrauns, 2012.

———. "Philology, Archeology and a *terminus a quo* for P's ḥaṭṭā't Legislation." In *Pomegranates and Golden Bells: Studies in Biblical, Jewish, and Near Eastern Ritual Law and Literature in Honor of Jacob Milgrom*, edited by David P. Wright et al., 29–38. Winona Lake, IN: Eisenbrauns, 1995.

———. *The Religions of Ancient Israel: A Synthesis of Parallactic Approaches*. London: Continuum, 2001.

———. "What A Difference a Year Makes." *HS* 47 (2006) 83–90.

20

שֶׁמֶן תּוּרַק *šɛmɛn turaq* (Song 1:3)

Gary A. Rendsburg and Ian Young

RUTGERS UNIVERSITY / UNIVERSITY OF SYDNEY

The first two poetic lines of Song of Songs (following the superscription) read as follows in the Masoretic Text (MT):

2 יִשָּׁקֵ֙נִי֙ מִנְּשִׁיק֣וֹת פִּ֔יהוּ כִּֽי־טוֹבִ֥ים דֹּדֶ֖יךָ מִיָּֽיִן׃

3 לְרֵ֙יחַ֙ שְׁמָנֶ֣יךָ טוֹבִ֔ים שֶׁ֖מֶן תּוּרַ֣ק שְׁמֶ֑ךָ עַל־כֵּ֖ן עֲלָמ֥וֹת אֲהֵבֽוּךָ׃

> 2 May he kiss me with the kisses of his mouth,
> for your love is better than wine.
> 3 To the scent of your good oils,
> *turaq* oil is your name;
> therefore the maidens love you.[1]

The meaning of the expression שֶׁמֶן תּוּרַק in v. 3 continues to elude scholars. Although the ancient versions, and more recently, the Qumran text 6Q6 = 6QCant have informed scholarly proposals in regard to the phrase, they are in fact of little help in understanding the meaning of the MT. In fact, the ancient witnesses are usually understood to reflect a variant text, as opposed to presenting an interpretation of the text which emerged as

---

1. For this translation, see Noegel and Rendsburg, *Solomon's Vineyard*, 189.

the MT.[2] Thus, the LXX μύρον ἐκκενωθὲν 'perfume poured out'[3] (lit. 'myrrh poured out'), the other Greek versions, Aquila and Origen's Quinta, ἔλαιον ἐκχεόμενον 'olive-oil poured out', and the Vulgate *oleum effusum* 'oil poured out'[4] are all understood as reflecting the graphically similar Hebrew word מוּרָק, the *Hoph'al* participle of the root ר-י-ק 'empty', hence 'poured out'.[5] The Peshitta's rendering משחא דמורא 'oil of myrrh' represents either yet another *Vorlage*, without the word in question, or an interpretation of the MT form as referring to a specific type of oil. Even further away from the MT, the corresponding part of the verse in 6QCant has been restored as מרֹ[קחת מורקה] 'an aromatic mixture poured out.'[6]

In this article our aim is not to discover the "original text" of this passage,[7] but simply to clarify what the MT offers at this point. Therefore, while it is obviously interesting, and important, that שֶׁמֶן תּוּרַק was not present in all ancient texts of the Song of Songs, this observation is not relevant to our attempt to elucidate the MT reading, unless it can be demonstrated that the MT is an obvious error for one of the other readings. We shall argue in what follows that it is better to view the MT phrase שֶׁמֶן תּוּרַק as a meaningful reading rather than as an error.

While there is no need to rehearse all of the many emendations and explanations offered for this phrase here,[8] a representative sampling follows

---

2. For a succinct presentation of the textual evidence, with commentary, see Dirksen, "Canticles," 11, 56*.

3. Thus the rendering in *NETS*, 662.

4. The highly paraphrastic Targum is also often considered to reflect this reading: "and your Holy Name was heard in all the earth, for it is choicer than the oil of anointment which is anointed (מתרבא) on the heads of kings and priests." For discussion, see Alexander, *Targum to Canticles*, 79–80.

5. Alternatively, these versions present an interpretation of the MT as a noun formed with *taw* from the same verbal root, literally 'oil of pouring out'.

6. Baillet, "Cantique des Cantiques," 113; cf. Dirksen, "Canticles," 56*.

7. Rendsburg tends to view the MT as close to the original text that left the pen of the author (see, for example, Rendsburg, *Psalms*, 16–17); whereas Young tends to see the MT as just one of the important late witnesses to the biblical text and usually puts the words "original text" in quotes (Rezetko and Young, *Historical Linguistics and Biblical Hebrew*, esp. 71–77).

8. We also do not mention the specific proposers of these suggested solutions, though we may direct the interested reader to the following summaries: Pope, *Song of Songs*, 300; Murphy, *The Song of Songs*, 125; Fox, *The Song of Songs*, 98; Garrett, *Song of Songs*, 125; Dirksen, "Canticles," 56*; Fishbane, *Song of Songs*, 29, 226. See also the dictionaries, Gesenius, *Handwörterbuch*, 6:1241; and *DCH*, 8:616, 758. For a detailed attempt to elucidate our word by an anonymous medieval Karaite grammarian writing in Judeo-Persian, see Khan, *Early Karaite Grammatical Texts*, 258–61, 304–5. For the most thorough treatment, with an albeit unacceptable (in our estimation) solution, see

below. As we shall see, the evidence of the versions informs some of the proposals suggested by modern scholars, though in some instances commentators have proceeded independently. Not all of the proposals surveyed here are, therefore, directly relevant to our narrower focus on the explanation of the MT. Nevertheless, it is important to get a grasp on the range of proposals, including their strengths and weaknesses. Here, then, the representative sampling of proposals, as promised above:

- a. תּוּרַק is the 3rd fem. sg. *Hophʻal* prefix-conjugation form of the root ר-י-ק 'empty', hence 'emptied' or 'poured out', in line with the Greek and Latin readings mentioned above.[9] This understanding, however, creates a grammatical incongruence, since שֶׁמֶן 'oil' is masculine, whereas the proposed תּוּרַק 'poured out' is feminine.[10] While lack of gender agreement occurs sporadically in the Bible,[11] one should be careful not to introduce another instance into the text unnecessarily.

- b. תּוּרַק should be emended to מוּרָק 'poured out', the *Hophʻal* participle of the aforementioned root, once more in line with the LXX and Vulgate renderings. This solves the lack of gender agreement mentioned above, though one must admit that *taw* and *mem* do not look alike in either the paleo-Hebrew script

---

Stoop – van Paridon, *The Song of Songs*, 28–30, 37–38.

9. The sense is that oil when decanted releases its scent, as noted by Rashi and Yosef Qimḥi, among others. Unless otherwise indicated, the comments of the medieval Jewish commentators cited in this footnote and the following one are accessed via Cohen, *Miqraʼot Gedolot ha-Keter: Ḥameš Megillot*, 4–7. For earlier rabbinic understandings of the word, based on the meaning 'poured out', and midrashic extrapolations therefrom, see Green, *Aroma of Righteousness*, 150–56.

10. As observed already by the aforementioned anonymous Karaite scholar, for which see Khan, *Early Karaite Grammatical Texts*, 258–9; and by several rabbinical commentators, such as Tobiah ben Eliezer (Leqaḥ Ṭov) and Isaiah di Trani (Rid), for which see Fishbane, *Song of Songs*, 29, 226, nn. 42–43. The efforts by both Isaiah di Trani and Abraham ibn Ezra to resolve the difficulty are, as one would expect from their pens, ingenious. The former considered תּוּרַק to be of the same *mišqal* as תּוֹשָׁב 'resident', the difference in the first vowel notwithstanding, with a nod to David Qimḥi, *Sefer ha-Šorašim*. The latter called attention to passages such as 2 Sam 17:12, Prov 2:18, Qoh 4:4, in which common masculine nouns appear to be treated as feminine.

11. See Rendsburg, *Diglossia in Ancient Hebrew*, 69–83. Note, however, that in almost all cases, it is the masculine form which replaces the feminine form; see, e.g., pp. 77–78 for a list of feminine nouns followed by masculine attributes (adjective or participle). In fact, we know of no instance in the Bible where a masculine noun is followed by feminine attribute (other than Gen 32:9, 1 Kgs 19:4K, which involve the numeral '1'), as would be required by this understanding of שֶׁמֶן תּוּרַק 'oil poured out'.

or the later square Hebrew script. Therefore it is unlikely that the MT reading is simply an erroneous version of the other. Instead, it must be treated as a reading in its own right, and an attempt must be made to explain it as meaningful. In addition, and this is relevant for both of these proposals, as Michael Fox observed, "but the oil's being poured out would not enhance the praiseworthiness of the boy's name."[12]

c. תּוּרַק should be emended to תַּמְרוּק 'cosmetics', especially since such are associated with women (Esth 2:3, 2:9, 2:12). To our mind, however, facile emendation in such drastic measure (introducing a *mem* and reversing the order of *waw-resh* to *resh-waw*) is uncalled for, especially if one can make sense of the current text.

d. The proposed restoration of 6Q6 = 6QCant 1:3 מר̇]קחת 'perfume', mentioned above, should be read.[13] Note, however, that this also entails deleting the word שמן, since the previous line ends with the phrase שמנים טובים (end of line 2), and then one reads מר̇] (start of line 3). It seems best to take this as simply a different text to the MT. It also should be noted, with Roland Murphy, "but it is quite difficult to discern support for the reading in the published photograph."[14] Regardless of the reading, this Qumran recension should be explained on its own merits—but to our mind it is not relevant to the elucidation of the MT.

e. תּוּרַק is to be derived from the root י-ר-ק, whence various nouns related to 'green, herbage, vegetation' are constructed, based on the fact that olive oil typically has a green hue. The quality of olive oil, however, is not determined by its color, but rather by other means and factors.

f. תּוּרַק is to be understood as a place name (thus already Tamakh = R. Abraham ben Isaac ha-Levi [Spain, d. 1393]). While naturally this is possible, we have no further evidence

---

12. Fox, *The Song of Songs*, 98. Perhaps, though, the reference is to the attractive scent released by the pouring of the oil, for which see above, n. 9.

13. Again, for the text and discussion, see Baillet, "Cantique des Cantiques," 113.

14. Murphy, *The Song of Songs*, 125. Upon inspecting the photograph published at the Leon Levy Dead Sea Scrolls Digital Library website (http://www.deadseascrolls.org.il/explore-the-archive/image/B-284841), we concur with Murphy's assessment.

for such a toponym, amongst the hundreds of such proper nouns in the Bible and cognate literature.

The best step forward, in our estimation, was taken by Marvin Pope, who, in his magisterial Anchor Bible commentary in 1977, pointed to the following line from a Ugaritic administrative text (*CAT/KTU* 3.13, line 20), within a list of commodities:[15]

> w . ṯn . irpm . w . ṯn . trqm

'and two (measures of) *irpm* and two (measures of) *trqm*'

The word *irp* almost undoubtedly means 'wine' (or refers to a specific type of wine), based on the Egyptian word *irp* 'wine'.[16] In parallel with this word, to quote Pope, "it seems likely that *trq* is a term for some type of high grade cosmetic oil, as suggested also by the context of its occurrence in the Song of Songs."[17] Note, incidentally, that the word *šmn* 'oil', with reference to ordinary oil presumably, also occurs in said Ugaritic text (lines 3 and 5, and perhaps to be restored in line 9 as well).[18]

We accept Pope's interpretation of both the Ugaritic document and Song 1:3, but this only raises the question: what, then, is the etymology of the word *trq* / תּוּרָק ? Unrecognized until now is the presence of this root in the Karatepe inscription.[19] Azitawada boasts:

---

15. In earlier editions of *CAT/KTU*, the text was given the designation 4.123, and thus it is cited, accordingly, in earlier studies. The third (and most recent) edition of *CAT/KTU* (see pp. 235–6), however, has reclassified and hence has renumbered the text, so that it now bears the designation 3.13.

16. See Gordon, *Ugaritic Textbook*, 366, §19.371. For other suggestions, see *DULAT* 1:105.

17. Pope, *Song of Songs*, 300. For a similar comment, see Noegel and Rendsburg, *Solomon's Vineyard*, 189, n. b. For the most detailed study building upon Pope's discovery, see Loretz, "Die ugaritisch-hebräische Gefäßbezeichnung" – per the title of his article, note that Loretz considered *trq* to refer to a type of vessel, one that contained high-quality oil (see also next note).

18. For a presentation and translation of the text, see McGeough and Smith, *Ugaritic Economic Texts*, 378–9. Note that these scholars also (see previous note) understand both *irpm* and *trqm* as types of vessels. See similarly *DULAT* 2:879. The text receives brief mention in Heltzer, "Olive Growing and Olive Oil in Ugarit," 81, but the key word *trqm* is not discussed.

19. Or to be more accurate, quite obviously, experts have understood that the root ת-ר-ק occurs in the Karatepe inscription, and they have discerned the meaning from the context (see anon), but no one has connected this verb to the form תּוּרָק in Song 1:3 (see further anon).

Version A, col. 1, line 9: ותרק אנך כל הרע אש כן בארץ
'and I crushed all the evil which was in the land'
Version C, col. 1, lines 15–16: [ות]רקת כל הרע אש כן בארץ
'and I crushed all the evil which was in the land'

(The two versions read essentially the same; the only difference is the use of the infinitive absolute plus independent pronoun to express the past in Version A vs. the use of the 1st com. sg. suffix-conjugation verb in Version C.)

The verb ת-ר-ק occurs only here within the Phoenician corpus, and no one has proposed a certain etymology.[20] Its meaning, accordingly, must be derived mainly from the context, though there is a certain amount of consensus nonetheless. In fact, already the earliest interpreters of the Karatepe inscription were able to ascertain the meaning of the root ת-ר-ק. A. M. Honeyman rendered the word 'crushed',[21] with an eye to the byform ט-ר-ק, "which is known from later Hebrew, Aramaic and Arabic; translate 'pound, beat, crush.'"[22] Albrecht Alt left an ellipsis in his translation, but then proposed either 'ausrotten' or 'ausleeren' in his commentary, deduced primarily from context.[23] Dupont-Sommer rendered the word as 'détruire', with a nod to Aramaic ת-ר-ך 'drive out' (cf. Targum Onqelos to Gen 3:23) and Akkadian *tarāku* 'beat, strike' (on the issue of the *k/q* interchange, see below).[24]

More recent editions of the Karatepe inscription have, for the most part, repeated the interpretations of the earliest scholars who studied the text. François Bron also rendered the word 'détruire', and very helpfully included a summary of other early attempts.[25] J. C. L. Gibson translated

---

20. The parallel Hieroglyphic Luwian text is not a direct word-for-word counterpart of the Phoenician text, and thus it cannot always settle the question of the meaning of a Phoenician lexeme. Nevertheless, its evidence is potentially relevant. Unfortunately, the Hieroglyphic Luwian text is unclear at this point. One text (Hu) is broken, while the other (Ho) uses an unknown logogram. Hawkins, *Corpus of Hieroglyphic Luwian Inscriptions*, 50, 60, gives the rendering '[remov]ed' with the square brackets indicating the broken or unclear text. He has conjectured the meaning 'removed' in the Hieroglyphic Luwian text based on the preservation of the preverb ARHA 'away' and (at least in Ho) the ablative case of the word 'land'. The authors would like to thank Craig Melchert (UCLA) for his expert advice on the Hieroglyphic Luwian text.

21. Honeyman, "Epigraphic Discoveries at Karatepe," 26, 32.

22. Ibid. For Arabic *ṭ-r-q* 'beat, strike', see Lane, *Arabic-English Lexicon*, 1846. For Aramaic (JBA) *ṭ-r-q* 'bite, sting', see *CAL*, s.v. *ṭ-r-q*. The suggested Hebrew form is limited to a single attestation (according to Ma'agarim), to wit, b. B. Qam. 115b, though the meaning there appears to be 'stir, mix'.

23. Alt, "Die phönikischen Inschriften von Karatepe," 274, 281.

24. Dupont-Sommer, "Etude du texte phénicien: Des inscriptions de Karatepe," 122. For the Akkadian, see *CAD* T, 203–5. For the Aramaic, see *CAL*, s.v. *t-r-k*.

25. Bron, *Recherches sur les inscriptions phéniciennes de Karatepe*, 53.

the word 'drove out',[26] with the note, "otherwise unknown; perhaps cognate with Akkad. *tarāku* 'to beat, strike' or better Aram. תרך Pael, 'drove out' (Targum [Onqelos] Gen. iii 23)."[27] *KAI* suggested 'ausrotten' (?), with the additional comment "vgl. arab. *taraqa*?"[28]—though this Arabic verb is not widely attested.[29] Hans-Peter Müller rendered the word 'zerschlug', with the comment "vgl. akkad. *tarāku(m)* 'schlagen'."[30] *DNWSI*, in its usual comprehensive manner, surveyed these and many other proposals, with the comments "meaning derived from context . . . uncert. etymology," and with the following verbs all listed as possible options: 'destroy, drive out, strike, smash, remove, take away, crush, break, shatter'.[31] In the most complete treatment of the Karatepe inscription to appear in recent years, K. Lawson Younger rendered the word as 'crushed', with a footnote referring to much of what we have summarized here.[32] Wolfgang Röllig opted for 'extirpated', with the note "probable from the context but the etymology of the verb is uncertain."[33] Finally, the entry in Charles Krahmalkov's dictionary of Phoenician reads: "T-R-Q [?etym] v. *qal* ERADICATE (from context)."[34]

Of all these options, as argued below, we prefer the rendering 'crushed' for Phoenician ת-ר-ק, cognate to the byform represented by the Aramaic and Akkadian roots *t-r-k*, as proposed early on in Karatepe scholarship by Dupont-Sommer and at a later stage by Gibson (again, on the matter of *k/q* interchange, see below). The closest biblical passage, which may be used to substantiate this specific meaning, is Mal 3:21 וְעַסּוֹתֶם רְשָׁעִים 'and you shall crush the wicked', using the verbal root ע-ס-ס 'crush, squeeze'—with a context quite similar to that of the Karatepe inscription, that is, the removal of evil or the wicked from the land. This is the only instance of this verb in Biblical Hebrew, though the root is better known as the basis of the noun עָסִיס 'sweet-wine' (or some such type of wine), due to the fact that grapes are crushed or squeezed in order to produce wine.

This, in turn, brings us back to תּוּרַק, which should be understood as the Qal passive of the selfsame root ת-ר-ק, with cognates in Ugaritic and

---

26. Gibson, *Textbook*, 3:47.

27. Ibid., 3:57. Gibson did not cite Dupont-Sommer (see above, n. 24) explicitly, though clearly he was indebted to his approach.

28. *KAI* 2:40.

29. See Lane, *Arabic-English Lexicon*, 304.

30. Müller, "Phönizische historische Inschriften," 641.

31. *DNWSI* 2:1233–4.

32. Younger, "The Phoenician Inscription of Azatiwada," 15.

33. Röllig, "The Phoenician Inscriptions," 51, 59.

34. Krahmalkov, *Phoenician-Punic Dictionary*, 498.

Phoenician. The word means 'beaten, crushed', hence the phrase שֶׁמֶן תּוּרָק means 'beaten oil, crushed oil', on par with the more common expression שֶׁמֶן כָּתִית 'beaten oil, crushed oil' (Exod 29:40, Num 28:5, 1 Kgs 5:25; see also Exod 27:20, Lev 24:2). The aforecited Ugaritic *trq*, then, refers to the same high-quality oil, which apparently could be used without the broader noun *šmn* preceding.

Thus far the etymology of תּוּרָק and its Ugaritic and Phoenician congeners; we now turn to the form of the word. Since the Tiberian reading tradition often preserves much older linguistic information, we take seriously the specific form of the word as transmitted by the MT.[35] As indicated above, תּוּרָק 'crushed' is to be understood as the internal passive of the Qal, clear vestiges of which remain in the biblical text.[36] One difficulty emerges, however, for the Qal passive suffix-conjugation is formed with *pataḥ* in the second syllable (see, e.g., Gen 37:33 טֹרַף 'he was torn', along with those forms which are accommodated to the Puʻal, such as Gen 3:23 לֻקַּח 'he was taken'); while the participle of the Qal passive is formed with *qameṣ* (see, e.g., 2 Kgs 2:10 לֻקָּח 'taken'; others are in pause, so that *qameṣ* appears regardless, thus most famously perhaps Exod 3:2 וְהַסְּנֶה אֵינֶנּוּ אֻכָּל 'and the bush was not consumed'; again, these examples are accommodated to the Puʻal). According to these principles, the form תּוּרָק 'crushed' should be a suffix-conjugation form, and not a participle—though naturally one expects the latter form to serve as the attribute following שֶׁמֶן. One may wish to argue that in this particular case, the expected shift of *turaq > turāq* (due to the accented second syllable)[37] did not occur, perhaps due to the presence of the two consonants pronounced deep in the throat (uvular /r/ and velar /q/), though we ourselves find this explanation doubtful.

A better explanation, it seems to us, is to regard the phrase שֶׁמֶן תּוּרָק not as noun + participial attribute, but rather as a bare or asyndetic relative clause, hence, 'oil (which) has been crushed'.[38] The *ṭəʻamim* certainly suggest this, since simple noun + adjective combinations in Hebrew *always* constitute a single joined unit, with conjunctive accent on the first element (the noun) and disjunctive accent on the second element (the adjective);

---

35. On this issue in general, see Morag, "Historical Validity"; and Khan, "Biblical Hebrew."

36. For general discussion, see Joüon-Muraoka, *Grammar of Biblical Hebrew*, 166–8, §58; and Blau, *Phonology and Morphology of Biblical Hebrew*, 217–8, §4.3.5.1.2–§4.3.5.1.5.

37. See Blau, *Phonology and Morphology of Biblical Hebrew*, 218, §4.3.5.1.5.

38. We are grateful to Elizabeth Robar (Tyndale House and University of Cambridge) for this suggestion. For more on the subject, see Holmstedt, "The Relative Clause," 107–14; and Holmstedt, "Relative Clause: Biblical Hebrew," 352–3.

thus, for example, Gen 21:8 מִשְׁתֶּה גָדוֹל 'a large feast'; Exod 32:11 בְּכֹחַ גָּדוֹל וּבְיָד חֲזָקָה 'with great power and with a strong hand'; Deut 1:35, 3:25, 4:21 הָאָרֶץ הַטּוֹבָה 'the good land'; 1 Sam 19:5 בְּדָם נָקִי 'against innocent blood'; 2 Sam 23:10 תְּשׁוּעָה גְדוֹלָה 'the great salvation'; Isa 39:2 הַשֶּׁמֶן הַטּוֹב 'the good oil'; etc.[39] Since שֶׁמֶן תּוּרַק displays a different combination of *ṭaʿamim*, it should not be considered a noun phrase comprised of noun + adjective, but rather should be parsed per above. For additional instances of noun + null-relative-marker + SC verb, see, e.g., Ps 74:2 זְכֹר עֲדָתְךָ ׀ קָנִיתָ קֶּדֶם 'remember your congregation (which) you created long ago; Lam 1:21 יוֹם־קָרָאתָ 'the day (which) you announced'.

Next we turn to the question of the relationship between *t-r-q* / ק-ר-ת 'crush' in Canaanite and the proposed cognates Akkadian *tarāku* 'beat, strike', Aramaic ת-ר-ך 'drive out, divorce'.[40] This requires positing an interchange between the voiceless velar /k/ and its emphatic counterpart /q/. On the one hand, we could quote Pierre Swiggers on the matter, "in my eyes, this root [i.e., *t-r-q*—G.A.R. & I.Y.] must not be merged with the root *trk*."[41] On the other hand, we note that the related roots *t-r-q* / *t-r-k* include the sonorant /r/, so that the postulated interchange may thereby be explained.[42] A close parallel to the same interchange is found in the verb 'kill, slay' throughout Semitic:[43] Hebrew ק-ט-ל *q-ṭ-l*, Old Aramaic ק-ת-ל *q-t-l* (Samalian, Sefire,

---

39. We are exceedingly grateful to Joshua Harper (Africa International University, Nairobi) for conducting the research for us, via the BibleWorks 8.0 program. His investigation determined that *every* instance of simple noun + adjective (even when the noun phrase is definite or when the noun is preceded by a preposition) is marked with conjunctive and disjunctive accents, respectively. The examples listed here are but a few of the many present in the Bible. All possible exceptions which emerged from Dr. Harper's research are explicable: the phrase includes more than one adjective (e.g., Gen 41:6), a prepositional modifier occurs after the adjective (e.g., Amos 2:13), or the adjective is comprised of four syllables and thus bears two accent marks (Deut 10:10, Jer 29:17, Ezek 40:17, Qoh 7:10).

40. For ת-ר-ך 'divorce' in post-biblical Hebrew, see t. Giṭ. 4:5, y. Giṭ. 6:5, 48a—information via *Maʾagarim*. We consider any relationship with Arabic *ṭ-r-q* 'beat, strike', Aramaic (JBA) *ṭ-r-q* 'bite, sting', as proposed by Honeyman (see above, n. 21), to be possible, though in this case one needs to posit a /t/-/ṭ/ interchange of the sort represented in the words for 'kill, slay' listed below. Note, incidentally, that the Arabic verb is used mainly for striking with a hammer, while the Aramaic verb has yet a more distant connotation.

41. Swiggers, review of Bron, 338.

42. One also may wish to incorporate Old Akkadian *tarāqu* into the *t-r-q* / *t-r-k* picture, as proposed by Greenstein, review of Bron, 201, though to be sure the evidence for this lexeme is rather slim (see *CAD* T, 207).

43. For the different forms within Aramaic, see *DNWSI* 2:1006–7. For a summary of the cognate evidence throughout Semitic, see Gesenius, *Handwörterbuch*, 5:1162.

etc.) / ב-ט-ל *k-ṭ-l* (Nerab) / ק-ט-ל *q-ṭ-l* (Aḥiqar), and perhaps also ב-ת-ל *k-t-l* (Frahang), Arabic-Sabaic-Geʿez *q-t-l*—and once more we note the presence of the sonorant (in this case /l/) in the root.⁴⁴ In sum, we are inclined to accept the relationship of these different verbal roots, as proposed by Dupont-Sommer, Gibson, Müller, et al. (see above).⁴⁵

When Rendsburg sees a rare word (in this case a *hapax legomenon*) in a biblical composition which he considers to be written in Israelian Hebrew (IH),⁴⁶ with cognates in Ugaritic and Phoenician, he immediately ponders whether said lexeme is also not a feature of IH. In this case, that conclusion seems inescapable to him: one should consider the root *t-r-q* / ת-ר-ק 'crush', attested once each in Ugaritic, Phoenician, and Song of Songs to constitute a nexus between the Phoenic group⁴⁷ of Canaanite and northern Hebrew. As such, this item can be added to the list of items collected previously by Rendsburg.⁴⁸

Regardless of the matter raised in the previous paragraph, most importantly for this article generally: the three rare words—one a *hapax legomenon* in the Bible, one attested but once in the Ugaritic corpus, and one attested only once in the more limited Phoenician corpus—all mutually elucidate each other.

Finally, as previous studies have shown, rare words, including *hapax legomena*, frequently are employed by the biblical authors *alliterationis causa*.⁴⁹ Hence, when we encounter a word such as תּוּרָק within the phrase שֶׁמֶן תּוּרָק 'oil (which) has been crushed', our antennae go up wondering if the sounds of the phrase do not echo the sounds of nearby words. In this particular case, we propose that the poet employed the expression to evoke the sounds of מִנְּשִׁיקוֹת 'with the kisses' in v. 2. Note how the consonants of this word in v. 2, /m/-/n/-/š/-/q/-/t/, resonate with those of the key phrase in

---

44. For additional examples, see Brockelmann, *Grundriss*, 1:122, with most of the examples including the sonorant /r/ within the word.

45. We have decided to limit the discussion to what is presented here, without entering into the larger picture of which of the options may be the "original" root, in which way any assimilation or dissimilation may have occurred, to what effect Geers' Law may be present, etc., etc.

46. On Song of Songs as a northern composition, see Rendsburg, "Israelian Hebrew in the Song of Songs"; Noegel and Rendsburg, *Solomon's Vineyard*, 3–62; and Young, *Diversity in Pre-Exilic Hebrew*, 157–66. For Young's later change to greater caution in regard to Israelian Hebrew, see, for example, the references in Young, Rezetko and Ehrensvärd, *Linguistic Dating of Biblical Texts*, 193–5.

47. For this term, see Ginsberg, "The Northwest Semitic Languages," 104–6, 108–11.

48. See n. 46 above.

49. See, for example, Rendsburg, "Alliteration in the Exodus Narrative"; Rendsburg, "Alliteration"; and Noegel and Rendsburg, *Solomon's Vineyard*, 63–106.

v. 3, /š/-/m/-/n/-/t/-/r/-/q/. Every consonant in the former set finds its mate in the latter set; or to look at this in the opposite direction, every consonant but /r/ in שֶׁמֶן תּוּרַק is anticipated in מִנְּשִׁיקוֹת in the previous verse. This is what poets do: they use language for the creation of literature.

※

The reader will have recognized that the co-authors of this article take divergent positions on several issues. Another of these, not relevant to the present enterprise, is the question of Standard Biblical Hebrew (SBH) vs. Late Biblical Hebrew (LBH). Rendsburg accepts the common interpretation of a diachronic development from the former to the latter, while Young does not consider that the biblical manuscripts in our possession preserve evidence of the language of discrete historical periods. We are able to set aside these differences, however, for the larger goal, to honor our friend and colleague Ziony Zevit, who has done so much to advance the field of Biblical Hebrew philology throughout his distinguished career. As the knowledgeable reader will know further, our honoree has served as a bridge between the two schools mentioned above, through his organization of panels devoted to the question at SBL/NAPH conferences, and through his editing of the published papers in *Hebrew Studies*, vols. 46–47 (2005–2006), to which the two present authors both contributed.[50] It is in the spirit of the SBL/NAPH panels and the resultant *Hebrew Studies* volumes that we jointly offer this essay as a tribute to Ziony Zevit.

BIBLIOGRAPHY

Alexander, Philip S. *The Targum of Canticles*. The Aramaic Bible 17A. London: T. & T. Clark, 2003.

Alt, Albrecht. "Die phönikischen Inschriften von Karatepe." *Die Welt des Orients* I/4 (1949) 272–87.

Baillet, Maurice. "Grotte 6: Textes bibliques: Cantique des Cantiques." In *Les 'petites grottes' de Qumrân*, 112–14. DJD III. Oxford: Clarendon, 1962.

Blau, Joshua. *Phonology and Morphology of Biblical Hebrew*. Linguistic Studies in Ancient West Semitic 2. Winona Lake, IN: Eisenbrauns, 2010.

---

50. In the former volume, the published papers, including Zevit's comments, appear on pp. 321–76; in the latter volume, the published papers, including Zevit's comments, appear on pp. 83–210. The contributions of the present authors are Young, "Biblical Texts Cannot Be Dated Linguistically"; and Rendsburg, "Aramaic-Like Features in the Pentateuch." For yet a third editiorial effort from the desk of our honoree, see also Miller-Naudé and Zevit, *Diachrony in Biblical Hebrew*.

Brockelmann, Carl. *Grundriss der vergleichenden Grammatik der semitischen Sprachen*, 2 vols. Berlin: Reuther & Reichard, 1908–13.

Bron, François. *Recherches sur les inscriptions phéniciennes de Karatepe*. Hautes études orientales 11. Geneva: Droz, 1979.

Cohen, Menahem, ed. *Miqra'ot Gedolot ha-Keter: Ḥameš Megillot*. Ramat-Gan: Bar-Ilan University Press, 2012.

Dirksen, P. B. "Canticles." In *Biblia Hebraica quinta editione cum apparatu critico novis curis elaborato: General Introduction and Megilloth: Ruth, Canticles, Qoheleth, Lamentations, Esther*, edited by Adrian Schenker, 11–24, 8*–13*, 26*–28*, 38*–40*, 56*–64*. Stuttgart: Deutsche Bibelgesellschaft, 2004.

Dupont-Sommer, André. "Etude du texte phénicien: Des inscriptions de Karatepe." *Oriens* 2 (1949) 121–26.

Fishbane, Michael A. *Song of Songs*. The JPS Bible Commentary. Philadelphia: Jewish Publication Society, 2015.

Fox, Michael V. *The Song of Songs and the Ancient Egyptian Love Songs*. Madison: University of Wisconsin Press, 1985.

Garrett, Duane. *Song of Songs*. Word Biblical Commentary 23B. Nashville: Thomas Nelson, 2004.

Gesenius, Wilhelm et al. *Hebräisches und aramäisches Handwörterbuch über das Alte Testament*, 18th edition, 6 vols. Berlin: Springer, 1987–2010.

Gibson, John C. L. *Textbook of Syrian Semitic Inscriptions*, 3 vols. Oxford: Clarendon Press, 1973–1982.

Ginsberg, H. L. "The Northwest Semitic Languages." In *Patriarchs*, edited by Benjamin Mazar, 102–24, 293. World History of the Jewish People. New Brunswick, NJ: Rutgers University Press, 1970.

Gordon, Cyrus H. *Ugaritic Textbook*. Rome: Pontifical Biblical Institute, 1965.

Green, Deborah A. *The Aroma of Righteousness*. University Park, PA: Pennsylvania State University Press, 2011.

Greenstein, Edward L. Review of Bron, *Recherches sur les inscriptions phéniciennes de Karatepe*. *JAOS* 102 (1982) 200–01.

Hawkins, John David. *Corpus of Hieroglyphic Luwian Inscriptions*, vol. 1: *Inscriptions of the Iron Age*. Berlin: Walter de Gruyter, 2000.

Heltzer, Michael. "Olive Growing and Olive Oil in Ugarit." In *Olive Oil in Antiquity: Israel and Neighbouring Countries from the Neolithic to the Early Arab Period*, edited by David Eitam and Michael Heltzer, 77–89. History of the Ancient Near East, Studies 7. Padova: Sargon, 1996.

Holmstedt, Robert D. "The Relative Clause in Biblical Hebrew: A Linguistic Analysis." PhD diss., University of Wisconsin, 2002.

———. "Relative Clause: Biblical Hebrew." In *EHLL* 3:350–57.

Honeyman, A. M. "Epigraphic Discoveries at Karatepe." *PEQ* 81 (1949) 21–39.

Joüon, Paul, and T. Muraoka. *A Grammar of Biblical Hebrew*, 2 vols., 1st edition with corrections. Subsidia Biblica 14/1–2. Rome: Pontificio Istituto Biblico, 1996.

Khan, Geoffrey. "Biblical Hebrew: Linguistic background of Masoretic Text." In *EHLL* 1:304–15.

———. *Early Karaite Grammatical Texts*. Masoretic Studies 9. Atlanta: Society of Biblical Literature, 2000.

Krahmalkov, Charles. *Phoenician-Punic Dictionary*. Orientalia Lovaniensia Analecta 90. Leuven: Peeters, 2000.

Lane, Edward William. *Arabic–English Lexicon*, 8 vols. With Stanley Lane–Poole. London: Williams & Norgate, 1863–1893.
Loretz, Oswald. "Die ugaritisch-hebräische Gefäßbezeichnung trq/twrq in Canticum 1,3: Liebesdichtung in der westsemitischen Wein- und Olivenkultur." *UF* 36 (2004) 283–89.
Ma'agarim = *Ma'agarim: Mifʿal ha-Millon ha-Hisṭori la-Lašon ha-ʿIvrit*, online at http://maagarim.hebrew-academy.org.il/Pages/PMain.aspx.
McGeough, Kevin M., and Mark S. Smith, *Ugaritic Economic Tablets: Text, Translation and Notes*. ANESSup 32. Leuven: Peeters, 2011.
Miller–Naudé, Cynthia L., and Ziony Zevit, eds. *Diachrony in Biblical Hebrew*. Winona Lake, IN: Eisenbrauns, 2012.
Morag, Shelomo. "On the Historical Validity of the Vocalization of the Hebrew Bible." *JAOS* 94 (1974) 307–15.
Müller, Hans–Peter. "Phönizische historische Inschriften." In *Texte aus der Umwelt des Alten Testaments*, Band I, Lieferung 6, 638–45. Gütersloh: Gütersloher Verlagshaus, 1985.
Murphy, Roland. *The Song of Songs*. Hermeneia. Minneapolis: Fortress, 1990.
Noegel Scott B., and Gary A. Rendsburg. *Solomon's Vineyard: Literary and Linguistic Studies in the Song of Songs*. SBL Ancient Israel and Its Literature 1. Atlanta: Society of Biblical Literature, 2009 / Leiden: Brill, 2009.
Pope, Marvin H. *Song of Songs*. AB 7A. Garden City, NY: Doubleday, 1977.
Rendsburg, Gary A. "Alliteration." In *EHLL* 1:86–87.
———. "Alliteration in the Exodus Narrative." In *Birkat Shalom: Studies in the Bible, Ancient Near Eastern Literature, and Postbiblical Judaism Presented to Shalom M. Paul on the Occasion of His Seventieth Birthday*, edited by Chaim Cohen et al., 83–100. Winona Lake, IN: Eisenbrauns, 2008.
———. "Aramaic-like Features in the Pentateuch." *HS* 47 (2006) 163–76.
———. *Diglossia in Ancient Hebrew*. American Oriental Series 72. New Haven: American Oriental Society, 1990.
———. "Israelian Hebrew in the Song of Songs." In *Biblical Hebrew in Its Northwest Semitic Environment: Typological and Historical Perspectives*, edited by Steven E. Fassberg and Avi Hurvitz, 315–23. Publications of the Institute for Advanced Studies 1. Jerusalem: Magnes Press, 2006 / Winona Lake, IN: Eisenbrauns, 2006.
Rezetko, Robert, and Ian Young. *Historical Linguistics and Biblical Hebrew: Steps Toward an Integrated Approach*. Ancient Near East Monographs 9. Atlanta: SBL Press, 2014.
Röllig, Wolfgang. "Appendix I: The Phoenician Inscriptions." In Halet Çambel, *Corpus of Hieroglyphic Luwian Inscriptions*, vol. 2: *Karatepe-Aslantaş*, 50–81. Berlin: Walter de Gruyter, 1999.
Stoop – van Paridon, P. W. T. *The Song of Songs: A Philological Analysis of the Hebrew Book* שִׁיר הַשִּׁירִים. ANESSup 17. Peeters: Louvain, 2005.
Swiggers, Pierre. Review of Bron, *Recherches sur les inscriptions phéniciennes de Karatepe*. *BO* 37 (1980) 336–43.
Young, Ian. "Biblical Texts Cannot Be Dated Linguistically." *HS* 46 (2005) 341–51.
———. *Diversity in Pre-Exilic Hebrew*. FAT 5. Tübingen: J. C. B. Mohr (Paul Siebeck), 1993.
Young, Ian, Robert Rezetko, and Martin Ehrensvärd. *Linguistic Dating of Biblical Texts*, 2 vols. London: Equinox, 2008.

Younger, K. Lawson. "The Phoenician Inscription of Azatiwada: An Integrated Reading." *JSS* 43 (1998) 11–47.

21

On the Tolerative/Permissive *Hiphʿil*

Jeffrey H. Tigay

UNIVERSITY OF PENNSYLVANIA

The causative nuance of the *hiphʿil*, and of its Aramaic and Akkadian counterparts the *haphʿel* / *ʾaphʿel* and *šuprus*, respectively, includes not only actions in which the subject causes the object (another person or a thing) to do something, but a range of other ways in which the subject is responsible for the object's action, such as allowing it, enabling it, tolerating it, or granting permission to do it. That all these types of action can be seen as related is manifested, in a different way, in the fact that in certain Indo-European languages verbs meaning "let" connote both "cause" and "allow" (e.g. German *lassen*, French *laisser* and, sometimes, English "let").[1] To distinguish between verbs that are literally causative and the other nuances, I will term all the latter "tolerative."[2]

> *It is a pleasure to take part in this tribute to Ziony Zevit, a good friend and polymathic scholar from whom I have learned much. I am grateful to Richard Steiner, David Stern, Saul Wachs, and Cornelia Wunsch for advice on several points, and especially to W. Randall Garr for his good counsel and for valuable comments on a draft of this paper. Needless to say, any mistakes here are mine alone.
>
> 1. For "let" see, e.g., *Webster's New World Dictionary*, 775, s.v. "let": "5. to allow; permit . . . 6. to cause to; make: usually with *know* or *hear [let* me hear from you*]*."
>
> 2. Scholars sometimes refer to the tolerative nuances as "permissive," but since this term is related to permission, which is a specific verbal action, I prefer the broader term "tolerative" except in cases involving explicit grants of permission. This term is used in a

The tolerative nuance of the *hiph'il* is unevenly recognized in grammars of Biblical Hebrew. I have not found it mentioned by the medieval Hebrew grammarians, though Rashi recognizes it in his commentary to Exod 20:20.³ In modern times it was not mentioned even in König's massive reference grammar,⁴ let alone in GKC,⁵ Bauer-Leander,⁶ or Bergsträsser.⁷ On the other hand it was mentioned in Green's grammar,⁸ in Joüon's grammar and Muraoka's revision thereof,⁹ in Waltke and O'Connor's *Introduction to Biblical Hebrew Syntax*,¹⁰ and in student grammars, such as Lambdin's *Introduction to Biblical Hebrew*.¹¹ Some of the grammars that do mention it identify one or another semantic characteristic of its use, but they provide less than a handful of examples. The only systematic study I know of is that of Jean Margain, who studied the tolerative use of both *pi'el* and *hiph'il* and lists 44 instances of the latter, but he rarely indicates why he considers them tolerative.¹²

---

similar but distinct sense with reference to the tolerative *niph'al* (*niph'al tolerativum*, to allow something to happen to oneself, GKC § 51c; Joüon-Muraoka, *Grammar*, § 51c).

3. On the clause בְּכָל־הַמָּקוֹם אֲשֶׁר אַזְכִּיר אֶת־שְׁמִי, Rashi explains: אשר אתן לך רשות להזכיר שם המפורש שלי, "where I will give you permission to pronounce my proper name." See Levine, *Numbers 1–20*, 228: "In every cult site where I *allow my name to be pronounced*" [emphasis original – JHT]. This is a notoriously difficult clause. Elsewhere I have supported the view that the original reading of אַזְכִּיר was תַּזְכִּיר, as reflected in the Peshitta, some of the Targumim, and some passages in rabbinic literature; see Tigay, "The Presence of God and the Coherence of Exodus 20:22–26," 203–4. See also Glucker, *Mi-Silvester 'ad Ziqne Ṣiyyon*, 37–39, kindly brought to my attention by Alexander Rofé. However, understanding אַזְכִּיר as a tolerative *hiph'il* is an attractive alternative that has the virtue of preserving the reading of the MT and the Samaritan Pentateuch, which is also reflected in the LXX.

4. König, *Lehrgebäude*.
5. GKC § 52g does recognize the permissive *pi'el*.
6. Bauer and Leander, *Historische Grammatik*.
7. Bergsträsser, *Hebräische Grammatik*.
8. Green, *Grammar*, 110, sec. 79.1, n. a.: "The causative sense in both piel and hiphil is sometimes weakened into a simple permissive."
9. Joüon, *Grammaire*, 123, § 54d; Joüon-Muraoka, *Grammar*, 163, § 54d. Muraoka (164, n. 3) adds, "Margain [see below – JHT] seems to exaggerate slightly the notion of 'tolerative' hifil (and piel)." I agree that many of Margain's examples are unconvincing, but many others might be added.
10. Waltke and O'Connor, *Introduction*, 445–6, § 27.5, s.v. Modal Senses.
11. Lambdin, *Introduction*, 212.
12. Margain, "Causatif et toleratif." Margain describes the tolerative sense as an attenuation of the causative sense (pp. 25, 26). See also the brief discussion by Charlesworth, "Beth Essentiae." Charlesworth discusses a few examples and gives his reasons for preferring permissive translations in two cases. In the case of a Talmudic prayer (אל תביאני לידי חטא, b. Ber. 60b), "a literal translation, recognizing only the causative force of the H binyan, would be inelegant" and "[t]he syntax seems clear." In the case of the

Similarly regarding Akkadian, the tolerative nuance of the *šuprus* is not mentioned in *GAG*'s or Ungnad-Matouš's sections on the Š-stem,[13] but it is mentioned briefly by Huehnergard in his *A Grammar of Akkadian*.[14] It is not mentioned in the Aramaic grammars of Rosenthal[15] or Bauer and Leander,[16] but it is recognized in some citations in Muraoka and Porten's Egyptian Aramaic grammar.[17] In comparative Semitic grammars it is mentioned by Brockelmann ("Vergünstigung")[18] and by Kienast, who quotes Brockelmann and adds that "das Kausativ ist tolerativ."[19]

On the other hand, reference dictionaries that are attentive to nuances more frequently point out the tolerative sense.[20] But it is translators who, forced by context, have long translated many *hiphʿil* forms with a tolerative nuance. Even the KJV, which is much less inclined to "dynamic translation" than more recent translations, rendered the *hiphʿil* as tolerative in many verses.[21]

In order to learn more about how tolerative *hiphʿil* verbs function, I have gathered a number of examples and have made a very preliminary attempt to classify them. The present article is more a study of semantics than of grammar in the narrow sense, since tolerative *hiphʿil* verbs are not morphologically different from causative ones. The only guide to distinguishing between them is context, but determining what the context requires—or at least what is consistent with the context—can be a very subjective task. To assist in this task it is helpful to consult different translations of the same passage. For this purpose, in addition to gathering examples from grammars and dictionaries, I searched (though not systematically) the online

---

fifth petition of the Lord's Prayer he prefers the translation "do not allow us to enter into temptation" based on the afʿel form of the verb [תַעְלֶן] in the Old Syriac version, in place of the common translation "do not lead us into temptation" which he finds "theologically perplexing" (p. 78).

13. von Soden, *GAG*; Ungnad-Matouš, *Grammar*.

14. Huehnergard, *Grammar*, 301, § 27.2 (f). (Huehnergard adds: "Such renderings must be derived from context.")

15. Rosenthal, *Grammar*.

16. Bauer-Leander, *Grammatik des Biblisch-Aramäischen*.

17. Muraoka-Porten, *Grammar*, 190, § 49d, and 191, § 49f.

18. Brockelmann, *Grundriss*, vol. 1, 526, § 257 h β.

19. Kienast, *Historische semitische Sprachwissenschaft*, 214, § 188.1 (b).

20. See BDB s. vv. רשי, רעב, נפל, פדה, לעט, כרת, גמא and שוב. For Akkadian see the Š forms of the verbs *erēbu, kašādu, aḫāzu* and *ṣalālu* (see lexical section in the relevant *CAD* entries), and the Š forms of the verbs *etēqu, ḫalāqu, labāru, naparkû* II, *niāku, pašāḫu, rabāṣu,* and *ṣalālu* in *CDA*, pp. 84, 101, 174, 238, 251, 268, 293, 332.

21. See, for example, KJV at Gen 24:17; Gen 25:30; Exod 21:8; Lev 2:13; 1 Sam 3:19; 1 Sam 21:14; 1 Kgs 2:6; Ezek 39:7; Ps 107:38; Prov 10:3; Job 11:14; Song 2:14.

or electronic versions of KJV, RSV, NJPS, NAB, NRSV, and NJB for verbs such as "permit," "allow," "let" (when it has the same meaning),[22] and the like. In such a search one quickly discovers disagreements about whether a *hiphʿil* is tolerative in a particular passage, because the causative and the various tolerative meanings sometimes overlap[23] and because of different perceptions of what the context implies. At times it seems that translators were motivated, at least partly, by what sounds best, or reads most smoothly, in English,[24] rather than a conscious attempt to determine the precise category of *hiphʿil* that the context implies. In any case, the very disagreements between translations—and sometimes within the same translation—can sharpen the issues involved. Essentially, then, in what follows we will sometimes be trying to determine the intention of the Biblical authors and sometimes to divine the translators' thinking when they decided whether to translate a *hiphʿil* verb as causative or tolerative.[25] This is, in other words, as much a study of translations as it is a study of the Biblical text. Sometimes, what we are discussing is not necessarily what the context requires but what the context is patient of.

Here, then, are some examples that have been perceived as toleratives, gathered under three partially overlapping headings:

(1) Allowing the object to do what the root means, granting a request, explicit or implicit.[26]

(2) Enabling the object to undergo an experience that is "welcome or agreeable" to it.[27]

(3) Allowing the object to do something by (the subject's) refraining from a contrary action.

---

22. I.e., excluding cases where for example, it is used as an auxiliary or in translating a cohortative verb.

23. As Kienast observes, "'Der kausativbegriff kann sehr mannigfaltig gewandt werden,' wobei es gelegentlich Überschneidungen in der Interpretation sein kann." Kienast, *Historische semitische Sprachwissenschaft*, 214–5, § 188.1.

24. Cf. Charlesworth, "Beth Essentiae," quoted above, n. 12.

25. Once the translators have made this decision, those on either side of the issue basically agree in how they translate the passage in question, except for minor variations in wording. In general I have cited only one translation to represent each interpretation of a passage.

26. Joüon-Muraoka, *Grammar*, 163, § 54d.

27. Waltke and O'Connor, *Introduction*, 445–6, §27.5 , s.v. Modal Senses.

On the Tolerative/Permissive *Hiph'il*   401

(1) Allowing the object to do what the root means, granting a request, explicit or implicit.

Terms for "lend," literally "allow to borrow":[28]

> Deut 28:12, וְהִלְוִיתָ גּוֹיִם רַבִּים וְאַתָּה לֹא תִלְוֶה, lit. "you will let many nations borrow (לוה), but you will not borrow" (my translation).

> Deut 15:6, וְהַעֲבַטְתָּ גּוֹיִם רַבִּים וְאַתָּה לֹא תַעֲבֹט, lit. "you will let many nations borrow (עבט), but you will not borrow" (my translation).

> Exod 12:36, וַיהוָה נָתַן אֶת־חֵן הָעָם בְּעֵינֵי מִצְרַיִם וַיַּשְׁאִלוּם, "And the Lord had disposed the Egyptians favorably toward the people, and they let them have their request" (NJPS) ("prop. *let* one *ask* (שאל) [successfully]," BDB 982c s.v. "Hiph.").[29]

Further cases in which the *hiph'il* means granting a request:

Gen 24:18, וַתַּשְׁקֵהוּ, "she . . . let him drink (שקה)," granting the servant's request of v. 17, הַגְמִיאִינִי נָא מְעַט־מַיִם מִכַּדֵּךְ, "Please let me sip (גמא) a little water from your jar.'" (NJPS; in v. 45 the request is worded as הַשְׁקִינִי נָא, "please let me drink" [my translation]).

Deut 2:30: וְלֹא אָבָה סִיחֹן מֶלֶךְ חֶשְׁבּוֹן הַעֲבִרֵנוּ בּוֹ, "But King Sihon of Heshbon refused to let us pass through (עבר)" (NJPS).[30] Moses's request is quoted in 2:27 (אֶעְבְּרָה בְאַרְצֶךָ, "Let[31] me pass through your territory"). The same usage also appears in an Akkadian letter: *tamkaram ša ṭuppi šarrim našû nuba'ama nušetteq*[32] *tamkaram ša ṭuppi šarrim la našû ana Bābilim nutarrašu*, "a merchant who has a document from the king we examine and let pass (*etēqu*), a merchant who has no document from the king we send

---

28. Cf. Arabic *'adāna*, "lend," from *dāna*, "borrow," cited by Brockelmann, *Grundriss*, vol. 1, 526, § 257 h β.

29. השאיל could also mean "enabled them to borrow," derived from שאל = borrow as in in Exod 3:22; 22:13; etc., except that in the context of Exod 3 and 22 "it is . . . not clear that there was any pretext of mere temporary use" (BDB 981d).

30. The translation as tolerative (literally permissive) is confirmed – if it needs any confirmation – by the equivalent passage in Num 21:23: וְלֹא־נָתַן סִיחֹן אֶת־יִשְׂרָאֵל עֲבֹר בִּגְבֻלוֹ, "But Sihon would not let Israel pass through his territory." Essentially the same translation is already found in Targum Onkelos (ולא אבא סיחון מלכא דחשבון למשבקנא למעבר בתחומיה) and the Vulgate (*Noluitque Seon rex Esebon dare nobis transitum*).

31. Here "let" is used for a cohortative verb, not a permissive one.

32. *šūtuqu*, from *etēqu*, an Akkadian interdialectical semantic equivalent of עבר. See Cohen, "'Held Method," 12.

back to Babylon."³³ Here the merchants' request is implicit—they come to the officials asking to proceed and they present their royal *laissez passer*. Neh 2:7 likewise mentions a royal *laisser passer*: אִם־עַל־הַמֶּלֶךְ טוֹב אִגְּרוֹת יִתְּנוּ־לִי עַל־פַּחֲווֹת עֵבֶר הַנָּהָר אֲשֶׁר יַעֲבִירוּנִי עַד אֲשֶׁר־אָבוֹא אֶל־יְהוּדָה, "If it please the king, let³⁴ me have letters to the governors of the province of Beyond the River, directing them to grant me passage until I reach Judah" (NJPS). Here, too, the request to pass is implicit (though in this case the officials are in no position to refuse).

In Deut 34:4, in which God is the speaker, He says to Moses, הֶרְאִיתִיךָ בְעֵינֶיךָ וְשָׁמָּה לֹא תַעֲבֹר, which NJPS renders "I have let you see (ראה) it [the promised land] with your own eyes, but you shall not cross there." The tolerative translation (rather than causative "show") recognizes the fact that this an allusion to the dialog of 3:24–28 and that God is (partially) granting Moses's request of 3:25, "Let³⁵ me, I pray, cross over and see (אֶעְבְּרָה־נָּא וְאֶרְאֶה) the good land on the other side of the Jordan, that good hill country, and the Lebanon" (NJPS).³⁶

Ps 59:11, אֱלֹהִים יַרְאֵנִי בְשֹׁרְרָי, "God shall let me see (ראה) my desire upon mine enemies" (KJV).³⁷ The same idiom appears in the Mesha inscription, "because (Kemosh) let me see (my desire on) all my adversaries" (הראני, line 4), and in Aramaic, in a letter from Elephantine, "we were fasting and praying to Ya'u the Lord of Heaven, who let us see (our desire) upon that Waidrang" (החוין, Cowley 30:15–16).³⁸ In the Elephantine letter this explicitly comes as the direct result of a prayer (מצלין, line 15), implicitly to

---

33. Leemans, *Old-Babylonian Merchant*, 105 (translation slightly modified), also cited in *CAD* E, 393d, sec. 2' which defines *šūtuqu* 5, c as "to allow persons or boats to pass or pass through (customs)." The text is also cited also in *CAD* T (s.v. *tamkaru*), 134b, sec. 7.

34. Here "let" is used for a jussive verb, not a permissive one.

35. Here "let" is used for a cohortative verb, not a permissive one.

36. Three verses earlier (34:1) NJPS and others translate "the LORD showed him (וַיַּרְאֵהוּ) the whole land." I assume that the translators' choice is based on the assumption that in 34:1 the narrator is giving a more "neutral" description of the event than God does in v. 4. Only KJV translates the verb as causative in both verses: (1) the LORD shewed him all the land ... (4) I have caused thee to see it with thine eyes.

37. Our translations all agree that the idiom implicitly refers to seeing the discomfiture of one's enemies, though they express it differently: RSV/NRSV: "will let me look in triumph on my enemies;" NJB: "will let me feast my eyes on those who lie in wait for me;" NAB: "show me my fallen foes;" NJPS: "God let me gloat over my watchful foes." See also Pss 54:9; 92:12; 112:8; 118:7, as well as Mic 4:11; 7:10b.

38. *TAD* A4.7 lines 15–16 (*TAD* 1, 68–71), where it is translated "let us gloat over that Vidranga."

see the defeat of Waidrang; we may presume such prayers to be implied in Ps 59 and the Mesha inscription as well.³⁹

(2) Enabling the object to undergo an experience that is "welcome or agreeable" to it.

The *hiphʿil* of ראה is rendered "let see" in many other passages where the action of the subject (very often God) is not in response to a request. In some cases we may think of these cases as responses to an implicit hope, but many seem to bring us to a broader semantic situation in which the *hiphʿil* refers to letting or enabling the object experience something that is welcome or agreeable, pleasant, beneficial, or a privilege, without necessarily presupposing a request or hope.

In cases like these a causative construction of הראה would be expressed by "show" or the like instead of "let see." It is true that "show" can sometimes mean "allow to see" (*OED* and others), so that even when a translation uses "show" it is conceivable that the translators recognized the tolerative force of the *hiphʿil*. But at least when they use "let see" in contradistinction to their predecessors, or to their own translation of nearby or similar passages, it is reasonable to assume that they are trying to make their tolerative construction of the verb more explicit, to convey the sense of concession or benefaction.

In Gen 48:11, Joseph brings his sons to Jacob who expresses his gratification at the fact that, whereas he never expected to see Joseph again, רְאֹה אֹתְךָ לֹא פִלָּלְתִּי וְהִנֵּה הֶרְאָה אֹתִי אֱלֹהִים גַּם אֶת־זַרְעֶךָ, "God has let me see your children as well" (NJPS).⁴⁰

In 2 Sam 15:25 David, fleeing from Absalom, tells Zadok to take the Ark back to Jerusalem and explains, אִם־אֶמְצָא חֵן בְּעֵינֵי יְהוָה וֶהֱשִׁבַנִי וְהִרְאַנִי אֹתוֹ וְאֶת־נָוֵהוּ, "If I find favor with the LORD, He will bring me back and let me see it and its abode" (NJPS).

In Deut 3:24 Moses begins his plea to God אַתָּה הַחִלּוֹתָ לְהַרְאוֹת אֶת־עַבְדְּךָ אֶת־גָּדְלְךָ וְאֶת־יָדְךָ הַחֲזָקָה, which most of our translations render with a causative verb, such as "thou hast only begun to show thy servant thy greatness and thy mighty hand" (RSV). NJPS, however, renders with a tolerative verb: "O Lord GOD, You who let Your servant see the first works of Your greatness

---

39. Cf. Jeremiah's plea אֶרְאֶה נִקְמָתְךָ מֵהֶם, "Let me see Your retribution upon them" (Jer 11:20; 20:12); see also Ps 54:9 (וּבְאֹיְבַי רָאֲתָה עֵינִי "let me gaze triumphant upon my enemies"); 118:7 (יְהוָה לִי בְּעֹזְרָי וַאֲנִי אֶרְאֶה בְשֹׂנְאָי, "With the Lord on my side as my helper, I will see the downfall of my foes"); 143:12 (וּבְחַסְדְּךָ תַּצְמִית אֹיְבָי וְהַאֲבַדְתָּ כָּל־צֹרֲרֵי נַפְשִׁי, "As you are faithful, put an end to my foes; destroy all my mortal enemies").

40. Only KJV renders as a causative: "shewed me."

and Your mighty hand." I presume that NJPS's choice was motivated by the continuation of Moses's plea in the next verse, אֶעְבְּרָה־נָּא וְאֶרְאֶה, "Let[41] me, I pray, cross over and see." The context is patient of either translation.

Allowing agreeable experiences is by no means limited to visual ones. In Exod 21:8, all our translations render וְהֶפְדָּהּ as a tolerative, such as KJV: "then shall he let her be redeemed"—literally, "let (someone) redeem (פדה) her." It is to the girl's benefit and her family's to let her out of a situation in which her master broke faith with her.

(3) Allowing the object to do something by (the subject's) refraining from contrary action. (Possibly a subcategory of [2])

Num 22:33: the angel says to Balaam כִּי עַתָּה גַּם־אֹתְכָה הָרַגְתִּי וְאוֹתָהּ הֶחֱיֵיתִי, "surely just now I would have slain you and let her (Balaam's ass) live (חיה)" (RSV). In Aramaic the *haphʻel / ʼaphʻel* of חיה sometimes has the same nuance: (a) Dan 5:19,[42] דִּי־הֲוָה צָבֵא הֲוָא קָטֵל וְדִי־הֲוָה צָבֵא הֲוָה מַחֵא, "Whomever he (Nebuchadnezzar) willed, he would kill or let live" (NAB). (b) Elephantine *Aḥiqar*, col. 4, line 51: אף שגיא סנחאריב מלכא רחמני על זי החיתך ולא קטלתך, "Moreover, abundantly Sennacherib the king loved me because I let you live and did not kill you."[43] In these cases the verbs are clearly not causative (bring to life, restore to life, keep alive by feeding). The subject allows the object to live by refraining from killing it.

In 1 Kgs 2:6 David charges Solomon, וְלֹא־תוֹרֵד שֵׂיבָתוֹ בְּשָׁלֹם שְׁאֹל, "and let not his (Joab's) hoar head go down (ירד) to the grave in peace" (KJV)—that is, don't allow him the luxury of dying in peace by failing to send him to the grave with blood, as David commands regarding Shimei in v. 9 (וְהוֹרַדְתָּ אֶת־שֵׂיבָתוֹ בְּדָם שְׁאוֹל, "his hoar head bring thou down to the grave with blood" [KJV]).[44]

In the following examples the verbs mean "let the time for an action pass by not performing the requisite action":

Jer 46:17: קָרְאוּ שָׁם פַּרְעֹה מֶלֶךְ־מִצְרַיִם שָׁאוֹן הֶעֱבִיר הַמּוֹעֵד, "There they called Pharaoh king of Egypt: Braggart who let the hour [literally, set time] go by (עבר)" (NJPS).[45] This difficult verse apparently means that the

---

41. Here, as noted above, "let" is used for a cohortative verb, not a permissive one.
42. The more expected form is מַחְיֵא.
43. Porten and Yardeni, *TAD* 3, 32–33 (C1.1).
44. In all the other cases of this idiom the translation is causative: if disaster befalls Benjamin it will cause Jacob to die in grief (Gen 42:38; 44:29, 31).
45. עבר is likewise used in rabbinic Hebrew for the passing (i.e., missing) of the time (זמן, יום) set for an action.

Egyptian king missed his chance by some military miscalculation.[46] While the verb could be translated as a causative (postponing the set time), the tolerative translation is supported by an equivalent idiom in Akkadian, as in the following examples. (a) *warḫam ēribam ina* UD.14.KAM *nīq pagrā'i linnepi[š] mimma nīqam šētu la ušettequ*, "on the 14th day of the coming month let the *pagrā 'u* offerings be made, they must on no account let (the term of) that offering to pass (*etēqu*),"[47] that is, let the day pass [= let the deadline lapse] by failing to make the required offerings; (b) *ūmī eli warḫim ištēn ušētiqma*, "if he allows more than one month to elapse (without returning a fugitive slave or stray animal he has seized)" (LE 50).[48]

Lev 2:13, וְלֹא תַשְׁבִּית מֶלַח בְּרִית אֱלֹהֶיךָ מֵעַל מִנְחָתֶךָ, "you shall not let the salt of the covenant with your God be lacking (שבת) from your cereal offering" (RSV). Here the idea is "do not let the salt be lacking by failing to add it," as commanded in the preceding and following clauses. Elsewhere the *hiph'il* of שבת followed by מן (מן השבית) is causative, meaning "destroy," "put an end to," "remove what is there," none of which would make sense here; here the sense is "fail to add." As NJB paraphrases the verse:[49] "You will put salt in every cereal offering that you offer, and you will not fail to put the salt of the covenant of your God on your cereal offering; to every offering you will add an offering of salt to your God."

1 Sam 3:19, וְלֹא־הִפִּיל מִכָּל־דְּבָרָיו אָרְצָה, "and (the Lord) did let none of his words fall (נפל) to the ground" (KJV),[50] that is, God did not allow any of Samuel's words to go unfulfilled by failing to fulfill them. This is the *hiph'il* of נפל, "fall," used in the sense of allowing a prophecy to go unfulfilled.[51] The tolerative translation is preferable to a causative one ("[the LORD] did not cause any of his words to fall to the ground"), which would make the statement too obvious to require saying.

Ps 107:38, וַיְבָרֲכֵם וַיִּרְבּוּ מְאֹד וּבְהֶמְתָּם לֹא יַמְעִיט, "He blesses them and they increase greatly; and He does not let their cattle decrease" (NJPS). That is, God doesn't let their cattle decrease by failing to bless them (with fertility; cf. Deut 7:13–14; 28:4, 11; Ezek 36:11). A causative translation of יַמְעִיט

---

46. See Hoffmeier, "New Insight"; McKane, *Jeremiah*, vol. 2, 1129–30.

47. ARMT 26, 220:22, cited in *CAD* P, 11d s.v. *pagrā'u* (partly my translation). Cited previously in *CAD* E, 392d sec. 3' from the earlier edition ARM 2, 90:23.

48. Roth, *Law Collections*, 67 (also cited in *CAD* E, 392a with a less precise translation). Cf. the use of *etēqu* for a deadline (*adannu*) passing (*CAD* A1, 99ac; *CAD* E, 387cd); for letting the term of a loan pass, see *CAD* E, 392, f1'.

49. The full verse reads: וְכָל־קָרְבַּן מִנְחָתְךָ בַּמֶּלַח תִּמְלָח וְלֹא תַשְׁבִּית בְּרִית אֱלֹהֶיךָ מֵעַל מִנְחָתֶךָ עַל כָּל־קָרְבָּנְךָ תַּקְרִיב מֶלַח.

50. NJPS more loosely: "He did not leave any of Samuel's predictions unfulfilled."

51. For נפל, "fall" used in the sense of a prophecy or promise going unfulfilled, see Josh 21:45; 23:14 (2x); 1 Kgs 8:56; 2 Kgs 10:10.

would mean that God did not diminish the numbers of the cattle, and in a verse describing God's blessing it seems unnecessary to state that he did not act in such a punitive way.

Prov 10:3, לֹא־יַרְעִיב יְהוָה נֶפֶשׁ צַדִּיק, "The Lord will not let the righteous go hungry" (NJPS). That is, he will not allow the righteous to go hungry by failing to provide them food. A causative translation ("God will not make the righteous go hungry") would make the point of the verse too obvious to state.

(4) Ambiguous cases

If the above examples are (at least in my estimation) fairly unambiguous, in many other passages disagreements among translations, and seeming inconsistencies within the same translation, encourage speculation about the translators' reasoning and their exegetical decisions.[52] Here the subjectivity of the enterprise is apparent in full force.

Returning to *hiph'il* forms of ראה (see above)—if welcomeness is, indeed, the reason for a tolerative translation of הראה, we might expect less welcome experiences to be translated as causatives, e.g., "make see" or "show," which are more neutral. As indicated above, while these terms do not by themselves imply unwelcomeness, they avoid the impression of concession or benefaction that "let see" does. This might explain the following:

In Deut 3:24, as we saw, NJPS renders לְהַרְאוֹת in Moses's words as a tolerative, "You who let Your servant see the first works of Your greatness and Your mighty hand." In Exod 9:16, on the other hand, it renders a similar phrase in God's words to Pharaoh, וְאוּלָם בַּעֲבוּר זֹאת הֶעֱמַדְתִּיךָ בַּעֲבוּר הַרְאֹתְךָ אֶת־כֹּחִי, with a causative verb, "Nevertheless I have spared you [i.e., let you survive] for this purpose: in order to show you My power." In rejecting the option of "let see" here, the translators may have been motivated by the fact that whereas Moses regarded seeing God's power as a welcome experience, for Pharaoh the same experience was a disagreeable one.

Similar reasoning could likewise explain the difference between the way NJPS (following RSV) translates Deut 5:21 and 4:36 (NJPS's verse numbering). In 5:21 the people, after hearing the Decalogue, tell Moses: הֵן הֶרְאָנוּ יְהוָה אֱלֹהֵינוּ אֶת־כְּבֹדוֹ וְאֶת־גָּדְלוֹ, "The Lord our God has just shown us His

---

[52] To be sure, inconsistencies within a translation are not always intentional. Some may be due to the passage of time between the translation of one book and another, or to the fact that different parts of what is published as a single translation were done by different committees, or to simple forgetfulness. I have tried to limit the selections here to passages that were presumably translated by the same committee.

majesty Presence." As their following words indicate ("Let us not die, then, for this fearsome fire will consume us; if we hear the voice of the LORD our God any longer, we shall die"), to them this was not a pleasant experience, and the translators may have rejected a tolerative translation for that reason. On the other hand, in 4:36, where Moses reminds the later generation of the same event, NJPS (and others; see just below) translates the key verbs as toleratives: מִן־הַשָּׁמַיִם הִשְׁמִיעֲךָ אֶת־קֹלוֹ לְיַסְּרֶךָּ וְעַל־הָאָרֶץ הֶרְאֲךָ אֶת־אִשּׁוֹ הַגְּדוֹלָה, "From the heavens He let you hear His voice to discipline you; on earth He let you see His great fire." Perhaps the translators' reasoning was that, despite the frightening nature and disciplinary intention of the event (לְיַסְּרֶךָּ), from Moses's perspective the experience was—like the exodus (v. 34)—a privilege (as implied by 4:32b–33).

That we are not "parsing" the translators' choices too finely is suggested by a comparison of how various other translations rendered the verbs הראה and השמיע with reference to the experience at Mt. Sinai. Presuming that the translators of NRSV, NAB, NJB and NJPS were aware of what the KJV and RSV had done, we can regard their deviations from them as probably deliberate. What we find is the following patterns of translation:

> KJV (which, as mentioned above, was aware that *hiphʿil* verbs can be tolerative) renders all the verbs as causatives: made thee to hear, shewed thee (4:36), shewed us (5:21). NAB, on the other hand, follows RSV and renders the verbs as toleratives in 4:36 where Moses is the speaker, but it also does so in 5:21 where the people speak ("the Lord ... has indeed let us see"), suggesting that the event was welcome to the people, too, despite their fear. What is more, NAB—alone among all the translations considered—renders even אַתָּה הָרְאֵתָ in 4:35 as a tolerative: "you were allowed to see," emphasizing what a privilege the event was for the people. NRSV, on the other hand, reverts to a completely causative translation in 4:36 and 5:21: "made you hear," "showed you" (4:36), "shown us" (5:21). That this is a conscious choice, influenced by God's motive of disciplining the people, is suggested by NRSV's very free translation of לָדַעַת in 4:35 as "so that you would acknowledge"—as if the people needed to be disabused of any lingering polytheistic notions.[53]

In Judg 13:23,[54] in responding to Manoah's fear that he and his wife would die after seeing a divine being (אֱלֹהִים), referring to the angel, his

---

53. The only one of our six translations that does not seem to follow a discernable plan here is NJB, which translates "he made you hear," "he let you see" (4:36), "has shown" (5:21).

54. For the textual issues in this verse see the commentaries and Zakovitch, *Ḥayye*

wife reassures him, saying—referring to the angel's announcement that she would bear a child (Samson) and instructions about how they should raise him, and to the vision of the angel ascending in fire—לוּ חָפֵץ יְהוָה לַהֲמִיתֵנוּ לֹא־לָקַח מִיָּדֵנוּ עֹלָה וּמִנְחָה וְלֹא הֶרְאָנוּ אֶת־כָּל־אֵלֶּה וְכָעֵת לֹא הִשְׁמִיעָנוּ כָּזֹאת, "Had the LORD meant to take our lives, he would not have accepted a burnt offering and meal offering from us, nor הֶרְאָנוּ all these things; and He would not have הִשְׁמִיעָנוּ thus." RSV translates the two *hiph'il* verbs as causatives: "he would not have . . . shown us all these things, or now announced to us such things as these." NAB, on the other hand, renders them both as toleratives "Nor would he have let us see all this, or hear what we have heard," characterizing the entire revelatory experience as a privilege, a welcome and agreeable experience. NJPS, however, treats the two verbs differently: "He would not have . . . let us see all these things; and He would not have made such an announcement to us." Apparently the NJPS translators—perhaps prompted by the word וְכָעֵת separating the two verbs—perceive Manoah's wife as speaking differently about the two parts of their experience: she regards the supernatural visual experience accompanying their offering, when they realize that their visitor was divine, as a welcome privilege ("God let us see"), compared to which the visitor's earlier announcement and instructions concerning Samson—received when she and Manoah thought him human—diminishes in importance and becomes primarily information ("he announced"), welcome though it was.

Mic 7:9, יוֹצִיאֵנִי לָאוֹר. NRSV translates "He will bring me out to the light," but NJPS renders "He will let me out into the light." This seems to take its cue from v. 8: the people's suffering is like sitting in the darkness of prison ("Though I sit in darkness"), and their future redemption will be like a release from prison into the light. Cf. Isaiah 42:7: "(I the LORD) . . . Opening eyes deprived of light, Rescuing (לְהוֹצִיא) prisoners from confinement, From the dungeon those who sit in darkness" (NJPS).[55]

Job 10:18, וְלָמָּה מֵרֶחֶם הֹצֵאתָנִי, NJPS translates "Why did You let me come out of the womb?" whereas NRSV translates "Why did you bring me forth from the womb?" The tolerative rendering is consistent with the way that birth is described elsewhere in the Bible: the baby comes out (יצא) of its mother's womb rather than being taken out (by somebody such as a midwife).[56]

Šimšon, 54–58, 63, 68–69.

55. See Paul, *Isaiah 40–66*, 190.

56. Cf. Gen 25:25; 38:28–30; Num 12:12; Jer 1:5; 20:18; Job 1:21; 3:11; 38:29; Qoh 5:14. Ps 22:10 is uncertain: כִּי־אַתָּה גֹחִי מִבָּטֶן מַבְטִיחִי עַל־שְׁדֵי אִמִּי.

Ambiguous in an entirely different way is the translation of the *hiph'il* of שלט in Qoh 5:18 and 6:2: גַּם כָּל־הָאָדָם אֲשֶׁר נָתַן־לוֹ הָאֱלֹהִים עֹשֶׁר וּנְכָסִים וְהִשְׁלִיטוֹ לֶאֱכֹל מִמֶּנּוּ, "Also, whenever a man is given riches and property by God, and is also permitted by Him to enjoy them;" אִישׁ אֲשֶׁר יִתֶּן־לוֹ הָאֱלֹהִים עֹשֶׁר וּנְכָסִים וְכָבוֹד . . . וְלֹא־יַשְׁלִיטֶנּוּ הָאֱלֹהִים לֶאֱכֹל מִמֶּנּוּ כִּי אִישׁ נָכְרִי יֹאכְלֶנּוּ, "that God sometimes grants a man riches, property, and wealth . . . but God does not permit him to enjoy it; instead, a stranger will enjoy it" (NJPS; NRSV translates as "enable" in both passages). The *qal* form of the verb appears in 2:18–19, וְשָׂנֵאתִי אֲנִי אֶת־כָּל־עֲמָלִי שֶׁאֲנִי עָמֵל תַּחַת הַשָּׁמֶשׁ שֶׁאַנִּיחֶנּוּ לָאָדָם שֶׁיִּהְיֶה אַחֲרָי: וּמִי יוֹדֵעַ הֶחָכָם יִהְיֶה אוֹ סָכָל וְיִשְׁלַט בְּכָל־עֲמָלִי שֶׁעָמַלְתִּי וְשֶׁחָכַמְתִּי תַּחַת הַשָּׁמֶשׁ, "So, too, I loathed all the wealth that I was gaining under the sun. For I shall leave it to the man who will succeed me—and who knows whether he will be wise or foolish?—and he will control all the wealth that I gained by toil and wisdom under the sun" (NJPS). In 5:18 and 6:2, even if השליט has a tolerative sense, the question is whether that sense comes from the *hiph'il* or from the root שלט, the basic sense of which is to possess or have power over something. In that case, the *hiph'il* may be causative, "empower."[57]

(5) Passages concerning God and sin

A number of passages use *hiph'il* forms in connection with sin and raise theological questions concerning divine control of human behavior.

In several prayers people plead with God not to cause—or allow—them to sin:

Ps 119:10, אַל־תַּשְׁגֵּנִי מִמִּצְוֹתֶיךָ. Although this could be translated as a causative ("do not cause us to wander from your commandments")—an option that might be supported by reference to the nearly synonymous phrase in Isa 63:17 discussed below—all of our translations agree in rendering the verb as a tolerative: "O let me not wander from thy commandments" (KJV and RSV), "do not let me stray from Your commandments" (NRSV, NAB, NJB, NJPS).

---

57. Cf. KJV, RSV, NAB: "give/grant power." The use of שלט, and of השליט followed by a supplementary verb, in Ecclesiastes reflects the terms' long legal use, attested in Akkadian and Aramaic as well and continuing down through the Geonic period. See Goldstein, "Syriac Bill of Sale," 2 (lines 11–12), 11; Greenfield, *'Al Kanfei Yonah*, vol. 1, 14; vol. 2, 610–12, 640–43; Greenfield, "מחקרים במונחי משפט"; Gropp, "Origin and Development"; Hurvitz, *Concise Lexicon*, 228–30; *CAD* Š1, 240; *DJBA*, 1148. The legal usage is reflected particularly in Seow's translation "exercise proprietorship," "authorize" (Seow, *Ecclesiastes*, 118, 136, 202, 209). In 5:18 and 6:2, however, the context seems less formal, referring to the opportunity (not the right) to enjoy one's possessions. Cf. NJB: "the ability to enjoy them," "the chance to enjoy them."

Ps 141:4, אַל־תַּט־לִבִּי לְדָבָר ׀ רָע. Not only is a causative translation possible here, too, but KJV and others choose this option: "Incline not my heart to *any* evil thing." NAB and others, however, render the clause as tolerative, "Do not let my heart incline to evil," and the context favors this option, since in the preceding verse the psalmist asks God to control his speech, in other words to prevent him from sinning: "O LORD, set a guard over my mouth, a watch at the door of my lips."

In Ps 119:133, וְאַל־תַּשְׁלֶט־בִּי כָל־אָוֶן. A causative translation would be "do not cause iniquity to dominate me," but all of our translations agree on rendering the verb as tolerative, essentially "do not let iniquity dominate me" (NJPS).[58]

Both the causative and tolerative translations raise the issue of human freedom, each in a different way: The causative translation implies that God might cause people to sin, and the psalmists ask Him not to. The tolerative translation implies that God can prevent people from sinning, and psalmists ask Him to do so—to take away their freedom to sin.

The issue of divine causality is raised even more explicitly by Isa 63:17, in which the exiles living in Babylonia, or the prophet speaking for them, asks לָמָּה תַתְעֵנוּ יְהוָה מִדְּרָכֶיךָ תַּקְשִׁיחַ לִבֵּנוּ מִיִּרְאָתֶךָ. NJB renders the verbs as toleratives: "Why, Yahweh, do You let us wander from your ways and let our hearts grow too hard to fear You?" This absolves God of the charge of causing the people to sin. It implies that the people had been tempted or inclined to sin, and God did not prevent them from doing so. Most of our translations, however, render the verbs as causative: "Why, O LORD, do you make us stray from your ways, and harden our heart, so that we do not fear you?" (NRSV).[59]

The point I wish to make here is that, with the exception of Ps 141:4, the context does not seem to favor one translation over the other, and the translators opting for tolerative translations may well be motivated by a

---

58. For the reverberations of this clause in later Jewish texts, see Flusser, "Qumrân and Jewish 'Apotropaic' Prayers"; Greenfield, '*Al Kanfei Yonah*, vol. 2, 640–43. Certain later Jewish prayers that echo this verse avoid the implication that God causes sin by revising the verb to read ואל ישלוט בי/בנו, "may (an/the evil inclination) not rule over me/us" (see Flusser, "Qumrân and Jewish 'Apotropaic' Prayers," 199, n. 22).

59. NAB adds, in a footnote: "The hardening of the heart (Exod 4:21; 7:3 – JHT) serves to explain Israel's sins—a motif to induce the Lord to relent." Paul, *Isaiah 40–66*, 567, 568, 583–4, accepts the causative translation, but in his view it does not imply that God intentionally or directly causes sin, but that he was ultimately responsible for the people's continuing to sin after the exile because the destruction of the Temple and Judah led them to despair and stray from his path: "The following verses claim . . . that God's aloofness is the ultimate cause of their sins, to which they confess [64:4–6])" (quotation from p. 568).

theological concern to avoid implying that God might cause people to sin.⁶⁰ Theologically, it is preferable for worshipers to voluntarily waive their freedom to sin and ask God to prevent them from doing so than to imply that He might cause them to sin. If that is the translators' motive, however, it is undercut by numerous passages in the Bible that indicate that God sometimes does cause people to sin. As Kaufmann explains, citing Isaiah 63:17 and other passages:

> Isaiah . . . ascribes such activity to God in his inaugural vision (6:9 f.); the thought is expressed by Elijah (1 Kgs 18:37) and the second Isaiah as well (63:17) . . . [This idea] is the outcome of a desire to comprehend all phenomena as actions of the one God. *While it is axiomatic that sin is man's doing, the religious consciousness of the Bible was unable to reconcile itself entirely with this restriction of God's dominion. There is a tension here between the moral demand that sets limits to the working of God and the religious demand that subjects all to divine control.* This tension is resolved in the eschatological vision of the new heart that man is to get at the end of days which will render him incapable of sinning (Jer 31:31 ff.; 32:39 f.; Ezek 11:19 ff.; 36:26 f.).⁶¹

Eichrodt cites further examples and adds the observation that "Even the innermost life of Man was subjected to the all-pervading divine energy. It is not simply that God allows a man to think thus and not otherwise; he is himself also at work within these acts of personal freedom . . . One will never do justice to the profound grasp of the reality of God which is evinced in these statements by trying to explain them in terms of God's *permissive* [emphasis added—JHT] will."⁶²

Hence the fact that a causative translation of the *hiph'il* would contradict the idea of free will cannot by itself be grounds for ruling it out in these verses. Without that motivation, the verses in question (except for Ps 141:4) are patient of either interpretation.

Conclusion

The tolerative/permissive *hiph'il*, like its counterparts in Akkadian and Aramaic, is a well-attested phenomenon in Biblical Hebrew, as illustrated by unambiguous examples of different types in which the subject (1) allows the

---

60. Cf. Charlesworth cited in n. 12 above: "theologically perplexing".
61. Kaufmann *Religion of Israel*, 75 (emphasis added).
62. Eichrodt, *Theology*, vol. 2, 176–81 (the quotation is from p. 178). See also Greenberg, "ואתה הסבת את לבם אחורנית."

object of the verb to do what the root means, granting a request, explicit or implicit; (2) enables the object to undergo an experience that is "welcome or agreeable" to it; and (3) (perhaps a subcategory of [2]), allows the object to do something by (the subject's) refraining from a contrary action. Because the tolerative *hiphʿil* is morphologically indistinguishable from the causative *hiphʿil*, its identification depends on the ultimately subjective interpretation of the contexts in which it appears, a subjectivity often reflected in translators' conflicting renditions. In some cases translators' choices seem to have been influenced by their theological presuppositions rather than the immediate context of a passage. Certain verbs, such as הראה, החיה, and העביר and verbs for lending, may have been used as tolerative *hiphʿil* with greater frequency than others. Whether this is really so requires a more thorough study.

BIBLIOGRAPHY

Bauer, Hans, and Pontus Leander. *Historische Grammatik der hebräischen Sprache des Alten Testamentes*. Hildesheim: Olms, 1962.

Bauer, Hans, and Pontus Leander. *Grammatik des Biblisch-Aramäischen*. Hildesheim: Olms, 1962.

Bergsträsser, Gotthelf. *Hebräische Grammatik*. Hildesheim: Olms, 1962.

Brockelmann, Carl. *Grundriss der vergleichenden Grammatik der semitischen Sprachen*. Berlin: Reuther & Reichard, 1908–1913.

Charlesworth, James H. "The Beth Essentiae and the Permissive Meaning of the Hiph'il (Aphel)." In *Of Scribes and Scrolls: Studies on the Hebrew Bible, Intertestamental Judaism, and Christian Origins Presented to John Strugnell on the Occasion of his Sixtieth Birthday*, edited by Harold W. Attridge, John J. Collins, and Thomas H. Tobin, 67–78. Lanham, MD: University Press of America, 1990.

Cohen, Chaim. "The 'Held Method' for Comparative Semitic Philology." *JANES* 19 (1989) 9–23.

Eichrodt, Walther. *Theology of the Old Testament*, trans. by J. A. Baker. 2 vols. Philadelphia: Westminster, 1961–1967.

Flusser, David. "Qumrân and Jewish 'Apotropaic' Prayers." *IEJ* 16 (1966) 194–205.

Glucker, John (Yoḥanan). *Mi-Silvester ʿad Ziqne Ṣiyyon: Mavo' le-Filologya*. English title: *From Sylvester to the Elders of Zion: Introduction to Philology*. Jerusalem: Carmel, 2011.

Goldstein, Jonathan A. "The Syriac Bill of Sale from Dura-Europos." *JNES* 25 (1966) 1–16.

Green, William H. *A Grammar of the Hebrew Language*. New edition. New York: John Wiley, 1889.

Greenberg, Moshe. "(מל״א יח:לז) ואתה הסבת את לבם אחורנית." In *Studies in Aggadah, Targum, and Jewish Liturgy in Memory of Joseph Heinemann*, edited by Ezra Fleischer and Jacob J. Petuchowski, 52–62. Jerusalem: Magnes / Cincinnati: Hebrew Union College, 1981.

Greenfield, Jonas C. *'Al Kanfei Yonah: Collected Studies of Jonas C. Greenfield in Semitic Philology*. Edited by Shalom M. Paul, et al. 2 vols. Leiden: Brill / Jerusalem: Magnes, 2001.

———. "מחקרים במונחי משפט בכתובות הקבר הנבטיות." In *Sefer Zikkaron le-Hanoch Yalon*, edited by E. Y. Kutscher, et al., 79–82. Ramat-Gan: Bar-Ilan University Press, 5734 [= 1973–1974].

Gropp, Douglas M. "The Origin and Development of the Aramaic *Šallīṭ* Clause." *JNES* 52 (1993) 31–36.

Hoffmeier, James K. "A New Insight on Pharaoh Apries from Herodotus, Diodorus and Jeremiah 46:17." *JSSEA* 11 (1981) 165–70.

Huehnergard, John. *A Grammar of Akkadian*. 3rd edition. Winona Lake, IN: Eisenbrauns, 2011.

Hurvitz, Avi. *A Concise Lexicon of Late Biblical Hebrew: Linguistic Innovations in the Writings of the Second Temple Period*. Leiden: Brill, 2014.

Joüon, Paul. *Grammaire de l'hébreu biblique*. Rome: Institut Biblique Pontifical, 1923.

Joüon, Paul, and T. Muraoka. *A Grammar of Biblical Hebrew*. 2 vols. Rome: Pontifical Biblical Institute, 1991.

Kaufmann, Yehezkel. *The Religion of Israel*, trans. by Moshe Greenberg. Chicago: University of Chicago, 1960.

Kienast, Burkhart. *Historische semitische Sprachwissenschaft*. Wiesbaden: Harrassowitz, 2001.

König, Friedrich E. *Historisch-kritisches lehrgebäude der hebräischen sprache*. 3 vols., 1881–1897. Repr. Hildesheim: Olms, 1979.

Lambdin, Thomas O. *Introduction to Biblical Hebrew*. New York: Scribner, 1971.

Leemans, W. F. *The Old-Babylonian Merchant: His Business and His Social Position*. Leiden: Brill, 1950.

Levine, Baruch A. *Numbers 1–20*. AB 4. New York: Doubleday, 1993.

Margain, Jean. "Causatif et toleratif en Hebreu." *GLECS* 18–23 (1973–1979) 23–31.

McKane, William. *A Critical and Exegetical Commentary on Jeremiah*. 2 vols. International Critical Commentary. Edinburgh : T. & T. Clark, 1986–1996.

Muraoka, T., and Bezalel Porten. *A Grammar of Egyptian Aramaic*. 2nd edition. Leiden: Brill, 2003.

Paul, Shalom M. *Isaiah 40–66*. Grand Rapids: Eerdmans, 2012.

Rosenthal, Franz. *A Grammar of Biblical Aramaic*. Wiesbaden: Otto Harrassowitz, 1961.

Roth, Martha T. *Law Collections from Mesopotamian and Asia Minor*. 2nd ed. Writings of the Ancient World 6. Atlanta: Scholars, 1997.

Seow, Choon-Leong. *Ecclesiastes: A New Translation with Introduction and Commentary*. AB 18C. New York: Doubleday, 1997.

Tigay, Jeffrey H. "The Presence of God and the Coherence of Exodus 20:22–26." In *Sefer Moshe: The Moshe Weinfeld Jubilee Volume: Studies in the Bible and the Ancient Near East, Qumran and Post-Biblical Judaism*, edited by Chaim Cohen, Avi Hurvitz, and Shalom M. Paul, 195–211. Winona Lake, IN: Eisenbrauns, 2004.

Ungnad, Arthur. *Akkadian Grammar*, revised by Lubor Matouš. Translated by Harry A. Hoffner. Atlanta: Scholars, 1992.

Waltke, Bruce K., and M. O'Connor. *An Introduction to Biblical Hebrew Syntax*. Winona Lake, IN: Eisenbrauns, 1990.

Webster's New World Dictionary. 3rd College ed. New York: Webster's New World, 1988.

Zakovitch, Yair. *Ḥayye Šimšon*. English title: *The Life of Samson (Judges 13–16). A Critical-Literary Analysis*. Jerusalem: Magnes, 1982.

Index of Scholars Cited

Abdelhadi, Souad, 318
Abu-Rabia, Salim, 318
Achenbach, Reinhard, 377
Aderet, Avraham, 105
Adir, Zeev, 106
Aharoni, Yohanan, 106
Aharon-Peretz, Judith, 326
Aḥituv, Shmuel, 136–38
Aimé-Grun, Noele. 247
Alberts, Rainer, 127, 217
Albrektson, Bertil, 159
Albright, William Foxwell, xxi, 24, 27, 117
Alexander, Philip S., 384
Allen, Leslie, 152
Allen, James P., 233
Alon, David, 103
Alperin, Hayim, 100
Alt, Albrecht, 388
Alter, Robert, 4
Altmann, Alexander, 45
Ambos, Claus, 240
Amiran, Ruth, 80, 84–86, 90, 111, 126, 223
Amizur, Eliyahu, 100
Andersen, Francis I., 224–25
Anderson, Benedict, 93, 224
Andrews, Edna, 319, 328
Archer, Shirley, 327–28
Asaf, Amnon, 102
Aster, Shawn Zelig, 239
Attridge Harold W., 240
Aurant, Sarah, 22, 24, 26
Austin, John L., 220
Avitzur, Shmuel, 100–101
Ayalon, Etan, 22, 134, 140–42
Azulay, Ariela, 81

Bacher, Wilhelm, 264
Baentsch, Bruno, 354, 364, 368
Baillet, Maurice, 384, 386
Bandstra, Barry L., 288
Barak Moshe, 102
Barkay, Gabriel, 30, 140–41
Bar-Nathan, Rachel,
Bar-Oz, Guy 22, 80–82, 94, 96, 100
Barr, James, 7, 159, 206
Barstad, Hans, 6, 8
Barthélemy, Dominique, 161
Barthes, Roland, 7
Baudissin, Wolf W., 377
Bauer, Hans, 266, 294, 398–99
Baumgartner, Walter, 295, 297
Beck, Pirhiya, 124
Beckwith, Roger, 205
Beecher, Willis J., 206
Beelders, Tanya, 324
Beit-Arieh, Itzhaq, 223
Ben Eliezer, Tobiah, 385
Ben Isaac, Abraham ha-Levi, 386
Ben-Dor, Emanuel, 84, 86, 91
Ben-Eli, Arieh, 99
Ben-Ḥayyim, Ze'ev, 264
Ben-Shlomo, David, 22
Ben-Tor, Emanuel, 90
Benyamini, Chana, 115
Ben-Yehudah, Eliezer, 209
Ben-Zeev, Judah Leib, 267–68
Ben-Zvi, Z., 99
Bergh, Luna, 324
Bergsträsser, Gotthelf, 266, 398
Berlin, Adele, 348
Berman, Joshua, 203
Bernick-Greenberg, Hannah, 135
Bertholet, Alfred, 371

Bertolino, M.A., 95
Biale, David, 203
Biber, Douglas, 350
Biedert, Ralf, 333
Biemann, Asher D., 45
Bignamini, Ilaria, 45
Bintliff, John, 12
Biran, Avraham, 81, 89, 90, 92
Bland, Kalman P., 51
Blank, Sheldon H., 220, 223
Blau, Joshua, xxii. 235, 266, 390
Blenkinsopp, Joseph, 347
Bliss, Frederick, 78
Bloch, Ariel, xxii
Bonesho, Catherine, 173
Bouchnic, Ram, 22, 26
Bourdieu, Pierre, 221
Bowman, Raymond A. 247
Brandman, Shemuel, 105
Braun, Joachim, 122, 126
Braunstein, Susan L., 48
Breuer, Edward, 46
Breuer, Mordecai, 158, 167, 170–71
Brichto, Herbert, 215
Bril, Joel, 264, 268–70, 272, 278
Brockelmann, Carl, 347, 392, 399, 401
Broida, Marian W., 219–20
Bron, François, 388, 391
Broshi, Magen, 28, 89
Bunimovitz, Shlomo, 24, 25, 27, 31, 62
Burdeli, Hayim, 105
Burden, Terry L., 288
Buth Randall, 322, 340

Calmeyer, Peter, 239
Caquot, André, 224
Carasik, Michael, 204
Carmi, Israel, 142
Carpenter, J. Estin, 364
Cassuto, Umberto, 208
Castelhano, Monica, 330–31
Cavallo, Guglielmo, 207
Chafe, Wallace, 350
Charlesworth, James H., 398, 400, 411
Chomsky, William, 271

Ciancaglini, Claudia A., 311
Cimbalist/Zori, Nehemia, 99
Clark, Herbert, 78
Clines, David J.A., 225
Cobbing, Felicity, 78
Cogan, Mordechai, 273
Cohen, Chaim, 401
Cohen, Jonathan D., 329
Cohen, Maimon, 157, 159, 160, 162
Cohen, Menahem, 385
Cohen, Rudolph, 135
Cohen, Shabbatai, 209
Collins, John J., 7, 300, 309
Condé, Anne-Marie, 94
Conrad, Susan, 350
Cook, Edward, 309
Corcos, Evelyne, 326
Cornelius, Izak, 118, 123
Cowley, Roger W., 204
Coxon, Peter, 299–300
Creel, Andrea, 123
Croft, Paul, 26
Cross, Frank M., 290, 309, 358
Culley, Robert, 254
Curtis, Robert I., 128–129

Dagan, Yehuda, 23–24, 27–29, 32
Dalman, Gustav, 78
Dandamayev, Muhammad, 68
Darby, Erin, 120
David, Nir, 96
Davies, Philip R., 4–5
Day, John R., 118, 224
de Hamel, Christopher F.R., 207
de Miroschedji, Pierre, 24
de Rossi, Johannes Bernardus, 161
de Trani, Isaiah, 385
deClaissé-Walford, Nancy, 151–53
Dégh, Linda, 348
Dehaene, Stanislas, 322–23
Delcor, Mathiae, 250
Derrida, Jacques, 7
Dever, William G., 118–19, 125–26
Devreesse, Robert, 206
Dhorme, Édouard, 225–26
DiCastro, Daniela, 49
DiLella, Alexander A., 241
Dillmann, August, 354, 362

Index of Scholars Cited 417

Dirksen, Piet B., 384
Dobbs-Allsopp, F.W., 220
Dohovny, Moshe, 102
Dolansky, Shawna, 222
Dommershausen, Werner, 129
Donner, Herbert T., 240
Dotan, Aron, 172–72
Dothan, Trude, 28, 60, 61, 64, 69
Dothan, Moshe, 135
Douglas, Mary, 129–30
Driver, Samuel Rolles, 296, 308
Driver, Geoffrey R., 309
Duchowski, Andrew T., 333
Dupont-Sommer, André, 388–89, 392

Eagleton, Terry, 12
Ebeling, Erich, 240
Edelstein, Gershon, 22, 24, 26
Efron, Zusia, 82
Ehrensvärd, Martin, 392
Ehrlich, Carl S.,
Eichrodt, Walther, 411
Eissfeldt, Otto, 253
Elat, Moshe, 62
Eliav, Uri, 106
Elliger, Karl, 240, 364, 368
Elliott, James K., 205, 207
Ellis, John M., 12
Ellison, Rosemary, 129
Engle, James R., 118
Eph'al, Israel, 65
Epstein, Claire, 102
Eshel, Esther, 29, 136–38, 240
Eviatar, Zohar, 326–27
Ewald, Heinrich G.A., 359, 363
Eyal, Pirchiya, 22

Fales, F.M., 63
Fantalkin, A., 66
Farber, Walter, 220
Faust, Avraham, 11, 21–26, 28–33
Feldman, Yosef, 106
Feldman, Zev, 99
Feucht, Christian, 361, 362
Fiennes, Ralph, 283
Findlay, John M., 324
Fine, Steven, 44, 50, 57–59

Finkel, Irving, 66–68
Finkelstein, Israel, 25, 28, 136, 141, 143
Finn, James, 78
Fishbane, Michael A., 215, 220, 384, 385
Fitzmyer, Joseph A., 309
Flannery, Kent, 12
Fleming, Daniel E., 373
Flusser, David, xxi, 410
Fogelson, Yoav, 105
Folmer, Margaretha L., 294, 307, 308
Forni, G., 95
Foucault, Michel, 7
Fox, Michael V., 156, 160, 384, 386
Fox, Everett, 285, 286, 288, 289
Freedman, David Noel, xxii, 207, 223, 288
Freud, Liora, 134, 141
Friedman, Richard Elliott, 283, 290, 292
Frost, Ram, 321, 324
Fruzhinin, Yoel, 101
Fuchs, R., 78
Fuller, Russell E., 206

Gal, Zvi, 96, 106
Galil, Gershon, 21
Gamliel, Chanoch, 264
Garber, Zev, 178, 181, 183, 196, 199, 202
Gärdenfors, Peter, 325
Gardi, Tomer, 97, 105
Garfinkel, Yosef, 61, 69
Garr, W. Randall, 263, 291, 397
Garrett, Duane, 384
Geertz, Clifford, 15
Geltzor, Nimrod, 96
Gesenius, Wilhelm, 384, 392
Geva, Esther, 327
Gibson, Shimon, 23, 27, 78
Gibson, John C. L., 389, 392
Gil, Eli, 102
Gilboa, Ayelet, 25
Gilchrist, Iain M., 324
Ginsberg, H. L., 392
Ginsburg, Christian D., 205

418 Index of Scholars Cited

Gitin, Seymour, 60, 61, 63–66, 69, 70, 72
Givon, Shmuel, 23, 27
Glaser, Menahem, 103
Glucker, John, 398
Goetze, Albrecht, 266
Gold, Victor, xxii
Goldingay, John, 152
Goldman, Zev, 99
Goldschmidt, Daniel, 241
Goldstein, Jonathan A., 409
Goldstein, Kaylin, 89
Goodenough, Erwin R., 125, 129
Gophna, Ram, 100, 101
Gordis, Robert, 157–60, 172
Gordon, Cyrus H., 387
Goren, Avner, 139
Goren, Haim, 78
Goshen-Gottstein, Moshe, 208
Gould, Stephen Jay, 204
Grabbe, Lester L., 5, 8, 16, 295, 301, 311
Graf, Karl-Heinrich, 345, 362
Gray, George Buchanan, 354
Greaves, Sheldon W., 220
Green, Deborah A., 384
Green, William H., 398
Greenberg, Moshe, xxi, 218, 411
Greenberg, Raphael, 24, 25
Greenfield, Jonas C., xxii, 371, 409, 410
Greenstein, Edward L., 391
Gregory, Richard L., 329
Grelot, Pierre, 309
Gress, David, 12
Gropp, Douglas M., 409
Grunberg/Giveon, Raphael, 103
Guillaume, Philippe, 206
Gunkel, Hermann, 358
Gunneweg, Jan, 134
Gutman, Shmarya, 105
Guzetti, Andrea, 77

Habel, Norman C., 225–26
Hadley, Judith M., 123, 125
Hall, Terry, 203
Halliday, Michael, 350
Halpern, Baruch, 8

Haran, Menahem, xxi, xxii, 129, 346
Harford-Battersby, George, 364
Harper, Joshua, 391
Harrington, Daniel, 309
Harrison, T. P., 64
Hawkins, John David, 388
ha-Yaari, Yaacov, 105
Hayes, John H., 3
Ha-Yisraeli, Reuven, 102
Hecht, R., 104
Heckl, Raik, 250
Heltzer, Michael, 387
Hendel, Ronald, 130
Herbert, G., 78
Herdner, Andrée, 224
Herzog, Zeev, 28
Hess, Orna, 102
Heston, Charlton, 284
Hestrin, Ruth, 80, 81, 83, 91
Hiebert, Theodore, 224, 225
Hillers, Delbert R., 126
Hockett, Charles, xxii
Hodder, Ian, 14
Hoffmeier, J. K., 405
Hoftijzer, Jacob, 309
Holladay, John S. 62
Holm, Tawny, 247
Holmstedt, Robert D., 390
Holzinger, Heinrich, 354, 368
Honeyman, Alexander M., 388, 391
Höpfl, Hildebrand, 209
Hossfeld, Frank Lothar, 151, 153, 154
Houtman, Cornelis, 348
Huehnergard, J., 399
Hurowitz, Victor A., 348
Hurvitz, Avi, 347, 373, 377, 409
Hurwitz, Elimelech, 105
Hyrskykari, A. T., 330, 333, 337

Ibrahim, Raphiq, 326, 327
Iggers, George G., 10
Ilan, Eliyahu, 106
Ilan, David, 81
Iliffe, John H., 78
Inbar, Yehudit, 79–81, 91, 94–96, 98–104, 106–107
Inhoff, Albrecht-Werner, 330

Isbell, Charles David, 203
Israel, Manfred Moshe, 105

Jakobson, Roman, xxiv
James, Peter, 60, 61, 63–68, 72
Jenni, Ernst, 266, 267, 278
Johnson, Mark, 326
Jones, Barry Alan, 206
Jongeling, Karel A., 309
Joosten, Jan, 264, 347, 350, 362, 373
Joüon, Paul, 152, 267, 390, 398, 400

Kahane, Pinhas Penuel, 79, 81, 85, 86, 91, 98, 112
Kahn, Lily, 267
Kalaitzoglou, Georg, 69
Kalimowski, A.W., 92
Kaplan, Yaacov, 100
Karageorghis, Vassos, 122
Kark, Ruth, 89
Karlip, Joshua,
Katriel, Tamar, 81
Katz, Haya, 22, 24, 26–29, 31, 80, 84
Katz, Karl, 98
Kaufmann, Yehezkel, 411
Keel, Othmar, 118, 123, 126
Kelle, Brad E., 4
Kelley, Page H., 288
Kelm, George L., 70
Kempinski, Aharon, 100
Kennicott, Benjamin, 161
Khan, Geoffrey, 384, 385, 390
Kienast, Burkhart, 399, 400
Kilmer, Anne Drafkorn, xxii, 25
Kimberley, Webber, 95
Kingery, W. David, 13, 14
Kitchen, Kenneth A., 294, 295, 297–302, 307–13
Kitz, Anne Marie, 214, 216, 220, 223
Kletter, Raz, 78–80, 99, 100, 101, 103, 118, 119, 121, 124, 126
Kloner, Amos, 80
Klostermann, August, 347, 363
Kna'ani, Hayim, 106
Knauf, Ernst Axel, 8, 10
Knohl, Israel, 362, 363
Koch, Klaus, 348, 349, 368, 369, 376
Koenigsberger, Bernhard, 50

Kogan-Zahavi, E., 62
Koh, Andrew J., 353
Kol-Inbar, Yehudit, 94
König, Eduard, 398
Kootcscher, M., 100
Kossina, Gustav, 9
Kottsieper, Ingo, 247, 248, 250, 252, 255
Kraft, Robert A., 207, 209
Krahmalkov, Charles, 389
Kraus, Hans-Joachim, 229
Kress, Gunther, 317
Kuenen, Abraham, 345, 362
Kugel, James, 203
Kuhn, Lesley, 338
Kutscher, Eduard Y., xxii, 298–99, 309, 310

Lacan, Jacques, 7
Lakoff, George, 326
Lambdin, Thomas O., 266, 283, 288, 398
Landau, Sh., 101
Lane, Edward William., 398, 399
Langacker, Ronald W., 325, 326
Lapp, Paul, 126
Larsen, Peter, 77
Larson, John A. Jr., 248
Lauinger, Jacob, 65, 67
Leander, Pontus, 266, 294, 308, 398, 399
Lederman, Zvi, 24, 27, 62
Lee, Jennifer, 327
Leemans, Wilhelmus F., 402
Leeser, Isaac, 207
Leiman, Sid Z., 206
Lemaire, André, 353
Lemche, Niels Peter, 9, 203
Lenzi, Alan, 221
Leonard, Miriam, 40
Lernau, Hanan, 103
Leslau, Wolf, xxii
Leuchter, Mark, 352
Levin, Iris, 327
Levin, Saul, 159
Levine, Baruch A., 232, 252, 362, 364, 377, 398
Levinson, Bernard M., 360

Index of Scholars Cited

Lev-Tov, Justin, 25
Levy, Thomas E., 11
Lewis, Theodore J., 221–24, 228
Lie, Arthur Godfred, 253
Light, Laura, 207
Lin, Lin, 327
Linder, Elisha, 105
Lipschits, Oded, 23
Lishanski, Sarah, 103
Lissovsky, Nurit, 135
Liverani, Mario, 3
Livingston, Dennis H., 223
Livneh, Micha, 102
Loewenstamm, Samuel E., xxii, 358
Lohfink, Norbert, 346, 371
Lohmann, Ingrid, 51
Long, V. Phillips, 3
Longman, Tremper III,
Loretz, Oswald, 387
Löwe, Judah ben, 268
Lowenstein, Steven, 45
Löwisohn, Salomon, 264, 270–72, 278
Lubar, Steven, 14
Luigi, Paula, 333
Lundbom, Jack R., 129, 221
Luzzato, Samuel David, 242
Lyotard, Jean Francois, 7

Macknik, Stephen L., 330
Maeir, Aren M., 61
Maggi, Maurizio, 95
Maman, Aharon, 276
Manor, Giora, 103
Marcus, Joyce, 12
Mardiger, Noah, 99
Margain, Jean, 398
Margalioth, Mordecai, 50
Markus-Rabbani, Tirzah, 101
Martin, Andrew M., 11
Martinez-Conde, Sosana, 330
Master, Daniel M., 69, 70, 72, 73
Mastin, Brian A., 137–38
Matouš, Lubor, 399
Maycock, Sarah, 95
Mazar, Amihai, 5, 27, 70
Mazar, Binyamin, 92
McBride, S. Dean, 222

McCarter, P. Kyle, Jr., 218, 221, 223
McDonald, Lee Martin, 204–207
McEvenue, Sean E., 348
McGeough, Kevin M., 387
McKane, WcKane, 405
McLuhan, Marshall, 209
Meirhof, Ezra, 100
Melchert, Craig, 388
Mendelssohn, Moses, 44–51, 267, 268
Merlo, Paolo, 118
Meshel, Ze'ev, 134, 135–142, 228
Meshorer, Yaacov, 92
Mettinger, Tryggve N. D., 231
Meyers, Carol, 120, 122, 128–30
Milano, Lucio, 128
Milgrom, Jacob, xxii, 223, 240, 347, 361, 364, 367, 370, 373, 376, 377
Millard, Alan R., 64, 353
Miller, Earl K., 329
Miller, Jim, 350
Miller, John Miller, 3, 203
Miller-Naudé, Cynthia L., 319, 316, 393
Mitchell, Christopher W.,
Mizrahi, Noam, 347
Möller, Astrid, 66
Montagu, Jeremy, 121, 122
Moore, Megan B., 4
Moorey, Peter, 120
Morag, Shelomo, 390
Moran, William L., 230
Morrison, Robert E. 330
Moses, Walther, 100
Mrozowski, Stephen, 11
Muilenberg, James, xxii
Müller, Hans-Peter, 389, 392
Muraoka, Takamitsu, 152, 167, 291, 294, 390, 398–400
Murphy, Roland E. , 384, 386

Na'aman, Nadav, 23, 61–63, 66, 69, 73, 135, 353
Narkiss, Mordechai, 98
Nassaji, Hossein, 319
Naudé, Jacobus A. 316, 319
Naveh, Joseph, 64

Neustadt, Mordechai, 102
Newberry, Percy E., 247
Niccacci, Alviero, 291
Niditch, Susan, 353
Niehr, Herbert, 253
Nietzsche, Friedrich, 8. 12
Nihan, Christophe, 356, 361, 363, 370, 377
Nims, Charles, 245, 247, 248, 250, 253
Nishri-Hevron, Rina, 105
Nissinen, Martti, 229
Noegel, Scott B., 216, 383, 287, 392
Nogalski, James, 208
Nöldeke, Theodor, 346, 359
Noth, Martin, 21, 368
Nun, Mendel, 102

O'Connor, M., 152, 266, 398, 400
Oden, Robert A., 240
Oestigaard, Terje, 9
Ofer, Avi, 28
Ofrat-Friedlander, Gideon, 98
O'Leary, Amy, 209
Olsen, Bjørner, 12
Orlinsky, Harry M., 158, 159
Ornan, Tallay, 223
Oshima, Takayoshi, 240
Overland, Paul, 322, 340

Packman, Ann T., 318, 338
Paran, Meir, 347–48
Pardee, Dennis G., 380
Parpola, Simo, 240
Paul, Shalom, 242, 408, 410
Paz, Sarit, 117, 121, 122, 124–26
Pearce, Mark, 12
Peels, Hendrik G.L., 204
Peled, Ruth, 91
Pelli, Moshe, 270
Perfetti, Charles, 319, 320
Perlman, Isadore, 134
Perry, Noam, 89
Pfanner, Michael, 44
Phythian-Adams, William, 78
Piasetzky, Eliezer, 141, 143
Pilz, Edwin, 117
Pitard, Wayne T., 224, 353

Polak, Frank H., 348–50, 352–54, 358, 361, 369, 370, 371–73, 377
Pollastek, Alexander T., 330
Polzin, Robert, 347
Pope, Marvin H., 225–26, 384, 387
Porten, Bezalel, 64, 294, 399, 404
Posner, Raphael, 208
Postgate, J. Nicholas, 63
Preschel, Tovia, 51
Pretorius, Elizabeth, 331
Preucel, Robert W., 11
Pritchard, James B., 117
Propp, William H. C., 240, 285, 286, 289
Provan, Iain, 3
Prown, Jules David, 14, 15

Qimron, Elisha, 347

Rabin, Chaim, xxii
Raffaeli, Samuel, 78
Rahmani, Levi Yitzhak, 77, 80, 81, 89–92
Rainey, Anson F., xxi
Rajak, Tessa, 46
Rayner, Keith, 329–31
Reed, Stephen A., 128
Reland, Adriaan, 44–45, 47, 56
Rendsburg, Gary A., 226, 347, 383–85, 387, 392, 393
Rendtorff, Rolf, 349, 374, 375
Rezetko, Robert D., 384, 392
Robar, Elizabeth, 390
Roberts, Colin H., 207
Robertson, Tip, 327
Roche, Alexander, 79, 99
Rofé, Alexander, 204, 398
Röllig, Wolfgang, 240, 389
Romano-Hvid, Karmit, 97
Rösel, Martin, 248, 250
Rosenthal, Franz, 297, 399
Rosovsky, Nitza, 77
Roth, Martha T., 405
Roth, Yehuda, 100
Rouse, Mary A., 207
Rouse, Richard H., 207
Rowley, Harold H., 294–314

Index of Scholars Cited

Rubin, David C., 374
Rüger, Hans Peter, 204
Ryder, Stuart A., 266
Rynhold, Daniel, 44

Sachar, Edna, 60
Sadiel, Tehilah, 22
Sáenz-Badillos, Angel, 152
Safrai, Baruch, 104
Samuel, Delwen, 128, 129
Sanders, Seth L., 220
Sapir, Yair, 22
Sapir, Zvi, 102
Sapir-Hen, Lidar, 25
Sarna, Nahum M., 206
Sasson, Jack M., 183, 186, 188–89, 192
Satanow, Isaac, 268
Satlow, Michael L., 203
Saur, Markus, 250
Schaeder, Hans H., 297
Schaudig, Hanspeter, 240
Schick, Conrad, 78
Schiffer, Michael B., 15
Schmid, Anton, 270
Schmitt, Rüdiger, 120, 217
Schneerson, Menachem Mendel, 51
Schniedewind, William M., 136, 203, 207, 353
Schramm, Gene, xxii
Schuller, Eileen, 240
Schwartz, Karl, 98
Searle, John R., 220
Segal, Dror, 142
Seger, Joe D., 26
Segert, Stanislav, 250
Seow, Choon Leong 234, 409
Shabak, Yehuda, 106
Shai, Itzhak, 23, 27
Shalit, Israel, 105
Shamir, Orit, 92, 93, 96, 110
Shapira, Yariv, 103
Share, David L., 326, 327
Sharmin, Salina, 333
Shatil, Evelyn, 327
Shavit, Alon, 25
Shay, Oded, 78, 98, 100
Shelley, Percy, 193

Shiller, Ely, 79, 81, 91, 94, 96, 98–105
Shimron, Joseph, 327
Shinan, Avigdor, 203
Shirai, Yehuda, 106
Shreiber, Arieh, 106
Siegel, Linda, 327
Siegenthaler, Eva, 330
Silver, Daniel Jeremy, 207
Simon, Charles, 209
Singer-Avitz, Lily, 134, 141
Sivan, Tamer, 327
Skeat, Theodore C., 207
Skehan, Patrick W., 241
Smith, Charles M., 203
Smith, Frank, 322
Smith, Mark S., 118, 130, 224, 353, 358, 387
Smith, Morton, 206
Smith, Wilfred Cantwell, 207
Sørensen, Jørgen Podemann, 220
Soden, Wolfram von, 399
Sorkin, David, 45
Speiser, Ephraim A., 284, 285
Sperling, S. David, 209
St. Laurent, Beatrice, 78
Stackert, Jeffrey, 362
Stager, Lawrence E., 61, 63, 66, 68–70, 72, 73
Stefanovic, Zdravko, 295, 300
Stegemann, Hartmut, 240
Steiner, Richard C., 245, 247–48, 250, 253, 255, 397
Stekelis, Moshe, 104
Stern, David, 397
Stern, Ephraim, 68, 207
Sternberg, Meir, 4
Stiel, Otto, 103
Stoop-van Paridon, P.W.T., 385
Sugimoto, David T., 117, 121, 122, 124, 126, 127
Sukenik, Eliezer, 100, 101
Swanson, Theodore Norman, 209
Swiggers, Pierre, 391
Sznycer, Maurice, 224

Tadmor, Miriam, 120, 123–25
Taha, Haitham Y., 326

Index of Scholars Cited

Tal, Ehud, 100
Talmon, Shemaryahu, xxii
Tamir, Gershon, 101
Tappy, Ronald E., 23, 27
Tarnas, Richard, 12
Ta-Shema, Israel, 208
Taşkömür, Himmet, 78
Tawil, Hayim, 240
Thistleton, Anthony C., 220
Thompson, Thomas L., 5, 8, 9
Thureau-Dangin, François, 241
Tidhar, David, 103
Tigay, Jeffrey, 263, 398
Toorn, Karel van der, 130, 217, 254
Tov, Emanuel, 161, 162, 172, 206
Tubb, Jonathan, 78

Ucko, Peter J., 120
Uehlinger, Christoph, 118, 123, 126
Unger, Eckhard, 239
Ungerleider-Mayerson, Joy, 77
Ungnad, Arthur, 399
Ussishkin, David, 23, 27
Ustinov, Baron, 78

Van Buren, E. Douglas, 126
Van der Merwe, Christo H. J., 226
Van Leeuwen, Theo, 317
Van Rooy, Bertus, 331
Van Wieringen, Archibald, 151–53
Vanderhooft, David, 70
Vanstiphout, Herman L.J., 348
Varner, William M., 208
Vincler, John A. Jr., 248
Vleeming, Sven P., 245, 249, 250
Voight, Mary M., 120

Wachs, Saul, 397
Wagman, Aharon, 87, 99
Waldbaum, Jane C., 66, 69
Waltke, Bruce K., 152, 266, 398, 400
Walton, John H., 223
Ward, William A., 65
Ware, Colin, 317, 324–29
Warsaka, Elizabeth, 118
Weil, Gerhard E., 172
Weimar, Peter, 357
Weinert, Regina, 350

Weinfeld, Moshe, 250, 359
Weiss, Meir, xxii
Wellhausen, Julius, 345
Wells, Bruce, 234
Wesselius, Jan Willem, 245, 249, 250
Westbrook, Raymond, 234
Whitelam, Keith W., 5, 8, 9
Williams, Ronald, 266
Willows, Stanislas, 326
Wilson, Robert Dick, 295
Wilton, Andrew, 45
Windschuttle, Keith, 13
Winkworth, Kylie, 93, 95
Wiseman, D. J., 66, 310
Wolfsohn, Aaron, 268
Wright, J. Edward, xxix
Wunsch, Cornelia, 397
Wyatt, Nicolas, 256

Yaacobi, Avshalom, 105
Yadin, Yigael, xxi–xxii
Yankelovich, Daniel, 11
Yarden, Leon, 44
Yardeni, Ada, 294, 404
Yaskil, Avraham, 104
Yasur-Landau, Assaf, 25, 353
Yeda'aya, Moshe, 102
Yeivin, Ephrat, 91
Yeivin, Shemuel, 79, 84–88, 90, 91, 99, 101, 102, 104
Yemini, Y., 101
Young, Ian, 384, 392, 393
Younger, K. Lawson, Jr., 389

Zadok, Ran, 67, 68
Zaharoni, Menahem, 100
Zakovitch, Yair, 407
Zauzich, Karl-Theodor, 248
Zenger, Erich, 151, 153, 154
Zevit, Ziony, 116, 117, 130, 134, 137–38, 219, 223, 250, 278, 288, 316, 340–41, 346, 347, 352, 376, 377, 393, 397
Zias, Joe, 80
Zimhoni, Orna, 22
Zimmels, Hirsch Jakob, 209
Zuckerman, Bruce, 178, 181, 183, 186, 190, 193, 198, 199, 202

Index of Biblical Passages

GENESIS

1:1–19	356
1:1	204
1:2	282, 358
1:5	358
1:9–10	358
1:9	345
1:11–12	358
1:11	358
1:17	358
1:20—2:3	356
1:21	358
1:24	358
1:25	358
1:26	358
1:29–30	358
2:2–3	358
2:17	284
2:21–23	xxix, xxxii
3:4	284
3:12–13	291
3:16	xxxii
3:23	388–90
4:7	219
6–8	345
6	356
6:7	217
7–8	356
7:4	217
7:6	355
7:9	290
7:11	355, 358
7:13	355
7:14	355
7:16a	355
7:17a	355
7:18–21	355
7:24	355
7:15	290
7:23	217
8:21	183
8:1	355
8:2	358
8:2a	355
8:3b	355
8:4b	355
8:5	355
8:13a	355
8:14–19	355
9	345, 356
9:1–26	355, 359, 368
14:10	224
14:23	286–87, 292
14:24	292
17	345, 357
17:1–8	356–57
17:9–14	357
17:15–22	356–57
17:23–27	357
18:10	284
19:1b–3	353
20:18	284
21:8	391
21:33	231
22:2	178
22:17	285
23:1–16	355
23:1	354
23:5–11	354
23:19–20	355

Index of Biblical Passages

24:18	401
24:17	399
24:45	401
25	355
25:1–12	354, 359, 368
25:25	408
25:30	399
26:11	283, 285
28:1–9	345, 354–56
28:3	357
28:18	370
29:21–33	349–50
29:23	350
31:50	222
31:52	222
31:53	221–22
32:9	385
32:26–30	353
35:11	357
37:33	390
38:28–30	408
40:17	128
41:6	391
42:38	404
43:14	357
44:29	404
44:31	404
48:3	357
48:11	403
49:27	358

EXODUS

1:7	290
1:15	264
1:19	290
3:14	231
3:15	231
3:2	390
3:7	285
3:22	401
4:16	287
4:21	410
5:2	180
5:23	284
6–7	345, 356
6:2–13	354
6:26—7:6	354–56
6:3	357
7:8–13	354–56
7:3	410
7:16	356
8:17	265
9:8–12	354–56
9:16	406
12	345, 347, 365–67, 374, 376
12:1–14	366
12:6	363
12:7	371
12:13	401
12:15–20	366
12:36	401
14	355–56
14:1–4	354
14:8–10	354
14:15–18	354
14:22–23	354
14:27–29	354
15	xxxiv
15:1–12	227
15:20	122
16	354–56
16:33	371
17	345
17:14	217
20:3	231
20:7	221
20:10	152
20:13	201
20:20	398
20:24–26	xxviii
21:2–11	371
21:8	399, 404
21:11	371
21:12	285
21:15	285
21:17	221, 285
22–24	345
22:27 (ET 22:28)	221
23:13	231
25–31	346
25–29	368, 376
25	45, 346, 67
25:10–12	348

EXODUS (continued)

25:11	369
25:12	369
25:1–9	348
25:4–7	348
25:10–30	367
25:10–16	348
25:11	368
25:12	369
25:13	369
25:15	369
25:18–19	369
25:18	369
25:19	369
25:23–31	348
25:24–26	369
25:28	369
25:31	369
25:37	369
25:40	46, 369
26–27	367
26:31–27:5	367
27:20	390
28:36	240
28	346, 367–68
29	346, 369
29:1–24	367, 368, 370
29	368, 370, 374
29:1	370
29:7	369, 370
29:8–9a	370
29:15–18	369
29:16b	370
29:19–21	369
29:20	369
29:22–23	369–70
29:12–13	371
29:20	371
29:40	390
30:1–10	368
30:1–9	367
30:16	371
30:18–22	367
30:34–36	371
32:11	391
34:29–35	354, 355
34:20–35	356
34:29–35	356
35–40	346
35–39	369
35:1—36:7	354
35	356
36	355
37:2	369
37:3	369
37:4	369
37:7	369
37:8a	369
37:11–13	369
37:15	369
37:17	369
37:25—38:8	367, 368
39:30	240
40:20	371

LEVITICUS

1–8	373
1–7	366
1–5	346
1–4	376
1–3	340
1–2	366
1	366
1:1—4:21	366, 374
1:3–6	370
1:8–9	370
2	366
2:13	399, 405
3	366
3:1–17	366
4	366, 374
4:1–35	366
4:2–23	364
4:21	375
4:41	364
4:42	364
4:46	364
5–6	366
5	366
5:1–13	366
5:14–26	366
5:19	375
6–7	346
6	366

7	366, 374	14:32	375
7:1–34	366	14:39–57	364
7:34	371	14:57	375
7:35	375, 377	15:2–15	364
7:37	375	15:14	371
8	365, 366, 368, 370, 374	15:16–33	363
8:8	370	15:32	375
8:9	240, 370	16:30	201
8:12	370	16	346, 365–67, 374
8:15	371	16:1–17	366
8:18–21	370	16:5–8	371
8:19b	370	16:12–13	371
8:22	370	16:18–28	366
8:23	371	16:18	371
8:26–27	371	16:29–34	360
8:26	370	17–26	227
9–10	345, 367–68, 371	17	346, 347, 353, 359, 361–63, 372, 373
9	356	17:22, 24	362
9:1–24	367	17:3–4	362
10	356	17:7	362–63
10:1–10	356, 367	17:22	362
10:1	371	17:24	362
11–15	346, 353	18–27	359
11–13	345	18–26	346, 353
11:2–8	363–65, 372–73	18–23	362
11:9–47	364–65, 372	18–22	363
11:10–13	364	18–21	345, 363, 373
11:20	364	18–20	359
11:41–43	364	18–19	372
11:46	375	18	360–62
12	372	18:1–30	359
12:2–8	363	18:6–20	361
12:2	364, 365	18:21	235, 361
12:7	365, 375	19	360–62
13	364–65, 372–73	19:2–18	359
13:1–37	364	19:12	235
13:23–37	363	20	360, 361, 372
13:37	271	20:1–15	360
13:38–59	363–64	20:2–5	361
13:47–59	364	20:2	285
13:59	375	20:11–21	361
14–15	345, 364, 372	20:14–15	371
14:2–19	364	20:16–27	359
14:14	371	21	360–62, 372
14:15–17	371	21:1–24	359
14:20–38	364		
14:24–25	371		

LEVITICUS (continued)

21:6	235
21:23	362
22–24	372
22	361–63
22:2–16	360, 373
22:2	235
22:26–30	361
22:32	235
23	362, 363, 373
23:1–8	360–61
23:10–22	361
23:39–44	361
23:24–37	360–61
24	213, 214, 222, 227, 232–34, 361–63
24:1–23	360
24:2	390
24:3	363
24:5–7	371
24:5–6	129
24:9	129
24:10–23	214
24:10	231
24:11–12	214–15
24:11	213–15, 223, 232
24:13	234
24:15–22	213
24:15–20	234
24:15–16	214–15
24:16	213, 214, 216, 223
24:17	216
24:18	216
24:19–20	216
24:21a	216
24:21b	216
24:23	216, 234
25–27	345, 373
25:1—26:33	362
25	360, 361, 372
25:1–34	360
25:35–55	360
25:38	360
25:39–46	360
25:40	360
25:42	288, 292, 360
25:44–46	360
25:47–54	360
26	347, 348, 362
26:1–33	361, 363
26:1–13	360
26:3–45	362
26:3–33	362
26:14–33	359, 360
26:32–33	362
26:33–35	362
26:34–45	361–63, 372
26:34	362
26:36–42	362
26:37–38	362
26:39	362
26:40–43	362
26:43–44	362
26:44–45	362, 372
26:45	362
26:46	375
27	346, 353, 360–62, 372
27:1–33	359
27:11	265–66
27:34	375

NUMBERS

1–3	362, 374
3:47–51	371
4	345, 374
4:1–20	374
4:9–10	371
4:12	371
5–6	374
5:11–31	219, 233
5:17	371
5:29	375
6:2–21	362
6:13	375
6:21	375
6:18	371
6:19	371
6:22–26	222
6:27	222
7:5	371
7:6	371
8	374
8:16–26	362, 374

8:16	289, 292	18:6–7	371
8:18–19	371	18:8	377
9:1–14	362	18:17–32	362, 373, 374
10:11–28	362	18:21–32	347
10:28	375	18:26	371
10:35–36	228	18:28	371
11:2	219	19	362
11:15	186	19:2–3	371
12:12	408	19:17	371
13–14	355, 356	19:30	362
13:17b	354	20	354, 355, 356
13:18–20	354	20:8	371
13:21	354	22:2ff	178
13:22–24	354	21:23	401
13:26b	354	22:33	404
14:1	354	24:4	357
14:2	354	24:16	357
14:3–4	354	26:2	362
14:5–7	354	27:1–11	373
14:8–9	354	27:18–20	371
14:10	354	28:1–31	362
14:11–24	354	28:5	390
14:25	354	31	354, 355, 356
14:26	354	31:29	371
15	361–63, 373, 374	31:30	371
15:2–26	361	31:47	371
16–17	354	36	373
16	355, 356	36:1–12	362
16:1–11	354	36:13	375
16:1–2	354		
16:6–7	371	DEUTERONOMY	
16:12–15	354		
16:16–23	354	1–3	351
16:17	371	1:1–15	371
16:18	371	1:35	391
16:25	354	2:27	401
16:26a	354	2:30	401
16:26b	354	3:24–28	402
16:27–32a	354	3:25	391, 402
16:27a	354	3:24	403, 406
16:33	354	4:21	391
16:34	354	4:32b–33	407
16:35	354	4:34	407
17	355, 356	4:35	407
17:11	371	4:36	407
17:12	371	5:11	221
18	373	5:1	376
18:1–16	373	5:3	290, 292

DEUTERONOMY (cont.)

5:7	231
5:14	152
5:17	201
5:21	406, 407
6:14	231
6:17	284, 285
7:13–14	405
8:19	285
9–10	351
10:10	391
12	346
12:3	218
12:20–25	372
12:20–23	363
14	371
15	360
15:1–2	371
15:6	401
15:10–18	371
15:12–18	360, 371
15:13	371
15:16–17	371
15:16b	371
15:17	371
15:17b	371
16:20	289
19:1–9	373
21:1–9	xxvi
23:8	289
25:6	217
25:19	217
26:16–19	376
27:11–26	219
28:4, 11	405
28:12	401
28:58	228
28:69	375
29:4–5	351
29:8	351
29:15	287
29:19 (ET 29:20)	219
31:18	286
31:23	287, 292
31:24–28	331–32
32:8–9	153
34	351, 355, 356
34:1–10	355
34:1	402
34:4	402

JOSHUA

1:7–8	204
7–8	xxvii
10:34–36	21
12:12	21
15:39	21
21:45	405
23:14 bis	405

JUDGES

3–9	350
3:26	288
11:34	122
12–19	350
13:23	407–8
17:2	219
21:17	217

1 SAMUEL

1:11	284, 377
1:20	219
2:6	275–76
3:13–14	221
3:19	399, 405
4:7	232
6:8	371
10:1	370
13:14	274–75
14:24	219
17:45	229
18:6	122
19:5	391
21:3–7	129
21:14	399
23:9	274–75
25:3	160

2 SAMUEL

1:6–10	353
1:10	240

Index of Biblical Passages

3:6	152
3:21, 23	348
6:1–2	228
6:19	129
7:6	376
8:15	154
12	218
12:9	218
12:10	218–19
12:14	218–19
14:7	217
14:24	348
15:2	153
15:6	153
15:25	403
16:5–13	221
16:7	219
17:12	385
18:18	217
19:21–23	221
22:51	163
23:10	391
23:20	160
24	233

1 KINGS

2:6	399, 404
2:8–9	221
2:44–46	221
3–16	351
5:25	390
6:36	208
8:56	405
12—2 Kgs 17	xxvii
12	256
12:20	373
13:16–18	154
18:3	208
18:37	411
19:2–4	186
19:4	385
21:10	221
21:13	221
22:49	160

2 KINGS

2:9	404
2:10	390
2:24	222
7:12	274–75
8:1	275–76
9:3	370
9:6	370
10:10	405
11:2	240
12–25	351
12:10 (ET 12:9)	216
14:11–13	143
14:22	143
14:25	143, 187, 208
17:21	160
17:24–33	256
18:4	152
18:21	216
20:4	162
22–23	363, 373
24	363, 373
25	363

ISAIAH

1:18	271
2:19	222
2:21	222
4:5	358
6	192
6:9–10	191, 411
8:21–22	221
9:6	154
10:5	181
14:19	230
14:22	217
16:5	154
17:14	358
26:19	274–75
27:1	227
28–33	xxxiv
28:5	241
30:22	219
30:27–33	228
36:6	216
39:2	391

ISAIAH (continued)

40:2	191
40:26	358
40:28	231, 358
41:20	358
42:5	358
42:7	408
43:1	358
43:7	358
43:15	358
43:18–19	195
44:26	275–76
44:28	153
45:1–3	188
48:6	153
45:7–8	358
45:12	358
45:18	358
48:7	358
51:9–11	227
51:9–10a	226, 235
51:10	358
51:15	225
54:2	376
54:16	358
57:19	358
58:11	265
62:3	241
63:17	153, 409–11
64:4–6	410
65:17–18	358
66:10	154

JEREMIAH

1:5	408
7:9	234
7:18	129
10:11f	220
10:16	153
11:20	403
13:18	241
15:10	186
18:23	218
19:1–11	219, 233
20:9	177
20:14–18	186
20:12	403
20:18	408
21:12	154
26	351
26:18	152
29:17	391
30:18	153
31:4	122
31:13–34	194
31:22	358
31:31ff	411
31:35	225
31:38	153
32:39	411
36–43	351
39:1–10	363, 373
40:10	231
44:15–25	129
46:17	404
48:13	256
51:19	153
51:59–64	219, 233
52:4–11	363, 373

EZEKIEL

1:21	357
8:14	230
10:5	357
11:19ff	411
13:18–19	235
16:12	241
16:17	271
20:9	218
20:14	218
20:22	218
20:39	218, 235
23:42	241
26:1—28:9	177
26:15	235
28	232, 235
28:2	232
28:6	232
28:7	235
28:8	235
28:9	232, 235
28:13	358
28:15	358

Index of Biblical Passages 433

28:16	235
28:18	235
28:23	235
32	227
36:11	405
36:20–23	218, 235
36:21	218
36:26f	411
39:7	218, 235, 399
40–48	347
40:17	391
43:18–27	375
44:1–15	375
44:16–31	375

JOEL

2:8	196
2:12–14	186
2:13	186

AMOS

1:2—2:16	219
1:3—2:3	177
1:6–8	61
2:13	391
3:2	177
3:8	177
4:13	358
7:4	358
7:7–9	183
7:10–15	176
7:12–17	xxvi
7:12–13	181
7:16ff	176
7:17	178
9:11	275–76
9:14–15	194

OBADIAH

15–16	219, 233

JONAH

1–4	175–202

MICAH

4:11	402
7:8	408
7:9	408
7:10b	402
7:18–20	196

NAHUM

1:4	224
3:1–4	180

HABAKKUK

1:5	161
1:16	161
3:12–14,16	224
3:8–15	223–24, 227
3:8	225
3:14	233
3:9	223, 224
3:11	224

ZEPHANIAH

1:4	218
3:3	358

HAGGAI

1:6	216

ZECHARIAH

5:1–4	219
5:3–4	234
13:2	218

MALACHI

1:14	222
2:10	358
3:21	389
3:23 (ET 4:5)	205

PSALMS

Reference	Page
1:1	151
1:2	204
5:9	164
6:4	164
9:13	164
9:19	164
10	232
10:5	163
10:10	161, 163, 164
10:12	163
11:11	164
17:11	163
17:13–14	219
17:14	163
18:51	163
18:55	163, 168
20	xxiv, xxvii, 244–57
20:2 (ET 20:1)	222, 229
20:6 (ET 20:5)	229
20:8 (ET 20:7)	229
20:10 (ET 20:9)	229
21	239
21:4b	239
22:10	408
24:6	163
26:2	163
29	227
29:1–2	228
30:4	163
30:6	358
34:21	265
35:1–8	219
36:7	358
38:21	163
39:1	164
39:5	275–76
41:3	164
42:9	163
42:3	231
48:13–14	154
49:15	164
51:4	164
51:12	358
54:7	163
54:9	402, 403
55:10 (ET 55:9)	219
55:16 (ET 55:15)	161, 163, 219
55:18	358
56:7	164
58:8	164
59	403
59:11	164, 402
59:16	164
60:7	164
65:9	358
69:5 (ET 69:4)	218, 219
69:15–16 (ET 69:14–15)	218, 219
69:23–29 (ET 69:22–28)	218, 219
71:12	164
71:20	163, 164, 172
72:17	164
73:2	164
73:10	164
73:16	164
74:2	153, 391
74:6	164
74:11	163
74:12–17	227
77:1	164
77:12	164
77:17–21 (ET 77:16–20)	227
77:20	163
78:45	265
78:60	376
79:10	163
79:10b–12	219, 233
84:3	231
85:2	164
89:13	358
89:18	164
89:20b–25	229
89:29	163
89:40	240
89:43	265
89:48	358
90:2	231
90:6	358
90:8	164
91:1	357
92:12	402
92:16	164
93:1–4	227
93:4	224
100:3	164

101:5	163	**PROVERBS**	
102:4	164	1:27	160, 166
102:19	358	2:7	166, 172
105:18	164, 170	2:8	165
105:28	164	2:18	385
105:40	163	3:15	166
106:45	164	3:27	166
106:9	224	3:28	166
106:38	399	3:30	166
107:38	405	3:34	166
109	219	4:9	241
109:2–3	218	4:16	166
109:9	218	6:13	166
109:13	218	6:14	166, 172
109:15	218	6:16	166, 169, 172
109:16–18	218	8:17	166
109:17–19	217	8:35	166, 172
109:31	218	10:3	399, 406
112:8	402	11:3	166
118:7	402, 403	11:26	215
118:17	274–75	12:4	241
119:10	409	12:14	166
119:79	164	13:20	166
119:133	410	14:21	166
119:147	163	15:14	166
119:161	163, 172	16:19	166
122	149–54	16:27	166
123:4	161–64	16:31	241
129:3	163	17:6	241
129:5	154	17:13	166
132:18	240	17:27	160, 166
137	149, 152	18:17	166
137:1	192	18:19	166
137:7–9	219, 233	19:7	166
139:6	163	19:16	166
139:16	164	19:19	160, 166
140:10–12 (ET 140:9–11)	219	20:4	166
140:10	163	20:16	160, 166
140:11	164	20:21	160, 166, 169
140:13	164	20:30	166
141:4	410, 411	21:19	166
143:12	403	21:29	166
145:6	164	22:3	166
147:19	164	22:8	166, 168, 172
148:2	164	22:11	166, 168
148:5	358		

PROVERBS (continued)

22:20	166
22:25	166, 167
23:6	160, 166
23:26	160
23:31	166
23:5	166
23:6	167, 169
23:24	166, 167
23:26	167
23:29	167
23:31	160, 167
24:1	166
24:17	166, 169, 172
25:24	167
26:2	160, 167
26:21	166, 167
26:24	167
27:10	167
27:15	167
27:20	166
27:24	167
28:8	167
28:16	167
30:10	167
30:18	167
31:16	167
31:18	167
31:21	172
31:27	166, 167

JOB

1:10	165
1:21	164, 168, 171, 408
2:7	165
2:9	219, 234
3:1–24	186
3:8	215
3:5	216
3:11	408
5:18	165
6:2	164, 167
6:21	164, 169
6:29	165
7:1	165
7:5	165
9:13	164
9:30	165
10:18	408
10:20	165
11:14	399
13:15	165
14:5	164
15:15	164, 168
15:22	165
15:31	164, 165
16:6–14	234
16:16	165
19	219
19:29	165
20:11	164, 167
21:13	164
21:20	165
24:1	165
24:6	165
24:10	265–66
26:1	225
26:12–13	225, 226, 227, 235
26:12	165, 225, 226
26:13	226
26:14	164, 165
27:15	165
29:8	274–75
30:11	164, 165, 169
30:22	165
30:28	266
31:11	165
31:20	164
33:19	165
33:21	165
33:28	165
36:15	265
37:12	165
38:1	165
38:4	165
38:12	165, 168, 171, 275–76
38:29	408
39:12	165
39:26	165
39:30	165
40:6	165, 168
40:7	165
40:24–26 (ET 40:24—41:2)	225, 233

41:4	165
42:2	165
42:10	165
42:11	165
42:16	165

SONG OF SONGS

1:2	383
1:2	393
1:3	383–93
1:8	376
2:14	399

RUTH

4:10	217

LAMENTATIONS

1:21	391
2:5	154
2:7	154
2:8	154
2:17	265
4:7	271

ESTHER

1:11	241
2:3	386
2:9	386
2:12	386
6:8	241
8:15	240

ECCLESIASTES

1:9	279
2:18–19	409
4:4	385
5:14	408
5:18	409
6:2	409
7:10	391

DANIEL

2:1	307
2:10	307
2:27	307
2:43	307
3	308
3:2–3	308, 310
3:5	308
3:7	308
3:10	308
3:15	308
3:17	307
3:29	307
4:15	307
4:34	307
5:16	307
5:19	404
6:5	307
6:21	307
7	xxvi
7:1	307
8:1	xxvi
9:21	xxvi
10:12	219

EZRA

3:8–13	363, 373

NEHEMIAH

2:7	402
6:19	152

1 CHRONICLES

18:14	154
21:1ff	233
28:1–11	363, 373
29:1–25	363, 373

2 CHRONICLES

24:20–22	205
28:5–14	363, 373
30:1–27	363, 373
36:22–23	204

www.ingramcontent.com/pod-product-compliance
Lightning Source LLC
Chambersburg PA
CBHW021926290426
44108CB00012B/741